D1197573

QUEBEC QUESTIONS

Quebec Studies for the Twenty-First Century

Edited by

Stéphan Gervais
Christopher Kirkey
Jarrett Rudy

OXFORD
UNIVERSITY PRESS

OXFORD
UNIVERSITY PRESS

8 Sampson Mews, Suite 204, Don Mills, Ontario M3C 0H5
www.oupcanada.com

Oxford University Press is a department of the University of Oxford.
It furthers the University's objective of excellence in research, scholarship,
and education by publishing worldwide in

Oxford   New York
Auckland Cape Town Dar es Salaam Hong Kong Karachi
Kuala Lumpur Madrid Melbourne Mexico City Nairobi
New Delhi Shanghai Taipei Toronto

With offices in
Argentina Austria Brazil Chile Czech Republic France Greece
Guatemala Hungary Italy Japan Poland Portugal Singapore
South Korea Switzerland Thailand Turkey Ukraine Vietnam

Oxford is a trade mark of Oxford University Press
in the UK and in certain other countries

Published in Canada
by Oxford University Press

Copyright © Oxford University Press Canada 2011

The moral rights of the author have been asserted

Database right Oxford University Press (maker)

First Published 2011

All rights reserved. No part of this publication may be reproduced, stored in a retrieval system, or transmitted,
in any form or by any means, without the prior permission in writing of Oxford University Press, or as expressly
permitted by law, or under terms agreed with the appropriate reprographics rights organization.
Enquiries concerning reproduction outside the scope of the above should be sent to
the Rights Department, Oxford University Press, at the address above.

You must not circulate this book in any other binding or cover
and you must impose this same condition on any acquirer.

Every effort has been made to determine and contact copyright holders. In the case of any omissions,
the publisher will be pleased to make suitable acknowledgement in future editions.

Library and Archives Canada Cataloguing in Publication

Quebec questions : Quebec studies for the twenty-first century / editors Jarrett Rudy,
Stephan Gervais & Christopher Kirkey.

Includes bibliographical references and index.
ISBN 978-0-19-543248-0

1. Québec (Province)—History. I. Rudy, Robert Jarrett, 1970–
II. Gervais, Stéphan III. Kirkey, Christopher John, 1962–

FC2911.Q85 2010   971.4   C2010-902958-5

Cover image: Panoramic Images/Getty
This book is printed on permanent (acid-free) paper ∞.

Printed and bound in Canada.

1 2 3 4 — 13 12 11 10

Contents

PART D: CITIZENSHIP   227

PART E: QUEBEC MODELS   305

PART F: QUEBEC INTERNATIONAL   383

Acknowledgements

Collectively, we would like to express our appreciation to many who share our enthusiasm for Quebec, its history, and its people. First off, editing a book that gathers such a great list of scholars is a unique privilege. We would like to thank them for sharing their expertise, giving us their confidence, and for responding quickly to our seemingly endless demands. We would also like to thank Oxford University Press (Canada) for immediately recognizing the tremendous value a multidisciplinary book focused on Quebec would have. Most especially, we are grateful for all the efforts of the editorial team at Oxford, including Jodi Lewchuk, Jacqueline Mason, Leslie Saffrey, Katherine Skene, and Phyllis Wilson. It has been a rare privilege for the three of us to work on this project together, exchanging and assessing ideas and perspectives. These countless interchanges have led to a close personal and professional friendship.

This book would never have been realized without the generous support, financial and otherwise, of several key offices. Above all else, significant support for this volume was provided by the Ministère des Relations internationales du Québec. Specific funding was made available to the Institute on Québec Studies at SUNY Plattsburgh through a Québec Research Initiative grant. The Government of Canada also provided important funding in the form of a conference grant, to support an authors' colloquium in Montreal at McGill University. Further support for *Quebec Questions* was kindly provided by the Secrétariat aux Affaires intergouvernementales canadiennes (Programme de soutien à la recherche en matière d'affaires intergouvernementales et d'identité québécoise), the Association internationales des études québécoises, the Ministère des Ressources naturelles et de la Faune, the Ministère de la Justice, the Dean of Arts Development Fund at McGill University, and the United States Department of Education.

We would like to acknowledge the extraordinary work of our translator, Cynthia Kelly, on nine of the chapters in this volume. Her conscientious collaboration with the authors and editors brought great clarity to these texts. Ms Kelly was backed by the invaluable talents of her colleagues Glenn Clavier, Maxine Cutler, and Donald McGrath, and by the sage linguistic advice of Brigitte Côté, Lisa Dillon, Cécile Latizeau, and Valerie Vanstone.

Many individuals have contributed over the years to giving us the personal and intellectual strength to cultivate our passion for Quebec. Of course, we will not be able to thank them all.

Stéphan would like to thank his parents, Louis Gervais and Lise Lafleur Gervais, for being such great role models and especially his mother for valuing the power of education and teaching him to have, to rephrase a Quebec expression, a 'quiet confidence' in himself. He also thanks his wife, Julie, for always being there next to him. Several others have also been inspirational. For many years he had the pleasure of working with Alain-G. Gagnon at the McGill Quebec Studies Program. Alain's will to 'set the record straight' on Quebec has been a great source of strength. Several encounters with the late Claude Ryan were also memorable. The venerable journalist and politician told him that he should be aware and proud of the possibilities of promoting a better understanding of Quebec to a Canadian and international audience by using McGill's reputation and tradition. Finally, he thanks Marc Walker for his timely and insightful editing.

Chris extends the most heartfelt thanks to the Kirkey and McCartney families, both with deep-seated family roots in Quebec. Their support over the years has been irreplaceable. For instilling in him a sharp desire and appreciation for the study of Quebec, he would like to express gratitude to two special colleagues, Louis Balthazar and Alain-G. Gagnon, both of whom encouraged and supported this intellectual voyage. To the true believers and supporters of SUNY Plattsburgh's Institute on Québec Studies, Michel Constantin, Yanick Godbout, Patrick Muzzi, Frédéric Tremblay, Robert Keating, and Robert Laliberté—a very large thank you for everything you have done. Finally, no statement can fully express the love, gratitude, and respect he wishes to extend to his wife, Donna.

Jarrett would like to thank his parents, Bob and Joan Rudy, for starting his interest in Quebec. He would also like to thank a number of other families who took him into their Quebec homes and taught him more about Quebec than any boy from Ontario could have hoped to learn. Important here are the Guindons of Saint-André-Avellin, the Nadeaus of Rivière-du-Loup, and the Groleaus of Sainte-Thècle. In the academic world, he would like to thank the members of the Montreal History Group for their intellectual support and their commitment to research that has gone a long way to making Quebec History a world-class field. Finally, he thanks his wife, Cynthia, for her love and patience.

Contributors

Stéphan Gervais is the coordinator of Quebec Studies at McGill University. His research interests include ethnocultural diversity, citizenship, and language issues in Canada. He is a founding member of *Globe: Revue internationale d'études québécoises* as well as *Les cahiers du 27 juin,* and with Dimitrios Karmis and Diane Lamoureux he has recently edited the book *Du tricotté serré au métissé serré ? La culture publique commune au Québec en débats* (Les Presses de l'Université Laval, 2008). He is currently working on Native Peoples issues in Quebec.

Christopher Kirkey is the Director of the Center for the Study of Canada and the Institute on Québec Studies at State University of New York College at Plattsburgh, where he holds a concurrent position as Full Professor in the Department of Political Science. He also holds an appointment as Adjunct Associate Professor at the School of International and Public Affairs at Columbia University, and formerly served as Associate Professor of Political Science and Canadian Studies at Bridgewater State College. He holds a Ph.D. in Politics from Brandeis University, serves on the editorial boards of *Canadian Foreign Policy* and *The American Review of Canadian Studies,* and served as Mine Action Scholar-in-Residence at the Canadian Department of Foreign Affairs and International Trade. A scholar of comparative foreign policy and international relations theory, Kirkey is the author of several journal articles and commissioned reports. His most recent work is the co-edited issue 'Canada's Commitment to Afghanistan', of *The American Review of Canadian Studies,* Vol. 40, No.2, Summer 2010.

Jarrett Rudy is an Associate Professor in the History Department at McGill University as well as the Director of the Quebec Studies Program at McGill. He teaches and researches nineteenth- and twentieth-century Quebec and Canadian social and cultural history. More specifically, he is interested in everyday interactions between cultural groups in Quebec and their relationships to larger economic and political structures. He is the author of *The Freedom to Smoke: Tobacco Consumption and Identity* (McGill-Queen's University Press, 2005) and a member of the Montreal History Group.

Brett Rushforth is an Assistant Professor of History at the College of William and Mary. He is the author of *'Like Negroes in the Islands': Indians and the Making of Racial Slavery in French North America* (UNC Press, forthcoming) and is currently at work, with Christopher Hodson, on a history of the French Atlantic world from 1400 to Haitian independence.

Donald Fyson is a Professor in the Department of History at Université Laval in Quebec City and co-director of the Centre interuniversitaire d'études québécoises. His latest book is *Magistrates, Police, and People: Everyday Criminal Justice in Quebec and Lower Canada, 1764–1837* (Osgoode Society / University of Toronto Press, 2006). His current research projects include violence between men in Lower Canada and the nature of penal justice in Quebec City, 1840–1965.

Brian Young is an Emeritus Professor of History at McGill University. He is the author of many works on

Quebec history, including *A Short History of Quebec* with John Dickinson (McGill-Queen's University Press, 4th Edition, 2008). He is presently completing a comparative study of the grande bourgeoisie in nineteenth-century Quebec.

Garth Stevenson is a Professor of Political Science at Brock University and the author of *Parallel Paths: The Development of Nationalism in Ireland and Quebec* (McGill-Queen's University Press, 2006), which won the Donald Smiley prize in 2007. His current research deals with immigration and cultural diversity in Canada, Quebec, and the United States.

Alexis Lachaîne obtained his Ph.D. in History from York University in 2007. His doctoral dissertation examined French Canadian nationalist writers, decolonization, and revolutionary nationalism in Quebec in the 1960s. He currently teaches at York University and the University of Toronto, and has published on various aspects of the history of Quebec and French Canada.

Yvan Lamonde is an Emeritus Professor of Literature and History at McGill University. Author of many works on Quebec intellectual history, including *Histoire sociale des idées au Québec,* with two volumes published, and a third volume to follow in September 2010, he was the co-general editor of *History of the Book in Canada.*

Michel Biron is a Full Professor of French and Quebec Literature at McGill University. Author of many works on Quebec literature, including *Histoire de la littérature québécoise* with François Dumont and Élisabeth Nardout-Lafarge (Boréal, 2007), he is presently researching the Quebec contemporary novel.

Martin Papillon is an Assistant Professor of Political Science at the University of Ottawa. His current research focuses on Indigenous self-government in Canada, more specifically on the role of Indigenous governments in Canadian federalism. He is also working more broadly on Indigenous rights, on nationalism in Quebec, and on issues of citizenship in multinational states. He is the Director of the Forum for Aboriginal Research at the University of Ottawa. Micheline Milot is a Professor in the Department of

Sociology at the Université du Québec à Montréal. She is the author of several works on religious pluralism and secularism. She is presently working with the French historian Jean Baubérot on a book about the sociology of secularism and secular states.

Jocelyn Maclure is a Professor in the Faculty of Philosophy at Laval University, where he teaches ethics and political philosophy. His current work focuses on secularism and multiculturalism. He published, with Charles Taylor, *Laïcité et liberté de conscience* (Boréal, 2010) and *Quebec Identity: The Challenge of Pluralism* (McGill-Queen's University Press, 2003). He worked as an analyst and expert writer for the Bouchard-Taylor Commission on Accommodation Practices Related to Cultural Differences in 2007–8.

Chantal Bouchard is a Linguist who teaches out of the French Language and Literature Department at McGill University. She is the author of an essay on the Sociolinguistic History of Quebec (*Obsessed with Language,* Guernica, 2008). She is presently working on the linguistic changes of French during the Revolutionary Period and their consequences on the status of Quebec French.

Martin Lubin is an Emeritus Professor of Political Science at the Plattsburgh campus of the State University of New York. Author of many articles on Quebec Politics and their linkages with the United States, he is currently working on the life and times and intellectual development of Camille Laurin as a vehicle for understanding the transformations of Quebec society and politics associated with the Quiet Revolution and its aftermath.

Linda Cardinal teaches in the School of Political Studies at the University of Ottawa and is holder of a Research Chair on la francophonie. Author of many publications on the relationship between language, politics, and citizenship, she has recently edited *Le fédéralisme asymmétrique et les minorités linguistiques et nationales* (Prise de parole, 2007).

Daniel Weinstock holds the Canada Research Chair in Ethics and Political Philosophy in the Department of Philosophy at the University of Montreal and is director of the Centre de recherche en éthique de l'Université de Montréal (CREUM). He has published many articles on the ethics of nationalism, problems of justice and stability in multinational states, and the foundations of international ethics.

Christopher M. Jones is a Teaching Professor of French and Francophone Studies at Carnegie Mellon University. A regular publisher on Quebec popular music since 2000, his current project concerns the evolution of country music in Quebec.

Denyse Baillargeon is a full professor of History at Université de Montréal. Author of *Babies for the Nations: The Medicalization of Motherhood in Québec, 1910–1970* (Wilfrid Laurier University Press, 2009), she is currently working on the fundraising drives of the Hôpital Sainte-Justine, a pediatrics hospital in Montreal, between 1929 and 1970.

Raffaele Iacovino is an Assistant Professor at the Department of Political Science at Carleton University. His research interests include Canadian and Quebec politics, federalism, citizenship and immigration, and citizenship education. He has recently published with Alain-G. Gagnon, *Federalism, Citizenship and Quebec: Debating Multinationalism* (University of Toronto Press, 2007).

Maryse Potvin is a Professor in Education at Université du Québec à Montréal and the Director of the *Discriminations & Insertion* axis at the Centre d'études ethniques des universités montréalaises (CEETUM). She is the author of many scientific works on ethnic relations (racism, youth of immigrant origin, antiracist and democratic education, critical media analysis, social discourses analysis, social and scholar inequalities), and of many expert reports, including *Measurement of Discrimination* for the European Commission (2004), and on Media and Reasonable Accommodations for the Bouchard-Taylor Commission (2007–8).

Marie McAndrew is a full professor in the Department of Educational Administration and Foundations and holds the Canadian Research Chair on Education and Ethnic Relations at the University of Montreal. Her research interests include minority education, intercultural education, ethnic relations and comparative educational policies.

Diane Lamoureux is a Full Professor in the Department of Political Science at Laval University, where she teaches political philosophy. She is the author of many books and articles on the Feminist Movement in Quebec. Her research interests include citizenship and democracy issues in contemporary Western societies.

Antonia Maioni is the Director of the McGill Institute for the Study of Canada, and an Associate Professor of Political Science and William Dawson Scholar at McGill University. She has published widely in the fields of Canadian and comparative politics, with a particular focus on health and social policy.

David Massell is an Associate Professor of History at the University of Vermont, where he teaches courses on the history of Canada, the United States, and the North American environment. He is the author of *Amassing Power: J.B. Duke and the Saguenay River, 1897–1927* (McGill-Queen's University Press, 2000) and *Quebec Hydropolitics: The Peribonka Concessions of World War Two* (McGill-Queen's University Press, forthcoming).

Peter Graefe is an Associate Professor in the Department of Political Science at McMaster University. His research on political economy and public policy has included work on Quebec's economic and social development policies, including policies to develop the social economy.

Gilbert Gagné is an Associate Professor of Political Studies at Bishop's University in Sherbrooke. Specializing in international political economy and North American integration, he has published many works on Quebec and international relations.

Nelson Michaud is a Full Professor and Vice-rector (Teaching and Research) [Directeur de l'enseignement et de la recherche] at the École nationale d'administration publique in Québec. His research interests focus on the international role of federated entities as well as on Canadian foreign policy.

Mark O. Rousseau is a Professor of Sociology at the University of Nebraska-Omaha. He is the co-author of *Regionalism and Regional Devolution in Comparative Perspective* (Praeger, 1987). He has authored and co-authored numerous articles on French and Quebec political economy with recent work focused on Francophonie.

Jody Neathery-Castro is an Associate Professor of Political Science and Women's Studies at the University of Nebraska-Omaha. Her research interests include Quebec, French, and Francophone politics and culture, with current work examining the role of culture in global trade.

Louis Balthazar is Professor Emeritus at Laval University. He is also president of the Center for US Studies, Raoul-Dandurand Chair, at the Université du Québec à Montréal. He has published extensively on United States foreign policy, Canadian-American relations, Quebec nationalism, and other topics. Among his recent books are *La politique étrangère des États-Unis: fondements, acteurs, formulations* with Charles-Philippe David and Justin Vaïsse (Les Presses de Science Po, 2008) and *Le Québec dans l'espace americain* with Alfred O. Hero Jr. (Québec-Amérique, 1999).

Earl Fry is a Professor of Political Science and Endowed Professor of Canadian Studies at Brigham Young University. Over the past three decades, he has written extensively on Quebec-US economic and political relations. He is also a former Special Assistant in the Office of the US Trade Representative.

Sylvain Schryburt is an Assistant Professor of Theatre at the University of Ottawa. Editor in Chief of *L'Annuaire théâtral* and occasional theatre critic for *les Cahiers Jeu*, he is presently working on the dynamics of international theatre festivals and the globalization of Quebec theatre.

Alain-G. Gagnon is Canada Research Chair in Quebec and Canadian Studies and a Professor in the Political Science Department at Université du Québec à Montréal. His research and writing has concentrated on Quebec and Canadian politics, with a special emphasis on multinational federalism, nationalism, identity politics, and party politics. In 2010, he is a Visiting Professor at the University Carlos III in Madrid, where he was awarded a Chair of Excellence in the Department of International Law, Ecclesiastical Law, and Philosophy of Law.

General Introduction

Stéphan Gervais, Christopher Kirkey, and Jarrett Rudy

Since the 1960s the most basic question asked by Quebecers and other Canadians alike, 'What does Quebec want?', has been central to any number of discussions about life in Quebec and in Canada. Over time and through numerous political crises, this question has transformed and many others have been added. Is Quebec distinct? What makes it distinct? Are its gender and class relations distinct? What of its political economy? What is Quebec culture, and how can this culture be protected? Is Quebec a nation? Who is included in this nation? Who supports Quebec sovereignty? What is its relationship with Canada? With the United States? What is Quebec's place on the international stage? In this era of globalization, it turns out that the issues raised by these questions have great currency elsewhere. What is the relationship between states and nations? How do we address national and cultural pluralism? What has been the impact of colonialism? In the end, it is no hyperbole to say that 'Quebec questions' share much ground with debates taking place around the world.

This book brings together leading scholars from Quebec, the rest of Canada, and the United States to shed light on these and other 'Quebec questions'. Students should find these essays valuable for several reasons. First, the essays go beyond case studies to provide a broad overview of key issues, individuals, and events in understanding Quebec. Each contribution provides tools that allow students to expand their research on and interest in Quebec through further readings and useful Internet sites. Second, as a multidisciplinary collection that spotlights research in history, sociology, literature, political science, the performing arts, public administration, and philosophy, this collection gives readers an entry into these disciplines and a sense of how different disciplines ask different questions about similar issues. With a sense

of these various perspectives, students can develop a dynamic interdisciplinary approach to thinking about Quebec. And third, these chapters can provide a lens for comparative analysis as readers may see links between themes presented here and their readings and research on other places.

It is well known in the social sciences and humanities that questions are framed by the time and place of those who pose them, and there is no way we would want to hide this. Contexts are important. For example, two works published in 1969 by authors of different political interests both sought to explain the rising malaise in Quebec. In his classic *Quebec in Question*, Marcel Rioux argued that French Quebecers were becoming conscious of the fact that through a process of economic, political, and cultural colonization they had become a dominated ethno-class. By the late 1960s they were taking action to liberate themselves. In his anthology *French-Canadian Nationalism*, Ramsay Cook's goal was 'to understand the complex minds and emotions of French Canadians as they debate the question that has been central to their entire history—*la survivance*.' By explaining the central beliefs of French-Canadian nationalism, Cook also sought to provide a context for what was happening in the 1960s.[1]

Our own context in the early twenty-first century is decidedly different from that of 1969. In the aftermath of 11 September 2001, some have embraced an 'us and them' world view, resulting in military engagements in Afghanistan and Iraq and questions as to whether people of Muslim and non-Judeo-Christian faiths should be able to emigrate to Western countries. Similarly, Quebecers have debated whether certain expressions of religious faith, such as wearing a hijab or kirpan, are compatible with 'Quebec values'. To some extent these debates have fuelled the fascination with cultural contact presented in this collection. They push us to think about the many ways in which different cultures make contact and about the resulting conflict, accommodation, assimilation, or hybridity. Questions of cultural contact highlight the dynamic nature of culture itself, casting doubt on the validity of an 'us and them' perspective. They also sharpen our analysis of the power relations that have been so important to the study of Quebec since the late 1960s, as class and gender analysis came to the fore.[2] It is not surprising then that most of the articles here focus to some extent on contact among the diverse groups of people who have lived in Quebec.

The questions we ask here are also influenced by when we were born. As academics born in the 1960s and 1970s, we were not actors in the Quiet Revolution that culturally, economically, and politically transformed Quebec, and which is discussed in many of the articles in this collection. We came of age following the Charter of the French Language (1977). For both the anglophone and francophone editors of this volume (the anglophones born in Ontario), Quebec is recognized as a province where the common public language is French—indeed, it is the language of the majority—that is home to peoples of diverse ethnic backgrounds and identities. For most of our adult lives there has been something close to peace between Quebec's linguistic communities. This does not mean there have been no conflicts. Nor does it mean that French will remain a vibrant language without a certain amount of vigilance. What it does mean is that concerns about the future of the French language are somewhat different than in 1969, when Rioux and Cook were writing.

Belonging to a post–Bill 101 generation has also affected how we answer the question 'Who is a Quebecer?' For much of our adult lives, a significant part of the Quebec population has viewed the term *Quebecer* as referring to all people living in Quebec who choose to identify themselves as such. We share this view of an inclusive and civic national identity, although we are not seeking to imperialistically declare that everyone who has ever lived in what is Quebec today is a Quebecer.

Most of this volume focuses on the period following the creation of the Province of Quebec by British

Royal Proclamation in 1763. There are several excellent surveys of Quebec history from pre-Contact Aboriginal peoples until today that should be read alongside this collection.[3] In terms of geography, *Quebec Questions: Quebec Studies in the Twenty-first Century* centres on the territory of the Province of Quebec, though the identity of the majority of Quebecers has not always corresponded with the borders of the province; at times, therefore, the analysis follows the French-Canadian diaspora to the United States. Other articles explore Quebec's cultural, political, and economic relations with the broader international community.

We believe that *Quebec Questions* will prove useful to many around the world who look to study, teach, and conduct research on Quebec. Since at least the late 1970s (see Alain-G. Gagnon's afterword in this volume), Quebec has increasingly become an object of study and a dedicated part of curricula in educational institutions far from its borders.[4] Interest was first fed through Canadian Studies centres and especially French Language and Literature departments. It was further promoted though the establishment of the American Council for Quebec Studies, the institutional and financial support of the Ministère des Relations internationales du Québec (Quebec ministry of international relations), the foundation of the Association internationale des études québécoises (International Association for Quebec Studies),[5] and the increased emphasis recently given to Quebec by the Association for Canadian Studies in the United States.[6]

With established and growing interest in Quebec as a field of multidisciplinary (and increasingly interdisciplinary) study, we realized that an appropriate English-language text for students, teachers, and researchers featuring a comprehensive overview on Quebec simply did not exist.[7] Current English-language introductions to Quebec are grounded in distinct political science or historical perspectives; the most important being *Québec State and Society* by Alain-G. Gagnon; *The Québec Democracy* by Guy Lachapelle, Gérald Bernier, Daniel Salée, and Luc Bernier; and John Dickinson and Brian Young's *A Short History of Quebec*.[8] While there is no question that these works serve as essential course materials for professors teaching Quebec politics and history, it is clear that present-day research and teaching on Quebec Studies can also be served by a multidisciplinary volume. In addition, existing multidisciplinary texts dedicated to the study of Canada or Canada–United States relations do not provide a substantive review of Quebec issues.[9]

This book is the direct result of a long conversation between the Quebec Studies Program at McGill University and the Institute on Québec Studies at SUNY Plattsburgh about how to address this specific need; a conversation that concluded with a joint commitment to craft a timely and comprehensive volume that, above all else, would teach Quebec Studies to international, Canadian, and Quebec students. Specific discussions about this collection began when the Institute on Québec Studies convened a colloquium on 11 October 2006 called *The Future of Quebec Studies in the United States: Enriching a Vibrant Community*, at the Weatherhead Center for International Affairs at Harvard University.[10] With the support of the Ministère des Relations internationales du Québec, the Government of Canada, the Association internationales des études québécoises, the Dean of Arts Development Fund at McGill University, and the Programme de soutien à la recherche en matière d'affaires intergouvernementales et d'identité québécoise, a contributors' conference was organized in Montreal in October 2008. For the conference we challenged authors to write 'spirited surveys' of current research in their fields. Papers were discussed across disciplines: for example, a historian of New France was asked to comment on a paper on Quebec–US economic relations and an art historian commented on the work of a specialist in Quebec diplomacy. In many ways, this mirrored our vision of interdisciplinary studies, where practitioners of different disciplines exchange insights on a common subject.

Like the conference, *Quebec Questions* is organized to promote discussion across disciplines. Contributions are divided into six interconnected thematic sections: memories, identities, language, citizenship, and Quebec international. These themes not only represent important current paths of research in Quebec, they also seek to allow scholars studying other parts of the world easy access for useful comparisons with Quebec. Each section begins with a brief introduction followed by essays. Accompanying most essays is a chronological timetable; a 'Biography' of a notable person mentioned in the chapter; and a 'Snapshot'—an in-depth examination of a key event, all of which complement the narrative. Each essay ends with study questions designed to promote classroom discussion, a list of relevant websites, and a brief bibliography.

Some readers might notice that certain themes, such as nationalism or Anglo-Quebecers, are not explicitly represented among the themes we have chosen. In fact, nationalism is an issue that enters into all sections of the book, just as it enters most areas of Quebec life, and Anglo-Quebecers appear in numerous chapters. That said, there are of course subjects that do not appear here: Quebec visual arts; cultural industries like television, radio, film and video, new media, and journalism; or minority cultures, the cultural geography of Quebec, or its historical demography. Readers also might find that the book focuses too much on political, cultural, economic, and social elites and not enough on everyday people and how they contribute to Quebec society. As a one-volume project committed to providing contributing authors sufficient space to make substantial contributions, difficult decisions had to be made; we hope that this book can lead to further projects which bridge different parts of society.[11]

To conclude, the goal of this collection is not to launch a grand theory of Quebec society or to say 'how it should be'. Rather, we look at the territory of Quebec and ask a series of questions across disciplines about the population that lives there, using a set of themes we find useful. As co-editors of this project, we believe that available scholarly materials for students, professors, and researchers are key to promoting sustained curricular and research efforts in Quebec Studies and thus expanding interest in Quebec. *Quebec Questions: Quebec Studies for the Twenty-first Century* is designed to serve this purpose.

Notes

1. First published in French as *La question du Quebec* (Paris: Seghers, 1969) and translated into English by James Boake (Toronto: James Lorimer, 1971); Ramsay Cook, ed., *French-Canadian Nationalism: An Anthology* (Toronto: Macmillan of Canada, 1969), 14.
2. For an impressive bibliography of this research, see John Dickinson and Brian Young, *A Short History of Quebec*, 4th edn (Montreal and Kingston: McGill-Queen's University Press, 2008).
3. The best English-language survey is Dickinson and Young, *A Short History of Quebec.*
4. See Fernand Harvey 'Le développement des études québécoises dans le monde' *Globe. Revue internationale d'études québécoises* 4, 2 (2001): 59–81.
5. The international network of academics formed by the Association internationale des études québécoises numbers close to 3,000 researchers.
6. See David Cameron, *Taking Stock: Canadian Studies in the Nineties* (Montreal: Association for Canadian Studies, 1996) and Patrick James and Mark Kasoff, eds., *Canadian Studies in the New Millennium* (Toronto: University of Toronto Press, 2008).
7. In French a number of works, published with an international audience in mind, have been published that offer a multidisciplinary introduction to Quebec civilization. See François Tétu de Labsade, *Le Québec. Un pays, une culture*, 2nd edn (Montreal: Boréal, 2000); Marcel Rioux, *Les Québécois*, 2nd edn (Paris: Seuil, 1980); Jacques Bouchard, *Les 36 cordes sensibles des Québécois* (Quebec City: Les Éditions Heritage, 1978); Marie-Christine Weidmann Koop, ed., *Le Québec aujourd'hui : identité, culture et société.* (Saint-Foy: Les Presses de l'Université Laval, 2003) and the recent Robert Laliberté, ed., *À la rencontre d'un Québec qui bouge. Introduction générale au Québec.* (Paris: Comité des travaux historiques et scientifiques), 2009.
8. Alain-G. Gagnon, ed. *Québec State and Society*, 3rd edn (Peterborough: Broadview Press, 2004); and Guy Lachapelle, Gérald Bernier, Daniel Salée, and Luc Bernier, *The Québec Democracy: Structures, Processes & Policies.* (Toronto: McGraw-Hill Ryerson, 1993). See footnote 2 for Dickinson and Young.
9. Patrick James and Mark Kasoff, eds., *Canadian Studies in the New Millennium* (Toronto: University of Toronto Press, 2008); David Taras and Beverly Rasporich, eds., *A Passion for Identity: Canadian Studies in the 21st Century*, 4th edn (Scarborough: Nelson Thomson Learning, 2001); Kenneth Pryke and Walter Soderlund, eds., *Profiles of Canada* (Toronto: Canadian Scholars' Press, 2003); and David Thomas and Barbara Boyle Torrey, eds., *Canada and the United States: Differences that Count* (Peterborough: Broadview Press, 2008).
10. The colloquium expressly focused on the identification and evaluation of the current state of teaching, research, publishing, and program activities on Quebec Studies in the United States.
11. See Denise Lemieux, ed., *Traité de la culture* (Ste-Foy: Les Presses de l'Université Laval, 2002) and the Quebec Government website, Observatoire de la culture et des communications, www.stat.gouv.qc.ca/observatoire/default_an.htm to find research on these issues.

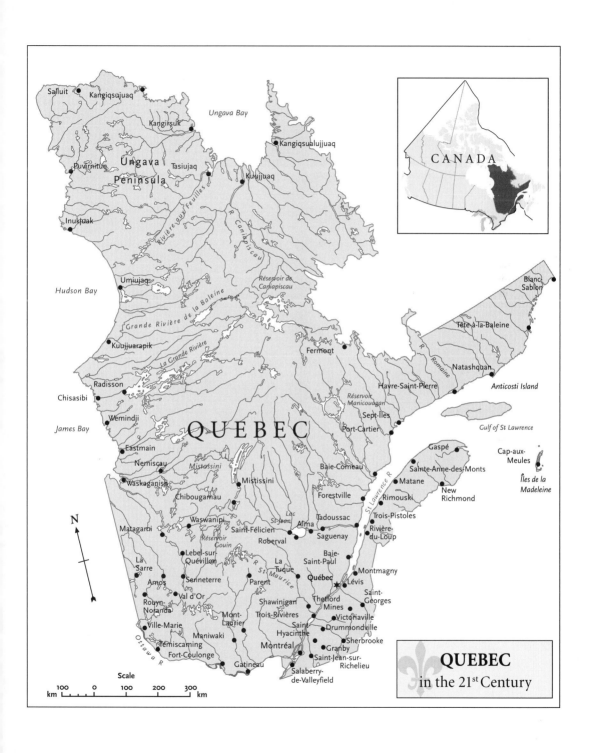

Salluit

Kangiqsujuaq

Ungava Bay

Kangirsuk

Kangiqsualujjuaq

Puvirnituq

Ungava Peninsula

Tasiujaq

Kuujjuaq

Inukjuak

Rivière aux Feuilles

R Caniapiscau

Réservoir de Caniapiscau

Umiujaq

Hudson Bay

Blanc-Sablon

Grande Rivière de la Baleine

Tête-à-la-Baleine

R

Romaine

Kuujjuarapik

Fermont

Natashquan

La Grande Rivière

Radisson

Havre-Saint-Pierre

Anticosti Island

Chisasibi

Réservoir Manicouagan

Wemindji

Sept-Îles

James Bay

QUEBEC

Port-Cartier

Gulf of St Lawrence

Eastmain

Gaspé

Cap-aux-Meules

Nemiscau

Mistassini

Baie-Comeau

Sainte-Anne-des-Monts

Waskaganish

Mistissini

Matane

Îles de la Madeleine

Chibougamau

Forestville

New Richmond

Rimouski

Lac St-Jean

Trois-Pistoles

Matagami

Waswanipi

Tadoussac

Saint-Félicien

Alma

St Lawrence R

Rivière-du-Loup

Réservoir Gouin

Roberval

Saguenay

N

Lebel-sur-Quévillon

Baie-Saint-Paul

La Sarre

La Tuque

Montmagny

St Maurice

Amos

Senneterre

Parent

Québec

Lévis

Rouyn-Noranda

Val d'Or

Saint-Georges

Shawinigan

Thetford Mines

Ville-Marie

Mont-Laurier

Trois-Rivières

Victoriaville

Témiscaming

Maniwaki

Saint-Hyacinthe

Drummondville

Fort-Coulonge

Montréal

Sherbrooke

Ottawa R

Granby

Gatineau

Saint-Jean-sur-Richelieu

Salaberry-de-Valleyfield

CANADA

Scale

100   0   100   200   300

km   km

QUEBEC
in the 21st Century

PART A
MEMORIES

INTRODUCTION

The past is particularly alive in Quebec. We see flashes of it in newspaper editorials, political speeches, debates about history curricula in schools, and even on Quebec license plates, which announce *Je me souviens*—'I remember'. But what is remembered? There is enormous debate about the past and 'collective memory'. How collective is memory? How can anyone really have a memory of events that occurred hundreds of years ago? How is collective memory produced? And what is the relationship between the production of historians and collective memory? Articles in this section implicitly and explicitly come up against these issues as they tell stories about Quebec's past.[1]

Some authors present new interpretations based on a shift in perspectives—in a sense challenging collective memory. This is what Brett Rushforth does in his chapter on New France. While technically this chapter goes beyond the temporal boundaries of this volume, today the memory of New France profoundly shapes many Quebecers' sense of themselves, making

questions about New France particularly important 'Quebec questions'. Rushforth presents a version of the history of New France that is innovative on at least two counts. First, he places European discovery of New France within a dynamic multi-national Atlantic world where ships crossed the ocean far more frequently than previously thought and France's colonial eye went far beyond the St Lawrence Valley. Second, he evokes the work of a growing number of historians who have shown that Native peoples, for their own reasons, played a decisive role in France's imperial venture in North America. When the fate of the colony rides on the military force of Native allies to the point that French laws did not apply to Natives and the Crown underwrote losses of French merchants to maintain positive economic relations with their Native allies, one has to think about the character of empire and how it was affected by local contexts. And, one might ask, how does seeing the Native and Atlantic contexts of New France relate to today's 'collective memory'?

The second article in this section is more explicit about the impact of public memory on social and political relations today. Donald Fyson shows that numerous views of the impact of British Conquest on *les Canadiens* are front and centre in political debates today. Yet he also shows that in this case the relationship between the past, as historians understand it, and collective memory, is tenuous at best. Professional historians no longer see the Conquest as a decapitation of the social structure of New France or as an event which brought enlightenment through the benevolence of the British crown. Instead, their assessments are far more ambivalent and nuanced, as Fyson's article shows through looking at key areas of Canadiens' activity in the economy and their interaction with the new colonial state. Few historians, however, have given renewed attention to the immediate post-Conquest period, and the decapitation thesis dominates popular understandings of the Conquest in Quebec, despite the important published studies, including Fyson's own.

Using the past to take political positions echoes in Brian Young's article on power relations in the period between the Lower Canadian Rebellions (1837–8) and Canadian Confederation (1867). Young finds uses of the past in numerous areas of power relations from francophone–anglophone relations, to the social relations of religion, to gender relations. In the realm of politics, the claim of Lord Durham (whose report to the British crown was supposed to explain and provide solutions to the problems that brought about the Rebellions) that French Canadians were a people without history still infuriates Quebecers today. In religion, it is hard to think of a more striking way of calling on the population to maintain Catholic tradition than through using the 'old bones' of Bishop Laval, as Archbishop Elzéar-Alexandre Taschereau did in 1878. And patriarchy can be reinforced by calling on women to live up to the example set by the Virgin Mary. Yet, Young's article demonstrates that memory is not the only way in which the past is active in today's political world. The past is part of our present through political structures, systems of land tenure, and the law. And ultimately power in Quebec, Young argues, is about more than the cultural clash of the national question—it is also about transforming class relations and gender inequalities—all of which are prominent in the transformations of this period.

Divergent views of Confederation have profoundly shaped politics in Quebec and Canada. In looking at how the federal government has attempted to 'accommodate' Quebec nationalism, Garth Stevenson's article highlights the historical development of different views of Canadian federalism, and the transformation of French-Canadian and Quebec nationalism since Confederation. The failures of successive federal governments' attempts to come to terms with Quebec nationalism have become part of Quebec nationalist collective memory. Indeed, though people can long argue about whether Quebec Premier René Lévesque would ever have signed Quebec on to a new Canadian Constitution or who was to blame for the failure of the Meech Lake Accord, the meaning of these events, much like the meaning of the British Conquest itself, has been transformed by larger political narratives, and their memories have overshadowed the details of the events themselves. What we remember is frequently more about who we are and what we want to be than the importance given to events by the actors of the past.

Notes

1. Notable studies on memory in Quebec include Jacques Mathieu, ed., *La mémoire dans la culture* (Saint-Foy: Les Presses de l'Université Laval, 1995); Patrice Groulx, *Pièges de la mémoire : Dollard des Ormeaux, les Amérindiens et nous* (Hull: Vents d'Ouest, 1998); and Colin Coates and Cecelia Morgan, *Heroines and History: Representations of Madeleine de Verchères and Laura Secord* (Toronto: University of Toronto Press, 2002). For a sociologist who asserts the importance of memory to the national project, see Jacques Beauchemin, *L'Histoire en trop: La mauvaise conscience des souverainistes québécois* (Montreal: VLB Éditeur, 2002), and for an opposing view see Jocelyn Létourneau, *A History for the Future: Rewriting Memory and Identity in Quebec*, trans. Phyllis Aronoff and Howards Scott (Montreal and Kingston: McGill-Queen's University Press, 2004).

CHAPTER 1

The Establishment of a French Empire in North America

Brett Rushforth, The College of William & Mary

— TIMELINE —

1440s–1480s Portuguese, French, and Italian explorations of eastern Atlantic.

1490s Columbus 'discovers' Americas; cod fishing begins near Newfoundland.

1504 French reach Brazil and begin dyewood trade.

1524 Giovanni da Verrazzano explores the North American coast for François I.

1534–42 Jacques Cartier explores St Lawrence Valley.

1555–65 Abortive French attempts to settle in Brazil and Florida.

1604 France establishes its first North American settlement at Port Royal.

1608 Champlain establishes Quebec.

1609–15 Champlain leads French–Native assaults against Iroquois.

1626–35 First French Caribbean colonies settled at St Christophe, Martinique, and Guadeloupe.

1629–32 Quebec taken over by British privateers and recovered by France.

1642 Jeanne Mance and Paul de Chomedey de Maisonneuve establish Montreal.

1649–66 Iroquois Wars—most Hurons killed, captured, or scattered.

1663 Royal takeover of New France and Caribbean colonies.

1670s–1680s French establish trade and mission posts in Great Lakes region and Mississippi Valley.

1689–1713 Imperial wars fought in North America; ending with Treaty of Utrecht.

1701 Great Peace of Montreal—treaty council confirming Iroquois neutrality.

1710s–1740s Mesquakie (Fox) and Chickasaw Wars; Native slave trade expands.

1751 The Marquis de la Galissonière argues for Canada's continued importance to France.

1752 French–Odawa raid on Pickawillany begins armed struggle for Ohio Valley.

1754–63 France, Britain, and Spain battle around the globe in Seven Years' War.

1755 France's native allies defeat General Braddock in Battle of the Monongahela.

1759 Battle of Plains of Abraham results in sur-render of Quebec.	**1763** Treaty of Paris confirms British control of Canada; French reclaim key Caribbean holdings.
1760 Montreal surrenders, completing British victory in North America.	

INTRODUCTION

As part of a complex and competitive North American continent, Quebec is connected to Europe, Africa, the Caribbean, and Latin America by commerce, migration, cultural exchange, and shared environmental challenges. Far from new, these connections date to the first decades of exploration and settlement that created a French presence in North America. French settlers came to Quebec not to create an independent French outpost, but to establish one of many links in a trans-Atlantic network of settlements tied to an expanding global economy. Tracing these complex and cosmopolitan beginnings will help us to understand Quebec's place in the global twenty-first century. But we must also remember the importance of Quebec's Native peoples to its history. Native peoples were both the lifeblood of New France's economy and the heart of its military defence, giving essential protection that allowed the colony to survive a century of colonial wars. Without their willing trade and military alliance there could have been no French presence in North America, and there would be no Quebec today. The households of Montreal and Quebec were also served by thousands of Native slaves, whose domestic and commercial labour subsidized the merchant community and propped up the status of town elites. Whether through labour, trade, diplomacy, or warfare, then, Native peoples helped lay the foundations of Quebec society. From the first voyages of exploration in the 1530s to the imperial warfare that gave Britain control of the region in 1763, Quebec was intimately tied to developments throughout Native North America and the Atlantic world.

ENCOUNTERS AND DISCOVERIES

The earliest French activities in the Atlantic, like the colonialism that would follow, were part of a wider pattern of European expansion involving collaboration of investors, mariners, cartographers, and monarchs in most of Western Europe. French efforts to profit from New World discoveries, motivated by international competition, paradoxically relied on international connections for their success. In the fifteenth and sixteenth centuries it was difficult to disentangle the activities of one kingdom from those of another, not least because most Atlantic activity was private rather than state sponsored. Nearly a century before Columbus crossed the Atlantic, French mariners worked with Iberian partners to explore the eastern Atlantic, the first step in an incremental expansion that resulted in American discovery. In 1402, for example, a Norman captain, Jean de Béthencourt, worked alongside Portuguese mariners to map and conquer the Canary Islands, rich in dyes, fish, and enslavable labour. Rather than claiming the islands for the king of France, Béthencourt established his own fiefdom there, drawing heavy taxes from European settlers and merchants who profited from his conquest. Successes such as this inspired investors to take incremental risks, little by little venturing further into the Atlantic in search of new places and peoples. From the 1430s through the 1480s, Portuguese investors—famously including Prince Henry, 'the Navigator'—sponsored the lion's share of these voyages, but French sailors and ships continued to play an important role even in ventures thought to be Portuguese or Spanish. Trading gold, bullock hides, ivory, and slaves between northwestern Africa and Europe, these voyages brought handsome returns to investors seeking Atlantic fortunes. Only by building on these more proximate successes could Christopher Columbus set a bolder course across the Atlantic. Columbus's accidental 'discovery' of the

Americas in 1492, followed by the more northerly explorations of John Cabot in 1497, set off a flurry of activity that shifted many French ships from African to trans-Atlantic trade.

News of Columbus's discovery spread rapidly in France, especially in port cities already linked to Iberian maritime activities. These connections immediately and extensively involved the French in New World commerce. Within a decade of Columbus's return to Europe, dozens of French ships—often with multinational crews—had sailed for the Americas. Extracting rich dyewoods from Brazilian forests, mostly with indigenous labour, French investors established a foothold in South America no later than 1504, alternately co-operating and competing with the Portuguese, who claimed Brazil as their exclusive territory. Norman craftsmen—such as the famous cloth makers of Rouen—used these new dyes to create highly desirable fabrics, in demand by mid-century throughout Europe, Africa, and the Americas.

Although far less glamorous than Spanish gold or silver, the most profitable New World commodity in the first half of the sixteenth century was cod, which teemed in vast quantities off the coasts of Newfoundland. Often imagined as an English enterprise controlled by Bristol merchants, French ships actually dominated the industry in the sixteenth century, outnumbering English vessels at least three to one. After mid-century as many as 500 French ships sailed annually for the fisheries, returning with millions of pounds of dried fish that stocked French larders and stimulated the production of French merchandise. As in Brazil, Newfoundland fishing crews rarely had a single national identity: Basques, Italians, Portuguese, Azoreans, Normans, and Englishmen sailed, worked, lived, and died together.

The Spanish discovery of gold on the island of Hispaniola, and their subsequent conquest of the Aztec and Incan empires brought fame and wealth to conquistador and crown alike, overshadowing earlier French activities and inspiring new ones. Envious of Spain's success—and fearful of the power a rival kingdom could derive from American wealth—the French crown began to take an interest in the Americas, which had until the 1520s been largely left to private initiative. Only two years after learning of Spain's 1521 conquest of the gold-rich Aztec capital of Tenochtitlan, King François I commissioned an Italian mariner, Giovanni da Verrazzano, to explore the coast of North America. Hoping to find either a passage through the Americas to Asia or another wealthy Native empire, Verrazzano found neither. Returning with a fairly detailed map of the North American coast and a description of coastal Native peoples, Verrazzano's voyage was only a limited success. A decade later, in 1534, Jacques Cartier obtained a similar commission, charged first with finding a passage to Asia and second, with finding sources of wealth along the way. Cartier had much experience in American navigation. He had personally shipped fish from Newfoundland and dyewoods from Brazil, and he had good relationships with Basque, Spanish, Portuguese, and English sailors who had frequented the mouth of the Bay of St Lawrence since the 1490s. Cartier even kept a Brazilian Native girl at his home in St Malo whom he had bought or kidnapped on an earlier dyewood expedition.

Cartier's international experience qualified him to sail Atlantic waters and explore the lands west of Newfoundland, but he was ill-prepared for the complex cultural currents he would navigate through the indigenous world he encountered in North America. Like Europeans, Natives had their own political, military, and cultural structures that would shape French colonialism as much as those of the Europeans. Cartier established a pattern of French–Native relations that would characterize the history of New France for more than two centuries. He first ignored Native peoples, then attempted to dominate them by force. Realizing that neither of these approaches could yield the results he needed, he settled on a policy of grudging cooperation that allowed Natives as much as the French to dictate the terms of their relationship.

Cartier and his contemporaries were initially quite dismissive of Native culture and accomplishments, calling Labrador 'the land God gave to Cain', and its indigenous inhabitants 'the sorriest folk . . . in the world'.[1] Seeking passage through—rather than to—America, Cartier pried for geographical information about the hoped-for water route across the continent to the Pacific. When such information failed to materialize, he moved on. Frustrated by his inability to find a passage to Asia, Cartier turned to violence. Stopping to glean information from the people of Stadacona, near modern-day Quebec City, Cartier found them eager to trade. He was not interested. After a brief, tense exchange with their chief, Donnacona, Cartier seized the chief and his sons, threatening to kill anyone who tried to free them. Releasing the father, Cartier returned to France with the sons as proof of his explorations and as possible sources of information and leverage. But Cartier's original commission could not be achieved by random acts of violence, so he returned with his captives to the St Lawrence a year later, hoping that he could persuade their father to help him in exchange for their release. Naturally wary of the treacherous foreigners, Donnacona nevertheless accepted his sons' return and provided more information to Cartier. Heading farther up the St Lawrence, Cartier encountered the village of Hochelaga, on the island of modern Montreal, where he found a thriving village surrounded by vast corn fields. At Hochelaga, Cartier portrayed himself as the Natives' saviour ('one would have thought Christ had come down to earth to heal them'),[2] but in reality Natives often saved him and his crew from disaster, providing them with food, essential geographical information, and especially a life-saving herbal remedy for a scurvy outbreak that nearly killed all of Cartier's men.

French reaction to Cartier's discoveries was mixed, but by 1541 the French crown sponsored a scheme to settle the St Lawrence Valley. Led by Cartier and his newly appointed superior, Jean-François de la Rocque de Roberval, the first French settlement in the St Lawrence was a short-lived failure. As they entered the Bay of St Lawrence they passed 13 ships: five Spanish, seven Portuguese, and one English. Cartier may have asserted exclusive right to the bay and the lands along the river that flowed into it, but his crew and the others he encountered there reflected the multinational nature of early Quebec exploration. Finding no diamonds, gold, or spices, the colony had to rely on trade with their Native neighbours, who were reluctant to welcome this settlement by people who had bullied and enslaved their kin. Within two years the enterprise folded and its few survivors returned to France. In the absence of precious minerals or easy routes to Asia, Cartier's successors instead tapped into the indigenous world of trade, providing France with valuable furs and skins that were in high demand in over-hunted Europe. Rather than dismissing or dominating Native peoples, the French could succeed only if they adapted to indigenous demands. Algonquians and Iroquoians would therefore play a prominent role in establishing permanent French settlement. Although it ended in short-term failure, what began as a mission to bypass North America sowed the seeds of French colonization that would grow in the seventeenth century.

In the second half of the sixteenth century French attention returned to the Newfoundland fisheries and Brazilian forests. In 1555, a French settlement near Rio de Janeiro on Brazil's Atlantic coast lasted only a few years before Portuguese competitors overcame a colony internally divided by religious conflict. Refugees from the Brazil experiment tried again in Florida, establishing two settlements to challenge the Spanish claim to North America's eastern seaboard. In 1565 the Spanish brutally crushed their French rivals in a one-sided campaign that left France with no permanent settlements in the Americas at the very time that Iberian New World expansion was reaching full stride. Spain found vast wealth in gold and especially silver, while Portugal's Brazilian settlers expanded the dyewood trade and built massive sugar plantations worked by both Native and African slaves. French involvement in the Americas continued for the final third of the sixteenth century in many uncoordinated but significant private ventures intent on extracting American resources. French port cities developed thriving industries associated with the New World, despite the absence of official or permanent French settlements there. These commercial connections, together with the geographical and nautical knowledge that made overseas commerce possible, created networks that would prove essential to France's seventeenth-century expansion throughout the Atlantic world.

CREATING NEW SOCIETIES

At the beginning of the seventeenth century, France—like England—took renewed interest in

North America as a land of vast resources and a strategic site to harass their Spanish rivals. Unable to gain a foothold in Florida or other southern locations, France built on its longstanding presence in the St Lawrence Valley, exploring and eventually settling there at the same time the English were establishing their first permanent North American colony at Jamestown in Virginia. Both projects drew inspiration from the work of Richard Hakluyt, an English promoter of American colonization who spent significant time in France. American settlements, he wrote in the late sixteenth century, 'will yelde unto us all the commodities of Europe, Affrica, and Asia, as farr as wee were wonte to travel, and supply the wants of all our decayed trades'. Significantly, it would also 'be a great bridle to the Indies of the Kinge of Spaine'.[3] Hakluyt's time in France had convinced many that for all their differences, the two kingdoms shared these goals: grasping overseas riches and reining in their Spanish competitor.

The most important architect of France's seventeenth-century colonization in North America was Samuel de Champlain, a skilled cartographer whose account of a 1603 visit to Canada sparked a passion for exploring and settling the region. Characteristic of France's New World projects, Champlain's first interest in the Americas centred on the tropics, and his first voyage to the New World took him to the Caribbean and Mexico rather than to Canada. Acting in part the curious scholar and in part an unofficial spy against Spain, Champlain gleaned both experience and knowledge that laid the groundwork for his Canadian endeavours. Many other Frenchmen trolled Caribbean waters at the beginning of the seventeenth century, most of whom were pirates harassing Spanish ships sailing from Mexico and Panama. The island of Hispaniola (later to become Haiti and the Dominican Republic) was home to perhaps hundreds of French, English, and Dutch pirates, a population that would grow into a powerful force by the later seventeenth century.

Champlain's Caribbean voyage signalled the centrality of Spanish competition in French colonial beginnings, and his vision for Canada retained much of that character. Between 1603 and 1607 Champlain traveled three times to the St Lawrence Valley, gathering important information about the lands and peoples of the region and circulating his findings in accounts and maps, both published and unpublished. Champlain improved upon the sixteenth-century charts from Cartier's time, and he mapped islands and coastlines in modern Quebec and New England. But perhaps his most startling reports detailed a remarkable demographic shift over the past half century. Although the French presence in the St Lawrence Valley during the 1500s was limited and generally seasonal, it had profoundly affected the region's Native peoples. Between Cartier's departure in the 1540s and Champlain's arrival in the early 1600s the Iroquoian people of Stadacona, Hochelaga, and other riverside villages had all but disappeared. Although little evidence survives to tell us why, the most likely explanation is a combination of disease brought by the Europeans and warfare sparked by competition for lucrative trade downriver. Whatever the cause, this depopulation opened opportunities for other Native peoples—the Montagnais, Algonkin, and Huron—to engage in French trade and to seek French alliances. During the 1580s and 1590s, as these groups solidified their trade relationship with the French, they also formed military partnerships. In the indigenous cultures of the northeastern woodlands, trade and alliance were inseparable. The friendship and trust that facilitated the exchange of goods also obliged mutual military protection in the face of common enemies. By 1600, French traders had established agreements with Montagnais, Algonkin, and Huron traders that, in exchange for furs, the French would give not only trade goods but also military assistance against their most feared enemies: the Iroquois nations south of the St Lawrence in modern New York. Drawn by trade, French adventurers were thus drawn into Native geopolitics. Indigenous commerce and alliance would dominate the colonial world of the seventeenth century.

In 1608, Champlain established a permanent settlement at Quebec from which he could trade with Native peoples and search for a passage to Asia. His original plans were fantastic, promising the French king massive revenue from a wide range of sources. In addition to millions of *livres* from eels, sturgeon, salmon, cow hides, and timber, the most dramatic revenue would come from levying customs duties on ships that sailed the St Lawrence to and from China, 'which would surpass in value at least ten times all those levied in France, inasmuch as all the merchants of Christendom would pass through the passage'.[4] The colony would also serve as an outpost in a great commercial war being waged by English and Flemish merchants, whose North American presence threatened to shut down France's very real profits from the cod and whale industries.

As for the country's Native peoples, Champlain's proposals ranged from paternalistic toleration of his Algonquian and Huron allies to unrestrained violence against his Iroquois enemies—a strategic rather than a moral distinction, as he believed that they all lived 'like brute beasts' more than men, and that they were 'given to revenge, and are great liars'.[5] Attacking the Iroquois in 1609, 1610, and 1615, Champlain introduced a newly destructive form of warfare to a conflict that had remained in relative equilibrium throughout the known past. French, and then Dutch, guns and metal weapons rendered warfare more deadly and started the first American arms race.

As the decades wore on, Champlain found neither a passage to China nor vast wealth in eels, leaving him by the late 1620s in charge of a faltering settlement inhabited by fewer than 80 French colonists. Recognizing the settlement's weakness, and asserting older English claims to the St Lawrence based on their presence at the fisheries, a group of privateers took over Quebec in 1629 as Champlain surrendered without a fight. After three years of negotiations, France regained control of the settlement in 1632 with a mere 43 inhabitants. Bolstered by Champlain's arrival with supplies and settlers the following year, Quebec was still only a small collection of scattered buildings and just over a hundred French settlers when Champlain died there in 1635.

The fur trade provided an economic base for French expansion, growing steadily over the next generation. At the heart of the fur trade, of course, were the Huron, Montagnais, Algonkin, and other Native peoples who supplied the furs in exchange for European manufactured goods. Building on patterns of trade established in the 1500s, these peoples brought thousands of beaver pelts, and many other

animal skins, to Quebec every year. The European goods they desired fit well within their own value systems, with the highest demand for practical items like wool cloth, metal cutting edges, and metal tips for arrows used for hunting as much as for war. But there was no denying the wartime advantage of iron weapons and guns, both of which remained in high demand in the face of Iroquois aggression.

Although undertaken for commercial profit, the colony at Quebec also had a religious purpose, supporters of which helped to fund the colony when commerce fell short. Although the Jesuits receive the most attention, many of the most influential religious figures in early New France were women. Two influential women arrived shortly after Champlain's death. The first, Marie Guyart (better known as Marie de l'Incarnation), arrived in 1639 following mystical visions of bringing Native children to Christ. She established a boarding school for French and Native girls, organized public relief efforts, and interacted intensively with her Native students' families. She learned to speak Algonquian and Iroquoian dialects, and anticipated later Jesuit efforts by translating religious materials into both languages. Jeanne Mance, also moved by dreams of heavenly glory, arrived in New France in 1641 and helped to found Montreal (then called Ville-Marie) in 1642. Quebec's community of women, though small, stood at the heart of the colony's social and political world and left some of the best surviving descriptions of this period. Until the late 1600s French men would far outnumber French women in Canada, but this small and powerful cadre of women leaders were among the colony's most important founders. Between Marie de l'Incarnation's arrival and her death more than 30 years later, she and her Ursuline colleagues contributed to the colony's development at least as much as Champlain.

These women considered converting the Natives a genuinely sacred mission; others took a more secular approach, using Christianization as a means to a commercial end. For both reasons Quebec's administrators required Native people involved in French trade to host missionaries in their villages, and by the mid-1630s Jesuit priests were preaching Christianity to Algonquian and Huron villages some distance from Quebec. Living in a land controlled in every way by their Native hosts, Jesuits had no choice but to adapt. As one Jesuit wrote, 'a missionary does not fear to make himself a savage, so to speak, with them, in order to make them Christians'.[6] Living in Native villages, Jesuits witnessed firsthand the destruction wrought by European diseases like smallpox and influenza, which claimed thousands of lives across the St Lawrence and Great Lakes regions. Weakened by disease, the Hurons were ill-prepared to face an Iroquois threat that had been fuelled by French violence and rendered more deadly by Dutch weaponry. In the late 1640s, Iroquois warriors spread out across the Great Lakes region to attack their enemies, striking with special force against their Huron antagonists. Village after village fell under the onslaught, scattering survivors in all directions. They then turned to the Hurons' French allies, nearly destroying the tiny village of Trois-Rivières and threatening the survival of the whole colony. Although under threat themselves, Algonkins, Montagnais, and surviving Hurons fought alongside French militia to protect their fledgling settlements. But for their support, the French would most likely have been destroyed or forced to leave. As they had many times in the past, Native peoples proved essential to the colony's survival.

Yet within the larger world of French overseas expansion, the St Lawrence colony remained marginal at best. As Jesuits and a handful of fur traders struggled to survive in North America, costing most investors more than they earned, French investments in the Caribbean began to pay stunning dividends. With permanent settlements founded on St Christophe in 1626 and Martinique and Guadeloupe in 1635, French settlement in the Caribbean quickly outpaced and overshadowed activities in Canada. French settlement on these tiny islands more than doubled that of New France, and when slaves are included the ratio rises to four to one. But it was economic output that gave the Caribbean such an edge, with tobacco profits supplemented after the 1650s with rapidly growing revenues from sugar. Importing Native slaves from South America and African slaves through Dutch merchants, France's Caribbean colonies became intimately linked to Africa, which had its first French settlement in 1638 at the mouth of the Senegal River. This would grow into France's most important African colony, supplying slaves, animal hides, gums, ivory, and a little gold throughout the eighteenth century. By 1660, France had growing colonies in Senegal, Martinique, Guadeloupe, St Christopher, Guiana, St Domingue, and Canada.

FACING EAST, FACING WEST

Between 1660 and 1740, Canada grew more important to France and its expanding imperial ambitions. Despite a low population and an unstable economy, because it controlled access to the most strategic waterways in North America—the St Lawrence and Mississippi rivers and the Great Lakes—New France could play a significant role in the geopolitics of empire. This role required the colony to develop along two different but complementary paths. Facing east toward the Atlantic, the colonial capital at Quebec became the key centre for French administration and the point of exchange for most French merchant ships coming from Europe or the Caribbean. Facing west toward the vast North American continent, Montreal became the primary site of trade and diplomacy with Native peoples. Exclusive suppliers of the colony's only profitable export—beaver pelts—Native nations also served as the colony's most important military defence against European rivals. The Atlantic and indigenous orientations of Quebec and Montreal worked in tandem to provide profits to France and allies to a strategic, but always vulnerable, colony.

In 1660 Canada's French population had not yet reached 3,000, dwarfed by the nearly 70,000 settlers in the English colonies just to the south. The colony's fur trade brought a few individuals great wealth but failed to provide significant returns to either the investment companies that controlled the colony or the French kingdom itself. A nearly constant state of war with the Iroquois threatened the colony's total ruin. Success elsewhere in the Atlantic world—in the French Caribbean as well as in Spanish, English, and Portuguese colonies—caught the attention of Louis XIV and his finance minister Jean-Baptiste Colbert, prompting a plan to reinvigorate the French colonies and to channel their profits away from private individuals and toward the state. After assuming personal rule of France in 1661, as part of a larger restructuring of France itself, the king and his minister took direct control of France's overseas colonies from the private companies that had governed them since their inception. They appointed royal governors and *intendants* (civilian governors responsible for law and finance) to represent the king in the colonies, and a 'sovereign' or 'superior' council of local elites that answered to the *intendant*. Overturning an already successful Caribbean model, the crown met great resistance to its intrusion there, but faltering Canada largely welcomed the move, receiving its first royal governor and seating its first superior council in 1663.

Colonists hoped that royal support could finally secure them from the Iroquois threat. As Canadian Pierre Boucher told Louis XIV during a 1662 visit to Paris, 'we have an enemy who keeps us pent up in a little corner and prevents us from going about and making discoveries; and so he will have to be destroyed'.[7] Over the next five years, Iroquois raids hit the French and their Native trading partners dozens of times, striking fear into colonists and interrupting the fur trade. Royal control of the colony brought with it the promise of French military support, which came slowly but surely. By 1666, two massive parties of French soldiers overwhelmed the easternmost Iroquois villages, destroying several Mohawk towns and impressing on the others the colony's increased power. Facing raids from French allies to the west and New England Natives to the east, the Iroquois agreed to a peace that lasted nearly 20 years.

Having provided a measure of security, the French crown also began subsidizing migration to Canada by paying for the trans-Atlantic passage of workers, a few families, and a large group of single women. Within three years New France's population doubled, but in the long term as many as two-thirds of new migrants to Canada returned to France or headed for the warmer and more prosperous Caribbean. In France itself, potential migrants had many other options than North America: they could join the king's ballooning army, or simply head south to Spain, paths taken by about half a million people in the seventeenth and eighteenth centuries. In contrast, a mere 10,000 colonists stayed permanently in Canada during the same two centuries. The colony's population reached 15,000 in 1700, but even with very high natural growth there was no chance of catching the English colonies, which the same year boasted more than 235,000 settlers and 30,000 slaves.

Nearly all French colonists lived in a narrow band of settlement described by an eighteenth-century visitor as 'one continued village' stretching along the St Lawrence from Montreal to the settlement of Quebec (and a little beyond). At its east end, about 280 kilometres from Montreal, Quebec was the colonial capital and the centre of trans-Atlantic commercial and political activity. Home to about 2,000 people in 1700, Quebec grew to about 5,000 by the 1740s. With the highest proportion of French-born residents anywhere in the colony, and with a powerful merchant class tied to French port cities, Quebec was a thoroughly Atlantic town, oriented eastward toward France and the wider Atlantic world. Headquarters of the governor, *intendant*, and a superior council that served as both legislative body and appeals court, Quebec housed the colony's most influential families. Quebec's governors, *intendants*, bishops, and Atlantic merchants all moved readily between what were often temporary posts in Canada and those in the Caribbean or France. Situated where the St Lawrence narrows from a wide bay to a river, Quebec became the logical point to exchange French goods arriving on ocean-going vessels for North American commodities brought from Montreal and the West. To attract European goods and to find buyers for American furs and skins, the town's major merchants drew on trans-Atlantic family networks that linked ports in northern and western France with those in Canada, West Africa, and the Caribbean. Although France's Atlantic colonies developed along distinct economic and social lines, familial and commercial ties wove a complex web of connection among them.

At the west end of the 'continuous village' sat Montreal, the name of both a compact colonial town and the much larger island on which it was built. By the 1660s the town became the centre of the colony's fur trade. Initially this meant that Native traders brought their skins and furs to Montreal, but after the Iroquois scattered France's nearest allies, French traders ventured westward to meet the Natives in their own villages. From the 1660s to 1680s, French traders and missionaries established trading posts and missions near Native settlements throughout the western Great Lakes and upper Mississippi Valley. The Natives' culture of linking trade and diplomacy, which had drawn the French into war with the Iroquois, worked in France's favour in this case, making military allies of indigenous trading partners eager for European goods. By 1680, a powerful network of alliances had developed with key nodes of trade in modern Ontario, Michigan, Wisconsin, Illinois, and Indiana. These alliances demanded mutual cultural accommodation and innovation by both Natives and French. Native women married French men, creating exclusive, kin-based claims to French trade, a practice that helped the French gain support for their diplomatic agendas as well. Western posts were linked to the colony through Montreal, which remained the nerve centre of Native trade and diplomacy, if not always its geographic centre. Most fur-trade voyages were outfitted on the island with trade goods from the town's warehouses, which swelled with furs and the goods used to procure them. Most traders and contracted servants came from the parishes on and around the island; thus over time a significant proportion of the area's men had personal experience with Native trade, diplomacy, and sometimes warfare. Rather than a simple exchange of guns and alcohol for beaver pelts, by the early 1700s Native trade had matured and diversified. The most common exchange by far was of European cloth for the hides and furs of moose, deer, and other animals, rather than beaver pelts.

Although colonial officials were pressured by their superiors to draw back from the West to the more defensible St Lawrence, Native allies made it clear that they would no longer travel all the way to Montreal for trade. They expected the French to come to them. To meet this request, and to prevent the English from taking their place in western trade, French officials established Detroit in 1701. Southern complements were founded along the Gulf of Mexico at Biloxi in 1699 and Mobile in 1702, from which the French built a southern alliance along much the same lines as in the Great Lakes. New Orleans would follow in 1718 and together they formed the separate but theoretically subordinate colony of Louisiana. With a longer growing season and excellent Mississippi delta soils, the site promised agricultural products as well as Native trade.

Despite the growth of trade, Canada still cost the French crown more than it earned from taxes, rents, and other revenues. Wanting to avoid the expense of a large standing army, French officials began to subsidize the fur trade so the colony could benefit from the alliances that came with it. The strategy paid off during two successive imperial wars between France and England from 1689 to 1713. Vastly outnumbered by their English enemies, the French survived the wars only because allies came to their assistance in large numbers. Seeing the war as an opportunity to weaken their own enemies, especially the Iroquois, Natives joined the French in campaigns that struck English colonial towns and Iroquois villages along the New York and Maine frontiers. By 1696 the Iroquois agreed to make peace with New France and its Native allies and to remain neutral in future wars between France and England. The agreement was formalized at a massive conference that convened at Montreal in 1701. With over a thousand representatives from 38 Native nations, the negotiations enacted on a grand scale what had been occurring in Native villages all around the Great Lakes. French and Native customs merged, and innovative hybrids arose to bridge the divides among the many cultures present. Iroquois neutrality was neither complete nor perfect, but it proved important to New France's ability to battle the English to an inconclusive draw in 1713.

The following period of relative calm witnessed the colony's most sustained growth and stability, lasting through the mid-1750s. During these years the colony grew to about 70,000 inhabitants (but fell much farther behind the British, who by midcentury had nearly 1.5 million colonists in North America). Sometimes called 'the long peace' due to the absence of European wars, this was still a time of almost constant violence on New France's western frontier. A series of wars with the Mesquakie (or Fox) and Chickasaw nations kept French soldiers and Native allies engaged in war for most of these years. French households also began buying Native slaves, who performed domestic and other menial tasks. French demand for slaves complicated and often undermined the colony's diplomatic agenda in the West, even as it gave Native allies an opportunity to weaken their own indigenous enemies by selling them to the French. The slave population in Montreal

PHILIPPE DE RIGAUD DE VAUDREUIL[8]

Louis-Philippe, eldest son of Philippe de Rigaud de Vaudreuil, Governor General of New France. Louis-Philippe distinguished himself commanding warships in the Marine royale française. The portrait does not show the subject wearing the characteristic white cross of the Order of Saint-Louis, which means it probably predates 1721, when he was made a member.

Source: Bibliothèque et Archives Canada, no d'acc 1989-518-15
Droit d'auteur: Expired / Périmé

Philippe de Rigaud de Vaudreuil (*c.*1643–1725) was governor of New France from 1704 until his death in 1725. He was, according to his biographer, an 'unspectacular' administrator with very limited education: he could not spell, his grammar was atrocious, and he owned only five books. But by mastering the indigenous and international worlds of New France he became a remarkably effective leader, successfully guiding the colony through a major war while expanding a Native alliance that would secure Canada for decades to come.

Born into a noble family from southern France, Vaudreuil gained distinction in European warfare as a member of Louis XIV's musketeers. In 1687, Vaudreuil translated his European experience into a post as commander of France's Canadian troops, a position that offered more upward mobility than he could hope for in Europe. When war with the Iroquois merged with the Nine Years' War in 1689, Vaudreuil's eventual success against a longstanding Iroquois enemy brought him prestige and earned him an appointment as governor of Montreal. In

1701, when western Native allies and the Iroquois met in Montreal to negotiate a truce and to guarantee Iroquois neutrality in imperial wars, Vaudreuil participated and as governor facilitated many of the local arrangements that made the conference a success. Because of his extensive military experience and his knowledge of Native diplomacy he was appointed governor of New France in 1704.

Vaudreuil's political enemies accused him of operating an illegal fur and alcohol trading business, and of allowing widespread smuggling between Montreal and the English colony at Albany. The charges were likely true, but they illustrate the degree to which France's international objectives in Canada depended on maintaining good relations with Native peoples. French demand for furs was at an all-time low when Vaudreuil took office, threatening to undermine the diplomatic alliances that were linked to the fur trade. By bypassing normal channels, Vaudreuil was able to give Natives both a better price for their furs and alcohol, legally forbidden to them. By allowing French merchants to sell their furs to the English, Vaudreuil kept Natives coming to Montreal instead of Albany, securing for New France the alliances that allowed it to survive the War of the Spanish Succession intact. Although he was frequently criticized, his strategy of working outside the law to facilitate Native alliances proved successful. During his governorship the French population of the colony almost doubled, from 16,000 to 30,000, and the colony entered its most sustained period of growth and stability. Vaudreuil's success brought prestige and opportunity to his family as they spanned the Atlantic in the French army and navy, and in the colonial administration of Louisiana, St Domingue, and New France. His son, Pierre, governed Louisiana in the 1740s and then, in 1755, became governor of New France at the outbreak of the Seven Years' War (see Snapshot box).

and Quebec never approached the numbers found in the Caribbean, but several thousand slaves lived in the colony in the eighteenth century.

Despite the westward drift of trade and diplomacy, visitors to Montreal would have encountered hundreds, and at certain times of the year thousands, of

Natives. Several Native villages, often called 'missions' because they had a priest and a small chapel, dotted the island and the shores on either side of the St Lawrence. More than 2,000—and at times as many as 3,000—Natives lived in permanent settlements on and around Montreal, a number that in some years approached one-third of the island's French population. Natives from elsewhere in the St Lawrence and many from northern and western regions came annually to the town to meet with traders and conduct business. The governor and *intendant* would spend several weeks each summer in Montreal meeting with visiting Native delegations. The combined effect of these three types of Native presence—slaves, local residents, and periodic visitors—profoundly influenced Montreal. Someone passing through the merchant district in the 1740s would have found a Native slave in nearly half the households, Native boarders in several others, Native day labourers loading and unloading goods in merchants' warehouses, and Native hawkers selling meat and produce at the market square. Among them would have been a few dozen English captives, seized in raids on New England and New York, many of whom had adopted Catholicism and married into French families, and even a handful of enslaved Africans. It is impossible to gauge the numbers of these people, who were not counted in French censuses, but it is reasonable to estimate a summer non-French presence about equal to the French who permanently lived in the town.

Quebec and Montreal may have been the most important nodes of economic and political life in New France, but most French Canadians lived in rural villages along the St Lawrence. From a relatively small foundation this rural population grew quickly through large families with survival and life-expectancy rates as high as any pre-industrial society could hope for. With abundant land available even to relatively poor inhabitants, most families farmed their own land and lived free of the harsher demands of seigneurial life in rural France. Most of these people experienced the international aspects of New France only indirectly, when they bought French soap or drank brandy or rum. They would have seen Native people more often than French merchant ships or Caribbean plantations, but they likely did not understand how intricately their lives were bound to people they called *les sauvages*.

Thus for 150 years New France prospered by embracing its international and indigenous contexts, becoming a strategic node in a trans-national web of empire that linked Europe, Africa, and the Americas long before anyone coined the term 'globalization'.

SNAPSHOT

The Seven Years' War

Between 1689 and 1763, New France fought four major imperial wars that began in Europe but drew in competing colonies in the Americas. In the Nine Years' War (1689–97), a coalition of European nations joined to resist the expanding power of the French Louis XIV. In the War of the Spanish Succession (1702–13) the same coalition—minus Spain—fought to keep Louis XIV from making his grandson the king of Spain and thereby threatening all of Europe with the combined forces of France and Spain. In the War of the Austrian Succession (1744–48) France and Prussia fought England and the Netherlands over who would become the monarch of Austria. In the misnamed Seven Years' War (1754–63), France, England, and Spain squared off in a global contest that merged European territorial battles with a fight for overseas power in North and South America, India, and the Pacific Rim. The end of this war brought the end of French colonial rule in New France, as the colony was ceded to Britain in the 1763 Peace of Paris.

In all of these wars, New France was called upon to attack England's interests in North America, raiding English settlements with Native allies and defending their own frontiers with local militia supplemented by a small number of French troops. In every case, the European treaties concluding these wars exchanged some colonial territories among European kingdoms, but left others untouched. At the end of the War of the Spanish Succession, for example, Louis XIV yielded Acadia to Britain but made his grandson king of Spain. After the War of the Austrian Succession, Britain returned the captured fortress of Louisbourg to France in exchange for a French-controlled settlement in India. At the end of the Seven Years' War, France yielded Canada to Britain so it could recover the Caribbean islands of Guadeloupe and Martinique. In this respect, the end of French control in Canada was similar to many earlier bargains struck by European kingdoms. New France had finally lost the imperial game that had sustained its place in the French kingdom despite its drain on French finances. But in another respect the Seven Years' War was different. Although it became a global war—with fighting in the Americas, Europe, India, and the Philippines—it began in North America.

Even after New France's impressive performance during the first half of the eighteenth century, many compared the colony to France's Caribbean and African interests and found it wanting. In 1751 Canada's governor, the Marquis de La Galissonière, acknowledged the central imperial concern: 'it cannot be denied that this colony has always been an expense to France, and that there is every appearance that it will long remain on the same footing.' Colonies were supposed to make money for the mother country, but from the beginning the French crown had lost more than it invested. Yet the governor reminded his superiors in France that preserving Canada was worth the cost, urging the king 'to omit no means, and to spare no expense, to assure the preservation of Canada, since only through it can America be enslaved to English ambition; and the progress of their empire in that part of the world is what is most likely to give them the upper hand in Europe'. By restricting the British colonies to the Atlantic seaboard, New France could keep them from the continent's vast resources and prevent their eventual expansion into Mexico, both essential to check British wealth and power.

According to the governor, the key to containing England's control of North America was the Ohio River Valley, which linked France's colonies in Canada and Louisiana and provided a barrier to English expansion. France and England both claimed the territory and had conducted trade there throughout the eighteenth century, but it remained under the control of independent Native 'republics', as the French derisively called them. Native villages along the Ohio, strategically placed to allow trade with both English and French colonies, drew suspicion as well as goods. One village in particular, called Pickawillany, began as a Miami settlement but quickly drew in a wide range of Natives with uncertain British and French allegiances. Growing in only one year from a small homogenous village into a large town with over 400 families, Pickawillany struck fear into the French for its potential to draw English influence into the Ohio Valley. Because trade and military alliance were so closely tied, France feared losing not only profits from the trade but their entire means of colonial defence. They responded with decisive force. Leading a group of Odawa, Métis, and French warriors, the Métis military commander Charles-Michel Mouet de Langlade crushed the town when many of its men were away hunting.

If Native trade in the Ohio Valley frightened the French, an armed attack there sounded alarm bells in the English colonies and put them on the defensive. When rumours spread about a French fort being built at the Forks of the Ohio (modern Pittsburgh, Pennsylvania), England responded with a reconnaissance mission. In 1754, an inexperienced George Washington marched to the Forks to monitor French activity. Before he could grasp the situation, Washington and his men fired on a French envoy and wounded him and several other men. One of Washington's allies, Tanaghrisson, killed the wounded French officer who had asked for quarter, hoping to spark a conflict that had already begun to smoulder. Tanaghrisson was successful. The French quickly retaliated, leading the governor of Virginia to warn of the total loss of North America and all its potential wealth unless the French could be chastened. Full-scale war broke out over control of the Ohio Valley, so central to the expansion and defence of both empires' North American holdings.

In North America, France won nearly all of the early campaigns, relying on Native warriors who killed or captured hundreds of British colonists in small but demoralizing raids all along the frontier. In a major victory for France, a force of western Natives and French soldiers routed General Edward Braddock and his army at Monongahela in 1755, eye-opening proof that indigenous ways of war could be highly effective against even a professionally led British army. Through 1757 the war went well for France, which seemed in little danger of losing Canada during the conflict. Two things turned the tide: shifting British strategy and the loss of France's Native allies. First, in England William Pitt began to devote remarkable sums of money to fight the war in North America, wielding the power of Britain's mighty navy and more than 40,000 ground troops to secure British colonies against New France's deadly attacks. Second, Louis-Joseph de Montcalm and other French military leaders alienated Native allies by treating them like subordinates and by overturning previous promises of captives and looting—western Natives' primary reward for risking their lives to defend New France. Angry and insulted, the Odawas, Ojibwas, and other allies returned to their villages in the Great Lakes region, unwittingly taking the smallpox virus back to their villages. During the fall of 1757 hundreds died. Unwilling to take such risks again for so little reward, the colony's Native allies stayed home. The tide of the war turned permanently in 1758, when huge infusions of British troops met French soldiers minus their key allies. Forts fell quickly in a series of demoralizing British victories that culminated in the 1759 surrender of Quebec after the Battle of the Plains of Abraham, and the 1760 surrender of Montreal. The war ground on for three more years in Europe and Asia until, in 1763, France's crushing losses brought the parties to the negotiating table.

The British were unsure whether Canada was the best reward for defeating France, and they seriously considered returning the colony to French control. Like France, they recognized the superior position and profitability of the Caribbean, where they had taken several French and Spanish islands, and they worried about taking on a colony that was losing money. After long deliberation, Britain opted to retain control of Canada and return the sugar islands of Martinique and Guadeloupe to France (and Cuba to Spain). Britain's decision was based on the same strategic reasoning that had prompted France to invest in New France over the previous century. Both France and Britain viewed Canada as a strategic pawn in a global chess game where the reward was European, not colonial, power. Located to ensure access to the continental interior, the St Lawrence colony ensured Britain's control of the Great Lakes and Ohio River Valley, both crucial to the security of Britain's North American colonies and to their future hopes of colonial expansion. The 1763 Treaty of Paris therefore ended French control of its former colony along the St Lawrence River. But no treaty could end the French presence there. Nearly all of the 70,000 French colonists remained, adapting to a new colonial regime but retaining many of their daily patterns of life.

QUESTIONS FOR CONSIDERATION

1. What role did New France play in the trans-Atlantic empire established by France from the sixteenth through the eighteenth centuries?

2. Discuss the importance of Native peoples in the history of New France. How did they shape the colony? How did the process of colonization affect them?

3. Should the Seven Years' War be considered a war of conquest in Canada? Who would favour, and who would oppose, this description and why? What historical evidence could help us answer this question?

NOTES

1. Ramsay Cook, ed. and trans., *The Voyages of Jacques Cartier* (Toronto: University of Toronto Press, 1993), 10, 24.
2. Cook, *Voyages of Jacques Cartier*, 64.
3. Richard Hakluyt, 'Discourse on Western Planting, Written in the Year 1584', in *Documentary History of the State of Maine*, ed. Charles Deane, vol. 2 (Cambridge: John Wilson and Son, 1877), 3.
4. Henry Percival Biggar, ed. and trans., *The Works of Samuel de Champlain* vol. 2 (Toronto: The Champlain Society, 1971), 331.
5. Biggar, *Works of Samuel de Champlain*, vol. 1, 110–11.
6. Reuben Gold Thwaites, ed., *The Jesuit Relations and Allied Documents*, vol. 51, (Cleveland: Burrows Brothers, 1899), 265.
7. Pierre Boucher, *Histoire veritable et naturelle des moeurs & productions du pays de la Nouvelle France, vulgairement dite le Canada* (Paris, 1664).
8. Drawn from Yves Zoltvany, 'Rigaud de Vaudreuil, Philippe de, Marquis de Vaudreuil,' *Dictionary of Canadian Biography*, vol. 2 (Toronto: University of Toronto Press, 1969).

RELEVANT WEBSITES

NEW FRANCE-NEW HORIZONS/NOUVELLE-FRANCE-HORIZONS NOUVEAUX: www.archivescanadafrance.org/english/accueil_en.html

VIRTUAL MUSEUM OF NEW FRANCE, CANADIAN MUSEUM OF CIVILIZATION: www.civilization.ca/cmc/explore/virtual-museum-of-new-france

LA FRANCE EN AMÉRIQUE/FRANCE IN AMERICA (LIBRARY OF CONGRESS/BIBLIOTHÈQUE NATIONALE): http://memory.loc.gov/intldl/fiahtml/fiahome.html

THE WAR THAT MADE AMERICA (SEVEN YEARS' WAR DOCUMENTARY WEBSITE): www.thewarthatmadeamerica.org/

DICTIONARY OF CANADIAN BIOGRAPHY ONLINE: www.biographi.ca/index-e.html
Thousands of biographical sketches from all phases of Quebec's history, with remarkably full coverage from the French colonial period.

SELECT BIBLIOGRAPHY

Anderson, Fred. *Crucible of War: The Seven Years' War and the Fate of Empire in British North America, 1754-1766.* New York: Vintage, 2001.

Boucher, Philip. *France and the American Tropics to 1700: Tropics of Discontent?* Baltimore: The Johns Hopkins University Press, 2008.

Brandão, José António. *Your Fyre Shall Burn No More: Iroquois Policy toward New France and Its Native Allies to 1701.* Lincoln: University of Nebraska Press, 1997.

Cook, Ramsay, ed. *The Voyages of Jacques Cartier.* Toronto: University of Toronto Press, 1993.

Dechêne, Louise. *Habitants and Merchents in Seventeenth-Century Montreal.* Trans. Liana Vardi. Montreal and Kingston: McGill-Queen's University Press, 1992.

Dickason, Olive P. *The Myth of the Savage and the Beginnings of French Colonialism in the Americas.* Alberta: University of Alberta Press, 1997.

Eccles, W.J. *The French in North America, 1500–1783.* East Lansing: Michigan State University Press, 1998.

Fischer, David Hackett. *Champlain's Dream: The European Founding of North America.* New York: Simon & Schuster, 2008.

Gauvreau, Danielle. *Québec: Une ville et sa population au temps de la Nouvelle France.* Québec: Presses de l'Université du Québec, 1991.

Grabowski, Jan. 'The Common Ground: Settled Natives and French in Montreal'. PhD dissertation. Université de Montréal, 1993.

Greer, Allan. *The People of New France.* Toronto: University of Toronto Press, 1997.

Havard, Gilles. *Empire et métissages: Indiens et Français dans le Pays d'en Haut, 1660–1715.* Paris: Presses de l'Université Paris-Sorbonne, 2003.

Lavallée, Louis. *La Prairie en Nouvelle–France, 1647–1760: étude d'histoire sociale.* Montreal: McGill-Queens University Press, 1992.

Mapp, Paul W. 'British Culture and the Changing Character of the Mid-Eighteenth-Century British Empire'. In Warren R. Hofstra, ed. *Cultures in Conflict: the Seven Years' War in North America.* Lanham, MD: Rowman & Littlefield, 2007, 23–59.

Pope, Peter. *Fish into Wine: The Newfoundland Plantation in the Seventeenth Century.* Chapel Hill: University of North Carolina Press for the Omohundro Institute of Early American History and Culture, 2004.

Pritchard, James. *In Search of Empire: The French in the Americas, 1670–1730.* Cambridge: Cambridge University Press, 2004.

Richter, Daniel K. *Facing East from Indian Country: A Native History of Early America.* Cambridge, Mass.: Harvard University Press, 2001.

Rushforth, Brett. "'A Little Flesh We Offer You": The Origins of Indian Slavery in New France'. *William and Mary Quarterly* 60 (October 2003): 777–808.

Taylor, Alan. *American Colonies.* New York: Viking, 2001.

Thornton, John. *Africa and Africans in the Making of the Atlantic World, 1400–1800.* Cambridge: Cambridge University Press, 1998.

Trigger, Bruce. *Natives and Newcomers: Canada's 'Heroic Age' Reconsidered.* Montreal and Kingston: McGill-Queens University Press, 1985.

White, Richard. *The Middle Ground: Indians, Empires, and Republics in the Great Lakes Region, 1650–1815.* Cambridge: Cambridge University Press, 1991.

CHAPTER 2

The Canadiens and the Conquest of Quebec: Interpretations, Realities, Ambiguities[1]

Donald Fyson, Université Laval/Centre interuniversitaire d'études québécoises

The singular goodness and kindness with which we have been governed by His Most Gracious Majesty King George III since, by force of arms, we became subject to his dominion . . . will no doubt be sufficient to arouse your thanks and your zeal in support of the interests of the British Crown.

—JEAN-OLIVIER BRIAND, BISHOP OF QUEBEC,
ENJOINING THE CANADIENS TO RESIST THE AMERICAN INVASION OF 1775[2]

. . . the province . . . subjected to British empire, has been, since the period of subjugation, nothing other than a province of misfortunates and slaves . . . the conquering nation, by the hands of its national individuals, immediately invaded almost all of the positions in the conquered country; in other words, by this usurpation, the Canadiens were declared strangers, intruders, civil slaves, in their own country . . .

—PIERRE DU CALVET, FORMER MAGISTRATE IMPRISONED BY GOVERNOR HALDIMAND,
IN *Appel à la justice de l'État*, 1784[3]

The Conquest took place a quarter millennium ago. For how many centuries will we still resent the British? . . . if there was the Conquest, there was also the 1774 Quebec Act, that guaranteed the Canadiens the maintenance of the Catholic religion and of the civil law . . . Quebec today is impregnated with English values, institutions, architecture . . . the heritage of that period is far from being exclusively negative . . .

—ANDRÉ PRATTE, EDITOR OF *La Presse*,
DENOUNCING CRITICS OF PAUL MCCARTNEY'S SHOW ON THE PLAINS OF ABRAHAM IN
2008[4]

. . . whatever the revisionists say, the military conquest of New France by England and the avowed intent of the colonial power to assimilate the francophones can never be considered pleasant memories by the Québécois people. In our collective unconscious, the Conquest has the same meaning as a rape. Some act as if nothing happened and try to minimize the event, but others will never forget.

—BIZ, MEMBER OF THE SOVEREIGNIST RAP GROUP LOCO LOCASS, *Le Devoir*, 2007[5]

— TIMELINE —

1759   Defeat of French forces at the battle of the Plains of Abraham and British occupation of Quebec City.

1760   Final surrender of French forces at Montreal; fall of New France.

1763   Treaty of Paris: New France formally ceded by French to British.

Royal Proclamation: creation of the Province of Quebec.

1764   Beginning of British civil administration of new Province of Quebec.

1774   Quebec Act (fully in force from 1775).

1775   Beginning of American War of Independence and invasion of Quebec

1783   Treaty of Paris: end of American War of Independence; portion of Quebec south of Great Lakes ceded to new United States; arrival in Quebec of Loyalists (American colonists who remained loyal to the British crown, known in the United States as Tories).

1791   Constitutional Act: Province of Quebec divided into two separate colonies (Lower Canada and Upper Canada, essentially the southern portions of modern-day Quebec and Ontario respectively), each with an elected Assembly.

INTRODUCTION

Despite the rhetorical certainty of those quoted at the beginning of this chapter, spanning more than two centuries, the British Conquest of Quebec is a profoundly ambiguous event. Were the new British masters guided by kindness and gentleness towards their new subjects, as Briand suggests, or did the conquered Canadiens (francophone Catholics) become slaves in their own land, as Du Calvet charged? Should today's francophone Quebecers stop making such a big deal out of the Conquest, as Pratte would like, or should they follow Biz in treating it as rape?

At its simplest, 'the Conquest' (almost always capitalized) refers to the military defeat of the French and their Native allies by the British, first at the battle of the Plains of Abraham in 1759, which led to the fall of Quebec City, and then at the final rendition of French forces at Montreal in 1760. This military victory gave Britain control over the former French colonial possessions in northeastern and central North America, part of what was known as New France. In what is now Quebec, this was the end of what Europeans call the Seven Years' War, what Americans call the French and Indian War, and what is often called in Quebec the *Guerre de la Conquête*, the War of the Conquest. The Conquest can also refer more generally to the transition of the colony and its Canadien population from one empire to another, including the military actions of 1759–60, the 1763 Treaty of Paris by which the French crown formally ceded most of New France to the British, and the 1763 British Royal Proclamation that created the Province of Quebec. By extension, the decades following this event are often discussed in terms of 'the effects of the Conquest', it being seen as the major traumatic event that shaped the colony's subsequent history. Indeed, according to a commonly held view, the Conquest founded modern Quebec; it was the point of departure of Quebec's contemporary history and the source of both Quebec's current unequal status within Canada and francophones' continuing status as a colonized people; one might almost talk of a continuous Conquest, right down to today. The Conquest, in short, is a very elastic concept.

The nature of the conquered entity is also open to interpretation. What exactly was conquered? New France? Canada? Quebec? The French? The Canadiens? None of these are particularly satisfying.

'New France' is too broad and 'Canada' (as used by the French at that time) is too narrow. New France properly referred to the entirety of French possessions in North America at that time, including not only what is now central and maritime Canada but also what is now the midwestern and (in part) southern United States. Not all of this territory was conquered by the British. 'Canada' properly referred only to the main French settlements in the St Lawrence Valley, essentially the south of modern-day Quebec, which was only part of what the British 'conquered'. Neither Canada (in its modern sense) nor Quebec existed at the time. The French officers and soldiers who defended the colony lost the battles, but were not themselves conquered, as most returned to France. Contrarily, some have long contended that it was not the Canadiens who were conquered, who lost the colony, but rather, those same French. Finally, what of New France's Native populations, allied to the French, but who did not consider themselves to have been conquered by the British?

As this chapter focuses on the effects of the Conquest on the francophone population of what is now Quebec, it adopts the shorthand 'Conquest of Quebec'. Although it is an anachronism, this term nevertheless has the satisfying effect of making clear that this series of events was not only the Conquest of a historical political entity, but is also a locus of historical memory that belongs to a particular society.

The Conquest remains a significant subject of public interest and discourse in Quebec even today. For example, it appeared recently that the Conquest and other potentially conflictual events might be downplayed in a new high-school history curriculum proposed by the Quebec government, with the Conquest integrated into a section entitled 'The Accession to Democracy'. A general public outcry and much heated public debate ensued, leading to a partial government retreat on the matter. In 2008, the participation of the Governor General, the Queen's representative in Canada, in the 400th anniversary celebrations of Quebec City was denounced by many Quebec nationalists as the very incarnation of the British Conquest. Even a concert by Paul McCartney on the Plains of Abraham was viewed by some as a 'new conquest'. More recently, in early 2009, plans to commemorate the 250th anniversary of the Battle of the Plains of Abraham with, among other things, a re-enactment and a masked ball, raised such a storm of protest that the re-enactment was cancelled and other events were substantially reshaped so as to avoid accusations of 'celebrating' the French defeat. More generally, a keyword search in the electronic archives of major francophone Quebec newspapers for names, events, and dates related to the Conquest brings up hundreds of articles, editorials, and letters just over the last few years.[6] Many contain only passing references, but a substantial number take the Conquest as the central subject, as seen in the citations from Pratte and Biz above. It is a theme that regularly leads to flights of rhetorical excess, with hard language, such as 'the holocaust of 1760', not uncommon. Most of the controversy stems from the widely divergent interpretations of the Conquest, and their current political usage.

INTERPRETATIONS OF THE CONQUEST

Most of the basic facts about the former French colony in the decades following the Conquest have been largely accepted, at least by professional historians, for quite some time (see Snapshot box). However, in interpreting the Conquest and its effects, there is and always has been far less agreement. Debates around Canadien adaptation to the new realities in the decades following the Conquest have long been a constant in Quebec and indeed Canadian history. Even the use of the term itself is contested. In French, at least, there are alternatives. *La Conquête* (or 'the Conquest') is the standard historiographical term, used by almost all anglophone historians and in much of the French-language literature as well. But many writers, especially more nationalist ones, see the term as inherently adopting the perspective of the Conqueror—the British. As an editorialist for *Le Soleil* described it recently, it is a 'contemptuous way of evoking the taking of possession of the soul and the body of an entire people'.[7] For the French, after all, it was not a conquest. Since the nineteenth century, some francophone writers have instead used the term *la Cession*. For some, this was a way to soft-peddle the Conquest so as to reconcile French- and English-Canadians. For others, though, the term underscored the fact that it was not the Canadiens who lost the colony, but rather France, which ceded it to Great Britain. This draws on deep resentment in Quebec towards France for abandoning Quebec: first, by not sending enough troops to defend New France during the war; then, by not attempting to retake Canada once it had fallen to the British; and finally, in 1763, at the peace talks, by giving up Canada in exchange for Guadeloupe, Martinique, and other considerations. Though not in common use today, *la Cession* is still used by some pre-eminent historians. Finally, since about the 1960s, some nationalist writers have used the term *la Défaite*, thus adopting the perspective not of the victors but rather of the vanquished, and seeking to keep ever fresh the memory of an event that has become a cornerstone of the sovereignist trends in current Quebec nationalism. For example, it was used (though not capitalized) in the 1994 program of the Parti Québécois, the main Quebec sovereignist party, just before the 1995 referendum on Quebec independence. Scholarly use of this term is less frequent, however, and even in popular writing, *la Conquête* remains by far the most usual term.

Whether called Conquest, or Cession, or Defeat, the meaning of the event to the Canadien population is open to interpretation. Take, for example, the question of how ordinary Canadiens reacted to the change in allegiance. According to an older, nostalgic Tory school, epitomized by such historians as A.L. Burt or Donald Creighton, ordinary Canadiens were either indifferent to the change, since they were ignorant peasants, or, at best, passively contented to see French autocracy disappear and British liberties arrive. In contrast, according to neo-nationalist historians associated with the University of Montreal in the 1950s and 1960s, such as Michel Brunet and Maurice Séguin, ordinary Canadiens reacted by retreating into largely passive and defensive resistance to the hated Conqueror. The two views are of course incompatible. In them we see summed up the two basic competing interpretations: the beneficial Conquest, and the disastrous Conquest; what one might call the 'jovialist' and the 'miserabilist' views. These two opposing views were present almost right from the start, as we can see in the quotations from Briand and Du Calvet, and continue to this day, as expressed by Pratte and by Biz.

The jovialist notion that the Conquest was beneficial for the Canadien population has a long history, stretching back to the initial declarations of the first British administrators, such as James Murray. At first, Canadiens such as Briand expressed it in vague terms, as a way of coping with the fact of defeat and coming to terms with the new colonial masters. But the revolutions in Europe at the end of the eighteenth century provided a more potent argument, with the development of the notion of the providential Conquest. The idea was simple: as revolution swept through France, conservative public figures in Quebec, such as Chief Justice William Smith or future Bishop Joseph-Octave Plessis, argued that by allowing the Conquest, God had miraculously preserved Quebec from the revolutionary and democratic horrors of its former motherland. This interpretation was taken up by the conservative, clerical historians of the nineteenth and early twentieth centuries, such as the abbé Henri-Raymond Casgrain. He wrote in 1891 that had New France remained French, it would have been subject to the abuses which destroyed France 'until it had fallen, with this last, into the abyss of Revolution',[8] and added, in a nod to social Darwinism, that the Conquest had weeded out the weaker elements of Quebec society.

By the second half of the twentieth century, this interpretation had largely declined, but another long-present variant continued. This interpretation had its roots in the British belief in the absolute superiority of their civilization: the Conquest had brought significant benefits to Quebec, such as parliamentary democracy, the printing press, a British-inspired entrepreneurial spirit, and so on. Often present in the writings of earlier generations of English-Canadian historians, in recent years this interpretation has largely disappeared from the historiographical landscape, at least in French, but is kept alive in the writings of historians such as Marcel Trudel, who has written pieces with titles such as 'The Conquest of 1760 also had its advantages', as well as by anti-sovereignist editorialists such as Pratte.

In contrast, there is the miserabilist idea that the Conquest was a total disaster for the Canadiens and subsequently the Quebec people. This too has long roots, associated with a nationalist interpretation of Quebec history that stretches back to writers such as Du Calvet and beyond. Its first real expression by a historian came from François-Xavier Garneau, often seen as the first influential francophone historian of Quebec, in the middle of the nineteenth century. Following the same line of argument as Du Calvet, Garneau declared that under the new British regime, 'every day the Canadiens felt more and more the scope of the misfortune of foreign subjugation, and that the sacrifices they had made were nothing in comparison with the suffering and moral humiliation that was being prepared for them and for their posterity.'[9] This notion of national disaster continued in the writings of the founder of scientific history in Quebec, the influential Lionel Groulx, in the first half of the twentieth century, to whom the Conquest was the 'supreme catastrophe'. It persisted in the writings of the historians of the neo-nationalist Montreal school in the 1950s and 1960s such as Brunet and Séguin, students of Groulx, and those of nationalist Marxists in the 1960s and 1970s such as Stanley Ryerson and Gilles Bourque. Ryerson and Bourque associated the colonialism inherent in the Conquest with the colonialism at that time being strongly contested elsewhere in the world, as in Africa. Although now far less explicitly in academic circles, the 'Conquest as disaster' still informs much of the discussion of Quebec history.

One aspect of the miserabilist view that deserves particular attention is the so-called 'decapitation thesis'. In this view, dating back to Garneau and beyond, the Conquest led to the disappearance of the colony's francophone elites, most of whom left the colony after the Conquest. The sociologist Marcel Rioux wrote in 1969, 'the *habitants* [farmers] and the *curés* [priests] remained alone (or thereabouts) in Voltaire's acres of snow, coming to grips with the English, the long winters, poverty and survival. This was the beginning of Quebec's long hibernation.'[10]

Very much the minority opinion in Garneau's time and up to the early twentieth century (Groulx, for example, did not embrace the decapitation thesis), this view was revived in a more sophisticated form in the mid-twentieth century by Brunet, Séguin, and other neo-nationalist historians of the Montreal school. To

explain why francophone Quebecers in the 1950s were economically dominated by their anglophone counterparts, they sought to portray New France as a normal society, developing its own entrepreneurial class. But this class was suddenly cut off by the disaster of the Conquest. The entrepreneurs left, went bankrupt, or were simply shifted aside by the anglophone merchants (largely American and Anglo-Scottish) favoured under the new system. The Canadiens retreated into agriculture, leaving the economic field to the British. Thus the Conquest of 1759–60 led to the economic inferiority of francophone Quebecers two centuries later.

To this neo-nationalist version of the decapitation thesis, the Marxist historians of the 1960s and 1970s added the notion of class: the Canadiens, shorn of their bourgeoisie (the entrepreneurial class), became the working class, while the English merchants and administrators who came into the colony (these writers generally used English and British interchangeably) became the ruling class, a structure which had persisted in Quebec ever since. Class and ethnicity became one; to quote Rioux again, 'all Quebec became a dominated ethnic class.'[11]

The decapitation thesis did not go uncontested. Historians such as Fernand Ouellet and Jean Hamelin, of Laval University, argued instead that, first, there was no real entrepreneurial class in New France, and second, the Canadiens could not adapt to the changes wrought by the Conquest, largely due to cultural inadequacies inherited from the French regime, such as little entrepreneurial spirit. This view gained very few adherents in Quebec, as it called into question the nature of current Quebec francophone society.

In current popular discourse on the effects of the Conquest, the disaster/decapitation thesis dominates (for an example see Chapter 11 in this volume). In major francophone newspapers over the last few years, perceptions of the Conquest, if not neutral are almost always negative, with few positive discussions. These negative portrayals of the Conquest range from general statements about its bad effects to hard-hitting attacks on the Conquerors, such as this reference to 'Dorchester and other "conquerors" whose design [was] to annihilate the French-Canadian people, beginning with their language and their identity.'[12] (Dorchester was one of the early governors of Quebec and an architect of the Quebec Act, which many historians consider one of the factors that allowed for Canadien cultural and linguistic survival.) The notion of a continuous Conquest, resonating down to today, is a strong theme; as the leaders of a radical wing of the sovereignist Parti Québécois declared, 'More than 250 years of domination have convinced us of the relentless desire of the governments that have dominated us and that still dominate us to update for their own period the fundamental aspects of the British conquest.'[13] Or even more clearly, as one more radical sovereignist writer, René Boulanger, put it, 'the Us of 1759 and that of 2006, is the same'.[14] Few are those who, like Pratte, venture to say that the Conquest was a good thing, or tell francophone Quebecers to just 'get over it'. Among professional historians, on the other hand, what seems to have gained sway in the last two or three decades is the notion that the Conquest led to rather less substantial change than was previously postulated. The notion of continuity was already present in the work of historians writing in the late nineteenth and early twentieth centuries, such as Thomas Chapais, but came into its own with the rise of historical study, beginning in the 1970s, that is less interested in politics than in broader social and economic conditions. For example, studies of Quebec agriculture or the seigneurial system in the eighteenth century rarely give 1759–60 as a pivotal date; instead, they tend to treat the entire century as a fairly unified period. A clear example is John Dickinson and Brian Young's *Short History of Quebec* (2003), which, in striking contrast to previous works, includes both New France and immediate post-Conquest Quebec in a single period stretching from the 1650s to the 1810s. The Conquest, in effect, is eliminated as a major structural event. Partly due to this perspective, very few professional historians today, whether francophone or anglophone, study the Conquest as such, leaving thinking and writing about it to scholars in other fields or to the broader public.

REALITIES AND AMBIGUITIES

To put it mildly, opinions on the effects of the Conquest on the Canadien population vary. What then is the truth behind these different assertions?

How can we reconcile them with reality as we know it, based on empirical historical research? There is as yet no definitive recent synthesis discussing the subject in depth; nor is there space in this chapter to examine all of the ramifications of the Conquest for the Canadien population. The main conclusion to emerge from recent empirical studies is that the effects of the Conquest were ambiguous, and that neither the miserabilist nor the jovialist interpretation is persuasive. This can be illustrated by looking at two key themes: the economic effects of the Conquest on the Canadiens, and the relationship of the Canadiens to political and state power in the post-Conquest period.

Economic Effects

As we saw, the most fundamental debate on the economic effects of the Conquest on the Canadiens is that between continuity and change. The notion of a radical change long dominating and pushing the Canadiens back into agriculture was replaced more recently by the notion of continuity. This is largely a question of perspective. Clearly, there was little structural change in the colony's fundamental economic structures after the Conquest. The same products dominated (furs for the commercial economy, agricultural products such as wheat and livestock for the subsistence economy), and the relationship between the colony and its European metropolis remained one of subordination; the mercantilist principles favoured by both France and England allowed trade only within each empire, and each empire used colonies essentially as sources of raw materials. But detailed study reveals that the situation was much more complex. For the economic elites of the French regime, it is clear that the Conquest was a short-term disaster. Many merchants had invested heavily in French paper money, which the French government largely refused to reimburse after the Conquest, leading to heavy losses. Canadien fur traders and import-export merchants, previously linked to French markets and credit networks that they knew well, suddenly found their French business links broken, since all transactions had to go through England or its possessions. They also had to compete with newly arrived British merchants (both from the American colonies and from Britain itself) with well-established credit and business relationships within the British empire. As a result, progressively over the decades following the Conquest, British merchants replaced Canadiens in the colony's international trade. Canadien seigneurs and nobles also feared for their prosperity and social status, since they were largely excluded from government and military positions. Even the Roman Catholic Church in the colony felt menaced, fearing the seizure of its properties by the Protestant English crown. As a result, many French economic elites did indeed leave the colony and return to France soon after the Conquest.

As we saw, this return to France, evident in the contemporary records, led some historians to postulate the decapitation of Canadien society. However, the empirical data do not support this thesis, at least not in its more extreme form. Studies clearly show that most of the pre-Conquest elites, such as seigneurs and merchants, remained in the colony, especially those born in New France. They found it more profitable to deal with the new regime rather than leave for an uncertain future in France. The decapitation was thus at most a partial one, although a very real loss nevertheless. Those that remained had to work hard at adapting to their new situation. For example, Canadien fur merchants faced difficult times immediately after the Conquest, with many retiring from the trade and most no longer involved in international exchanges. However, by re-orienting themselves to controlling the trade toward the interior of the continent, and especially through their relationships with the Natives who supplied the furs, Canadien merchants adjusted to the new regime. At the end of the 1760s, a decade after the Conquest, most canoes engaged in the fur trade leaving Montreal for the Western interior were financed by Canadien merchants. It was not until the late 1770s, after the outbreak of the American War of Independence, that the arrival of a new set of British fur-trading merchants and changes in the organization of the fur trade led to British almost completely replacing Canadien merchants, even in the interior trade. The change was thus gradual, giving Canadiens time to adapt.

Canadien merchants also invested in seigneuries, which remained mostly in Canadien hands; even in 1791, fewer than a third of the colony's seigneuries had passed entirely or partially into British control, including that of the British crown. As a result, two-thirds of the Canadien population had as their only seigneurs either Canadien elites or Catholic religious institutions (which owned a number of important seigneuries), and only about a sixth of Canadiens had as their only seigneur a member of the new British elite. Even in the cities, where the British population was concentrated, Canadiens dominated land-holding. Since property was to become an increasingly lucrative source of income in the nineteenth century, Canadiens property-holders had good long-term prospects. Largely forced out of international trade by the competition of the new British merchants (although there did remain a few important Canadien import-export merchants), Canadien merchants also re-oriented themselves toward internal trade: even in the 1790s, half of those in the colony identifying themselves as merchants were Canadiens.

The Canadiens thus adapted to the new economic order, rather than withdrawing into agriculture, as was once thought. At the same time, the impact of the Conquest and the arrival of British merchants is undeniable and cannot be minimized. The situation was, in short, complex.

Political and State Power

When we look at Canadiens and the imperial transition from the perspective of political and state power, we again find ambiguity. From either a pro- or an anti-nationalist stance, the Conquest was a fundamental turning point in the relationship between Canadiens and the state, in the British colonial administration. Here again, different historiographical visions clash. Notions of a reign of terror, of the crushing of Canadien rights, of their exclusion from power by an anti-papist government, are expressed by historians such as Garneau, Groulx, Brunet, and those of the Marxist school. In contrast, notions of a benevolent dictatorship designed for an unenlightened people are found in Creighton, Burt, and others. But almost always, the post-Conquest Canadiens are presented as a people excluded from power, attached to their traditional institutions such as civil law and the French language, and hence firm in their rejection of British institutions. This characterization, whatever the underlying ideology, presents a fundamentally conservative view of Canadiens.

Indeed, the most persistent image is one of radical political change effected by the transfer of power from one crown to another, such as the abolition of French civil law under the 1763 Royal Proclamation (which led to very strong complaints) and the imposition of a British-dominated administration on the francophone population. Certainly, at a constitutional level, the change was clear: through the Conquest and the change of allegiance, English public law (regulating the relationship between the crown and its subjects, and including criminal law) replaced French. But more fundamentally, France and England, despite some apparent differences, were quite similar in political organization and operation, both being *ancien régime* states with an emphasis on elite rule, little popular participation in the structures of power, and strong co-operation between Church and state. In Quebec for the first 30 years of British rule, the political structures were largely the same as under the French, with the colony ruled directly by a governor (in New France, a tandem of governor and *intendant*) aided by a council appointed from the colony's elites.

There was indeed significant continuity in how the colonial state dealt with the Canadien population. Take, for example, the administration of law. Even though French civil law was formally replaced by English common law in the 1763 Royal Proclamation, courts and notaries continued to follow French practices. The use of French civil law was acknowledged by British officials such as Lord Hillsborough, one of the principal architects of the Royal Proclamation, who wrote in 1768 that 'it never entered Our Idea to overturn the Laws and Customs of Canada, with regard to Property'. Further, despite assertions by some historians, there is no evidence that the Canadien population boycotted the new courts of the British colonial administration or that they used the courts any less frequently than under the French regime. Many of the court officials were Canadiens, although none of the judges were Catholics, and the courts operated in both languages. Even in the criminal courts, where English criminal law definitively replaced its French predecessor, the proceedings in most cases were similar to those under the French regime. Many

court proceedings and documents were in French and jurors were drawn from both linguistic communities. Thus the Quebec Act of 1774 formalized a de facto situation when it restored French civil law (while maintaining English law for criminal cases). In the end, the British population of Quebec probably had to adapt to the legal traditions of the Canadiens as much as vice versa.

The same complexity is seen in the everyday administration of the colony. Despite early attempts to emulate British institutions, a significant part of local administration returned to French practices soon after the Conquest. For example, under the French regime, the militia had been the principal means of organizing the population to do the bidding of the state, with every male of fighting age being enrolled. The residents of each parish were organized into one or more companies under the direction of a captain, who was also one of the principal agents of the colonial state for non-military matters. The militia was abolished at the beginning of British civil administration in 1764, and replaced by a system of locally elected bailiffs. However, this system lasted only a decade, and the militia was restored in 1775 under the threat of American invasion. Once again, the militia captains served as government representatives in the rural parishes. Roads continued to be built and repaired under the existing French system of co-opting the labour of those who lived along them, under the supervision of an officer called the *Grand Voyer*, or chief roads inspector, a position retained from the French regime. Policing functions such as arrests were carried out by professional bailiffs who occupied essentially the same positions, and were very often the very same men, as during the French regime. Even the Catholic parish was adopted as the basic administrative unit, an incongruous choice for a supposedly anti-Catholic empire, where the Anglican Church was the official church.

If the nature of the colonial state did not change much, what of the persistent notion of the exclusion of Canadiens from power? The classic example, brought up again and again, is the 1763 Royal Proclamation. The Proclamation introduced anti-Catholic measures such as the Test Acts, applied in England and in most of the American colonies, which required Catholics to renounce their faith if they wanted to participate in public administration. It is undeniable that these measures existed, but much qualification is needed. First, these measures did not specifically target the Canadiens as a conquered people with the object of crushing and assimilating them. They were rather an extension of the domestic and colonial policy of English anti-Catholicism, which was closely paralleled by anti-Protestant measures in France and in pre-Conquest New France. As well, the British colonial administrators quickly realized that in a colony that was over 95 per cent Catholic, excluding Catholics from all public functions was impossible. They thus found the means to circumvent the anti-Catholic measures. For example, Catholics were accepted on juries as early as 1764, while they were still excluded at least in part in England; Catholics were also permitted to serve in subordinate public positions, such as court personnel, notaries, and lawyers, and even in some important positions such

as *Grand Voyer*. Further, a few francophones in the colony were Protestants, mostly Huguenots, officially banned but unofficially tolerated in New France; the British administrators placed several of them in high public office, notably as judges and magistrates. Finally, the whole policy of formal exclusion of Catholics from public life was abandoned from 1775 under the Quebec Act, which contributed to the American colonies' resentment of Britain and helped lead to the American War of Independence.

It is not enough, however, to say that the Canadiens could have access to all government positions from 1775; the important question is, did they? Here again we find complexity. It is clear that the British significantly predominated in the higher positions in the colonial administration: most often, two-thirds or more British to one-third or less Canadiens. However, two points are important to note. First, the British domination could be seen instead as the usual domination of metropolitans over colonials in both the French and

Luc de La Corne

Anonymous, London, Portrait of Luc de La Corne Saint-Luc (1711–1784), about 1778, 76.2 cm x 63.5 cm.

Montreal, Musée du Chateau Ramezay, in the Montreal Archive, 1998.898. Photo by Robert Derome.

Luc de La Corne (1711–1784), generally known as La Corne Saint-Luc, is a good example of the adaptation of Canadien elites to British rule after the Conquest. Born in New France into a noble family, La Corne Saint-Luc had a profitable career as a colonial military officer and fur-trade merchant under the French regime. During the War of the Conquest, he used his extensive ties to Native groups, including his

mastery of several Native languages, to lead Native allies into battle against the British, winning several notable successes. For these exploits, he was awarded the Croix de Saint-Louis (Cross of Saint-Louis), one of the highest honours available to nobles in New France. He fought in the final major battle between the British and the French in Quebec, the 1760 Battle of Sainte-Foy (near Quebec City), a French victory rendered irrelevant by the French government's failure to send enough reinforcements to follow up.

One might expect that the Conquest represented disaster for La Corne Saint-Luc, and that the British would have little desire to see him stay. His first inclination was indeed to return to France, as did a significant part of the French colonial nobility and officer class. He left Quebec in 1761, but the ship on which he was travelling, the *Auguste*, was wrecked off the northern tip of Nova Scotia, killing many Canadien nobles and officers and their families. La Corne Saint-Luc was one of the few survivors (he lost two children in the wreck, along with his eldest brother), and made his way back to Quebec. He later wrote a rousing and somewhat self-aggrandizing account of the wreck and his trip back, which was published in Montreal in 1778.

La Corne Saint-Luc stayed in Quebec and accommodated himself very well to the new regime. Although as a Catholic he no longer could hold a military or other official position, he remained one of the wealthiest Canadiens in the colony, with a fine house in Montreal, a retinue of slaves, and an expensive lifestyle. His main income derived still from trade and despite not being a seigneur, he was considered part of the seigneurial class, a group whom the British colonial administrators saw as natural allies. Two of La Corne Saint-Luc's daughters married British officers, and Governor Carleton (later Lord Dorchester) thought well enough of him to name him to the Legislative Council of Quebec in 1775. On 17 August 1775, with six fellow Canadien councillors, La Corne Saint-Luc took the oath specially designed for Catholics in the Quebec Act that replaced the anti-Catholic measures in the Test Acts. In Council, he was an active member from the beginning, faithfully present at almost every session. He was also a staunch supporter of the French Party, which generally tended to support autocratic and conservative measures. La Corne Saint-Luc, for example, along with the other members of the French Party, voted in 1782 to refuse a law which would have introduced habeas corpus (the right to contest unwarranted imprisonment) into the colony. Further, when a habeas corpus law passed in 1784, he showed his religious conservatism by proposing a measure that would disallow the right to habeas corpus for members of religious orders who had taken vows—a measure that even the Catholic bishop of Quebec opposed.

La Corne Saint-Luc was not simply a British toady, and acted against the interests of his former foes when it served his purposes. In the early 1760s, he was accused of fomenting discord among France's former Native allies, who in 1763 rose against the British in Pontiac's Rebellion. Later, at the beginning of the American War of Independence, in the fall of 1775, when American troops invaded Quebec and Montreal was about to fall, La Corne Saint-Luc indirectly contacted the rebel general, Richard Montgomery, to offer secret terms of surrender—only a few weeks after he had been sworn in as a legislative councillor and taken an oath of loyalty to the King! Montgomery did not trust him, describing him as 'a great villain and as cunning as the devil', and the Americans eventually imprisoned La Corne Saint-Luc for a short time in New York. After his release, he again became a loyal British subject and participated with his Native allies in Gen. John Burgoyne's ill-fated 1777 campaign against the rebels, which ended in disaster at Saratoga. Burgoyne in part blamed La Corne Saint-Luc for his defeat, describing him as 'by nature, education, and practice, artful, ambitious, and a courtier'. Burgoyne was not the only British official suspicious of La Corne Saint-Luc. Carleton's successor, Governor Haldimand, named him his aide-de-camp, but was too suspicious of his changeable loyalties to promote him in the militia as he had requested. Indeed, La Corne Saint-Luc maintained commercial and personal links with France.

But this did not prevent La Corne Saint-Luc benefitting from the British presence. All in all, for him the Conquest was no disaster, although it did significantly upend his life. Like many of his fellows, he became a staunch defender of the Quebec Act. In one of his last actions in the Legislative Council, he proposed a motion to the King for the preservation of the Quebec Act, which was then under fire from reformers, including some members of Council. The motion in its original form stated that the Council 'wished nothing more strongly than to be able to transmit [the Act] to posterity as a precious charter that will ensure the enjoyment of the privileges and the religion of the peoples of this province. [We are] convinced by the experience and the changes that have occurred since the Conquest that the Canadiens will live happily under this Act, and will be in short order indissolubly incorporated into the British nation.'[15] On this at least, he and Bishop Plessis were in perfect harmony.

British empires, including the American colonies. Public offices were often lucrative positions doled out as patronage to those well-connected in the metropolis. Indeed, when the bureaucracies of New France before the Conquest and Quebec after 1775 are compared, the proportion of high positions such as judgeships, seats on Council, and the like that were held by people born in the colony (both British and French) is similar, about a third. Second, and more importantly, the further down one looks into the government bureaucracy, the more Canadiens one finds. Take for example the justices of the peace, the judges who dealt with most criminal cases and handled most local administration in the cities. As soon as the restrictions on Catholics were lifted, Canadiens were quickly in the majority in this important office. This meant that the public face of criminal justice and local administration in Quebec was at least as French as English; again, a most ambiguous situation for a conquered colony.

It must not be thought, however, that the French participation in administration was due to benevolence on the part of British administrators. It partly stemmed from conflicts within the British elite itself, divided between, on the one hand, the governors, colonial administrators, and army and, on the other hand, the British merchants (who before 1775 included many Americans). Neither group appreciated the other: the governors, all aristocrats and former military officers, disdained the merchants' commercial pursuits and sought to maintain autocratic control, while the merchants urged a more democratic form of government, with the formation of a house of assembly (although to be reserved for Protestants only). In this context, Canadien elites, notably the seigneurs and nobles, became important allies of the governors. After all, they shared the same aristocratic and autocratic ideals. British governors kept French aristocratic traditions alive in the colony, living in the same residence as their French predecessors, the Château Saint-Louis in Quebec City; they were fond of French fashions and cooking, to the extent of importing French chefs; all spoke fluent French; and most attempted to reproduce some aspects of courtly life in the small elite society of Quebec City, with balls, banquets, and the like to which the seigneurs and nobles were invited. The wife of Guy Carleton, Lord Dorchester, the longest-reigning

governor, had been educated in part in the court of Marie-Antoinette at Versailles. This partnership of British and French elites led to the British governors and their entourage becoming the firmest supporters of the rights of the Catholic Canadiens, around what was known as the 'French Party' (mostly composed of British administrators) which dominated the appointed colonial legislature through to the end of the 1780s.

But more importantly, the British had early learned that the best way to maintain effective control over a colony was to co-opt local elites and even popular classes into local government, while ensuring that ultimate power rested with British colonial administrators; this is the fundamental principle of 'indirect rule'. The English state used this model in England itself to administer local populations as well as in many of its other colonies. In Quebec, then, it was natural that colonial administrators would put local administration in the hands of the local population, including Canadiens. The importance here is that this principle created a political space that Canadiens, largely marginalized at the upper levels of political power, were able to occupy. For example, as noted above, in the first decade of British civil rule, the colonial administration established a system of local officials in rural areas, the bailiffs. These were derived from the English system of parish constables, where every year, heads of households elected one of their own to serve as constable (responsible for far more than just policing). The annual bailiff election records show that almost all the bailiffs were Canadiens, and that Canadiens participated quite willingly in elections—in theory a new practice for them, though it also had roots in pre-existing forms of local governance such as parish assemblies. Thus, even ordinary Canadiens adapted rapidly to the new system.

CONCLUSION

Overall, the Conquest was and still is profoundly ambiguous. The effects of the Conquest and the regime change on the Canadien population varied considerably according to social group. Without doubt, the elites were far more affected than ordinary Canadiens, the farmers and other members of the popular classes. For the latter, life did not change dramatically; they were excluded from economic and political power before the Conquest, and largely remained so after it. The new British masters preserved the same autocratic structures and, after a few years of uncertainty, confirmed the seigneurial system; some themselves became seigneurs. Socially and economically, the colony remained primarily agricultural. On the other hand, a new group of British, largely Anglo-Scottish elites, arrogated to themselves a significant portion of the political and economic power previously held exclusively by the Canadien elites. It is nevertheless very difficult to talk of any 'decapitation' of Canadien society through the departure or decline of its elites; the great majority of them remained in the colony and even in the immediate post-Conquest years retained considerable social and economic power, to which they added political power, at both the colonial and the local level, after 1775. What changed for them was their relative power; from essentially dominating under the French regime, these men had to cede much of their place to the new British elites. Further, by the end of the 1780s, the Canadien population, both elite and popular class, once again faced challenges similar to those that had appeared so daunting in the 1760s. These challenges were a rapid influx of British Loyalist settlers from the former American colonies, a decline in the relative economic position of Canadien merchants, and a partial return in the 1790s and early 1800s to an official policy of cultural assimilation. But the more complicated, ambiguous legacy of the period of imperial transition up to the mid-1780s allowed them to adapt to the new regime and to survive the harsh impositions of colonialism that were to come in the nineteenth century, such as the military repression of the Rebellions of 1837–8 and the forced union with Upper Canada in 1841, with the express goals of submerging, assimilating, and anglifying the Canadien population. Still, both popular-class and elite Canadiens were not simply passive spectators of British domination: both adapted themselves, pragmatically, to the new situation.

Nevertheless, the prime importance of the Conquest rests not only in its immediate effects, but also in its long-term consequences. First, the Conquest evidently led to the integration of this francophone society into a larger anglophone milieu, first the British Empire and then, progressively from 1841, Canada. This led to considerable and persistent interethnic tensions, expressed in dramatic events such as the Rebellions of 1837–8, the anti-conscription crises in Quebec during both world wars, or the violent activities of the Front de libération du Québec in the 1960s and the subsequent October Crisis in 1970. Most significant is the key place that the Conquest holds in the collective memory and constructed identity of francophone Quebecers today: the sense of abandonment by France, still seen in the (now diminishing) popular phrase *maudit Français* ('damn Frenchman'); the continuing association of anglophones with the conqueror; finally, the profound sense of collective injustice that still pervades parts of Quebec society. Biz, quoted at the beginning of this chapter, was not wrong: the Conquest is indeed one of the founding moments in the collective memory of francophone Quebecers, one of the historic events that comes up again and again in public discourse (though whether it can be called 'rape' is less clear). It is in this sense that the empirically verifiable effects of the Conquest on the Canadien population explored in this chapter are perhaps less important today than how the Conquest is perceived in contemporary Quebec's collective memory.

SNAPSHOT

The Aftermath of the Conquest in Quebec

In the short term, the Conquest led to a series of dramatic and seemingly perilous changes for the European colony and its French inhabitants. The colony's name changed from Nouvelle-France (or Canada) to the Province of Quebec, and it became a royal colony under the direct control of the British crown. New

France had theoretically covered most of the interior of North America, down to Louisiana (though most of its territory was in practice largely controlled by France's Native allies), with its capital at Quebec City. As of 1763, the new Province of Quebec was limited to a small rectangle along the shores of the St Lawrence River. The colony's 65,000 or so francophone, Catholic inhabitants, or Canadiens, become subjects of the British crown, and were compelled to take an oath of allegiance. They had reason to be nervous about the transition. The British state was officially Protestant, anti-Catholic, and very publicly anti-French. The Catholic Church, which had dominated religion in New France, was thus in a precarious position. So too were elites such as seigneurs (major landowners) and nobles, who had depended on government patronage and support before the Conquest and were faced with a new colonial regime where traditional avenues of advancement, such as the army, were essentially closed to them. Canadien merchants were also concerned, especially those engaged in the import-export trade, mostly exporting furs and importing manufactured products and consumption goods. British imperial policies meant they could no longer trade directly with France. Even ordinary Canadiens had reason to fear. During the siege of Quebec, British forces had burned hundreds of farms in a deliberate policy of terror. In England and most of her American colonies, Catholics were excluded from most positions of public trust and subjected to many restrictions on their civil rights. Further, just a few years earlier in Nova Scotia, the British army of occupation had deported the entire Acadian (French-Catholic) population. Even private property was under threat. Though most was guaranteed under the terms of the 1760 articles of surrender, it appeared that the laws regulating property would be British. This, it was feared, would lead to the disappearance of the colony's landholding system, the seigneurial system, whereby the territory was divided into large landed estates owned by seigneurs and held by habitants, semi-independent farmers who worked for themselves but paid dues to the seigneurs. In short, the Conquest was a pivotal event in Quebec's history, rife with potential negative effects on the Canadien population.

The actual effects were more complicated. Overall, between 1759 and 1791, we can distinguish three major periods, each representing a major shift in British imperial policy towards the colony (see Timeline). First, the military regime, 1759–64: the period when the conquered colony was under military rule by the army of occupation, awaiting the outcome of the war elsewhere in the world and of the subsequent peace negotiations. This was a crucial period, since it established mutual expectations between the Canadiens and their new colonial masters. Overall, these expectations were positive. While the period was highly disruptive to the colony's former elites, who lost their positions of power, its broader effects on the Canadien population as a whole were perhaps less dramatic than what one might expect from the words *military regime*. Thus, much of the Canadiens' habitual referents were preserved: the Catholic religion, including the right of the Church hierarchy to exercise its functions; property rights, including the seigneurial system, the property of religious orders, and private property, including slaves; the right of Canadien merchants to continue operating; French civil law; even certain pre-Conquest structures of authority, such as the Canadien militia officers who ran the lower courts, Canadien bailiffs who essentially continued to act as the strong arm of the law, and Canadien notaries who continued to practise, though now with commissions granted by the British military governors. There were of course some very important changes, such as the dismantling of the French administrative system, replaced by military councils and tribunals, and the de facto abolition of the military functions of the militia and the disarmament of the population. But in their dealings with the Canadien population, the new British administrators most often communicated in French (the international language of the elite at the time). The Canadiens thus seemed to have had little fear of forced assimilation or (their other great fear) deportation.

Under the Royal Proclamation of 1763, however, largely implemented between 1764 and 1775, the official British policy was assimilation, with apparently significant restrictions on the religious and political rights of the Canadiens. The objective was to replace the French, Catholic colony with a British, Protestant one. To this end, British authorities envisaged a two-fold approach: encourage British immigration, especially from the American colonies to the south, and assimilate the Canadiens. From this flowed measures such as the exclusion of Catholics from most high government offices; the wholesale replacement (in theory) of French civil and criminal law by English common and statute law; the intent to grant further land not in seigneuries but according to free and common socage (where farmers essentially owned their lands outright); the nomination of French-speaking Anglican curates with the express purpose of converting the Canadiens; the weakening of the Catholic Church by controlling its priests, no longer supporting its collection of revenues such as tithes, and abolishing the powerful male religious orders (the Jesuits and the Recollets); and even the amputation of the interior territory, which sought among other goals to sunder links between the Canadiens and their former Native allies in the interior. Here was ample fodder to feed the fears of the Canadien population. However, put simply, this policy, designed in London, did not work. Few British colonists came to the colony, with semi-permanent immigration largely limited to colonial officials, American and British merchants eager to profit from the new opportunities of a colony suddenly open for trade, and a few artisans and labourers. The drying up of direct French immigration thus had little effect on the ethno-religious composition of the colony's population. Further, almost all of the British settled in the three main towns, Quebec City (still the capital), Montreal, and Trois-Rivières, rather than in the rural areas of the colony, where 85 per cent or so of the population lived and which remained almost exclusively Canadian, at least until the mid-1780s. British imperial administrators on the spot found it more practical to attempt to solidify the loyalty of the Canadiens, and notably their elites, by essentially putting aside the policies of assimilation and by replacing them with a policy of appeasement, introducing flexibility as much as possible into their dealings with Canadiens and especially Canadien elites. For example, French civil law continued to hold sway de facto, with the tacit approval of

the colonial administration, and early governors such as James Murray and Guy Carleton gave more support to the Catholic Church than to the fledgling Anglican establishment, as when they allowed the consecration of a new Catholic bishop in 1766. As well, from a purely practical point of view, administrators continued the practices of official bilingualism already initiated under the military regime, for example publishing all their official notices in both English and French and replying in French to correspondents who addressed them in that language.

Finally, under the Quebec Act of 1774, appeasement became official imperial policy, despite secret instructions which appear to have preserved the idea of assimilation. Thus, from 1775, French civil law was definitively restored, though with some modifications; most of the religious and political restrictions on Catholics were lifted; Catholics were allowed to occupy almost any government position, with a number of Canadiens from the seigneurial class named to the colony's appointed legislature; the right of the Catholic Church to collect the tithe was reaffirmed; and a significant part of the interior of the continent was re-attached (formally at least) to the colony (essentially, most of present-day southern Quebec and Ontario, and the Great Lakes basin). This was in part due to the troubles in the American colonies, building toward revolution since the early 1770s. Britain thus found itself in the ironic position of having to count on the loyalty of its newly conquered Canadien subjects to counter the American subjects, largely on whose behalf the Conquest of Quebec had been undertaken 15 years before. This proved a very weak reed. When the American colonies launched their revolutionary war in 1775, one of their first military actions was to invade Quebec. Despite the efforts of Canadien religious leaders and most of the seigneurs, favoured by the Quebec Act, the Americans met little resistance from the Canadien population, although the Canadiens gave little active support either. The British defeat of the invasion was largely due to a combination of luck, American strategic problems, and the arrival of British reinforcements. Still, the spirit of the Quebec Act remained official policy through to 1791.

QUESTIONS FOR CONSIDERATION

1. Was the Conquest a disaster for the Canadien population of Quebec?

2. Why did the British treat the conquered Canadiens less harshly than had been feared?

3. What do Quebecers think of the Conquest today?

NOTES

1. My thanks to Robert K. Whelan, Brian Young and Thomas Wien for their comments. All translations in the text are my own.

2. H. Tétu and C.-O. Gagnon, eds., *Mandements, lettres pastorales et circulaires des évêques de Québec*, vol. 2 (Quebec: A. Coté, 1888), 264–5.

3. Pierre Du Calvet, *Appel à la justice de l'État* (London: 1784), 135.

4. André Pratte, 'Le calumet de paix', *La Presse*, 19 July 2008, A29.

5. Biz, 'La célébration de l'aliénation québécoise', *Le Devoir*, 22 December 2007, B5.

6. This is based on searches in the Eureka.cc database, for articles from *Le Devoir*, *La Presse*, *Le Soleil* and *Le Droit*, and in canoe.ca for articles from the *Journal de Montréal* and the *Journal de Québec*, from the beginning of 2005 to mid-2009.

7. Didier Fessou, 'La Conquête, prise 2', *Le Soleil*, 18 December 2005, C1.

8. H.-R. Casgrain, *Guerre du Canada, 1756–1760: Montcalm et Levis*, vol.2 (Quebec: L.-J. Demers, 1891), 235.

9. François-Xavier Garneau, *Histoire du Canada depuis sa découverte jusqu'à nos jours*, vol.2, 2nd edn (Quebec: John Lovell, 1852), 378.

10. Marcel Rioux, *La Question du Québec* (Paris: Éditions Seghers, 1969), 41.

11. Ibid.

12. Francine Lavoie, 'Un symbole de notre statut minoritaire', *Le Devoir*, 25 September 2007, A6.

13. Pierre Dubuc and Marc Laviolette, 'Pour la relance du Parti québécois', *Le Devoir*, 19 May 2007, B5.

14. René Boulanger, *La bataille de la mémoire: Essai sur l'invasion de la Nouvelle-France en 1759* (Quebec: Éditions du Québécois, 2007), 23.

15. *Journals of the Legislative Council of Quebec*, 21 April 1784, Library and Archives Canada, R10808-4-X.

RELEVANT WEBSITES

THE CANADIAN ENCYCLOPEDIA: www.thecanadianencyclopedia.com
Articles covering in greater detail many of the events and ideas discussed here.

DICTIONARY OF CANADIAN BIOGRAPHY ONLINE: www.biographi.ca/index-e.html
Biographies of many of the major historical actors of the period (the discussion of La Corne Saint-Luc in this chapter, for example, is based largely on the biography by Pierre Tousignant and Madeleine Dionne-Tousignant).

CANADA IN THE MAKING: www.canadiana.org/citm/index_e.html
Detailed explorations of the period, with primary source illustrations.

DONALD FYSON, LA HAUTE SOCIÉTÉ AU QUÉBEC, 1759–1793: http://telequebec.tv/sites/marie-antoinette/
Part of the Marie-Antoinette website of Télé-Québec (use the website Menu to locate the article).
In French only, this illustrated article directly addresses the question of Canadien elite adaptation.

SELECT BIBLIOGRAPHY

A significant part of the relevant historiography is in French but is not presented here. The older

French-language historiography is partially summarized in Miquelon, Neatby, and Nish. .

Brunet, Michel. *French Canada and the Early Decades of British Rule, 1760–1791.* Ottawa: Canadian Historical Association, 1968. Available at: www.collectionscanada.gc.ca/cha-shc/008004-111.01-e.php?q1=H&interval=100.

Fyson, Donald. *Magistrates, Police, and People: Everyday Criminal Justice in Quebec and Lower Canada, 1764–1837.* Toronto: Osgoode Society/University of Toronto Press, 2006.

———. 'The Canadiens and British Institutions of Local Governance in Quebec, from the Conquest to the Rebellions'. In Nancy Christie, ed., *Transatlantic Subjects: Ideas, Institutions and Social Experience in Post-Revolutionary British North America* (Montreal and Kingston: McGill-Queen's University Press, 2008): 45–82.

Igartua, José. 'A Change in Climate: The Conquest and the Marchands of Montreal'. *Historical Papers* 1974: 115–34.

Lawson, Philip. *The Imperial Challenge: Quebec and Britain in the Age of the American Revolution.* Montreal and Kingston: McGill-Queen's University Press, 1989.

Miquelon, Dale ed. *Society and Conquest: the Debate on the Bourgeoisie and Social Change in French Canada, 1700–1850.* Toronto: Copp Clark, 1977.

Neatby, Hilda. *Quebec: The Revolutionary Age, 1760–1791.* Toronto: McClelland & Stewart, 1966.

———. *The Quebec Act: Protest and Policy.* Scarborough: Prentice-Hall, 1972.

Nish, Cameron, ed. *The French Canadians, 1759–1766: Conquered? Half-Conquered? Liberated?* Toronto: Copp Clark, 1966.

Tousignant, Pierre. 'The Integration of the Province of Quebec into the British Empire, 1763–91. Part I: From the Royal Proclamation to the Quebec Act'. *Dictionary of Canadian Biography* IV(1979): xxii–xlix.

CHAPTER 3

Thinking about Power in Post-Rebellion Quebec, 1837–1867

Brian Young, McGill University

Why in 1878 would the most important religious leader in Canada, Elzéar-Alexandre Taschereau, organize an elaborate procession through the Quebec capital to re-bury the bones of his predecessor Bishop François de Laval, dead some 170 years? And, in a Victorian age that featured change, the photograph, the telegraph, and the Darwinian theory of evolution, what might explain his determination to impose the doctrine of Immaculate Conception (1854) across Catholic Quebec? From our standpoint in the twenty-first century, his concerns might seem like necrophilia, narcissism, or an anachronism from a more devout time. Or, these actions might alert us to the fact that the Cardinal, far from being effete, was living up to his reputation as a very practical 'Prince' with Machiavellian goals, focused on wielding power and authority in Quebec society. Indeed, his connecting of the dots of memory around old bones of religious heroes and his aggressive sortie to control women, their sexuality, and their visions of conception illustrate the complexity of power in mid-nineteenth century Quebec. Marx and Engels, now out of favour but seasoned observers nonetheless of matters of power, may not have had it entirely right, at least for the Quebec example, in arguing that by creating modern industry and world markets, the bourgeoisie have 'conquered . . . exclusive political sway'.[1] In this brief discussion we want to broaden our view of power to include priests, fathers, and yes, professors, journalists, and other purveyors of information.

Political interpretations of the mid-nineteenth century are readily available. Those that treat Quebec often use a neo-Marxist analysis to show the power of a developing professional and industrial bourgeoisie and its frequent use of police or military to carry out state violence.[2] Politics in the sense of constitutions and parliaments will have an important place below but if we look below the surface, and think about the significance of old bones, Virgin Birth, or in our times, power over the life of the unborn, we see that power in society is also hugely influenced by the Church, by law, and by gender and culture. Think for example, of a father's control in the family, of the authority of a priest, teacher, or doctor in a church, school, or hospital, of the position of manager or foreman in businesses such as a bank or factory, of judges and jailers through the law, its courts, prisons, or gallows, or of publishers and editors through the media and the control of information.

ERUPTION, REPRESSION, AND RECONCILIATION

Given the breadth of these power relations, historians try to organize their explanation by situating power into defined periods of time and space. Among the schemas used to define periods in Quebec's history are:

- constitutional landmarks in Canada's progress from colony to nation-state;
- the transition to modernity;
- the evolution of Quebec from a feudal to an industrial economy; and
- the stages in the evolution of women's rights.

In all of these schemas, the Rebellions of 1837–8 in Lower Canada (or Quebec) and the Canadian Confederation in 1867 are central events, making them useful bookends for examining how political, state, institutional, and family powers were transformed. The first decade, 1837–49, was characterized by eruption and repression. For eruption we have the Rebellions, the suspension of the Legislature and imposition of a Special Council and, later in the decade, the burning of the Parliament building in Montreal and publication of a manifesto of annexation to the United States. Repressive measures in the late 1830s and in the 1840s included imprisonment, exile, and execution of rebels, or Patriotes as they were called by the French Canadians. Also repressive, although Lord Durham would undoubtedly have denied it, was his Report (1839). Appointed governor to inquire into the Rebellions, he reduced French-Canadian nationality to the state of being 'destitute' and its people as having 'no history and no literature'. By suspending the Patriote-dominated assembly following the rebellions, the governor and his Special Council held direct power. Finally, the union of Lower Canada with Upper Canada (the southern portion of Ontario) in 1840 suggested the subordination and even assimilation of francophones into a larger English Canada.

As early as the mid-1840s however, measures of reconciliation counterbalanced these tendencies. The state, whatever its historical suspicions of ecclesiastical power, enabled the Roman Catholic Church to increase its power in Quebec society. Bicultural political alliances were also established. Francophone leaders such as Louis-Hippolyte LaFontaine and George-Étienne Cartier sought alliance with Upper Canadian, English-speaking Protestant counterparts such as John A. Macdonald, later Canada's first prime minister. This coalition would play a central role in achieving responsible government, building a federal state, deconstructing seigneurialism, and fundamentally revising customary, mortgage, and contract law. At the same time, this group successfully marginalized liberals, Tories, nationalists, and religious zealots, both Protestant and Catholic. Thus until the mid-twentieth century, nationalist parties such as the Bloc Populaire or Bloc Québécois, whatever the strengths of their social programs, were doomed to minority status.

It may also be useful to think of this pattern of eruption, repression, and reconciliation recurring in Quebec history. Can it be compared, for example, to the period after the Conquest of 1759–60 or to the period marked by the independence movement and referendums in the last quarter of the twentieth century?

After the Conquest, repressive measures to deport French Catholics (as had been done with the Acadians in the Maritimes), to assimilate them, or to impose British law, institutions, and a Church of England Protestantism were quickly abandoned as impractical both for demographic reasons and out of respect for

GEORGE-ÉTIENNE CARTIER

Portrait of George-Étienne Cartier, image 142 x 97 mm: on mount 181 x 130 mm Positive Paper Silver–albumen

Notman & Son/Library and Archives Canada/C-06166

I first took up study of Cartier, a leading Quebec politician and a Father of the Canadian Confederation, as a graduate student interested in industrialization in Quebec, railways, and Cartier's involvement in the Pacific Scandal.

When I published what I thought was an innocuous study of his political defeat in the federal elections of 1872, I was shocked to receive a sharp rebuttal from Michel Brunet, nationalist historian at the Université de Montréal.[3] That episode brought home to me the complexity of issues around identity in Quebec and the sensitive relationship between History and the 'National Question'. My interest piqued, I set out to write a full biography of Cartier poking at the vicissitudes of his career, his place among the Patriotes of 1837, and his role in the founding of what would become the Conservative Party. I was struck by the complexity of his political milieu, his combination of being a francophone Montrealer and a pan-Canadian federalist, and his defence of the Catholic Church despite being a strong free thinker.

I was writing in the heyday of Pierre Elliott Trudeau, and I was struck by how these two Montreal politicians, albeit separated by a century, faced similar issues around individual mores, nationality, identity, and biculturalism. Cartier's own papers were largely destroyed following his death in 1873, but a few letters in archives in Montreal and Ottawa, the diaries of relatives, collections of his speeches, and the records of public debates in Ottawa and Quebec gave me adequate primary sources to construct a biography, *George-Étienne Cartier: Montreal Bourgeois*, published in 1981.

Cartier was born in Saint-Antoine sur Richelieu in 1814. His parents' decision to baptize him 'George' in honour of King George III, rather than the French 'Georges', was symptomatic of the politicization that would dog him throughout his life. At age ten, he was sent to the Collège de Montréal, a classical college run by the Sulpician priests. Trained in the law, in the 1830s Cartier was attracted to the Patriote cause of Louis-Joseph Papineau. He joined the Sons of Liberty and fought at the battle of Saint-Denis in October 1837; charged with treason, he fled to the United States.

With the annulment of the charges against him, Cartier was soon back in Montreal practising as a well-connected lawyer. He was an early supporter of Louis-Hippolyte LaFontaine and his alliance with Anglophone reformers in Upper Canada. In

1848 he was elected to the Legislative Assembly, by 1854 he was in the cabinet, and two years later he was Canada's second-ranking politician as John A. Macdonald's Quebec lieutenant. In the administrative structuring of Canada in this period, Cartier played a major role in legislation affecting education, municipalities, seigneurialism, and particularly the codification of Quebec civil law. Affable, capable in ethnic politics, and able to bridge the gap between religious minorities—Protestants in Quebec and Roman Catholics in the rest of Canada—he used his political connections well in acting for both the land interests of the Sulpicians and the industrial projects of the Grand Trunk Railway.

It was as a Father of Confederation that he takes his place in Canadian history. A conservative and a strong believer in the British balanced constitution, particularly its emphasis on an appointed upper house, he feared republicanism and American models that emphasized democracy or the 'melting pot'. As early as 1858, he adopted federalism as the best constitutional solution to Canada's political impasse and his discourse bears comparison with that of Trudeau:

> . . . historical facts teach us that French-Canadians and English-Canadians should have for each other a mutual sympathy, having both reason to congratulate themselves that Canada is still a British colony . . . If we unite, we will form a political nationality independent of the national origin and religion of individuals.[4]

He agreed to sit in a coalition government in 1864 and represented Quebec at conferences in Charlottetown and Quebec City where the Quebec Resolutions were hammered out into what would become the British North America Act. After the Confederation of Canada in 1867, Cartier served in the first Macdonald government as Minister of Militia and Defence. By now, far from his Patriote sympathies in the Rebellions of 1837, Cartier insisted on a British aristocratic rank and in 1867 he was made a baronet. In the same year and, benefiting from the double mandate (the right to stand for office at two levels of government), 'Sir' George-Étienne Cartier was elected to both the Canadian Parliament and the Quebec Legislative Assembly. His career however, was winding down. As Quebec's most prominent federalist, he was unable to defend effectively a French-Canadian, Catholic identity in divisive issues like Catholic schools in New Brunswick and Riel's first rebellion in Manitoba (1869–70). Tension from industrialization, ethnic intolerance, and increasing British immigration weakened his projects for ethnic equality and for a federation in which French Canadians might jump at his cry of 'All Aboard for the West'. The rigidity of Ultramontanist Catholic leaders like Bishop Ignace Bourget of Montreal and the rise of a liberal movement weakened his Montreal base of support. In the 1872 election, his enemies brought him down over his involvement in the Canadian Pacific slush fund.

These are the political ups-and-downs associated with hard-rock politics in Montreal. But his life has many other elements to interest the historian. A quintessential French Montrealer, Cartier was cultural and intellectual heir of a French America centred on Montreal, from New Orleans and Acadia, and from Paris and the Caribbean. Political leader of Canada's most important and most bicultural city, he was on the cusp of French–English relations. To the chagrin of nationalists, Cartier was a committed anglophile, shopping for clothes and titles in London. He had a positivist vision of a pan-Canadian society that, through a federal balance of powers and construction of a new 'political nationality', might protect its political minorities. But competing visions were evident in his own home. His wife, Hortense Fabre, 14 years his junior, was connected to French intellectuals and ultramontane clerics.

It is perhaps fitting that the anglophile Cartier died in May 1873 in London, seeking remedies for his kidney disease. His body was returned to Canada for a triumphant funeral in Notre Dame Church and burial in the parish cemetery Notre Dames des Neiges. He is memorialized in Montreal with a huge winged statue on Mount Royal (the base of the statue is now the site for inter-cultural smoking and drumming in Sunday afternoon 'tam tam jams'). Hortense Fabre retired to France following Cartier's death, and died in Cannes in 1898.

British liberties. Instead, the Quebec Act (1774) and Constitutional Act (1791) represented imperial recognition of Quebec institutions and of a certain legal geography for French Canada, albeit always assuming that French Canadians would ultimately be a minority in the envisioned larger, English-speaking Canadian state.

Can a similar pattern be seen in the aftermath of the narrowly failed 1995 referendum on Quebec sovereignty? First reactions of the Canadian federalist majority include the Clarity Act (2000) which gives Ottawa scrutiny over questions posed in future sovereignty referendums and over the validity of referendum results. More recently, Ottawa has made gestures of reconciliation including financial measures to give Quebec more autonomy in social programs, immigration, and health, and recognition of Quebec as a 'nation', albeit a minority nation within a larger, multicultural, English-speaking Canada.

There is a final caveat to understanding power relations in both mid-nineteenth century Quebec and across the entire span of Canadian history from 1760 to the present. We must understand the centrality of the institutions of *ancien régime* France and more important, the priority of the British constitutional and cultural systems over republican models erected in France and the United States. Any tendency to republican governance was purged by the abortive Rebellions of 1837–8 and by the failure of the short-lived American annexation movement. The parliamentary, party, and cabinet system, the established (state-supported) Roman Catholic and Anglican churches, and Quebec's judicial and administrative structures took their inspiration from Britain. British constitutional practice and its Canadian imitations were resolutely pragmatic, compromising, and much less theoretical than the models of intellectuals like Charles Louis de Montesquieu or Thomas Jefferson.

The dominance of British culture had strong implications for communication in Quebec. From our own school and tourist experiences with other languages, we know that mastery of language tilts power, be it that of a waiter or judge! Failure of nationalism or independence in 1837, the subsequent reinforcement of British tradition, and the ongoing economic integration of Quebec with the dominant culture of North America, all meant increasing power for English as both a language and a way of thinking, even though the vast majority of Quebecers, then and now, were French speaking.

CHANGING FORMS OF POLITICAL POWER

Before the 1840s, Quebec was overwhelmingly rural, and imposing authority on its frequently unruly peasantry was a primary concern. Rural power in both New France and in Lower Canada had been concentrated in the hands of Crown officials and an aristocracy that exerted seigneurial control along the St Lawrence River and its tributaries. Other groups exercising significant power included the parish clergy and, in Montreal and Quebec City, the great merchants, whose wealth was derived from staple trades like furs, from importing goods from Britain and the Caribbean, or from trading locally in food, alcohol, or firewood. To give face to these groups, we can think of Sir John Colborne, Governor of British North America and representative of Queen Victoria during the rebellions, Louis-Joseph Papineau, seigneur and leader of the Patriote movement, and Peter McGill, importer, banker, and land developer. (These men can be easily researched in the *Dictionary of Canadian Biography*.)

These groups—Crown officials, seigneurs, and merchants—lost power in the decades following 1837. The dismantling of the British mercantile system in favour of free trade encouraged Britain to step back from direct political control of the colony; Britain transferred power and the expenses of the colony from the Governor and Colonial Office into the hands of Canadian authorities. The power exercised by governors like Colborne and his successors Lord Durham and Lord Elgin, diminished after the 1850s. In the late 1840s, an end came to a half-century struggle between the legislature and executive for control of the taxation purse. The granting of responsible government, the development of party and cabinet systems, and the alliance of centrists in Quebec and Ontario brought about the dependence of the executive branch on a bi-national majority in the legislative assembly. Papineau, leader of the movement for national liberation, anti-English and elitist, could never aspire to majority status in this structure. Nor would Peter McGill and his generation of Tory and anti-French merchants remain important players in centrist politics and in establishing state structures to promote the railways and factories that would industrialize Quebec.

Let us briefly examine how political power evolved over the 1840s and 1850s. Martial law was proclaimed after the first Rebellion in 1837 and the assembly was suspended. After the second wave of rebellions in 1838, harsher punishments were imposed. Some 850 Patriotes were arrested and 108 court-martialled, 99 of whom were condemned to death. Twelve were actually hanged and 58 deported to penal colonies in Australia. The pain of this failure and punishment, and its heightening in Lord Durham's Report has marked Quebec history every since. Nationalist historian Maurice Séguin, for example, has not been alone in interpreting the period as 'serfdom' under 'British occupation'.[5] Without doubt, the Rebellions facilitated a purging of nationalists, an accession to power by a new moderate and bi-ethnic group of moderates, and the expansion of conservative controls imposed by the Catholic Church. The Special Council, dominated by members of the anglophone elite, legislated for the colony between 1838 and 1841, and set in place a new institutional framework that included asylums, Catholic classical colleges, rural police, circuit courts, and literary societies. It began the breakdown of old seigneurial controls and the stranglehold of a religious order on land in Montreal, offering the city's landowners the right to commute their lands into freehold tenure. It further reassured capitalists through a Registry Act (1841), which forced the public registration of contracts such as land sales and mortgages. Finally, it accorded social and corporate powers to the Catholic Church, allowing existing religious communities to admit new members, permitting entry into Quebec of orders from France and Ireland, and exempting the property of religious institutions from taxes.

The Act of Union of 1840, one of Lord Durham's proposals, did permit a legislative assembly which would replace the Special Council. The assembly had 42 seats each for the newly named Canada East and Canada West (formerly Upper and Lower Canada), an apparent measure of equality that masked the fact that Canada East had a population of 650,000, compared to Canada West's 450,000. Power in this political structure inevitably shifted away from regional or nationalist parties to pragmatic, bicultural political alliances. Quebec leaders like LaFontaine and Cartier found common ground with their Ontario counterparts around a program of canals, railways, and economic development. They agreed to leave provocative national issues such as schools and social institutions to separate, autonomous treatment in both Canada East and Canada West. This separation into provincial jurisdiction of controversial religious and social issues would be echoed later in Confederation. The formation of this centrist party, known first as the Reform Party and ultimately as the Conservative Party, coincided with the repeal of the British Corn Laws and Navigation Acts after 1846, as Britain embraced free trade and re-evaluated the worth of settler colonies like Canada. In 1847, Governor General Lord Elgin accepted the principle of responsible government, calling on LaFontaine and Robert Baldwin to form a government after they won an election majority. Passage of the Rebellion Losses Bill, which compensated Patriotes for their losses in the Rebellions, enraged the anglophone elite. In April 1849 they were at the core of an angry mob that torched the Parliament building while other commercial leaders called for annexation to the United States.

Although Quebec politics would remain deeply fractured, with strong liberal and nationalist tendencies, the LaFontaine-Cartier Reformers kept themselves at centre stage. In the larger politics of Canada, they espoused liberal capitalism, free trade, and immigrant labour while, at home, they shored up their Quebec base by encouraging an expanding institutional and ideological place for the Catholic Church. They paid careful attention to regional concerns, subsidizing local colonization and roads and railways into frontier zones, and using government patronage to good effect. Conscious of Quebec sensitivities and power structures, they responded slowly to capitalist demands to dismantle seigneurialism, seeking support in particular from the Catholic clergy, proprietors of some of the largest seigneuries. They also understood the economic and regional importance in Montreal and the Eastern Townships of Quebec's English-speaking community, its conservatism, and its fears as an ethnic minority. Reform leaders made important concessions; Quebec would be officially bilingual with English increasingly dominant in business and equal as a language in government and in the law. Speaking in English, moderates like Cartier emphasized their British loyalty, love of things British, and their trust in the building of a bicultural, pan-Canadian state. They were also attentive to the future of English Montreal's university and to English school, benevolent, and social institutions; and in the federation negotiations after the mid-1850s, Quebec's English-speaking minority was given assurances concerning its schools and rights to a fixed number of seats from the Eastern Townships.

Whatever its attraction to capitalists and central Canadian moderates, Confederation was never an easy sell in French Quebec or, for that matter, in parts of the Maritimes. Regionalism, increasing ethnic tensions, the concentration of power in Ottawa, and fears of being swamped by a Protestant and potentially racist English Canada tested federalist leaders like Cartier. While his opponents accused him of putting in place a legislative union rather than a federation and of leaving the French-Canadian population 'fast asleep', Cartier, whatever his private cynicism, spoke of a political dream. In the old order, one's place depended on position in a hierarchy that was rooted in feudalism, while in the republican model, citizenship and constitutional rights guaranteed liberty and equality. Cartier suggested a third possibility, promoting a vision of identity, and ultimately of sovereignty, that was more layered, more intricate, and perhaps unattainable! He pointed to the model of existing autonomous jurisdictions in religious and ethnic matters such as education. He described the federation as potentially a new 'political nationality' and, standing Durham on his head, described a society in which both French and English would remain intact and in which the common good would result from competition and imitation among Races, Nations, and Religions:

> We would form a political nationality with which neither the national origin, nor the religion of any individual would interfere . . . We were of different races, not for the purpose of warring against each other, but in order to compete and emulate for the general welfare.[6]

At Confederation negotiations in Charlottetown and Quebec City in 1864, delegates from Quebec accepted a highly centralized state, with protection of French-Canadian interests in Ottawa largely delegated to an upper house or senate that had no financial control and whose members were appointed for life. The financial terms of the British North America Act, which enacted Confederation, reinforced Quebec's subservience to Ottawa, since more than half of the province's income was a federal subsidy. Centralization was, however, entirely within the logic of Canadian capitalism and the province's bankers, shippers, and industrial producers had access to strengthened, integrated markets. Quebec did retain much autonomy in powers that included education, social services, and natural resources. This would be important for the Church and for a local professional elite.

POWER AND THE CHURCH

Legislative politics and constructing the Canadian federation, as we have suggested by our reference to 'old bones', were however, only pieces in Quebec's larger power puzzle. While the French and American republics and, to a lesser extent, English Canada emphasized the secular in modernizing and industrializing societies, Quebec took a distinct route. You may have noticed that the Roman Catholic Church, except for its parish role, was not particularly emphasized in our description of the dominant forces in Quebec before the Rebellions. True, the Church had been a loyal supporter of the Crown stretching back through the War of 1812 with the United States, through the horror for Catholics of the French Revolution, and through its comfortable connivance with both British and French officials across the eighteenth century. But the Church had had difficulty recruiting and training priests, and the peasantry had remained wary of the clergy's ambitions and controls. The Church's influence however, had been particularly critical in the Rebellions of 1837–8, with bishops describing the insurrections as 'criminal in the eyes of God'. In rural parishes, the Church used its muscle to defuse unrest among the peasantry while priests from the Seminary of Montreal discouraged Montreal's growing Irish-Catholic working-class population from assimilating the rebellions to their historical struggle against British exploitation. A grateful Quebec elite returned the favour in the 1840s, granting the Church power to develop schools, hospitals, and other social institutions for the Catholic population.

Membership of female religious communities, which had remained steady before 1840, doubled in the 1840s. Twelve male orders (most imported from Europe) were established in Quebec in the second half of the nineteenth century. The Church was given virtual autonomy in teaching Catholic children, training teachers, curricula, and textbooks, and powerful authority over the flow of information through books, clubs, and newspapers. Whereas only 36 per cent of the parishioners at Montreal's Notre Dame Church took Easter communion in 1839, virtually all of the Catholic population of the diocese of Montreal did so in the 1860s. With this expanded role, the Church used its power to shape Quebec in conservative directions, becoming more moralistic, more disciplinary of women, and emphasizing Quebec's separateness from the secular and materialistic culture of English-speaking North America. Adding to this growing moral and social authority, the Church, in the void left by the collapse of Papineau's Patriote movement, successfully portrayed itself as the primary defender of a French-Canadian nation. This orientation and insularity from North American society had effects stretching perhaps to the present in issues like immigration and integration. Catholic Quebec, with the singular exception of Irish Catholics, did not encourage a pluralist vision, tending instead to a defensive and exclusive corral protecting faith and nation. Intermarriage, American or English-Canadian trade unions, and Protestant university teachers posed difficulties, as we see below in the story of Elzéar-Alexandre Taschereau. Later in the century, newcomers such as Jews and other non-Catholic immigrants would gravitate to Protestant, English-speaking institutions. Nor was the Catholic Church immune from internal division between ultramontanists who believed in the superiority of the Pope and those, led by the archbishop of Quebec, who gave predominance to the Church as a national institution.

SNAPSHOT

The Consecration of Archbishop Taschereau, Quebec City, 20 March 1871

When I think of major ceremonial events which have marked the immediate past, an Olympic opening, a Super Bowl game, or the funeral of Diana, Princess of Wales, comes to mind. Each had its pageant, banners, fly-pasts, and rituals, its speeches, royal boxes, and 'big shots', its rock-star music from Bruce Springsteen to Elton John, and its rush of journalists and photographers. In their wake and in our cities and cupboards are stadiums, mementoes, and 'Lady Di' coffee cups. Similar public events were staged in nineteenth-century Quebec around events like the British victory at Waterloo, the opening of Montreal's Victoria Bridge, or the funeral of Albert, Prince Consort to Queen Victoria. Elzéar-Alexandre Taschereau was consecrated as Archbishop in the Basilica of Quebec City, 20 March 1871. The extravagant ceremony included a papal bull, the display of coats of arms, uniforms, ecclesiastical robes, and flags; and the presence of bishops, justices, senators, and other notables from around the Atlantic world. Banquets, concerts, and symbolic processions through city streets and specially-constructed triumphal arches culminated in a mass, communion, and bestowal of the ring and mitre on the new Archbishop. The event was commemorated in paintings, special tokens, photos (thanks to new daguerreotype technology), and later in front of the Basilica, a memorial statue of the Archbishop.

Taschereau was a media star of his day, distinguished, cultured, and available for interviews and photos. Of the fourth generation in an aristocratic family, he was the son of a judge and seigneur. While his brother chose law, rising to sit in the Supreme Court of Canada, Elzéar-Alexandre was drawn to the priesthood, the career of three of his uncles, including the Bishop of Quebec. Trained in the classical-college tradition with an excellent education in the sciences, literature, and philosophy, he took a Grand Tour of Europe before being ordained a priest in 1842. Instead of serving as a parish priest, he spent his career as an intellectual and administrator; he taught at the Seminary of Quebec, took a doctorate in theology in Rome, and served as superior of the Seminary and rector of Laval University.[7]

Occurring at the time of the new Quebec Civil Code, the Confederation of Canada, and the turbulence surrounding Louis Riel and the future of French Canadians in the West, his nomination for Bishop was part of the affirmation of a Quebec national identity rooted in the Roman Catholic Church, elite families, and historical legal, seminary, and convent institutions. His four-hour consecration was a major celebration. The Basilica was lavishly decorated for the occasion, with an artist from the *Illustrated News* capturing the scene for an audience throughout the British world. Journalists drew particular attention to the chandeliers above the altar from which hung the Archbishop's coat of arms. The ceremony began with a triumphant procession, which began next door to the Basilica at the Archbishop's Palace, but wound by a circuitous route past the city's most important institutions. It was officiated by the Archbishop of Toronto who was seconded by eight bishops. Witnessing in front pews were 150 priests, the professoriate from Laval University, and political, diplomatic, and judicial notables. Among Taschereau notables present were his brother, Judge Jean-Thomas Taschereau, and Major Eugène-Arthur Taschereau, aide-de-camp to the Lieutenant Governor. After the granting to him of the ring, mitre, gloves, and pastoral baton of an archbishop, the bestowal of the kiss of peace from each of his episcopal colleagues, and the singing of a Te Deum, 'His Grandeur' blessed the congregation:

A sentiment of profound respect marked each bowed head and a shiver of joy and of immense religious enthusiasm could be felt through the immense crowd. There was something infinitely solemn in this majestic benediction even if it had the familiarity of the blessing a father might give his children. It was in fact a moment of profound veneration and of the most respectful love typical of the great moments of affection stamped with the seal of religion.[8]

Taschereau used his office as archbishop and then as Canada's first cardinal (1886) to consolidate Roman Catholic institutions and to position the Church at the core of a French-Canadian national identity. He oversaw the establishment of some 40 new parishes, 30 missions, and regional classical colleges. He worked to strengthen Laval University as a Catholic university and introduced several teaching orders into Canada including the Marist brothers and the clerics of Saint-Viateur. His funeral was held in the Basilica in April 1898, the same space where he had been consecrated archbishop and cardinal. The family biographer described the funeral ceremony as 'the most impressive ever held in our country'.[9] In 1923, with his nephew, Premier of Quebec Louis-Alexandre Taschereau looking on, a grateful province dedicated a statue in the archbishop's honour in the square in front of the Basilica. Designed and cast in bronze in Paris, the statue gave physical permanence to the ceremony and his career in Church, seminary, and university. While the religiosity, emphasis on death, and masculine dominance in the Taschereau consecration perhaps differentiate it from Olympic opening ceremonies, Super Bowl victory celebrations, and Elton John praising Diana's beauty, these are all 'theatre', as the wise Edward P. Thompson pointed out, spectacles that use public space to reinforce values and hierarchies.[10]

POWER, LAW, AND SEIGNEURIALISM

Our discussion of power in mid-nineteenth century Quebec must next consider the fundamental changes that occurred around historical systems of law and landholding. As a result of the Quebec Act (1774), the British had permitted jurisdiction of the family, social relations, and seigneurial lands to continue under French customary law, a system summed up in the sixteenth-century Custom of Paris. The present can be described as 'a charter age' and we look for our legal rights in the Canadian or Quebec Charter of Rights or the American Bill of Rights. The customary law of mid-nineteenth century Quebec was different, less specific, less tightly written, and more a sense of historical maxims, what a sage called 'the spirit of the centuries'. Montesquieu used that same word in his *Spirit of the Laws* (1748) and other French legal thinkers related law to 'natural order'; feminist historian Bettina Bradbury alludes to the medieval hierarchies of that law, referring to the 'superior chivalry of French law'. At the time of the Rebellions, there was no official Quebec version of the Custom.

Customary law in outlining seigneurialism did not give absolute rights in property, insisting instead on the priority of the family and of vulnerable widows or children. This clashed with the principles of a modern, capitalist state in which the individual can contract his labour or property apart from family needs and in which registered creditors have priority. A final frustration for those who favoured a rational, scientific, and uniform system across Quebec was the fact that English, and sometimes American, common law applied in English-speaking regions. Wills, for example, could be prepared under the English system, while in the Eastern Townships, a Vermont-style contract for the sale of a horse sealed by a handshake rather than a written agreement might be valid. Power and right in these polyjural situations was difficult to determine and remote from modern concepts of the law as an ordered and predictable science and discipline.

Since at least the beginning of the nineteenth century, feudal (and that is the correct term) institutions like customary law and seigneurialism in Quebec faced various attacks. These accelerated with capital accumulation in projects like railways or industries and with the prospect of geographical expansion into a broader Canadian state. Although wealthy English Quebecers had been major purchasers of seigneuries, their community regularly attacked it as effete and obstructive to capitalist development. Seigneurialism applied to urban centres as well as the rural parishes, and the big industrial millers and land developers in Montreal chafed at its milling monopoly and its *lods et ventes* (sales taxes) on improvements. Capitalists and industrial producers demanded an end to seigneurial and customary rights in favour of a 'free' market in land and labour. In the new legal and property regimes resulting from codifying the civil law and dismantling seigneurialism, individual rights, freedom of contract, and freehold property took precedence over family and community priorities that reached back to early Christian and medieval concepts of family and social relations. A universal education system; a province-wide judicial infrastructure of courthouses, jails, and police; new municipalities; and new forms of taxation were other pieces in this puzzle of changing relations of power.

The 1850s were the critical period in Quebec legal history. Faculties of law, schools in which law would be treated as a scientific discipline, were established at McGill and Laval universities in 1853–4. In 1854, the Seigneurial Act dismantled seigneurialism across Quebec, taking land from its entwined and feudal context and making it a specific and distinct commodity that an individual could freely buy and sell. 1857 was probably the critical year with Attorney General Cartier establishing a Codification Commission of three senior judges. Cartier pointed out that 'the code will be written in both languages'. The Commission had power to determine which French laws were still in effect and how they had been affected by legislation since the Conquest. They would have huge influence in establishing new definitions of contract, of settling issues like divorce in Catholic society, and of reshaping the place of women. In 1866, one year before Confederation, the transformation of the Custom of Paris into the Civil Code was complete, and the Civil Code took effect in Quebec.

POWER OVER WOMEN

Gender is a fundamental locus of power relations, and the feminist movement has struggled to place this reality as central in the history of Quebec. Authors like Bettina Bradbury and Cecelia Morgan give particular importance to the mid-nineteenth century, emphasizing a slippage in the place of women, what Morgan and others call the 'masculinization' of Canadian society after the Rebellions.[11] This could be seen in the factories, where women usually represented a reserve army of labour. Women who owned property could vote until 1849, when a law was rewritten to exclude them; women did not regain that right in Quebec provincial elections until 1940. Although few women had had the right to vote, those who could played a decisive role in some urban ridings:

> It is odious, Papineau argued for example, to see women dragged up to the hustings by their husbands, girls by their fathers, often against their will. The public interest, decency, and the modesty of the fair sex require that these scandals cease.[12]

In the same critical period in the mid-nineteenth century, administrative laws concerning registry, mortgages, and contracts were systematically adjusted to subordinate the rights of the wife to capitalist relations. Just as important as these changes in state regulation were private relations and legal and social customs deeply rooted in both Protestant and Catholic society in Quebec. To describe this power, we cannot do better than quote historian Bettina Bradbury:

> Power and rights were not evenly distributed at this time. In working-class families wage dependency locked wives and children to husbands and fathers in a relationship that was at once mutual and complementary, yet hierarchical and dependent. Women were legally incapacitated upon marriage. This meant that most had no rights to administer property or even their own wages.[13]

Law in Western society, whether English common law or the Custom of Paris, subjugated the wife to her husband. In Quebec, he had entire financial authority, he established the family home, he had rights to discipline his wife, and he had rights to infidelity as long as he did not bring a lover into the family home.

Wives had always assisted their husbands in the boutiques, market stalls, and artisanal shops, and many operated businesses of their own such as grocery stores, taverns, and dressmaking shops. But a married woman who wanted to operate independently in trade and enter into contracts or hire employees could do so under article 179 of the Civil Code only with the formal authorization of her husband.

Marta Danylewycz has pointed out that, as they were excluded from the professions, middle-class women had few work options outside marriage.[14] Catholic women in Quebec increasingly turned to the convent for careers of authority and relative autonomy from male control. Twenty-five female religious communities were established in Quebec in the second half of the nineteenth century. Women also faced strong moral and behavioural censure. While the world of law and university was increasingly influenced by rationalism and science, there was growing cultural pressure on Catholic women to assume the mysticism, suffering, and obedience of models like Mary:

> Mothers, why not imitate the Blessed Virgin? a Montreal priest wrote in an 1871 sermon. . . . You sweep the floor, you cook the dinner, you mend your children's clothes, you keep things in good order in the house. Why not do all this in a spirit of love of God. All those actions the Blessed Virgin performed. There were very ordinary actions but they were sanctified by the spirit of love and charity which animated the Blessed Virgin.[15]

CONCLUSION

How can we relate these issues of power and authority to our own times and to other periods of Quebec history? Can we join the dots between the doctrine of Immaculate Conception as an example of nineteenth-century clerical power and Cardinal Jean-Claude Turcotte's decision in September 2008 to renounce his membership in the Order of Canada, in protest against the naming to the Order of Henry Morgentaler? Morgentaler was a major force behind the liberalization of Canadian abortion laws and giving women the power to determine the fate of a fetus they carry. As with the doctrines of the Virgin Birth and the Immaculate Conception, and the issues of secularism we saw in the 1850s, Cardinal Turcotte insists that power does not rest in the hands of individual mothers-to-be: 'we are not masters of human life, it rests in the hands of God'.

We also suggested that power in the mid-nineteenth century shifted from aristocrats and seigneurs to a new bourgeoisie that held power in government and business. Women and workers made little headway in the mid-nineteenth century and most of their gains

toward equality occurred in the twentieth century. But traditional hierarchies and forms of power are tenacious. As recently as 2001, for example, Conrad Black, English Quebec's most powerful capitalist native son, chose to renounce his Canadian citizenship so that he could sit in the British House of Lords as Lord Black of Cross Harbour. We can conclude then that the nineteenth-century forms of power that we have examined here are not nostalgic but real and ongoing.

QUESTIONS FOR CONSIDERATION

1. What comparisons can be made with the themes developed here and other experiences across Canada in the same period?

2. Can you compare the role of the Catholic Church in Quebec to its place in France in the same period, in the United States, or in another country with which you are familiar?

3. Using the Notman Collection of Photographs at the McCord Museum of Canadian History website, can you develop a portfolio of images that support or contradict the main arguments of this chapter?

NOTES

1. See for example Marx's *Communist Manifesto*, describing conditions in the very period we are examining!

2. Examples include John Dickinson and Brian Young, *A Short History of Quebec* (Montreal and Kingston: McGill-Queen's University Press, 2008), 154–97; or Paul-André Linteau, Jean-Claude Robert and René Durocher, *Quebec: A History, 1867–1929* (Toronto: Lorimer, 1983).

3. 'The Defeat of George-Étienne Cartier in Montreal-East in 1872'. *Canadian Historical Review* 51(4) (December 1970), 386–406. Excerpted in Marlene Shore, ed., *Reading Canada's History: The Contested Past* (Toronto: University of Toronto Press, 2002), 224–32.

4. Cited in J.-C. Bonenfant, 'George-Étienne Cartier', *Dictionary of Canadian Biography*. Cartier's ideology is most accessible in Joseph Tassé, ed., *Discours de Sir Georges* [sic] *Cartier* (Montreal 1893).

5. Maurice Séguin, *L'idée d'indépendance au Québec: Genèse historique*. (Trois-Rivières: Boréal, 1970), 250.

6. Young, *George-Étienne Cartier: Montreal Bourgeois* (Montreal and Kingston: McGill-Queen's University Press, 1981), 81.

7. For his career, see his biography by Honorius Provost available online in the *Dictionary of Canadian Biography*.

8. 'Un sentiment de respect le plus marqué inclina toutes les têtes et l'on sentit comme un frémissement de joie et d'enthousiasme religieux agir sur l'immense assemblée. Il y avait là quelque chose d'infiniment plus solennel encore que cette bénédiction, pourtant si auguste

du père de famille bénissant ses enfants. C'était une vénération plus profonde, un amour plus respectueux, comme toutes les grandes affections empreintes du sceau de la religion'. *Le Nouveau Monde*, 21 March 1871.

9. Pierre-Georges Roy, *La famille Taschereau* (Lévis: Mercantile, 1901), 'les plus imposantes qui aient jamais été faites dans notre pays', 137.

10. Edward Thompson, *Making History: Writings on History and Culture* (New York: New Press, 1994), 208.

11. Lykke de la Cour, Cecilia Morgan, and Mariana Valverde, 'Gender Regulation and State Formation in Nineteenth-Century Canada' in Allan Greer and Ian Radforth, *Colonial Leviathan: State Formation in Mid-Nineteenth-Century Canada* (Toronto: University of Toronto Press, 1992), 163.

12. Allan Greer, *The Patriots and the People: The Rebellion of 1837 in Rural Lower Canada* (Toronto: University of Toronto Press, 1993), 206.

13. Bettina Bradbury, *Working Families: Age, Gender, and Daily Survival in Industrializing Montreal* (Toronto: McClelland & Stewart, 1993), 220.

14. Marta Danylewycz, *Taking the Veil: An Alternative to Marriage, Motherhood, and Spinsterhood in Quebec, 1840–1920* (Toronto: McClelland & Stewart, 1987).

15. Cited in Brian Young, *In its Corporate Capacity: The Seminary of Montreal as a Business Institution, 1816–1876*. (Montreal and Kingston: McGill-Queen's University Press, 1986), 155.

Useful Websites

Dictionary of Canadian Biography:
www.biographi.ca/index
A very useful site for researching the prominent
people of the period.

McCord Museum: www.mccord-museum.qc.ca/en/
For interesting archival collections as well as
historical objects.

Musée de l'Amérique française: www.mcq.org/fr/
maf/index.html
Canadiana: www.canadiana.org/eco.php
Documents on the period.

Select Bibliography

Christie, Nancy, ed. *Transatlantic Subjects: Ideas,
Institutions, and Social Experience in Post-Revolutionary
British North America.* Montreal and Kingston: McGill-
Queen's University Press, 2008.

Curtis, Bruce. *The Politics of Population: State Formation,
Statistics, and the Census of Canada, 1840–1875.*
Toronto: University of Toronto Press, 2001.

Danylewycz, Marta. *Taking the Veil: An Alternative to
Marriage, Motherhood, and Spinsterhood in Quebec,
1840–1920.* Toronto: McClelland & Stewart, 1987.

Fecteau, Jean-Marie. *La liberté du pauvre: Sur la régulation
du crime et de la pauvreté au XIXe siècle québécois.*
Montreal: VLB, 2004.

Greer, Allan and Ian Radforth. *Colonial Leviathan: State
Formation in Mid-Nineteenth-Century Canada.*
Toronto: University of Toronto Press, 1992.

CHAPTER 4

Canadian Federalism and the Search for Accommodation of Quebec Nationalism

Garth Stevenson, Brock University

— TIMELINE —

1864   Quebec conference on proposal for federation of British North America adopts Quebec resolutions, outlining main provisions of federal constitution for Canada.

1865   Quebec resolutions adopted by Canadian Parliament after debate.

1867   British North America (BNA) Act comes into effect.

1873   George-Étienne Cartier dies.

1878–9   Letellier controversy erupts when Liberal Lieutenant-Governor dismisses Conservative government of Quebec. When federal Conservatives return to office, Lieutenant-Governor is dismissed.

1882   T.J.J. Loranger's letters on BNA Act expound compact theory of Confederation.

1887   Honoré Mercier becomes Quebec's first nationalist premier.

1896   Wilfrid Laurier becomes Canada's first francophone prime minister.

1917–8   Francoeur resolution introduced and debated in Legislative Assembly.

1927   Judicial Committee of Privy Council (JCPC) awards all of Labrador to Newfoundland. Beginning of efforts to agree on an amending formula for BNA Act.

1932   JCPC decides that air transport and broadcasting fall under federal jurisdiction.

1936   Maurice Duplessis becomes premier for first time.

1940   Quebec, under Liberal government, agrees to constitutional amendment placing unemployment insurance under federal jurisdiction.

1944   Duplessis returns to office after five years in opposition.

1948   Quebec adopts its own official flag, first province to do so.

1951   Duplessis agrees to constitutional amendment sharing jurisdiction over pensions between provincial and federal governments.

1954   Quebec imposes provincial income tax. Federal government agrees that part of it can be credited against federal income tax.

1956 Report of Tremblay Commission calls for fundamental changes in Canadian federalism.

1957 Federal government begins to make equalization payments to Quebec and other provinces.

1960 Jean Lesage becomes premier. Beginning of 'Quiet Revolution'.
Rassemblement pour l'indépendance nationale (RIN) established.

1964 Federal–Quebec compromise allows establishment of two parallel pension plans.

1965 Preliminary report of The Royal Commission on Bilingualism and Biculturalism says Canada 'is passing through the greatest crisis in its history'.
Quebec rejects Fulton-Favreau constitutional amending formula.
Union Nationale leader Daniel Johnson publishes *Égalité ou Indépendance*.

1966 Johnson becomes premier.

1967 René Lévesque publishes *Option Québec*, leaves Liberals, and forms Mouvement Souveraineté-Association (MSA).

1968 MSA merges with RIN to become Parti Québécois (PQ).

1970 Robert Bourassa becomes premier. PQ wins second-largest share of popular vote.
October crisis. FLQ kidnaps and kills Pierre Laporte. War Measures Act proclaimed.

1974 Bill 22 makes French official language of Quebec.

1976 Lévesque becomes premier, forms first PQ government.

1977 Charter of the French Language adopted.

1980 Referendum on sovereignty-association; 40 per cent vote in favour.

1981 Federal government and all provinces except Quebec agree to new constitutional amending formula and Charter of Rights and Freedoms, which protects English-language education in Quebec.

1982 Supreme Court rules that Quebec never had veto over constitutional change.

1985 Robert Bourassa again becomes premier.

1987 Meech Lake Accord recognizing Quebec as 'distinct society' is agreed to by all provincial premiers.

1990 Meech Lake Accord unravels as Manitoba and Newfoundland refuse to ratify it.
Lucien Bouchard resigns from federal government and forms Bloc Québécois.

1991 Allaire Report and Bélanger-Campeau Report are published.

1992 Quebec and Canada reject Charlottetown Accord in simultaneous referendums.

1994 Jacques Parizeau becomes premier.

1995 Referendum on sovereignty; 49.4 per cent vote in favour.

1998 Supreme Court rules that Quebec has no automatic right to secede, but that federal government would have to negotiate if 'a clear majority' of Quebec voters supported sovereignty.

2000 Clarity Act imposes rigid conditions on Quebec's ability to secede.

2006 Canada's Parliament recognizes Québécois as a nation.

Whether and how Quebec nationalism can be accommodated within the Canadian federal state is the most important question in Canadian politics. Certainly it has lasted longer than any other political controversy in Canada, and it is safe to say that more writers have written more extensively about it than any other Canadian topic. Yet no consensus about it has ever developed, either in Quebec or elsewhere, and it remains imperfectly understood, at least by Canadians outside of Quebec. Part of the reason for this is the language barrier. Quebec's political discourse is of course conducted mainly in French, and only about one-tenth of Canadians outside Quebec understand that language. But another reason is the ambiguity of the term *federalism* itself, and its relationship, in Canada, to different kinds of nationalism.

TWO CONCEPTS OF FEDERALISM

Alain-G. Gagnon has suggested that there are two different concepts or understandings of federalism, which he calls the 'American' and 'European' versions.[1] Using this terminology, it is probably safe to say that most Canadians outside Quebec have an American understanding of the word *federalism* while most francophones in Quebec have a European understanding of it.

The American concept of federalism was set out by James Madison, Alexander Hamilton, and John Jay in *The Federalist*, a series of essays designed to persuade the voters of New York to accept the then-new Constitution of the United States. It views federalism as an institutional framework which divides authority between two levels of government for two primary purposes: to govern a large territory in an effective and efficient manner, and to protect individual freedom and property by avoiding the concentration of authority in any single person or institution. Although some of the units of the federation may have distinct identities, cultures, or traditions, the argument for a federal form of government can be sustained independently of these differences. The United States Constitution, which the three authors of *The Federalist* helped to draft, is based on this concept of federalism, and it has been subsequently imitated to varying degrees in a variety of places including Australia, Brazil,

Germany, and Mexico. Such federations may be more or less decentralized, in theory and in practice, but the distribution of powers between the two levels of government is based on functional criteria—which level can do the job best. American-style federalism is also characterized by symmetry: each province or state has exactly the same status and the same degree of autonomy as all the others.

The origins of the European concept of federalism are somewhat less clear, and the concept is not clearly embodied in the constitution of any European state. However, its essential purpose is clear enough. That purpose is to allow distinct nations or cultural communities occupying different but neighbouring geographical spaces to preserve their identities, languages, cultures, and traditions within their own spaces while delegating some authority to common institutions for purposes primarily of economic growth and military security. It is often associated with the principle of subsidiarity in Catholic political thought, which states that no function should be entrusted to a higher authority if it can be effectively performed by a lower authority: this is, in other words, the decentralization of power. The European Union, which appears to be developing gradually into a federation, is the best example of this kind of federalism.

For most Canadians outside Quebec, federalism means essentially what it means to Americans. Most Canadians outside Quebec like the province in which they live, if only because those who don't can quite easily move to one that they like better; but the emotional involvement with the province, if any, is not usually very deep, except in Newfoundland and Labrador, which was a separate colony until 1949 and retains a fairly strong sense of distinct identity. In a vast country that extends through several time zones, it makes sense to have a more local government deal with local concerns, rather than having all decisions made in Ottawa. Local control may also have economic advantages, particularly where natural resources are involved. The division of responsibilities between the two levels of government is not usually seen as ideological, but rather as pragmatic and functional. Few Canadians outside Quebec object to the federal government spending money in their province on matters that are constitutionally under provincial jurisdiction.

Particularly since 1982, when the Charter of Rights and Freedoms came into effect, most Canadians outside Quebec are more concerned with their individual rights and freedoms than they are with the autonomy and collective 'rights' of the province in which they happen to live. Finally, most Canadians outside Quebec believe that all Canadian provinces, large or small, are equal to one another in status and that none should be given special rights or privileges.

Quebecers' view of federalism is quite different. Of course federalism itself is a contested and controversial concept in Quebec, with many people (sovereignists) arguing that no kind of federalism suits Quebec's needs and that nothing short of complete independence will suffice. But even those Quebecers (usually the majority) who are federalists justify their choice quite differently than people in other parts of Canada, who take federalism for granted. For most Quebec federalists, Quebec, rather than Canada, is their primary source of political identity and allegiance. They accept Canada because its existence is believed to be good for Quebec, rather than vice versa. In defending their federalist preferences, they argue that Canadian federalism enables Quebec to make its own decisions about education, health, justice, language policy, the environment, and other important subjects while giving it certain economic benefits. But they also are wary of any intervention by the federal government in fields of provincial jurisdiction. If the federal government spends money in such fields, they are likely to think that the federal government has more money than it needs and should give that money directly to the provincial governments with no strings attached. Finally, most Quebec federalists believe that Quebec differs from the other Canadian provinces in being the homeland of a distinct people with its own language and traditions, based on 400 years of history. Therefore, it makes sense to them that the government of Quebec should have some powers and responsibilities that the other provincial governments do not have.

These different perspectives are not new. They reflect not only that Quebec has a different and longer history than the rest of Canada, and that Quebecers predominantly speak a different language, but also that Quebecers, and the francophone population of Canada generally, are a small and shrinking minority in Canada and North America. If Canada had only one English-speaking province and the predominant language in North America was French, the people of that English-speaking province would probably be similarly preoccupied with provincial autonomy.

QUEBEC AND FEDERALISM: 1867 TO 1960

Canada became a federation in 1867 because the experiment of governing central Canada as a unitary state had proved unworkable. George-Étienne Cartier, Quebec's Conservative leader, supported the new arrangement because it would give French Canadians in Quebec control over education, social services, municipal affairs, and civil law, even though the federal government would have the primary responsibility for economic development. It was Cartier who insisted that a long list of 'Exclusive Powers of Provincial Legislatures' be included in the constitution. His Liberal opponents argued that the powers given to the province were inadequate and that the addition of Nova Scotia and New Brunswick to Canada would make French Canada an even smaller minority in a larger country. Most of the Catholic clergy were Conservatives and agreed with Cartier that Confederation's advantages outweighed the disadvantages.

In the 1880s a Quebec judge, T.J.J. Loranger, expounded what is called the 'compact theory' of Confederation, arguing that the formation of the federal state was the result of a treaty or compact among the provinces and that no changes in the constitution, particularly changes that would increase the power of the central government, could be made without their unanimous consent.[2] Maurice Duplessis, premier of Quebec from 1936 to 1939 and from 1944 to 1959, made the same point more pithily when he said that the federal government was the child of the provinces, not their father. The Tremblay Commission of Inquiry on Constitutional Problems, appointed by Duplessis in 1953 and reporting three years later, recommended a drastic revision of Canada's constitution. It would have required the federal government to give up all involvement in social and cultural policy, to abstain from imposing income tax, to spend only in areas of its own exclusive jurisdiction, and to share its macroeconomic powers and responsibilities with the provinces.[3] Duplessis himself made little effort to promote the ideas of the report, although he established a provincial income tax and refused to allow some federal spending programs within Quebec such as hospital insurance, the Trans-Canada Highway, and grants to universities.

Nonetheless, from 1867 until about 1960 federalism (variously defined) was taken for granted almost as much in Quebec as in any other part of Canada. Sovereignty for Quebec, although advocated occasionally by a few individuals, and perhaps secretly dreamed of by others who prudently remained silent, was not considered a realistic or serious option. Anglophone Canadians and francophone Quebecers were then probably more different in culture, and as socially isolated from one another as they are now, but the legitimacy of Canadian federalism was not threatened. Quebec, of course, had its disputes with the federal government, but most of them were not significantly different from those of other provinces. In fact, until Duplessis formed his second government in 1944, it was Ontario, not Quebec, that was most militant (and most successful) in defending its autonomy against the federal government.

This apparent stability was largely the result of the fact that the national aspirations of both anglophone and francophone Canadians were not as closely associated with different levels of government as they are today. First, governments had fewer functions than they have now and were mainly concerned with maintaining law and order, regulating foreign trade, and building and maintaining the infrastructure of transportation and communication. Second, the nationalism, if such it could be called, of anglophone Canadians was focused as much on the British Empire and Commonwealth as on Canada itself. Third, the nationalism in Quebec, although powerful, was largely focused on an ethno-cultural group (French-speaking Catholics) who were widely dispersed outside of Quebec (including substantial numbers in the northeastern United States) and by no means as predominant within Quebec as they became later. Fourth, the prevailing ideology of francophone Quebec tended to downplay the importance of the state (including Quebec's provincial government)

in relation to other institutions such as the Catholic Church, the family, and associations representing occupational or interest groups.

Thus, the issues that divided anglophone from francophone Canadians, at least until 1945, were mainly external relations and defence, especially participation in British wars and the imposition of conscription, or about the rights and privileges of the francophone and Catholic minorities in provinces other than Quebec, especially with regard to education. (These francophone minorities grew rapidly after Confederation, and by 1921 almost a quarter of Canada's French-speaking population lived outside of Quebec.)

There was little the government of Quebec could do about foreign policy, and Quebec's influence, such as it was, could best be exercised through Quebec's federal members of Parliament, most of whom were usually supporters of the government party. Decentralization of the federal system would not have solved the problems faced by the minorities, since the other provinces were using their autonomy to curtail the use of French in the schools and elsewhere. On the other hand, if Quebec had advocated coercive federal action to support the minorities in other provinces, it might have created a precedent that would endanger Quebec's control over its own educational system and culture. Thus there was *French-Canadian* nationalism, but not much *Quebec* nationalism centred around the institutions of the Quebec 'state'. Francophones in Quebec were actually the most enthusiastic supporters of *Canadian* nationalism, in wanting to substitute distinctively Canadian national symbols for British ones and to increase Canada's independence from British foreign policy.

THE AGE OF CONSTITUTIONAL UNCERTAINTY

All of this changed dramatically with the 'Quiet Revolution', which is usually said to have begun after Duplessis died in 1959 and the Liberals took power in 1960. It was essentially completed over the next two decades. During this period Quebec changed from a strongly Catholic and socially conservative society to an aggressively secular and socially liberal

one. In the process it built a modern interventionist welfare state ('the Quebec model') within the
framework of Canadian federalism. The 'state' (a
term rarely used in Quebec before the 1960s) sub-
stituted itself for the Catholic Church as a provider
of education, health care, and social services, and it
also undertook initiatives in economic and language
policy that undermined the power and influence of
Quebec's anglophone minority, which had dominated the province's economy for two centuries. As a
result, Quebec francophones began to identify with
their Quebec 'state' more than with Canada, with
their Church, or with a francophone collectivity that
lacked clear geographical boundaries. They began to
refer to themselves not as 'French Canadians' but as
'Québécois'. (Prior to the 1960s this term, if used at all,
would have referred only to a resident of Quebec City.)

The rather sudden emergence of state-centred
Quebec nationalism, and of an effective Quebec
public service and other institutions through which
it could be expressed, was the first significant threat
to the legitimacy, and even to the survival, of the
Canadian federal state since Confederation in 1867.
Quebec neo-nationalists began to view the existing
Canadian federal state as an obstacle to satisfying
Quebec's collective needs and to fulfilling Quebec's
ambitions. Some of them began to think that a fully
independent and sovereign Quebec might be the only
appropriate solution. A number of pro-sovereignty
parties and movements were formed in the early
1960s, ranging from moderate right-wing to extreme
left-wing. Other nationalists believed and hoped that
in some way Canadian federalism could be reformed
to accommodate Quebec's needs, perhaps by giving Quebec a 'special status' with more powers and
responsibilities than the other provinces, or perhaps
by transferring some federal powers and responsibilities to all of the provinces.

In the period just before and during Quebec's Quiet
Revolution, the rest of Canada was also changing in
ways that Quebecers sometimes failed to appreciate,
complicating the task of accommodating a changing
Quebec within the Canadian federation. Large-scale
immigration, at first from Europe and later from
other continents, made Canada, and particularly
Ontario, a multicultural, rather than a 'British',

society. Increasingly Canadians focused their attention on their own federal state and their own continent, rather than on Britain and the Empire.[4] The
Canadian federal state in the 1940s, like the Quebec
provincial state two decades later, had developed an
effective public service and greater sources of revenue. It demonstrated its capabilities by effectively
participating in two wars (1939–45 and 1950–3),
establishing state enterprises and social welfare programs, controlling both inflation and unemployment, and persuading Newfoundland to join Canada
as a tenth province in 1949. In the same year Canada
abolished constitutional appeals to the Judicial
Committee of the Privy Council in England, which
had often defended the autonomy of Quebec and
other Canadian provinces.

The Canadian federal state also began, ominously
for Quebec nationalists, to involve itself in matters
from which it had previously abstained, such as
health, education, and cultural policy. Canadians
outside Quebec, perhaps particularly those who had
chosen Canada as their new country, were not at all
inclined to place these policy achievements at risk
by drastically reshaping Canada to accommodate
Quebec's wishes, nor did they understand why anyone
would wish to do so. As they heard about Quebec's
demands for change, they began to ask 'What does
Quebec want?', at first out of genuine curiosity but
increasingly out of exasperation. Quebecers had
often urged other Canadians to become Canadian
nationalists rather than British imperialists. When
they got their wish, they soon discovered that they
would have been better off if the rest of Canada had
not become nationalists; when Canadians turned
their attention to their own federation, the central
government became stronger, which worked against
Quebec's nationalistic interests.

The premiers who governed Quebec between 1960
and 1976 faced a difficult task. Most of the intellectual and media elites, and some crypto-sovereignists
within their own governments, urged them to be
more militant and aggressive in their dealings with
the federal government, to demand fundamental
changes in Canada's constitution, and to use Quebec's
existing powers to the fullest extent. Most of the business community, more conservative elements of the

population, and Quebec's anglophone minority tried to pull the government in the opposite direction.

The premiers had to make important choices regarding tactics and strategy. First, in seeking incremental and informal changes to Quebec's relations with the federal government, they had to choose whether to rely mainly on bilateral discussions with the federal government, on alliances with the governments of other provinces, or on recourse to the judiciary in its role as the interpreter of Canada's constitution. Second, they had to decide whether to depend solely on these informal and incremental changes, which might be undone by a later federal government, or to insist on formal constitutional changes, which would be permanent and would provide significant symbolic benefits and possibly satisfy at least some of the sovereignists.

After Lester Pearson became Prime Minister of Canada in April 1963, Premier Jean Lesage, who had been Pearson's colleague in an earlier federal government, tended to emphasize bilateral dealings with the federal government. Thus, he gained certain advantages for Quebec, including the right to opt out of certain federal programs in return for an increased share of direct tax revenue and the compromise by which Quebec established its own contributory pension plan when the federal government established a parallel plan for Canadians in the other provinces. Pearson, who was sympathetic to the Quiet Revolution, also established a Royal Commission on Bilingualism and Biculturalism to investigate the causes of Quebec's discontent and recommend possible solutions.

After Lesage was defeated in 1966 by Duplessis' old party, the Union Nationale, Premier Johnson, followed by Premier Bertrand, had less rapport with the federal Liberals, and gave more attention to alliances with the other provinces. Pearson was followed as prime minister in 1968 by Pierre Trudeau, who despite, or perhaps because of, being a francophone Quebecer himself, rigidly opposed any concessions to Quebec nationalism. Trudeau's attitude reinforced the rift between the federal government and Quebec. It largely continued after 1970 under Robert Bourassa who, although a Liberal, had no personal ties with the federal Liberal government and had a poor relationship with Trudeau.

The strategy of seeking provincial allies, however, had its problems. Claude Morin, who played an important part in Quebec's intergovernmental relations as a civil servant in this period and later as a minister, concluded that the strategy was futile.[5] The most obvious ally for Quebec was Ontario, which had sometimes made common cause with Quebec against the federal government as far back as the 1880s. Premier John Robarts, in office from 1961 to 1971, was Quebec's ally to some extent, but his successor, Bill Davis, seemed less interested in this role and preferred a centralist and pro–federal government position. Alberta, which in the 1970s adopted a truculent anti–federal government position to protect its energy resources from federal interference, might have been an ally for Quebec, but its priorities and interests were different, and Alberta voters, few of whom had ever visited Quebec, were not particularly sympathetic. Probably Morin's conclusion was justified.

As for the courts, they had been little help to Quebec since the abolition of constitutional appeals to the Judicial Committee of the Privy Council in 1949. Duplessis once observed that the Supreme Court of Canada was like the Tower of Pisa, always leaning in the same direction, by which he meant that it always favoured the federal government over the provinces. In the 1970s the Quebec government commissioned an inquiry to determine whether this was in fact the case; its report concluded that it was, but blamed it on the terms of the constitution rather than on the preferences of the judges.[6] This conclusion provided ammunition to those who argued that a new constitution, or even Quebec sovereignty, was the necessary solution to Quebec's discontent with Canadian federalism.

At the time of the Quiet Revolution, Canada's constitution was still an Act of the British Parliament, and the most significant parts of it could be amended only by that Parliament, although by convention it always acted at Canada's request. In the early 1960s the federal government was engaged in the latest of several efforts (since 1927) to remedy this situation by patriating the constitution with an amending 'formula' that would provide a procedure for amending it without British participation. In consultation with the provinces, a formula was devised which would in effect have given every province a veto over most important amendments. Lesage at first accepted this formula, since it seemed to accord with Loranger's compact theory, but eventually rejected it, under pressure from Quebec's intellectual elites, because it would increase the difficulty of changing the constitution to make it more congenial to Quebec's needs.

Lesage himself seemed to have little interest in formal constitutional change, or perhaps he was simply realistic about its prospects and feared that a failed attempt would increase support for the sovereignty movement. (In the 1990s, after Lesage's death, this was exactly what happened.) His successor, Daniel Johnson, was apparently more hopeful and published a short book just before becoming premier, in which he argued that Quebec's choice was 'equality or independence'; either a radically revised constitution that would recognize Quebec as one of two equal nations, or else a sovereign Quebec.[7] Most Canadians outside of Quebec, as well as the federal government, saw little difference between these two alternatives, but Premier Robarts of Ontario responded to Johnson's concerns by hosting a 'Confederation of Tomorrow' conference in 1967, which Johnson and all the other premiers attended.

The federal government soon decided to seize control of the constitutional issue itself. It hosted a constitutional conference which met intermittently from 1968 until 1971. That conference finally ended in deadlock when a document known as the Victoria Charter, embodying as much decentralization as the federal government would concede, was rejected by Premier Bourassa after Quebec's intellectual elites, and some of his own advisors, deemed it to be inadequate. It proved to be the best deal Quebec would ever be offered; its amending formula, which gave vetoes to Quebec and Ontario but not to the other provinces, was soon afterwards rejected by Alberta's new government. Over the next few years Quebec and the federal government discussed constitutional changes that might take the wind out of the sails of the sovereignist Parti Québécois, but came to no agreement. None of the other provinces, after Robarts retired, showed much interest in participating in these talks.

Dramatic Developments, But No Solution

Constitutional discussions were suspended when René Lévesque and his Parti Québécois were elected to form Quebec's government in November 1976. Lévesque had been a minister in Lesage's government but had become increasingly disillusioned with Canadian federalism, and left the Liberal Party to form his own party in 1967. During his successful campaign in 1976, he promised to hold a referendum on 'sovereignty-association', an idea which he had outlined in a book in 1967.[8] He envisaged Canada and Quebec as two sovereign states sharing a common currency and some joint institutions, with free trade between the two. The referendum would ask whether the Quebec government should be given a mandate to negotiate sovereignty-association with the federal government. Although described as 'separatism' by its opponents, Lévesque's plan was little different in substance from Daniel Johnson's idea of equality or independence, although it was outlined in much greater detail. The main flaw in the plan was the unlikelihood that either the federal government or the other provinces would ever accept such a drastic change in Canada's constitution, regardless of the referendum result.

The Quebec Liberals were at that time led by Claude Ryan, a devout Catholic intellectual and the former editor of Montreal's nationalist daily, *Le Devoir*. Realizing that the constitutional status quo was no longer popular in Quebec, the party established a constitutional committee to produce a blueprint for reformed federalism as an alternative to the sovereignty-association proposed by the Parti Québécois. Usually known as 'the Beige Paper', from the colour of its cover, the Liberal document was released in January 1980.[9] It proposed transferring some federal responsibilities, such as unemployment insurance and penitentiaries, to the provinces, but was generally very moderate. Its most radical suggestion was that the Senate should be replaced by a council of provincial delegates, similar to the Bundesrat in the Federal Republic of Germany. 'Special Status' for Quebec, to which the Quebec Liberals had been theoretically committed since 1968, was not proposed.

The Lévesque government postponed its referendum, perhaps unwisely, until near the end of its first mandate. The wording of the question was designed to attract voters who were not necessarily committed to independence, or even sovereignty-association, but who merely wanted major changes in the constitution. That fact, and friction between the federal and provincial Liberals who were jointly campaigning against the proposal, seemed for a while to make success a realistic possibility, but the proposal was decisively rejected on 20 May 1980, with about 60 per cent of Quebecers voting against it.

Trudeau had promised Quebec that he would pursue (unspecified) constitutional changes if the referendum proposal was rejected by the voters. Most Quebec voters probably assumed that this was a promise to implement some of the ideas in the Beige Paper, or in the slightly more radical report of the Pépin-Robarts Task Force on National Unity, which his own government had established in 1977. However, Trudeau had other plans, and saw the decisive federalist victory in the referendum as a mandate to play hardball. He convened another constitutional conference and announced that he would seek patriation of the constitution with a new amending formula, and the entrenchment of a Charter of Rights which, among other purposes, would permit much of Quebec's language legislation to be struck down by the courts. There was no mention of additional powers for Quebec, or for any other province.

Only two provinces, Ontario and New Brunswick, supported Trudeau's plan, and the British government, which had to bring the proposal before its own Parliament, was unsympathetic for several reasons. The remaining eight provinces, including Quebec, formed an alliance against Trudeau's plan and tried to stop it by challenging it in the courts and by lobbying in Britain. Nonetheless, Trudeau eventually prevailed in November 1981, when he agreed to modify his proposals to make them acceptable to every province except Quebec. This ended a long-standing tradition that the British Parliament would not be asked to amend the constitution without Quebec's consent, a tradition that the Supreme Court of Canada subsequently ruled to have had no legal significance.[10] That Quebec could not rely on alliances with the other provinces was conclusively demonstrated.

The humiliating outcome eventually led to the resignation of Lévesque and the disintegration of his government. Trudeau retired in 1984 and the federal Liberals lost the election later that year, losing most of their Quebec seats in the process, although they had won 74 of Quebec's 75 ridings in 1980. (In fact they have never won a majority of Quebec ridings since the patriation of the Constitution, although they did so routinely for almost a century before that event, a contrast which suggests Quebec's disillusionment.) The new prime minister was a Quebec anglophone, Brian Mulroney, who had promised during the campaign to make constitutional changes that Quebec could accept 'with honour and enthusiasm'. His attempt to fulfill this promise led to the Meech Lake Accord, which is discussed in the Snapshot box in this chapter.

The failure to adopt the Meech Lake Accord led several members of the federal Parliament, headed by Mulroney's friend and former lieutenant Lucien Bouchard, to form a new Quebec nationalist party at the federal level, the Bloc Québécois. From 1993 to 1997 the Bloc would be the second-largest party in the House of Commons, and thus Her Majesty's Loyal Opposition. It also led to a resurgence of support for sovereignty in Quebec, which reached record levels in

SNAPSHOT

The Meech Lake Accord

The Meech Lake Accord was perhaps the closest Quebec and the rest of Canada have come to agreeing on a revision of the Canadian Constitution that would satisfy, at least in part, the needs and aspirations of both communities. When it was drafted in 1987, and for a short time thereafter, it seemed almost certain that it would be incorporated into Canada's Constitution, since it was supported by the government of Canada, the premiers of every province including Quebec, and the principal opposition parties in both Quebec's National Assembly and Canada's Parliament. However, this anticipated outcome was not to be.

The origins of the Meech Lake Accord can be traced back to 1981–2, when the Trudeau government caused Canada's Constitution to be patriated and substantially amended without the consent of the government or National Assembly of Quebec. There was considerable resentment in Quebec over the Constitution. Many people outside of Quebec also agreed that it had been inappropriate to proceed without the consent of Quebec and that something must be done to restore the legitimacy of the Canadian Constitution in that province. During the federal election campaign of 1984 the Progressive Conservative leader, Brian Mulroney, promised to seek constitutional changes that Quebec could accept 'with honour and enthusiasm'.

Mulroney won the election, and his party won a majority of Quebec's votes and seats for only the second time in the twentieth century. Implementing his promise was made easier in the following year when the Quebec Liberals defeated the Parti Québécois and returned to office under Robert Bourassa. In the spring of 1986 Bourassa's minister of intergovernmental affairs, Gil Rémillard, delivered a speech to a conference at Mont Gabriel in which he set forth Quebec's terms for accepting the revised Canadian Constitution. These were explicit recognition of Quebec as a distinct society, guarantee of increased powers over immigration, limitation of the federal spending power, recognition of a right of veto for Quebec over constitutional changes, and participation by Quebec in the appointment of judges to the Supreme Court of Canada. Significantly absent from the list was any demand for changes in the Canadian Charter of Rights and Freedoms.

The Mulroney government was satisfied with Quebec's agenda, and began the process of sounding out the other provinces. It discovered that they were generally prepared to agree, provided that the concessions demanded by Quebec would, with the exception of recognition as a distinct society, be made available to all the provinces. Also, some provinces wanted provincial participation in the selection of senators to be added to the list, to which Quebec and the federal government agreed. In the spring of 1987 a first ministers' conference at the prime minister's summer residence of Meech Lake produced a first draft of the Accord embodying these proposals, and a subsequent conference in Ottawa hammered out the details of the final text. Besides recognizing Quebec as 'a distinct society', it increased the number of types of constitutional amendments that would require unanimous provincial approval, required the selection of senators and Supreme Court justices from lists of names submitted by the provinces, constitutionally entrenched an existing Canada–Quebec agreement on immigration, and provided that a province opting out of a federal cost-sharing program would receive financial compensation if it had a program of its own with similar objectives.

The Accord then had to be ratified by Parliament and all the provincial legislatures. Under Canada's complex constitutional amending formula, some parts of the Accord would require the unanimous approval of the provinces. At Bourassa's insistence it was agreed that it would have to be ratified in its entirety or not at all; the entire Accord would require unanimity. There was also a provision in the amending formula that ratifications must take place within three years, and although it is not clear that this was intended to apply to amendments requiring unanimity, it was decided that the time limit would apply in this case.

For a while everything seemed destined to proceed smoothly. Quebec was the first province to ratify, closely followed by Alberta and Saskatchewan. However, a ferocious attack on the Accord by former Prime Minister Pierre Trudeau, who repeated his objections in an appearance before a Senate committee, caused growing opposition to the Accord outside of Quebec, particularly within the various provincial wings of the Liberal Party. Opposition was also expressed, for various reasons, by some feminist groups in anglophone Canada, by First Nations, and by the right-wing Alberta-based Reform Party, which was committed to replacing the appointed Senate with an elected upper house. Some people in anglophone Canada, although very few if any in Quebec, complained that it was inappropriate for eleven men to negotiate fundamental changes in Canada's Constitution with little or no popular input or participation. Others feared that the clause recognizing Quebec as a 'distinct society' would weaken the effect of the Charter of Rights and Freedoms in Quebec. Sympathy for Quebec in anglophone Canada was also eroded by Premier Bourassa's decision to maintain restrictions on English-language commercial signs, and by his support for the Free Trade Agreement with the United States, which was widely opposed in Ontario. As the critics began to express their views, and as public opinion seemed to agree with them, some provincial governments hesitated to submit the Accord to their legislatures for ratification.

During the three years available for ratification, three premiers who had agreed to the Meech Lake Accord left office: Richard Hatfield of New Brunswick in 1987, Howard Pawley of Manitoba in 1988, and Brian Peckford of Newfoundland in 1989. Hatfield and Pawley lost elections and Peckford retired, whereupon his successor lost an election almost immediately. Hatfield had not had time to submit the Accord for ratification before his defeat and Pawley had hesitated because of growing opposition in his province. Peckford had succeeded in having it ratified, but the newly elected government led by Clyde Wells indicated that it would seek to rescind Newfoundland's ratification, a possibility that no one seems to have anticipated. Wells was a disciple of Trudeau and his constitutional advisor, Deborah Coyne, was Trudeau's intimate friend. Wells was determined that the Accord should fail to be adopted. The new premiers of New Brunswick and Manitoba, Frank McKenna and Gary Filmon, showed little inclination to ratify the Accord, although neither was as fanatical in his opposition as Wells.

As the June 1990 deadline for ratification approached, with three provinces in opposition, the federal government became increasingly apprehensive that its constitutional initiative would fail and began to consider how to make the Accord more palatable to its opponents. A parliamentary committee chaired by Jean Charest, who would become premier of Quebec several years later, suggested several additions to the Accord that might serve this purpose. Almost simultaneously, Gil Rémillard warned that rejection of the Accord might seriously impair Quebec's relationship with Canada. The Charest committee report provoked several Quebec members of Parliament to resign from the Progressive Conservative party , including Mulroney's friend and colleague Lucien Bouchard, who had helped to write the 'honour and enthusiasm' speech six years earlier. Subsequently these MPs formed a pro-sovereignty party in Parliament, the Bloc Québécois.

The Charest report persuaded McKenna to submit the report to the New Brunswick legislature for ratification. Wells, however, remained adamant, and in Manitoba, an Aboriginal member of the opposition, Elijah Harper, skilfully and unexpectedly used the legislature's rules of procedure to block ratification within the time limit.

The Meech Lake Accord thus expired at the end of the three years during which it had to be ratified. Its collapse persuaded many people in Quebec that the rest of Canada had little sympathy for, or understanding of, Quebec's aspirations, and led to significantly increased popular support for the sovereignty movement.

The failure of Meech Lake had many consequences, including the formation of the Bloc Québécois and the very close result of the second Quebec referendum on sovereignty in October 1995. It also revived Pierre Trudeau's popularity outside of Quebec; he had been very unpopular when he retired in 1984. Although the Mulroney government tried again to amend the Constitution with the Charlottetown Accord two years later, that agreement had little firm support either in Quebec or elsewhere and was probably doomed to fail. The Meech Lake experience persuaded many Canadians, both in Quebec and elsewhere, that discussions of constitutional reform were futile and more likely to do harm than good. It also contributed to an estrangement between Quebec and the rest of Canada that has never entirely ended.

ROBERT BOURASSA

Robert Bourassa jokingly strikes a Napoleonic pose in front of a statue of Napoleon in May 1983 as he mused on his intentions of returning to politics to lead the Quebec Liberals back into power—which he did.

CP Photo/Jacques Nadeau

Niccolò Machiavelli, who pioneered the systematic study of government and politics five centuries ago, wrote that a successful leader

> must imitate the fox and the lion, for the lion cannot protect himself from traps, and the fox cannot defend himself from wolves. One must therefore be a fox to recognize traps, and a lion to frighten wolves. Those that wish to be only lions do not understand this.[11]

Robert Bourassa, one of the most successful politicians in Quebec's history, understood this. Like most of the politicians who succeed in stable democracies, he was more fox than lion, and this quality helped him guide Quebec through some of the most turbulent times in its history. He led his party to victory in four elections, a record exceeded only by Maurice Duplessis.

Bourassa was born in Montreal in 1933, the son of an accountant. At the age of 12 he enrolled in Collège Brébeuf, a Jesuit institution and the most prestigious of Quebec's private 'classical colleges'. He went on to study economics, political science, and law, earning three degrees. He spent some time in Ottawa as a public servant and then returned to Quebec to serve as secretary and research director of a commission on Quebec's public finances. Impressed by Bourassa's work on the commission, Premier Jean Lesage had planned to make Bourassa his Minister of Finance if the Liberals remained in office after the 1966 election. However, they were defeated.

Bourassa was the youngest of the three candidates who sought the party leadership when Lesage announced his retirement in 1969. Lesage had a polling firm find out what qualities Quebec voters wanted in a premier—they wanted someone young and knowledgeable about economics. Bourassa, who fitted this description perfectly, was chosen as leader and led the party to victory in the election of 1970.

The four years in opposition had been a difficult time for the Liberal party, which had lost its nationalist wing, and its most popular personality, when René Lévesque left to form his own party. Bourassa, who was friendly with Lévesque, had tried to keep his friend in the Liberal party and had participated in the informal discussions that led to the idea of sovereignty-association. He eventually concluded that the idea was not practical, largely because in his view a sovereign Quebec could not realistically share a common currency with Canada.

Bourassa's first term in office was tumultuous and his government faced conflicts with the federal government, with revolutionary terrorists (the FLQ) and with organized labour. In October 1970 he had to seek federal help when the FLQ kidnapped the British trade commissioner and one of Bourassa's cabinet ministers, Pierre Laporte. Prime Minister Pierre Trudeau sent in the army and invoked the emergency powers of the War Measures Act, making it appear as if Bourassa had surrendered control of Quebec to the federal government. In the following year Bourassa reluctantly, and perhaps unwisely, rejected Trudeau's Victoria Charter, which would have given Quebec a constitutional veto and some additional legislative powers. (This episode began his engagement with constitutional reform, which would occupy him for much of the next 21 years.) In 1972 labour conflicts in the public sector escalated into a general strike, which ended with the imprisonment of the three principal labour leaders.

Although these events made Bourassa and his party appear both hostile to labour and excessively submissive to the federal power, Bourassa was neither. Furthermore, his first government had many significant achievements, including establishing medicare;

reorganizing social services; initiating the gigantic James Bay hydro-electric project and negotiating the agreement with the Cree nation that made the project possible; and adopting the Official Language Act (Bill 22), which made French Quebec's official language and included the first practical measures in Quebec's history to preserve and promote the language. Years later, Bourassa would tell an academic seminar that the Official Language Act was the achievement of which he was most proud.

With the defeat of his party in 1976, Bourassa's political career seemed to be over. He resigned as party leader and spent considerable time in Europe and the United States studying economics and European integration. But, when the Liberals led by Claude Ryan unexpectedly lost another election in 1981, Bourassa's prospects revived. He was again elected leader of the party in 1983 and led it to victory in 1985.

Bourassa's second, and longer, stint as premier of Quebec was dominated by constitutional reform. He had a much better relationship with Prime Minister Brian Mulroney than he had ever had with Trudeau, who was scornful of all Quebec provincial politicians. Bourassa was largely responsible for both the Meech Lake Accord of 1987 and the Charlottetown Accord of 1992. Both agreements reflected his talent for compromise and his desire to do what he perceived to be best for Quebec. Between these two events, he helped to lower the temperature when Quebecers reacted with bitterness and indignation to anglophone Canada's rejection of the Meech Lake Accord. Although a different kind of leader might have sought popularity by supporting independence for Quebec at this time, Bourassa was convinced that independence was not in Quebec's best interests. He also championed free trade with the United States and helped his friend Mulroney win re-election on this issue in 1988, when the Conservatives won their largest majority in Quebec since Confederation.

Bourassa attracted controversy in 1988 when he used the notwithstanding clause in the Canadian Charter of Rights and Freedoms to override a Supreme Court decision and maintain the requirement (introduced by Lévesque's government in 1977) that outdoor commercial signs be written in French only. This was bitterly resented by Quebec's anglophone minority, as his Official Language Act had been in 1974, and the three anglophones in his cabinet resigned. Five years later, however, Bourassa agreed to allow bilingual signs provided the French lettering was more prominent than the English, a compromise that satisfied most people.

Another crisis Bourassa faced was the massive protest in 1990 by members of the Mohawk First Nation against a proposal that a Mohawk burial ground in the town of Oka be used to enlarge a golf course. This led to the death of a police officer, a lengthy blockade of the Mercier Bridge connecting Montreal with its south shore suburbs, and the use of the Canadian army to aid the civil power in Quebec for the third time in 22 years, and the second while Bourassa was premier. His preoccupation with the Oka crisis contributed to his death, since during the crisis he delayed treatment of the skin cancer that eventually killed him in 1996, more than two years after his retirement.

When Bourassa died, *The Economist*, a British weekly that he read regularly for most of his adult life, called him 'everyone's idea of a decent Canadian, warm-hearted and conciliatory'.[12] His instinct was always to seek compromise and moderation, and to strike a balance between economic growth and social justice. Sadly, a proposal to name one of Montreal's major streets after him was rejected, although his sometime friend and rival, Lévesque, was honoured in this way, and the man who destroyed the Meech Lake Accord, Trudeau, had his name bestowed on Montreal's airport. Nonetheless, Bourassa deserves to be remembered.

the early 1990s. Even the Quebec Liberal Party was influenced by the shift in public opinion; in 1991 it debated a proposal by its constitutional committee, known as the Allaire Report, which was much more radical than the Beige Paper.[13] This proposal would

have transferred to the provinces practically all of the federal government's responsibilities apart from defence, currency, tariffs, and equalization payments.

Bourassa meanwhile appointed the Belanger-Campeau Commission, with representation from virtually every significant interest group and political party in the province, to sound out the opinions of Quebecers about Quebec's constitutional future. As he doubtless anticipated, this heterogeneous commission could arrive at no substantive consensus, but did propose that a referendum on sovereignty be held in either June or October of 1992. It also proposed that a committee of Quebec's National Assembly be formed to examine any proposal for constitutional change that might be made by the governments of Canada and of the other provinces.[14] The latter proposal was an implicit invitation to the Mulroney government to make another effort at constitutional reform, and thus provide Quebec with a credible alternative to the increasingly popular option of sovereignty.

The result of this invitation was the Charlottetown Accord, which would have given Quebec somewhat less than the Meech Lake Accord, apart from a new provision that Quebec's representation in the House of Commons would never be allowed to fall below 25 per cent of the total number of seats. The Parti Québécois, which had mildly supported the Meech Lake Accord, declared that the Charlottetown Accord was inadequate and campaigned against it. Bourassa's government, however, supported it and scheduled a referendum on the Charlottetown Accord (not on sovereignty, as the Belanger-Campeau Commission had suggested) for October 1992. Mulroney's government organized a simultaneous referendum on the Accord in the rest of Canada. The Accord went down to defeat on 26 October 1992, receiving only 42.4 per cent of the votes cast in Quebec and a slightly higher percentage in the rest of Canada.

Neither Canada's Progressive Conservative government nor Quebec's Liberal government long survived this defeat. The federal Liberals returned to office in 1993 under Jean Chrétien, who had been Minister of Justice at the time of patriation in 1982, and the Parti Québécois formed a government a year later under Jacques Parizeau, a more hard-line sovereignist than René Lévesque. Parizeau's government held another referendum on sovereignty in October 1995, assisted by Lucien Bouchard's Bloc Québécois and by Action Démocratique du Québec, a nationalist party that had been formed by dissident Quebec Liberals after Bourassa's party failed to endorse the Allaire report.

In contrast to 1980, the referendum question called for sovereignty whether or not the rest of Canada was willing to offer 'association' to a sovereign Quebec. Nonetheless, it was almost successful, and the federalist margin of victory on 30 October 1995 was barely more than one per cent of the votes cast. Premier Parizeau tactlessly but accurately noted in his concession speech that most francophone Quebecers had voted in favour and that sovereignty had been defeated only by 'money and some ethnic votes'.

As in 1980, the defeat of the referendum in 1995 weakened Quebec's bargaining power and led to a hardening of the federal Liberal government's opposition to Quebec nationalism. Their immediate response was to introduce the Regional Veto Act, prohibiting constitutional amendments without Quebec's consent, but this change of policy would not actually be incorporated in the Constitution and no other constitutional changes were offered. Subsequently, and more significantly, the Liberals sought an advisory opinion from the Supreme Court on the question of whether Quebec had a legal right to secede under either Canadian or international law.

In its response to this question the Supreme Court dismissed the relevance of international law and its principle of self-determination, since it said that Quebec was not a dependent territory or a colony and was not oppressed by the rest of Canada. It ruled that, according to Canadian law, Quebec could not secede unilaterally (as Parizeau had allegedly planned to do had his referendum succeeded) but only following negotiations with other Canadian governments and with due respect for such principles as democracy, federalism, and minority rights. However, the federal government would have an obligation to negotiate if a clear majority of Quebec voters supported a clear question on sovereignty.[15] In 1999 Chrétien's government responded by introducing the Clarity Act, which provided that Canada would negotiate with Quebec following a successful referendum on sovereignty only if Canada's Parliament was convinced that the referendum question had been clear and the victory decisive. The criteria by which Parliament would make these determinations were not specified.

The Parti Québécois suffered electoral defeat in 2003, but the Bloc Québécois continues to be

Quebec's most popular party at the federal level. In November 2006, the House of Commons adopted a resolution recognizing 'the Québécois' as a nation within Canada. The implications of this initiative, if any, remain to be seen. Some Quebec observers argued that it would have been more meaningful if it had recognized 'Quebec' as a nation.

Where Do We Go From Here?

Has the cycle of constitutional discussion and controversy that began with the Quiet Revolution really ended after the referendum result of October 1995 and the Clarity Act? Has Quebec's quest for sovereignty also ended after two referendum defeats in 1980 and 1995? Is Quebec reconciled, or at least resigned, to its present status within the Canadian federation? Is Quebec nationalism doomed to subside until it becomes only a faint memory, like the secessionist movements of the American South in 1861, Nova Scotia in 1867, or Western Australia in 1933? Many Canadians outside Quebec, and some within it, undoubtedly hope that the answer to all these questions is yes. However, it would be unwise to assume that this is the case. It is perhaps worth remembering that a book called *The Decline of Nationalism in Quebec* was published in 1981!

Quebec remains different from the other Canadian provinces, not only because its people speak a different language and its legal system is based on different principles, but because the majority of its people regard it as a national community and give their Québécois identity precedence over their Canadian identity, even though the latter is, for most of them, by no means negligible. The fact that Quebec's legislature is called the National Assembly, an obviously unthinkable possibility in any other province, should speak for itself. In these circumstances, Quebec's equal constitutional status with the other nine provinces seems anomalous and unlikely to endure indefinitely.

Admittedly Quebec's de facto situation is somewhat different from the others. Unlike other provinces, it has its own pension plan, selects its own immigrants, and collects its own personal income tax, powers which other provinces could exercise if they wished but which they are content to leave to the federal government. Unlike all provinces except Ontario, Quebec has a provincial police force of its own, rather than contracting with the federal force. Its influence on federal politics is far from negligible, and it probably benefits economically from its association with Canada, although less so than many Canadians outside of Quebec believe. Within Quebec the economic disparity between anglophones and francophones, which was very pronounced a few decades ago, has virtually disappeared.

However, none of these facts has fully reconciled Quebec to the constitutional status quo. What Quebec really demands is some formal constitutional *recognition* of its status as a distinct nation, albeit one that chooses, for the time being at least, not to be fully sovereign. It does not want to be told that it is 'equal' in status with Ontario, let alone with Prince Edward Island. It wants Canada to recognize its 'deep diversity', and not just the 'regional differences between provinces and states that exist in any federation'.[16] Unfortunately, this recognition is precisely what most of the people in other parts of Canada, and therefore the politicians who represent them, are unwilling to concede. As long as this mindset persists, the unresolved Quebec question will persist also.

Questions for Consideration

1. Why are Quebec and the rest of Canada unable to agree on constitutional issues when they share similar liberal and democratic values?

2. What changes in the two societies since the middle of the twentieth century have made accommodation between their constitutional preferences more difficult?

3. Would the Meech Lake Accord, if it had been adopted, have led to a lasting consensus between Quebec and the rest of Canada?

4. Following the defeat of two referendums on sovereignty, in 1980 and 1995, is Quebec likely to make another attempt to become a sovereign nation-state, or will it abandon that aspiration?

Notes

1. Alain-G. Gagnon, 'The political uses of federalism', in Michael Burgess and Alain-G. Gagnon, eds., *Comparative Federalism and Federation* (Toronto: University of Toronto Press 1993), 15–44, at 16.
2. T.J.J. Loranger, 'Letters upon the interpretation of the federal constitution known as the B.N.A. Act' (Quebec: Morning Chronicle, 1884).
3. Report of the Royal Commission on Constitutional Problems, volumes I–IV (Quebec: 1956). A very abbreviated version with an introduction by David Kwavnick was published in the Carleton Library series in 1973.
4. José E. Igartua, *The Other Quiet Revolution: National Identities in English Canada, 1945–71* (Vancouver: University of British Columbia Press, 2006).
5. Claude Morin, *Quebec versus Ottawa* (Toronto: University of Toronto Press 1976), 102–13.
6. Gilbert l'Ecuyer, *La cour suprême du Canada et le partage des compétences, 1949–1978* (Quebec: Government of Quebec, 1978).
7. Daniel Johnson, *Égalité ou Indépendance* (Montreal: Éditions de l'Homme, 1965).
8. René Lévesque, *An Option for Quebec* (Toronto: McClelland & Stewart, 1968).
9. Constitutional Committee of the Quebec Liberal Party, *A New Canadian Federation* (Montreal: Liberal Party of Quebec, 1980).
10. *Reference re. Quebec veto* (1982) 2 S.C.R. 793.
11. Niccolò Machiavelli, *The Prince* (1513), ch. 17.
12. *The Economist*, 12 October 1996, 95.
13. Constitutional Committee of the Quebec Liberal Party, *A Québec Free to Choose* (Montreal: Liberal Party of Quebec, 1991).
14. *The Political and Constitutional Future of Québec* (Québec: Quebec National Assembly, 1991).
15. *Reference re. Secession of Quebec* (1998), 2 S.C.R. 217.
16. For the concept of deep diversity, see Charles Taylor, *Reconciling the Solitudes: Essays on Canadian Federalism and Nationalism* (Montreal and Kingston: McGill-Queen's University Press, 1993), especially chapter 8, 'Shared and Divergent Values'.

Relevant Websites

Government of Quebec: www.gouv.qc.ca/portail/quebec

The Council of the Federation: www.councilofthefederation.ca

The Forum of Federations: www.forumfed.org

Institute of Intergovernmental Relations at Queen's University: www.iigr.ca

Intergovernmental Affairs Office (Government of Canada): www.pco-bcp.gc.ca/aia

Canadian Intergovernmental Conference Secretariat: www.scics.gc.ca

Supreme Court of Canada
Decisions since 1983: http://scc.lexum.umontreal.ca/en

Select Bibliography

Gagnon, Alain-G., and Raffaele Iacovino. *Federalism, Citizenship and Quebec: Debating Multinationalism.* Toronto: University of Toronto Press, 2007.

Lemco, Jonathan. *Turmoil in the Peaceable Kingdom.* Toronto: University of Toronto Press, 1994.

McRoberts, Kenneth. *Misconceiving Canada: The Struggle for National Unity.* Toronto: Oxford University Press, 1997.

Murphy, Michael, ed. *Quebec and Canada in the New Century.* Kingston: Institute of Intergovernmental Relations, 2007.

Resnick, Philip, and Daniel Latouche. *Letters to a Québécois Friend.* Montreal and Kingston: McGill-Queen's University Press, 1990.

Taylor, Charles. *Reconciling the Solitudes: Essays on Canadian Federalism and Nationalism* (Montreal and Kingston: McGill-Queen's University Press, 1993.

Weaver, R. Kent, ed. *The Collapse of Canada?* Washington: The Brookings Institution, 1992.

Part B
Identities

Introduction

This is the first of several sections in this collection which deals explicitly with questions of identity. Put most simply, identity can be defined as how we answer the question, 'Who am I?' Until relatively recently the answer to this question was obvious. Yet, increasingly academics and others have conclusively demonstrated that our individual notions of identity derive from culturally specific social processes and practices.[1] Though we are not always completely conscious of it, our diverse relations with others, both within and outside our own culture, shape the way we understand who we are and who we aren't.

One's individual identity is multi-layered: one has gender and sexual identity, class identity, racial, ethnic, and cultural identity, all helping to shape one's personal identity. The elements that one shares with others create a collective identity. In creating personal identities we emphasize some parts of our personal stories and downplay others. Our identities are also subject to external pressures; other people have ideas about who we should be, and there may be a social

price to play if we don't live up to its changing norms of, for example, what a women or a man should be, or what beliefs a Quebecer should hold. Our identities frequently shape the way people treat us, and they influence the way we treat others.

From several disciplinary perspectives, this section underlines how identity plays out in Quebec, particularly around land and religion.[2] In the first contribution, historian Alexis Lachaîne outlines three key points about identity in Quebec. First, the identity of the majority has changed. Indeed, until at least the Second World War, French-Canadian identity was based on the French language, Catholicism, and an agricultural way of life. In the late nineteenth century and into the twentieth, these ideals did not correspond with the experience of a growing number of French Canadians, and by the 1960s the majority reconstituted its identity, rejecting agriculture and Catholicism and focusing on the French language and the Quebec state.

Second, Lachaîne suggests that the traditional identity of French Canadians was a normative position.

It was an ideal that was not embraced by all French Canadians, especially those who in the late nineteenth and early twentieth centuries moved to the United States. Rather than embracing their identities as farmers or even French speakers, these French-Canadian men may have seen their identities as breadwinners as more important. To be true to this part of their personal and collective (male) identity they left the province of Quebec to find work. Third, Lachaîne examines the relationship of land and identity. He shows that the identity of the majority population in Quebec has not always been confined with Quebec's borders. Indeed, millions of French Canadians departed, and the land, both in terms of making a living through agriculture and of a sense of belonging within nation-state boundaries, faded as an element of their collective and individual identities.

Historian Yvan Lamonde's chapter on Quebec within the Americas also explores land and identity. For him, dominant francophone Quebec identities have been and still are deeply influenced by their 'Americanicity'. His chapter thinks through the numerous ways in which Quebec identities have been influenced by belonging to the Americas, from the earliest French colonial settlement, to US invasion during the War of Independence, to ideological influence on the Patriote movement, to American controlling interests in Quebec industry, to US influence over Quebec fashion and style. Over time, certain aspects of American influence have been rejected while others have been accepted wholeheartedly. The result, Lamonde submits, is that Quebec identity is pluralistic and profoundly post-modern—a hopeful sign for the future of the increasingly pluralistic Quebec society. Lamonde also asks whether the majority of Quebecers will take up the American passion for independence, in which case American influence on Quebec identity becomes even more fascinating.

Michel Biron continues this history of the idea of America in Quebec and its relationship to identity through exploring the boundaries of Quebec literature. His contribution shows that questions of who is included within the field of Quebec literature are as complicated as the question of who is a Quebecer. Biron shows that the answers to these questions change over time, with anglophone Quebecers, for example, considering themselves part of Quebec literature only from the 1980s on, and francophones outside of Quebec gradually disengaging themselves from Quebec literature when it no longer encompassed the identity of being French Canadian.

Biron's chapter focuses on the changing nature of three other boundaries. Looking south, Quebec novelists and poets are increasingly fascinated by the American literary tradition, though America continues to be seen as somewhat foreign. The second border he surveys is that between Quebec literature and French literature. While much self-defined Quebec literature shares a language with its former colonial parent, enthusiasm about France is limited. In fact, most Quebec authors have lost any strong feelings (either love or hate), for France; it is merely one country among many. The roles of France and America in Quebec literature have changed over time, but the third border, with the North, appears in Quebec literature as a surprisingly stable symbol of disorientation and rootlessness. Biron intriguingly suggests that this meaning of the North is particularly important to understand why, beginning in the 1980s, migrant writers were so quickly integrated into the Quebec literary canon.

The territory of Quebec is not only important to the identities of the francophone majority. For even longer it has been a key element in Aboriginal identities—a central point in political scientist Martin Papillon's discussion of the clash between francophone Quebec and Aboriginal nationalisms since the 1970s. Papillon shows that two transformations in identity shaped that clash. First, part of the way francophone Quebecers sought to redefine their collective identity was by taking the economy 'by the horns'. Hydroelectric development of the Quebec North was key. Inspired by international anti-colonial movements, Aboriginal peoples also began to present themselves in new ways and assert their collective identities in land and constitutional negotiations.

The chapter also emphasizes that the way we think we are presenting ourselves to the world is not always the way in which we are understood. Aboriginal people were seen by many of European background as children and uncivilized—certainly not how they saw themselves. Government policy was based on the European understanding of Aboriginal identities, to catastrophic ends. If it had not been clear before, we now see that identities are not only questions of imagination. They affect political and economic decisions and the structuring of everyday life.

Sociologist Micheline Milot examines identity in the relationship of politics and religion in Quebec. Milot looks at the process by which the Quebec and Canadian states stopped giving special rights, or stopped limiting the rights, of people of particular religious identities. This process she defines as 'laicization', and she argues that Quebec followed a timeline very similar (except in education) to that of other Canadian and American jurisdictions.

The model of laicization in Quebec is rooted in the British domination of French Canada and its co-opting of French-Canadian loyalty. Implicit and explicit freedom of religion and equality of worship were keystones that necessitated a neutral state, but not secular inhabitants. This freedom and equality has strengthened in the last 30 years with the rise of human rights legislation. Recently, however, Quebec's model of separation of the church and state has been challenged by those promoting a French model of a secular state over 'reasonable accommodation' of religious minorities.

Political philosopher Jocelyn Maclure uses the recent controversies about reasonable accommodation to outline two conceptions of Quebec identity: the 'civic pluralist' and the 'romantic conservative'. The civic pluralist views Quebec identity as being open to all immigrants in a pluralist society. The romantic conservative is more fearful of the impact of immigration on the French Canadian majority, and would require greater assimilation of immigrants to existing Quebec society. By showing the diversity of 'bedfellows' that opposed reasonable accommodation, Maclure looks to debunk the nationalist romantic conservative belief that this opposition represented the rise of the previously silent French Canadian majority and reassertion of their collective identity.

Questions of identity are important because they have ethical, moral, and political implications. Indeed, in Quebec much rides on the question 'Who am I?' This section largely focuses on land and religion, and their complicated role in constructing Quebec identities. Later sections will continue to investigate identity in Quebec through citizenship, language, and international relations.

NOTES

1. On the rise of identity in the humanities and a useful critique, see Rogers Brubaker and Frederick Cooper, 'Beyond Identity', *Theory and Society* 29 (2000): 1–47.

2. For those who would like to further explore issues of identity in Quebec, useful places to start are Mikhaël Elbaz, Andrée Fortin, and Guy Laforest, eds., *Les frontières de l'identité: Modernité et postmodernisme au Québec* (Saint-Foy: Les Presses de l'Université Laval and L'Harmattan, 1996); Jocelyn Létourneau, ed. *La question identitaire au Canada francophone. Récits, parcours, enjeux, hors-lieux* (Saint-Foy: Les presses de l'Université Laval, 1994); and Bettina Bradbury and Tamara Myers, eds. *Negotiating Identities in 19th- and 20th-Century Montreal* (Vancouver: University of British Columbia Press, 2005). This introduction is indebted to Karine Hébert's contribution to Bradbury and Myers as well as Létourneau's introduction to his volume.

CHAPTER 5

The Evolution of French Canada

Alexis Lachaîne, York University

— TIMELINE —

1867 British North America Act. Province of Quebec created as part of new Dominion of Canada.

1870 Province of Manitoba created with both French and English as official languages.

1885 Métis leader Louis Riel hanged for treason after a failed rebellion in Canadian Northwest. His execution sparks angry protests among French Canadians in Quebec.

1890 Manitoba Schools Question. Manitoba's provincial government abolishes French as official language and cuts off funding to province's Catholic schools.

1896 Wilfrid Laurier elected Canada's first French-Canadian prime minister.

1897 Laurier–Greenway Compromise instituted to resolve Manitoba Schools Question. The compromise infuriates French-Canadian nationalists everywhere.

1905 Provinces of Alberta and Saskatchewan created.

1910 Association canadienne-française d'éducation de l'Ontario (ACFEO) founded in Ontario to represent and defend rights of French Canadians in that province.

Independent Catholic newspaper *Le Devoir* founded in Montreal by nationalist Henri Bourassa.

1912 Regulation 17 passed by provincial government in Ontario. Beginning of Ontario Schools Crisis.

1917 Conscription Crisis divides French and English Canadians.

1926 Ordre de Jacques-Cartier founded: secret organization devoted to advancing French-language rights in federal civil service and solidarity of French Canadians.

1937 Second Congrès de la langue française au Canada held in Quebec City.

1942 Second Conscription Crisis in Canada, once again dividing French and English Canadians.

1944–59 Maurice Duplessis and Union Nationale government in power in Quebec.

1945 Gabrielle Roy's novel *The Tin Flute* published.

1960 Jean Lesage and Liberal party take power in Quebec. Beginning of Quebec's Quiet Revolution.

1963 Royal Commission on Bilingualism and Biculturalism established by Canadian Prime Minister Lester B. Pearson. André Laurendeau is co-chair of commission.	**1976** Election of René Lévesque and Parti Québécois in Quebec. **1980** Quebec referendum on sovereignty-association.

In March 1950, Jack Kerouac, a 25-year-old Franco-American, published his first novel, *The Town and the City*, to mixed but mostly positive reviews. Although the novel did not sell particularly well, and seven years would pass before he achieved literary fame and success with his cult classic, *On the Road*, Kerouac nonetheless had reason to feel proud. The son of immigrant French-Canadian parents from Quebec, the Lowell, Massachusetts–born writer had soared above the plight of most of his compatriots. He had written 'an American story' that, in the minds of many reviewers, betokened a promising future.

Shortly after *The Town and the City* was published, Kerouac read a favourable review of his novel in a Worcester, Massachusetts, newspaper called *Le Travailleur*. The review, written by Yvonne Le Maitre, a fellow Franco-American and journalist, touched him profoundly. On 8 September 1950, he rushed off a letter to 'Madame' Le Maitre in which he thanked her for her kind review and sheepishly excused himself for 'writing in English, when it would be so much better to address you in French; but I have no proficiency at all in my native language, and that is the lame truth'.[1]

Like many young Franco-Americans of his generation, Kerouac had been raised in French, not speaking English until he was six or seven years old. But now, unable to adequately express himself in his mother tongue, and perhaps to make up for writing his first novel in English, he went on to declare to Yvonne Le Maitre that even though at present he could not write in his native French anymore, and was amazed, as he put it, 'by that horrible homelessness all French-Canadians abroad in America have', that he would someday 'write a French-Canadian novel, with the setting in New England, in French'. All his knowledge, he declared, lay in his '"French-Canadianness" and nowhere else'.[2]

Kerouac had been pondering his 'French-Canadianness' for some time. While he felt hope and

exhilaration at the possibility of becoming a great American novelist like Herman Melville, Mark Twain, and Thomas Wolfe, he also felt striking guilt for being 'anglicized', and a profound longing to 're-frenchify' himself. In one particularly revealing entry in his journals, dated 19 March 1950, Kerouac recounts a 'tea-vision' in which his dead brother, Gerard, reminded him of his 'true self' and criticized certain aspects of his life, such as straying from his French-Canadian roots. Gerard, Kerouac recalled, had told him that he 'should not try to defrench' himself, and should 'go to church', and even hinted he 'should go to Lowell, or Canada, or France, and become a Frenchman again and write in French'. Kerouac believed his older brother, in this vision, represented his

> original self returning after all the years since I was a child trying to become 'un Anglais' in Lowell from shame of being a Canuck . . . He reminded me my father had started the same sad business in his own life, by mingling with 'les Anglais', which really means *non-French*. . . . Soon I will resolve the thing by Anglicizing my Frenchness, or Frenchifying my English, whichever way it works. There are pitfalls I will have to examine: for instance, getting a 'French wife' may only be regressive, like going back to the simple relationship with my sister, as kids. This may all only be interesting material, or madness, or as I hope, an eventual comedown to the roots of my true self.[3]

The journal entry ends with Kerouac saying he will bring his 'Road' manuscript with him on his trip, and promises his dead brother that he will settle things.

In many ways Jack Kerouac was not your typical French Canadian. As a writer, he spent a great deal of time thinking, jotting down notes, writing letters, and working on his novels; he never held a steady job, and rarely stayed in one place for long; and his growing reputation as a writer and spokesman for the beat generation gave him access to a world few French Canadians from Lowell, Nashua, or even Ottawa could dream of. But in other, equally significant ways, he was also typically French Canadian, particularly in trying to make sense of his 'French-Canadianness' and resolving the dilemma of his identity. Indeed, the very way in which Kerouac navigated his identity as a French Canadian mirrored countless other French Canadians' efforts to understand themselves in a world which saw them as a minority, an anomaly in the broader sea of English-speaking North America. The French-Canadian identity fit in no easy categories or definitions, and was often fashioned individually. It was something navigated every day, and there was nothing at all simple or assured about its meaning.

This chapter provides an overview of the evolution of 'French Canada' from its beginnings in the mid-nineteenth century to its disintegration and eventual demise by the late 1960s. Its focus is on Quebec, but it also examines that province's special relationship with French-Canadian communities beyond its borders, and how it both nurtured and impeded the dream and the reality of a broader French-Canadian collectivity in North America.

THE ORIGINS OF FRENCH CANADA

When the British North America Act was passed in 1867, most French Canadians lived within the territorial boundaries of the newly created province of Quebec. There were tiny pockets of French Canadians in other parts of Canada and even in the United States, but they were anomalous, scattered, and few. The French Canadian elites and Fathers of Confederation who had supported and helped negotiate the Canadian federation intended that the province of Quebec would be the homeland of the French-Canadian people. Within its boundaries, with its own institutions and laws, the French-Canadian nation could live according to its own distinct traditions, and survive.

What those French-Canadian elites had failed to understand, however, was that the province's walls were porous. Indeed, over the following decades, hundreds of thousands of French Canadians left the province to live and work—some temporarily, some permanently—outside its borders. It was a veritable

hemorrhage. Most emigrated to the United States, specifically New England; many migrated to neighbouring Ontario; and some settled in the western Canadian provinces of Manitoba, Saskatchewan, and Alberta. The causes of this migration were primarily economic and social: by the mid-nineteenth century the population of Quebec had exponentially increased, while land had become scarce. Moreover, changes in Quebec's rural economy in the latter half of the nineteenth century, brought about by industrialization and a shift from subsistence to commercialized agriculture, contributed further to French-Canadian families being phased out of the traditional rural parishes dotting the Quebec countryside. These families lost their foothold in this rapidly changing environment; their choice was between leaving their homeland and settling where land was more readily available, or selling their services and work as wage labourers, either in Quebec's industrializing towns and cities, or in those south of the border. It is estimated that between 1840 and 1930, close to 900,000 French Canadians settled in the United States, 150,000 or so moved to Ontario, and tens of thousands settled the Canadian West.

This out-migration, or 'exodus', of French Canadians from Quebec caused fear and consternation among the province's elites. As they watched Quebec's rural parishes become increasingly depleted, and found themselves unable to staunch the outward flow of French Canadians from Quebec, many priests, politicians, and even poets railed against the growing emigration. Using a heavy dose of morality and judgment to condemn their compatriots' reasons for leaving the province, they argued that choosing emigration was materialistic and base, and they appealed to the more 'noble' and patriotic sentiments of their French-Canadian brethren to try to keep them at home.

French Canada's elites did more than just excoriate those French Canadians who emigrated, however; they also promoted the colonization of Quebec's undeveloped hinterland as a possible solution to the emigration problem and generated a movement to repatriate those French-Canadian families that had already left the province. Through the valiant efforts of such famed figures as Antoine Labelle, a priest and avid promoter of the colonization movement, later appointed head of the provincial ministry of agriculture and colonization in the late 1880s, thousands of pioneering families opened up unsettled regions of Quebec. This movement was captured perhaps most famously in Louis Hémon's classic 1913 novel *Maria Chapdelaine*, set in the pioneering Lac St Jean region north of Quebec City. Such colonization schemes produced mixed results, however, and in stemming the tide of emigration and repatriating families who had already left, they proved a failure.

The life of the pioneering settler was marked by back-breaking work and the constant threat of crop failure, personal injury, and various other calamities. The illiterate Félix Albert, whose autobiography is an invaluable window into life in a colonizing settlement in the 1860s and 1870s, shows that emigration proved an alternative few colonizing settlers could turn down: 'When I thought about it, I realized that all this work was paying me very little; the harvest was small, the cost considerable, and troubles of one kind or another caused a great deal of difficulty. At that point I said to myself, "I'm going to leave this place".'[4]

Félix Albert, like countless other French Canadians in this period, chose emigration regardless of patriotic, religious, or cultural concerns. What counted most for migrant French Canadians, as historian Bruno Ramirez and others have shown, was the family economy and choosing the best for the family and its future.[5] Most migrants emigrated with their families, or their future families, in mind. And if many them felt that their work abroad was only temporary—to pay off debts or save enough money to settle on a piece of land back home—most stayed abroad, becoming acclimatized to their new abode. Quebec would always be the land of their birth, and they would maintain close relations with it, but home now lay beyond its borders.

This emigration of hundreds of thousands of French Canadians from Quebec in the decades following Confederation radically altered the dynamic of French Canada and how the French Canadian collectivity was imagined. If at the time of Confederation most French Canadians lived within the province of Quebec, by the turn of the century this was no longer the case. In 1901 the French-Canadian population and that of French-Canadian descent in North America was 2,413,090. The province of Quebec constituted 1,322,115, or 55 per cent of the total; there were 900,000 living in the United States, 158,671 in Ontario, and 27,700 in Canada's western provinces.[6] The boundaries of French Canada had grown, and now included portions of the northeastern United States, Ontario, and settlements dotting the Canadian prairies.

THE APOGEE OF FRENCH CANADA

In response to this new reality, the French-Canadian elites shifted gears. They put away their moralizing condemnations of emigration and focused instead on building an institutional and organizational network, based in Quebec, that would cross borders to encompass the changing French-Canadians outside of Quebec. Patriotic organizations such as the Saint-Jean-Baptiste Society and the Union Saint-Joseph founded chapters in cities as far away as Lowell, Massachusetts, and French-Canadian Catholic parishes and school systems appeared in the 'Little Canadas' in New England's textile towns and the minority francophone communities in eastern Ontario and the prairie provinces. Thus the emigrant communities had the same institutions as Quebec communities. Moreover, from the 1880s onwards, French-Canadian patriotic congresses provided an opportunity for French Canadians from Quebec and all parts of the diaspora to gather and affirm their common values, regardless of where they lived.[7]

The discourse surrounding these common values centred on the notion of survival, or *la survivance*. To survive amid English-speaking Protestantism, which was often equated with urbanization and the industrialized capitalist system, French Canada's elites promoted the values that set French Canadians apart: the French language, Roman Catholicism, and the ideal of an agricultural vocation. Moreover, to justify the presence of French Canadians beyond the borders of Quebec, the province's elites argued that the French Canadian people had a providential mission to spread Catholicism and the French language throughout North American, thus remaining true to their core values and furthering what was seen as 'God's design'. All of French Canada would thus have to be unified in common purpose to ensure the survival of French language and the Catholic religion in North America.

Several crucial events that directly threatened the survival of French Canadian populations outside of Quebec in this period reinforced the siege mentality inherent in the nationalist discourse and encouraged greater co-operation among the nationalist and clerical elites both in Quebec and throughout the French Canadian diaspora. As historian A.I. Silver has shown, the second Métis uprising against the Canadian government in the West in 1885, led by Métis Louis Riel, alerted French Canadians in Quebec to the plight of their French-speaking Métis brothers.[8] The second Riel Rebellion, as it came to be known, and particularly the hanging of Riel for treason after a widely publicized trial, was perceived as an affront to French Canada as a whole. French-Canadian tempers flared at the insensitivity of Conservative Canadian Prime Minister Sir John A. Macdonald and his government. In Quebec and French Canadian communities elsewhere, the day of Riel's hanging was a day of national mourning, and fiery speeches denounced the injustice of the 'murder'; indeed, even future Liberal Prime Minister Wilfrid Laurier—by no means a fervent nationalist—in an impassioned speech declared that, had he been present on the banks of the Saskatchewan River when the rebellion broke out, he himself 'would have taken up arms against the government'.

The 'Riel Affair' was the first of several events that helped open the eyes of French Canadians in Quebec to the threats facing French-speaking peoples beyond their borders. It was followed by a series of French-language school crises, most notably in Manitoba and later in Ontario, which pitted the French-Canadian nationalist dream of French-language rights across Canada against a dominant and increasingly intransigent anglophone majority. The latter half of the nineteenth to the early part of the twentieth century was the heyday of British imperialism and the nascent English-Canadian nationalism in the decades after Confederation tied itself to what it believed to be the superior values of Anglo-Saxon culture and civilization. State-building is a messy business, and the predominantly English-Canadian provinces sought increasing uniformity in culture and education.

The western province of Manitoba, officially bilingual when it was created in 1870, quickly moved to eliminate French language rights and ban French language education from its schools. Indeed, in 1890 the Manitoba government declared a virtual war on French Catholic institutions in the province, abolishing French as an official language in its parliament and courts, and cutting off public funds to its Catholic schools. Of course, this infuriated French Canadian nationalists in Quebec, and their ire had not subsided seven years later when Liberal Prime Minister Wilfrid Laurier struck a compromise with Manitoba Premier Thomas Greenway to allow one hour of religious instruction after school where demand warranted, and to allow bilingual instruction if 10 students in any school district spoke a language other than English. But French-Canadian nationalists were in no mood to compromise, and saw this as merely a slap in the face of their vision of a broader French-Canadian nation.

Following Manitoba's example, Ontario similarly restricted the right to French language education in its schools. In 1912, convinced that the quality of education in its bilingual schools did not meet provincial standards, the Ontario government passed its infamous Regulation 17, which made English the sole language of instruction after the first two years of primary schooling. French Canadians in Ontario mounted a campaign to resist what they perceived to be an odious restriction on their language rights. The Association canadienne-française d'éducation de l'Ontario (ACFEO), founded in 1910 and devoted to protecting French-language rights in Ontario, spearheaded this campaign. They sought the aid of Quebec's French-Canadian nationalist and clerical organizations. French Canadians in Quebec gave money in support of the struggle, Quebec's newspapers kept their readers informed of the events in the neighbouring province, and Quebec's government passed a motion condemning the regulation. This crisis was soon followed by the First World War and the ensuing conscription crisis, but many French-Canadian nationalists in Quebec remained convinced that the real threat to their survival was not on the battlefields of Europe, but rather in Ontario.

One of these French-Canadian nationalists was Henri Bourassa. Bourassa, the leading French-Canadian nationalist spokesman during the first two decades of the twentieth century, did much to promote French language rights in Canada by championing a bilingual and bicultural vision of Canada. According to Bourassa, Confederation had been a pact between two founding peoples, French and English Canadians, each with equal rights under that pact to protect their distinctive language and culture. Through his articles in the independent Montreal Catholic newspaper, *Le Devoir*, of which he was founder and editor, and as an independent member of Parliament, Bourassa tirelessly argued that an affront to French language rights anywhere in Canada was an affront to the rights of the French-Canadian nation itself and was an inherent contradiction of the very spirit of Confederation. Because Canada was a pact between two distinct peoples, and because the spirit of Confederation upheld the duality of culture and of language across the country, the support for the linguistic rights of French-speaking minorities outside of Quebec was of the utmost importance for French-Canadian nationalists.

HENRI BOURASSA (1868–1952)

Portrait of Henri Bourassa in July 1917 as it appeared on a mortuary card in 1952

Library and Archives Canada/C-009092

Henri Bourassa, a politician and journalist, was one of the most influential nationalists in the history of French Canada. His career spanned over three decades and, although his star began to wane among French-Canadian nationalists following the First World War, his legacy had tremendous staying power as his ideas continued to circulate widely long after he retired from public life. He staunchly defended Canada's independence from Great Britain at a time when British imperialism was at its height in English-speaking Canada, and tirelessly advocated for the rights of French Canadians not just in Quebec but across Canada. His crusade for a bilingual and bicultural Canada, based on the notion of a pact between two nations, helped define French-Canadian nationalism for over a generation.

If lineage means anything, it is no surprise that Henri Bourassa was destined for great things. His father, Napoléon Bourassa, was a renowned Quebec artist, and his grandfather on his mother's side was Louis-Joseph Papineau, the iconic political leader of the Patriote Party at the time of the Rebellion of 1837. Bourassa threw himself into politics at an early age, getting himself elected mayor of the town of Montebello in 1890 when he was only 22 years old. He won his first seat in federal Parliament as a Liberal in 1896, when the Liberals took power after many years in opposition and Wilfrid Laurier became Canada's first French-Canadian prime minister.

It did not take long for Bourassa to butt heads with Laurier and his conciliatory policies. By 1899 the young nationalist firebrand resigned his seat over Laurier's decision to send Canadian troops to South Africa to fight in the Boer War (1899–1902). Bourassa felt this set a dangerous precedent because he deemed the Boer War to be an imperial war, and because Laurier had sent the troops without consulting Parliament. Re-elected in a by-election the following year, he continued to make his voice heard in Parliament. His defence of Canadian sovereignty and greater independence from Great Britain would serve as a guiding principle throughout the rest of his political career.

Bourassa's vision of Canada lay in his firm belief that the country had been founded on a pact between two nations. He believed that French and English Canada held equal rights under the original meaning of the confederal agreement; this vision of a bicultural Canada was his justification of the defence of French-language rights across the country. In 1905 he waged a public campaign against Prime Minister Laurier's retreat on Catholic and French education rights in the new western provinces of Alberta and Saskatchewan. His stature as a nationalist leader in French Canada was further heightened when, in September 1910, he delivered a famous speech at the Eucharistic Congress in Montreal in defence of the French language. The French language, he argued to thunderous applause, was the best vehicle to preserve Catholicism in North America. For Bourassa, the French language and the Catholic faith went hand in hand: one was inextricable from the other. His star was on the rise.

In that same year, 1910, he founded *Le Devoir*, one of the most influential nationalist newspapers in Quebec to this day. As editor of *Le Devoir*, as in his political life, he argued for his vision of a sovereign bicultural Canada, and for the rights of the French-Canadian nation. In 1912, when Ontario passed the infamous Regulation 17, Bourassa threw himself headlong into the defence of the beleaguered French-Canadian minority of that neighbouring province. On the federal level, he attacked Prime Minister Laurier's decision to create a Canadian navy on the grounds that it could serve only the interests of Great Britain in time of war. As unofficial leader of a new generation of French-Canadian nationalists, he actively campaigned against the Laurier Liberals in the federal election of 1911, thus contributing to that party's defeat and the rise to power of Robert Borden and the Conservatives.

After the First World War broke out, Bourassa continued his campaign in favour of Canadian sovereignty and excoriated the Borden government during the war, which he saw as supporting only British imperialist ends. The ensuing crisis over conscription

in 1917 only further promoted Bourassa, a staunch anti-conscriptionist, as a leading figure in the French-Canadian nationalist movement. He led the charge against conscription, which was highly unpopular in French Canada, and continued to argue for French-language rights in Ontario. Why, he argued, should French Canadians go off to die in Europe when the real struggle was being waged across the border in Ontario, where French-Canadian rights were at stake? Being at the forefront of the nationalist movement in French Canada during the First World War made Bourassa highly unpopular among English Canadians, who labelled him a traitor.

After the First World War, Henri Bourassa became increasingly isolated in the intellectual and political landscape of French Canada. Although he remained editor of *Le Devoir* until 1932, and held a seat in the House of Commons from 1925 to 1935, his public campaigns increasingly dealt with issues of a purely Catholic and social nature. Uncomfortable with too close an association between nationalism and Catholicism among French Canadians, which he believed went against the Pope's direct instructions in the 1920s, Bourassa fell out of favour with the new generation of French-Canadian nationalists, led by historian and cleric Lionel Groulx, that came to dominate the nationalist movement in the interwar years. Bourassa did make a final public re-emergence during the Second World War when conscription once again came to be seen as a threat to French Canada. He died in 1952, a decade before the Royal Commission on Bilingualism and Biculturalism, which drew heavily on his vision of Canada and French Canada's place within it.

After the war, French-Canadian nationalist, historian, and cleric Lionel Groulx took over where Henri Bourassa left off, advocating for the rights of French language minorities outside Quebec. Although Lionel Groulx has primarily been understood as a Quebec nationalist, as historian Michel Bock argues, Groulx considered French-Canadian minorities outside Quebec inextricable from the French-Canadian

nation. In his vision of French-Canadian nationalism, which he promoted again and again from the 1920s to the 1950s, French-Canadian minorities outside Quebec were the ramparts of the French-Canadian nation: if they fell, the French Canadians in Quebec would also fall. Indeed, Groulx argued that French Canadians had a providential and historic mission to live and flourish on the North American continent.

They constituted, Groulx said, the vestiges of the great French Empire that once spread from Quebec City to Louisiana, from the Rocky Mountains to the Ohio Valley. Their ancestors had been the missionaries, explorers, colonizers, and soldiers who had opened up the continent and spread Christianity and civilization throughout North America, and because of this, Groulx insisted, the French-Canadian people possessed inalienable rights even in those areas where they constituted a minority.[9]

The Bourassa and Groulx visions of the French-Canadian nation were widely disseminated in the nationalist newspapers and networks throughout French Canada during the interwar period, both in Quebec and beyond. New organizations such as the Ordre de Jacques-Cartier (OJC) founded in Ottawa in 1926 with chapters in Ontario and Quebec sprang up to promote this ideal. Founded at the end of the battle against Regulation 17 in Ontario, the OJC was an elite organization that required its members swear an oath of secrecy. They were to work behind the scenes in French-Canadian organizations and institutions to promote the solidarity of French Canadians, and within the federal civil service to fight for the advancement of French language rights at the federal level. Moreover, this variant of French-Canadian nationalism was at the forefront in a number of important congresses that brought together French Canadians from Quebec and the diaspora to affirm their common values and promote the various struggles for *la survivance* across North America. An offshoot of these congresses was the Conseil de la vie française en Amérique (founded in 1937) which, like the OJC, sought to further develop ties between French Canadians, serve as a linchpin for the French-Canadian institutional network, and promote French language rights across the continent. Indeed, many people belonged to both these organizations.[10]

But if French Canada developed as a discourse and as an institutional and organizational network led by the French-Canadian elites in this period, and was profoundly marked by the linguistic conflicts that erupted in the latter half of the nineteenth and the early part of the twentieth century, to what extent did the average French Canadian, both within and outside of Quebec, participate in this process? Indeed,

to what extent did the average French Canadian's conception of French Canada reflect that of the elite? Unfortunately, little if any work has been done in this area, and we can only point to a few examples that might illustrate an alternate conception of the French-Canadian experience than the one which we so far have examined. Let us look for a moment at a few of these examples.

Groundbreaking work by historians in the study of the correspondence of French Canadians is emerging, painting a rich and varied picture of the French-Canadian diaspora.[11] One study in particular, by historian Marcel Martel, examines the correspondence between a French-Canadian father and son in New England from 1912 to 1929 and offers a fascinating window into the life of an average French-Canadian family of that time and place.[12] The father, Jean-Henri Frenière, was a middle-class entrepreneur and inventor who emigrated from Quebec to Rutland, Vermont in 1872. His son, Maxime-Ovila Frenière, an adult at the time the letters are exchanged, lived in Springfield, Massachusetts, and worked in industrial design. What emerges in this correspondence, aside from the primacy of the family economy over all other matters, is a picture of French Canadians who chose *not* to participate within the institutional network and instead actively engaged with the English-speaking community, for material advancement. Moreover, over half of the letters between them are in English, not French, illustrating the quick adaptation to the language of the majority. Interestingly, the son, whose command of the French language was tenuous at best, joined the Franco-American Union Saint-Jean-Baptiste d'Amérique and took French classes in an attempt to reclaim his French-Canadian heritage. His father had mixed feelings about this, writing that it was a little late in life for his son to be devoting his time to such activities, and that he would make better use of his time by devoting it to his work instead. As Martel points out, for Jean-Henri Frenière, language was not a part of his identity, but rather a tool for communication and social advancement. Aside from this brief but interesting exchange, there is little mention of the French-Canadian institutions and organizations in their correspondence, and religion and the Catholic Church are never mentioned at all.[13]

Another example that suggests an alternate under-standing of the French-Canadian identity is that of famed Franco-Manitoban author Gabrielle Roy's father, Léon Roy. Gabrielle Roy, author of classic French-Canadian novels including *The Tin Flute*, was born in St-Boniface, Manitoba, but her father, Léon, was born in Quebec, or what was then called Canada East, in 1850. Upon reaching adulthood, he fled his home province for the United States, working for a time in Lowell, Massachusetts where he opened a small restaurant with a friend. Eventually he sold his restaurant and returned to Canada, but not to Quebec, choosing instead to move to Manitoba where he met his wife and settled down to have a family. Léon Roy had learned to speak English; this helped him adapt to what was a predominantly English-speaking province, though he settled in a French-Canadian community and became a shopkeeper. Interestingly, in the early 1890s, as the Manitoba Schools Crisis raged, Léon Roy chose to publicly campaign for Wilfrid Laurier and the Liberal party, who would strike the compromise with Manitoba premier Thomas Greenway that angered

so many French-Canadian nationalists. Gabrielle Roy's father was a savvy character, however, and like Jean-Henri Frenière, he put his own ambitions and the interests of his family over any patriotic or reli-gious views. Indeed, because of his support for the Laurier Liberals, and in spite of attacks from the local French-Canadian elites and members of the clergy, he eventually got a well-paying and much sought-after government job as interpreter at Immigration Hall in Winnipeg, and later became Inspector of Colonies.[14]

What we see in both of these examples, then, is that the French-Canadian experience outside Quebec was not always a part of the traditional French-Canadian institutional or organizational network, and that French Canadians often navigated their French-Canadian identity on an individual basis. The French-Canadian identity, regardless of how the elites defined it, was not solely, or even always, based on language and religion. For many French Canadians there were other more important issues at stake. But let us now turn to the climax of the evolution of French Canada and its demise.

SNAPSHOT

Quebec and the Ontario Schools Crisis (1912–1927)

The Ontario Schools Crisis (1912–27) is widely seen as the foundational event of the Franco-Ontarian col-lectivity. The suppression of the French-language in Ontario schools by the Ontario government under the infamous Regulation 17 led Franco-Ontarians to form a common front and wage a campaign of civil disobedience, popular protest, and legal action in an attempt to overturn the unjust law. Thus Franco-Ontarians, united in a common objective, began to see themselves as a distinct collective group within the wider French-Canadian nation.

But if the Ontario Schools Crisis served to solidify the identity of French Canadians in Ontario, it also had important ramifications for French Canadians within Quebec. Indeed, the timing of the schools crisis, which took its most severe turn during the heady and divisive days of the First World War,

solidified French-Canadian nationalism within Quebec itself. French-Canadian nationalists in Quebec came to see linguistic rights in Ontario as inextricably linked to the broader struggle over conscription and French-Canadian rights throughout Canada. Quebec was the fortress of the French-Canadian nation, they believed, and French-Canadian minorities outside Quebec formed the outposts of that nation. Therefore an affront to the rights of French Canadians in Ontario was seen as an affront to the French-Canadian nation itself. If an outpost fell, it was believed, Quebec would soon follow.

The origins of the Ontario Schools Crisis lay in the large number of French-Canadians who migrated to Ontario, particularly to the eastern portions of the province, in the second half of the nineteenth century. These waves of French Canadians from Quebec pour-ing into the province were seen as a threat by many segments of Ontario's Anglo-Protestant majority. In the discourse of the time, which was heavily tinged with anti-Catholic prejudice and British imperialist sentiment, French Canadians were seen as backwards, disloyal, and foreign. In accordance with these views, the government of Ontario made English a compulsory language of instruction in its schools in 1885. In 1890 English became the only language of instruction in a school unless the number of French Canadians in the area made this impossible, in which case a bilingual school could continue to operate. In 1912, however, an unlikely alliance between the province's anti-Catholic Orange Order and the Irish Catholics led by Bishop Michael Fallon of the diocese of London, Ontario, pressured the government to make English the only language of instruction in the province's schools without exception after the first two grades of primary instruction—the infamous Regulation 17.

The French-Canadians of Ontario, using their institutional and organizational networks, including the Association canadienne-française d'éducation de l'Ontario (ACFEO) and newly founded Catholic French-language newspapers, such as *Le Droit*, mobilized themselves against Regulation 17 and sought to have it overturned. Protests and rallies were held, including a rally of 5,000 people on Parliament Hill in Ottawa in 1916. The ACFEO even went so far as to encourage francophone trustees of the Ottawa Separate School Board to purposely disobey the law; this caused the board to lose its subsidies from the provincial government. Tempers flared, and incidents of civil disobedience and even sporadic acts of violence occurred.

In the context of the First World War and the ensuing Conscription Crisis, French Canadians in Quebec came to the aid of their French-Canadian compatriots in Ontario in various ways. Quebec newspapers covered the Ontario Schools Crisis widely, keeping the population informed of the events taking place in the neighbouring province. A number of groups and organizations raised funds to help finance the resistance to Regulation 17. The Saint-Jean-Baptiste Societies of Montreal and Quebec City, along with the Société du parler français collected funds among Quebec's francophone population, as did the province's Catholic bishops

and primary francophone university, the Université Laval. Moreover, nationalist leaders such as Henri Bourassa, Armand Lavergne, and Olivar Asselin gave speeches pledging the province's support for the cause, and Quebec Liberal Premier Lomer Gouin even publicly called on Ontario's English-speaking majority to treat its French-Canadian minority with generosity and respect, a move which could easily have incited allegations of one province's political interference in another's affairs. Behind the scenes, Cardinal Bégin, Archbishop of Quebec, travelled to Rome to lobby the Vatican in support of French language rights in Ontario. Quebec's Catholic French-Canadian youth groups, such as the Association de la jeunesse canadienne française, also raised funds in support of the cause.

After the First World War, the conflict in Ontario was still unresolved, despite a Papal call for moderation on the issue and a ruling by the British Privy Council that upheld the legality of Regulation 17. Quebec's interest and participation in the Ontario Schools Crisis continued well into the 1920s as the new generation of French-Canadian nationalists in Quebec, spearheaded by historian and cleric Lionel Groulx and his nationalist Action française group, continued to militate in favour of French language rights in Ontario. Lionel Groulx, under the pseudonym Alonié de Lestres, even wrote a fiery novel on the Ontario Schools Crisis, *L'Appel de la race* (1922), and Action française bestowed an award upon Franco-Ontarian senator Napoléon Belcourt, president of the ACFEO.

As the 1920s wore on, however, the Ontario Schools Crisis wound down as the government of Ontario found Regulation 17 increasingly difficult to enforce. With both sides taking a more moderate course, Regulation 17 was ultimately abandoned in 1927, bringing the crisis to a close.

The Ontario Schools Crisis helped create important ties between French Canadians in Ontario and in Quebec, and these ties outlasted the crisis itself. One of its direct consequences was the creation of the Ordre de Jacques-Cartier, a secret society devoted to the advancement of French language rights in the federal civil service and to fostering greater ties among the organizational and institutional structures of French Canada.

The End of French Canada and the Rise of the Québécois Identity

Gabrielle Roy's *The Tin Flute*, published in 1945, is widely thought to be the first truly urban and modern novel by a French-Canadian writer. It vividly captured the changes in Quebec during the tumultuous years of the Second World War. Focusing on the problems of a working class French-Canadian family, with a stunning cast of characters, it heralded a new dawn in French-Canadian literature, and catapulted its young Franco-Manitoban author to national and international fame. Quebec sociologist Jean-Charles Falardeau, writing about the transformations taking place in his province in that period, describes the novel's setting: 'The daughter of Maria Chapdelaine who was an ammunition-factory worker at Valcartier during the war now lives with her own family of five children in the Rosemount ward of Montreal. Maria's married brothers are employees of the Aluminum Company at Arvida and Shipshaw after having been workers at the Jonquière pulp plant.'[15] By the Second World War, it was clear that Quebec was primarily an urban and industrialized society, and that the province's French Canadians had largely become wage earners. As historian Ramsay Cook put it, 'the Quebec of Louis Hémon has moved forward to the Quebec of Gabrielle Roy—and beyond'.[16]

It took time for Quebec's government to catch up to this new social structure. Under Premier Maurice Duplessis, whose Union Nationale party ruled the province from 1944 to 1960, a conservative view of Quebec society was upheld, promoting the basic tenets of traditional French-Canadian nationalism: a French, Catholic society with an agricultural vocation and a docile workforce. Duplessis' government, profoundly non-interventionist, played a negligible role in Quebec's social and economic matters, and the Church's hegemony was unchallenged.

But in this period, referred to as *La grande noirceur* ('The Great Darkness'), traditional French-Canadian nationalism in Quebec was increasingly challenged. Believing that it did not reflect an urban and industrialized Quebec, a new generation of nationalists,

or neo-nationalists, re-invented French-Canadian nationalism to make it modern and relevant. The major players in this neo-nationalist movement were intellectuals, such as André Laurendeau, editor of *Le Devoir* during the 1950s, and the historians of the 'Montreal school'—Michel Brunet, Guy Frégault, and Maurice Séguin—all previously disciples of Lionel Groulx. They argued that French-Canadian nationalism needed to be modernized, and the Quebec government needed to play a greater role.[17]

André Laurendeau and other neo-nationalists attacked the corrupt and retrograde ideology and practices of Maurice Duplessis and the Union Nationale, and argued that their province needed to catch up to the rest of the world, lest it forever remain 'backwards'. While Laurendeau continued to support the rights of French-Canadian minorities outside of Quebec, taking the appointment of Co-Chair of the federal Royal Commission on Bilingualism and Biculturalism when it was created by Canadian Prime Minister Lester B. Pearson in the early 1960s, the other neo-nationalists took an increasingly opposing course. Believing French-Canadian minorities outside of Quebec were doomed to irreversible assimilation and could no longer be helped, they argued that the survival of French Canada could only be maintained within Quebec itself, where an activist government could adequately promote and defend its existence.

French-Canadian identity in Quebec was changing. Jean Lesage and the Liberals came to power on 22 June 1960, ushering in a period of state-building and rapid reforms that has come to be known as the Quiet Revolution. At first the Lesage Liberals attempted to champion the cause of French-Canadian minorities outside of Quebec through initiatives such as the Service du Canada français d'outre-frontières to facilitate relations between Quebec and the diaspora; however, such initiatives quickly turned to disenchantment.[18] During the Quiet Revolution, the Quebec government focused on building their own province and the plight of French Canadians within its borders.

This new concept of the Quebec state had profound ramifications for the notion of French Canada. In the 1960s, a decisive shift came as French-Canadian nationalists within Quebec refashioned the French-Canadian identity into the Québécois identity. It was the heyday of decolonization movements around the world, and many French-speaking Quebecers, influenced by the decolonization discourse and national liberation struggles abroad, came to equate the term *French Canadian* with a colonial status within Quebec and Canada. The rising Quebec independence movement in this period fed off the decolonization discourse and argued passionately that the French-Canadian identity would forever mean second-class status, and that it was only through complete independence—political, social, economic, and cultural—that French-Canadians in Quebec could truly shake off their colonial status and assume their full identity as Québécois. No longer prepared to define their identity based on the pillars of the French language, farming, and Catholicism, the new Québécois identity would be based on linguistic and territorial lines.

This, of course, profoundly affected French-Canadian minorities outside of Quebec who were excluded from the new territorial dimension of the Québécois identity. Left to their own devices, they turned to an increasingly active federal government for language-rights protection to support their future struggles for language rights. In the minds of Quebec francophones, French Canada had broken up into distinct parts and had dissolved. The election of the Parti Québécois in 1976, and the subsequent Quebec referendum on sovereignty-association in 1980, served only to exacerbate this break. There were no more French Canadians; henceforth there would only be Québécois, Franco-Ontarians, Franco-Manitobans,

and so forth. French Canada, which had lasted just over a century, had ended.

On 7 March 1967, two years before he died, Jack Kerouac was invited to travel to Montreal to be interviewed on a French-language television show called *Le Sel de la Semaine*. The interview was conducted entirely in French, and the interviewer asked Kerouac about his French-Canadian family, his upbringing in Lowell, and if he had gone to a French school. Indeed, he seemed genuinely surprised when Kerouac explained that he had not learned to speak English until he was six years old. Kerouac went on to explain in his thick Franco-American *joual*:

> We spoke French in the shack . . . in the house. Also, it was a neighborhood, all French, Beaulieu Street and Boisvert Street, and . . . and the club, it was all old Frenchmen who played cards, who played pool, and . . . . Christmas, New Year, they made meat pies and they screamed their heads off. . . . And, ah . . . once a year, Canadians would come down . . . from Quebec . . . in dog sleighs in the snow, to celebrate. Did you know that? To Lowell![19]

Speaking to a modern Québécois audience, Kerouac, despite his literary fame and success, seemed to feel it necessary to justify his French-Canadian identity. To the audience his accent and his recollections of his French-Canadian upbringing seemed quaint, and even faintly humorous. Jack Kerouac and his memories of French Canada embodied a world that, for many Quebecers in the late 1960s, no longer existed.

Questions for Consideration

1. To what extent was French Canada the product of nationalist and clerical elites? Did their dream correspond with the reality of everyday French Canadians?

2. What role did Quebec play in the evolution of French Canada, and its eventual demise?

3. What is the heritage of French Canada today?

Notes

1. Jack Kerouac, *Selected Letters: 1940–1956*, ed. Ann Charters (New York: Viking Penguin, 1995), 227.
2. Ibid., 228.
3. Ibid., 258–9

4. Félix Albert, *Immigrant Odyssey: A French-Canadian Habitant in New England*, ed. Frances H. Early, trans. Arthur L. Eno, Jr (Orono, Maine: University of Maine Press, 1991), 65.

5. See, for example, Bruno Ramirez, *On the Move: French-Canadian and Italian Migrants in the North Atlantic Economy, 1860–1914*, (Toronto: McClelland and Stewart, 1991) and Yukari Takai, *Gendered Passages: French-Canadian Migration to Lowell, Massachusetts, 1900–1920*, (New York: Peter Lang, 2008).

6. These figures are cited in Yves Roby, *Histoire d'un rêve brisé? Les Canadiens français aux États-Unis* (Sillery: Septentrion, 2007), 7.

7. For a history of these patriotic congresses as they pertain to Franco-Ontario, see for example, Gaétan Gervais, *Des gens de résolution: le passage du 'Canada français' à 'l'Ontario français'* (Sudbury: Institut franco-ontarien/Prise de parole, 2003), 17–106.

8. A.I. Silver, *The French-Canadian Idea of Confederation 1864–1900* (Toronto: University of Toronto Press, 1982), 150–79.

9. See Michel Bock, *Quand la nation débordait les frontières: les minorités françaises dans la pensée de Lionel Groulx* (Montreal: Les Éditions Hurtubise HMH, 2004).

10. See Marcel Martel, *Le deuil d'un pays imaginé: rêves, luttes et déroute du Canada français* (Ottawa: Les Presses de l'Université d'Ottawa, 1997) and Marcel Martel, *French Canada: An account of its creation and break-up, 1850–1967*, Canada's Ethnic Group Series Booklet No. 24 (Ottawa: The Canadian Historical Association, 1998).

11. I am referring particularly here to Yves Frenette, Marcel Martel, and John Willis, eds., *Envoyer et recevoir. Lettres et correspondances dans les diasporas francophones* (Sainte-Foy: Les Presses de l'Université Laval, 2006).

12. Marcel Martel, '"Gardons contact": l'expérience épistolaire de Jean-Henri et de Maxime-Ovila Frenière en Nouvelle-Angleterre, 1912–1929,' in ibid., 175–97.

13. Ibid, 191–2.

14. On Roy, see François Ricard, *Gabrielle Roy: A Life*, trans. Patricia Claxton (Toronto: McClelland and Stewart, 1999), 3–22.

15. Quoted in Ramsay Cook, *Canada and the French-Canadian Question* (Toronto: Macmillan of Canada, 1966), 80.

16. Ibid.

17. See, for example, Michael D. Behiels, *Prelude to Quebec's Quiet Revolution: Liberalism versus Neo-Nationalism, 1945–1960* (Kingston and Montreal: McGill-Queen's University Press, 1985) and Jean Lamarre, *Le devenir de la nation québécoise selon Maurice Séguin, Guy Frégault et Michel Brunet, 1944–1969* (Sillery: Septentrion, 1993).

18. A discussion of the SCFOF can be found in Martel, *Le deuil d'un pays imaginé* (see footnote 10).

19. Paul Maher Jr, ed., *Empty Phantoms: Interviews and Encounters with Jack Kerouac* (New York: Thunder's Mouth Press, 2005), 268.

RELEVANT WEBSITES

MULTICULTURAL CANADA: http://multiculturalcanada.ca Multiculturalism and ethnic groups in Canada. See specifically the entry on French Canadians in the Encyclopedia of Canada's Peoples by historian Yves Frenette.

LA FRANCOPHONIE EN AMERIQUE DU NORD: www.cefan.ulaval.ca
Laval University website on the North American Francophonie. This website is in French only.

THE CENTRE FOR RESEARCH ON FRENCH CANADIAN CULTURE OF THE UNIVERSITY OF OTTAWA: www.crccf.uottawa.ca

STATISTICS CANADA: www.statcan.ca
See specifically the latest census information on the linguistic portrait of Canada today.

SELECT BIBLIOGRAPHY

Albert, Félix. *Immigrant Odyssey: A French-Canadian Habitant in New England*. ed. Frances H. Early, trans. Arthur L. Eno, Jr. Orono, Maine: University of Maine Press, 1991.

Behiels, Michael D. *Prelude to Quebec's Quiet Revolution: Liberalism versus Neo-Nationalism, 1945–1960*. Kingston and Montreal: McGill-Queen's University Press, 1985.

Bernard, Roger. *Le Canada Français: entre mythe et utopie*. Hearst: Le Nordir, 1988.

Bock, Michel. *Quand la nation débordait les frontières: les minorités françaises dans la pensée de Lionel Groulx*. Montreal: Les Éditions Hurtubise HMH, 2004.

Cook, Ramsay, ed. *French Canadian Nationalism: An Anthology*. Toronto: Macmillan, 1969.

———. *Provincial Autonomy, Minority Rights and the Compact Theory, 1867–1921*. Ottawa: Queen's Printer, 1969.

Frenette, Yves. *Brève histoire des Canadiens français*. Montreal: Boréal, 1998.

———,Marcel Martel, and John Willis, eds. *Envoyer et recevoir. Lettres et correspondances dans les diasoporas francophones*. Sainte-Foy: Les Presses de l'Université Laval, 2006.

Gaffield, Chad. *Language, Conflict, and Cultural Conflict: The Origins of the French-Language Controversy in Ontario*. Kingston and Montreal: McGill-Queen's University Press, 1987.

Gervais, Gaétan. *Des gens de résolution: le passage du 'Canada français' à 'l'Ontario français'*. Sudbury: Institut franco-ontarien/Prise de parole, 2003.

Horton, Donald. *André Laurendeau: French-Canadian Nationalist 1912–1968*. Toronto: Oxford University Press, 1992.

Jaenen, Cornelius, ed. *Les Franco-Ontariens*. Ontario Historical Studies Series. Ottawa: Les Presses de l'Université d'Ottawa, 1993.

Lamarre, Jean. *Le devenir de la nation québécoise selon Maurice Séguin, Guy Frégault et Michel Brunet. 1944–1969*. Sillery: Septentrion, 1993.

Levitt, Joseph, ed. *Henri Bourassa on Imperialism and Bi-culturalism, 1900–1918*. Toronto: Copp Clark, 1970.

Louder, Dean R. and Eric Waddell, eds. *French America: Mobility, Identity, and Minority Experience Across the Continent*. trans. Franklin Philip. Baton Rouge and London: Louisiana State University Press, 1993.

Martel, Marcel. *Le deuil d'un pays imaginé: rêves, luttes et déroute du Canada français*. Ottawa: Les Presses de l'Université d'Ottawa, 1997.

———, *French Canada: An Account of its Creation and Break-up, 1850–1967*. Canada's Ethnic Group Series Booklet No. 24. Ottawa: The Canadian Historical Association, 1998.

Ramirez, Bruno. *On the Move: French-Canadian and Italian Migrants in the North Atlantic Economy, 1860–1914*. Toronto: McClelland & Stewart, 1991.

Roby, Yves. *Histoire d'un rêve brisé? Les Canadiens français aux États-Unis*. Sillery: Septentrion, 2007.

———, *Les Franco-Américains de la Nouvelle Angleterre. Rêves et réalités*. Sillery, Septentrion, 2000.

Silver, Arthur. *The French-Canadian Idea of Confederation 1864–1900*. Toronto: University of Toronto Press, 1982.

Takai, Yukari. *Gendered Passages: French-Canadian Migration to Lowell, Massachusetts, 1900–1920*. New York: Peter Lang, 2008.

Wade, Mason. *The French Canadians 1760–1967*. 2 vols. Toronto: Macmillan, 1968.

CHAPTER 6

Quebec's Americanicity

Yvan Lamonde, McGill University

— TIMELINE —

1774–5 American revolutionary propaganda distributed in Quebec and province invaded by American Revolutionary Army.

1791 England grants Lower Canada its House of Assembly.

1812 United States invades Canada for second time.

1830 Patriotes make increasing reference to US republican independence.

1837 US support for Patriote cause comes from inhabitants on Canada–United States border, but not from American states or US federal government.

1838 Unsuccessful rebellion of some hundred exiled Patriotes originates in United States.

1849 After resistance of 1837, rebellion of 1838, and initiatives to repeal union of Upper and Lower Canada are all defeated, minority of francophone and anglophone Lower Canadians (British Tories and French-Canadian Democrats) draft plan for annexation with United States.

1859 Edmé Rameau de Saint-Père introduces notion that French Canada has spiritual or providential vocation in Americas.

1866 Abbé Henri-Raymond Casgrain grafts idea of moral vocation in Americas onto notion of providential vocation of French Canada.

1872 Trade Union Act recognizes right of workers to associate in Canada, and US unions begin to organize in Canada and Quebec.

1896 In his book *L'avenir du peuple canadien-français*, Edmond de Nevers foresees '[North] American continental union' which would include 'small nations'.

1902 Msgr Adolphe Pâquet delivers his famous speech on future of French race in North America, breathing new life into Rameau de Saint-Père's vision, just as Vatican begins to consider repudiating Catholic vocation of French Canadians in North America.

1928 Based on his observations of increased US investment and penetration of US business and media culture into Quebec, businessman Beaudry Leman says of American civilization: 'We can't live with it and we can't live without it'.

1945 Increasingly, French Canadians adopt materialist 'American way of life', abandoning their ascetic spiritual self-image.

1961 Quebec's General Agency in New York (which hired its first Agent General in 1943) becomes General Delegation of Quebec in New York (now the Quebec Government Office in New York).

1970 More and more US counterculture embraced in Quebec, and place of Quebec in Americas and Quebec's Americanicity examined more intensively.

Quebec's 'Americanicity' may seem obvious to a student from Boston or a professor from Seattle. Quebec is in North America; therefore, in the geographical sense of the word, it is American. It is 'Americanized,' hence it is 'American'. In contemplating The Declaration of Independence or the famous speech by Ralph Waldo Emerson, 'The American Scholar',[1] our student or professor might even conflate Canada's and Quebec's experiences with a wider emancipation process involving other societies in the Americas. They might consider for a moment, in the spirit of the Monroe Doctrine (1823) or of their compatriot John Louis O'Sullivan (1845), that the United States has a 'Manifest Destiny'[2] in the Americas. But by the same token, our American scholars might well wonder what 'destiny' the other societies of this hemisphere have followed. What destiny, what concept of their place, and what perception of their role might these societies, who share the continent of South and North America, have had in the past or have today?

Understanding the Americanicity of a society outside the United States but 'inside' the Americas (a continent with a history that has not always been associated with or reduced to the US nation-state), requires us to embrace revelations and reorient our preconceptions about identity. With this in mind, let us start by trying to understand what is meant by *Americanization*.

TWO MEANINGS OF *AMERICANIZATION*

The first meaning of *Americanization* dates back to America's earlier origins. In fact, all the societies that make up 'the Americas' are new societies[3] in that they were shaped by the contact between European immigrants and the Aboriginal peoples of the continent.[4] All the colonial settlers had to adapt to the New World, its inhabitants, its climate, and its constraints. By taking up residence in the Americas, they became Americans. Most significantly, these newcomers (profoundly influenced by the Aboriginal peoples they met) underwent an Americanization that lasted fully two centuries before the United States was born.

The second meaning of *Americanization* lies in the United States' rise to power and its international expansionism at the end of the nineteenth century. The domination of Canada and other countries in the Americas by foreign US capital investment beginning around 1920; the spread of US culture throughout the Americas through technology and media such as the popular press; the near-monopoly of the US film industry after the First World War; and the emergence after 1945 of the notion of an 'American' way of life—these are all milestones in the process of Americanization. Indeed, the commanding power of the economy, military, technology, and media culture that flowed out of the United States has profoundly affected culture and behaviour in countries around the world.

Societies in the Americas have therefore undergone two forms of Americanization; but the second form cannot erase the historical and enduring first form. Indeed, US press, cinema, radio, architecture, television, diet, and attire—the second form—greatly contributed to the Americanicity of French Canada and Quebec. But Americanicity cannot be reduced to Americanization. In Quebec, as in Mexico, (and here we have the full definition of Americanicity), there is a consciousness of belonging to the New World that precedes and transcends the relationship with United States; there is an attendant propensity to observe the political and cultural consequences of belonging to the American hemisphere; and all societies of the New World have the history of their relationships with the Old World, the memory of their 'Europeanicity'.[5] This said, the United States was the main catalyst in Quebec's historical relationships within the Americas for two reasons: its immediate geographic proximity as Quebec's neighbour, and its very early and successful colonial emancipation, which later became a model for Europe and the Americas alike.[6]

QUEBEC'S AMERICANICITY AND THE WAR OF INDEPENDENCE

The words *Quebec's Americanicity* convey an unfashionably historical phenomenon. French Quebec's long history of continental Americanicity began with the struggles of colonial settlers from France, who had to adapt to life in the New World. By the end of eighteenth century, the telltale (political) signs of Americanicity were increasingly numerous. In 1774, 11 years after France ceded its American territory to England in the Treaty of Paris, the First Continental Congress (of what would become the United States) mandated Fleury Mesplet, a francophone printer in Philadelphia, to print pamphlets for distribution in the Province of Quebec. The pamphlets invited the inhabitants of Quebec to join the 13 American rebel colonies in their very just cause, urging 'your Province is the only missing link that remains to complete the strong and shining chain of their Union.'[7] For six months, troops from the rebel colonies occupied Quebec before being pushed back from the shores of the St Lawrence River at Quebec City by the British regiments that arrived in the spring of 1776.[8] But by that time, there had been ample opportunity for the notion of American republicanism to be disseminated. In 1777, the governor of Britain's new colony recognized that 'for years, the manner in which this people has been governed has not been sufficiently firm, whence the penetration of American ideas of emancipation and independence'.[9] In the same vein, the Bishop of Quebec City lamented the increased flouting of authority, along with the subversive forces at work in 1790:

> have we not the right to blame the advancement of this spirit of liberty and independence among our [French] Canadians, [a spirit] initially brought to us through the distribution of Anglo-American manifestos at the beginning of the last war, and propagated through the multiplication and the licence of our newspapers and by the liberties taken in conversations about political affairs?[10]

The groundwork for US anti-colonial republican ideas was clearly being laid and would continue to influence political life in Lower Canada. This was particularly true after 1823, when Louis-Joseph Papineau came back disappointed from London, where he and John Neilson had gone on behalf of Lower Canada (now part of Quebec) to register their opposition to a prospective Union with Upper Canada (now part of Ontario). By 1830, the Parti patriote founded in 1826 (or the 'Patriot Party' to its anglophone members, inspired by the US Patriots of 1776), was making increasing reference to the success of American Independence and the US model of republican government. The party was especially interested in applying the electoral model of the US state Senates to the Legislative Council of Lower Canada. This was then the exclusive preserve of the British colonial authorities, who typically appointed anglophones who supported their policies, thereby giving the British the means to oppose legislation passed in Lower Canada's elected House of Assembly.

THE CLAWS OF THE BRITISH LION OR THE TALONS OF THE AMERICAN EAGLE?

Louis-Joseph Papineau (see Biography box) was not the only thinker to develop an 'American' vision for the future of Lower Canada. Étienne Parent, editor of the Quebec City newspaper *Le Canadien*, was of the same mind in an editorial of 21 May 1831:

> There is not, to our knowledge, a French people in this Province, but rather a Canadian people, a religious and moral people, a people both loyal and liberty-loving, capable of enjoying these things; this people is not French, nor English, nor Scottish, nor Irish, nor Yankee, but Canadian. It can and must take pride in its origins and congratulate itself on its current union, which, we hope, will n'er be torn asunder by violence; yet the situation of this land, its statistics, its resources and a thousand other circumstances, must needs convince any attentive observer that (barring measures of violence and extermination) the people of Canada, embracing a vast share of the American hemisphere, has quite another destiny before it.

Nonetheless, Parent was not in favour of Lower Canada joining the American Union and compared Quebec's situation with that of Louisiana when it entered the Union in 1812. With this precedent in mind, Parent feared for the French language (doubting it would be used in Congress), for the legal system, and for some French colonial institutions such as the seigneurial regime. Moreover, he predicted that if Lower Canada joined the Union, the ensuing flood of Americans pouring into Quebec would be so great that French Canadians would run the risk of losing 'their political preponderance as a distinct people'.

Parent, who would break ranks with Papineau and the Parti patriote in 1836, advised party members to spend more time studying the situation of Louisiana than that of Poland. On 22 February 1832, he wrote in *Le Canadien* that he did not believe

a people of six thousand and some souls capable of maintaining its independence and its nationality.

Assuredly not at the very doorstep of a powerful and enterprising nation . . . . It is for this reason that we have always maintained that the clear interest of England and of Lower Canada was that the nationality of the Canadian people be preserved and nurtured until it was in a state to defend itself from the encroachments of its neighbours.

LOUIS-JOSEPH PAPINEAU (1786–1871)

Louis-Joseph Papineau, ca. 1852

Photograph attributed to T.C. Doane / Library and Archives Canada / C-066899

Papineau would have been a Washington or a Bolivar if Lower Canada had succeeded in achieving independence in 1837 or 1838. But this was not to be and, for much of his political life he in fact became the scapegoat for political failures, the frustrations of some, and the resentments of others. Today, Papineau is remembered as the greatest politician Lower Canada would see in the first half of the nineteenth century.[11] Indeed, his vision of Lower Canada's destiny in the Americas would be the most sustained and consistent of any politician, both before and after the resistance of 1837 and the rebellion of 1838.

The son of Joseph Papineau (one of the members of the first House of Assembly of Lower Canada in 1792), Louis-Joseph Papineau was called to the bar in 1810, two years after he was first elected to the Assembly. An articulate, self-assured orator, he was soon elected Speaker of the Assembly (1815) and took over as the clear leader of the Parti canadien (later the Parti patriote) in 1817. It was Papineau who, from 1815 to 1837, championed controversial parliamentary and

constitutional struggles on behalf of the citizens of Lower Canada. His chief struggle was the demand that residents of Lower Canada enjoy the full range of freedoms that the British constitutional monarchy was required to afford its subjects. But Papineau's visit to London in 1823 opened his eyes to a number of discouraging circumstances: the British government's lack of interest in its colony, the social misery caused by industrialization, and the strategic waffling in the politics of the metropole. To his dismay, he found that the House of Commons Select Committee on the Civil Government of Canada conducted its affairs in much the same way in 1828. By 1831, Papineau was looking elsewhere for inspiration:

it is therefore not to the mother country [England] any more than to the rest of Europe (where the social orientation is completely different and where the distribution of wealth is very unequal), that one must look for examples; it is instead to America, where one sees neither colossal fortunes nor degrading poverty, where men of genius move through the different ranks of society, unobstructed.[12]

Refusing to see the imperial, class-bound House of Lords reproduced in the colony, Papineau vigorously denounced Lower Canada's appointed (predominantly anglophone, British loyalist) Legislative Council and demanded that its members be elected. He was developing a vision for Lower Canadian society in the context of the Americas:

There must needs be a king in Europe, where he is ensconced by monarchies . . . . The same does not apply here, for we do not have and cannot have an aristocracy; we have no need of these magnificent attributes. We do need a simple [form of] government, like that of the United States.[13]

In 1833, his criticism of the monarchy and the aristocracy led him to praise the American republic:

Of all these governments, those whose regime is unrivalled in producing the most delightful fruits, have been [part of] the pure or slightly modified republicanism of the confederated states of New England. . . . [Republicanism] has produced, in its inhabitants' way of life, an improvement that is palpable and visible to this day.[14]

Papineau was certain that 'before long, all of the Americas must be republican', later asserting confidently, 'We need only be mindful of the fact that we are living in the Americas and mindful of how we have been living here.' In 1834, he and other members of the Parti patriote drafted the famous Ninety-Two Resolutions, a political inventory of Lower Canada's grievances, demands, and aspirations, which were passed in the House of Assembly and submitted to the imperial government. Some of the Ninety-Two Resolutions (numbers 31, 41, 43, 45, 46, 48, 50, and 56) had obvious revolutionary overtones, presenting the United States as a democratic model for preventing abuses of power, underscoring social differences between England and the Americas, recalling the importance of representation by population, and evoking the imminent threat of annexation to the United States. The Russell Resolutions, London's response to these demands, categorically refused all of Lower Canada's resolutions.

Public outrage over the rejection of the Ninety-Two Resolutions and the popularity of Papineau's leadership during this period would be the most crucial factors in the months that followed. By May 1837, Papineau was keenly aware of both. Careful not to make any overt threats, he declared that if no significant changes were made, 'the history of the former [American] plantations will once again [take its course], with the same inevitable result'.[15] It was not long before these weighty words came to fruition.

The repression that followed the armed Patriote resistance of November 1837 forced Papineau and a number of Patriotes into exile in the United States. Papineau wrote to his friend, American historian Georges Bancroft, upon his arrival in the United States:

[Our] society in the Americas is constituted differently from that of Europe. By all the laws of Nature, we are detached from Europe and attached to the United States, and our unanimous wishes call for this Union [with the United States].[16]

Papineau and his right-hand man, Edmund Bailey O'Callaghan, did not raise enough money to purchase arms and munitions for the Patriote cause, nor were they able to persuade the US authorities, including President Van Buren, to lend any form of support. The 1837 Patriote resistance and the rebellion of 1838, from which Papineau publicly dissociated himself, subsequently met with defeat.

Worse yet, Papineau would see his attempts to oppose the Union between Lower Canada and Upper Canada definitively quashed by a decree from London (following Lord Durham's 1839 *Report on the Affairs of British North America*). A proposal supporting Lower Canada's annexation to the United States, which he helped draft, also failed, since political backing from the colony's British Tories (disappointed by the repeal of the Corn Laws in 1846) and radical Whigs proved too limited and contradictory to move the initiative forward.

In February 1839, Papineau went to France under exile for his role in the Patriote cause. In 1845 he was pardoned and, upon his return to Lower Canada, re-entered political life, only to be marginalized by Louis-Hippolyte LaFontaine's 'reformers'. In 1854, Papineau left public life to develop his large estate, La Petite-Nation, a former seigneury which had just been abolished and re-established (with payment of compensation) as a freehold property.

The recent publication of Papineau's correspondence gives us a privileged glimpse into the intellectual and political development of a man who would remain a fierce proponent of the annexation of Lower Canada to the United States for the rest of his life. As of 1854, we see that Papineau did not embrace the emergent 'mixed, neo-Canadian' national identity, preferring instead a mixed nationality of the Americas, which he called 'Columbian,' or 'pan-American'. He envisioned 'a State of Quebec' within the Union; the annexed territory of Lower Canada would be twice the size of New York state and would constitute three states. Papineau supported annexation because he was convinced that the US style of federalism would be more open than that of Canada. Both before and after Canadian Confederation in 1867, annexationists in Lower Canada and (later) Quebec continued to be fascinated by the prospect of creating a flourishing state that would enjoy greater freedom from central authority. Shortly before his death, Papineau would speak of the same annexationist vision, in a 'global confederation of the northern continent'.[17]

THE 'VOCATION' OF FRENCH CANADA IN THE AMERICAS

The failure of the Patriote resistance in 1837, the rebellion in 1838, the campaign to repeal the Union of Upper and Lower Canada proposed by Lord Durham, and the initiative to annex Lower and Upper Canada to the United States in 1849–50,[18] elicited new questions: What would the destiny of French Canada be in the Americas? How would it deal with the presence and influence of the United States? Étienne Parent provided the first insight into both of these questions in his writings, and French author Edmé Rameau de Saint-Père examined them more thoroughly in a chapter about the moral and intellectual future of Canadians in the Americas in his book *La France aux colonies* (1859).

The notion of a collective 'vocation' was embraced by French Canadians with relative ease, owing in part to the familiar foil of 'American immorality'. In *Le Canadien* of 28 November 1807, anticipating a change of allegiance, an anonymous author named 'Canadiensis' wrote:

If unfortunately, with the passing of time, Canada should fall under American domination, it would not be long before we felt the Americans' greed and monopolizing spirit, born in the bosom of commerce, and avaricious for all forms of power.

Thus, while the discourse around the new ruralist and agriculturalist vision for French Canadians was tinted with a degree of rosy Jeffersonianism, the Americans' spirit of debauchery, the poison of their 'equality', and their mercantilism were typically condemned in the same breath. On 17 July 1837 in *Le Canadien*, Parent wrote that he expected no more from the Americans than 'the sentiment that can result from a rule of arithmetic'. By contrast, French Canadians had become a 'providential people' (yet another familiar representation) uninfected by crass mercantilism and spared the horrors of the French Revolution, thanks to the prophylactic Conquest of the British.

In his book *La France aux colonies* Rameau de Saint-Père proposed that

national repulsion, better than a customs barrier, place an embargo on anything that remotely resembles Americanism at the border of Canada's land, that each person take heed and ward off the baneful contagion of this unwholesome civilization . . .

According to Rameau de Saint-Père, US civilization was based on 'a lowly shopkeeper's calculations,' the 'worship of money,' material well-being, and creature comforts. As to the moral future of French Catholic Canada, he believed it would lie elsewhere:

while in the United States, minds are being absorbed by the exhausting enterprises of business, industry and the worship of the golden calf, it is Canada's enterprise to build for herself, unselfishly and with a noble pride, the intellectual, scientific and artistic side of the American movement, preferably devoting herself to the worship of sentiment, thought and refined aesthetics.[19]

Conservative Catholic circles, eager to halt any annexation initiatives, wasted no time in transposing Parent's and Rameau de Saint-Père's spiritualist future into a Catholic future. Indeed, it was the Church's anti-annexationist discourse on the providential vocation of French Canadians in the Americas, used to spread the Catholic faith across the continent (reprised by Abbé Henri-Raymond Casgrain, and in part by Edmond de Nevers, Msgr Louis-Adolphe Pâquet, Olivar Asselin, Victor Barbeau, and the Tory discourse calling for the promotion of traditional values) that would define French Canadians for an entire century.[20] This discourse continued in flagrant disregard of direct edicts handed down from the Vatican during the early 1920s (downplayed by the Catholic authority in Quebec at the time), which clearly stated that in Canada and the United States, proselytizing was to be led by Irish anglophone Catholics. But these edicts went unheeded and the ideology of the 'vocation of the French race in America' prevailed until the end of the Second World War.[21]

While Quebec's anti-American religious discourse was being undermined from within the Vatican hierarchy, it was also being challenged by the circumstances of the times. From 1830 to 1930, both in spite of and because of the 'golden calf' ideology in the United States, hundreds of thousands of French Canadians emigrated to the land of factories and materialism in search of work; from 1872 onward, US labour unions would dominate Canadian and French-Canadian syndicalism; and the US culture of circuses, amusement parks (for example, Montreal's Sohmer Park 1889–1909), burlesque shows, silent motion pictures (1895), and the talkies (1929) reigned supreme. Commenting on the impact of American civilization in 1928, businessman Beaudry Leman declared: 'We can't live with it and we can't live without it'.[22]

Over the years, depictions of this evolving American civilization became increasingly prominent in the works of Quebec writers such as poet Alfred Desrochers and novelists Jean-Charles Harvey and Philippe Panneton (who went by the pen name 'Ringuet'). Following the Second World War, the predominant American consumer society effectively supplanted the ideology of a French-Canadian, Catholic spiritual vocation in the Americas (see Snapshot box).

SNAPSHOT

Americanicity and Postwar Consumption in Quebec

After the deprivation of the Depression, and the rationing, scrimping, and saving that took place throughout the Second World War, consumer spending skyrocketed in North America in the postwar era. The United States, Canada's wartime ally, pumped an average of 74 per cent of foreign investment into the Quebec economy from 1945 to 1960. Simultaneously US goods were consumed en masse, and with them came American influences and standards of living rose. For instance, during the same period, 64 per cent of feature films shown in Quebec theatres were made in the United States. In 1953, 34 per cent of Quebec households owned an automobile and by 1960, 49 per cent did. The car to person ratio was one car for every 15.2 people in 1939, which rose to one per 10.1 people in 1949, one per 9.1 people in 1954, and reached one per 6.3 people by 1959.

In 1953, 37.4 per cent of Quebec households owned an electric vacuum cleaner, compared with 57.8 per cent in 1960. These households, 82 per cent of which were already equipped with an electric washing machine in 1953, were even more likely to have one in 1960 (89 per cent). While most dwellings in Quebec contained an electric refrigerator in 1953 (68.4 per cent), this appliance had become the norm by 1960 (94 per cent). But for many households, the electric stove was the most striking new addition: found in only 22.7 per cent of kitchens in 1953, it was in 50.2 per cent of them by 1960.

The boom in the ownership of communications and entertainment equipment generally progressed in keeping with the age of the medium. Telephone ownership grew from 52.5 per cent in 1941 to 77.2 per cent in 1951, and then to 84.3 per cent in 1960. Radios, found in 92.6 per cent of households in 1941, had a 97.3 per cent penetration rate by 1960. From a marketing perspective, television was a relatively fast-track technology. Whereas radio took 15 years (1922–37) to reach most homes, television caught on in just four years: 9.7 per cent of households had a TV set in 1953, 27.8 per cent in 1954, 48.5 per cent in 1955, and 64.2 per cent in 1956.[23] With so many major everyday, domestic lifestyle changes in Quebec resembling those taking place in the United States, the question soon became: Is modernization synonymous with Americanization?

All told, retail sales leapt from $245.71 per person in 1941 to $600.86 in 1951 and had reached $781.19 by 1960. Another indicator of new levels of consumption was the rising number of advertising agencies, which grew from 22 Canada-wide in 1941 to 61 in 1961. Meanwhile, periodicals sold $100 million worth of advertising in 1948, compared with $300 million in 1960.[24] As these trends continued, the growing need to measure the Americanization of Canadian culture culminated in the Royal Commission on National Development in the Arts, Letters, and Sciences (also known as the Massey-Lévesque Commission), held from 1949 to 1951.[25]

The clear acceptance of consumerism and an 'American' way of life was significant on two levels in Quebec. First, it tended to narrow the gap between middle-class and working-class perceptions of the United States and Americanization.[26] Second, the self-representation of French Canadians as the standard-bearers of spiritualism and Catholic asceticism became both anachronistic and contradictory after the cumulative effects of the Depression and the Second World War turned them into 'materialists'. Once again, French Canada would embark on a quest for its destiny in the Americas.

WRITERS AND THE DEVELOPMENT OF AMERICANICITY

As the Second World War drew to a close, it was Quebec essayists and novelists who would detect contradictions and formulate entirely new representations of their cultural identities. It was during a polemical discussion with writers from France that Quebec novelist and publisher Robert Charbonneau first became conscious of belonging to the American continent. 'We are not Frenchmen; our life in America, our cordial relations with our English-speaking compatriots and Americans, our political independence, have made us different,' he declared. Charbonneau proposed that his fellow writers discover what it meant to be American by exploring 'the American side as much as at the French side' and by sampling the vintages of both 'the Californian vineyard of Mr. Steinbeck' and 'the vineyard of Racine' in France.[27]

But it was French-Canadian essayist Jean Le Moyne who truly established Quebec's relationships with the Americas and with Europe as undisputed subjects of study. An avid reader of Henry James and F. Scott Fitzgerald, Le Moyne recognized that the Americas were invented by Europe and that, in his view, his people were very much connected with their 'first-degree European relatives':

. . . the Americas are an invention, the posterity of Europe, and in relation to Europe, American societies are without exception marsupial foetuses, unequally developed, but all attached to the teat. As Americans, nothing really distinguishes us but geography. Notwithstanding our European heredity, an irresistible differentiation has begun, occurring on all levels at the same time. We are slowly working on [developing] our difference, we are gradually crafting ourselves a new identity.[28]

Henry James showed Le Moyne that Americans had a 'double identity', while F. Scott Fitzgerald taught him that 'France is absent and the United States is far away' from Quebec. Above all, Le Moyne admitted that he no longer believed that French Canadians could ever entirely define themselves in French,

because of one overriding fact: the invention and the form of the Americas are not French. As a result, we are subjected to an osmotic pressure that no fortifications could contain. The only obstacle [to this pressure], given [Quebec's] geographic location and indistinct borders, would be the one thing that we will never have: large numbers.[29]

The writers and critics who followed Le Moyne on his imaginary 'Oregon trail' (to the 'great American promised land') would recast this ambiguity and contribute to naming the variable that is Quebec identity.

This literary journey was unfolding around 1970, at a time when the US counterculture had reached Quebec and the beat generation was being expressed by poets and writers.[30] This was also the era of bohemian 'Californian dreaming' in the Quebec novel.[31]

Playwright Jacques Languirand explored the symbolic and political relationship of Quebecers of French-Canadian ancestry with the Americas, and how the repressed aspects of their Americanicity manifested themselves:

> To be frank, I had the impression that the more French Canada defined itself as being independentist-separatist at a conscious level, the more it became annexionist at a sub-conscious level.[32]

Jacques Godbout investigated the cultural aspects of this double identity, relating it (like Le Moyne) to Quebec's relationships with France and with America. His 1965 novel *Le couteau sur la table* (*Knife on the Table*) begins by taking a stand: 'rather than being *French*, in a very personal way, we now prefer to be *ourselves*, in French'. Godbout's abiding fascination for this American vein of identity and Quebec's collective imaginings come to life in his novels, essays, and in his film *Will James*.

Essayist Jean Larose, who has looked closely at the challenge of being French or francophone in the Americas, has commented 'it is easy, crossing Washington Square [in New York City] or Place du Panthéon [in Paris], to imagine that we have found peace in our mixed identity'. Larose regards Quebecers' indecision about their identity as rich in potential and holds that Quebecers of French-Canadian origin must move away from their double negation (being neither French nor American) and toward a double assertion of self.[33]

In 1995 the study of Americanicity in Quebec literature was authoritatively established with the publication of Jean Morency's brilliant work, *Le mythe américain dans les fictions d'Amérique de Washington Irving à Jacques Poulin*, in which Morency evokes the imaginary realm common to culturally dualistic American societies that belong to both 'the European sphere and that of the New World [which is] in the process of inventing itself'. To Morency 'the splendid autonomy of the continental imagination' was

revealed in the grand narrative of 'an intellectual history [involving] the metamorphosis of humankind upon contact with the American continent'.[34]

A current perspective on Quebec's Americanicity is found in the surveys and reflections of Guy Lachapelle and Gilbert Gagné. Guy Lachapelle surveyed Quebecers' feelings about belonging to Canada and the Americas and their perceptions of the United States. Overall, he found that Quebecers jealously guard their language and universal health care system; favour continental economic relations; and have joined the US media and business culture, adopting and often adapting US content, formulas, and formats. Gilbert Gagné has examined the effects of globalization on Quebecers' perceptions of the United States and, in particular, on strategies to promote and defend cultural difference and diversity.[35]

OBSTACLES TO ENGAGING WITH THE CONCEPT OF AMERICANICITY IN QUEBEC

Perceptions of Quebec's relationship to the Americas, and especially Quebec's relationship with the United States, are not unanimous. For instance, anti-capitalist and socialist Quebecers may identify with Latin American experiences, but these may not be the sole or the most vital way for them to remember that they belong to the *entire* American continent and to embrace their Americanicity.[36] On the other side of the same fence, José Marti in Cuba (*Nuestra America*, 1891), José Vasconcelos (*La raza cosmica*, 1925) and Leopoldo Zea in Mexico, and Domingo Faustino Sarmiento in Argentina are Latino thinkers and writers of the Americas who have sought to further articulate this multi-layered relationship.

Historically, there are five main reasons why Quebecers of French-Canadian ancestry have not been able to fully accept or engage with the concept of Americanicity. First, it is not easy to grasp that Americanicity flows from everyday, lived experiences rather than being consciously or intelligibly pondered. For Quebecers to accept their Americanicity they would have to acknowledge Quebec's similarities and differences vis-à-vis an entire continent. It would mean confronting the fact that, like the societies that surround it, Quebec is also a 'new society,' shaped by various waves of immigration (1815, 1900, 1945, and 1970 until today), which did not opt for the US melting pot or for Canadian multiculturalism, but for a policy of integrative interculturalism that is still in its ill-defined infancy.[37]

Second, since the 1930s francophilia (i.e., exaggerated veneration for France and all things French) has overshadowed Quebec's American origins. For Quebecers of French-Canadian ancestry to engage with the concept of their Americanicity, they would have to accept their Europeanicity, and particularly, the traditional relationships that Quebec has been maintaining with France, Britain, and Rome and the Vatican. My mnemonic formula for this *external* heritage is: $Q = - F + GB + US^2 - R$, as explained in my book, *Allégeances et dépendance.*

Third, even after 1945, embracing Quebec's Americanicity would have undermined the notion of 'French America', whereby the French race had an exclusive, providential vocation in the Americas. Being a francophone meant being a good French-Canadian Catholic. Significantly, this 'American' Francophonie was often ignored in academe, except in discussions of French-Canadian emigration to the United States since 1830. But resistance to embracing Americanicity abated in Quebec after the Estates General of French Canada (1967). At these meetings it became clear that francophone Quebecers and French Canadians outside of Quebec had different interests and, for the most part, these groups would no long be represented by the same organizations. The notion of 'French Canada' subsequently began its decline[38] and took on another meaning for those who began to call themselves 'Québécois'—no longer Frenchmen and Frenchwomen living in the Americas, but the francophones of the Americas.[39] From this point on in Quebec's development, the notion of French America could no longer be

contemplated as anything but a curious cultural artifact.

Fourth, although for years openly accepting Quebec's Americanicity was perceived as a tacit endorsement of annexationism, this perception has also clearly fallen by the wayside. After over a quarter-century of promoting free trade in the Americas as an economic imperative, both the Parti Québécois and the Liberal Party of Quebec have established the conviction among Quebecers that it is possible to be continentalist without being annexationist.

Fifth, recognizing that Quebec belongs to the American continent does not mean that Quebecers unconditionally accept all of the ideological positions, economics, technology, and military stances that define the United States, nor does it mean that they reject their ties with Europe. In fact, on both counts, some measured resistance to embracing Americanicity remains.

Understanding Quebec's Americanicity requires us to break free of our preconceptions, a notion which is itself characteristic of the American experience. But the notion of breaking free is complicated by Quebec's status within Canada. It would seem that placing any conceptual distance between Quebec and France or England requires a reconceptualization of Quebec's relationship with Canada. It is not my contention that sovereignty is a prerequisite for recognizing Quebec's Americanicity. I would simply suggest that for Quebecers to recognize themselves as full-fledged denizens of the Americas, cultural and political choices will have to be made.

One thing is certain—the heritage of Americanicity is worth knowing, recognizing, and metabolizing properly if Quebec's self-image is to be commensurate with reality. Understanding Quebec's Americanicity means situating our identity within postmodernism, in the plural, without giving up anything of ourselves, and embracing the broad diversity of heritages that enrich a new, intercultural generation of Québécois citizens.

QUESTIONS FOR CONSIDERATION

1. What is the difference between 'Americanization' and 'Americanicity'?

2. What kept the notion of the 'vocation of the French race in the Americas' alive and why did this notion lose its relevancy?

3. What were the components of Quebec's new 'destiny' in the Americas?

4. Why has it been so difficult for some Quebecers to accept or engage with the concept of their Americanicity?

NOTES

1. This speech was translated in Quebec by Sylvie Chaput. (Quebec: Éditions du Loup de gouttière, 1992).
2. An expression coined by O'Sullivan in the *Washington Democratic Review* (Summer 1845), which he founded in 1837.
3. Gérard Bouchard, *Genèse des nations et cultures du nouveau monde : essai d'histoire comparée* (Montreal: Boréal, 2001).
4. The first studies on Quebec's Americanicity predate 1992, the five hundredth anniversary of Columbus' discovery of the Americas. For the moment, these studies borrow little from New American Studies, a field which provides greater perspective on the Eurocentric narrative of the Americas and is mindful of the place of the Aboriginal peoples of the Americas pre- and post-Columbian history. For a pioneering study, see Denys Delâge 'L'influence des Amérindiens sur les Canadiens et les Français au temps de la Nouvelle-France', in *L'acculturation, Lekton*, 2, 2 (automne 1992): 103–91. His article was translated into English and published as 'Aboriginal Influence on the Canadians and French at the Time of New France,' in Gordon Christie, ed., *Aboriginality and Governance: A Multidisciplinary Perspective*, (Penticton BC: Theytus Books, 2006), 79–139. The original French version of this article is available online on the website Les Classiques des sciences sociales at: http://classiques.uqac.ca/contemporains/delage_denys/delage_denys.html
5. In the United States, the work of Henry James provides an apt illustration of this last point.
6. This concept is developed in Yvan Lamonde, *Allégeances et dépendances. Histoire d'une ambivalence identitaire* (Quebec: Éditions Nota bene, 2001), chapitre II; For a bibliographical update on studies in Quebec's Americanicity, see Yvan Lamonde, 'Les appropriations culturelles du nouveau continent au Québec (1800–1960)', in Gérard Bouchard and Yvan Lamonde, *Québécois et américains. La culture québécoise aux XIXe et XXe siècles* (Montreal: Fides, 1995), 395–418.
7. 'Aux Habitants de la Province de Québec', 26 October 1774, in Gustave Lanctôt, *Le Canada et la Révolution américaine (1774–1783)* (Montreal: Beauchemin, 1965), 281–91, our translation.
8. For an examination of writing on the American presence in the eighteenth century, see Pierre Monette et al, *Rendez-vous manqué avec la révolution américaine : les adresses aux habitants de la province de Québec . . .* (Montreal: Québec-Amérique, 2007).
9. Governor Carleton to Lord Germain, 9 May 1777, in Adam Shortt and Arthur G. Doughty, eds., *Documents Relating to the Constitutional History of Canada, 1759–1791*, Part II (Ottawa: Taché Printer of the King, 1918), 676.
10. Yvan Lamonde, *Histoire sociale des idées au Québec, I : 1760–1896* (Montreal: Fides, 2000), 31–3, our translation.
11. The Quebec expression 'avoir la tête à Papineau', evokes the reverence many Quebecers had for Papineau's intelligence. The English equivalent of this expression would be 'a true Einstein'.
12. 'Correspondance de *La Minerve*'. M. Papineau, *La Minerve*, 17 February 1831.
13. Ibid.
14. 'Correspondance de *La Minerve*'. L'hon. Orateur L.-J. Papineau, *La Minerve*, 21 January 1833, our translation.
15. Louis-Joseph Papineau, *Procédés de l'Assemblée des Électeurs du Comté de Montréal*, Montreal, May 1837, 11, our translation.
16. The references to the documents of this period may be found in Yvan Lamonde, *Allégeances et dépendances*, op. cit., 38–40, 44–6.
17. Yvan Lamonde, 'Introduction', in Louis-Joseph Papineau, *Lettres à ses enfants*, vol. I: 1825–1854, ed. Georges Aubin and Renée Blanchet (Montreal: Les Éditions Varia, 2004), 22–4.
18. Henry David Thoreau would tour through Lower Canada six years thereafter. See the most recent version of *A Yankee in Canada* (1856), Henry David Thoreau, *Excursions*, edited by Joseph J. Moldenhauer (Princeton: Princeton University Press, 2007).
19. Edmé Rameau de Saint-Père, *La France aux colonies* (Paris: Jouby, 1859), 269.
20. For information on their writing and positions, see Yvan Lamonde, *Allégeances et dépendances*, op. cit., 59–82.
21. On this question, see chapter V, 'Rome et le Vatican : la vocation catholique de l'Amérique française ou de l'Amérique anglaise?' in Lamonde, *Allégeances et dépendances*, op. cit.
22. Beaudry Leman, 'Les Canadiens français et le milieu américain', *Revue trimestrielle canadienne* 14, 5 (septembre 1928): 263–75.
23. Jean-Pierre Charland, *Système technique et bonheur domestique. Rémunération, consommation et pauvreté au Québec (1920–1960)* (Quebec: Institut québécois de recherche sur la culture, 1992), 147, 148, 150, 152, 156; Yvan Lamonde and Pierre-François Hébert, *Le cinéma au Québec. Essai de statistique historique (1896 à nos jours)* (Quebec: Institut québécois de recherche sur la culture, 1981), 165.
24. Jean-Guy Daigle and Luc Côté, 'La sollicitation marchande dans la vie privée : les annonces du jeudi dans

les quotidiens québécois (1929–1957)', *Recherches socio-graphiques* XXXIII, 3 (1992): 369–406; From the same authors, see 'Publicité de masse et masse publicitaire dans la presse quotidienne au Québec (1929–1957)', in Pierre Lanthier and Guildo Rousseau, eds., *La culture inventée. Les stratégies culturelles aux XIXe et XXe siècles* (Quebec: Institut québécois de recherche sur la culture, 1992), 247–66.

25. Paul Litt, *The Muses, the Masses, and the Massey Commission*, Toronto, University of Toronto Press, 1992.

26. Yvan Lamonde, 'Le regard sur les Etats-Unis : le révélateur d'un clivage social dans la culture nationale québécoise', *Journal of Canadian Studies/Revue d'études canadiennes* 30, 1 (printemps 1995): 69–74.

27. Robert Charbonneau, *La France et nous. Journal d'une querelle* (Montreal: L'arbre, 1947), 23, 32, 34, 40, 49, 53.

28. Jean Le Moyne, 'Ringuet et le contexte canadien-français', *Revue dominicaine* (février 1950): 83.

29. J. Le Moyne, 'Lectures anglaises', in *Convergences* (Montreal : Hurtubise HMH), 27.

30. For two different readings of the beat generation, see Pierre Nepveu, *Intérieurs du Nouveau Monde : essai sur les littératures du Québec et des Amériques* (Montreal: Boréal, 1998) and Jean-Sébastien Ménard, 'Parler de l'Amérique d'une certaine manière : la Beat Generation au Québec', PhD dissertation (Langue et littérature françaises), McGill, 2008.

31. René Labonté, 'Québec-Californie : la Californie à travers la fiction québécoise', *The French Review* 62, 5 (April 1989) : 803–14.

32. Jaques Languirand, 'Le Québec et l'américanité', in *Klondyke* (Montreal: Cercle du livre de France, 1971), 219–37; repris dans *Études littéraires* 8, 1 (April 1975): 143–57.

33. Jean Larose, *La petite noirceur* (Montreal: Boréal, 1987), 70–1, 192, 175–6; *L'amour du pauvre* (Montreal: Boréal, 1989), 94.

34. Jean Morency, *Le mythe américain dans les fictions d'Amérique. De Washington Irving à Jacques Poulin*

(Québec: Nuit blanche éditeur, 1995), 11–12, 17, 225–6; Also see Yvan Lamonde, 'Pour une étude comparée de la littérature québécoise et des littératures coloniales américaines', *Journal of Canadian Studies/Revue d'études canadiennes* 32, 2 (été 1997): 72–8 and Jean-François Chassay, *L'ambiguïté américaine : le roman québécois face aux Etats-Unis* (Montreal: XYZ, 1995).

35. See for example Guy Lachapelle et Gilbert Gagné, 'L'Américanité des Québécois ou le développement d'une identité nord-américaine', *Francophonies d'Amérique* 10 (2000): 87–99; also see 'Intégration économique, valeurs et identités : les attitudes matérialistes et postmatérialistes des Québécois', *Politique et Sociétés* 22, 1 (2003): 27–52.

36. On the subject of the anti-Americanism of *Parti pris* and *Socialisme* in postwar Cuba and during the war in Vietnam, see Yvan Lamonde, *Allégeances et dépendance*, 97. For information on the anti-Americanism of prominent essayist and union activist Pierre Vadeboncoeur, and on the resistance of sociologist Fernand Dumont, see ibid., 104–7.

37. François Rocher, Micheline Labelle, Ann-Marie Feld and Jean-Claude Icart, *Le concept d'interculturalisme en contexte québécois : généalogie d'une néologisme* (Montreal-Ottawa: UQÀM-Université d'Ottawa, Centre de recherche sur l'immigration, l'ethnicité et la citoyenneté, 21 December 2007), report submitted to the Bouchard-Taylor Commission, available online at www.accommodements.qc.ca/documentation/rapports-experts.html.

38. The decline of French Canada is brilliantly analyzed by Marcel Martel. His work, *Le deuil d'un pays imaginé. Rêves, luttes et déroute du Canada français. Les rapports entre le Québec et la francophonie canadienne (1867–1975)* (1997) is summarized in a brochure, *French Canada: An Account of Its Creation and Break-up, 1850–1967* (Ottawa: The Canadian Historical Association, 1998).

39. Guy Rocher, 'Les conditions d'une francophonie nord-américaine originale', in Guy Rocher, *Le Québec en mutation* (Montreal: Hurtubise, 1973), 89–107.

SELECT BIBLIOGRAPHY

Bouchard, Gérard. *Genèse des nations et cultures du nouveau monde : essai d'histoire comparée.* Montreal: Boréal, 2000.

Chassay, Jean-François. *L'ambiguïté américaine : le roman québécois face aux Etats-Unis.* Montreal: XYZ, 1995.

Lamonde, Yvan. 'Les appropriations culturelles du nouveau continent (1800-1960)'. In Gérard Bouchard and Yvan Lamonde, *Québécois et américains, La culture québécoise aux XIXe et XXe siècles.* Montreal: Fides, 1995, 395–418.

———. *Allégeances et dépendance, Histoire d'une ambivalence identitaire.* Quebec: Éditions Nota bene, 2001.

Morency, Jean. *Le mythe américain dans les fictions d'Amérique. De Washington Irving à Jacques Poulin.* Quebec: Nuit blanche éditeur, 1995.

Nepveu, Pierre. *Intérieurs du Nouveau Monde : essai sur les littératures du Québec et des Amériques.* Montreal: Boréal, 1998.

Rocher, Guy. 'Les conditions d'une francophonie nord-américaine originale'. In G. Rocher, *Le Québec en mutation.* Montreal: Hurtubise, 1973, 89–107.

CHAPTER 7

The Frontiers of Quebec Literature

Michel Biron, McGill University

— TIMELINE —

	Politics and Culture	Literary Works
1534	Jacques Cartier's first voyage to Canada. He claims territory on behalf of King of France.	
1632–9		Jesuit Paul Le Jeune writes annual instalments of his *Relation du voyage de la Nouvelle-France*.
1632		Marie de l'Incarnation begins to write her *Écrits spirituels*, which she will complete in 1654.
1744		*Histoire et Description générale de la Nouvelle-France avec le journal historique d'un voyage fait par ordre du roi dans l'Amérique septentrionale* by François-Xavier de Charlevoix.
1763	Signing of Treaty of Paris seals Britain's victory in New France.	
1764	*La Gazette de Québec/The Quebec Gazette* officially launched.	
1806	First issue of *Le Canadien* newspaper begins circulation 22 November.	
1814	Louis-Joseph Papineau becomes leader of Canadian Party.	
1837–8	Patriote rebellions of Lower Canada.	First French-Canadian novel published: *L'Influence d'un livre* by Philippe Aubert de Gaspé, fils.
1839	After visiting Canada for six months, John George Lambton (Lord Durham) writes report in which he concludes it is necessary to assimilate French Canadians, 'a people with no literature and no history'.	

	Politics and Culture	Literary Works
1845–52		*Histoire du Canada depuis sa découverte jusqu'à nos jours* by François-Xavier Garneau published in four volumes.
1860	Beginning of patriotic literature movement in Quebec, spearheaded by Abbé Henri-Raymond Casgrain.	
1862		*Jean Rivard, le défricheur canadien* by Antoine Gérin-Lajoie published in *Les Soirées canadiennes*.
1863		*Les Anciens Canadiens* by Philippe Aubert de Gaspé, pere
1873		*Chroniques, Humeurs et Caprices* by Arthur Buies
1881		*Angéline de Montbrun* by Laure Conan
1882		*Œuvres complètes* by Octave Crémazie
1887		*La Légende d'un peuple* by Louis Fréchette
1895	Foundation of École littéraire de Montréal.	
1896		*L'Avenir du peuple canadien-français* by Edmond de Nevers
1904		*Émile Nelligan et son œuvre*, compiled and edited by Louis Dantin Camille Roy's presentation 'La nationalisation de la littérature canadienne' published in *Bulletin du parler français au Canada*.
1916		*Maria Chapdelaine* by Louis Hémon (first released 1914 in *Le Temps* in Paris) published in Quebec.
1918		*Manuel d'histoire de la littérature canadienne-française* by Camille Roy
1920		*Les Atmosphères* by Jean-Aubert Loranger
1929		*À l'ombre de l'Orford* by Alfred DesRochers
1937		*Regards et Jeux dans l'espace* by Saint-Denys Garneau
1938		*Trente Arpents* by Ringuet
1944		*Les Îles de la nuit* by Alain Grandbois
1945		*Bonheur d'occasion* by Gabrielle Roy
1947		*La France et nous* by Robert Charbonneau

	Politics and Culture	Literary Works
1948		*Refus global.*
1953	Foundation of Éditions de l'Hexagone in Quebec.	*Le Tombeau des rois* by Anne Hébert
1955		*Rue Deschambault* by Gabrielle Roy
1958		*Agaguk* by Yves Thériault *Poèmes de l'Amérique étrangère* by Michel Van Schendel
1960		*Le Libraire* by Gérard Bessette
1962		*Contes du pays incertain* by Jacques Ferron
1963		*La Ligne du risque* by Pierre Vadeboncœur
1965	Term *littérature québécoise* featured prominently in *Parti pris* magazine in manifesto issue entitled 'Pour une littérature québécoise'.	*Prochain Épisode* by Hubert Aquin *L'Âge de la parole* by Roland Giguère
1966	Marie-Claire Blais receives Prix Médicis for her novel, *Une saison dans la vie d'Emmanuel.*	*L'Avalée des avalés* by Réjean Ducharme
1967	On 24 July, General de Gaulle declares 'Vive le Québec libre!' from balcony of Montreal City Hall. Opening of first CEGEPs (collèges d'enseignement général et professionnel).	*Salut Galarneau!* by Jacques Godbout
1968		Michel Tremblay's *Les Belles-Sœurs* performed for the first time. Michèle Lalonde writes poem 'Speak White' for *Poèmes et Chants de la résistance* show.
1970	In October, FLQ kidnaps British diplomat James Cross and Quebec Minister of Labour, Pierre Laporte. Federal government invokes War Measures Act. Pierre Laporte killed. First *Nuit de la poésie* held on stage of Théâtre Gesù.	*L'Homme rapaillé* by Gaston Miron *L'Amélanchier* by Jacques Ferron *Kamouraska* by Anne Hébert
1971		*Le Réel absolu. Poèmes 1948–1965* by Paul-Marie Lapointe
1972	First Rencontre québécoise internationale des écrivains organized by *Liberté* magazine.	
1973		*L'Hiver de force* by Réjean Ducharme

	Politics and Culture	Literary Works
1974		From 1974 to 1976, volumes of André Major's *Histoires de déserteurs* successively released.
1976	On 15 November, René Lévesque's Parti Québécois elected.	*Le Roman à l'imparfait* by Gilles Marcotte
1977	Union des écrivains québécois (UNEQ) founded. Hubert Aquin commits suicide.	
1978		*Les Deux Royaumes* by Pierre Vadeboncœur *Monsieur Melville* by Victor-Lévy Beaulieu *La grosse femme d'à côté est enceinte* by Michel Tremblay, first novel of Montreal series *Chroniques du Plateau Mont-Royal*.
1979	Antonine Maillet receives Prix Goncourt for *Pélagie-la-Charrette*.	
1981		*Vie et Mort du Roi boiteux*, play by Jean-Pierre Ronfard *Le Matou* by Yves Beauchemin
1982	Anne Hébert wins Prix Femina for *Les Fous de Bassan*.	
1983	*Vice versa*, a magazine about transcultural issues, launched in Montreal.	*Maryse* by Francine Noël
1984		*Moments fragiles* and *Agonie* by Jacques Brault *Volkswagen Blues* by Jacques Poulin *La Détresse et l'Enchantement*, Gabrielle Roy's posthumous autobiography *Kaléidoscope ou les Aléas du corps grave* by Michel Beaulieu
1985	First Trois-Rivières International Festival of Poetry.	*Comment faire l'amour avec un nègre sans se fatiguer* by Dany Laferrière *La Trilogie des dragons*, theatrical show by Robert Lepage
1986		*Surprendre les voix*, a posthumous essay collection by André Belleau *Le Souffle de l'harmattan* by Sylvain Trudel
1988		*L'Écologie du réel* by Pierre Nepveu
1989		*La Rage* by Louis Hamelin *Le Vieux Chagrin* by Jacques Poulin
1990		*Dévadé* by Réjean Ducharme

	Politics and Culture	Literary Works
1991		*Le Bruit des choses vivantes* by Élise Turcotte *L'Obéissance* by Suzanne Jacob
1993		*Genèse de la société québécoise* by Fernand Dumont
1995		*L'Ingratitude* by Ying Chen *Soifs* by Marie-Claire Blais
1996	Poet Gaston Miron dies 14 December; state funeral services held.	
1997		*Littoral*, play by Wajdi Mouawad, performed at Théâtre La Licorne.
1998		*La petite fille qui aimait trop les allumettes* by Gaétan Soucy *Intérieurs du Nouveau Monde* by Pierre Nepveu
1999		*Mille eaux* by Émile Ollivier
2001		*Putain* by Nelly Arcan *Rouge, mère et fils* by Suzanne Jacob
2005	Opening of Grande Bibliothèque de Montreal.	*Le Siècle de Jeanne* by Yvon Rivard
2006	Mavis Gallant becomes first anglophone to win Prix Athanase-David.	

When the term *Quebec literature* made its debut in the mid-1960s, it marked a new beginning. Its predecessor, *French-Canadian literature*, had become incompatible with the assertions of the Québécois nationalist project that epitomized the Quiet Revolution. Consequently, *Quebec literature* (*littérature québécoise*) was minted to turn the page on Quebec's former minority status as a national culture vis-à-vis both Canada and France. The name change soon entered into circulation and, by the beginning of the next decade, was widely embraced in intellectual circles, which set about breathing new life into the new nomenclature.

Taught extensively in schools and universities, Quebec literature has since established its institutional legitimacy, but to this day, its frontiers remain nebulous. The frontiers of literature, we should keep in mind, do not abide by the same laws as those of politics and are certainly not framed in the same terms. In politics, there are rules that establish who has the right to vote and

who is a full-fledged citizen. In literature, these kinds of exclusive rules would be meaningless, as the frontiers of national literature are often implicit and shifting.

For example, in the 1970s, it would have been unthinkable to include anglophone writers in the history and canon of Quebec literature. A few decades later, anglophone writers like Frank R. Scott, Mavis Gallant, and Mordecai Richler are part of Quebec's literary landscape. Conversely, we might also ask whether Canada's francophone authors living outside of Quebec, like Acadian poet Gérald Leblanc or Franco-Ontarian novelist Daniel Poliquin, should also be included within the corpus of Quebec literature. Again, in the 1970s, this question would have been considered nonsensical. But today, with the emergence of Acadian and Franco-Ontarian literatures, it would be bad form for a literary historian hailing from Quebec to ignore what distinguishes these literatures from Quebec literature. These examples give us an idea of just how ambiguous the expression 'Quebec literature' can be, so why even attempt to define literary frontiers?

Defining literary frontiers would be of little interest if it simply involved demarcating the limits of a national literature by drawing up a list of what it includes and excludes. But when national frontiers show how a corpus of literary texts interacts with the world around it, frontiers become much more fertile subjects for discussion. In the early days of literary criticism, there was a penchant for linking the distinguishing colours of a literature to its geographical environs. Today, critics who automatically equate a given landscape or climate with specific styles of writing tend to draw bemused smiles. But, setting aside the reductionist/determinist aspects of this early analysis for a moment, it could be argued that a geography of literature exists in conjunction with a sociology of literature. The idea here is not to attach a book to a mighty mountain range or to endless prairie skyland, but to recognize that a literary text bears the imprint of the neighbourhood and community from which it has sprung.

Quebec literature is a particularly salient case in point, as its striking geographical frontiers have made a lasting impact on its sociology. Although of the French language, Quebec literature is nonetheless separated from Paris by a vast ocean and has developed independently from its mother literature. Based in North America, it is also isolated by a linguistic frontier and belongs to a tradition that is foreign to the references that inform English-language Canadian and American literatures. Quebec's geographic and linguistic frontiers are often cited by literary critics to explain the two-fold marginality of its literature in relation to both France (or La Francophonie) and North America. But there is a third, invisible frontier that gives specific meaning to the ever-shifting relations that Quebec authors have with France and with North America: the legendary frontier to the North, which still lies wide open to unknown possibilities. Regardless of their era and of the meaning they attributed to this abstract frontier, in their mind's eye, Quebec authors have always been able to envision the broad, desert-like expanse of horizon that might allow them to escape and start life with a clean slate elsewhere. There is a part of Quebec literature that simply cannot be understood without getting to know this third side of the triangle.

A Long Way from Paris

As with all other French-language literatures outside of France, Quebec literature has an ambiguous and problematic relationship with Paris. That said, Quebec's relational ambiguities are not the same as those observed in francophone regions to the south, be it the French West Indies, the Maghreb, Lebanon, or sub-Saharan Africa. Unlike these regions, in Quebec French is the official language, mother tongue of the majority, and dominant language of the culture, as it is in the European Francophonie (Belgium, Luxemburg, and Switzerland). Where language conflicts do exist between France and Quebec, they tend to play out within the French language itself, much as conflicts between American and British English do. Indeed, George Bernard Shaw's famous witticism about the United States and England could be transposed here to describe this relationship: Quebec and France are two nations 'separated by the same language'.

SNAPSHOT

Literary Turf War between Montreal and Paris

The Second World War was a watershed era in the literary evolution of Quebec. During this short interval of time circumstances dramatically changed for French Canadian authors, leading them to hope they could make a career of their writing. As newspapers and magazines continued to expand their readerships, they solicited the services of French-Canadian writers to attract readers. The radio, very much part of everyday life (having appeared on the scene one decade earlier), allowed many authors to earn additional income by writing radio dramas. Together, these media gave their work a wider distribution than it would ever have had otherwise, given the limited size of the literary community and the weaknesses of editorial infrastructures.

Indeed, from the nineteenth century until the 1930s, literary publishing remained extremely limited in French Canada. In 1936, there were still only six publishers. However, in 1940, when France surrendered to the invading Nazi German forces, the situation quickly changed. As imports originating from enemy or enemy-occupied countries were declared illegal, Canada could no longer import books from France. Canada's Mackenzie King government therefore gave Canadian publishers exceptional licences to reprint all of the French books that were no longer available in Canada, provided they paid for the copyright fees through the Office of the Custodian of Enemy Property. In so doing, it handed over the reins of an immense publishing market to Quebec and brought about a veritable editorial boom.

The first to benefit from this particular situation were a handful of established Montreal publishing houses (for example, Éditions Beauchemin, Éditions Fides, and Éditions Valiquette). But new publishing operations soon sprang up, including Éditions Variétés, Éditions Pony, and notably, Éditions de l'Arbre in 1941, followed (between 1943 and 1945) by eight other publishers (Parizeau, Société des Éditions Pascal, Serge, Marquis, Lumen, Mangin, B.D. Simpson, and Pilon). This sudden literary gold rush was followed by an equally swift reversal of fortunes. By the end of the war, licences for new publishing houses were no longer being granted, thereby depriving publishers of their main tool for development and causing about a dozen Quebec publishers to cease operations between 1946 and 1949. Only academic publishers like Beauchemin, Granger et frères, and Librairie générale canadienne survived, along with Édition Fides (which specialized in religious books). Since literature no longer offered any return on business investment, the annual number of literary publications gradually declined, for lack of a viable market. By the 1950s, as Jacques Michon has noted, an average of 11.9 novels were published annually, a significant drop from the 1940s, when the average number of annual releases stood at 14.5.

Despite its brevity, the publishing boom between 1940 and 1946 considerably altered the literary landscape of Quebec. It allowed Montreal publishers to forge direct links with many authors from France, who had taken refuge from the war in New York City. At the same time, many writers also chose to take up residence in Montreal, including the likes of Antoine de Saint-Exupéry, Georges Simenon, and Jacques Maritain. Quebec publishers released works by Paul Claudel, Julien Green, François Mauriac, Pierre Emmanuel, Pierre Seghers, Paul Éluard, Georges Bernanos, and many others during this vibrant period. New editions of the classics were re-released. For instance, in 1944 Bernard Valiquette released Victor Hugo's complete poetic works in a single-volume edition. Many other authors whose mass distribution had previously been blocked by the Catholic Church's Index of Forbidden Books were also published. In fact, Balzac, Baudelaire, Verlaine, Rimbaud, Proust, and Gide made their belated literary debuts in Quebec around this time. These books, published in Quebec, were then distributed in many parts of the world. Montreal publishers, spurred on by the nationalist elite, also published French-Canadian authors. For instance, Roger Lemelin's Au pied de la pente douce[1] was released by Éditions de l'Arbre, and Gabrielle Roy's Bonheur d'occasion[2] was published by Société des éditions Pascal. Because many of these books appeared side by side with prestigious works formerly published in France, they acquired a new-found legitimacy. Some authors, like Lemelin and Roy, sold very well, proving that there was a market for French-Canadian literature.

But by 1946, during the postwar Reconstruction period in France, normal operations were restored and Paris eagerly rushed in to snatch back the reins of French-language publishing. From that time onward, an acrimonious conflict pitted Montreal against Paris or, more precisely, it pitted two clans of intellectuals from French Canada and France against each other. On the one hand, there were those who held that French-Canadian literature existed independently of French literature, while on the other, there were those who believed that Quebec literature was simply a branch of literature originating from France. Very quickly, the debate turned to issues of identity, a sore point which led (by association) to the irksome issues of the autonomy of French-Canadian literature and of French Canada itself in relation to France.

Quebec literary scholars Gilles Marcotte and Elisabeth Nardout-Lafarge recount and analyze the impassioned turf war (*querelle*) that ensued.[3] It began on 8 March 1946, when Louis Aragon, a member of the Comité national des écrivains (CNÉ) in France, launched an attack on Montreal publishers in *Les Lettres françaises* (the literary paper of the Resistance in France). Aragon lambasted these Quebec houses for publishing authors from France accused of collaborating with the Nazis during the Second World War. Secretly founded during the war by an underground group of authors, critics, and antifascist Resistance intellectuals, the CNÉ enjoyed considerable legitimacy in the newly liberated postwar France, casting itself as a fearless moral arbiter, determined to purge the literary world of its unworthy wartime traitors. But while authors such as Maurras, Drieu LaRochelle, and Jouhandeau were being systematically blacklisted in France, they continued to be published in Quebec. It was Quebec's ideological 'complacency' toward fascism and Nazi-collaborator authors that Aragon hotly denounced in *Les Lettres françaises*. Robert Charbonneau was the first Quebec publisher to respond to these accusations in Montreal's literary review, *La Nouvelle Relève*, deeming his reputation to be beyond reproach. Charbonneau, who had always opposed Hitler and Nazism, had also belonged to the *Relève* group of authors who had taken a public stand in 1936 in support of the Spanish Republicans fighting the civil war in Spain. Not only did he believe his positions to be ideologically unassailable, but he was speaking to the issue as a publisher who had been victimized by the cavalier actions of his French counterparts, who had been only too eager to brusquely snatch back their market shares after the war with no regard for Quebec publishers. As with almost all new Montreal publishers, Charbonneau's company (Éditions de l'Arbre) had been effectively pushed to the brink of bankruptcy as a result. He emerged embittered and disillusioned by his experiences, concluding that maintaining equitable relations with France was impossible.

In the same breath, the sense of dispossession among French-Canadian authors prompted Charbonneau to argue that French Canada's prospects for development would hinge upon overcoming a number of ingrained, culturally driven preconceptions. He named several, including the belief that action was more worthwhile than intellectual work; the Jansenist view that the reading of fiction should be held suspect; the Canadian inferiority complex regarding national publications, judged (at that time) to be inferior to foreign offerings; the enduring resonance of Parisianism among French-Canadian authors; and the foregone conclusion that the quality of Quebec French and the province's small literary community made it impossible to create its own home-grown literature.

Charbonneau maintained that the autonomy of French-Canadian literature was no longer tied (as the regionalists would have claimed) to a territory or a race, but more to Joyce, Kafka, Dos Passos, and Faulkner. He also frequently argued that the most innovative literary works, particularly novels, would no longer come from Paris. Looking to France for literary models or examples would therefore be of little interest to French-Canadian authors, in his opinion; they would do better to look elsewhere, beginning with the United States and the rest of Canada. The universalism, or more specifically, the Americanicity that Charbonneau was calling for, was immediately interpreted by Montreal literary critics like René Garneau as an offensive mounted against the culture of France.

The central issue discussed in the collection of articles that Charbonneau assembled about this pitched battle, entitled *La France et nous : Journal d'une querelle*, was Quebec's autonomy. But this rare polemic between intellectuals from Quebec and France also revealed how intensely defensive and centralist reactions became when Quebec authors used their circumstances in North America to stake out their claim on France's time-honoured literary turf. The dashed hope of seeing Quebec culture recognized by France and the strong desire to embrace Americanicity experienced during this conflict established a twofold relationship with literature that continues to haunt Quebec authors to this day.

While the linguistic situation in Quebec and Acadia may be comparable to that of francophone European countries, the geographic distance that separates the North American Francophonie from Paris has, nonetheless, had an obvious and important impact. This cultural distance was already palpable in the days of New France, when the French voyageurs observed a number of unusual characteristics in Quebecers, ranging from their hardy physical endurance to their somewhat casual attitudes regarding social hierarchy. After New France was ceded to Britain in 1763, the effect of distance was amplified and manifested itself in a multitude of ways, most often through various forms of resentment in francophone Canada toward the French motherland. So it was that Louis-Joseph Papineau, the future leader of the rebellious Lower-Canadian nationalist Patriotes, extolled the virtues of the freedoms afforded by British parliamentarianism and was distrustful of the French political model, which he held was prone to serious authoritarian abuses, like France's Reign of Terror in 1793. The same British liberalism influenced François-Xavier Garneau, French Canada's own celebrated 'national' historian and author of the four-volume *Histoire du Canada* (1845–52), which emerged as the first great French-language intellectual oeuvre in Canada. It has become customary to cite this monumental work as the French Canadian people's proud collective response to Lord Durham's denigrating report on their society.[4] Garneau is cited far less frequently for the fact that his monumental *Discours préliminaire* was penned for French-Canadian readers, rather than for readers in France. His narrative of the burgeoning French-Canadian nation was set within the vast historical framework of the Americas, underscoring Quebec's distance from the *mère-patrie* by placing its people's history under the banner of a new national consciousness.

From a literary perspective, no nineteenth-century French-Canadian work challenged the literary tradition in France. The notion of creating a national literature had occurred to many, but was stymied by cultural and demographic realities; despite significant growth in the number of well-read individuals throughout the century, the potential for establishing authorship as a true vocation was still lacking. It was not until the beginning of the twentieth century that Quebecers established

themselves in such vocations, attracted by Paris and European Modernism. These were the days when Émile Nelligan became synonymous with French Parisianism. He, better than anyone, exemplified the ideal of the misunderstood poet or bohemian author in Canada. As an imitator of Baudelaire and French Symbolism, Nelligan was also out of step with the Parisian works of his time, and hence an unwitting example of the cultural desynchronization that persisted between modern France and Quebec. From 1910 onward (and even more so after the First World War), Quebec authors began to sojourn in France and familiarized themselves with contemporary French literature as it was being written. Poets like Jean-Aubert Loranger and Alain Grandbois were directly inspired by Modernist poets from France. More often than not, however, relations with France were academic and laden with psychological complexes. It was rare to see a French-Canadian author integrate—much less blend—into French literary life as Belgian or Swiss authors did. It was not until Gaston Miron's generation appeared on the literary scene that personal and professional links with major authors from France were forged. In 1999, Miron was the first Quebec poet to be published in the prestigious *Poesie* collection of Gallimard in Paris.

Along with this development, a growing, long-standing malaise was taking hold behind the scenes. Since the end of the Second World War, Robert Charbonneau and other French-Canadian intellectuals had rejected the metaphor of 'the tree and the branch' when discussing the literary relationship between France and French Canada. They contended that literature from Quebec was a tree unto itself, growing far removed from the old tree that gave it life. According to them, in the future the rejuvenation of Quebec literature would have to be nourished by literatures *outside of* France. Strained relations with France manifested themselves in various ways thereafter, notably with the advent of *joual*, which made its sensational literary debut in the 1960s. It was in theatre, with the performance of Michel Tremblay's *Les Belles-Sœurs* (1968) ('The Sisters-in-Law') that the clash over *joual* reached its most spectacular heights. Among novelists, some authors associated with the magazine *Parti pris* tried (less successfully) to integrate *joual* into their works. Yet another, distinctly different, linguistic tack was taken by Réjean Ducharme in his very first novel (*L'Avalée des avalés*, 1966) (*The Swallower Swallowed*), which he wrote in original, slice-of-life prose that was not *joual*, but that consciously challenged major works in French literature.

After that point, rare were the Quebec authors who would measure their talents against those of their literary contemporaries in France or succeed as brilliantly as Ducharme in their experimentation with linguistic and cultural encounters between the two peoples. Many simply chose to substitute France's language and culture for their own, while a few continued to imitate its literature. Réjean Ducharme was alone in his radical approach, pushing as far as he could the eternal conflict that both separated and united Quebec and France. Gradually, this epic conflict waned as Quebec's progressive detachment from France gained momentum, mitigated by the implementation of reforms in

teaching and education at the end of the 1960s, but also by a broader trend towards cultural pluralism in the contemporary world. As times changed, the focus shifted away from Paris, as demonstrated by *Liberté*, a Quebec arts magazine. Whereas 'Haïr la France?' (literally, 'Hate France?') was emblazoned on the cover of an issue in the early 1980s, some 20 years later the cover headline was purely descriptive: 'Lettres de la France' ('Letters from France'). The latter issue presented contemporary literature from France just as it would Portuguese or German literature: it was a literature that had become foreign to Quebec. While literature from France was still part of the arts landscape, it incited little debate as it had simply become one point of reference among others.

The view that French literature had become relatively inconsequential for Quebecers was perhaps best

LITERARY ICONOCLAST RÉJEAN DUCHARME

Réjean Ducharme, shown in this undated photo, is one of the French language's greatest living literary stylists. He has lived in Montreal as a hermit for more than 30 years. Six of his works have been translated into English.

CP PHOTO/Files

Relatively little is known about Réjean Ducharme's life, apart from the fact that he was born in 1941, in Saint-Félix-de-Valois. Biographical sources do not tell us a great deal about Ducharme and are generally limited to reproducing the information provided by the author himself in a derisory autobiography included with his first novel, *L'Avalée des avalés* (*The Swallower Swallowed*):

I was only born once. That was done in Saint-Félix-de-Valois, in the province of Quebec. The next time that I die, it'll be the first time. I want to die vertically, head down and feet up.

. . .
I suffered through six months at École Polytechnique de Montréal. At last upon my deliverance [from school], I took myself for an office clerk and still take myself for one today. But the people who hire office clerks don't want to take me for an office clerk. I don't always work and don't always work as an office clerk. One month out of two, I am out of work.

I was in the Arctic with Canadian Aviation, in 1962. No one will believe me. I do not know why. I say, 'I was in the Arctic.' They answer, 'No way.' In 1963, 1964 and 1965, I hitch-hiked in Canada, the United States and Mexico. That's tiring.[5]

Well before *L'Avalée des avalés* was released in the fall of 1966, journalists and columnists caught wind of what was in the works: a totally unknown, young 24-year-old Quebecer was about to publish his first novel with Gallimard, the most prestigious publisher in France. Around that time, publishers in France and Quebec started to cast doubt on the author's true identity, igniting the short-lived 'Ducharme affair'. It began with a series of outlandish rumours, some intimating that a famous writer was using Ducharme's name as a front. Since the young unknown refused to grant any interviews with the media, the intrigue around his person grew ever thicker, forcing Gallimard to dispatch philosopher Clément Rosset to Ducharme's home to prove that he really existed and was, in fact, the author of his writing. In Quebec, the affair gained even more momentum when it was reported that Ducharme had, at first, unsuccessfully submitted one of his manuscripts (*L'Océantume*) to Montreal publisher, Pierre Tisseyre. From that point forward, Quebec critics and journalists could not get enough of the fabulous stories of the young Quebec writer, rejected at home, only to be published in Paris.

In reality, Gallimard had received, not one, but three manuscripts in the mail, one after the other: *L'Océantume*, *Le nez qui voque*, and *L'Avalée des avalés*. It was this third manuscript that the publishing house chose to release first, sensing that it would be a contender for the Prix Goncourt. Ducharme just missed the mark, but the novel struck an enthusiastic chord with critics on both sides of the Atlantic Ocean.

His success grew the following year with the release of *Nez qui voque* (1967), which was a clear testament to the novelist's talent. *L'Océantume* (1968) was the next to appear, then a fourth novel, *La Fille de Christophe Colomb* (1969) (*The Daughter of Christopher Columbus*), written in a bizarre style of verse which demonstrated the extent to which Ducharme's work was moving away from established models and was destabilizing ways of reading.

Like the American authors Thomas Pynchon or J.D. Salinger, Réjean Ducharme has always refused to speak publicly, except at the very beginning of his career, when he responded to Pierre Tisseyre's insinuations that his manuscript had been considerably reworked by Gallimard. Since that time, Ducharme has never strayed from his initial line of conduct: 'I don't want to be taken for a writer; I never want my face to be recognized.'[6] While managing to remain a 'phantom' author, he fast became a classic figure in Quebec literature. During the 1970s, Ducharme's reputation continued to flourish, notably after the publication of two other novels, *L'Hiver de force* (1973) (*Wild to Mild*) and *Les Enfantômes* (1976), which used the same emotionally charged language, incorporating

adult-child characters whose lucid thinking shone a black light on the words and deeds of the society that surrounded them.

During the same period, Ducharme also gained renown as a playwright, scriptwriter, and lyricist. In 1968, he was one of the first playwrights (along with Michel Tremblay) to introduce *joual* into theatre, with *Le Cid maghané* (1968), a parody of Corneille's classic. Ten years later, he wrote his strongest play, *HA ha!* . . . (published in English as *HA! HA!*), directed by Jean-Pierre Ronfard. He also wrote several film scripts, including *Bons Débarras* (Francis Mankiewicz, 1980), which became a resounding success. A friend of popular singers Robert Charlebois and Pauline Julien, he wrote the lyrics to a number of their songs.

From 1980 onward, Ducharme became increasingly reclusive, to the point that the media, on constant alert for the slightest rumours about him, wondered what had become of him. As it turned out, he had been holding exhibitions of found-object collages in various Montreal galleries under the pseudonym 'Roch Plante'. Many of the artist's *trophoux* (a play on the word *trophy* that sounds like *too crazy* in French), as he called them, were a reflection of his taste for punnery, as evidenced by their titles ('Le déjeuner sous l'herbe', 'Chemin de fer à repasser').

Ducharme resurfaced in 1990 with his seventh novel, *Dévadé*, to become the very first winner of the new Prix Gilles-Corbeil, the highest literary honour in Quebec. True to form, he refused to attend the awards ceremony, once again eliciting a flood of commentary from journalists and critics. The novelist's 'big comeback' crystallized in 1994 with the publication of *Va savoir* (*Go Figure*) followed by *Gros mots* in 1999.

Ducharme is primarily known for his inimitable relationship with language. In his literary works, he has never ceased to deconstruct clichés and reinvent the power of emotions. More than any other Quebec writer, Ducharme has profoundly influenced the writers of generations to come. A true iconoclast of his times, he has even been featured as a character in several contemporary novels, including *Le cœur est un muscle involontaire* (2002) (*The Heart Is an Involuntary Muscle*) by Monique Proulx and *Ça va aller* (2002) by Catherine Mavrikakis.

expressed by novelist and critic Louis Hamelin (born in 1959), who commented:

> It doesn't happen so often anymore that I take a peek at what is being written over in France. I am reassured by reminding myself that there are people who are paid to do that sort of thing. (*Le Devoir*, 7 January 2004)

In the present era of globalization, commentary about France or French literary personalities involved in literary production is frequent, but in each instance, the cultural frontier is clearly evident. Some novelists have even made the figurative distance between Quebec and France a prominent theme in their writing. In *Le Siècle de Jeanne*, Yvon Rivard creates an author protagonist who writes postcards to his granddaughter from Paris. Rivard himself was well acquainted with France, since he, like many Quebec writers, had lived and studied in Paris in his twenties. The protagonist writes as though he has known the people of France forever, introducing them to his granddaughter with a mixture of respect and irony, as an ethnological curiosity.

In *Le Manuscrit Phaneuf*, by Gilles Marcotte, the narrator describes a Quebec publisher (the central character) and his favourite travel destinations:

> . . . parts of the Middle East and North Africa, a few countries in Europe. With the exception of France, which he had deliberately side-stepped, like a trap, the trap of his fellow creatures, the trap of recognition, of the encounter. Later on, he would have to go to Paris—*profession oblige*—but never stayed around there for long.[7]

This publisher, from a company renowned for its 'young' literature, viewed his trips to Paris with marked reluctance. A trip to Paris had become customary practice and no longer elicited any particular expectations in this era of travel beyond the boundaries of the Western world (circa 1985). Indeed, at a time when it was more accessible than it had ever been, the city of lights inspired neither love nor hate: Paris, evermore, was merely 'business as usual'.

AMÉRIQUE ÉTRANGÈRE: STRANGERS IN THEIR OWN LAND

By contrast, in recent decades the draw of the south (meaning, first and foremost, the United States) has grown ever more powerful. France seems to have progressively faded from the collective consciousness of Quebec authors, while the United States and the Americas in general have acquired a captivating cachet in contemporary literary writing. A propos, Louis Hamelin (alluded to earlier) is a contemporary author who has shifted his interest from France to better pursue his passion for American literature, assiduously chronicling its evolution in his columns for publications like *Le Devoir*. Of course, this interest in US culture is nothing new: in the nineteenth century, many French-Canadian journalists, historians, and authors made abundant reference to their neighbours to the south, from François-Xavier Garneau (mentioned earlier) to Antoine Gérin-Lajoie in his two *Jean Rivard* novels (in 1874 and 1876). After the Union Act of 1840, many of French Canada's liberal thinkers even expressed their support for annexing Quebec to the United States. In 1900, essayist Edmond de Nevers devoted a long essay to the American soul (*L'Âme américaine*). In the 1920s and 1930s, while his friend Louis Dantin was living in Cambridge, Massachusetts, poet and journalist Alfred DesRochers became a fan of American poetry. At the same time, Rosaire Dion-Lévesque was translating Walt Whitman. Moreover, after the Second World War, publisher and novelist Robert Charbonneau proposed that American novelists be translated and published in Montreal, rather than in Paris.

By the mid-1960s, the term 'Americanicity' had entered into usage at the same time that the expression 'Quebec literature' was endorsed and promoted by the young, politicized intellectuals of the magazine *Parti pris*. The concomitance of these concepts was significant, as the initiative to found a 'literature of Quebec' was based on an emergent identification of a people with their territory—with a homeland, a nation, and a continent. Quebec authors also began to identify more clearly with the frontier to the south, which had appeared far away and impassable in the time of Louis Hémon's novel, *Maria Chapdelaine* (1914). By the 1930s, the threshold of America was no longer regarded as a threatening entity; it emerged instead as a solution to unemployment. For example, Ringuet's *Trente arpents* (1938) (*Thirty Acres*) reaches its conclusion when old Euchariste Moisan, having sold his land, leaves Quebec and finds safe haven with his exiled son, living in New England. In *Bonheur d'occasion* (1945) (*The Tin Flute*) by Gabrielle Roy, there is no need to leave Quebec to live like an American: Montreal offers all the charms of a modern, American-style metropolis. Even when Quebec publishing house Éditions de L'Hexagone (founded in 1953) promoted the poetry of Quebec, its 'poésie du pays' did not constitute a patriotic poetry, but a home-grown poetry of North America. Pierre Nepveu's *Intérieurs du Nouveau Monde*, which would become a landmark essay in Quebec Studies, demonstrated the extent to which this poetry (and Quebec literature as a whole) shared with other literatures in the Americas a specific relationship not only with space, but also with time, while remaining at arm's-length from America itself (like Franco-Belgian poet Michel Van Schendel described in *Poèmes de l'Amérique étrangère* [1958]).

Americanicity, strange and fascinating, would begin to enter Quebec literature through every possible avenue in the 1960s. The urban experience (so common to US literature) was the most prevalent Americanized theme to be found in scores of fictional or poetic writing. Jean Basile was among the Quebec novelists who celebrated Montreal's St Lawrence Boulevard —'the Main'. In *La Jument des Mongols* he declares, 'Without the Main, my children, I do believe that I would detest Montreal.'[8] Gaston Miron was also among the Quebec poets who would write about his city, expansively proclaiming, 'Montreal is as big as universal disorder.'[9] Paul-Marie Lapointe associated the city with its most primitive and most modern elements: 'small prehistoric men walking / between the buildings / in a rain that is loaded with missiles'.[10]

'America' presupposed travelling, a kind of nomadism, manifested as a Kerouacian wanderlust *On the Road*. In *Volkswagen Blues* (1984) (Quebec's best known road novel, by Jacques Poulin), Jack Waterman (the author's alter ego) and an Aboriginal woman cross the entire continent to find Jack's estranged brother, who has disappeared without a trace. But the goal of this quest becomes much less important here than the quest itself, a re-enactment (two or three centuries later) of the crossing of the continent by French explorers. In this case, the extreme mobility of Poulin's character is fuelled by his search for his roots. Since no one had ever introduced Jack to his roots, it seemed they had to be retraced and regrown. In contemporary

Quebec literature, the characters who disappear into the woodwork are, more often than not, parents who leave their children to fend for themselves.

In parallel with America's beat generation and counter-culture, which became mainstays in Quebec's cultural landscape, some Quebec writers also identified with an older literary tradition. In 1978, for instance, novelist Victor-Lévy Beaulieu devoted three volumes to Melville, commenting on his life and works. At one time, Beaulieu even claimed to identify more closely with Melville than with any other French-language writer. Many other Quebec writers found their literary models in American literature. Jacques Poulin's complete works are regarded (by the critics and by himself) as being strongly influenced by the US novel and, more specifically, by the novels of Ernest Hemingway. In *Le Vieux Chagrin* (1989) (*Mr Blue*), Poulin writes:

> In fact, all I knew about the art of writing I'd picked up from reading interviews with Ernest Hemingway, which I'd actually read before I myself was a writer: at the time I'd been a professor, a Hemingway specialist.[11]

The main thing Poulin learned from Hemingway was a basic rule of writing that he sought to apply to his own works: always write about the subjects you know best. But in no way could Poulin ever be mistaken for Hemingway himself. Hunting, bullfighting, big cities, female conquests, male camaraderie, military exploits, alcohol, boxing—none of these manly experiences entered into Poulin's world. In his novel, when he asks what the author of *The Old Man and the Sea* would have answered if he found himself before Marika (a mysterious female character), Poulin playfully cites a virile and gallant quip from Hemingway, but only to deride his own inadequacies. In fact, Poulin's copious references to this American author effectively deepen the divide that separates him from Hemingway's America, which remains decidedly foreign, whatever his claims on the subject. The same could also be said of the way in which Victor-Lévy Beaulieu depicts Melville, who is evoked in his novel only to impress upon the reader how hopelessly impossible it is for a Quebec writer to lay full claim to 'America'.

Up North: The Frontier of Freedom and Solitude

Most curiously, time and again, Quebec authors have turned their backs on the 'real American experience,' much as they have turned their backs on French literary tradition. It is not that contemporary Quebec authors are trying to cast themselves in a superior light by contrasting their national virtues with those of United States, as was the case in the era of Abbé Casgrain and Monseigneur Roy. They simply have their characters leave the American experience behind by escaping to the north country. Pierre, the protagonist in Gabrielle Roy's *La Montagne secrète* (1961) (*The Hidden Mountain*), chooses the silence of the Great White North, and André Major's numerous deserters (*Histoires de déserteurs*, 1974–6) start life anew on the outskirts of the city as marginal members of society. Ducharme's *Dévadé* (1990) paints the individual as a perpetual 'de-escapee', trapped, but forever fleeing.

While waves of perception about the Quebec–France and Quebec–US literary frontiers have ebbed and flowed from one era to the next, the frontier of the North has been a bulwark that remained the same, thereby affecting the other frontiers with an equal but invisible force. Two novels, written respectively around the beginning and end of the twentieth century, embody this phenomenon: the first, *Maria Chapdelaine* (an old classic), was ostensibly traditional, the second, *Le Vieux Chagrin* (*Mr Blue*), was associated with the renewal of contemporary literature.

Louis Hémon, the author of the first novel, was clearly intrigued by Maria's father, Samuel, a secondary character. Samuel Chapdelaine belongs to the breed of land-clearing pioneers who colonized northern Quebec. The novel transports us northward, to the remote region of Lac-Saint-Jean at the end of the nineteenth century, when the tracts of land advertised in a colonization campaign have still only attracted a trickle of settlers. Samuel proves to be an anti-social man who chooses to build a home for his family, miles away from the nearest village. His actions are not motivated by a desire to build a fiefdom unto himself, but by an acute aversion to any form of community outside of his immediate family.

The pater familias Chapdelaine was a pioneer and, as such, could have been one of the most celebrated folk heroes in Quebec's nationalist discourse, had he not been possessed by a pining to move (the anglicism *mouver* is used in the novel) constantly, further and further north. This pining greatly displeased his wife, who had dreamt all her life of living well ensconced in a parish she could call home. When she dies, we see Samuel confess to his daughter his hatred for society—any form of society—and declare that he is insane. Neither France nor the United States, nor even his own nation held any attraction for him that could compare to the land of the North, his true home.

In the second novel, Jacques Poulin's *Le Vieux Chagrin* (*Mr Blue*), a former professor of literature describes the old frame house that had belonged to his father and was passed down to him. It was an aged, expansive house, and the reader can imagine that it was there the protagonist connects with his roots and childhood memories, much like the characters recounted in *Rue Deschambault* (1955) by Gabrielle Roy (one of Poulin's favourite writers, along with Hemingway). The many patch-ups the house had undergone over the years make it look odd and mismatched—ruins, renovated piecemeal, over and over again. But the strangest part was that the house itself (a home that was never meant to be moved) was literally uprooted by his father, who transported it from one shore of the St Lawrence River over to the other, where there were no people, to get some peace and quiet.

Though the days of Quebec's lumberjacks had passed, when we juxtapose the two stories, it becomes clear that the father of Poulin's protagonist is a direct literary descendant of Samuel Chapdelaine, hauling his household far from the village, away from other folks, to get some peace.

Similar examples are easy to find in contemporary Quebec literature. *Va savoir* (*Go Figure*) by Réjean Ducharme introduces us to Rémi Vavasseur. Rémi's wife leaves him and he fills the void by renovating the little place she had just bought in the Laurentians, north of Montreal. In Louis Hamelin's first novel, *La Rage* (1989), which takes place in the same region, the narrator is a former biology student who turns his back on workaday life, becoming a plane spotter at Mirabel airport. The surrounding countryside looks like the Sahel desert, he tells us. He rides his bicycle around the area in his search for a stream and, showing a blithe disregard for all fences blocking his way, takes hardy possession of this empty territory. The relatively recent *La petite fille qui aimait trop les allumettes* (1998) (*The Little Girl Who Was Too Fond of Matches*) by Gaétan Soucy (one of Quebec's most critically acclaimed novels at the time of its release), takes place in an isolated house in the middle of a pine forest, far removed from civilization. Here as well, the father in the story leaves a curious legacy of madness (a paternal death is a frequent motif in contemporary Quebec literature), after raising his two children in seclusion, as though he wanted to shield them from any and all social contact. As in Poulin's novel, the house becomes a retreat and writing space, a kind of postmodern ivory tower, crammed with books, where reality is shaky. From their respective towers, Poulin cites Hemingway; Ducharme cites Balzac; Soucy cites the Bible, Spinoza, and the dictionary; Hamelin cites Malcolm Lowry, and he too the dictionary—the only book that his character brings on his retreat.

All of these postmodern characters rekindle relationships with old stock figures (for example, the coureur des bois) and reactivate the theme of exile that has transcended the history of Quebec literature. Almost invariably, these characters inhabit a barren, marginal space on the fringe of society, where they are guaranteed immense freedom, but condemned to solitude. They live in poverty, luxury items being a rarity. They share a common literary culture, which distinguishes them from their predecessors. But, most importantly, while going about their business, they observe each other with an inexhaustible curiosity, driven by the desire to give the narrative of their lives an improbable coherence. The traditional poles of identity—including family, friends, social class, generation or nation, are not enough, nor are they truly determining factors. The past is as vague as the future. Naturally, the open frontier of the North has expanded, but in fact all frontiers are opening up with every step these characters take, pledged to boundless mobility. Regardless of where their focus may lie, they feel highly detached from any form of social life, which they find consistently underwhelming. They are not as attached to others as they are to the signs of their negligible

presence. It is as though they are always surveying the land, searching for traces of their origins. In *Lignes aériennes* (2002) (*Mirabel*), a prose poem that unfolds like a personal narrative, Pierre Nepveu returns to the expropriated land in the region of Mirabel, where his own family used to live. He talks to himself as though he were alone in the world:

> today it was
> that I bent down
> over my black shoes
> and spoke to them like a pair of dogs,
> ordering them outside
> was scraping over the damp grass,
> I lay down at the foot of a tree,
> although I have few roots
> for probing my life[12]

In fact, the observation in this poem about having 'few roots' may be emblematic of all contemporary Quebec literature.

From the nineteenth-century works of Abbé Casgrain to the poetry of the 1960s, the literati who have traditionally described Quebec literature have adopted the vantage point of one people or 'la nation', often redoubling their efforts to assert its specificity and centricity. But since 1980, the new theme of *dépaysement* or decentring has been redefining Quebec literature as a significant influx of Quebec authors with origins that span the globe are producing what has been called 'migrant writing'. Bilingual and bicultural Montreal has evolved into multicultural Montreal, as Emile Ollivier, a Haitian novelist, explained to a compatriot:

> I also told him that to really write about Montreal, [he] should begin with contextualizing nomadic discourse, migrant discourse and [the discourse] that both share, discourse from nowhere, discourse from elsewhere, discourse that is not quite from here, not quite from elsewhere; I told him that this city has four solitudes—francophone, anglophone, immigrant and Black—[he] must show how our presence jostles and tropicalizes Montreal, splashes it with bright colours. As Borges said of Buenos Aires, *the only beauties are involuntary*.[13]

In this new space, splashed with bright colours, the very notion of a 'frontier' loses part of its meaning. Present-day Montreal no longer bears any resemblance to the Montreal of *Bonheur d'occasion*. Former notions of Quebec's 'people' and 'nation' now coexist with a growing collective awareness of multi-faceted cultural diversity. Without a doubt, Quebec's 'national consciousness' is being forced to reconceptualize itself. But even in this vastly altered landscape, some familiar points of reference have remained.

For one thing, the same twofold marginality vis-à-vis France and the United States that has characterized

Quebec literature since its inception is still an influential reality. For another, Quebec's northern frontier has kept its exotic magnetic pull. It has repeatedly reconciled Quebecers' sense of *pays* (their people, nation, homeland) with their openness to *dépaysement* (decentring). Indeed, the rapid success of migrant writing in Quebec may be owed to the fact that it confirms (more than it contradicts) this self-made spirit of new beginnings in the open north—a world view shared by generations of Quebec authors.

QUESTIONS FOR CONSIDERATION

1. Historically speaking, how would you say France and North America have been diametrically opposed in relation to Quebec literature?

2. Why do Quebec authors often represent 'America' as a foreign entity?

3. In what way has the northern frontier marked literary works from Quebec?

NOTES

1. Translated as *The Town Below* by Samuel Putman (Toronto: McClelland & Stewart, 1967).
2. Translated as *The Tin Flute* by Hannah Josephson (Toronto: McClelland & Stewart, 1947).
3. Gilles Marcotte, 'Robert Charbonneau, la France, René Garneau et nous . . . ,' in *Littérature et circonstances*, ' Essais' collection (Montreal: L'Hexagone, 1989), 65–84; Élisabeth Nardout-Lafarge, 'Histoire d'une querelle,' in Robert Charbonneau, *La France et nous. Journal d'une querelle* (Montreal: Bibliothèque québécoise, 1993), 7–26.
4. In his report to the Crown, this British emissary suggested that since the French Canadians were a people with no history or literature of their own, they ought to be assimilated.
5. Our translation. Ducharme's autobiography was not included in the English translation of his novel by Barbara Bray, Hamish Hamilton, London: 1968.
6. Our translation of *Le Devoir*, 14 January 1967.
7. Our translation and italics. Gilles Marcotte, *Le Manuscrit Phaneuf* (Montreal: Boréal, 2005), 113–14.

8. Our translation of Jean Basile, *La Jument des Mongols* (Montreal: Éditions du Jour, 1964), 10.
9. Our translation of Gaston Miron, 'La marche à l'amour', in *L'Homme rapaillé*, coll. 'Poésie', (Paris: Gallimard, 1999), 62.
10. Our translation of Paul-Marie Lapointe, 'Le temps tombe', in *Le Réel absolu. Poèmes 1948–1965* (Montreal: L'Hexagone, 1971), 220.
11. *Mr Blue* was translated from the French by Sheila Fischman (Montreal: Vehicle Press, 1993), 22. Original work by Jacques Poulin, *Le Vieux Chagrin* (Montreal/Arles: Leméac/Actes Sud, 1989), 23.
12. Judith Cowan's translation of *Mirabel* (Montreal: Vehicle Press, 2004), 11. Original by Pierre Nepveu, *Lignes aériennes* (Montreal: Éditions du Noroît, 2002), 11. Excerpt used by permission from Mirabel by Pierre Nepveu, translated by Judith Cowan and published by Signal Editions, Véhicule Press.
13. Our italics and translation of Émile Ollivier, *La Brûlerie* (Montreal: Boréal, 2004), 55–6.

RELEVANT WEBSITES

L'ÎLE: L'INFOCENTRE LITTÉRAIRE DES ÉCRIVAINS QUÉBÉCOIS: www.litterature.org

CENTRE DE RECHERCHE INTERUNIVERSITAIRE SUR LA LITTÉRATURE ET LA CULTURE QUÉBÉCOISES: www.crilcq.org

BIBLIOTHÈQUE ET ARCHIVES NATIONALES DU QUÉBEC: www.banq.qc.ca/portal/dt/accueil.jsp

UNION DES ÉCRIVAINES ET DES ÉCRIVAINS QUÉBÉCOIS: www.uneq.qc.ca

Service documentaires multimedias:
www.sdm.qc.ca/Produit.cfm?P=9&M=3

Érudit: www.erudit.org/index.html
Database of French-language articles.

Access to research at Université de Montréal,
Université Laval, and Université du Québec à
Montréal

Select Bibliography

Beaudoin, Réjean. *Le Roman québécois.* Montreal: Boréal,
    1991.
Biron, Michel, François Dumont, and Élisabeth Nardout-
    Lafarge (with the assistance of Martine-Emmanuelle
    Lapointe). *Histoire de la littérature québécoise.*
    Montreal: Boréal, 2007.
Bourassa, André G. *Surréalisme et littérature québécoise
    : histoire d'une révolution culturelle.* Montreal: Les
    Herbes rouges, 1986.
Brossard, Nicole, and Lisette Girouard, eds. *Anthologie de
    la poésie des femmes au Québec : des origines à nos jours.*
    Montreal: Éditions du Remue-ménage, 2003.
Dumont, François. *La Poésie québécoise.* Montreal: Boréal,
    1999.
Fortin, Marcel, Yvan Lamonde, et François Ricard, *Guide
    de la littérature québécoise.* Montreal: Boréal, 1988.
Gallays, François, Sylvain Simard, and Robert Vigneault,
    eds. *Le Roman contemporain au Québec (1960–1985).*
    Archives des lettres canadiennes, Tome VIII. Montreal:
    Fides, 1992.
Gauvin, Lise, and Gaston Miron. *Écrivains contemporains
    du Québec : anthologie.* Montreal: L'Hexagone, 1998.
Godin, Jean Cléo, and Dominique Lafon. *Dramaturgies
    québécoises des années quatre-vingt.* Montreal: Leméac,
    1999.
———, and Laurent Mailhot. *Théâtre québécois I.
    Introduction à dix dramaturges contemporains.* New
    edition. Montreal: Bibliothèque québécoise, 1988.
———. *Théâtre québécois II. Nouveaux auteurs, autres
    spectacles.* Montreal: Hurtubise HMH, 1980.
Hamel, Réginald, John Hare, and Paul Wyczynski.
    *Dictionnaire des auteurs de langue française en Amérique
    du Nord.* Montreal: Fides, 1989.
*Histoire du livre et de l'imprimé au Canada. Volume I : Des
    débuts à 1840.* Eds Patricia Fleming, Gilles Gallichan,
    and Yvan Lamonde, 2004. *Volume II : 1840–1918* Eds
    Yvan Lamonde, Patricia Fleming, and Fiona A. Black,
    2006. *Volume III : 1918–1980.* Eds Carole Gerson and
    Jacques Michon, forthcoming. Montreal: Presses de
    l'Université de Montréal.
Lafon, Dominique, ed. *Théâtre québécois 1975–1995.*
    Archives des lettres canadiennes, Tome X. Montreal:
    Fides, 2001.

Lemire, Maurice, ed. *Dictionnaire des œuvres littéraires du
    Québec.* 8 volumes: I (up to 1900), II (1900–1939), III
    (1940–1959), IV (1960–1969), V (1970–1975), VI (1976–
    1980), VII (1981–1985), VIII (1986–1989). Montreal:
    Fides, 1978–2005.
———, and Denis Saint-Jacques, eds. *La Vie littéraire au
    Québec.* 5 volumes: I (1764–1805), II (1806–1839), III
    (1840–1869), IV (1870–1894), V (1895–1918). Quebec:
    Presses de l'Université Laval, 1991–9.
Lepage, Françoise. *Histoire de la littérature pour la jeunesse
    (Québec et francophonies du Canada).* Orléans, Ont.:
    Éditions David, 2000.
Linteau, Paul-André, René Durocher, Jean-Claude Robert,
    and François Ricard, *Histoire du Québec contemporain,*
    vol. I, *De la confédération à la Crise;* vol. 2, *Le Québec
    depuis 1930.* Montreal: Boréal, 1989.
Lord, Michel. *Anthologie de la science-fiction québécoise
    contemporaine.* Montreal: Bibliothèque québécoise,
    1988.
Madore, Édith. *La Littérature pour la jeunesse au Québec.*
    Montreal: Boréal, 1994.
Mailhot, Laurent. *L'Essai québécois depuis 1845 : étude et
    anthologie.* Montreal: Hurtubise HMH, 2005.
———. *La Littérature québécoise depuis ses origines.*
    Montreal: Typo, 1997.
———, and Pierre Nepveu. *La Poésie québécoise, des
    origines à nos jours. Anthologie.* Montreal: Typo, 2007.
Marcotte, Gilles, ed. *Anthologie de la littérature québécoise.*
    Vols. 1 and 2 (1534–1895); vols. 3 and 4 (1895–1952).
    Montreal: L'Hexagone, 1994.
Michon, Jacques, ed. *Histoire de l'édition littéraire au
    Québec au XXe siècle.* Vol. 1 *La naissance de l'éditeur
    1900–1939;* Vol. 2 *Le temps des éditeurs 1940–1959.*
    Montreal: Fides, 1999, 2004.
New, William H. *A History of Canadian Literature.*
    Montreal and Kingston: McGill-Queen's University
    Press, 2003.
Pellerin, Gilles. *Anthologie de la nouvelle québécoise actuelle.*
    Quebec: L'Instant même, 2003.
———. *Dix ans de nouvelles : une anthologie québécoise.*
    Quebec: L'Instant même, 1996.
Royer, Jean. *Introduction à la poésie québécoise : les
    poètes et les œuvres des origines à nos jours.* Montreal:
    Bibliothèque québécoise, 2009.

CHAPTER 8

Aboriginal Peoples and Quebec: Competing or Coexisting Nationalisms?

Martin Papillon, University of Ottawa

— TIMELINE —

1100s   Aboriginal settlements in St Lawrence Valley.

1534   French explorer Jacques Cartier lands on Gaspé Peninsula where he is met by Iroquoians from St Lawrence Valley.

1608   Samuel de Champlain establishes first permanent French settlement at what is now Quebec City.

1615   Allied with Champlain, Algonquin, Innu, and Hurons defeat Iroquois contingent in northern New York state, setting stage for French–Iroquois conflicts.

1701   Great Peace of Montreal. Iroquois establish peace and friendship alliance with French and their Aboriginal allies, ending almost a century of wars.

1763   Royal Proclamation. Following Britain's victory in Seven Years' War, colony of Quebec passes to British control. George III limits settlements on Indian lands.

1867   British Parliament adopts British North America Act, creating Canadian federation. No Aboriginal representatives invited to conferences leading to creation of this new federal union.

1876   First Indian Act adopted by federal Parliament. It consolidates various colonial laws

and policies regarding management of Indian lands and communities.

1815–1923   Land cession treaties are negotiated with First Nations in most of Ontario and Prairie provinces. No such treaties are signed in Quebec.

1960   Status Indians gain right to vote in federal elections.

1969   Federal government's *Statement on Indian Policy* (White Paper) proposes abolition of Indian Act and dismantling of reserve system in order to further integrate First Nations into mainstream Canadian society.

1975   James Bay Crees and Inuit of Nunavik sign first 'modern treaty', James Bay and Northern Quebec Agreement, with Quebec and federal government.

1982   'Aboriginal and Treaty Rights' recognized in Constitution Act, 1982.

1990   Oka Crisis. Standoff between Mohawks and Canadian military ends after 78 days.

1991–4   James Bay Crees organize successful international campaign against Great Whale hydroelectric project.

1992   Charlottetown Accord, which proposed that Canadian Constitution recognize Aboriginal peoples' inherent right to self-government, defeated in pan-Canadian referendum.

1995   Quebec referendum on sovereignty-partnership. Many Aboriginal leaders raise possibility of partition in event of 'yes' vote.

2001   Quebec government and James Bay Crees sign Paix des Braves agreement, ending

years of conflict over interpretation of James Bay and Northern Quebec Agreement.

2007   Quebec, federal government, and Inuit sign agreement-in-principle for creation of regional government in Nunavik.

We often forget that in the early days of Canada, politics was at least a three-way affair between the French, the British, and the various Aboriginal nations who dominated the land beyond the major European settlements. The first inhabitants of the continent established themselves as power brokers between British and French forces.[1] They negotiated military and economic alliances with the colonial powers, bargained access to the key fur trade routes, and eventually positioned themselves strategically as key actors in the battles for North America. Of course, this trilateral relationship did not last; once the French colonies fell into British hands, Aboriginal peoples lost their position as intermediaries between European powers. They were themselves progressively subjected to British colonial rule.

Today, even if Aboriginal peoples form a relatively small minority in what has become Canada, the idea of sovereign Aboriginal nations coexisting with the descendants of French and English settlers remains a powerful one. Like francophones in Quebec, Aboriginal peoples seek to protect their cultures, languages, and distinctive identities. And like many francophone Quebec nationalists, they challenge the political foundations, legal institutions, and geographic scope of Canadian sovereignty. Of course, unlike Quebec sovereignists, very few Aboriginal nations actually seek complete independence from Canada, given their small size and limited resources. They have nonetheless adopted a very similar discourse, seeking greater recognition of their status as distinct polities engaged in a nation-to-nation relationship with Canada.

Sharing similar goals, Aboriginal and Quebec nationalisms recently have collided as they often compete for control over the political agenda and challenge each other's legitimacy. The conflict has

been especially salient for Aboriginal nations whose traditional territory is in Quebec. As the core vehicle of Quebec nationalism, the provincial government is particularly sensitive to any challenges to its territorial jurisdiction and to the sovereignty of its Parliament, the National Assembly.

I suggest in this chapter that the specific context in Quebec, where sovereignty and national identities are constantly debated and challenged in public discourse, has opened opportunities for Aboriginal peoples to redefine their relationships with Quebec and Canada. After discussing the origins of Aboriginal nationalism in the colonial past of the Canadian state, this chapter examines the various moments of tensions between Quebec and Aboriginal peoples to show how these overlapping nations are slowly learning to coexist on a shared territory.

ABORIGINAL PEOPLES AND COLONIALISM IN CANADA AND QUEBEC

There are today over one million Aboriginal people in Canada, representing 4 per cent of the total population. It is a highly diverse population, with more than 1,500 communities, some of them linked through ancient or more recent political ties, forming approximately 60 self-defined nations speaking as many as 50 languages.[2] While more than half of Aboriginal people in Canada now live in cities and towns, many remain closely attached to the land, which is central to their culture and traditions.

In Quebec, there are approximately 82,000 Aboriginal people, representing 0.8 per cent of the population of the province. There are 11 Aboriginal nations formally recognized by the government of Quebec (see Table 1). Most Aboriginal people in Quebec live in sparsely populated rural areas that are rich in natural resources. The Inuit live in the north-ernmost part of the province, where they make up the majority. The Huron and Mohawk nations live in small communities near Quebec City and Montreal respectively and have much closer daily interaction with the francophone majority of the province.

There are some parallels in the history of Aboriginal peoples and French Canadians; the main one is that both groups were reduced to minority status within a predominantly British North America. But British colonial rule operated very differently for the two groups. Very early on, British colonial authorities saw their interest in maintaining good relationships with the descendants of French settlers. Their reli-gion, legal institutions, and civil society were recog-nized and protected in the Quebec Act of 1774. Their continued presence as a distinct people was one of the main reason for the creation of a federal, rather than a unitary, state in 1867. George-Étienne Cartier and other French Canadians played a leading role in the creation of the Canadian federation.

TABLE 8.1 Aboriginal Populations in Quebec

Nation	Population
Abenaki	2,091
Algonquin	9,645
Attikamek	6,321
Cree	16,151
Huron-Wendat	3,006
Innu	16,199
Inuit	10,464
Maliseet	786
Mi'kmaq	5,104
Mohawk	16,727
Naskapi	673
Total	**87,167**

Source: Ministère des Affaires indiennes et du Nord cana-dien, Registre des indiens, 31 décembre 2007.Ministère de la santé et des services sociaux du Québec, Registre des bénéfici-aires cris, inuits et naskapis de la Convention de la Baie-James et du Nord québécois et de la Convention du Nord-Est québé-cois, 31 janvier 2007

Aboriginal peoples met with a different situation in British North America. The Royal Proclamation of 1763 recognized their presence and rights to the land, but it also clearly established them as subjugated nations under the 'protection' of the British crown. In most of what is now Ontario and the Prairie prov-inces, colonial authorities negotiated land cession treaties through which Aboriginal peoples agreed to the presence of settlers on their traditional territor-ies in exchange for smaller tracts of lands reserved for their benefit and protected from the encroach-ment of settlers. In northern territories and what is now Quebec, no such treaties were signed; Aboriginal peoples were simply ignored and marginalized in the new dominant order.

The Indian Act was adopted in 1876 under the authority of the newly constituted federal govern-ment. The Act had the explicit objective of facilitat-ing colonial expansion to the West and 'preparing' the Aboriginal population for its eventual assimila-tion into the dominant society. The annual report of the Department of the Interior in 1876 illustrates the philosophy behind the Indian Act:

> Our Indian legislation rests on the principle, that the aborigines are to be kept in a condition of tutel-age and treated as wards or children of the State . . . . The true interests of the aborigines and of the State alike require that every effort should be made to aid the Red man in lifting himself out of his condition of tutelage . . . and through education and every other means, to prepare him for a higher civiliza-tion by encouraging him to assume the privileges and responsibilities of full citizenship.[3]

Until they were judged 'emancipated' by the Canadian government, Aboriginal peoples were con-fined to limited reserves, small pieces of lands under federal jurisdiction where they were treated as chil-dren under the benevolent protection of the govern-ment. Such reserves were first established in what is now Quebec under the French regime, but most iso-lated Aboriginal communities were spared until the federal government systematically applied the policy in the early twentieth century.[4] Many Aboriginal nations in Quebec were then forced to leave their traditional hunting grounds to make room for the always-expanding Euro-Canadian settlements. The

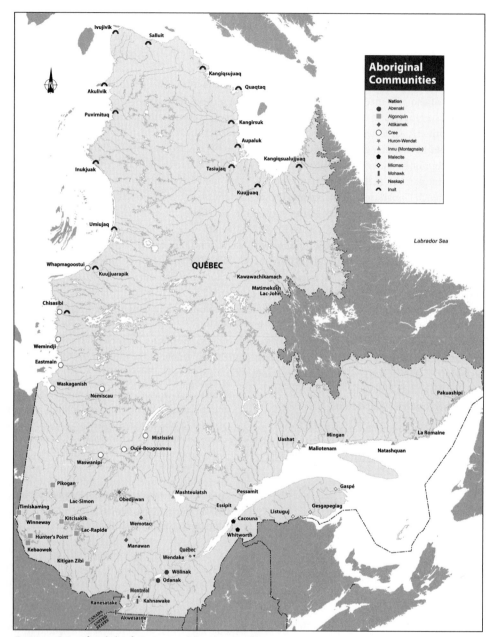

FIGURE 8.1 Aboriginal Communities in Quebec

Source: Based on the map *Les Autochtones du Québec*, produced by the Secrétariat des Affaires autochtones du Québec, 2008 (www.autochtones.gouv.qc.ca).

Algonquin who once dominated the Ottawa River Valley, for example, were confined to remote areas of limited interest to settlers.[5] The federal government also sought to speed up assimilation through the infamous residential schools system, in which Aboriginal children were educated according to the values of Western societies. Many such schools were established in Quebec.

Sociologist Jean-Jacques Simard[6] aptly describes the logic behind the policies and administrative structures set in place to control the Aboriginal populations as a process of geographic, economic, cultural, and political 'reduction'. Previously self-governing and culturally distinct societies were progressively contained geographically, subjugated politically, and forced to adopt the cultural codes, norms, and social practices of the dominant society. Aboriginal communities thus became, and largely remain to this day, *internal colonies* of the Canadian state.

BEYOND COLONIALISM: THE RISE OF THE ABORIGINAL SELF-DETERMINATION MOVEMENT

The model of internal colonialism established in the nineteenth century came under stress in the aftermath of the Second World War. At a time when liberal ideals of equality and universal human rights were spreading in Canada and around the world, the discriminatory Indian Act and the various policies designed to 'civilize' Aboriginal peoples became increasingly difficult to defend. The poor socio-economic conditions in Aboriginal communities were also gathering growing media attention. As a result, the federal government progressively expanded most benefits of citizenship—including full access to social programs and the right to vote—to Aboriginal people.

Making Aboriginal people citizens like all others was the stated intention behind the now infamous federal White Paper, *Statement on Indian Policy*, of 1969. To break with its colonial past, the federal government proposed the abolition of the Indian Act as the revocation of treaties that were seen as a source of exclusion from full citizenship. Aboriginal people reacted strongly to the White Paper. Many rejected its philosophy of egalitarian citizenship, which was viewed as a new form of forced assimilation into the majority society. Aboriginal organizations started to develop an alternative discourse based not on equality between individuals, but equality among *nations*. Building on examples of Third World decolonization

and similar indigenous movements in the United States, Aboriginal leaders in Canada explicitly used the language of international human rights and national self-determination to assert their claims for proper protection of their distinctive cultures and languages, for control over their lands, and for political recognition as distinctive national communities.

Given the relatively small size of Aboriginal communities, which now coexist on the territory with a far larger non-Aboriginal population, self-determination is not generally understood as a process by which an independent state with the classic attributes of sovereignty is created. Aboriginal self-determination is rather generally understood as a process by which a nation or a community regains *control* over its own political destiny and renegotiates with the state the terms and conditions of its relationship with and participation in the dominant societies' institutions. Not surprisingly, the federal and provincial governments in Canada have resisted Aboriginal assertions of their right to self-determination as a form of shared sovereignty. This is especially true in Quebec, where Aboriginal self-determination claims clash with similar claims from another minority nation challenging the boundaries and legitimacy of Canadian sovereignty.

Early Encounters Between Aboriginal and Quebec Nationalisms

Under the Canadian Constitution (the British North America Act of 1867 and the Canadian Constitution of 1982), the federal government inherited the British crown's responsibility for relations with 'Indians'. Aboriginal peoples thus have tenuous relationships with Canadian provinces. This is true of Quebec. Until the 1960s, the provincial government showed little interest in establishing its presence in Aboriginal communities. Except for Inuit communities in the northernmost part of the province, services in Aboriginal communities, including elements of provincial jurisdiction, such as education, health, and welfare, were provided through the federal Department of Indian Affairs. The emergence of modern Quebec nationalism in the 1960s transformed this dynamic.

With the Quiet Revolution, the Quebec state became the main vehicle of the newly assertive nationalist francophone elite. Through the provincial govern-ment, this elite engaged in a significant nation-building exercise, constantly seeking to consolidate the territorial and social boundaries of the political community and expand the provincial state's influence in various areas of public policy. This was true for Quebec's Aboriginal policy. While elsewhere in Canada provinces are still often unwilling participants in Aboriginal govern-ance, the Quebec government has adopted an activist stance, seeking simultaneously to assert its authority over Aboriginal peoples within its territorial bound-aries and gain legitimacy as their primary interlocutor in negotiating the conditions of exercise of their rights and political autonomy.[7] Not surprisingly, Quebec and Aboriginal nationalisms rapidly collided in this context.

A key element of Quebec's national project has been to assert the authority of the provincial state over its resource-rich northern lands, a territory annexed to Quebec in 1912 but largely ignored by subsequent provincial governments. In the words of Quebec Premier Robert Bourassa (premier from 1970–6 and 1985–94), northern Quebec was a 'vast reservoir of untapped resources' that 'had to be conquered' for the benefit of all Quebecers.[8] Energy production and the expansion of the mining industry were central ele-ments of the province's state-led economic develop-ment strategy in the 1960s and 1970s. Linking the remote North to the rest of the province, however, was more than an economic enterprise. In establishing its presence on its entire territory, the Quebec govern-ment was also symbolically taking ownership of the land on behalf of the francophone majority.[9] It is in this context that the Bourassa government launched the James Bay hydroelectric project in 1971.

Previously, Quebec had largely treated as unimport-ant the presence of Aboriginal people on lands and riv-ers slated for hydroelectric development. For example, Innu communities were simply moved to other loca-tions without any sort of consultation when the large Manicouagan complex was developed on their traditional lands in the 1960s. This time however, Aboriginal people affected by the James Bay project reacted strongly. A group of young Cree leaders, sup-ported by the Indians of Quebec Association, chal-lenged the legitimacy and legality of Quebec's unilateral action. They won an important court battle to stop the project until their claims to the land were settled. While this court decision was overturned in appeal, it eventu-ally forced Quebec to negotiate a settlement.

This settlement, signed in 1975 by Quebec, Canada, the Crees, and Inuit became the first 'modern treaty' in Canada, the James Bay and Northern Quebec Agreement. This was a significant achievement for Aboriginal people. Like its federal counterpart, the provincial government was forced to acknowledge not only the existence of Aboriginal rights limiting its territorial sovereignty, but also the political relevance of Aboriginal peoples as distinct communities that could not simply be dissolved in the newly assertive provincial nationalism.

Battles over Constitutional Recognition

Aboriginal and Quebec nationalisms continued to intersect during the constitutional debates that dominated Canadian politics for most of the 1980s. Aboriginal people took advantage of Quebec's chal-lenge to the constitutional order to engage in their own form of constitutional politics. They even gained sufficient support across Canada for the inclusion in the Constitution Act (1982) of a general provision for the recognition of Aboriginal and treaty rights. While section 35 is worded very generally, it nonetheless rec-ognizes that Aboriginal peoples have specific rights because of their unique status and history in Canada.[10]

Quebec rejected the 1982 constitutional package for reasons that had little to do with the recognition of Aboriginal rights. The Aboriginal leadership in the province nonetheless sought clarifications on the government's position regarding the recognition of their rights in the province. In its 1983 response, the Parti Québécois government established 15 princi-ples guiding its relationship with Aboriginal peoples. Among others, the Quebec government stated that it:

> Recognizes that the Aboriginal peoples of Qué-bec constitute distinct nations, . . . having the right to determine the development of their own culture and identity.

> Recognizes the right of Aboriginal nations, within the framework of Québec legislation, to govern themselves on the land allocated to them.

Considers that these rights are to be exercised as part of the Québec community and hence could not imply rights of sovereignty that could affect the territorial integrity of Québec.[11]

The policy statement illustrates the ambiguous position of the provincial government on the recognition of Aboriginal rights. On the one hand, Quebec embraced the idea of Aboriginal nations as distinct collectivities. On the other hand, it clearly established the limits of this recognition. Self-government was to be exercised 'within Quebec' and was not to affect the territorial integrity of the province. Today this ambiguous position continues to form the backbone of Quebec's Aboriginal policy.

The province's position was put to the test in no small fashion in the following decade as Quebec and Aboriginal recognition claims collided again on the constitutional front. In 1987, the federal government and the provinces, including Quebec, negotiated the Meech Lake Accord, which would enable Quebec to endorse the 1982 Constitution. The centrepiece of the Accord was the inclusion in the Canadian Constitution of an interpretative clause recognizing Quebec as a 'distinct society' within Canada. Aboriginal peoples strongly opposed the agreement, as they felt their own recognition claims were being ignored. As public opinion in English Canada rose up against the Accord, Aboriginal leaders reminded Canadians that if there were any distinct society in Canada, it was the Aboriginal nations, not Quebec.

The collapse of the Meech Lake Accord in 1990 and the ensuing debates over Quebec's and Aboriginal peoples' place in the federation resulted in a war of words over boundaries of political communities, nationhood, and democratic legitimacy. Ovide Mercredi, the Grand Chief of the Assembly of First Nations, one of the main national Aboriginal organizations, provoked dispute when he declared before Quebec's National Assembly that Quebec did not have the right of self-determination 'since it does not constitute a single people'. 'To deny our right to self-determination in the pursuit of your aspirations,' he added, 'would be a blatant form of racial discrimination'.[12] Quebec Premier Robert Bourassa replied that 'no matter Quebec's future, the rights of Aboriginal peoples must be exercised within the jurisdictional boundaries of the National Assembly'.[13]

By associating their own claims to self-determination with those of Quebec, Aboriginal leaders positioned themselves as legitimate constitutional actors on par with Quebec and other provinces. Their success in this respect was confirmed in the next round of constitutional negotiations, as major national Aboriginal organizations sat at the table as full negotiating partners with the federal government, the provinces, and the territories. The outcome was the Charlottetown Accord of 1992. One of its proposals was to include in the Constitution Aboriginal peoples' inherent right to self-government. The Accord also proposed to recognize Aboriginal governments as a third order of governments in the Canadian federation.

Despite the defeat of the Charlottetown Accord in a pan-Canadian referendum, Aboriginal peoples gained considerably in the process. They were now considered full constitutional actors, holding what amounts to a de facto political veto on constitutional changes affecting their rights. Their constitutional claims could also no longer be simply ignored. In the aftermath of the Charlottetown negotiations, it was clear that any future attempt to recognize Quebec's status in the Constitution would involve a similar recognition for Aboriginal peoples. In many ways, Aboriginal peoples succeeded in placing their claims for constitutional recognition on par with those of Quebec, linking their future status in the federation to that of the francophone province.

A NEW CHAPTER: COMPETING SOVEREIGNTIES

If the 1980s were dominated by struggles over recognition in the Canadian Constitution, in the 1990s there were more direct conflicts between Aboriginal and Quebec nationalisms over the boundaries of the political communities coexisting on Quebec's territory. The Oka Crisis of the summer of 1990 (see Snapshot box) was the first major conflict. When a group of Mohawk activists resisted the construction of a golf course on a traditional cemetery adjacent to the community of Kanesatake, police intervention rapidly turned into an armed standoff lasting several weeks and necessitating the intervention of the Canadian Armed Forces. For the Mohawks, the construction of the golf course without their consent, and the provincial police intervention in support of the construction, were attacks on

their authority over the land and their very existence as a distinct nation. Similarly, for Quebec nationalists, the Mohawks' resistance and the ensuing intervention of the Canadian army were reminders of the fragility of their own claim to territorial sovereignty.

SNAPSHOT

The Oka Crisis

What started as a relatively peaceful act of resistance by the Mohawk community of Kanesatake, near Oka, just north of Montreal, against the expansion of a local golf course on their traditional lands, rapidly worsened when the Quebec provincial police intervened to forcibly remove the protesters. Violence erupted, gunfire was exchanged, and a police officer was killed. Militant Mohawks and self-described traditional Warriors of the old Haudenosaunee (Iroquois) Confederacy had erected a barricade on a provincial road nearby, blocking access to many residents of the area. In solidarity, a second group blocked access to a major bridge connecting the island of Montreal to the suburbs near another Mohawk community, Kahnawake.

Tempers flared on both sides of the barricades. Militants and Warriors, some of them armed with semi-automatic weapons and wearing army fatigues, challenged the police force to intervene again, threatening retaliation. As expressions of intolerance from the non-Aboriginal francophone population affected by the blockade reverberated and were amplified in the media, the conflict evolved into a bitter battle between two nations, both claiming sovereign authority over the land and negating the other's legitimacy. The blockade was portrayed in Quebec media as an unlawful action, a challenge to the rule of law by a group of radical militants with ties to organized crime. By contrast, the Mohawk protesters saw themselves as asserting sovereignty, a legitimate act of self-defence in the face of an intolerant provincial government. As the conflict dragged on, the Quebec government asked the federal government for military support. During that fateful summer, 2,500 soldiers from the Canadian Armed Forces, a powerful

symbol of Canadian sovereignty, were deployed near the barricades and the surrounding areas.

Images of Mohawk children playing near the barricades, a few metres away from Canadian tanks and heavily armed soldiers, received worldwide media attention. The standoff lasted 78 days. On 26 September, after increasing pressure from the military, the remaining protesters left their compound peacefully and the barricades were dismantled, without a clear resolution to the crisis.

Twenty years later, the events of Oka still elicit strong emotions in Canada, in Quebec, and, especially, in Mohawk communities. For many in Canada, the Oka Crisis was an awakening, a realization that a profound gap remained between Aboriginal people and other Canadians. The events in Oka led to the federal government's Royal Commission on Aboriginal Peoples, whose 1996 report revisited our shared history, pointed to the painful legacy of past policies, and proposed a radical agenda for change based on the recognition of Aboriginal peoples as equal partners in a nation-to-nation relationship with Canada.

In Quebec, especially for nationalists, the episode was a reminder that not everyone agrees on the territorial boundaries of the political community, nor on the role of the provincial state as the legitimate source of authority in that territory. The presence of Aboriginal peoples, with their own national aspirations, could no longer be ignored.

For Mohawks, the events of 1990 have left a bitter taste. In both Kanesatake and Kahnawake, the two communities most affected by the crisis, wounds are only slowly healing. Tensions with the local non-Aboriginal population are dissipating, 20 years later, but a general distrust of government authority remains. The Quebec police rarely venture into the communities. In Kanesatake, the epicentre of the crisis, the golf course was never built, and some of the disputed land was bought by the federal government for an eventual transfer to the Mohawks. But the Mohawk land is intertwined with non-Aboriginal private properties, making its management as a coherent territory almost impossible and its development difficult. The community is divided on its future course. Sadly, criminal elements are taking advantage of the vacuum created by the divisions and the uncertain legal status of the territory, further complicating reconciliation between Mohawks and their Québécois neighbours.

The Oka Crisis was fresh in the collective memory when Quebec faced another direct challenge to its territorial authority. The second phase of the James Bay hydroelectric project on the Great Whale River was launched in 1988. The James Bay Crees, who mobilized against the first project in the 1970s, opposed this new development on their traditional hunting grounds. Allied with a network of environmental groups, the Crees put together a highly effective international campaign, portraying the project as 'a new Amazonian catastrophe' and decrying Quebec's lack of respect for their rights as the first inhabitants and caretakers of the land.

The Great Whale battle once again pitched Quebec's conception of its territorial sovereignty and economic interests against those of a small group of Aboriginal people asserting its own rights and authority on the land. And Quebec lost the international public relation battle. The Quebec state looked just like any other western capitalist government, obsessed with its economic interest and little concerned about the environment and the rights of minorities. Fearing that this negative image would prejudice the international community against an eventual recognition of Quebec sovereignty, the newly elected Parti Québécois government shelved the project on the eve of the 1995 sovereignty referendum.

These conflicts underline the potential volatility of the nationalist encounter in Quebec, but also the influence of Aboriginal peoples when political boundaries and self-determination are publicly debated. In a sense, Aboriginal peoples have taken advantage of the political dynamics caused by Quebec nationalism to make gains of their own.

During the 1995 referendum campaign the tensions between Quebec and Aboriginal nationalisms reached their apex. Aboriginal representatives boycotted the consultations leading to the referendum, arguing the province-wide process was a violation of their own right to self-determination.[14] The Crees and Inuit organized their own referendum, while the Mohawks did not allow Quebec election officials onto their territory. In Aboriginal communities that participated in the referendum, the sovereignty option was massively rejected. Aboriginal leaders were again challenging political boundaries and asserting their own notion of their place in Canada through the political debates in Quebec. The will of the majority in Quebec could not be imposed on their people. Matthew Coon Come, the Grand Chief of the James Bay Crees, put it in plain language in a conference in Washington that received plenty of media attention in the months preceding the referendum:

> We conceive of ourselves as one people, tied together by the land we share and care for . . . . Now, the government of Québec proclaims the Québécois—that is anyone who may presently reside in the province, including Cree—a people. The Parti Québécois claims for that people the right to self-determination, while in the same breath denying the Crees the same right. If the separatists win the referendum, we will stay in Canada with our territory.[15]

As this quote suggests, Aboriginal leaders, with the support of some English-Canadian media, also started to evoke the possibility of partition. If Quebec voted 'yes' to separation, they argued, Aboriginal peoples could very well refuse to join the new independent state and stay in the Canadian federation with their territories. The federal government embraced this argument, thus impressing upon Quebec voters the possible consequences of a 'yes' vote.[16]

MATTHEW COON COME

Matthew Coon Come was elected Grand Chief of the Grand Council of the Crees, a position he held for more than 10 years before winning the leadership of the Assembly of First Nations (AFN) in 2000.

CP Photo/Andrew Vaughan

Born in a tent on his father's trapline near the Cree community of Mistissini in 1957, Matthew Coon Come became one of the most recognized and controversial Aboriginal leaders in Canada. Like most Aboriginal children of his generation, Coon Come attended a residential school. He pursued his formal education at Trent University and McGill where he studied law in the 1980s and became familiar with Canada's legal system and the emerging jurisprudence on Aboriginal and treaty rights. He returned to his community to run for office as a band councillor before he finished his law degree. Part of a young generation of Cree leaders who came of age with the James Bay and Northern Quebec Agreement, Coon Come emerged as a strong advocate of Cree rights. He rapidly distinguished himself as an astute negotiator and political strategist in relations with governments.

Matthew Coon Come was elected Grand Chief of the Grand Council of the Crees in 1987. Under his leadership, the Grand Council launched a very successful public relations campaign against the second phase of the James Bay hydroelectric project on the Great Whale River. At the heart of the campaign was a clever association of Cree rights on the land to be flooded with the protection of the rivers and forests of northern Quebec, allowing a fruitful alliance

with environmentalist groups in Canada and, perhaps more importantly, in the United States, where the electricity produced by the future hydroelectric complex was to be sold. The highlight of the campaign was a canoe trip down the Hudson River to Manhattan, where Coon Come made a speech in front of thousands of sympathetic New Yorkers on Earth Day in 1991. The ensuing media attention allowed Coon Come to speak to legislators in New York and other New England states about the environmental and human consequences of the hydroelectric project. The Quebec government finally cancelled the Great Whale project in 1994.

Coon Come and the Grand Council of the Crees took advantage of the international network built during the Great Whale campaign to mobilize against yet another project of the nationalist government in Quebec: a referendum on the separation of the province from Canada. While the Parti Québécois assumed that a sovereign Quebec would maintain its existing boundaries, Coon Come argued that the Cree nation could not be forced to follow Quebec down the path of independence. In a series of speeches at Harvard University, in Washington, and in Europe, Coon Come challenged the legitimacy of a Quebec secession from Canada without Cree consent. The Grand Council organized its own consultation on the future of the Cree nation a few months before the Quebec referendum, and a resounding 96 per cent of those who voted in Cree communities opted to stay in Canada.

Coon Come's politics have certainly put the Crees on the map, but his very direct style and colourful language have had consequences. During the referendum campaign, he did not hesitate to accuse Quebec nationalist leaders of racism. He even described the treatment of the Cree nation by the provincial government as cultural genocide. Not surprisingly, such strong words did not make him a popular figure in Quebec. Francophone media portrayed him as an English-speaking Aboriginal leader with little understanding of Quebec, or even the supreme insult, as an agent of the federal government. Relations with Quebec would remain tense for the duration of his tenure as Grand Chief.

After more than 10 years as the head of the Grand Council of the Crees, Matthew Coon Come was elected as Grand Chief of the Assembly of First Nations (AFN) in 2000. The AFN is the main Aboriginal organization representing the interests of First Nations living on reserves at the federal level in Canada. He narrowly defeated the previous Grand Chief, Phil Fontaine, by criticizing his conciliatory approach with the federal government. Promising a more assertive and critical leadership, Coon Come focused his energies on treaty rights and the development of a nation-to-nation relationship between the federal government and the AFN. Under his leadership, that relationship rapidly soured and he eventually lost support among the more moderate First Nations leadership, losing his bid for re-election in 2003. After a few years working behind the scenes,

Coon Come was again elected Grand Chief of the Grand Council of the Crees in 2009.

Coon Come is perhaps best described as a Cree nationalist: a nation builder who presided over much of the Crees' own, not so quiet, revolution. Despite his strong political views and sometimes confrontational language, Coon Come is also pragmatic, capable of compromise when necessary. Under his leadership, and despite very public confrontations with Quebec nationalists, the Grand Council of the Crees negotiated several agreements with the provincial government over compensation for hydroelectric development, water contamination resulting from the flooding, and development in the communities. Charismatic in his own way, Coon Come personifies the current generation of Aboriginal leaders: educated, astute in using the legal and political resources available to Aboriginal people, at ease in the hallways of political and economic power in Montreal, Toronto, or New York, but always aware of his roots in the small Cree community where he was born.

CONTEMPORARY DYNAMICS: MUTUAL RECOGNITION?

Throughout the 1980s and 1990s, Aboriginal peoples gained a place as constitutional actors, and challenged Quebec's assumption about the unity of the province as a single national political community. The scale and boundaries of the Quebec nation could no longer be taken for granted, as Aboriginal peoples clearly established their own self-determination claims as territorially organized and historically constituted nations.

In the aftermath of the 1995 referendum, with the close results in mind and an acute understanding of the legitimacy gained by Aboriginal peoples during the process, the Parti Québécois government sought to rebuild the bridges after a decade of tense relations. In a policy orientation document released in 1998, the government reaffirmed its recognition of Aboriginal nations and its commitment to self-government 'as a means to reconcile aboriginal aspirations with those of Quebecers as a whole, while maintaining the territorial integrity of Quebec'.[17]

Again, the provincial government rejected the principle of an inherent Aboriginal authority overriding the territorial and jurisdictional boundaries of the province. But in the same document, the government also insists on the need to 'develop and improve Quebec-Aboriginal relations'.[18] The policy document proposed concrete steps to achieve this goal: most importantly, the negotiation of bilateral Quebec-Aboriginal agreements of 'mutual understanding' and the delegation of 'contractual jurisdiction in areas of relevance for Aboriginal social, economic and cultural development'.[19] This form of delegation doesn't come close to fulfilling Aboriginal self-determination claims, but Quebec was the first provincial government in Canada to develop such a comprehensive approach to bilateral relations with Aboriginal peoples.

Perhaps more significantly, Quebec clearly established in its 1998 policy orientation a bilateral conception of Aboriginal-Quebec relations. The federal government is barely mentioned despite its constitutional jurisdiction over Aboriginal peoples. The objective for Quebec was to establish privileged channels with Aboriginal nations in order to move the centre of gravity of Aboriginal-state relations from Ottawa to Quebec City.

To reinforce the construction of more direct bilateral bridges, the provincial governments proposed a permanent forum through which Aboriginal leaders in the province could sit with elected members of the government to discuss issues on the policy agenda. The Conseil Conjoint des Élus was to operate as a nation-to-nation conduit between the government and Aboriginal peoples. The Conseil, however, has not produced the expected results for Aboriginal peoples. Meetings are sporadic, and it remains strictly a consultative body. Too often, consultations on key policies affecting Aboriginal interests in the province take place only after the policy is established.

In other ways, however, Quebec's 1998 policy led to significant developments for Aboriginal peoples. In what is perhaps the most striking development in Aboriginal-Quebec relations since the 1995 referendum, Premier Bernard Landry and the Grand Chief of the James Bay Cree Nation, Ted Moses, announced in 2001 they had reached an agreement to end the protracted disputes on the interpretation of the James Bay and Northern Quebec Agreement (JBNQA). The Agreement Respecting a New Relationship between the Cree Nation and the Government of Quebec, also known as the Paix des Braves, established the framework for what the parties called a 'new era of mutual recognition and nation-to-nation cooperation between the Crees and Quebec'.[20]

The Paix des Braves established co-management for the exploitation of forestry, a main area of conflict between the Crees and Quebec. Quebec also agreed to transfer its economic and social development obligations to Cree communities under the JBNQA to Cree authorities. One important innovation of the agreement is the mechanism for transferring economic development funding to the Crees. The basic amount transferred for 50 years ($70 million annually) is indexed to the annual value of natural resource extraction (including forestry, mining, and hydro-electric production) on Cree territory. The Crees agreed to withdraw all judicial proceedings against Quebec in matters relating to the agreement, but more importantly, they agreed to new hydroelectric developments (the Eastmain 1-A/Rupert diversion project) on their traditional lands.

The Paix des Braves is not revolutionary. It is not a new treaty nor does it recognize any form of shared sovereignty over the territory. It is essentially an agreement on regional economic development and natural resource extraction. Quebec was under pressure to open up the territory for resource extraction and obtain guarantees for forestry exploitation and hydroelectric development. But it was clear that Quebec could no longer deal with the Crees as an 'administered' group and simply impose its will from above. It had to recognize the mutual nature of the relationship. In this respect, despite their many concessions, the agreement was a victory for the Crees: their political status and legitimacy as a distinct nation were acknowledged by Quebec.

This is reflected in the process that led to the Agreement as well as in its language. As in international diplomatic relations, the Paix des Braves was negotiated in secrecy at the highest level, directly between the elected Cree leaders and the office of the Premier of Quebec. All other parties interested in the development of the region were excluded. Few members of the provincial cabinet were even aware of the negotiations. Thus the two parties used nation-to-nation language in promoting the agreement.

The Paix des Braves also had an impact on the political dynamic between the Crees and Ottawa. Cree leaders used the Agreement to obtain similar recognition from the federal government. Ironically, the same Cree leaders who denounced Quebec's colonial practices internationally during the Great Whale and referendum episodes toured Europe with Quebec officials selling the virtues of their new partnership while attacking the federal government for its 'old colonial mentality'.[21]

The strategy eventually paid off for the Crees, as the federal government responded to the pressure of this new political dynamic. In July 2007, the Crees and the federal government announced they had signed a draft agreement for their own 'Paix des Braves'. The federal government agreed to pay $1.4 billion to settle outstanding obligations under the JBNQA and establish new joint governance for the next 20 years. The agreement also established a negotiation agenda towards drafting a Cree constitution and the creation of a Cree Nation government with an elected regional assembly.

The Inuit of Quebec are also adapting their existing governance structures to consolidate their regional autonomy. Unlike the future Cree government which will operate under federal legislation on the fairly limited territory of the communities, the government of Nunavik, the Arctic area of Quebec, will be a regional public government with powers delegated from the province to run most government programs north of the fifty-fifth parallel. The creation of Nunavik as an autonomous region is a major reconfiguration of the political map of the province, which further confirms the re-emergence of Aboriginal nations as distinct political communities within, or in relation to, Quebec. It also confirms the growing recognition by the government and nationalist forces in the province of the permanent presence of Aboriginal nations coexisting with the Quebec nation.

Conclusion

The result of the past 30 years of encounter between Quebec and Aboriginal nationalisms may surprise an outside observer. On the one hand, there were numerous conflicts as Aboriginal peoples and Quebec competed for constitutional recognition, democratic legitimacy, and territorial authority. The boundaries of what are in effect overlapping political communities have been the object of battles, especially in 1995, when Aboriginal peoples refused to be bound by the result of the Quebec referendum on sovereignty.

At the same time, Quebec nationalism has opened many opportunities for Aboriginal peoples to make

significant political gains in the past few decades. By taking Quebec to task on its assertion of its own right to self-determination, Aboriginal peoples have forced Quebec to recognize their presence and political legitimacy as distinct political communities. 'If Quebec can secede from Canada, then why can't we secede from Quebec?' they argued.

Recent developments in Aboriginal-state relations in Quebec suggest much remains to be done to move beyond the heavy legacy of past colonial practices. Aboriginal peoples largely do not have the jurisdictional tools, resources, and political clout of a large provincial government like Quebec. But it is increasingly hard for the provincial and federal governments to ignore Aboriginal peoples and their claims to self-determination. The Paix des Braves and the agreement with the Inuit of Nunavik are striking examples of progress in Aboriginal self-determination in Quebec.

What does this mean for the current relationships among Aboriginal peoples, Quebec, and Canada? The recent retreat of the sovereignty option in Quebec may well reduce the visibility of Aboriginal demands as their own claims lose their strategic importance for both the federal government and Quebec. But the gains made remain significant and are likely here to stay. It will be politically hard for Quebec to retreat from existing agreements or to ignore Aboriginal peoples in its future economic, social, and political development strategies.

Questions for Consideration

1. Why are many Aboriginal nations challenging the legitimacy of Canadian sovereignty on their lands?
2. What are the sources of the conflict between Aboriginal peoples and the Quebec government? How has this conflict evolved in recent decades?
3. What are the similarities and differences between Quebec and Aboriginal nationalisms?

Notes

1. In Canada, the term *Aboriginal peoples* is often used instead of the more internationally recognized term *Indigenous peoples* to designate the first inhabitants of the land. According to the Constitution Act, 1982, Aboriginal peoples comprise three groups, the First Nations or American Indians, the Inuit, and the Métis. I use *Aboriginal peoples* to refer to all three groups in this text and make the distinction when necessary.

2. For historical details about ancient and contemporary nations, see Volume 1 of the Final Report of the Royal Commission on Aboriginal Peoples (RCAP).

3. Department of the Interior, *Annual Report for the year ended 30th June, 1876*, in RCAP vol. 1, 345.

4. Claude Gelinas, *Les Autochtones dans le Québec post-confédéral, 1867–1960*. (Québec: Septentrion, 2008).

5. For a history of the Algonquin people, see the film *The Invisible Nation* by Richard Desjardins and Robert Monderie, distributed by the National Film Board of Canada.

6. Jean-Jacques Simard, *La réduction: l'autochtone inventé et les Amérindiens d'aujourd'hui* (Sillery, Que.: Septentrion, 2003).

7. Daniel Salée, 'The Quebec State and Indigenous Peoples', in Alain-G Gagnon, ed., *Quebec: State and Society*, Third edition (Peterborough, Ont.: Broadview Press, 2004).
8. Robert Bourassa, *La Baie James* (Montreal: Editions du Jour, 1973), 12.
9. Caroline Desbiens, 'Producing North and South: A Political Geography of Hydro Development in Québec' *The Canadian Geographer* 48, 2 (2004): 101–18.
10. Section 35(1) reads: 'the existing aboriginal and treaty rights of the Aboriginal peoples of Canada are hereby recognized and affirmed.' In a later amendment, it was specified that rights defined in a land claim settlement were considered treaty rights under the Constitution.
11. The National Assembly reaffirmed these principles in a motion adopted in 1985.
12. Denis Lessard, 'Pour Mercredi, il n'y a pas de peuple québécois', *La Presse*, 12 February 1992, A1.
13. Normand Delisle, 'Le droit à l'autonomie gouvernementale ne mène pas à la souveraineté territoriale', *La Presse*, 6 March 1992, B14.
14. Philippe Cantin, 'Un déni du droit des autochtones', *La Presse*, 7 December 1994, B4.
15. Matthew Coon Come, 'The Status and Rights of the James Bay Cree in the Context of Quebec Secession', Prepared for the Conference of the Centre of International Studies, Washington, September 1994.
16. Ronald Irwin, 'Cree Have the Right to Remain Canadians', *Ottawa Citizen*, 24 April 1994, A4.
17. Secrétariat aux affaires autochtones, *Partnership, Development, Achievement* (Quebec: Ministère du Conseil exécutif, Gouvernement du Québec, 1998), 12.
18. Ibid., 15.
19. Ibid., 22.
20. Secrétariat aux affaires autochtones, 'Signature d'une entente de principe entre le grand conseil des Cris et le Gouvernement du Québec', press release, 23 October 2001, available at: www.autochtones.gouv.qc.ca/centre_de_presse/communiques/2001/saa_com20011023.htm.
21. Grand Council of the Crees, *Report to the Council/Board on Federal Negotiations*, 23 July 2003.

RELEVANT WEBSITES

ABORIGINAL CANADA PORTAL: www.aboriginalcanada.gc.ca/

ASSEMBLY OF FIRST NATIONS: www.afn.ca

CBC NEWS ABORIGINAL PEOPLES: www.cbc.ca/news/aboriginals/

GRAND COUNCIL OF THE CREES: www.gcc.ca/

INDIAN AND NORTHERN AFFAIRS CANADA: www.ainc-inac.gc.ca/index-eng.asp

INDIGENOUS STUDIES PORTAL: http://iportal.usask.ca/

NUNAVIK PORTAL: www.nunavik.ca/en/index.html

SECRÉTARIAT AUX AFFAIRES AUTOCHTONES (QUEBEC GOVERNMENT): www.saa.gouv.qc.ca/index_en.asp

TREATIES AND LAND CLAIM AGREEMENTS IN CANADA: www.ainc-inac.gc.ca/al/index-eng.asp

SELECT BIBLIOGRAPHY

Alfred, Taiaike. *Wasáse: Indigenous Pathways of Action and Freedom*. Peterborough, Ont.: Broadview Press, 2005.

Beaulieu, Alain. *Les Autochtones du Québec: des premières alliances aux revendications contemporaines*. Montreal: Fides, 1997.

Bourassa, Robert. *La Baie James*. Montreal: Editions du Jour, 1973.

Cairns, Alan. *Citizens Plus*. Vancouver: University of British Columbia Press, 2000.

Desbiens, Caroline. 'Producing North and South: A Political Geography of Hydro Development in Québec'. *The Canadian Geographer* 48, 2 (2004): 101–18.

Dickason, Olive, and David T. McNab. *Canada's First Nations: A History of Founding Peoples from Earliest Times*, 4th edn. Toronto: Oxford University Press, 2008.

Gelinas, Claude. *Les Autochtones dans le Québec post-confédéral, 1867–1960*. Québec: Septentrion, 2008.

Grand Council of the Crees (of Québec). *Sovereign Injustice: Forcible Inclusion of the James Bay Crees and Cree Territory Into A Sovereign Québec*. Nemaska: Grand Council of the Crees, 1995.

Ivison, Doug, Paul Patton, and Will Sanders, eds. *Political Theory and the Rights of Indigenous Peoples*. Cambridge: Cambridge University Press, 2001.

Jenson, Jane, and Martin Papillon. 'Challenging the Citizenship Regime: James Bay Cree and Transnational Action'. *Politics and Society* 28, 2 (2000): 245–64.

Salée, Daniel. 'The Quebec State and Indigenous Peoples'. In Gagnon, Alain-G., ed., *Quebec: State and Society*, 3rd. Ed. Peterborough, Ont.: Broadview Press, 2004.

Secrétariat aux affaires autochtones. *Partnership, Development, Achievement*. Quebec: Ministère du Conseil exécutif, Gouvernement du Québec, 1998.

Simard, Jean-Jacques. *La réduction: l'autochtone inventé et les Amérindiens d'aujourd'hui*. Sillery, Que.: Septentrion, 2003.

Royal Commision on Aboriginal Peoples (RCAP). *Final Report*, 4 vols. Ottawa: Canada Communication Group Publishing, 1996.

York, Geoffrey, and Loreen Pindera. *People of the Pines, the Warriors and the Legacy of Oka*. Toronto: Little, Brown & Company, 1991.

CHAPTER 9

That Priest-Ridden Province? Politics and Religion in Quebec

Micheline Milot, Université du Québec à Montréal

— TIMELINE —

1608 Foundation of Quebec City by Samuel de Champlain. French *ancien régime* alliance between Catholic Church and French state takes root in Quebec City.

1763 Treaty of Paris. After British Conquest of 1759, France cedes New France to England. Catholic Church loses its status as established Church.

1774 First constitution, the Quebec Act, grants Catholics freedom of worship and abolishes requirement that Catholics take Test Oath to hold public office.

1791 Constitutional Act marks beginning of parliamentarianism and division of Canada into two provinces. Section 21 stipulates that ministers of religions, be they Catholic or Anglican, cannot be elected as members of Houses of Assembly in both Upper and Lower Canada.

1832 House of Assembly of Lower Canada adopts legislation to guarantee persons professing the Jewish religion equal rights.

1854 Legislation to abolish financial privileges of Anglican Church passed.

1866 Legislation on divorce passed, despite Catholic Church's resistance.

1867 Canada's Confederation. Constitution Act (also called the British North America Act)

adopted; no privileges granted to churches, except for protection of school administration for minority populations of Protestants and Catholics in Quebec and Ontario.

1869 Catholic Church refuses to bury Joseph Guibord in a Catholic cemetery because he refused to renounce his membership in Institut canadien, which promoted liberal ideas.

1875 Judiciary Committee of the Privy Council in London dismisses Church's appeal in the Guibord case and orders that his remains be interred in a Catholic cemetery.

1901 Superior Court of Quebec rules in Delpit-Côté case that the civil bond of marriage takes precedence over the religious bond.

1964 Ministère de l'Éducation du Québec created. The state takes charge of education, but Catholic and Protestant churches still have a major role to play within government structures.

1968 Federal Omnibus Bill decriminalizes homosexuality and authorizes civil marriage.

1975 Quebec Charter of Human Rights and Freedoms adopted by the National Assembly. As a supra-legislative instrument, this charter affords broad protection for equality and freedom of conscience and of religion.

1997 Quebec National Assembly obtains constitutional amendment to repeal special protection for religious school administrations.

1999 Task Force created on religion in school, and recommends complete laicization of school system.

2000 Law abolishes religious status of all public schools. Rights of churches within state structures also abolished.

2005 Federal Civil Marriage Act recognizes civil marriages between same-sex spouses.

There is strong opposition from some Catholic and Protestant groups.

2007 Consultation Commission on Accommodation Practices Related to Cultural Differences established to shed light on debate around accommodations granted on religious grounds in public sphere.

2008 Religious courses in public schools abolished in Quebec. A non-religious course on ethics and religious culture becomes mandatory for all students.

For a long time, Quebec was perceived as 'that priest-ridden province' in Canada, caught in the powerful grip of the Catholic clergy, which exerted its influence in all spheres of society and especially in political life. Was Quebec's situation exceptional compared with the United States or with Canada's anglophone provinces, which were predominantly Protestant? Was the Catholic Church more inclined than Protestant churches to impose religious norms on political power?

While the propensity of the Catholic Church to control politics in Quebec was undeniably strong, I submit that the situation was far more complex and nuanced. To this end, we will examine relations between Quebec's political, juridical, and religious institutions since the eighteenth century. At that time Quebec had to find ways of adapting to religious (albeit mainly Christian) diversity to facilitate political governance, as did the United States and Canada's anglophone provinces. All three of these societies went through a similar process; while they progressively recognized religious freedom and equality of worship (for all denominations), the state acted independently in relation to all churches. But Quebec is exceptional in North America for its unusually early adoption of explicit measures to safeguard tolerance.

Laicization describes the process by which the Quebec state asserted itself and recognized religious freedoms, a process that differs from *secularization*.

Here we are specifically addressing the process of laicization that has taken place since the British Conquest of New France in 1759. This date is important for our topic, because it marks the end of the *ancien régime* in New France, under which a strict Catholic Church–French state alliance prevailed. What the Conquest itself meant to the French Canadian population is a different topic, and is dealt with extensively in Chapter 2.

SECULARIZATION AND LAICIZATION

The place ascribed to religion in various societies has undergone major transformations over the past two centuries. On one level, everyday social and cultural norms around religion have changed, while on another level, public institutions and the state have made rules and protocols to both effect and prevent change. The term *secularization* has often been used in English to describe both levels of change. But in 1957, American sociologist Talcott Parsons proposed that in the United States the secularization of *values* or types of social behaviour be distinguished from the secularization of *institutional structures*. The notion of laicization allows us to define this second institutional level of change so that it is not confused with the first. Since this chapter specifically focuses on structures and institutional decisions, the term *laicization* will be used to more accurately identify the process being examined.

Secularization occurs when religion progressively loses its relevance as a social and cultural framework for defining moral values and social conduct. In a largely secular society, religion may still hold relevance for individuals and command social legitimacy, but it can no longer impose a single moral code prescribing norms for all members of that society. By contrast, laicization is a process by which the state deliberately distances itself from religion on an institutional level. Indeed, for the state to ensure that individuals and different religious convictions are treated equally (within prescribed legal limits), it must be free to formulate collective norms, and therefore no religion or set of convictions can be allowed to control the political order. Implicit to state independence is the dissociation of civil legislation from religious edicts. This dissociation demands that the state abstain from favouring or disfavouring one or several religions. In sum, I define laicization as a state-driven political and juridical adjustment process which, by virtue of guaranteeing equal justice for all, seeks to ensure freedom of conscience and religion under a state that is neutral with regard to different coexisting individual moral codes and beliefs about how to live a 'good life'[1] in society.[2]

In this chapter, we will examine several political and juridical decisions that illustrate how equality of worship and freedom of conscience and religion were established, both through a framework of political neutrality and through a de facto (never constitutionally explicit) separation of Church and state in Quebec. With this historical background in mind, we will examine how these principles were developed up to the beginning of the twenty-first century.

FROM TOLERANCE TO LAW: 1759–1867

The colony of New France, as noted earlier, was an extension of the *ancien régime* in France, in which the Catholic Church and French state had forged a firm alliance. This model could not survive the British Conquest in 1759 and the new socio-political situation generated by a henceforth linguistically, religiously, ethnically, and culturally mixed society. On a political level, post-Conquest French Canada was subject to British governance, which maintained close ties with the Church of England (Anglicanism). But the newly conquered territory was exceptional for its time in that its political conflicts did not lead to entrenched religious conflicts or to the specific repression of any religion. In this sense, the new Province of Quebec was an extraordinary society in an era when religions in colonized territories were being politically repressed. Its departure from contemporaneous European models of relations between Church and state ushered in a novel approach to political regulation. These parameters for laicization were sketched out gradually in Quebec, through a process that, in many ways, was unfolding ahead of its time.

Freedom of Worship

With the Royal Proclamation of 1763 (establishing a basis of government in the territories formally ceded by France to Britain in the Treaty of Paris), Catholic French Canadians became British subjects and as such their religious freedom was eventually protected under British law. This fundamental freedom, which some in Europe, torn apart by hundreds of years of religious wars, had long sought to establish, was entrenched in two constitutional acts adopted in the eighteenth century: the Quebec Act of 1774 and the Constitutional Act of 1791. The Catholic Church, which had been highly intolerant of Huguenots and Jews under the French regime, was protected by the rights enshrined in these constitutional documents.[3] The British government even granted the Catholic Church the right to collect its traditional tithes, thereby ensuring the clergy's subsistence and facilitating freedom of worship. Thus, the first cornerstones of laicization were set in place in the New World. Freedom of worship would no longer depend on the arbitrary benevolence of those controlling political governance. In other British territories and even in the United States, Catholics would not enjoy similar freedom for several decades.

This was a context of political domination, after a military conquest and at a time when religious pluralism was not yet widely tolerated. In the years following the Conquest, as a prerequisite to holding public office, the new British regime required Canadian Catholics to swear the Test Oath, in which they renounced allegiance to the Pope (along with the doctrine of transubstantiation and the cult of the Virgin). Over a decade after the Test Oath was proclaimed, the Quebec Act expressly abolished this practice. Under the Act, only a simple Oath of allegiance to the King was required for any British subject in Quebec to hold public office.

In the United States, the Religious Test was abolished when the First Amendment of the American Constitution was introduced, but only within the federation, which meant that the Test continued to be mandatory in some states, such as Massachusetts, until 1821. The American approach to this tended to be steeped in ethical or philosophical justifications, like those of Thomas Jefferson, who held up tolerance as a virtuous and positive value that strengthened the social cement of the nation.[4] By contrast, in Quebec, the British crown's pragmatic political and economic concerns far outweighed its need for philosophical debate. Given that the former French colony occupied a strategic territorial position in North America and that maintaining the loyalty of its Catholic majority was crucial to ensuring the conquered territory's stability, British governors proceeded with care in matters of religion. Recognizing religious freedom as a right had the immediate advantage of currying favour with the population, but it also established and important bench mark and structured Quebec's development for years to come.

Equality of Worship

Abolishing the Test Oath was not just a religious matter, but also a question of juridical equality for the Crown's subjects. It marked a breakthrough in the progress of tolerance and began the process of ending deeply ingrained practices of discrimination. So while it was true that in practice British colonists could more easily attain high-ranking positions in the years that followed the Test Oath's abolition, this inequality was not so much a consequence of religious affiliation as it was the product of political domination.

At this point, equality of worship was still incomplete, since the state had reserved the right to support and maintain the Protestant clergy under section 36 of the Constitutional Act of 1791, an economic advantage that the Catholic Church did not enjoy. The Catholic Church had lost its civil recognition (London had prohibited any papal jurisdiction in the territories of the British Empire), but still had clear autonomy in internal ecclesial management and the right to collect its 'accustomed Dues and Rights' (section 35) from its parishioners.

Gradually, equality of worship was written into nineteenth-century law. In 1832, the House of Assembly of Lower Canada passed 'An Act to declare persons professing the Jewish religion entitled to all the rights and privileges of the other subjects of His Majesty in this Province'. The Union Act of 1840, joining Upper and Lower Canada, reiterated colonial state protections for freedom of worship. Under the Union Act, religions were to be treated without discrimination and Lower Canada's Legislative Council and the House of Assembly were mandated accordingly:

> [No] Bill or Bills shall be passed containing any Provisions which shall in any Manner relate to or affect the Enjoyment or Exercise of any Form or Mode of Religious Worship, or shall impose or create any Penalties, Burdens, Disabilities, or Disqualifications in respect of the same. . . (Art. 42)

In 1851, the legislature of the United Province of Canada passed the Freedom of Worship Act, which more explicitly recognized equality of worship. Thus, despite the influence of Catholicism and the Church of England (the two majority faiths in Lower and Upper Canada respectively), no political rights or official status was afforded to either as a state religion.

Separating Powers

In Quebec, as in the rest of Canada, no constitutional law proclaimed the separation of Church and state. However, the separation of powers was distinctly implied as a concept in Quebec's constitutions and legislation. In the Quebec Act of 1774, there was no mention of any established Church. Nonetheless, section 6 provided for the 'accustomed Dues and Rights, for the Encouragement of the Protestant Religion, and for the Maintenance and Support of a Protestant

Clergy'. In reality, it was the Anglican Church (the Church of England) that benefited from this constitutional privilege. As a province of England (whose official church was ruled by the King), Quebec was being governed with an apparent bias. Without a clear separation between Church and state, the government lost credibility as an impartial entity capable of providing equal protection to persons of all faiths. For this reason, other Protestant denominations rallied to demand the abolition of Anglican economic privilege, supported by the Anglican Church itself. Consequently, the government adopted legislation in 1854 to eliminate the Anglican Church's economic privileges, a move that more clearly defined Church–state power relations.

The Constitutional Act of 1791 marked the beginning of a vital political phase as it introduced a parliamentary political system, based on the British model, in a colony still in the embryonic stages of becoming a democratic regime (which would take several decades to grow to maturity). Section 21 of the Act, regarding representation by religious leaders in Canada's Houses of Assembly, stipulated

> That no Person shall be capable of being elected a Member to serve in either of the said Assemblies, or of sitting or voting therein, who shall be a Member of either of the said Legislative Councils to be established as aforesaid in the said two Provinces . . . who shall be a Minister of the Church of England, or a Minister, Priest, Ecclesiastic, or Teacher, either according to the Rites of the Church of Rome, or under any other Form or Profession of religious Faith or Worship.

Two provisions in this section of the Constitutional Act significantly influenced the development of relations between the churches and the state. First, the fact that no privileges were conceded to ministers of the Anglican Church in elective politics effectively separated the institutional role of politics from that of religion—a major break with the British model. Secondly, the disqualification from holding public office affected Anglican clergy as much as it did Roman Catholic clergy, thereby instituting equality between churches in politics. It is also worth noting that none of the constitutions adopted in the eighteenth century made any specific explicit reference to God or contained any

express provisions regarding the establishment or dis-establishment of religion. Here we could say that there was a tacit or a de facto separation of powers.

Political Neutrality in Religious Matters

All of the New World societies were faced with the daunting challenge of ensuring that the sparks of dogmatic rivalries from Europe did not reignite in North America. There was a clear impetus to start afresh in the New World and construct politics on new foundations. But the scope of choices available for this construction was limited.

> Either the State would be constructed by borrowing its legitimacy from a source other than the insurmountable multiplicity of interpretations of the Sacred Text, or from one of these [interpretations]—a particular denomination, an interpretation that is controversial but provisionally dominant in terms of power relations—would seize control of [the state]. [5]

Indeed, the state did not arbitrate in disputes between the existing dogmas and clearly did not rely on any of them to legitimize its authority. Instead, state legitimacy was largely determined by its willingness to act as a neutral authority in Quebec.

The first Neutrality Act was passed in the United States in 1794. This legislation clearly distinguished between the neutrality of the state and the freedom of its citizens, who were not required to observe moral neutrality. It also provided an innovative perspective in the Western world, although it did not prevent religion from holding considerable sway in American society. In Canada, this neutrality was established as much by what was contained in constitutions as by what was not, for it was through the state's constitutional recognition of religious freedom and equality of worship that various political bodies established a degree of neutrality. But it was also because the successive constitutions made no explicit reference to an official state religion that the government of Quebec was able to build credibility as a neutral entity. The abolition of the Anglican Church's financial privileges that began in 1854 was also a step towards political neutrality in state relations with different churches.

For years of course, government neutrality was tested by French Canada's Catholic clergy, a formidable pressure group in its drive to influence politicians. Through their near-monopoly over essential local services—notably, schools, hospitals, and charities—Catholic religious communities played a central role in shaping the moral and cultural consciousness of Quebec's demographic majority. But government policy and juridical rulings clearly diverged from the Catholic Church's agenda, despite its best efforts to influence political decisions and preach moral prescriptions.

FROM THE CANADIAN FEDERATION TO QUEBEC'S QUIET REVOLUTION

The Constitution adopted at the time of Confederation, on 1 July 1867, more clearly articulated the emerging tradition of religious tolerance and political neutrality and marked the birth of modern Canada. Four provinces were created by Confederation: Quebec, Ontario (these two having been the former Province of Canada), New Brunswick, and Nova Scotia. The British North America Act of 1867 (BNA Act) distributed powers in two tiers: a central federal authority and provincial authorities. The provinces acquired jurisdiction over social affairs, including education, civil law, and public health. The BNA Act, much like the constitutions that preceded it, did not provide a complete framework for relations between churches and the state. It did not mention the separation of Church and state, or laicism (or secularism), much less a union of Church and state, and made no reference to God. The 1867 Constitution Act relied *implicitly* on the principles of neutrality and the separation of the churches and the state. Nonetheless, it made provision for special protections that applied exclusively to the administration of Catholic and Protestant schools in minority contexts, both in Quebec and Ontario (this protection has not applied in Quebec since 1997). No financial support was guaranteed to Quebec's churches, the state did not promise to collect any taxes for redistribution to the religious communities, and there

was no express provision regarding freedom of religion. However, prior legislation on freedom of worship was recognized under section 129 of the BNA Act. Measures prescribed by the Union Act of 1840 regarding worship and religious groups therefore remained in effect for each province.

Blurred Boundaries between Politics and Religion

During the second half of the nineteenth century, French Canadians in Quebec expressed a particularly strong desire to ensure their survival as a cultural minority or 'nation' in the Americas. French-Canadian national and clerical interests converged at a common crossroads:

> *Political* conservatism would strive to 'conserve' [French Canadian] nationality, language, laws, social mores and religion. *Religious* conservatism would strive to 'conserve' an almost identical nationality and, most importantly, it would defend, in keeping with its spiritual and temporal interests, first religion, then language, laws and social mores.[6]

The Catholic Church's social 'works' (like those of several other faiths in Quebec) were widespread, often highly efficient and a source of development, establishing its own schools, hospitals, farming cooperatives, journalism, and farmers' unions, effectively relegating the state to an auxiliary role in the areas of education, health, and social welfare. Things might have been different had the Quebec government taken charge of education and health institutions when the BNA Act gave it those powers. Later attempts at state intervention were rebuffed by the Church, which had invested extensively in these areas. Such was not the case in the English-speaking Protestant and Jewish communities of the same era in Quebec, where the institutional network for anglophones had been laicized for years. To create viable institutions within the province's faith-based social framework, anglophones had to maintain a peaceable coexistence with other faiths. Moreover, the (Protestant) anglophone bourgeoisie had established its power in business by keeping it very clearly separate from religion, an attitude that the Catholic Church hardly encouraged.

Civil Law Puts a Damper on the Catholic Church's Social Control

Not surprisingly, the Catholic Church's attempts to orient social and political norms often ran afoul of the juridical interpretation of civil law. Among the many events illustrating a distancing of powers between Church and state was the famous Guibord affair, described in detail in the Snapshot box. In 1869, the Bishop of Montreal, Msgr Bourget, refused to grant a Catholic cemetery burial to Joseph Guibord, who had worked for a group of liberal thinkers. The Bishop was dealt a resounding blow when the Privy Council in London ruled against him on the matter. In its precedent-setting 1875 judgement, it deemed that

SNAPSHOT

The Guibord Affair (1869–1875)

The Guibord Affair was a landmark event in Quebec's religious history. Joseph Guibord was a printer and a member of the Institut canadien in Montreal. Upon his death, the Ultramontane Catholic Bishop of Montreal, Msgr Bourget, refused to bury him in a Catholic cemetery, sparking a protracted series of sensational court battles. Repeated appeals by his widow culminated in a trial before the highest court in the land, the Judicial Committee of the Privy Council in London (there was no Supreme Court of Canada at that time).

Guibord's legal case held special significance because it took place at a time when the conservative forces of the Catholic clergy were virulently opposing liberal thinking. Thus, a simple dispute over refusing to bury a man created widespread controversy over both the dissemination of modern, liberal ideas in a very conservative society and the separation of Church and state. But to fully grasp what motivated the Bishop's decision and the significance of the legal confrontation it provoked, some background is required on the Institut canadien and Ultramontanism.

Institut canadien

The Institut canadien opened its doors on 17 December 1844 in Montreal. It was devoted to the free flow of ideas and was a gathering place for intellectuals, artisans, business employees, lawyers, and doctors who subscribed to the ever-expanding realm of liberal thinking in Quebec. Public lectures and intellectual debates were held there, it had a well-stocked library, and foreign newspapers were available to members and subscribers. Thanks to these resources, the men of the Institut canadien could follow events in the European revolutions including the notable social unrest fomenting in France, or learn about the advent of democracy in several countries. Some of the more radical members rejected the Church's interference with freedom of thought and were even in favour of Quebec's annexation to the United States. It was not long before their overt liberal and annexationist ponderings brought the Conservative Party and the Catholic clergy to unite against them.

Ultramontanism

Ultramontanism was a Catholic doctrine that made its first appearance during the French Revolution and took root in Quebec between 1820 and 1830. Its followers categorically rejected any compromise between Catholicism and the modern thinking of liberalism. They even contended that religious society should entirely dominate civil society and that the state should submit to the Church. Of course, the Ultramontanes firmly believed that the Pope's authority was unassailable and his judgement infallible. Many of the initiatives launched by radical Ultramontanes failed, but the Ultramontane school of thought would continue to influence Quebec in various ways until the mid-twentieth century.

Msgr Ignace Bourget, the Bishop of the diocese of Montreal from 1840 to 1876, was the most emblematic figure of Quebec Ultramontanism. He believed that the existence of the Institut canadien and the new ideas that it promoted challenged the 'absolute' authority of the Church and represented a threat to the faith of French Canadians. In fact, the Institut and the Church competed for the public sympathy. Many Institut canadien members belonged to the Parti rouge, a political party that was promoting democracy and aiming to secure a dominant political influence over French-Canadian society. Meanwhile, under Msgr Bourget's leadership, the clergy's moral control over French Canadians was increasing substantially. It seemed that a confrontation was inevitable.

The Conflict

Msgr Bourget fought the Institut with threats, in his sermons at various churches, and even through edicts obtained from the Vatican. In 1858, the Bishop succeeded in convincing 138 members to leave the Institut canadien. Rome condemned the Institut in 1868, placing its Yearbook, printed by Joseph Guibord, on the Vatican's List of Forbidden Books for its faithful. Mgr Bourget delivered the following edict:

> He who persists in the desire to remain in the said Institut or to read or merely possess the above-mentioned yearbook without being so authorized by the Church deprives himself of the sacraments at the hour of his death.[7]

Bourget was referring to the Catholic of rite of 'extreme unction', in which sacraments are administered to the gravely ill before death to absolve the faithful of all their sins. Prohibiting this essential sacrament to Catholics and thereby jeopardizing the peace of their immortal souls was a very serious measure for the Bishop to take, especially at this time in history.

In July 1869, with the support of Rome, the Bishop proclaimed an ordinance against the Institut canadien, effectively discrediting it in the eyes of all Catholics. Four months later, on 18 November 1869, Joseph Guibord had a stroke and later died. But while Guibord was a member of the Institut, he was also a devout Catholic and not anti-clerical. Abbé Andreé-Marie Garin, a missionary in northwestern Canada had even entrusted Guibord with printing the catechism in an Aboriginal language in 1854. But Guibord

refused to renounce his membership in the Institut. For this reason, the Church denied him its extreme unction, which meant that his body could not receive Catholic religious rites, including burial in a Catholic cemetery. This would be the last time Msgr Bourget would assail the Institut canadien.

The Legal Saga Around the Refusal of Burial

Joseph Guibord's widow, Henriette Brown, and some of his friends subsequently launched legal proceedings against the Bishop and the Fabrique de la Paroise de Notre-Dame de Montreal (the organization that should have been responsible for Guibord's funeral) to appeal the refusal to bury Guibord. The case was heard before the courts of Quebec, and was appealed as far as the Judicial Committee of the Privy Council in London. Years passed as the case went through the rigours of the legal system, while Guibord's remains lay in a Protestant cemetery.

On 21 November 1874, five years after Joseph Guibord had died , the Judicial Committee ruled that the Catholic Church should not only bury Guibord in consecrated ground at a proper and convenient time,[8] but that it also defray all legal costs. When the belated burial was first attempted on 2 September 1875 at Côte-des-Neiges Catholic cemetery in Montreal, a crowd of Catholics prevented Guibord's remains from being interred. The undertakers involved in the second attempt came prepared with reinforcements and on 16 November 1875, with the protection of 1,255 soldiers, a full six years after he had passed away, Joseph Guibord's remains were laid to rest. His grave was said to be covered with protective layer of cement in order to prevent any desecration. Still determined to register the Church's disapproval, Msgr Bourget made use of the very last power at his disposal, deconsecrating the site of interment as prohibited to Catholics and separate from the rest of the cemetery.

Although the Church held that Catholic burials fell entirely under its jurisdiction, this event established the precedence of civil law over the laws of the Church—a major setback for a religious institution accustomed to controlling every aspect of its parishioners' lives, from cradle to grave.

cemeteries fell under civil jurisdiction, even though churches held the right to keep civil status registries on behalf of the state. Other incidents clearly marked the divide between the aspirations of ecclesial powers and their denial by the civil state. In 1871, the Church tried influencing conservative members of the legislature directly, lobbying them to promote the 'Catholic program' and commit to defending Catholic morals. The Church canvassed candidates in anticipation of the 1871 provincial election, and of the very few who signed on to the Catholic program, only one managed to get elected.

In 1875, the government of Quebec took action to disentangle the Church from state affairs. In an amendment to the Quebec Election Act, it prohibited 'undue influence' (section 258) to eradicate intimidation, threats, or any other means of coercion being used by priests (the main targets of the legislation) to influence how their congregations would vote. In 1900, the moral ground held by Quebec's Bishops shifted yet again when two Catholics were married by a Protestant pastor in the Delpit-Côté affair. The Catholic Church legally invalidated the marriage, but some months later, the case was heard before the Superior Court of Quebec, where Judge J.S. Archibald stunned and overruled the Bishopric. His ruling determined that marriage was governed primarily by *civil law* in Quebec. A hierarchy of jurisdiction over the religious aspect of marriage was thereby established by the court: the *form* of a ceremony would no longer determine the validity of a marriage contract. Notably, the government of Quebec did not invalidate the civil status of religious unions or introduce mandatory civil marriage, as was the case in France. Indeed, in Quebec civil marriage was not instituted as such until 1969, meaning that until that time, a religious ceremony was the only legal means of getting married.

FROM THE QUIET REVOLUTION TO THE BEGINNING OF THE TWENTY-FIRST CENTURY

Quiet Revolution is an expression that may require some clarification outside of Quebec. In fact, the

'revolution' that began in 1960 did not involve the violent overthrow of a political regime, but a modernization of Quebec's institutions and the role of the state. After 15 years of an unusually authoritarian administration under Premier Maurice Duplessis, whose close connections with the Catholic Church greatly emboldened his style of governance, the province was breaking free of its political and religious constraints. Economic prosperity and ideas of social reform had already been remodelling institutional structures for some time in most Western societies. But in Quebec, reform happened so quickly that it seemed the province had made a radical, revolutionary break with past social and political patterns.

Following the Second World War, the modernization, industrialization, and urbanization of Quebec proceeded at a pace so accelerated that traditional frameworks founded on family and parish could not keep up with the new demands of modern living. Churches and congregations found it increasingly difficult to secure enough personnel and materials for the schools, hospitals, and charities that they ran. The institutions that they had been managing for over a century were quickly laicizing, a trend that soon came to be perceived as being an unavoidable social necessity. But the laicization of institutions did not pit believers against non-believers, nor liberal thinkers against Catholics. In fact, most of the writing and discussions about, and initiatives in favour of laicization came from Catholic groups and even from within religious ranks, and it was these activities that led them to play an important role in Church renewal. In 1958, the Ministry of Youth and Social Welfare was created, in 1961 the Hospital Insurance Act entered into force, and in 1964 the Ministry of Education was founded. From 1964 forward, a new middle class began to administer large institutions, taking over from clerics and members of religious orders, who were seeing their recruitment numbers plummet.

Schools: The Church's Bastion of Resistance

In Quebec the first real public debate on the roles of Church and state in education dates back to 1963, when the Royal Commission of Inquiry on Education in the

Province of Quebec (called the Parent Commission) took place. Following the Commission's recommendations, Bill 60, or An Act to Establish the Ministry of Education and the Superior Council of Education, was passed in 1964, bringing education under the provincial government's jurisdiction. Successive Catholic bishops had staunchly opposed the creation of this ministry since the end of the nineteenth century, fearing that if the state took control of education 'majority rule' would lead to a rapid laicization of the school system. The Assembly of Quebec Catholic Bishops lobbied the government to change Bill 60 so that the Church would be ensured the right to continue adminstering its own schools. The resulting legislation, adopted six months later, was a compromise between state prerogatives and the interests of the Catholic Church: the Ministry of Education would oversee the administration of the school system, but the system would remain bi-denominational—Catholic and Protestant. The Catholic and Protestant churches were thereby seated in the upper echelons of the Ministry of Education and the Superior Council of Education, where they both served.

The discriminatory aspects of this faith-based arrangement soon came to light: only two faiths had been given the right to a school system, and that system was out of step with the degree of secularization in Quebec society. Meanwhile, the groundwork laid for policy orientations during the Quiet Revolution was already shaping areas such as cultural diversity, social integration, and equality among citizens. In 1999 widespread public debate over the place of religion in public schools was triggered by a report from the Task Force on the Place of Religion in Schools entitled *Religion in Secular Schools: A New Perspective for Quebec*. In its report, the Task Force recommended that the government laicize the entire public school system based on two considerations: the importance of recognizing fundamental human rights and the need to adapt to the cultural and religious secularism and pluralism of Quebec's evolving social landscape. On 1 July 2000, all public schools in Quebec were laicized and by 2008 religious instruction in Catholic and Protestant doctrine *was abolished*. The government introduced a mandatory new course on ethics and religious culture for all students to promote their understanding of various religious and secular world views while encouraging dialogue.

The Importance of Fundamental Human Rights

In the last quarter of the twentieth century, recognition for fundamental rights and freedoms progressed significantly owing to the adoption of the Quebec Charter of Human Rights and Freedoms in 1975 (and the Canadian Charter of Rights and Freedoms in 1982). To a large extent, the moral foundations of a society shaped by longstanding Christian values were being rebuilt. Indeed, the value system expressed in the Charter became the touchstone of good citizenship. With the adoption of the Charter, equality and freedom of conscience and religion acquired supralegislative status: no laws or public regulations could violate these principles.

Today, Quebec's justice system, like that of all contemporary democratic societies, is theoretically free of any expressly discriminatory provisions, and does not favour any religious group. But in practice, religions and beliefs are treated differently and unequally because laws are uniformly enforced and designed for all citizens, regardless of the specific needs of particular groups. A rule or a universal law which applies uniformly to all members of society can have unintended discriminatory effects when, for example, restrictions affect the practice of one faith but not that of another. These are cases of 'indirect discrimination'.

In Canada and in Quebec, a legal obligation exists to correct indirect discrimination: reasonable accommodation.

> In certain cases, the obligation of accommodation forces the State, persons or private businesses to change norms, practices or legitimate and justified practices or policies, which apply to all without distinction, to take into account the particular needs of some (especially ethnic or religious) minorities.[9]

Reasonable accommodation is an instrument that promotes peaceable social negotiation and assists institutions and employers, encouraging them to adapt to social diversity.

This type of accommodation is not new and has established itself as a tradition in North America. However, in Canada and Quebec accommodation is a *legal obligation*—the equivalent of a conferred right to equality. Its underlying principle: Freedom of religion presupposes the right to freely practise a religion. But this practice may be infringed upon or restricted by general norms set in place for the majority. (A clear example of this is the general restriction on carrying weapons infringing on the Sikh practice of wearing a kirpan, a small knife.[10]) According to this juridical perspective, it is not enough to create theoretical rights; the state and its public institutions must ensure that reasonable accommodation is expressed in concrete policies and practices so that rights may be respected.

Debates on the Expression of Religious Affiliation in the Public Sphere

Since 1975, Quebec's institution of fundamental human rights has affected many aspects of public life and presented some challenging problems. Most of these problems have tended to involve established individual freedoms rather than the rights conceded to churches. Indeed, although Quebec society has laicized considerably, some Quebecers would prefer to prohibit any display of religious affiliation in public institutions. There are also those who object to the notion of over-accommodation with regard to the wearing of religious symbols (such as the Muslim hijab or the Sikh kirpan), adapting work schedules to religious practices, or providing spaces at work or school for prayer. And there are those Quebecers who fear that the expression of identities and values that differ from those of the Christian majority will harm Quebec's heritage of identity. Ironically, in practice, most requests for 'reasonable accommodations' on religious grounds come from Christians rather than from religions that are newer to Quebec.[11] Nonetheless, identity and accommodation have established themselves as a highly charged political issues, especially among many 'old-stock' Quebecers of French-Canadian origin, who see themselves as a majority in Quebec but a minority within Canada.

THE FRENCH MODEL VS. THE TRADITION OF ACCEPTING DIVERSITY

In 2007, the government of Quebec struck a Consultation Commission to compare the merits of two opposing models for accommodating religious diversity.[12] The first is the model of laicism adopted in France, which prohibits wearing any religious symbol in public institutions and makes no religious accommodation in the workplace. Its goal is to clearly demarcate the separation between Church and state. The second is the Quebec tradition of religious plurality, in which religious freedom necessarily includes the freedom to express religious affiliation. The second model, favoured by the Consultation Commission, recognizes the importance of the neutrality of the state and its institutions along with the equally important right to freedom of conscience and religion, which allows citizens to express their religious convictions, provided that this expression does not infringe upon the freedoms of others. In this second model, it is institutions and not individuals who are laicized. Expressed in broader terms, the second model emphasizes individual competency and the quality of the goods or services those individuals provide to society rather than their religious identity. The impassioned intensity of this debate, which is also taking place in other pluralistic and sometime highly secularized societies, clearly illustrates that the issue of religious freedoms remains a sensitive subject in Quebec.

CONCLUSION

In Quebec, relations between religious tradition and the state have been defined more by praxis than by Constitution. Indeed, today most modern democracies are founded on principles that dissociate the state from any specific religion or religious norms. From their inception, New World societies have grappled with issues around religious plurality, but mainly with regard to Christian plurality. These societies have become increasingly diversified as their citizens' ever-expanding world views have shaped institutions,

Louis-Antoine Dessaulles (1818–1895)

Louis-Antoine Dessaulles, reproduction of an 1861 original print

Studio Notman & Son, Montréal / Bibliothèques et Archives nationales du Québec

Louis-Antoine Dessaulles was one of the many citizens of Lower Canada who significantly contributed to advancing modern ideas during the nineteenth century. Born in Saint-Hyacinthe on 31 January 1818, this intellectual was interested in politics, but never held a prominent political position. It was as an activist that he distinguished himself and epitomized the political vibrancy of the era in which he lived. Indeed, tensions ran high during the second half of the nineteenth century as the free flow of liberal ideas made the conservative Catholic Church fear the worst for the future of the Roman Catholic religion and the French-Canadian nation.

Inspired by the French writer Lammenais's later work, Dessaulles was a polemicist renowned for his liberal spirit and anticlericalism. A member of the Institut canadien, he served as its president three times between 1862 and 1867 and gave a number of lectures there. At its inception, the Institut accepted only Catholics into its membership, but under Dessaulles' presidency, men of other religious affiliations and atheists were also accepted. The Ultramontane Bishop of Montreal, Msgr Ignace Bourget, vehemently opposed the 'religious mixing' within the Institut, which he perceived as a threat to the faith and the Catholic national identity of French Canadians.

Throughout his life, Dessaulles stressed the importance of clearly separating Church and state and called for laic, republican schools. In Quebec, as in Europe and the Americas, modern ideas were circulating as never before. The Vatican reacted by publishing Pope Pius IX's *Quanta cura*, an encyclical letter, and the Syllabus in 1864, denouncing the key 'errors' of modernity, including a notable condemnation of the separation of Church and state.

Dessaulles's life story had its contradictions. For instance, although he was a staunch defender of 'modern' freedoms, he owned a seigneury and thereby perpetuated the old seigneurial regime. He also extolled the virtues of universalism, human solidarity, and freedom of expression in his famous speech on tolerance in 1868. In fact, Dessaulles, who never denied that he was Catholic, deliberately included references to the Bible in this speech. Like a preacher, his discourse was based on the principles of Christian tolerance and charity. He hoped to teach religious authorities a lesson by using scripture to prove that religion and religious freedom were not incompatible. While he fought Ultramontanism and was openly anticlerical, he was not antireligious. After Dessaulles's speech on tolerance was published in the Yearbook of the Institut canadien in 1868, Msgr Bourget demanded that Rome place the publication in the Index of Forbidden Books and condemn the Institut. The next year, when Msgr Bourget refused Joseph Guibord a Catholic burial, Dessaulles ardently defended the civil burial rights and was a witness in the legal proceedings brought by Guibord's widow.

Dessaulles also belonged to the Parti rouge, a radical liberal party, and favoured annexing Quebec to the United States. To him, the American republic represented freedom from British royalty and was a truly democratic society in which Church and state were separated and the yoke of the Catholic Church carried no weight. Dessaulles published *Six lectures sur l'annexation du Canada aux États-Unis* in 1851. In his discussion of democracy, freedom, and religion he asserted that:

It was from the evangelical principle that all men are born equal that civilization drew a [fundamental] conclusion (a conclusion rejected by Ultramontanism in its stubborn interest and hunger for power), namely: that each individual possesses moral independence which results in his individual sovereignty as a member of society . . . . But man's individual and native sovereignty, inherent to his nature as a thinking being, *necessarily* flow from the sacred dogma of the *sovereignty of the people*, a dogma uncontested on the free soil of the American continent, even by the Catholic Hierarchy.

There is no doubt that Louis-Antoine Dessaulles contributed to laicization that was already underway

in Lower Canada. His battles, seen in the context of his era, presaged the current battles we see between people of faith and atheists, and battles for 'laic democracy' (although this term was not used in Dessaulles's time). At the end of his speech on tolerance in 1868, Dessaulles categorically condemned intolerance and the submission of the mind as the 'enemies' of democracy.

After some time spent in exile in Belgium and France, Louis-Antoine Dessaulles died in Paris in 1895.

laws, and public policies. Nonetheless, they naturally still bear the imprint of their Christian heritage, and in Quebec some citizens would like these values to take precedence in areas like societal development and the determination of individual rights. This view has fuelled a plethora of 'rights' debates concerning abortion, gay and lesbian couples, and the wearing of religious symbols in public. Clearly, authorities in Quebec and North America are better equipped than they ever have been to tackle these controversies head on. Backed by the considerable gains of laicization, they should be implementing an ethic of recognition for the diversity of moral codes and religious beliefs that exist in our society.

Questions for Consideration

1. What were the defining characteristics of the process of laicization undertaken by the state in Quebec?

2. Has the Catholic Church really been an influential power in all of the social and political aspects of life in Quebec?

3. How can we differentiate between processes of secularization and processes of laicization in democratic societies?

Notes

1. John Rawls, *A Theory of Justice* (Cambridge: Harvard University Press, 1832).

2. Micheline Milot, *Laïcité dans le Nouveau Monde. Le cas du Québec* (Turnhout, Belgium: Brepols Publishers, 2002), 34.

3. French Protestants who were members of the Reformed or Calvinistic communion of France in the sixteenth and seventeenth centuries. J.-L. Lalonde, *Des loups dans la bergerie : les protestants de langue française au Québec, 1534–2000* (Montreal: Fides, 2002).

4. D. Lacorne, 'Tolérance, républicanisme et laïcité. L'exemple américain', in P. Statius and P. Bachelard, eds., *Actualité de l'école républicaine?* (Caen: Centre régional de documentation pédagogique, 1998), 85–93.

5. Guy Haarscher, *La laïcité* (Paris: PUF, 1996), 94.

6. Yvan Lamonde, *Histoire sociale des idées au Québec (1760–1896)* (Montreal: Fides, 2000), 319.

7. Available at www.biographi.ca/009004-119.01-e. php?&id_nbr=4470&&PHPSESSID=6e8mbcgk3u0b2c vpnd6eqebf65, accessed 10 April 2009.

8. Lord Selborne, *Affaire Guibord: jugement des Lords du Comité Judiciaire du Conseil Privé sur l'Appel de Dame Henriette Brown vx. Les Curé et Marguillers de l'œuvre et de la Fabrique de Notre-Dame, au Canada*, 21 November 1874, 10.

9. José Woehrling, 'L'obligation d'accommodement raisonnable et l'adaptation de la société à la diversité religieuse', *Revue de droit de McGill/McGill Law Journal* 43 (1998): 328, our translation.

10. The case of Gurbaj Singh Multani is a classic illustration of general restrictions infringing on religious practice. This case began in Montreal in 2001 and wound up before the Supreme Court of Canada in 2006. See Chapter 19 for discussion of this case.

11. Commission des droits de la personne et des droits de la jeunesse, *Les plaintes de discrimination fondée sur la religion*

portées devant la Commission des droits de la personne et des droits de la jeunesse Montreal: CDPDJ, 2006.

12. The Consultation Commission on Accommodation Practices Related to Cultural Differences, in 2007, Co-Chaired by Gérard Bouchard and Charles Taylor. Their final report was entitled, *Building for the Future: A Time for Reconciliation*, 2008.

RELEVANT WEBSITES

THE CONSULTATION COMMISSION ON ACCOMMODATION PRACTICES RELATED TO CULTURAL DIFFERENCES, 2008: www.accommodements.qc.ca/index-en.html

ETHICS AND RELIGIOUS CULTURE PROGRAM, MINISTÈRE DE L'ÉDUCATION DU QUÉBEC: www7.mels.gouv.qc.ca/DC/ECR/index_en.php

RELIGION IN SECULAR SCHOOLS: A NEW PERSPECTIVE FOR QUÉBEC (1999): www.mels.gouv.qc.ca/REFORME/religion/html-ang/ang/index.htm

COMMISSION DES DROITS DE LA PERSONNE ET DE DROITS DE LA JEUNESSE, QUÉBEC: www.cdpdj.qc.ca/

SELECT BIBLIOGRAPHY

Bramadat, Paul, and David Seljak, eds. *Christianity and Ethnicity in Canada*. Toronto: University of Toronto Press, 2008.

Carignan, P. *De la Charte québécoise des droits et libertés : origine, nature et défis*. Montreal: Éditions Thémis, 1989.

Eid, Nadia F. *Le clergé et le pouvoir politique, une analyse de l'idéologie ultramontaine au milieu du XIXe siècle*. Montreal: Hurtubise HMH, 1978.

Hamelin, Jean, and Nicole Gagnon. *Histoire du catholicisme québécois. Le XXe siècle, t. I: 1898–1940*. Montreal: Boréal Express, 1984.

Lamonde, Yvan. *Histoire sociale des idées au Québec (1760–1896)*. Montreal: Fides, 2000.

Lemieux, L. *Histoire du catholicisme québécois. Les XVIIIe et XIXe siècles, t. I: Les années difficiles (1760–1839)*. Montreal: Boréal, 1989.

Lyon, David, and Marguerite Van Die, eds. *Rethinking Church, State and Modernity—Canada between Europe and America*. Toronto: University of Toronto Press, 2000.

Milot, Micheline. *Laïcité dans le Nouveau Monde. Le cas du Québec*. Coll. Bibliothèque de l'École des Hautes Études, Turnhout, Belgium: Brepols Publishers, 2002.

Rocher, Marie-Claude, and Catherine Drouin. *Un autre son de cloche. Les protestants francophones au Québec*. Quebec: CEFAN, 1993.

Trudel, Marcel. *Mythes et réalités dans l'histoire du Québec*. Montreal: Hurtubise HMH, 2001.

Voisine, Nive. *Histoire de l'Église catholique au Québec (1608–1970)*. Commission d'étude sur les laïcs et l'Église. Première annexe au rapport. Montreal: Fides, 1971.

CHAPTER 10

Quebec's Culture War:
Two Conceptions of Quebec Identity

Jocelyn Maclure, Université Laval

INTRODUCTION

Quebec society is not torn by public morality issues such as abortion, birth control, same-sex marriage, crime and punishment, and gun control. The pro-choice position on abortion is widely accepted, birth control is promoted and available, same-sex couples can marry, tough talk on 'law and order' does not fly and virtually no one thinks that most civilians should be allowed to carry guns in the street. While some Quebecers hold different views, few are ready to defend the conservative side on these issues. In light of the 'culture wars' fought in the United States between Progressivism and Orthodoxy (following James Davison Hunter's terminology), it appears that the progressive agenda has carried the day in Quebec.[1] It would, however, be hasty to conclude that Quebec does not have its own 'culture war'. I want to suggest in this article that the debate over the meaning, contours, and fate of Quebec's collective identity is in some ways similar to the American culture wars, in its disagreements over worldviews, values, and political agenda.

I attempt to reconstruct the debate between two dominant current conceptions of Quebec identity, those with a significant number of adherents among intellectuals and opinion-makers. (There are many conceptions of Quebec identity, some more widespread than others. I do not attempt to thoroughly map out all these conceptions here, and neither do I try to update the conceptual framework I proposed in a previous book.[2]) The two dominant conceptions tend to give rise to conflicting political visions and

programs and consequently to ethical and political disagreements, and therefore merit discussion.[3]

I call these two conceptions the 'romantic-conservative' and the 'civic-pluralist' conceptions of Quebec identity. I will first present the civic-pluralist conception, as the romantic-conservative is largely a reaction against it. Although this distinction somewhat resembles one more commonly made, between 'ethnic' and 'civic' nationalism, I argue that this more common distinction fails to grasp the substance of what is probably the most salient identity-related disagreement in Quebec today.

THE DEBATE BETWEEN 'CIVIC PLURALISTS' AND 'ROMANTIC CONSERVATIVES'

The Civic-Pluralist View

The civic-pluralist conception of identity holds that all inhabitants of Quebec that recognize themselves as Quebecers *are* Quebecers.[4] Being a Quebecer is predicated upon neither French-Canadian origin nor assimilation to the majority. Identity choices are left to the individual; it is up to the newcomer to decide whether to keep aspects of his or her cultural origins alive or not. The emphasis is on the civic framework or 'common public culture' that sets the terms of social co-operation. The civic-pluralist vision is at its core a *liberal* one: individuals have basic human rights that limit what the state can do in the name of the common good (liberalism in this sense relates to the rights and freedoms of individuals, not necessarily leaning toward the left or right side of the political spectrum).[5]

There are debates and disagreements among civic pluralists. Some of these are 'liberal neutralists' (or 'difference-blind' liberals), believing that the state should guarantee the same basic individual rights to every citizen and adopt a 'hands-off' approach to culture and identity. The state ought to fight against ethnic and religious discrimination and promote tolerance, but it should not put forward what has been called a 'politics of recognition' or a policy of multiculturalism that confers special recognition and specific rights to cultural minorities.[6] As liberal pluralists, they don't see cultural diversity as a threat that needs to be contained—quite the opposite, they most likely rejoice in the diverse lifestyles that immigration has brought to Quebec.[7] But they do not think that group-specific rights or policies should be designed for cultural minorities. They are not likely to support, for instance, religion-based accommodations in the workplace or in the delivery of public services. They see fairness as the identical treatment of all citizens by the state.[8] Citizens are free to engage in the cultural and religious activities of their choice in their private lives and in civil society, but the state should not implement policies and programs designed to support minority cultures.

On the other hand, some civic pluralists are 'liberal multiculturalists'.[9] They think that fairness towards cultural and religious minorities sometimes necessitates differential treatment. Liberal multiculturalists favour, for instance, the reasonable accommodation of minority religious beliefs and practices and the recognition of the collective rights of Aboriginal peoples. The debate between liberal neutralists and liberal multiculturalists is a political philosophy debate; they differ on the meaning and conditions of social justice or fairness under conditions of cultural diversity.

For both liberal neutralists and liberal multiculturalists, Quebec identity is open to all Quebec citizens. Civic pluralists conceive cultural diversity as an asset for Quebec society. They see a multicultural Quebec society as good for the economy, the arts, and social interactions, insofar as new Quebecers are willing to

lead their lives within the parameters of the common civic framework.

Civic pluralists (both liberal neutralists and liberal multiculturalists) are less likely to feel that Quebec identity is weak, fragile, threatened, and perhaps slowly disappearing. From their perspective, the Quiet Revolution succeeded in turning Quebec society into a strong, civic, outward-looking nation. They see Quebec society as strong enough to integrate and value cultural diversity. They see national identities as internally diverse and under continuous transformation. This vision is widespread among younger generations.

The Romantic-Conservative View

The romantic-conservative conception holds that the shift from French Canadian identity to Quebec identity was not completely positive—something important was lost along the way. They believe that the 'historical majority' (Quebecers of French-Canadian origins) somehow lost its political empowerment and assertiveness as it opened up to plurality. This, they argue, was caused not by conscious and voluntary decisions, but by a combination of the unhappy consciousness of a self-effacing majority that zealously wants to avoid xenophobia and ethnic nationalism and of the successful imposition of a pluralist ideology by the intellectual and political elites. Conservative nationalists therefore generally think that Quebecers of French-Canadian origins ought to start re-asserting themselves and invite newcomers to rally behind them.[10] Romantic conservatives tend to worry about the fate of the older French-Canadian identity within the new civic Quebec identity.[11] In this regard, they are carrying out the legacy of the late sociologist Fernand Dumont.

The main contention of the romantic conservative seems to be that French Canadians (and those who assimilated to them) fought for their survival throughout history. They were the driving force behind the Quiet Revolution, but their affirmation and empowerment has somehow waned. They see 'political correctness' and the prevailing pluralist ideology preventing the 'silent majority' from asserting itself and pursuing its legitimate goals and interests.

The 2006–8 'reasonable accommodation crisis' is seen as a romantic-conservative reaction against pluralism[12]— the majority allegedly has re-asserted itself, shaken off political correctness, and loosened the grip of the pluralist ideology.

Why the majority is faced with this predicament is not clear. It is hard to pin down the argument made by romantic nationalists without reverting to philosophical concepts drawn from Hegel, Marx, and the Frankfurt School. They appear to argue that the self-consciousness of Quebecers seems to have been altered by a mix of superstructure and alienation/false consciousness. In this view, Quebecers' self-consciousness was influenced by the pluralization, fragmentation, and individualization of the superstructure, the general framework of society; this process is seen in many liberal, late-modern democracies. These forces make it difficult to maintain the republican idea of a people united by a shared vision of the common good. [13] The romantic conservative further argues that alienation and false consciousness have come into play; under the influence of a 'cosmopolitan elite' promoting a pluralist ideology, Quebecers have been led to believe that they were xenophobic and not open enough to cultural diversity. Thus they would have internalized a distorted image of themselves and, in doing so, lost sight of their best self-interest.[14] In keeping with the 'Critique of Ideology' program of the early Frankfurt School, romantic nationalists set themselves to criticize the prevailing pluralist or cosmopolitan ideology and help the 'silent majority' to rediscover its voice.[15]

As I suggested in the introduction, the 'civic–ethnic' nationalism distinction fails to capture the nature of the debate over Quebec identity. Conservative nationalists are not ethnic nationalists in the strictest sense. Ethnic nationalism is defined by the belief that ethnicity ought to be the sole criterion of citizenship. But romantic conservatives allow the possibility that newcomers can gradually come to identify with the experience and aspirations of the majority, that is, French Canadians. As Jacques Beauchemin writes:

> How should the idea of the Franco-Quebec majority be understood? Does it only include Quebecers of French-Canadian ancestry? They, as we know, have integrated [into their society] a great

many individuals from other cultures who, for a very long time, have been part of the historical journey of French Canadians. It would not occur to us to consider the Ryans, Johnsons, Kellys and countless others in any other way. But we must also consider as an integral part of this majority those who, for one reason or another—such as language, cultural affinities or their belief in Quebec's common values—have boarded the train of Quebec history as it rolls along.[16]

The meaning of 'boarding the train of Quebec's history' is, of course, very nebulous. One of the fault lines between romantic nationalists and civic pluralists most probably lies in what is expected from new Quebecers. Whereas conservative nationalists tend to favour a 'cultural convergence' model of integration—which most probably involves substantial cultural assimilation on the part of the immigrant—pluralists or interculturalists will generally value and recognize cultural differences and leave identity choices to the immigrant.

ENGAGING ROMANTIC-CONSERVATIVE NATIONALISM

As readers may have guessed, I am an engaged participant in this debate rather than a neutral observer. I have tried to defend liberal pluralism both as a political philosophy and as an integration model for societies such as Quebec. I now want to sketch out what I see as some of the most important problems in the romantic-conservative conception of Quebec identity.

First, I do not agree that the political affirmation process launched in the late 1950s has come to a halt. Conservative nationalists lose sight of one crucial sociological fact, one that is probably obvious to external observers of Quebec society: nationalism is the dominant political paradigm in contemporary Quebec. To use a Wittgensteinian formulation, Quebec nationalism is a 'background agreement' against which political disagreements are played out.

It is safe to say that an important majority of Quebecers and virtually all political leaders endorse the following two propositions: (1) Quebec is a nation and, as such, (2) it has a right to self-determination (which can take a variety of forms).[17] Accordingly, all significant political parties, including federalist ones, seek to consolidate or expand Quebec's political powers, and claim to be the best defenders of Quebec's national interests. Take as a case in point the newspaper *La Presse*. The opinion section of *La Presse* is driven by a group of very assertive and energetic federalist political writers who nonetheless all claim to be Quebec nationalists. And they are! One need not be a sovereignist to be a nationalist. These 'federalist-nationalists' disagree with sovereignists on what political form best serves Quebec national interests, but they don't deny that Quebec is a nation that should enjoy much political autonomy. Antinationalist thought in Quebec is marginal. Who are its spokespersons? It dawned on me recently that the chapter on antinationalist thought among Quebec intellectuals in my 2000 book[18] was in fact an obituary!

It would perhaps help to distinguish here between an inflationist and a deflationist notion of nationalism. Here, it is sufficient to note that the inflationist view holds, à la Ernest Gellner, that nationalism means that all nations should have their own state.[19] The deflationist view holds that nationalism lies in the identification with a distinct and bounded national identity and in the belief that nations have a right to some political autonomy.

I fail to see what facts derived empirically from the social sciences support the claim that Quebec nationalism, and in particular the political affirmation of francophone Quebecers, has stalled. One would want to ask romantic-conservative nationalists: Does the fact that Quebec sovereignty was not achieved prove that Quebec nationalism is on the backburner?[20] If so, this would mean that Quebec, Catalonia, and Scotland could effectively promote their own national identities and expand or consolidate their self-governing powers only if they secede and become fully sovereign countries—a statement that is empirically false.[21]

Second, the implicit philosophy of history that the romantic-conservative position seems to presuppose is suspect. It appears to be a teleological conception of Quebec history—a belief that we can discern in the past and the present the stages of a purposeful development process leading up to a final destination.

Take, for instance, another quotation from Jacques Beauchemin:

While subscribing to this conception of democracy, built on openness to minorities and the recognition of multiple identities, the first thing that the Franco-Quebec majority must do is to assert itself as a majority. A society, any society, cannot be constructed and advanced if it is not driven by the will of the majority, constituted as a political subject.

The Quiet Revolution would not have been possible without the momentum garnered from the national awakening that occurred among Quebecers. In the same way, the future of Quebec, within the context of globalization and interdependence in which the fate of nations is playing out today, depends on its capacity to rally as a political subject, capable of speaking on [its own] behalf . . . .

Quebecers must give themselves permission to do so. They must go back to their history, acknowledging the road [they have travelled] and, without any pangs of conscience, embrace their desire to extend it further. Essentially, this road remains that of the Franco-Quebec majority. [This majority] can legitimately wish to pave the way to Quebec's future constitution.[22]

What does it mean for Quebecers to 'give themselves permission'? Should we not assume that they have already done so? If they have not, is it because they are blinded by false consciousness? And how are we to interpret the idea that Quebecers 'must go back to their history, acknowledging the road [they have travelled] and, without any pangs of conscience, embrace their desire to extend it further', if not in terms of a philosophy of history predicated on the belief that Quebecers can extract from the past what they need to build their future?

What we ought to do here and now cannot really be directly inferred from the past. On the one hand, the past is rife with tensions and is interpreted in various, contested ways. Which events tell us what we must do now? Which interpretations of the past must we favour? On the other hand, and more importantly, just because X happened in the past does not imply that we need to pursue X or its correlates in the present or future. The fact that a nation was xenophobic at a given moment of its history obviously does not mean it ought to be the same in the present. The past simply does not generate that type of moral obligation. Leaving aside the 'was/ought' distinction that still keeps philosophers busy today, we can first note that the past cannot by itself provide us with the answers to our current challenges and predicaments. Moreover, is it hard to see the principle by which current generations would be morally obligated to simply reproduce the identity they inherited from their predecessors. It is precisely because we have to create a future for ourselves out of what we have inherited that we can enjoy a degree of freedom, that we can be the co-authors of our collective life. As the communitarian critics of liberalism have pointed out, it is true that identities do not emerge in a vacuum and are not strictly the result of autonomous will. We are 'embedded' selves.[23] But the proposition that we are not free-floating agents is ontological; it describes a basic aspect of human nature. It is not a normative or a moral proposition—it does not prescribe how we ought to act. That identities are built with material inherited from the past does not generate a duty to be faithful a given interpretation of our history. What we ought to do here and now does not mechanically unfold from what happened in the past. Invoking history can never replace reasoning together about what we want to become. Since normative judgments (what we should become) cannot be directly inferred from descriptive judgments (what happened in the past), conservative nationalists will have to provide their fellow citizens with reasons and arguments for their vision of the future.

THE DEBATE OVER RELIGIOUS ACCOMMODATIONS: THE STRANGE BEDFELLOWS THESIS

Earlier in this chapter, I contested the idea that the francophone majority's political resolve faded as Quebec society opened itself to the world and became internally diverse. But conservative nationalists maintain that the recent commotion over the accommodation of religious minorities confirmed the identity-affirmation deficit of the majority and coincided with the beginning of its political reassertion.

The problem with this interpretation is that it greatly homogenizes the opposition to accommodating religious diversity. As I alluded to above, some neutralist liberals and civic nationalists are also opposed to the legal accommodation of minority religious beliefs and practices. However, their reasons are very different from those of the conservative nationalists. Their claim is that religious accommodations are incompatible with civic values such as gender equality, the separation of Church and state, fairness among co-workers, interculturalism, and so on. Such public values can be endorsed by all Quebecers, *regardless of their cultural origins.* Many people who are generally well disposed toward cultural diversity and who favour interculturalism as an integration model nonetheless hold that the proper place of religion is in the private sphere and that no accommodations should be granted to the members of religious minorities.

Conservative nationalists see the reaction against religious accommodations as a reassertion of the historical majority's 'identity', 'culture', or 'customs and ways'. According to this view, Quebecers of French Canadian origins would have seized the occasion of the reasonable accommodation debate to reassert themselves and stop bending too much in trying to accommodate immigrants. I would not want to deny that some Quebecers rebelled against religious accommodation because they saw it as a threat to the traditions and customs of the majority, but I think that a fair analysis of the debate leads us to conclude that the conservative reaction against religious accommodation was considerably less prevalent than the civic or liberal critique of reasonable accommodation.[24]

These two often-stated but mutually incompatible positions show the heterogeneity of the opposition to religious accommodation:

1. It is only recently and as a result of painful struggles that Quebecers were able to achieve a true separation between the Church and the state. *Laïcité* (secularism) is one of the Quiet Revolution's greatest achievements. It is now threatened by the religious practice of minorities. They need to accept that religion, in Quebec, belongs to the private sphere. We should not let

religion sneak back into the public sphere through accommodation measures.

2. Quebec is a Catholic (or, more inclusively, Christian) society. Catholicism is an integral part of Quebec history and identity. The Quiet Revolution threw the baby out with the bathwater. Catholicism ought to have a special status within our collective life. It cannot be put on a par with the other religions brought to Quebec through immigration.

These two positions are mutually incompatible. Normally at war with one another, liberal neutralists and conservative nationalists both found reasons to oppose religious accommodation, leaving liberal pluralists caught in the middle. I call this the 'strange bedfellows thesis' of the religious accommodation debate.[25] This unlikely and unpremeditated alliance between liberal neutralists and conservative nationalists created the illusion of a self-conscious and united majority reasserting itself. This belief, however, is an illusion. The background political philosophies of the two camps are irreconcilable, as are the political prescriptions stemming from them. The liberal pluralist position is the mean between neutral liberalism and romantic-conservative nationalism.

CHARLES TAYLOR

by François Côté-Vaillancourt, MA Candidate, Faculty of Philosophy, Université Laval

Charles Taylor in his office at McGill University. Taylor was awarded the Templeton Prize on 14 March 2007 and will use it to advance his studies on the relationship of language to art and technology.

McGill News

Charles Taylor was born in 1931 in Montreal. Although he held the Chichele Chair in Social and Political Theory at All Souls College, Oxford, from 1976 to 1981, he taught for most of his career at McGill University. One of the few modern philosophers who dared to enter Quebec's political debate, he invested himself deeply in shaping Quebec's future. He ran for the (progressive, social-democrat) New Democratic Party in four federal elections in the 1960s, participated in government consultations after the failure of the Meech Lake Accord for constitutional reform, and recently co-presiding over the Consultation Commission on Accommodation Practices Related to Cultural Differences.

He holds a PhD in philosophy from Oxford University. His thesis was published under the title *The Explanation of Behaviour* (1964). While more epistemological than his other writing, this book already presents a criticism of simplistic approaches to the human subject based only on brute facts and causal arguments, and puts forth an explanation involving the deeper roots and motives for human actions. His work reached its peak with the publication of *Source of the Self* (1989), in which he examines the modern conception of the subject, which he describes as the combination of the 'value of ordinary life', centred on family, work, love, and so on, and of an 'ethic of authenticity', an urge felt by each person to realize his or her own potential in a unique and authentic way.

Born from the union of an English-speaking Protestant and a French-speaking Catholic, and living in Quebec, Taylor's philosophy is sensitive to difference and to the importance of culture and language and their appropriate recognition—matters that post–Second World War American liberal thinking tends to obscure. In his view, identity is a complex construction forged in dialogue and social interactions, involving 'strong evaluations' that are not on par with more superficial and instrumental reasons for action. Thus, the 'disengaged self'—the notion that one can fully define oneself through the exercise of one's rational faculties—is, according to him, a misconception.

Against this philosophical background, Charles Taylor turned his focus to political philosophy and articulated a response to the framework set out by John Rawls in his famous book *A Theory of Justice*. Taylor's critique included an argument suggesting that the simplistic conception of the self found in liberal thinking is a consequence of the 'atomistic' view borrowed from modern science. Yet, despite his appeal for a more holistic approach, Taylor (and most other so-called 'communitarian' thinkers) does not repudiate liberalism as a whole and is in no way suggesting that the interests of the community have more weight than individual rights and freedoms. In fact, most of them even reject the 'communitarian' denomination.

Taylor's contribution to the 'liberal-communitarian debate' also includes a rejection of the dominant 'procedural' theories of justice. These theories are based on the honourable idea that if a community proclaims X as good, all its members who do not accept X would be second-class citizens. Therefore, the state should limit itself in defining justice and make sure that everyone has the opportunity to pursue his or her goals, whatever they may be. This position is often presented as 'the priority of the just over the good'. While having some merits, these theories would abandon too much to achieve formal equality and individual freedom. Taylor points out that such a position presupposes a conception of 'the good', and wants to reintegrate discussion of collective identity and common goals within debates on justice. Another of Taylor's concerns is that procedural liberalism ends up reducing politics to the judiciary process.

With that in mind, Taylor argues that the culture and language of some communities can be legitimately viewed as equally important to justice, Quebec being the prime example of a society that cannot bring itself to function under a purely procedural paradigm. As he observes, the political debate resulting from the emergence of 'the good' alongside 'the just' inevitably means that complex political disagreements cannot be solved by the simple application of a theory of justice such as Rawls', and that difficult choices and sacrifices will have to be made.

While drawing heavily from Continental Europe thinkers—including Rousseau, Herder, Hegel, Heidegger, and Merleau-Ponty—Taylor writes in the clear manner of Anglo-American philosophers and primarily for that audience, making him the ideal bridge-builder between these two great traditions of contemporary Western philosophy and, indeed, a central figure for any accurate understanding of a society such as Quebec that defines itself by referring to both traditions.

Snapshot

The 2007–2008 Bouchard-Taylor Commission
by François Côté-Vaillancourt, MA Candidate, Faculty of Philosophy, Université Laval

Summary of the Events
Following months of public discontent over the accommodation of religious minorities, on 8 February 2007 Quebec Premier Jean Charest announced the establishment of the Consultation Commission on Accommodation Practices Related to Cultural Differences. Since the recognition of an obligation to accommodate by Canadian and American courts, debates on the legitimacy of religious accommodations have continued both in political philosophy and in the public sphere, and the discontent had seized the general public through overwhelming media coverage. Cases such as the Canadian Supreme Court's decision to allow a young Sikh to wear his religious

dagger (kirpan) at school (the Multani Affair—see Chapter 19) fuelled the controversy.

The Consultation Commission mandate included:

- taking stock of accommodation practices in Quebec;
- analyzing the attendant issues, bearing in mind the experience of other societies;
- conducting extensive consultation on this topic; and
- formulating recommendations to the government to ensure that accommodation practices conform to Quebec's values as a pluralistic, democratic, egalitarian society.

While it could have interpreted this mandate in the narrower sense of a strictly legal inquiry, the Commission chose to address the broader issue of Quebec's sociocultural integration model. This audacious choice was of course consistent with the appointment of the Commission's co-chairs, the philosopher Charles Taylor and the historian Gérard Bouchard, two leading intellectuals renowned for, among other things, their work on identity and cultural diversity.

The investigation was based on different sources, including research projects conducted by academic researchers, meetings with experts and representatives of sociocultural organizations, but also—what came to be the most visible part of the Commission—public consultations held all across Quebec. For weeks, Quebec's attention—through the press as well as live coverage on TV—turned to the odyssey of these 'two modern wise men' crossing the land in pursuit of the perceptions and opinions of the average citizen.

The subsequent work of the Commission led to the publication of a thorough report named *Building the Future: A Time for Reconciliation* (see Relevant Websites at the end of this chapter for a link to the report). While anchored in Quebec's situation, the Report develops numerous concepts and tools that transcend the context in which they were formulated and are likely to enrich the debates on the challenges of cultural and religious diversity taking place all across the Western world. Therefore, one possible reason for the popular attention given to the Commission is probably the notion that other societies facing similar fears and uncertainty could learn from a small, peripheral nation like Quebec.

The Two Sources of the Crisis

The Commission's first conclusion was to confirm the asymmetry between the real scope and impact of cultural accommodations and the widespread popular perception of their effects. In addition to showing that the reasonable accommodation of minorities poses no threat to the foundation of collective life, the Commission was able to prove that the degree of media coverage on reasonable accommodation did not correlate with a sudden increase in its practice. Perhaps the most shocking element discovered was that in 15 of the 21 cases at the core of the controversy, there were striking discrepancies between public perception and the facts. With these findings, it was then possible to characterize the crisis as a 'crisis of perception'.[26]

The second conclusion, however, tempers the idea of a political or media-led plot to foment public discontent, as the crisis of perception could not have caused such discontent without some sort of pre-existing widespread anxiety over the fate of Quebecers' shared identity. Many citizens, for instance, expressed anxiety over the possible loss of core values established during the Quiet Revolution, such as secularism and gender equality. The Commission clearly points out the strangeness of a situation in which 'the members of the ethnocultural majority are afraid of being swamped by fragile minorities that are worried about their future'.[27] Although these concerns are rooted to some extent in the minority status of French-Canadian Quebecers in North America as a whole, it is nonetheless observable all across the Western world.[28]

The Three Social Norms of Quebec's Common Public Culture

One of the goals of the Commission was to provide guidelines for reasonable accommodation, a task that involved for the most part a reconstruction of the values, norms, and institutions already present in Quebec's common public culture.

- The first element is the integration model: *interculturalism*. Often seen as distinct from Canadian multiculturalism, interculturalism aims to preserve Quebec's national character—for example, based on French as the common public language—while allowing and protecting cultural and ethnic diversity in conformity with liberal values. The focus is on integration, interaction, and sharing, whereas multiculturalism, as it is commonly interpreted, could be satisfied with a peaceful co-existence between hermetic communities.
- The second element relates to what the report calls 'harmonization practices' and the need to negotiate when, for example, cultural customs or values conflict, rather than to launch a legal battle. The report characterizes the 'legal route' as 'codified' and 'rigid', and as creating winners and losers. It recommends that a dispute be negotiated through the 'citizen route', which uses less formal procedures to reach a compromise that both sides are happy with. It thus offers an effective way to solve problems in accordance with values of dialogue, negotiation, and reciprocity that we find at the centre of Quebec's integration model.
- The third element deals with deep-seated convictions, whether religious or secular. Behind any secular system there is a deliberate balance between four principles—the moral equality of persons, freedom of conscience, the separation of Church and state, and state neutrality with respect to convictions of conscience. The Commission argues in favour of a conception of the secular state that they call *open secularism*. This system's primary virtue is to depart from a rigid model of secularism as seen in France, where the respect of the first two principles leads to actions directed against religion and its manifestations—as exemplified by the legislation that banned wearing visible religious symbols at school—a path that is deemed by the Commission as incompatible with a true neutrality of the state, as well as with attaining integration through diversity.

Recommendations

While we have looked mainly at the conceptual content of the Commission's report, it also includes the following practical recommendations:

- In response to possible clashes between accommodation and gender equality, the Commission insisted in its first recommendation that, while general norms would exclude most instances of such a conflict, all requests in the public-service sector that would bestow upon a woman an inferior status to that of man are to be disqualified.
- Consistent with the guidelines for accommodation practices and in a spirit of reciprocity, it also stated that the practice of saying a prayer in some municipal council meetings should be abandoned and the crucifix, an explicit symbol of Christianity, should be removed from the wall of the Quebec National Assembly. It is to be noted that this recommendation was voted down unanimously by the members of the National Assembly a few minutes after they received the report, in an act that seems explicable only as a message to voters that accommodation issues are exclusively the concern of cultural minorities and will not require any change for the majority.
- In contrast, according to the Commission's open interpretation of secularism and to be fair and inclusive, it recommended that society should respect dietary prohibitions of different cultures or faiths, and also allow the wearing of Islamic headscarves, Sikh turbans, or Jewish kippas in class, in athletic events, and at work for most civil servants, since the principles in these situations do not concern the separation of Church and state.

- Finally, it was reaffirmed that requests for legitimate accommodation must seek to protect or restore a right, such as time off for a non-Christian religious holiday, and that accommodation cannot be used to suppress someone else's rights. For example, a child cannot be denied the right to study science or to receive a life-saving blood transfusion in order to accommodate a parent's religious beliefs.
- In order to give more precise guidelines to legislators, civil servants, and concerned citizens, the report suggests that the Quebec government produce 'a white paper on secularism' to review the tradition of open secularism in Quebec and ensure its clear articulation in debates to come. Fulfilling this recommendation does not yet appear to be on the government's agenda. Without agreed-upon, well-publicized guidelines to secularism, matters such as the wearing of the Islamic headscarf in the public sphere are still likely to launch heated debate.

Despite the work that is yet to be done to fulfill its recommendations, the Commission was successful in ending the popular crisis surrounding the practice of accommodation.

Conclusion

It is important to get a clearer view of the contrast between the civic-pluralist and the romantic-conservative conceptions of Quebec identity chiefly because this contrast generates substantial political disagreement about the nature of citizenship and integration. Those who adhere to the romantic-conservative view tend to favour a more conformist conception of the common public culture and a more assimilative integration model: immigrants ought to endorse a particular interpretation of the past as well as a particular vision of the common good.

Those who hold the liberal and civic view defend a pluralist model of integration which seeks to strike an appropriate balance between respect for cultural diversity and the demands of social co-operation. Integration, seen from that standpoint, does not require assimilation. Liberals continue to debate among themselves what form and degree of recognition and accommodation ought to be granted to cultural minorities. As it is solidly anchored in deep philosophical and political disagreements, Quebec's homebrewed 'culture war' will most likely give intellectuals, elected officials, and citizens plenty of debate material in the years to come.

Questions for Consideration

1. What are the positions in your own society about what should be expected or required from immigrants?
2. Where do the views of 'difference-blind' liberalism and multicultural liberalism diverge?

Which one is, in your opinion, the most congruent with the spirit of liberalism?

3. What is the role of political philosophy? Why, do you think, is Quebec society a fertile ground for political philosophy?

Notes

1. It will be interesting to see whether President Obama's more dialogue-based, less Machiavellian approach to politics will soften the edges of the culture wars in the United States. See William Saletan, 'This is the Way the Culture Wars End', *The New York Times*, 21 February 2009, available at www.nytimes.com/2009/02/22/opinion/22saletan.html.

2. Jocelyn Maclure, *Quebec Identity: The Challenge of Pluralism* (Montreal and Kingston: McGill-Queen's University Press, 2003).

3. As John Rawls put it, 'we turn to political philosophy when our shared political understandings, as [Michael] Walzer might say, break down, and equally when we are torn within ourselves.' John Rawls, *Political Liberalism* (New York: Columbia University Press, 1993), 44.

4. Since identities are in part matters of self-recognition and self-description, we must allow for the possibility that a Quebec *citizen* does not recognize himself as a Quebecer. For example, think of someone who would describe him- or herself exclusively as a Cree, a Canadian, or a citizen of the world.

5. As Yael Tamir and David Miller have argued, liberalism and nationalism are not incompatible, as the political community within which liberal institutions are set out is most commonly a *national* political community. I will not address here the liberal nationalists' additional argument that liberal institutions *necessitate* or *presuppose* the nation-state. It suffices for my purposes to point out that liberalism and nationalism are not logically incompatible. See Yael Tamir, *Liberal Nationalism* (Princeton: Princeton University Press, 1995) and David Miller, *On Nationality* (Oxford: Oxford University Press, 1995). For a critique of liberal nationalism, see Geneviève Nootens, *Désenclaver la démocratie : Des huguenots à la paix des Braves* (Montreal: Québec Amérique, 2004).

6. Charles Taylor, *Multiculturalism and The Politics of Recognition* (Princeton: Princeton University Press, 1992); James Tully, *Strange Multiplicity: Constitutionalism in an Age of Diversity* (Cambridge: Cambridge University Press, 1995); Will Kymlicka, *Multicultural Citizenship* (Oxford: Oxford University Press, 1995).

7. Jeremy Waldron, 'Minority Cultures and the Cosmopolitan alternative', *University of Michigan Journal of Law Reform* 25 (1991): 751.

8. Brian Barry, *Culture and Equality: An Egalitarian Critique of Multiculturalism* (Cambridge, Mass.: Harvard University Press, 2001).

9. I will not address here the debate over the similarities and differences between 'multiculturalism' and 'interculturalism'. See Chapter 17 for Rafael Iacovino and Charles-Antoine Sevigny's excellent presentation of the Quebec intercultural model of integration.

10. As we will see, this most probably means that immigrants should assimilate, but the formulations are usually very vague.

11. According to historian Éric Bédard, conservative nationalists are 'as preoccupied with the defensive survival of Quebec as they are with the political status of Quebec.' Their nationalism is driven by the 'haunting anxiety of seeing their culture disappear'. Éric Bédard, 'La colère "bleue" des nationalistes', *Le Devoir*, 26 April 2007.

12. See the Snapshot box on the Bouchard-Taylor Commission.

13. For a clear and accessible analysis of these societal transformations, see Charles Taylor, *The Ethics of Authenticity* (Cambridge, Mass.: Harvard University Press, 1992).

14. The idea that Quebecers of French-Canadian origins are somehow alienated is a common theme among conservative nationalists in Quebec. See Maclure, *Quebec Identity. The Challenge of Pluralism*, Chapter 1.

15. The striking similarities between conservative nationalism and the Freudian-Marxism of some members (Marcuse, Fromm) of the early Frankfurt School never fail to surprise me.

16. Jacques Beauchemin, ' La mauvaise conscience de la majorité franco-québécoise', *Institut du Nouveau-Monde*, available at www.vigile.net/article4044.html (accessed on 13 September 2007, our translation). For Beauchemin, 'évoquer la majorité franco-québécoise, c'est donc désigner le rassemblement de tous ceux, Canadiens français de souche et compagnons de route, qui se sentent appartenir au Québec non pas seulement du point de vue des droits que procure la citoyenneté, mais de celui de ce sentiment collectif qui rend solidaire d'une aventure commune'. This is, again, very vague. We would need to know more about the meaning of the 'collective sentiment' and 'common adventure' to tease out the real implications of Beauchemin's position.

17. Robert Bourassa's reaction after the failure of the Meech Lake Accord as well as the conclusions of the Bélanger-Campeau Commission were probably instrumental in the crystallisation of that background consensus.

18. Jocelyn Maclure, *Récits identitaires : le Québec à l'épreuve du pluralisme* (Montreal: Éditions Québec Amérique, 2000). The English translation is cited in note 2.

19. Ernest Gellner, *Nation and Nationalism* (Ithaca, N.Y.: Cornell University Press, 1983).

20. See Jacques Beauchemin, 'La souveraineté au nom de la mémoire', in Jocelyne Couture, ed., *Redonner sens à l'indépendance – Les intellectuels pour la souveraineté* (Montreal: VLB Éditeur, 2005).

21. Michael Keating, *Nation Against the State: The New Politics of Nationalism in Quebec, Catalonia and Scotland*, 2nd edn (New York: Palgrave MacMillan, 2001).

22. Beauchemin, 'La souveraineté au nom de la mémoire', our translation.

23. Michael Sandel, *Liberalism and the Limits of Justice*, 2nd edition (Cambridge: Cambridge University Press, 1998).

24. I developed that position in 'Le malaise relatif aux pratiques d'accommodement de la diversité religieuse. Une thèse interprétative', in Paul Eid, Jean-Sébastien Imbeault, Marie McAndrew, and Micheline Milot, eds, *L'accommodement raisonnable et la diversité religieuse à l'école publique. Normes et pratiques* (Montreal: Fides, 2008).

25. Maclure, *Quebec Identity*.

26. Gérard Bouchard and Charles Taylor, *Building the Future: A Time for Reconciliation* (Quebec: Gouvernement du Québec),18.

27. Ibid.

28. Ibid, Chapter 9, Section C.

Relevant Websites

Commission de consultation sur les pratiques d'accommodement reliées aux différences culturelles: www.accommodements.qc.ca/index-en.html

Institut du Nouveau Monde: www.inm.qc.ca/english.html

University of Ottawa Centre for Interdisciplinary Research on Citizenship and Minorities: www.sciencessociales.uottawa.ca/circem/index_e.asp

Centre d'études ethniques des universités montréalaises: www.ceetum.umontreal.ca/english/home.htm

UQÀM Centre de recherche interdisplinaire sur la diversité au Québec: www.cridaq.uqam.ca/

Les Cahiers du 27 juin: www.cahiersdu27juin.org/

L'Action nationale: www.action-nationale.qc.ca/

Select Bibliography

Barry, Brian. *Culture and Equality: An Egalitarian Critique of Multiculturalism*. Cambridge: Polity Press, 2001.

Beauchemin, Jacques. *L'histoire en trop. La mauvaise conscience des souverainistes québécois*. Montreal: VLB Éditeur, 2002.

Dumont, Fernand. *Raisons communes*. Montreal: Boréal, 1995.

Hunter, James Davison. *Culture Wars: The Struggle To Control The Family, Art, Education, Law, And Politics In America*. New York: Basic Books, 1992.

Kymlicka, Will. *Multicultural Citizenship*. Oxford: Oxford University Press, 1995.

Maclure, Jocelyn. *Quebec Identity. The Challenge of Pluralism*. Montreal and Kingston: McGill-Queen's University Press, 2003.

Taylor, Charles. *Multiculturalism and The Politics of Recognition*. Princeton: Princeton University Press, 1992.

Thériault, Joseph Ivon. *Critique de l'américanité. Mémoire et démocratie au Québec*. Montreal: Québec Amérique, 2002.

Venne, Michel, ed. *Vive Quebec! New Thinking and New Approaches to the Quebec Nation*. Toronto: Lorimer & Company, 2001.

PART C
LANGUAGE

INTRODUCTION

Could a book about Quebec's history and society not have a section dedicated to the question of language? Quebecers are admittedly obsessed with language.[1] The early twenty-first century situation, characterized by linguistic peace, contrasts sharply to that of only a few decades ago. The French language presence in North America has always been an object of curiosity and fascination.

In his 1831–2 tour of America that led to the publication of the book *Democracy in America*, French thinker Alexis de Tocqueville wrote:

> Canada piques our curiosity keenly, [as] the French nation has kept itself intact there. They have the customs and language of the century of Louis XIV.[2]

Language has always been a central theme of debate and discussion within the different political and social circumstances of New France, the Province of Quebec, Lower Canada, United Canada, Quebec, and Canada. For example, language was one of the first matters raised by the newly elected members in the Lower Canada Parliament (1792–3) and of the new 1867 Dominion of Canada. Parliamentarians pondered: What would be the language of debates and of the laws within parliamentary and political institutions? Although the questions have differed from one century to the next, the importance of language in both Quebec and Canadian history has been constant. Examining the language theme in the context of Quebec raises questions that relate to all the themes of this book: memory, identity, citizenship, Quebec models, and Quebec in the international sphere.

Much international interest in Quebec focuses on language. It is striking to see, for example, in academic readers on language and society, how often Quebec is used as a case study for language policy and planning, language conflict, language and identity, bilingualism and bilingual education, language and ethnicity, language rights, linguistic minorities, language and nationalism, and second language acquisition.[3]

Following a multidisciplinary approach, this section examines the language question through the lens of a sociolinguist, a political scientist, a sociologist, a philosopher, and a writer. These different approaches provide us with insightful perspectives on Quebec history and society while raising important questions about the use of language in society.

First we have a sociolinguistic examination of descriptive aspects of French in Quebec. To paraphrase sociolinguist J.A. Fishman, it seeks to answer the question: Who speaks (or writes) what language (or what language variety) to whom and when and to what end?[4] Chantal Bouchard's article asks: Is Quebec French considered the equivalent of Parisian French and how has the perception of French changed over time? The reader gains a historical overview of the perceived quality of French in Quebec. Starting with the French regime, Bouchard shows that various European observers perceived French in New France to be very similar to metropolitan French, differing only in vocabulary. This perception would, however, change. In the nineteenth century, Europeans and Canadiens (descendents of French settlers in New France) called New World French 'gobbledygook'. What explains this change from 'pure' language to 'corrupt' language usage? Why did this devaluation occur? Bouchard shows how key political and historical moments influenced this perceptual transformation. For example, how did the Conquest and the British Regime affect language? Ties with France gradually waned and French in Quebec was isolated and threatened. Bouchard asserts, for example, that the linguistic insecurity of francophone Quebecers began in 1841, with the Union of Upper and Lower Canada. She evaluates the extent to which periods of anglicization in the sociolinguistic history contributed to self-depreciation.

During the 1960s and 1970s, however, a new protagonist took the stage on the language front: the Quebec state. Martin Lubin highlights the different linguistic challenges during the Quiet Revolution. Lubin's chapter looks at the dynamics of the sociology of language in Quebec in response to the question: What accounts for differential changes in the social organization of language use and behaviour toward language?[5] As Lubin points out, during the Quiet Revolution, provincial and federal Commissions revealed that French Canadians were economically and socially disadvantaged. How would French Canadians try to reverse this situation? As a political scientist, Lubin describes the attempts of the Quebec state to take control of the language issue. Lubin gives an excellent overview of the nationalist path taken by Quebecers trying to elevate their status and that of the French language. We see the majority assert itself politically, culturally, and linguistically. In the early twenty-first century, we see the making of a language planning process in Quebec. Given the dominance of English in Montreal, one wonders how advocates could reclaim it as a French city. How was this change perceived by francophones and anglophones? What about the allophones, those whose mother tongue was neither French nor English? Finally, how did linguistic peace emerge?

While focusing on Quebec, Linda Cardinal examines a broader context: federal government involvement in language planning and its impact on Quebec language laws. Cardinal argues that to understand policymaking in Quebec and Canada, we need to look at Canada-Quebec political power relations. To identify major trends, Cardinal examines Canada's demolinguistic profile over the last half century.[6] She notes that English has made net gains in Canada, because increasingly those whose mother tongue is not English now use it most often at home. In addition, Cardinal sees no signs for optimism for the French language outside Quebec, citing the continuing decline in French both as a mother tongue and as a spoken language. Thus she asks: What is the impact of federalism on language planning in Canada? What are the policy milestones in Canadian language planning that have had an impact on Quebec language policymaking? Cardinal proposes two different but interacting visions: a territorial model (Quebec's approach) and a personality principle (Canada's approach). For Cardinal, appreciating these tensions between Canadian and Quebec language policies is vital to understand the normative debate on identity and national unity in Canada. Both federal and Quebec language laws have framed this debate.

Daniel Weinstock focuses on the Quebec language policy issue from a political philosophy perspective. To contextualize the Quebec situation, Weinstock examines some language-related challenges for Quebecers and Catalans. Weinstock's chief question is: How can language policies favour a popular convergence around a regional majority language, which is itself a minority language in the larger regional context?

Francophone Quebecers faced the dilemma of opting either for a laissez-faire approach that might jeopardize the vitality of their language or for a legislative approach that aims to protect the language but risks infringing on individual rights. This building tension between collective and individual rights raises the question: Can a society with strong collective goals be liberal?

French in Quebec has always been much more than a medium of communication. It was a central part of Canadien and French-Canadian identity and culture. With the Quiet Revolution and the decline of Catholicism, French became even more important to the new Quebec identity. Language became the focus of political life in Quebec in the 1960s as legislation began what Weinstock calls the 'politics of language'. Weinstock points out that interpretation of the language debate in Quebec varies greatly. Indeed, how do the perspectives of Canadian francophones, anglophones, and allophones inside Quebec vary, and compare to each other and to those of Canadians outside Quebec? Weinstock suggests two important concepts for understanding this situation from the perspective of political philosophy: identity and liberal justice. French as the official and common public language helps to establish French as a new pillar of the territorially based Quebec identity; but to non-francophone Quebecers, the mandatory use of French might seem exclusionary. Weinstock reflects on how language policies can achieve balance and justice. Finally, he considers how perceptions of language policies in Quebec have changed. What could explain the linguistic peace in Quebec for almost 20 years? Why are anglophones and allophones not contesting Bill 101, as they did when the law was adopted in 1977? Weinstock suggests that the key lies in identity issues around the question: Who is a Quebecer?

We then shift focus to language and identity issues as expressed in Quebec music and song lyrics. What is the importance of language in defining a Quebec song? Christopher Jones asks: What is unique about popular music in Quebec in the North American context? How does popular music shape the way Quebecers think about themselves? Jones starts his musical journey of periods, genres, and celebrities in 1945 when Félix Leclerc and Raymond Lévesque, the first icons of Quebec chansons (French songs whose lyrics are most important) made their mark on the public sphere. He notes several factors in the emergence of this unique Quebec voice in chansons: radio and television programs devoted to chansons, popular venues, contests, and the influence of key individuals. We discover that the road to the recognition of Quebec's voice in chanson first passed through Paris. Jones then takes us to the 1960s and the Quiet Revolution, examining the role of songwriters in this period of intense social change. In a period that poet Roland Giguère calls '*l'âge de la parole*', we find, not surprisingly, a boom in Quebec chansonniers (songwriters) and a proliferation of popular music houses called *boîte à chansons*. Songwriters lent their voices to the evolving discourse on nationalism, identity, and language. We also find an American influence in the 1950s and 1960s and the chanson of this era shared the popular success and spirit of the *yé-yé* movement. Like Quebec literary writers, by the end of the 1960s Quebec songwriters had to choose between standardized French or the colloquial Québécois *joual*. Songwriters in the 1960s and 1970s felt the pulse of Quebec society and contributed to its nationalism, and a new generation of bands took over from the chanson pioneers. These artists benefited from government policy in the 1970s that mandated a high level of French-language content for radio music.

The 1980s brought tough economic times and a post-referendum effect, which caused national identity and language to languish in Quebec popular culture. English lyrics not about Quebec became common. In the 1990s, the Quebec music scene expanded into hip hop, country, and Anglo-rock. The chanson tradition was revived with the work of bands like Les Colocs, who integrated various musical genres with playful French lyrics containing popular Québécois colloquialisms. Jones's chapter shows how a Quebec-based musician belongs to a diverse, multilingual community of musical genres, where French is key.

The music scene faces many of the French-language questions that Quebec society does: Is French as the common public language of Quebec encompassing Quebecers of all origins? Will French be the medium that can promote interactions among all Quebecers for the development of Quebec society?

NOTES

1. Taken from Chantal Bouchard's book title: *Obsessed with Language: A Sociolinguistic History of Quebec* (Toronto: Guernica Editions, 2008).
2. Alexis de Tocqueville, to his mother, 19 June 1831, Yale Tocqueville collection.
3. See for example: Chrstina Brett Paulston and G. Richard Tucker, *Sociolinguistics: The Essential Readings* (Toronto: Wiley-Blackwell, 2003), and Florian Coulmas, ed. *The Handbook of Sociolinguistics* (Toronto: Wiley-Blackwell, 1998).
4. J.A. Fishman, 'The Sociology of Language' in Pier Paolo Giglioli, ed., *Language and Social Context* (Penguin, 1972), 46.
5. Ibid., 47.
6. See Statistics Canada publications, *Canadian Demographics at a Glance*, available at: www.statcan.gc.ca/pub/91-003-x/91-003-x2007001-eng.pdf ; and *Evolving Linguistic Portrait, 2006 Census*, available at: www12.statcan.gc.ca/english/census06/analysis/language/pdf/97-555-XIE2006001.pdf.

CHAPTER 11

The Sociolinguistic History of French in Quebec

Chantal Bouchard, McGill University

— TIMELINE —

1763   Treaty of Paris: France cedes Canada to England. After surrender of New France three years earlier, most schools close their doors.

1791   Constitutional Act: Canada divided into two provinces, Lower Canada, which is mainly French, and Upper Canada, which is mainly English.

1831   Étienne Parent relaunches newspaper *Le Canadien*, under motto 'Our Institutions, Our Language and Our Laws!' Alexis de Tocqueville comments on language of French Canadians.

1837   Patriote rebellion violently repressed by the British army.

1840   Union Act unites Upper and Lower Canada, further to recommendation of Lord Durham, who also advised linguistic assimilation of French Canadians. Section 41 (repealed only eight years later) makes English only official language of United Province of Canada.

1867   British North America Act: Section 133 institutes bilingualism in Canada's federal Parliament, Quebec's legislature, and in courts of every province.

1902   Société du parler français au Canada founded, begins to publish *Bulletin du parler français au Canada* goes on to organize

large-scale 'Congresses' on French language. (The first takes place in 1912; the fourth, and last, in 1956.)

1937   Second Congress on the French Language: Participants call for creation of Office de la langue française and Comité permanent de la survivance française established.

1961   One year after Liberal Party of Jean Lesage elected and Quiet Revolution begins, Office de la langue française created.

1968   Gendron Commission of Inquiry on the Position of the French Language struck. St Leonard school crisis begins.

1974   Bill 22 adopted by Liberal government of Robert Bourassa, proclaiming French as official language of Quebec.

1977   René Lévesque's Parti Québécois government adopts Bill 101, Charter of the French Language and founds Conseil de la langue française, the Commission de toponymie, and Commission de protection de la langue française.

2001   Commission of the Estates General on the Situation and Future of the French Language in Quebec, chaired by Gérald Larose, tables its report.

If ever there was one central issue, one nerve centre, in Quebec history, it would be language. The French language that was transplanted to the banks of the St Lawrence River in the early seventeenth century thrived there unhindered until the middle of the eighteenth century. At that time, it was the language of the Canadiens, the name given to the French colonists who were born in New France. It was also the same prestigious parlance spoken not only in Paris and in all of France's major cities, but also in cultivated circles throughout Europe. It was after 1763, when the colony was ceded to Britain in the Treaty of Paris, that the trouble with language began.

The Paradox of *Bon Usage* and Devaluation

After the British takeover, with each passing era perceptions of the French language changed remarkably among Quebecers of French-Canadian (Canadien) origin. For years now, I have studied their political, economic, and social history, asking questions about how this history has shaped linguistic identity. One question I have asked is why francophone Quebecers in the 1950s and 1960s were so negative in their opinions about the French they spoke. Through my research, I was able to convincingly demonstrate that their opinions were directly linked to the development of a negative self-image, which began to emerge toward the end of the nineteenth century.[1] My political, economic, and social analyses proved this point.

Politically, I found that French Canadians saw themselves as a dominated, poor, and ignorant people, condemned to a mediocre destiny. This collective identity had been forged over time by weighty events (the British Conquest, the Rebellions of 1837–8 and the ensuing repression, the Durham Report, the Union Act, and Canadian Confederation) over time. Each of these events disempowered French Canadians and underscored their political status as minority people.

Economically, I found that their most striking change in self-image came with a massive change of vocations and context. As the population grew and arable farm land became correspondingly scarce, the province's peasant farming class, the habitants, flocked to the city to take on jobs and underwent a large-scale proletarization. These erstwhile farmer-landowners, who had not been rich but had enjoyed relative independence up to that point, thereby became dependent, waged urban labourers and employees at the service of their English bosses. The under-education of the peasant and working classes was clearly not conducive to their social mobility. Neither was the fact that anglophones controlled the industrial and business sectors. These factors only exacerbated the feeling among French Canadians that they were being blocked at every turn, caught in an inferior social position from which they were ill-equipped to break free.

Socially, this decline in class status followed the same downward curve as opinions on language, with both reaching their lowest point around 1950–60. Newspapers, books, and public presentations about language, fed much of my post-Conquest analysis. But I was not able to examine opinions on language prior to 1840 since the first documentation of this kind appeared around that time. Therefore, it is impossible to know first-hand what the Canadiens of 1800 might have thought about their language and whether they deemed it legitimate or not. This said, there are many documents dating from the time of New France and the first decades of the British regime, written by foreigners who were merely passing through. By all of these visitors' accounts, the French spoken in New France was faithful to the *bon usage* (correct use of language) for that era and judged in a very positive light. Differences were remarked upon in some cases, but mostly pertained to vocabulary. Neither pronunciation nor syntax seemed to diverge from the norm. A few concurrent usages were noted, but these simply reflected language variations that also existed in France. It was toward the mid-nineteenth century that a negative discourse about the language of the Canadiens began to surface and would virtually establish itself as the rule. Erudite French-Canadian 'men of letters' began to disparage the language of their compatriots in their writings on the subject—and they were not alone in their opinions. The British, the Americans, and Anglo-Canadians also heaped derogatory criticisms on the language spoken by French Canadians, often claiming it was nothing but a French *patois* (dialect). As comment upon comment accumulated, the French spoken in Quebec was devalued. Within little more than half a century, how could such a remarkable reversal of opinion occur?

Certainly, after the Conquest, the British presence in Quebec had been making its mark on the language of the Canadiens. But how could a few dozen borrowed English words lead to such a dramatic loss of status, especially at a time when borrowings from English were common enough in France? To answer this question it is important to understand the importance of contact with France. When contact was broken, the linguistic changes taking place in France no longer had any direct bearing on the inhabitants of its former colony. Consequently, it took less than two generations for Canadien French to lose its legitimacy—an abrupt, if not brutal, turn of events. Certainly, no other rational explanation for this reversal of opinion may be found by examining the internal development of French in Quebec. There is, in fact, every reason to believe that the early Canadiens were very conservative in their language use. We may surmise that, between 1793 and 1830 a trickle of anglicisms likely found their way into common parlance, but such utterances were still relatively limited. It also appears that the departure of a large segment of the upper class during the 1763 regime change in Quebec fostered the dissemination of some popular or provincial vocabulary, to the detriment of normative or *bon usage* French words.[2] However on the whole, these changes were too modest to account for the loss of legitimacy suffered by French in Quebec, as manifested in the criticisms of the French Canadian, British and American intelligentsia.

In any event, these exceptional anglicisms and incorrect locutions should not have sufficed to discredit the language of French Canadians such that it could be justifiably labelled a 'French-Canadian *patois*', as the British and Americans would unrelentingly claim. As for the unfavourable opinion of French-Canadian men of letters, my research has shown that two main factors came into play. First, they feared that anglicization, which was spreading throughout the nineteenth century, would bastardize French (and they soon launched an ambitious newspaper campaign against it). Second, their perception of deviations from the *bon usage* was predicated on the normative standard of contemporaneous Parisian French. Since, as I have previously pointed out,

Canadian French had evolved very little since 1763, it had to be the changes in Parisian usage that ultimately produced these perceived deviations. It was this historical progression that the intellectual elite of 1840 failed to acknowledge and elucidate to others.

What, in fact, have intellectuals said about the 'deviations' that occurred from 1763 to 1840? Through its research (in the early twentieth century), the Société du parler français au Canada (SPFC) established that many of the Canadianisms in Quebec pronunciation and vocabulary were in fact archaisms with respect to normative French. In other words, as abundantly illustrated by Jules-Paul Tardivel, they were very much in keeping with the *bon usage* of their time.[3] SPFC researchers Adjutor Rivard and Louis-Philippe Geoffrion also highlighted the etymological similarities between France's regional vernaculars and the Quebec lexicon. In fact, claims that French has remained in a very pure state in Quebec, and that Canadien French is the language of the *Grand Siècle* of Bossuet and Racine are not hard to find. Defenders of Canadien French would say that it remained 'legitimate' because it complied with the *bon usage* of the eighteenth century and that of the *ancien regime*. Viewed in this way, the linguistic conservatism of French Canadians was eminently praiseworthy, buttressed by the indisputable prestige of French literature and culture during this period and by a widespread distrust of the innovations of the Republic, the Empire, and (in literary matters) Romanticism. But it is here that we encounter the thorny notion of 'legitimacy'. Louis Fréchette, Arthur Buies, and many other writers and intellectuals ridiculed such claims, saying their proponents were 'puffed up with crass ignorance'.[4] These detractors (and like-minded critics in the nineteenth century) argued that conformity to contemporary standards was the sole measure of linguistic legitimacy; hence any of the archaisms, anglicisms, or other uses of their compatriot's language that these men perceived as being inaccurate were judged illegitimate.

As for vocabulary, over the years the question of legitimacy has focused minds, intellectual or not, on various categories of Canadianisms and has been addressed somewhat differently. While everyone agrees that anglicisms should be rejected in French, positions on other categories have varied considerably. Because the first systematic research into the origins of Canadianisms began only in the twentieth century, distinctions remain unclear between archaisms that were part of the norm in the seventeenth and eighteenth centuries, provincialisms brought over from Poitou or Normandy, and neologisms of form or meaning created to name the discoveries of the New World. What we do know, as evidenced by the Quebec newspaper columns on the French language at the end of the nineteenth century, is that people tended to reject a word or expression when they discovered its 'Canadian' origins and realized that it competed with/deviated from standard language use. Similarly, language columnists typically accepted only Canadianisms that expressed concepts exclusive to North America. In short, the scope for lexical creativity remained exceedingly narrow in Quebec until 1900.

The paradox before us is astonishing. After just two generations, a language variety that had changed very little was almost entirely devalued. The political and economic circumstances of French Canadians weighed significantly in the balance since the prestige of a language variety is inextricably linked to the social position of its speakers or, as Pierre Bourdieu would say, 'a language is worth what those who speak it are worth'.

The Impact of the Conquest

In 1763, New France was ceded to England in the Treaty of Paris. The population of the colony, some 65,000 souls of French origin, was entirely French speaking since emigration conditions and the situation in the colony did not allow for the transmission of any other European languages at the time. Linguistic unity was achieved quickly and without the need for the any intervention, since *patois d'oïl* and the other languages spoken in eighteenth-century France died out with the first generation of Canadiens.

What sort of French did Quebecers speak as new British subjects? Various sources provide valuable insight into this question. By way of comparison, we may look at the comments made by foreign visitors to New France and (later) to the new Province of Quebec, under the British regime. About a dozen

descriptions of New France are left to us by these foreigners, providing telling observations about the language spoken by French Canadians.[5] The concordance between their comments is remarkable, as all agreed that the Canadiens spoke a very pure French with no accent and that there were no *patois* in Canada. Even the Marquis de Montcalm remarked that 'the peasants speak French very well'.[6] Another dozen or so accounts from foreign visitors[7] were written about the Province under British rule from 1763 to 1853, essentially confirming observations from the previous period, but including a few remarks on the influence of English. With the passage of time, this influence would become more pronounced.

Toward the beginning of the nineteenth century, the archaizing (increasingly outdated) characteristics in Canadian French are first mentioned and they too became increasingly pronounced over time. By 1833, Isidore Lebrun spoke of the 'strong imprint of the refugee style'[8] in Quebec. He was referring to the style of exiled Protestant writers who, cut off from the evolution of the language in France, used turns of phrase and expressions that seemed outmoded in the mother country. In an article that appeared in an 1850 edition of the *Revue des Deux Mondes*, writer Théodore Pavie undoubtedly best articulated the feeling that must have overtaken most cultivated Frenchmen when they recognized jargon among Canadiens that had not been used for a generation or two in France:

> They speak an old and relatively inelegant French; their thick pronunciation, devoid of accentuations, is not so far removed from that of the Lower Normans. Talking with them, one soon realizes that they were separated from us before the period in which everyone in France began to write and engage in discussion.[9]

The historic period alluded to here was, of course, that of the French Revolution. Jean-Jacques Ampère, who was also a writer, struck another note entirely in his comments, expressing his pleasant surprise at overhearing local lingo in Montreal that appeared to come straight out of Molière's time.

Observations about pronunciation and accents followed a similar path. Many of the pronunciations generally used in Quebec had come to be associated with popular or regional uses in France, and owing to their exclusion from the 'sophisticated' register of France, they came to be regarded as archaisms of pronunciation. But no major differences in pronunciation between the social strata were apparent within Quebec, where society was not highly stratified at that time. During the first half-century of the English regime, after the departure of the French elites, this relative similarity in pronunciation was even more apparent. By the first half of the nineteenth century, comparisons with the accent from Normandy had become increasingly frequent. In her detailed and comprehensive study of observations written by foreigners in the seventeenth, eighteenth, and nineteenth centuries, Marie-France Caron-Leclerc found that few concrete examples of pronunciation were given to substantiate these comparisons. Moreover, Caron-Leclerc has rightly underscored the fact that, in the eighteenth and nineteenth centuries, the slightest departure from the reference accent was considered to be either Norman or Gascon. The so-called 'Gascon' accent was undoubtedly a catch-all category for the full range of accents in the Midi region (in the south of France). The 'Norman' accent was used in reference to all of the supposed provincial accents in northern France. These somewhat impressionistic accounts from the first half of the nineteenth century show that foreigners perceived a difference in Canadian pronunciation, which was usually somewhat analogous to that found in the cities of northwestern France. '[They] speak French with the Norman accent of the middle classes',[10] said Tocqueville of Quebec lawyers, aptly capturing the essence of an accent not of the Norman peasants but of the inhabitants of Norman towns and villages. It should be pointed out that accents in Quebec at that time had likely not reached present-day levels of homogeneity, whereby only a few characteristics now enable us to distinguish between regional varieties. In short, some accents most likely incorporated traits of pronunciation that had become archaisms in the reference French of the times (but had survived in Quebec and the provinces of France), which led foreigners to conflate Canadian and Norman accents.

Ideally, to complete this sociolinguistic overview and gain some insight into French at the beginning of the nineteenth century, we would listen to what the Canadiens themselves had to say about the language they were speaking. But since few metalinguistic documents predate 1840, Jacques Viger (1787–1858) (the first mayor of Montreal and a learned scholar), provides us with one very instructive and exceptionally non-judgmental resource. In 1810, Viger set about compiling a collection of French-Canadian neologisms, including variants in pronunciation, new accepted meanings for existing French words, and borrowings from English and Amerindian languages.[11] Since this collection was only published a century later, it could not have influenced the perception that Viger's contemporaries had of their language. Nonetheless, it does show that, in certain circles, Canadians were aware of the original nature of their French.

Scholars studying sociolinguistics can now describe with some accuracy the language spoken by French Canadians in the early nineteenth century. As to their vocabulary, it seems that the consequences of the Conquest, notably the departure of the French elite and the collapse of the education system (which caused a dramatic drop in literacy rates), led to a reduction in lexical variation. Claude Poirier has pointed out that popular language clearly gained ground as many words found in the writings of New France disappeared and were replaced by competing regional or popular expressions.[12] Also, from 1763 onward, as British and French-Canadian populations mingled, an increasing number of English borrowings were added to the original lexical base. The vocabularies of politics and the law were the first to be affected, as French Canadians had to adapt to these new institutions, but some observations show English words from other language categories were also being borrowed with increasing frequency in everyday language.

THE PECULIARITIES OF CANADIEN FRENCH

The vocabulary of Canadianisms used by the Canadiens may be classified into a number of subsets, depending on their origins. In the original lexical base of French origin, there are *archaisms*, words from standard seventeenth- and eighteenth-century French that fell out of use in France but remained current in Quebec. There are *provincialisms*, words or expressions brought over by the colonists from their various provinces of origin. Also worth noting, within the vocabulary of French origin are scores of existing words that took on one or more new meanings. In many cases, these were the *semantic neologisms*, which assigned new meanings to flora and fauna whose names, in France, designated other, often similar, species.

Certainly, it was natural that a population transplanted to a new continent and living in circumstances very different from those of their ancestors would feel the need to coin words to designate new things and concepts with *morphological neologisms*. A wide variety of geographic, climatic, and cultural phenomena would be named in this way. The Canadianisms of the New World also included a major class of words, called *borrowed neologisms*. These were words borrowed from foreign tongues, the oldest of which came from Amerindian languages. While *Amerindianisms* were not numerous, they established themselves in the language very quickly. Most provided names for plants and animals, although some pertained to elements of material culture.

Of course, the largest class of *borrowed neologisms* was English borrowings. Within this class, it is important to distinguish between words or expressions that constitute *formal borrowings*, whose form is English but meaning is not, and those that are *semantic borrowings*, whose form is French but whose meaning is English. Also included in this category are *calques*, which result from the translation of the elements of a compound word or expression.

English borrowings only gradually made their way into Canadien French and, apart from neologisms, have been the only class of words to undergo constant development since 1763. By contrast, a number of archaisms, provincialisms, and Amerindianisms progressively faded out of use. Before the nineteenth century drew to a close, a whole host of Amerindianisms had been dropped from Canadien French. As for archaisms and provincialisms, harsh condemnations from language columnists likely contributed to their gradual demise and to the pursuant adoption of words from standard French. However, with the founding of the Société du parler français au Canada in 1902, a movement was launched to rehabilitate archaisms and provincialisms, which were declared legitimate because they were French in origin. English borrowings, for their part, would remain subject to general reprobation and continue to be perceived today as the chief threat to the quality of French in Quebec.

THE SELF-CONSCIOUSNESS OF LANGUAGE (1841–1842)

For some 80 years after France broke contact with its former colony, French in Quebec evolved in a vacuum. In reality, apart from the growing influence of English, little had changed, although pronunciation undoubtedly became more uniform. For most French Canadians, whose literacy rate remained markedly low, language transmission had been oral. Under the French regime, overall literacy was 23 per cent and as high as 45 per cent in Quebec City, but by 1779 it had fallen to 13 per cent and had inched up to 27 per cent by 1849.[13] Only a few men of letters, such as Michel Bibaud and Jacques Viger, seem to have been aware of specific and manifest divergences between the French spoken in Quebec and that spoken among the educated classes in France. It was therefore in a context of sheltered ignorance that a small textbook for college students suddenly questioned the legitimacy of Canadian usage of French and gave rise to a controversy that would have enduring repercussions. Published by Abbé Thomas Maguire in 1841, the *Manuel des difficultés les plus communes de la langue française, adapté au jeune âge, suivi d'un recueil de locutions vicieuses*, was a sort of dictionary of language problems. From this time forward, Quebec's own francophone elite, Anglo-Canadians, the British, and the Americans would question the legitimacy of Canadian French with growing stridency and regularity. In fact, this very public rejection of the language spoken by Quebecers would mark a point of origin for the insecurity about language that would follow in Quebec.

Quebec's Infamous *Manuel* and its Proponents

Abbé Thomas Maguire

Abbé Thomas Maguire, the author of the *Manuel* that sparked the language debate, was born in Philadelphia in 1774 to parents of Irish and British origin. His family settled in Halifax in 1776 (at the time of the American War of Independence) since his parents were United Empire Loyalists. At the age of 13, Maguire was sent to Quebec City to study under the Jesuits, with whom he completed his education. Ordained into the priesthood, he was appointed curate of the parish of Notre-Dame de Québec and then served various other parishes. In 1828, he was appointed Principal of Collège de Saint-Hyacinthe, and was later sent on a mission to France to resolve a problem regarding funds that belonged to several religious communities and that were confiscated during the French Revolution. He stayed in France for six months. A year after returning to Quebec, Abbé Maguire left his position at Collège de Saint-Hyacinthe and settled in Quebec City, where he taught philosophy at the seminary. He was subsequently named Chaplain to the city's Ursuline Order of nuns, a position he would hold until his death in 1854. In 1829, he went on another European assignment, this time in Rome. Abbé Thomas Maguire published several works on Catholicism. The *Manuel des difficultés*, which appeared in 1841, was his last publication.

Abbé Jérôme Demers

The Abbé Jérôme Demers was the author of 'Remarques sur le "Manuel des difficultés les plus communes de la langue française"', which appeared in the *Gazette de Québec* in April and May of 1842. Born in Saint-Nicolas, Quebec to a farming family in 1774, he studied first at the Petit Séminaire de Québec and then in Montreal, before returning to Quebec City and the Grand Séminaire. Demers began teaching before completing his studies and became Director of the Petit Séminaire in 1802. There, until 1849, Demers was by turns Director, Superior, and Procurator, while continuing to teach and produce student textbooks, of which there was great need at the time. For 50 years, he devoted himself almost exclusively to the education of young people and thereby helped train a large segment of the French-Canadian elite during the first half of the nineteenth century. Narcisse-Eutrope Dionne, who devoted a monograph to the controversy surrounding Maguire's *Manuel*, wrote that the reach of Demers's authority was considerable, well beyond the Petit Séminaire:

> How could things have been otherwise when he was known to have trained 10 bishops, 200 priests, 60 lawyers, 40 doctors, 30 notaries, and when the list of his former pupils included Quebec notables like Louis-Joseph Papineau, Jacques Labrie, Louis Moquin, Joseph Parent, René-Édouard Caron, Joseph Lagueux, Augustin-Norbert Morin, Zéphyrin Nault, Pierre Chauveau, Jean-Thomas Taschereau, Joseph Cauchon and Octave Crémazie? So you see, it is hardly surprising that the advice of the Abbé Demers was considered equivalent to that of an oracle—his word was law.[14]

Jérôme Demers died in 1853.

Comparing the Protagonists

It is striking to note that the two main protagonists in this debate were born in the same year, received very similar educations in most of the same institutions (the Petit Séminaire and the Grand Séminaire in Quebec City), and must have known one another. The tone of their attacks and retorts even suggests a possible mutual dislike. As to their perceptions of language, two biographical details may have played a role in their respective positions. First, Maguire's mother tongue was English and he had spent a significant amount of time in Paris. These factors probably enabled him to be more detached in his appraisal of the language spoken by French Canadians. Second, Demers came from a modest background but was renowned for his vast erudition. Having never left the province, he had to rely on books published in France for his authoritative knowledge of standard French. Indeed, he made abundant use of such sources in his *Gazette* articles.

Inside the Debate

Now for a closer look at some of the other authors who commented on the debate that pitted Maguire against Demers. The editor of the *Gazette de Québec* penned several lines at the end of Demers's last letter, as an introduction to the article that appeared in *Le Canadien*. He also wrote an editorial note in support of Demers' position on the use of the Amerindianism *atoca* (cranberry), citing an excerpt from a dictionary. The author of these editorial remarks was most likely Ronald Macdonald. Born in Prince Edward Island in 1797, Macdonald began his studies in a Quebec City seminary at the age of 15 and must have studied under—none other than Joseph Demers.

Étienne Parent, editor of *Le Canadien*, contributed much more substantially to the debate. He wrote an article directly critiquing Maguire's *Manuel*, making no allusions to Demers' letters. The article argued in favour of many of the Canadianisms condemned by Maguire. Born to a farming family in 1802, Parent studied at the Collège de Nicolet, and then at the Grand Séminaire in Quebec City. He soon became a journalist and spearheaded many debates, all of which focused on the defence of the French-Canadian nation. Although an ally of Papineau and the Parti patriote, he rejected calls for rebellion. In 1831, he relaunched the newspaper *Le Canadien* and gave it its celebrated motto: 'Our Institutions, Our Language and Our Laws!'[15]

Michel Bibaud was the last, but not the least ardent debater, to pronounce on Maguire's *Manuel* and the polemics surrounding it. Born in 1782 to a Côte-des-Neiges farming family, he studied at Montreal's Collège Saint-Raphaël, initially devoting himself to teaching. He launched his career in journalism at *Le Spectateur canadien* and helped to found *L'Aurore* in 1817. *L'Aurore* was the first paper to publish a column discussing the French language, written by a French Canadian. In it, Bibaud denounced borrowings from English. He then wrote for *Le Spectateur canadien* (which merged with *L'Aurore*) until 1822 and also published numerous school textbooks and authored the first book of poetry in Quebec's literary history, *Épîtres, Satires, Chansons, Épigrammes, et Autres Pièces de Vers*, released in 1830. Bibaud founded several monthly papers, notably, *La Bibliothèque canadienne* in 1825, *Le Magasin du Bas-Canada* in 1832. In 1842, he established *L'encyclopédie canadienne, journal littéraire et scientifique,* which featured his critique of Maguire's *Manuel* and of the polemics that pitted Maguire against Demers. Throughout his long career, Bibaud strove to enhance the cultural enlightenment of French Canadians. His background differed from those of the other protagonists in the language debate. He was the only Montrealer among them and the only one with no connection to a seminary in Quebec City. By the time Maguire's *Manuel* appeared, Bibaud had been writing articles on Canadian French for 20 years, persistently criticizing the anglicization of the language, especially in the field of law.

SNAPSHOT

The Origin of Doubt about French in Quebec: Maguire vs. Demers

Some 80 years after relations with France were broken off, only a few French-Canadian men of letters seem to have been aware of the discrepancies that were beginning to appear between the French spoken in Canada and that spoken by the educated class in France. Oblivious to this ever-widening divide, Abbé Thomas Maguire published a small textbook for college students that questioned the legitimacy of some Canadian French and thus unwittingly

unleashed a storm of polemics whose repercussions would shape a generation of thought. Published in 1841, the *Manuel des difficultés les plus communes de la langue française, adapté au jeune âge, suivi d'un recueil de locutions vicieuses,* was a sort of dictionary of language problems. In it, Maguire addressed a variety of linguistic issues, from idioms and difficult conjugations to shades of meaning between words. Most of the entries were merely explanations based on similar textbooks, dictionaries, and grammar books from France. But Maguire's *Manuel* differed from these publications in that it often adopted a peremptory tone and denounced language usage that could be collectively described as 'Canadianisms'. This term encompassed a multitude of linguistic sins, including variant pronunciations, morphosyntactic variations, French-Canadian neologisms, formal and semantic borrowings from English, archaisms, provincialisms, nautical terms whose meanings had been stretched, and words or expressions from popular vernacular. A few weeks after Maguire's *Manuel* was released, an anonymous author published a long article in the pages of the *Gazette de Québec,* criticizing it. Maguire wrote a reply and the anonymous author, who would soon be revealed as the Abbé Jérôme Demers, responded in kind. The editor of the *Gazette de Québec* appended to the end of Demers' response a commentary by the editor of another newspaper, *Le Canadien*. It was at that point that Michel Bibaud commented on the debate and on the *Manuel*, in several issues of his new monthly newspaper, entitled *L'Encyclopédie canadienne*.[16]

Historical context also played an important role in this language debate. For French Canadians demanding truly representative democracy, 1837–8 was a pivotal time in their political agitating. Louis-Joseph Papineau's Parti patriote led the people into a rebellion that was violently repressed by the British army. In the wake of this devastating civil unrest, the British government sent Lord Durham to conduct an inquiry. In an infamous report, Durham recommended that the two colonies of Upper and Lower Canada be united for the avowed purpose of making the French Canadians a minority, the better to shepherd their linguistic assimilation towards English. His description of French Canadians as 'a people with no history, and no literature' shocked and offended the province's educated elite, particularly Étienne Parent, who published his translation of Durham's report in the pages of *Le Canadien* newspaper. Despite the opposition of most members of the French-Canadian educated class—including journalists, politicians, and legal experts—the Union Act of Upper and Lower Canada was adopted in 1840 by the British Parliament. Section 41 of the enabling legislation made English the only official language of the United Province of Canada, a provision that would not be repealed until 1848. The dramatic failure of the 1837–8 rebellion had so weakened the position of French Canadians that they were unable to muster any effective opposition to the new political structure that had made them a minority. A morose atmosphere of collective defeat and bleak prospects for the nation weighed heavily in the years that followed. In these disheartening circumstances, the publication of a work that denounced—often in highly condescending terms—many of the most current linguistic habits of French Canadians (thereby attacking one of the building blocks of their identity) was perceived as a slap in the face. Maguire's *Manuel* effectively confirmed Lord Durham's views by characterizing French Canadians as ignoramuses who could not even master their mother tongue. Worse, by denying legitimacy to most Canadianisms, this publication essentially stripped French Canadians of their right to linguistic creativity. At a time when French Canadians, sorely tried by political events, who were struggling to define themselves within a state structure not of their choosing and feeling threatened by the minority status it had imposed upon them, this sudden attack on *their* French hit a raw nerve.

LANGUAGE LAWS AND LANGUAGE BATTLES

The creation of the Office de la langue française in 1961 was the Quebec government's response to an increasingly urgent popular demand. The idea behind this demand was first articulated at the second Congress on the French Language in 1937, when the Société du parler français au Canada recommended that a government body be created to address the deterioration it had observed in the quality of French in Quebec. But it was only after the Second World

War that Quebec francophones seriously considered using their government as an instrument in the service of their language. It was then that a new kind of consciousness grew among French Canadians regarding their cultural dispossession and linguistic alienation. This consciousness reached unprecedented levels in 1960, culminating a state of crisis and the public debates that raged over *joual*.[17]

Despite the efforts that were made to promote French in Quebec, the language seemed to be steadily deteriorating. French-Canadian society had undergone profound changes since the latter part of the nineteenth century. The anglicization of culture and language in Quebec started with the transition from a rural/agricultural to an urban/industrial society, and continued to manifest itself increasingly in a pervasively English environment, among a population whose levels of education remained limited until the 1960s.

During the 1920s and 1930s, in an effort to legitimize Canadian French and to combat the myth of a French Canadian *patois*, the members of the SPFC celebrated the virtues of the peasant language as an expression of the nation's values, emphasizing how unaffected it had been by the 'sin' of anglicization in the 'language of the cities'. After the Second World War, as the exodus from the countryside to the city continued in Quebec, a potentially catastrophic situation had to be confronted once again, according to some authorities: In a nutshell, French is dying out in Canada.[18]

Newspaper columnists, educators, journalists, and writers all persistently sounded the alarm. In 1952, at the third Congress on the French Language, the seemingly unstoppable deterioration of the language was highlighted yet again, making past remedies (individual efforts and education) appear increasingly futile. The decisive year for changing the attitudes of opinion leaders appears to have been 1956. It was then that the fourth Congress called for the establishment of an Office du vocabulaire français in Quebec's Department of Public Instruction. From that time on, the discourse from all sides in colloquia, congresses, reports, conferences, and newspaper articles invariably called on the Quebec government to take decisive action to promote French. But these appeals were met with obvious political inertia. The

failure of Premier Maurice Duplessis's government to act exasperated a generation of young intellectuals, growing increasingly impatient with the social obstacles imposed on francophones.

In October 1959, jouurnalist André Laurendeau sparked a virulent debate on the controversial subject of *joual*. In a letter to the newspaper *Le Devoir* regarding the quality of the French spoken by the teenagers he knew, he lamented that 'almost all of them speak joual'.[19]

A Catholic brother and teacher, operating under the pen name of Frère Untel (later translated as 'Brother Anonymous' in English) concurred on this point in another letter to the editor: 'Our pupils talk joual, they write joual. . . . Joual is their language'. Brother Anonymous continued, 'I hear talk of a Provincial Office of Linguistics. I am all for it. THE [FRENCH] LANGUAGE IS PUBLIC PROPERTY and the State should protect it as such'.[20]

This exchange between Laurendeau and Brother Anonymous prompted an extraordinarily spirited reaction. A shockwave ran through the public, as though the very act of naming *joual*, the cultural outcome of generations of hard urban living, had crystallized the longstanding apprehensions of the francophone intellectual elite. It had also heightened a consuming collective consciousness regarding the gravity of the situation.

In the early 1960s, the Lesage government announced that it was creating a Ministry of Cultural Affairs. Journalist Gérard Fillion commented on this plan as follows:

> The government has just announced the creation of a Ministry of Cultural Affairs. This is all well and good. But by what concrete measures does the Quebec State intend to protect the French language—the same way it proposes to put an end to forest depletion and water pollution? . . . It should know in advance that [whatever] concrete measures it does adopt, however rigorous they may be, they will resonate deeply with both the people and the intellectual class.[21]

Faced with the fact that the many measures taken by civil society groups and movements to promote French in the early twentieth century had failed to slow its perceived degradation, on 24 March 1961, the Quebec government created the Ministry of Cultural Affairs and the Office de la langue française (OLF). In an era when some people even questioned whether 'Quebec French' could be considered French at all, the Quebec government appeared to be the only body powerful enough to rectify this situation. The first step it took was having the OLF 'define a linguistic model'. Public pressure continued for the government to address the cause–effect relationship between the status of the language and the inferior economic and social position of French Canadians. However at its inception, the OLF had no means by which to address these causes of linguistic deterioration, so integrally linked to the inferior status of French. Plainly, there was much work to be done before the government would be able to turn the tide in linguistic development.

The debate about *joual* served to expose the imbalance between the strength of English in relation to French, showing that despite Quebec's strong francophone majority, English was continuing to gain ground. In the late 1960s, the realization grew among Quebec francophones that the anglicization of immigrant children via the school system also seriously threatened their majority status. The Catholic–Protestant division imposed by the education system had long segregated students according to their religious backgrounds. Newcomers from southern Europe, being mostly Catholic, generally sent their children to French-language Catholic schools, whereas new Quebecers of most other religious affiliations attended English-language Protestant schools, which were more open to religious diversity. A Catholic English-language system also served many Quebecers of Irish origin. Until 1930, immigrant children were divided almost equally between English-language and French-language schools. But some 30 years later, in 1961, over 90 per cent of children of immigrant origin were being educated in English. Montreal had long been 65 per cent francophone, but English was disproportionately represented everywhere—in business, in public signage, and in the workplace. In many of Montreal's neighbourhoods, it was difficult to find services in French. English was an essential qualification for employment, even for subordinate positions, and the average income of unilingual francophones

was lower than that of all other social groups, including immigrants. The prospect of Quebec's metropolis being overrun by the English language was perceived as a real and present danger for the future of francophone society in Quebec and for the survival of its culture.

In 1968, against this volatile backdrop, a controversy broke out regarding the schools of St Leonard, Montreal. The local school board had decided to eliminate their bilingual curriculum and offer French-only courses. This move prompted anglophone Quebecers and immigrant associations to launch a broad-based protest movement and the ensuing battle remained heated for months on end. Various francophone groups supported the school board's decision and broadened their lobby for new regulations to require that immigrants to Quebec attend French-language schools. Quebec's Union Nationale government reacted by adopting Bill 63, effectively making language of instruction a matter of free choice, but this law did not resolve the problem. It was not until Bill 22 was adopted in 1974 by Robert Bourassa's Liberal government that more effective measures were taken to integrate foreign-born students into francophone society. Bill 101, adopted in 1977 by the Parti Québécois government under the leadership of René Lévesque, would further strengthen these measures.

Bill 22, which became the Official Language Act, made French the official language of the Quebec government. Bill 101, which became The Charter of the French Language, was more ambitious and much wider in scope, seeking to make French the common public language of all Quebecers.

QUEBEC FRENCH COMES INTO ITS OWN

For years, in other Canadian provinces, francophone Quebecers had witnessed the unremitting erosion of French-Canadian communities that had assimilated to English in droves. Even in their majority position in Quebec, francophones recognized that their demographic predominance was seriously threatened and, overcome with an intense feeling of linguistic alienation, reacted by trying to take control of all the political ground at their disposal.

Still working through this difficult process, francophone Quebecers (and the rest of the Western world) experienced faster and more pervasive communications through modern technology. First radio, then (especially) television, brought the news of the day into homes in the most remote regions of the countryside, establishing widespread daily contact with standard French. Moreover, as trips and visits abroad increased, and more francophone immigrants and travellers came to Quebec, Quebecers began to break out of the isolation they had experienced since the late-eighteenth century. In Quebec as elsewhere, all of these phenomena combined led to a relative levelling of dialects. Many of the traits of pronunciation and some of the vocabulary, including borrowed English words or local, twentieth-century vocabulary, that previously had characterized Quebec French were gradually replaced by their standard French equivalents from one generation to the next. And as might be expected, broad swaths of vocabulary pertaining to traditional peasant life fell into disuse, due to urbanization and the modernization of agricultural techniques.

These transformations had an even greater effect on the entire panoply of words influenced by English. Indeed, everyday Quebec French of the 1960s was teeming with these *formal borrowings* or *loan words* from English, which, being *doubly* stigmatized, were ripe for elimination. De-anglicizing Quebec French undoubtedly brought it more in line with standard French, even though standard French (in France) had paradoxically begun to borrow more and more from Anglo-American vocabulary. Semantic borrowings from English accounted for another source of divergence from standard French, and were a growing trend among the increasingly bilingual francophone Quebecers. More recently, over the past two decades, I have observed a sharp rise in the use of *faux amis* ('false cognates') in France, particularly in the nation's newspapers and electronic media. A recent study conducted by Marie-Éva de Villers, who systematically compared the vocabulary used in the French newspaper *Le Monde* with that used in several Quebec dailies, indicated that over 80 per cent of their content shared the same lexical usages. As for the Quebec print media, recently created neologisms formed the largest category of non-standard usage. We may therefore infer that, when it comes

to naming new objects and concepts, francophone Quebecers are now allowing themselves a greater margin of lexical innovation than they did in the past. Other indicators show that while the resemblance between spoken French in Quebec and Europe has increased, in recent decades certain facets of Québécois pronunciation and vocabulary have also acquired a legitimacy that they never enjoyed before. Far from being signs of linguistic regression, over time they have come to be valued as positive, identity-enriching social assets. In fact, observations of diction among Quebec radio and television anchors (the standard-bearers of oral French) reveal phonetic traits distinctive to Quebec, traits that used to be systematically eradicated in the media. It seems that francophone Quebecers, heartened by 40 years of collective successes, now have a much higher opinion of their distinctive culture and language, a positive sense of their identity, and are therefore exercising some autonomy vis-à-vis the prevailing normative reference. This new linguistic norm has yet to be clearly defined and its departures from the European standard are neither numerous nor very pronounced. But simply put, a distinctly Québécois variety of French now exists and its use is socially valued, a fact that will doubtless have a formative effect on the future development of the language.

Some might contend that current prevailing trends—the relative levelling of dialects and the emergence of a new linguistic norm for Quebec—are potentially contradictory. In fact, this is not so: the reason Quebecers can allow themselves to appreciate a distinctly Québécois variety of French today is that Quebec usage is now close enough to other varieties of French that it will not lead to misunderstandings and is not becoming a distinct language, contrary to the fears voiced half a century ago. Simply put, Quebec's language policy, combined with developments in communications technology, has actually succeeded in turning the tide in linguistic development.

FRENCH AS A COMMON PUBLIC LANGUAGE

Over 25 years after the adoption of the first measures to make French the official language of Quebec and to integrate immigrants into French-language schools, a 1997 report by the Conseil de la langue française, *Le français langue d'usage public au Québec*, noted that while French had indeed become the language of public life in Quebec, it remained weak in some areas, including the workplace. Moreover, the report held that the level of francization among newcomers to the province was not yet satisfactory.

The findings in this report for Quebec as a whole may seem reassuring since they showed that 88 per cent of Quebecers were using French in their public activities. But predictably, a regional breakdown of statistics for respondents who used French almost exclusively or as the main language of their public life dropped to 78 per cent in the Greater Montreal area and to 71 per cent for the Island of Montreal. Clearly, Greater Montreal is the place where the stakes are highest, where the vast majority of anglophone Quebecers live and where most immigrants have settled. The behaviour of these two groups will therefore determine whether French will progress, stagnate, or regress as the common language of Quebec in the future.[22]

If the current behaviour of younger generations of allophone and anglophone Quebecers is any indication, the public use of French has a good chance of gaining ground in Quebec's metropolitan area, since these young people now far outnumber their parents in their mastery of French. In fact, 80.8 per cent of young adult anglophones now have a fluent command of the language.[23] However, the new immigrants who settle in Montreal each year, many of whom do not speak French upon arrival, must also be factored into the linguistic equation. In most other regions of Quebec, where French predominates, these linguistic shortcomings may be addressed through varying degrees of institutional involvement, but half-measures will not suffice in the Greater Montreal area, where newcomers are more likely to choose English over French for a multitude of reasons. Failure to integrate newly arrived Quebecers into the francophone community is likely to have lasting, long-term repercussions. Therefore, it is no longer enough to send foreign-born children to French-language schools. Quebec must also promote and protect classes for learning French as a second language for adult immigrants as an equally important part of consolidating the use of French as the language of public life.

Conclusion

From 1760 to 1960, the sociolinguistic history of Quebec followed a long downward spiral of degradation. With Quebec's loss of political status, insecurity about the French language grew increasingly strong. By contrast, since the 1970s, French has seen a steady improvement in its status within Quebec society. Language legislation has successfully mitigated the sense of alienation it was designed to address. In 2010, francophone Quebecers have a much higher opinion of their language, which they now regard as being legitimate. The fact that newcomers now adopt French as the language of their public lives is accepted as a matter of course. But given that some stagnation in the everyday use of French has been observed in recent years (especially in Montreal), francophone Quebecers are still on their guard. Without fail, each new statistical report on language is immediately and meticulously analyzed. Each line is sure to be dissected, scrutinized, and commented on. Indeed, it may truly be said that very few societies in the world are as passionate about language issues as Quebec, as language indisputably remains one of Quebec's most distinguishing cultural characteristics.

Questions for Consideration

1. How can we account for the differences between standard French and the French spoken in Quebec over the years?

2. Francophone Quebecers had a very negative opinion of their language from about 1850 to 1960. What social factors contributed to this opinion?

3. To what can we attribute the much more favourable opinion that francophone Quebecers now have of their language at the beginning of the twenty-first century?

NOTES

1. See Chantal Bouchard, *Obsessed with Language: A Sociolinguistic History of Quebec* (Toronto: Guernica Editions, 2008).
2. See Claude Poirier, 'Une langue qui se définit dans l'adversité', in Michel Plourde, ed., *Les français au Québec, 400 ans d'histoire et de vie* (Montreal: Fides/ Les publications du Québec, 2000), 111–22.
3. Tardivel delivered a lecture to this effect in 1901. Jules-Paul Tardivel, *La langue française au Canada*, la Compagnie de publication de la Revue canadienne (1901), reproduced in *Le Devoir*, 22 June 1912.
4. Louis Fréchette, *La Patrie*, 4 August 1874.
5. All of these observations may be found in Marie-France Caron-Leclerc, 'Les témoignages anciens sur le français du Canada (du XVIIe s. au XIXe s.) : édition critique et analyse', PhD Thesis, Université Laval, 1998.
6. Montcalm, *Journal du marquis de Montcalm*,[témoignage de 1756] in Caron-Leclerc, 'Les témoignages anciens', 65.
7. John Lambert, *Travels through Canada...*, [témoignage de 1807] in Caron-Leclerc, 'Les témoignages anciens', 73–4.
8. Isidore Lebrun, *Tableau statistique et politique des deux Canadas* [témoignage de 1833] in Caron-Leclerc, 'Les témoignages anciens', 101.
9. Théodore Pavie, 'L'Amérique anglaise en 1850', *Revue des Deux Mondes* 8, 15 December 1850, 992, in Caron-Leclerc, 'Les témoignages anciens', 116.
10. Alexis de Tocqueville, in Caron-Leclerc, 'Les témoignages anciens', 90.
11. Jacques Viger, 'Néologie canadienne ou dictionnaire des mot créés en Canada et maintenant en vogue;—des mots dont la prononciation et l' orthographe sont différentes de la prononciation et orthographe françaises, quoique employés dans une acception semblable ou contraire, et des mots étrangers qui se sont glissés dans notre langue', in *Bulletin du parler français au Canada* VIII (1909–1910).
12. Claude Poirier, 'Une langue qui se définit dans l'adversité', in Michel Plourde, *Les français au Québec*, 111–22.
13. Claude Galarneau, 'Évolution de l'alphabétisation au Québec', in Michel Plourde, ed. *Les français au Québec*, 103.
14. Our translation. Narcisse-Eutrope Dionne, *Une dispute grammaticale en 1842* (Quebec: Typ. Laflamme & Proulx, 1912), 34.
15. 'Nos institutions, notre langue et nos lois!'
16. Demers' first letter to the *Gazette de Québec* appeared on 23 April 1842. Maguire's reply was published on 28 April, and Demers' final text in early May. Michel Bibaud's commentaries in *L'Encyclopédie canadienne* appeared in Book 1, Volume 3 (May 1842), Volume 4 (June 1842), Volume 6 (August 1842) and Volume 7 (September 1842). Bibaud also reprinted the article from *Le Canadien* in Volume 9 (November 1842).
17. *Joual*: The name given to the type of working-class language developed in cities among former peasants who became urban labourers and worked under anglophone bosses around the end of the nineteenth century. The progressive anglicization that characterized *joual* reached its apex in the 1960s, when heated debates over its legitimacy led writers like Michel Tremblay to reclaim and celebrate this popular vernacular in their various works. With the language laws of the 1970s; the adoption of French as the common language of public life; and vastly improved levels of education overall, the anglicization of French has subsided significantly in Quebec.
18. Pierre Baillargeon, column, 'Quelle langue parlons-nous?', *La Patrie*, 26 October 1947.
19. André Laurendeau, 'La langue que nous parlons', *Le Devoir*, 21 October 1959.
20. Jean-Paul Desbiens (Frère Untel), 'Je trouve désespérant d'enseigner le français', letter to the editor, *Le Devoir*, 3 novembre 1959. For English translation see: Frère Untel, *The Impertinences of Brother Anonymous*, tr. Miriam Chapin (Montreal: Harvest House, 1962). Uppercase typography has been used, as in the original French version.
21. Gérard Fillion, 'Le règne du joual-vapeur', *Le Devoir*, 23 November 1960.
22. Paul Béland, *Le français, langue d'usage public au Québec en 1997*, rapport de recherche (Quebec: Conseil de la langue française, Gouvernement du Québec, 1999).
23. Madeline Gauthier and Mégane Girard, *Caractéristiques générales des jeunes adultes de 25–35 ans au Québec* (Quebec: Observatoire Jeunes et société, Institut national de la recherche scientifique, prepared for Conseil supérieur de la langue françaises, May 2008), 89.

RELEVANT WEBSITES

CONSEIL SUPÉRIEUR DE LA LANGUE FRANÇAISE:

www.cslf.gouv.qc.ca

Research publications on the situation of the French language.

SECRÉTARIAT À LA POLITIQUE LINGUISTIQUE DU QUÉBEC—CORPUS LEXICAUX QUÉBÉCOIS:

www.spl.gouv.qc.ca/corpus/index.html

Many articles on different subjects concerning the French language in Quebec and a database.

Centre interdisciplinaire de recherches sur les activités langagières, université Laval:
www.ciral.ulaval.ca
  Useful website for finding research material on different language topics.

Office québécois de la langue française:
www.olf.gouv.qc.ca
  Research publications on many aspects of the French language in Quebec.

Histoire de la langue française au Québec:
www.tlfq.ulaval.ca/axl/francophonie/hislfrnqc.htm
  A history of the French language in Quebec by Jacques Leclerc.

SELECT BIBLIOGRAPHY

Bouchard, Chantal. *Obsessed with Language: A Sociolinguistic History of Quebec.* Toronto: Guernica, 2008.

Corbeil, Jean-Claude. *L'embarras des langues.* Montreal: Québec Amérique, 2007.

de Villers, Marie-Éva. *Le vif désir de durer.* Montreal: Québec Amérique, 2005

Gendron Jean-Denis. *D'où vient l'accent des Québécois? Et celui des Parisiens?* Ste-Foy: Presses de l'Université Laval, 2008.

Georgeault, Pierre, and Michel Pagé, eds. *Le français, langue de la diversité québécoise.* Montreal: Québec Amérique, 2006.

Mougeon, Raymond, and Édouard Béniak, eds. *Les origines du français québécois.* Ste-Foy: Presses de l'Université Laval, 1994.

Plourde, Michel, and Pierre Georgeault, eds. *Le français au Québec, 400ans d'histoire et de vie.* Montreal: Conseil supérieur de la langue française/ Fides, 2008.

Stefanescu, Alexandre, and Pierre Georgeault, eds. *Le français au Québec : les nouveaux défis.* Montreal: Fides, 2005.

CHAPTER 12

The Politics of Language in Quebec

Martin Lubin, SUNY Plattsburgh

— TIMELINE —

1910 Quebec Liberal government of Premier Lomer Gouin regulates language practices of railways, telephone, and electric power companies, which had previously often operated solely in English.

1937 Premier Duplessis and his Union Nationale (UN) government adopt law declaring that only French text of Quebec legislation is authoritative.

1951 Debut in Montreal of Radio-Canada, French-language television network of Canadian Broadcasting Corporation.

1955 Ligue d'action nationale collects 200,000 signatures, supporting French name Le Château Maisonneuve instead of The Queen Elizabeth for downtown Montreal complex of offices, shops, and hotel. English name prevailed.

1956 Premier Duplessis appoints provincial Royal Commission on Constitutional Problems.

1960 Founding of Rassemblement pour l'independance nationale (RIN) which advocates political independence of Quebec and French as sole official language of Quebec.

The Programme of the Quebec Liberal Party calls for establishment of Quebec Ministry of Cultural Affairs and 'Office de la langue française'.

Election of Premier Jean Lesage and Quebec Liberal Party (QLP) majority government.

Quebec's Quiet Revolution begins; Duplessis era of 'Quebec politics' ends.

1961 Lesage government establishes Quebec Department of Cultural Affairs within which is Office de la langue française.

1962 RIN pamphlet entitled *Le bilinguisme qui nous tue* argues bilingualism in Montreal is inherently unequal and strength of English in Montreal threatens survival of French language and culture.

1963 Province-wide Société Saint-Jean-Baptiste endorses policy designating French as Quebec's 'official language of work, education, and public administration'.

1966 Election platform of QLP promises to make French principal language of work and communications. Lesage QLP loses; UN forms majority government under leader Daniel Johnson.

1968 UN government of Premier Jean-Jacques Bertrand establishes Commission of Inquiry on the Position of the French Language and French Language Rights in Quebec (Gendron Commission).

Bertrand UN government introduces Bill 85 in attempt to regulate linguistic conflict by affirming linguistic freedom of choice in education, but due to fierce opposition, it is soon withdrawn.

1969 Bertrand UN government adopts Bill 63 as first step towards making French priority language in Quebec while guaranteeing freedom of linguistic choice in education.

Coalition of francophone Québécois nationalists and leftists, including organized labour and Front de libération du Québec (FLQ) members mobilizes 15,000 demonstrators to protest English character of McGill University, a core anglophone Montreal institution.

1970 Robert Bourassa and QLP form majority government. FLQ October Crisis takes place soon after.

1972 Gendron Commission submits its report to Bourassa QLP government.

1973 Bourassa QLP majority government re-elected on platform containing vague references to French as language of work and 'cultural sovereignty'.

1974 Bourassa government passes Bill 22, which among other things required school boards to assign children to English or French.

1976 Réne Lévesque leads Parti Québécois (PQ) to power for first time, forming majority government.

1977 Camille Laurin, PQ Minister of State for Cultural Development, directs drafting of the White Paper 'Quebec's Policy on the French Language'; declares 'there will no longer be any question of a bilingual Quebec'.

Premier Lévesque's PQ government introduces Bill 1, based on Camille Laurin's White Paper, which ultimately becomes law as Bill 101, Charter of the French Language.

1979 Supreme Court of Canada declares invalid provisions in Bill 101 making French sole official language of provincial courts and National Assembly.

1983 Bill 57 allows bilingualism in English-language schools, hospitals, and social service agencies.

1984 Supreme Court of Canada extends right to English-language education to include children of anglophone parents educated in English anywhere in Canada.

1986 Quebec Court of Appeal confirms 1984 decision of Quebec Superior Court that Quebec government could not prohibit use of English in commercial signs and advertising.

1988 Supreme Court of Canada rules that Bill 101 unconstitutionally proscribes bilingual signs. QLP Premier Bourassa invokes the 'notwithstanding clause'.

1993 QLP majority government adopts Bill 86, which states that French must predominate on all public signs, posters, and commercial advertising.

2002 Bernard Landry PQ majority government adopts Bill 104, which integrates Commission de protection de la langue française with Office de la langue française. It also disallows children who had attended private English-language schools from later enrolling in public English-language schools.

2007 Quebec Court of Appeal invalidates Bill 104 because it contravenes Section 23 of Canadian Charter of Rights and Freedoms.

2008 Supreme Court of Canada agrees to hear appeal regarding provisions of Quebec's language law, which impose strict limits on who can attend English language schools in Quebec.

2009 Supreme Court of Canada rules that private English-language schooling should be taken into account when a child's eligibility to enrol in a public English-language school in Quebec is being assessed.

INTRODUCTION

The issue of language is never far from the centre of Quebec politics. As always, the French-speaking community in Quebec faces the major challenge of how best to protect and promote the French language through collective political action in an era of increased globalization in a predominantly anglophone North America. How far could and should Quebec go to protect and promote the French language and thereby reinforce recognition of Quebec as a distinct society or nation either within or outside the Canadian federal system? What are the implications for Quebec's anglophone and other minority communities?

This chapter first presents a broad framework for understanding how French language questions are rooted in the Quiet Revolution and the social and political context within which Quebec addressed these issues in the 1970s. It then discusses three crucial milestones in the politics of language in Quebec after 1960: the formation of Quebec's first-ever provincial Ministry of Cultural Affairs in 1961, the adoption of Bill 22 in 1974, and the adoption of Bill 101 in 1977. The chapter concludes with a brief account of the impact of Quebec's 1970s language policies on francophone and anglophone communities today.

BEFORE THE QUIET REVOLUTION: RELIGION, LANGUAGE, AND THE POLITICAL ECONOMY OF NATIONAL IDENTITY

Before the Quiet Revolution, guarding the French language was firmly in the hands of the Catholic Church. After the defeat in the Patriote Rebellions in 1837–8, the Catholic Church built a broad network of social welfare and educational institutions, which constituted the heart of French Canada's cultural heritage. For over 100 years, government in Quebec limited itself to dealing with other sectors; language and social policy were virtually non-existent.[1] The economy was dominated by British, anglophone Canadians, and American capitalists to whom the provincial government sold off natural resources within its borders. Paralleling the

francophone-Catholic social structure, anglophone ethnic and religious associations established their own network of hospitals, schools, and social welfare.

From the Conquest in 1760 to the Quiet Revolution beginning in1960, English (Canadian, British, and US) control over capital, land, and surplus value ensured that French Canadian Quebecers would be greatly underrepresented among the financial and industrial bourgeoisie in the province, and substantially over-represented among the unskilled and semi-skilled categories of the workforce. The English–French cultural division of labour[2] was a classic colonial pattern, where Anglo-Canadian, British, and US capitalists had no incentives whatsoever to change the rules of the game. The Roman Catholic Church establishment[3] did not want to upset the social order because their interests meshed nicely with those of the anglophone authorities in a convenient relationship of elite accommodation.[4] The traditional petite bourgeoisie in Quebec (lawyers, doctors, and priests), who numerically dominated the ranks of French-Canadian nationalists, opposed both federal and provincial government expansion into social policy. They called on French Canada to maintain the traditional agrarian way of life and social order, and resist assimilation through their traditional institutions; at the same time anglophone groups were orchestrating the industrialization of Quebec.

MODEST BEGINNINGS: JEAN LESAGE, THE QUIET REVOLUTION, AND THE POLITICS OF BUREAUCRATIZATION OF LANGUAGE POLICY

The Quebec Liberal Party (QLP) triumph over the Union Nationale (UN) on 22 June 1960 marked the beginning of the Quiet Revolution. Over the following 20 or so years, a new technocratic middle class spearheaded Quebec's noisy evolution from traditional French Canadian nationalism into Québécois neo-nationalism.[5] Spurred on by the belief that the provincial government could be a key actor in transforming Quebec society, neo-nationalist technocrats produced a torrent of Quebec provincial public policy initiatives including the prioritization of the French language.[6] The Quebec provincial government capitalism that they created actively promoted the emergence of a stronger, more competitive, francophone financial and industrial bourgeoisie in the private sector.

As the Quiet Revolution unfolded, mainstream neo-nationalist politicians, policy-makers, and opinion leaders, and a growing new generation of young street demonstrators built up a list of longstanding concerns about Quebec society that needed to be addressed through political action. These included:

- The subordination of French Canadians in the Quebec economy;
- Anglo-Quebec economic elite resistance to French Canadian claims to equality of opportunity in the economic and industrial development of Quebec;
- The need for French-Canadian workers in Quebec to have some fluency in English, whether for external communications with their own company's head offices, clients, competitors, or suppliers, or whether for technical and instructional communications, even in those firms where French was the internal language of communication;
- The tendency of immigrants to choose English as the language of daily use in homes, workplaces, schools, and on the street;
- The little need that anglophone Quebecers historically had for French, and their lack of motivation for learning it; and
- The failure of institutions of higher learning in Quebec to train many French Canadians to be technologically sophisticated business managers and leaders of Quebec's commercial and industrial decision-making elite.[7]

Such an agenda was a clarion call for a neo-nationalist coalition of working class people, new private and public sector middle-class people, and an emerging industrial and financial bourgeoisie to mobilize around promoting the French language.

Early in the Quiet Revolution, neo-nationalists started pondering how the province could promote Quebec culture. Before 1960, UN Premier Duplessis had merely paid lip service to preserving French-Canadian culture and made little public policy to promote specific cultural activities. He denounced Ottawa's Royal Commission on National Development in the Arts, Letters, and Sciences (Massey Commission 1951) as unconstitutional federal interference in provincial autonomy, but later he failed to develop a policy on Quebec culture even though it had been recommended in the 1956 report of his own provincial Royal Commission of Inquiry on Constitutional Problems (popularly known as the Tremblay Commission).[8]

Yet a more interventionist position on Quebec culture was not necessarily forthcoming with the change in government. The premier of the new QLP government, Jean Lesage, had a more voluntarist view of culture. As head of the Official Opposition, Lesage had deplored the quality of popular spoken French and the generally low level of cultural awareness in Quebec, but he doubted whether public policy could make the significant improvements for which francophone intellectuals and groups were beginning to call. His preferred approach stressed personal activity and improving the economic, social, and educational contexts in which cultural achievements could flourish. Before becoming QLP leader in 1958, Lesage had been a federal cabinet minister and had supported the Canada Council to support arts and social science research.

Lesage saw the establishment of a Quebec Ministry of Cultural Affairs as a way for the Quebec government to carry out its constitutional obligations under Sections 92 and 93 of the 1867 British North America Act. The first article of the 1960 QLP platform committed the party to establishing a Ministry of Cultural Affairs, which it did in 1961. Rather than practising 'state interventionism' the new department would 'try . . . to co-ordinate the activities of organizations working for the expansion of Quebec's culture'. A poorly mastered, imprecise language prevented intellectual and scientific progress; French Canadians would cease to exist as such if they did not preserve their language. Because culture is a function of language, the new department would have under its jurisdiction an Office de la langue française (OLF) to ensure the quality of French spoken in the province. Methods used could vary in 'intensity and scope' according to circumstances.

Yet Lesage's orientation on culture was at odds with the more nationalist members of the QLP. Conflict over different visions of the state role in promoting culture played out over the question of language and came to a head under Quebec's second Minister of Culture, Pierre Laporte. Laporte ordered a White Paper defining Quebec's cultural policy and setting out a plan of action. While the final paper was a compromise between Laporte's statist and Lesage's voluntarist positions, the 1966 QLP election platform showed a significant move towards the nationalist, interventionist position. A section entitled 'Le Quebec français' guaranteed the vitality of French and maintained that the state would 'enable the majority of the population to live in French'. French would be 'the principal language of work and communications' and have 'prior place' in all sectors of society. Quebec's 'true French image' would be ensured by making French predominant on public signs. And a QLP government, if re-elected, would develop an immigration policy to encourage the integration of 'neo-Canadians into the francophone mainstream of Quebec society'.[9]

Early on, anglophone responses to the establishment of the OLF were muted, few, and far between. This minority community (and to a lesser degree its institutionally distinctive Jewish[10] and anglophone-Catholic[11] components) had become accustomed to its own autonomously managed health, educational, and social services institutions. Elite accommodation, rather than noisy organized political demonstrations or confrontations, had long been the weapon of choice in defending anglophone social institutions. The passive anti-statist posture of traditional French-Canadian clerical nationalism before the Quiet Revolution had promoted such accommodation. Despite Quiet Revolution campaigns of economic nationalism and the uncertain future of non-confessional educational and social services, anglophones generally welcomed the early reforms.

THE SOCIAL AND POLITICAL CONTEXT, LANGUAGE, AND THE ARTICULATION OF POPULAR DEMANDS FOR CHANGE

In the 1960s, English–French tensions over language grew in Montreal. Nationalist voices began to loudly call upon the Quebec government to provide visible symbols of the French character of Quebec and her metropolis; these calls included a demand for French unilingualism. A new political party, the Rassemblement pour l'independence nationale (RIN), founded in 1960, called for Quebec to separate from Canada and for French to become the only language of the new state. At its founding convention, the party resolved that: 'Once independence is established, only the French language will be official in Quebec' and that the Quebec government should proclaim itself as unilingually French immediately, not unlike the governments of the other provinces which were unilingually English.[12] This minor separatist political party ultimately merged with the Parti Québécois (PQ), which was founded in 1968.

French unilingualist practitioners of both 'street' and conventional electoral politics, such as the RIN, disagreed over how rapidly a French-only policy should be put into effect and over the place of English-language schools. Whereas the 1965 RIN program proposed a system of French-only public education, René Lévesque, then the most nationalist member of the Lesage QLP cabinet and the future Parti Québécois sovereignist premier of Quebec (1976–85), favoured French as the priority language but without imposing French unilingualism on the anglophone minority.[13] Nevertheless, one common idea prevailed: a fundamentally unequal bilingualism must be abandoned, because the system of linguistic dualism in Quebec promoted the degradation of French.

By 1963 the Société Saint-Jean-Baptiste (SSJB) also supported French unilingualism. Founded in 1834, the Société Saint-Jean-Baptiste de Montréal, representing mainly Montreal francophone doctors, lawyers, shopkeepers, and Roman Catholic clerics, had frequently voiced its concern about the corrosive impact of English on the French character of the city. French-Canadian nationalist groups like this had focused on prohibiting English unilingualism on anything that reaches the public: billboards, stamps, cheques, money, and the like. But in 1963, the province-wide SSJB supported a policy whereby the provincial government would designate French as Quebec's 'official' language of work, education, and public administration.[14] In doing so, the SSJB turned away from its previous advocacy of a bilingualism wherein English would be tolerated but French would be the priority language.

The emerging new francophone middle class, largely those whose occupations dealt with knowledge and information—teachers, administrators, journalists, and policy analysts—broadly supported this novel Québécois nationalist-statist language position. The push for language policies promoting the status of French had distinct cultural roots; but the material interests of the new middle class of francophones would also clearly be well served by policies promoting the use of French in all sectors of Montreal life.[15] Thus, the interests of the old SSJB-oriented unilingualism and the new middle classes converged around promoting the French language, helping to legitimize this francophone common front.

Mass political mobilization on both sides of the English–French linguistic divide intensified after a September 1969 riot in St Leonard, then an independent municipality on the Island of Montreal, between Catholic Italian Quebecers who wanted an English education for their children, and francophone parents and nationalist activist members of the Ligue pour l'integration scolaire. The latter demanded that the children of immigrants (known as 'allophones', whose mother tongue was neither French nor English) be integrated into the francophone school system. At that time, immigrants to Quebec could choose the language of instruction for their children, and 75 per cent were choosing English schools.[16] Following the decision of the local public Catholic school board to impose French instruction on allophone children, Italian parents in St Leonard refused to send their children to public Catholic schools.[17]

Badly underestimating the linguistic insecurity of the francophone population, in 1969 the UN majority government of Premier Jean-Jacques Bertrand passed Bill 63, 'An Act to promote the French language in Quebec', which reaffirmed the principle of parental freedom of choice in education. Nationalist unilingualists thought that this principle would hasten the trend toward francophones becoming a minority in their own province, and a series of mass demonstrations by increasingly numerous and vociferous Québécois nationalist groups followed.

In December 1968, Bertrand's government established a Commission of Inquiry on the Position of the French Language and Language Rights in Quebec, known as the Gendron Commission. The Commission addressed French as the language of work, the integration of new Quebecers into the francophone community, and the language rights of the francophone majority and non-francophone minorities.[18] The commission made many recommendations in its final report in 1972. Foremost, it called on the provincial government to aim to make French the common language of Quebecers: that French be proclaimed the official language of Quebec while retaining the status of English in the courts and legislature of Quebec consistent with section 133 of the 1867 British North America Act; that French gradually become the language of internal communication in the workplaces;[19] that a working knowledge of French should henceforth be a condition for admission to the practice of any trade or profession;[20] and that consumers have the right to be served in French.[21]

The Commission did not recommend any coercive measures to make immigrant or any other children attend French schools. Instead, it suggested that making French the dominant language in the Quebec economy would induce immigrants to choose to educate their children in French, provided that English was taught adequately as a second language. Most children from homes where neither English nor French was spoken attended anglophone Catholic schools in Montreal; such children far outnumbered those in these schools who spoke English at home. The commission attributed this pattern of allophone linguistic choice to three factors: the perception that English was more useful in the Quebec economy, the fact that English as a second language was badly taught in the French schools of the Montreal Catholic school system, and the perception that francophone Quebec had not always made immigrants feel welcome.

THE POLITICS OF BILL 22 (1974)

Before the final report of the Gendron Commission was tabled, the political landscape in Quebec had changed dramatically. In 1970, the QLP returned to power with Robert Bourassa (see Biography box in Chapter 4) at its head, a newly constituted pro-sovereignty PQ ran candidates for the first time in a Quebec provincial election, and the FLQ October Crisis had shaken the entire country.[22] The QLP platform contained ambiguous references to French as the language of work and to 'cultural sovereignty'—Quebec's freedom to protect and develop the French language.[23]

Following the re-election of his government in 1973,[24] Bourassa introduced Bill 22 as a middle ground between anglophones, francophones, and allophones. This Official Language Act made provisions to promote French in business and the economy, though these provisions were significantly weaker than those recommended by the Gendron Commission. For example, the law did not indicate how rigorously the OLF would enforce the criteria for granting private firms 'francization' certificates that would allow them to receive Quebec subsidies or other benefits and to conduct business with the Quebec government. The OLF could choose whether or not to take into account the structure of each firm and the unique circumstances of its head office, subsidiaries, and branches.[25]

On the other hand, provisions of Bill 22 for language of education did not follow the Gendron recommendations. Rather than relying on the progress of French as the priority or common language in the workplace to encourage immigrant allophone families (6 per cent of Quebec's population in 1974) to choose French schools for their children, Bill 22 outlined a more coercive approach. Access to English-language education would be open only to allophone children who could, before entering kindergarten at five years old, demonstrate proficiency in English in government-administered tests.[26] The nine-member OLF regulatory agency advised the Minister of Education; cooperated with businesses to implement programs for greater use of French in their operations; investigated whether the law was being followed; awarded certificates of 'francization' to businesses that successfully upgraded their use of French; and improved the quality of the French language itself by various measures, including steps to standardize vocabulary used in Quebec and to accept or reject new expressions.[27]

People from all language groups found reasons to oppose Bill 22. Francophone nationalist groups like the unilingualist umbrella group Mouvement du Québec français (MQF), which brought together teachers, unions, and nationalist groups, saw Bill 22 proposals as a Trojan horse for the anglicization of the province. The MQF and other unilingualists criticized Bill 22's concessions to bilingualism and the continuation of English-language education as a right, rather than as a privilege, for genuine English speakers. Anglophone groups such as the Montreal Board of Trade, the Association of English Speaking Catholic Teachers, the Canadian Jewish Congress (CJC), and the Provincial Association of Protestant Teachers were shocked by the significantly diminished status of English proclaimed in the bill. They denounced the reversal of previously unrestricted access to English schools, and especially the linguistic proficiency testing of small children, as a discriminatory denial of both the basic universal rights of individual anglophone Quebecers and the historically acquired anglophone community–specific rights based on custom and tradition.[28] Allophones were stunned that the future of their children's education would be decided by a test when they were only five years old.

FROM LANGUAGE LAWS TO A CHARTER OF THE FRENCH LANGUAGE: THE CREATION OF BILL 101 (1977)

On 15 November 1976 Quebec elected a PQ majority government with René Lévesque as premier (see Biography box in Chapter 22). Its top legislative priority early in its mandate was not sovereignty but a comprehensive language policy to affirm the pre-eminence of French in Quebec. The PQ Minister of State for Cultural Development Camille Laurin (see Biography box) supervised the delineation of the main features of the Charter of the French Language which first saw light in the White Paper on Quebec's Language Policy (March 1977), Bill 1 (April 1977), and finally Bill 101 (August 1977). The far-reaching and controversial policy proposals of the White Paper were based on the assumption that if language is the core of collective culture, then francophone Québécois culture could not endure within a bilingual framework. In other words, whatever the historical traditions of toleration

CAMILLE LAURIN[30]

Camille Laurin entering the National Assembly in Quebec City on 27 April 1977 to introduce the government's French language law.

CP Picture Archive/
Louise Bidault

The life and times of Camille Laurin (1922–1999), chief architect of the Quebec Charter of the French Language (Bill 101, 1977—see Snapshot box) provide a useful lens through which to view the complex process of modernization in Quebec during the latter half of the twentieth century. Catholicism, nationalism, and Freudian psychiatry constitute a triad of Laurin's salient formative influences, which at various stages had a profound impact upon his core economic, social, and political beliefs. The theme of continuity and change is central to understanding the intellectual odyssey of Camille Laurin. Beginning as an insular, clerical, conservative, French-Canadian nationalist, he became a secular, statist, Québécois neo-nationalist public intellectual and a Parti Québécois (PQ) government cabinet minister.

Laurin was born in 1922 in Charlemagne, then a small French-Canadian village at the extreme east end of the Island of Montreal, coincidentally only a few months before René Lévesque, the father of the contemporary Quebec sovereignty movement. At that time, the Roman Catholic Church and its health, educational, and social-welfare institutions dominated French Quebec society. Anglo-Canadian and US capital dominated the primary natural resources and rapidly growing secondary manufacturing sectors of the Quebec economy. The Laurin family were devoutly Catholic in a community where social ties developed principally around the Church and numerous religious holidays. Laurin's father Eloi, a

director of the local branch of the Provincial Bank of Canada was a petit bourgeois French-Canadian economic nationalist, a fervent supporter of *achat chez nous*—buy goods and services from *our own* French-Canadian merchants, not from *them*, the non–French Canadian non-Catholics—and an ardent defender of the French language. A long-time Quebec Liberal Party militant, Eloi in 1935 shifted his allegiance to Paul Gouin's l'Action liberale nationale, which advocated the nationalization of hydro-electricity; he detested Duplessis. It was Paul Gouin, son of former Quebec premier Lomer Gouin and grandson of Honoré Mercier, another former premier, and a member of the French-Canadian 'big bourgeoisie', who financially enabled Eloi's son Camille to continue his education from 1937 to 1941 at L'Assomption College. This school catered to children of less well-off French-Canadian merchants, workers, and farmers.

In his fourth year of classical college, at the behest of Abbé Armand Trottier, Camille joined St Mary's English Academy, a literary and oratory student club. His speech topics—in English—included 'School and Immorality', 'Struggles for Our Language', and 'Immigration is Detrimental to us'. This was his introduction to the English language and civilization. In 1940, Camille composed a song which contained the following lyrics: 'My dear friends, hang on to our language, let us never obey our oppressors, from our ancestors it is saintly heritage, our young hearts must remain French'. Meanwhile in the classrooms and corridors of this classical college, student Camille heard and did not disagree with lavish praise heaped upon both the Franco and Pétain fascist corporatist regimes in Spain and France.

His admission to the University of Montreal School of Medicine was delayed one year because he was not adequately prepared at L'Assomption College in the basic physical sciences. In 1947, Laurin became director of the university's student journal *Quartier Latin*. In these pages, perspectives of the emerging post–Second World War French-Canadian intelligentsia on Catholic social action were presented. Laurin wrote that neither Marx, Dewey, nor Freud were enemies of French Catholics. Frequent themes which Laurin addressed here include: 'The Role of the Church in Society'; 'Secularization of Education'; 'Workers' Conditions'; 'Social Policy'; 'Political Future of Quebec and Canada'; and 'International Issues'. As Director of the *Quartier Latin*, Laurin was also preoccupied with the journal's use of proper French—that worthy cause of the greatest French university in North America. Although French-Canadian nationalists (including Laurin) generally conflated anti-communism, defence of Catholicism, anti-conscription, and anti–English Canada themes, Laurin at this time wrote that French-Canadian nationalism was too much grounded in the traditional values of language and religion. To be relevant in the future, French-Canadian nationalism would have to refocus on new social values and the economic development of society. French-Canadian nationalism would continue to believe in a cultural and Catholic mission as a people; but Laurin thought it necessary to focus largely on issues such as workers' salaries, collective bargaining, housing, social insurance, taxes, popular education, and recreation.

In 1949, during his fifth and final year of general medicine at the University of Montreal, he decided to specialize in psychiatry rather than clinical medicine. In 1950, he did a 12-month residency in psychiatry at Queen Mary Veteran's Hospital in Montreal. He chose Queen Mary because he judged that anglophone hospitals were more advanced than francophone institutions, with more emphasis on psychological causes than the physical and physiological roots of mental disorder stressed in French hospitals in Quebec. To realize his dream of becoming a fully accredited psychoanalytic psychiatrist, he

had to pursue further study in the United States or Europe, because in Montreal, francophone psychiatrists were resistant to modern trends in the field. In French Quebec generally at this time, mental illness was widely stigmatized. Quebec was far behind also in teaching methods in psychiatry and in patient care in psychiatric hospitals. Thus, Laurin began to see himself as a future psychiatrist, teacher, administrator, and reformer of Quebec psychiatry.

Despite decades of use in Europe and the United States, even the most advanced thinkers among French Quebec psychiatrists feared Freud's theories. In Laurin's eyes, Freud was a genius; his discoveries were essential to understanding and treating the human mind. He went to Boston until 1952, when US conscription law forced him to go to France to complete the arduous prerequisites to full certification as a psychotherapist. In 1957 he returned to Quebec to start a practice at the age of 35.

The Catholic, nationalist, and Freudian psychoanalytic cross-currents mesh in Laurin's analysis of what ailed the French Quebec people and what could be done to cure this collective disorder. He believed that the French Québécois suffered a deep and collective sense of powerlessness that only the liberating gesture of political independence would be able to correct. He saw his own Québécois people as sad, passive, resigned to their fate, and discouraged. The healthy part of their personality was affected by a significant loss of self-confidence and the sense of always being a small cog in the grand scheme of things. The remedy could only be the establishment of a strong Quebec state to overcome the enduring effects of the British Conquest.

In a sense, the story of modern Quebec is the story of Camille Laurin writ large.

for acquired linguistic rights, '. . . there will no longer be any question of a bilingual Quebec'.[29]

Many anglophone groups and institutions testified before the legislative committee that examined Bill 1 in June and July of 1977. The Canadian Jewish Congress and the Protestant School Board of Greater Montreal (PSBGM) claimed to support, at least in theory, the bill's objective of promoting the French language.

However, the PSBGM criticized the restrictive rules of access to English education and the provisions requiring predominantly anglophone school boards to write their internal and external communications in French. They went so far as to protest that Bill 1 threatened the survival of English-language education. The Canadian Jewish Congress reiterated criticisms of Bill 1 provisions on access to English schools, prohibition of

English on commercial signs, the requirement that anglophone school boards and municipalities communicate in French, and the abolition of official bilingualism in the courts and the Quebec National Assembly. They were particularly critical of a provision which would allow the Quebec government to override sections of the 1975 Quebec Charter of Human Rights and Freedoms. Business groups like the Royal Bank of Canada, the Montreal Board of Trade, and La chambre de commerce du district de Montréal contended that the francization program of the Charter would encourage capital flight and damage economic development. More polemically, some claimed that the bill was akin to 'cultural genocide'; some compared the PQ to Nazis.

On the other hand, the Montreal branches of the SSJB and the MQF, though generally supportive of the Charter, insisted that it did not go far enough limiting education in English. In belittling anglophone opposition, Camille Laurin warned that English-speaking Quebecers should learn to see themselves as a minority and not as part of an English-Canadian majority residing in Quebec. He disputed the contention that Quebec anglophones were struggling on behalf of universal human rights, because they did not take into account social inequalities which ought to limit recourse to absolute individual rights. But, in a series of *Le Devoir* editorials, Claude Ryan criticized Laurin for his division of Quebec into 'good' (pro-Charter) Quebecers (like himself) and 'bad' ones (anglophones and anti-Charter francophones).[31]

On 26 August 1977, the Charter of the French Language was adopted as Bill 101 in the Quebec National Assembly. What are the important principles behind Bill 101? What are its intervention domains? The preamble to Bill 101 proclaims the major principles of this law:

> The French language is the instrument by which [the Quebec] people has articulated its identity
>
> . . . Quebecers wish to see the quality and influence of the French language assured . . . [the Charter will] make of French the language of Government and the Law, as well as the normal and everyday language of work, instruction, communication, commerce and business

> . . . [the achievement of] this objective [should be] in a spirit of fairness and open-mindedness, respectful of the institutions of the English-speaking community of Québec, and respectful of the ethnic minorities;
>
> . . . Québec recognizes the right of the Amerinds and the Inuit of Québec, the first inhabitants of this land, to preserve and develop their original language and culture;
>
> . . . [these principles are] in keeping with a new perception of the worth of national cultures in all parts of the earth, and the obligation of every people to contribute in its special way to the international community.[32]

As for the scope of Quebec state intervention, Bill 101 tackles language in the following domains:

- the legislature and the courts (Chapter III)
- civil administration (Chapter IV)
- commerce and business (Chapter VII)
- labour relations (Chapter VI)
- instruction (Chapter VIII)
- semi-public agencies (Chapter V) [33]

To some extent, the PQ's Bill 101, the Charter of the French Language, was a continuation of the official unilingualism policy which the QLP's Bill 22 had begun three years earlier, when it proclaimed in a provincial statute for the first time that 'French is the Official Language of Quebec' (Title 1-1) and that therefore 'it is incumbent upon the government of the province of Quebec to employ every means in its power to ensure the pre-eminence of that language' (Preamble).[34]

Bill 101 reproduced provisions of Bill 22 on the language of public administration, labour, and business; but whereas Bill 22 relied on incentives and persuasion, the Charter relied more on coercion. Sections 7–13 of the Charter, unlike Bill 22, permitted only French in Quebec statutes and court judgments. This provision was declared invalid by the Supreme Court of Canada in 1979, which ruled that it violated Section 133 of the British North America Act. Section 45 provided that no employee could be dismissed, suspended, or demoted for inability to speak a language other than French. Section 53 stated that businesses must publish their catalogues, brochures, and flyers in French. Under Section 55 of Bill 101, businesses need not provide contracts in English, even if a customer so requests; Bill 22 had made English contracts obligatory upon request. Section 58 required that commercial signs must be in French only, although other sections allowed for exceptions in certain circumstances.

Section 136 of the Charter required all firms with 50 or more employees to acquire a certificate of francization; Bill 22 had limited these certificates to those receiving contracts, subsidies, concessions, or benefits from the government.[35] Bill 22, in Chapter II, Division 1, established a French Language Board (La regie de la langue française) to supervise and assist businesses in obtaining the certificates. If firms were not seeking provincial government contracts or subsidies, they could under Bill 22 avoid the costs of francization entirely. Bill 101 created three different boards to enforce the Charter and to carry out functions formerly assigned solely to the Régie de la langue française:

- the Office de la langue française to define and conduct policy, to approve francization certificates, to set up terminology committees, and to administer French proficiency tests.
- the Conseil de la langue française to monitor the progress of language planning and to advise the Minister of Education regarding interpretation of Bill 101.

- the Commission de surveillance et des enquêtes to deal with failures to comply with the Charter.[36]

On access to English-language education, the Charter rules were much more restrictive than those in Bill 22, even though the latter's controversial provision for testing of allophone children entering kindergarten was eliminated. In fact, there was no need for such a provision in Bill 101, as all immigrants, including those from English-speaking countries, were denied any right to educate their children in English. Section 73 of the Charter allowed only four categories of children to receive an English education:

. . . those whose father or mother had attended an English school in Quebec, those whose father or mother had attended an English school in another province and were already living in Quebec when the bill was adopted by the National Assembly, those who were legally enrolled in an English school in Quebec before the bill was adopted, and the younger siblings of those who qualified under the third criterion.[37]

Anglophone migrants from other provinces of Canada arriving after the adoption of the Charter were thus denied the right to send their children to English schools. This restriction was overturned in 1984, when the Supreme Court of Canada ruled that under Section 23 of the 1982 Charter of Rights and

SNAPSHOT

Bill 101: The Charter of the French Language

The National Assembly's adoption on 26 August 1977 of Bill 101 as the Charter of the French Language and its implementation illustrates the robustness of Quebec's democracy and its respect for the rule of law. There was intense controversy over the meaning of the principle of toleration of minority rights and how to apply it when a freely elected Quebec government tries to significantly invert power relations between minority and majority linguistic communities.

Before the Quiet Revolution, anglophone Quebecers, although numerically the minority, held a considerable economic majority, as they were disproportionately advantaged in education and business; francophone Quebecers made up over 80 per cent of the population, and yet they were the economic minority. The essence of politics is power—who gets what, when, and how. Politics entails the authoritative distribution of advantages to some and disadvantages to others in the name of the whole community. Politics also entails the displacement of emotional affect, rationalized as the public interest. And ultimately politics becomes the art of compromise, one hopes, between rival societal segments, because without conflict, there can be no politics—democratic or otherwise—and consequently no need for compromise. All these perspectives on politics come into play in some form when one tries to dispassionately assess the significance of the Charter of the French Language.

In looking back over the past 30 years, both sovereignist and revised-federalist francophone Quebec nationalists have come to consider the Quebec National Assembly's adoption of the Charter of the French Language, Bill 101, in 1977 to be essential in the perennial struggle to defend and promote the use of the French language. From this perspective, the Charter has permanently reversed long-term trends whereby the anglophone minority had perpetually dominated the francophone Quebecer majority. The experience and understanding acquired since 1977 will enable French Quebec society to serenely meet the challenges of a multimedia universe and computers. Bill 101 gave francophones the self-confidence necessary to face the future; and they will never return to the conditions which prevailed before 1976. Even though several major provisions of Bill 101 have been overturned by both the Quebec Court of Appeals and the Supreme Court of Canada, the language Charter has completely transformed the social structure of Quebec by francizing immigrants and putting political and economic power in the hands of francophones.

Yet, the law also has exacerbated the long-time linguistic fault line in Quebec society. Bill 101 did place what many would call stringent limits on using English outside the home, certainly more than Quebec's prior Official Language Act, the Quebec Liberal Party's Bill 22 (1974). Bill 101 was loudly denounced by its opponents, not all of them anglophones, both inside and outside the National Assembly, as useless, hypocritical, unconstitutional, and economically costly. The Charter was castigated as 'separatist' law which would eviscerate the historically acquired rights of the anglophone minority

in Quebec. Anglophone opponents predicted dire economic consequences for all Quebecers and the disappearance of the Quebec anglophone community. It was thought by many that the provisions of the Charter would arbitrarily be put into effect by faceless, unelected language bureaucrats in the Office de la langue française, to whom too much power was delegated by the Quebec legislature. But, some 30 years after adoption of the law, the anglophone community has not disappeared. In North America, of which Quebec is inevitably a part, the economic, cultural, and scientific prominence of English makes it unlikely that Quebec could ever be without a dynamic anglophone cultural community.

Bill 101 has limited anglophone rights and privileges, threatened English-language schools by significantly shrinking the number of students they can serve, and diminished the status of the anglophone community, especially in Montreal, from the historically dominant group to merely the most important of many minority cultural communities in a predominantly French-speaking society. Overwhelming opposition to every aspect of Bill 101 in the anglo-Montreal community remains deeply entrenched; though its intensity, as reflected in movements such as the now defunct Equality Party, has declined. Very few anglophones view the Charter as legitimate, though it is becoming increasingly clear that neither a PQ or QLP government in office in Quebec City will change the essentials. English Montreal and its institutions are largely accommodating themselves to the new Montreal, although not with much enthusiasm.

In most areas, the Parti Québécois's Bill 101 continued along the linguistic policy trajectory begun with Bill 22 under Robert Bourassa's Liberals. For example, the francization provisions of Bill 101 were only slightly more rigid than those of Bourassa's law. While Bill 101 was generally more restrictive than Bill 22 on language of instruction for immigrants, the PQ statute was more permissive in permitting the siblings of children already enrolled in English schools to receive instruction in English. Nevertheless, Bill 101 was clearly the policy of a political party dedicated to leading Quebec out of the Canadian federation to political independence. That law was a significant departure from Bill 22 with respect to French-only public signs and requiring French as the language of work in public institutions regardless of their linguistic composition.

Bill 101 is the most enduring public policy achievement of the PQ. It is the cornerstone of the Quebec sovereignty movement's claim to be the true heirs of the legacy of the Quiet Revolution of the 1960s, rather than the Quebec Liberal Party versions of revised federalism under Lesage, Bourassa, Ryan, and Charest. Ironically, the linguistic security provided by Bill 101 may have unintentionally attenuated francophone dissatisfaction with Canadian federalism, thus irreparably damaging the PQ's effort to secure majority support in the 1980 and 1995 Quebec referendums on sovereignty.

Freedoms, access to Quebec's English schools must be extended to children of anglophone parents educated in English anywhere in Canada.

CONCLUSION

Anglophones were angered as well as confused: English was the language of the demographic, economic, and political majority in Canada and indeed in North America. How could it be that *their* QLP provincial government in 1974—let alone the more draconian PQ administration to follow in 1977—restricted both the individual and acquired community rights of Canadian citizens residing in Quebec?

The 1976 PQ election victory and Bill 101 accelerated the departure of anglophones from Quebec. During the initial five-year mandate of the Levesque government (1976–81), the proportion of francophones grew from 80.7 per cent to 82.4 per cent of the total population of Quebec, and anglophones declined from 12.9 per cent to 10.9 per cent;[38] 131,500 anglophones left Quebec.[39] It is possible that anglophone departures were primarily based on purely economic rather than political and linguistic factors. However, Bill 101 did strongly influence the 'opportunity structure' in Montreal, increasing the value of French in the city's labour market and limiting the options open to unilingual anglophones. Associated with the departure of individual anglophones and contributing significantly to it through the relocation of jobs was the transfer of corporate head offices from Montreal to Toronto and other Canadian cities.[40] Yet most anglophones did not leave Montreal despite the 1981 re-election of the PQ only 11 months

after the 1980 Quebec referendum. Many chose to defy Bill 101, especially the education provisions (e.g., the Quebec Clause). And they sought to restore public display of bilingual commercial signs and guarantees of government services in English. But that 1981 election had effectively ended any hope of Montreal reverting to a pre-PQ laissez faire linguistic regime.

When in 1988 the Supreme Court of Canada ruled that Bill 101 unconstitutionally banned bilingual commercial signs, QLP Premier Bourassa invoked the 'Notwithstanding Clause', Section 33 of the federal Constitution Act, 1982. The latter permits provincial governments to override, for five years at a time, sections 2 through 7 and Section 15 of the Canadian Charter of Rights and Freedoms that might conflict with provincial law. The Quebec National Assembly adopted Bill 178, which maintained unilingual French signs outside of public buildings but permitted bilingual signs with French predominating inside. In protest, three anglophone QLP ministers resigned, claiming that Bourassa had reneged on 1985 election campaign promises; francophone nationalists strongly protested this dilution of Bill 101. And ultimately, this particular episode contributed in no small measure to English-Canadian backlash inside and outside Quebec which helped to bring about the June 1990 Meech Lake (dis)Accord.

Today is no longer 1977 or 1988. Linguistic tensions in Quebec have subsided somewhat. This is the result of a combination of factors: court decisions overturning some of Bill 101's more controversial provisions; the onset of constitutional fatigue over the question of Quebec's constitutional status after the 1995 referendum; non-francophone adaptation due to more familiarity; legislative and bureaucratic accommodations to specific provisions of the Charter (see Timeline). Moreover, thanks to Quebec government intervention, francophone Quebec society has been substantially transformed; Quebec's cultural division of labour has considerably narrowed; and the allophone 'children of Bill 101' are slowly integrating into French Quebec society. For example, in 1971, 90 per cent of allophone children were enrolled in English-language schools; by 1994–5, 79 per cent were enrolled in French-language schools.[41] Without the Charter's restrictions, allophone parents likely would not have chosen to enrol their children in French-language schools.

More recently, for the first time since 1976, the number of anglophones in Quebec modestly rose from 591,000 in 2001 to 607,000 in 2006. The population growth rate between 2001 and 2006 for anglophones (+2.7 per cent) was higher than for francophones (+2.0 per cent). In contrast to a decrease of 16,000 in the number of people who spoke English most often at home between 1996 and 2001, there was an increase of 40,000 between 2001 and 2006. For those whose primary home language is English, the 5.5 per cent increase since 2001 doubles that of the population whose main home language is French (+2.8 per cent).

The increase in Quebec's anglophone population is primarily due to many fewer anglophones leaving the province between 2001 and 2006 compared to the seven previous five-year periods. In particular, 34,000 anglophones left Quebec between 2001 and 2006. At the same time, 26,000 anglophones moved to Quebec, mostly from Ontario, resulting in a net loss of 8,000, in contrast to 1996–2001, when the net loss was almost 30,000. The number of anglophones moving to Quebec has not changed much since 1976, but the number of departures has clearly decreased. The net loss of 8,000 anglophones is the smallest since 1966.[42]

A recent study by the Conseil superieur de la langue française states that Quebecers aged between 25 and 35 acknowledge the relevance of Bill 101 and they attach much importance to the French language.[43] For anglophone Quebecers, however, the French language is merely a useful tool rather than a core element of their identity. An even more current poll in 2007, upon the thirtieth anniversary of Bill 101, shows that 79 per cent of francophones, compared to 57 per cent of non-francophones, believe that Bill 101 had a positive effect on Quebec society. That percentage goes up to 82 per cent for all Quebecers between 18 and 24 years old.[44]

Defining a modus vivendi between francophones and anglophones in Quebec continues to be a work in progress. The data above suggest that Bill 101 did create a framework in which more and more of Quebec's people of all ethnic and linguistic origins are beginning to feel more secure on the question of language. The climate in 2010 is better than it was in 1977—at least for now.

QUESTIONS FOR CONSIDERATION

1. How did it come to pass that, prior to the Quiet Revolution, in terms of the politics of language, the French-speaking 'majority' of the population in Quebec in fact had 'minority' status? In what respects? Explain and elaborate in some detail.

2. How did the French-speaking 'majority' overcome their pre-Quiet Revolution 'minority' status? In what respects? How did this happen? Explain and elaborate in some detail.

3. Largely on the basis of what you read in this chapter on the politics of language in Quebec, to what extent (if at all) do you feel that Quebec has struck a proper balance between the principle of respect for the rights of minority non-francophone language communities and the duty of any freely elected government to translate the democratic preferences of its francophone majority, which makes up more than 80 per cent of its population, into adequate protection and therefore active promotion of the use of French in Quebec? Why? Explain and elaborate in some detail.

Notes

1. On why the absence of a state intervention tradition in Quebec contrasted to Canada before the Quiet Revolution, see, Philip Resnick, *The Masks of Proteus: Canadian Reflections on the State* (Montreal and Kingston: McGill-Queens University Press, 1990), 207–20.

2. Kenneth McRoberts, *Social Change and Political Crisis* (Toronto: McClelland & Stewart, 1993), 25–7. See also Everett Hughes, *French Canada in Transition* (Chicago: University of Chicago Press, 1971), chapter VII, 'The Industrial Hierarchy', 46–64.

3. The Roman Catholic Church is not a monolith. Catholic social doctrine and its applications by Catholic lay and clergy activists in the 1940s and 1950s were at odds with the generally more conservative orientations of that institution's elites. Trudeau, P.E. *The Asbestos Strike*, (Toronto: James Lewis & Samuel, 1974), 13–18.

4. Kenneth McRae, ed., *Consociational Democracy: Political Accommodation in Segmented Societies* (Toronto: McClelland & Stewart, 1977), 240–4; 255–9.

5. Donald Cuccioletta, and Martin Lubin, 'The Quebec Quiet Revolution: A Noisy Evolution', *Quebec Studies* 36 (Fall 2003/Winter 2004): 130–2; 136.

6. Similar projects included the creation of Hydro-Quebec (1962); the establishment of a secular Quebec Ministry of Education (1965), and a Quebec Pension Plan (Regie des Rentes) in tandem with a Quebec Investment Fund (Caisse de depot et placement), also in 1965.

7. Extrapolated from Government of Quebec, *Report of the Commission of Inquiry on the Position of the French Language and on Language Rights in Quebec* (Gendron Commission) Vol. 2, *Language Rights* (Quebec: Official Publisher, 1972), 10–11.

8. Dale C. Thomson, *Jean Lesage and the Quiet Revolution* (Toronto: Macmillan, 1984), 311.

9. Thomson, ibid., 321. See also M.V. Levine, *The Reconquest of Montreal: Language Policy and Social Change in a Bilingual City* (Philadelphia: Temple University Press, 1990), 54–5.

10. See Martin Lubin, 'The Politics of Social Policy in Quebec: The Case of Bill 65 (1971) and the Jewish Community', *Quebec Studies* 1, 1 (Spring 1983): 43–70.

11. Garth Stevenson, *Community Besieged: The Anglophone Minority and the Politics of Quebec* (Montreal and Kingston: McGill-Queen's University Press, 1999), 102–3.

12. Levine, op. cit., 52.

13. See for example Smith, B. *La Loi 22: Le Parti Québécois, Aurait-il Fait Mieux?* (Montreal: Edition du jour, 1975). This hard-line *independantiste* unilingualism advocate denounces the PQ's misguided conciliatory third option, re: Bill 22 (1974).

14. Gouvernement du Québec, *Commission d'enquêtê sur l'éducation* (Parent Commission) Vol. 4 (Quebec, éditeur officiel du Québec, 1966), 119. See also Guy Lachapelle et al., *The Quebec Democracy: Structure, Processes, & Policies* (Montreal: McGraw-Hill Ryerson, 1993), 332.

15. Levine, 44.

16. G. Latif, *L'école québécoise et les communautes culturelles* (Quebec: Ministère de l'Education, 1988), 56.

17. Christian Rioux, 'The Quebec Language Question is back: From Saint-Leonard to the Bouchard-Taylor Commission', *Inroads* 22, (Winter-Spring 2008): 58.

18. Gendron Commission, Vol. 2, *Language Rights*, 5.

19. Ibid., Vol. 1 *Language of Work*, 291. See also Stevenson, 115–16.

20. Ibid., 294.

21. Ibid., 299.

22. Pierre Laporte, a member of then Quebec Premier Bourassa's post-1970 Quebec provincial election QLP cabinet was kidnapped by a Quebec Liberation Front (FLQ) cell and murdered. In turn, Canada's Federal Liberal Prime Minister, Pierre Trudeau, proclaimed the War Measures Act, 1914, to respond to '. . . an apprehended state of insurrection'.

23. Stevenson, op. cit., 117.

24. Due to the mathematical and geographical problematics of Quebec's single-member plurality district electoral system, despite an increase in PQ electoral support from 20 per cent to over 30 per cent, the PQ caucus in the National Assembly in fact declined from 7 to 6 seats.

25. McRoberts, 229–30.

26. National Assembly of Quebec, *Bill 22 Official Language Act, First reading*, Quebec: Official Publisher, 2nd session, 30th Parliament 1974, Ch. 5, S. 51, p. 10.

27. Ibid., ch. 2, Ss. 61–7, p. 13–14.

28. Levine, 102–5, and Stevenson, 120–1.

29. Levine, 114.

30. Sources: J.-C. Picard, *Camille Laurin: L'homme debout* (Montreal: Les Editions du Boreal, 2003); R. Filion, *Une Saison Chez Camille Laurin: Cornet d'UN Compagnon de route,* (Montreal: Isabelle Quentin, 2005); www.assnat.qc.ca/FRA/membres/notices/j-l/LAURC.htm; www.speedylook.com/Camille_Laurin.html.

31. Levine, 116–18.

32. www.olf.gouv.qc.ca/english/charter/preamble.html.

33. See the full text of the Charter at: www.olf.gouv.qc.ca/english/charter/preamble.html. See also Charter of the French Language, R.S.Q., Chapter C-11, updated to 1 February 1984.

34. See Bill No. 22, Official Language Act, First Reading, Title 1 and Preamble.

35. Stevenson, p. 145. See also Charter of the French Language, Title I.

36. Guy Lachapelle, 338–40. See also Charter of the French Language, Titles II, III, and IV.

37. Stevenson, 145–6.

38. Martin Lubin, 'Quebec Nonfrancophones and the United States' in A.O. Hero Jr. and M. Daneau, *Problems and Opportunities in U.S.–Quebec Relations* (Boulder, Colorado: Westview Press, 1984), 188–91.

39. See www12.statcan.gc.ca/english/census06/analysis/language/pdf/97-555-XIE2006001.pdf.

40. Stevenson, 152.

41. Ian Lockerbie et al., *French as the Common Language in Quebec: History, Debates and Positions* (Montreal: Les editions Nota bene, 2005), 104.

42. www12.statcan.ca/English/census06/analysis/language/anglo pop.cfm.

43. www.cslf.gouv.qc.ca/publications/PubF223.pdf.

44. Carole Topin, 'La loi 101 a la cote'. *La Presse*, 24 August 2007, 1, 6.

RELEVANT WEBSITES

L'AMÉNAGEMENT LINGUISTIQUE DANS LE MONDE: www.tlfq.ulaval.ca/axl/

Information about official language regimes in multi-lingual societies around the globe.

CONSEIL SUPÉRIEUR DE LA LANGUE FRANÇAISE: www.cslf.gouv.qc.ca/

This provincial governmental body advises the Minister responsible for the application of the Language Charter on cases involving potential infractions to the law. It usefully archives the Conseil's opinions.

DAVID CRYSTAL: www.davidcrystal.com/

David Crystal is one of the world's leading chroniclers of the world's endangered languages. The part of his website on 'language death and diversity' contains references to his major works on the subject.

DIVERSCITÉ: www.teluq.uquebec.ca/diverscite/entree.htm

An academic journal based in Quebec that publishes scholarly work on language trends as they affect minority languages in a context of globalization.

ETHNOLOGUE: www.cslf.gouv.qc.ca/

An indispensable clearing house of academic studies on the languages of the world. Its bibliography now runs to some 13,000 items.

OFFICE OF THE COMMISSIONER OF OFFICIAL LANGUAGES OF CANADA: www.ocol-clo.gc.ca/html/publications_e.php

This federal governmental body monitors the situation of Canada's two official languages, English and French. It is particularly concerned with the status of French outside Quebec, and of English inside Quebec. Its annual reports are available on the website, and give a good sense of trends as they develop over time.

OFFICE QUÉBÉCOIS DE LA LANGUE FRANÇAISE: www.olf.gouv.qc.ca/

This provincial governmental body is tasked with monitoring trends in the use of French in Quebec. The website regularly publishes reports on the province's linguistic situation, and contains many tools for the francization of businesses subject to the provisions of the Language Charter.

SELECT BIBLIOGRAPHY

Caldwell, Gary, and Eric Wadell, eds. *The English of Quebec: From Majority to Minority Status*. Quebec: Institut Québécois de recherche sur la culture, 1982.

Coleman, William D. 'The Class Bases of Language Policy in Quebec, 1949-1983' in Gagnon, A-G., *Quebec State and Society*. Toronto: Methian, 1984.

Fraser, Matthew. *Quebec Inc.: French-Canadian Entrepreneurs and the New Business Elites*. Toronto: Key Porter Books, 1987.

Garreau, Joel. *The Nine Nations of North America*. New York: Avon Books, 1981.

Keith-Ryan, Heather, and Sharon McCully. *Quebec Bonjour, eh? A Primer for English-Speakers*. Mansonville, Quebec: VOA Publications, 1996.

Mallea, John R., ed. *Quebec's Language Policies: Background and Response*. Publications of the International Centre for Research on Bilingualism, Quebec: Les Presses de l'Université Laval, 1977.

Milner, Henry. *The Long Road to Reform: Restructuring Public Education in Quebec*. Montreal and Kingston: McGill-Queen's University Press, 1986.

Provencher, Jean. *Rene Levesque: Portrait of a Québécois*. Markham, Ont.: Paperjacks, 1977.

Resnick, Philip. *Letters to a Quebec Friend*. Montreal and Kingston: McGill-Queen's University Press, 1990.

Ryan, Claude. *A Stable Society: Quebec after the PQ*. St. Lambert, Quebec: Les Editions Heritage, 1978.

Roussopoulos, Dimitrios I., et al., eds. *Our Generation: Quebec/Canada October Events* 7, 3 (October–November 1970).

Untel, Frere. *The Impertinences of Brother Anonymous*. Montreal: Harvest House, 1968.

CHAPTER 13

Language Planning and Policy Making in Quebec and in Canada

Linda Cardinal,[1] *University of Ottawa*

— TIMELINE —

1774 Quebec Act guarantees freedom of religion in Province of Quebec and restores French civil law while maintaining English criminal law.

1791 Constitutional Act divides Province of Quebec into Upper and Lower Canada. In Lower Canada, English and French are used in the Legislative Assembly and bills are prepared in both languages. In Upper Canada, French has no official status.

1839 Lord Durham presents his *Report on the Affairs of British North America*, which recommends reuniting the two provinces in order to assimilate French Canadians into English culture.

1840 Section XLI of Act of Union provides that all records and proceedings of Parliament of the United Province of Canada be in English only.

1867 Section 133 of British North America Act permits the use of French and English in parliamentary debates and in all federal courts, and for provincial statutes and in provincial courts in Quebec.

1870 Manitoba Act establishes dual system of Protestant and Roman Catholic schools. It also says that both English and French can be used in the Legislative Assembly as well as before the courts. Records and journals of Legislature must be prepared, and all laws must be published, in both languages.

1871 Common Schools Act provides for free education in New Brunswick, but abolishes public support of denominational schools.

1877 North-West Territories Act amended to specify that both English and French may be used in Legislature and before courts. Both languages shall be used in records, journals, and orders.

1890 Official Language Act in Manitoba provides that English be the only official language of that province. Public funding of Catholic schools abolished.

1892 French abolished de facto in North-West Territories Legislative Assembly. In following years, it is gradually abolished as language of instruction in the region.

1910 Lavergne Act, the first act regulating use of French in Quebec. It requires that bus, train, and tram tickets be printed in both English and French.

1912 In Ontario, Regulation 17 limits use of French as a language of instruction to first two years in elementary schools. It is amended one year later to permit French as subject of study for one hour per day.

1916 English made only language of instruction in Manitoba.

1931 English made only language of instruction in Saskatchewan.

1961 Creation of Office de la langue française.

1968 Ontario amends Education Act to recognize existence of French-language elementary schools and to authorize creation of French-language high schools.

Saskatchewan Education Act modified to allow establishment of designated schools that can teach as much as 80 per cent in French.

1969 Official Languages Act declares that English and French enjoy equal status, rights, and privileges in Parliament and government of Canada.

Quebec adopts Bill 63, which makes English schools available to any child upon parents' request. Curricula and examinations must ensure working knowledge of French for all Quebec children attending English schools.

1970 Act 113 restores status of French as language of instruction in Manitoba.

1974 National Assembly of Quebec adopts Bill 22. French proclaimed official language of the province.

1977 Bill 101, also known as The Charter of the French Language, adopted.

1981 An Act Recognizing the Equality of the Two Official Linguistic Communities in New Brunswick adopted.

1982 Government of Canada and nine provinces agree on patriation of Canadian Constitution. Charter of Rights and Freedoms is enshrined in new Constitution Act. Charter incorporates language rights of Official Languages Act and new rights related to official language minority education.

1986 Ontario adopts French Language Services Act, ensuring that government services are offered in French in 25 designated areas.

1988 In Alberta, Language Act reaffirms unilingual English nature of province while recognizing right to use French in Legislature and before certain courts.

Alberta School Act recognizes francophones' right to instruction in French.

1998 In *Reference re Secession of Quebec*, Supreme Court of Canada, in ruling on whether Quebec has right to unilateral secession, identifies protection of minorities as underlying constitutional principle.

In Quebec and Canada, language planning and policy-making is far from a neutral process devoid of political investment. Power relations between language groups influence language planning and policy-making and remind us that political and normative debates are linked to concrete political issues. States need to provide solutions to these political issues to bring about linguistic peace in one form or another. In discussing the crucial role that language, especially English and French, has played and continues to play in Canada and especially in Quebec, this chapter shows that much history and politics lie behind language planning and policy-making in both societies. Canadians like to think that their tolerance and respect for diversity are part of their cultural heritage; few would admit that it rests also on power politics. In other words, there is nothing 'natural' about the recognition of diversity or the promotion of languages.

Language planning and policy-making requires formal state intervention.[2] It involves making language laws and state intervention in areas strategic to the promotion of languages such as the economy, education, health, immigration, and justice. Therefore, language laws usually interact with planning and policy-making in other spheres of government intervention, and sociolinguists can advocate an integral or holistic approach to language planning and policy-making.[3] Planning is usually guided by two principles: personality and territoriality.[4] The personality principle is based on the idea that individuals have rights, including the right to speak the language of their choice. In contrast, the territoriality principle is based on the idea that a language is a collective good that needs to be protected or reinforced on its own territory.

Students of nationalism agree that the territoriality principle is more effective for promoting linguistic and national minorities.[5] However, language policies often borrow from both the territoriality and the personality principles. A language policy may be premised on the ideal of individual rights (the personality principle) but may only apply in certain areas where numbers warrant (the territoriality principle). This is a negative use of the territoriality principle; a more positive use would be to provide some form of territorial devolution or confer a special status on a particular group. Such a situation, however, may create minorities within the minority. In a liberal framework, a language law that reinforces the language of a majority in a given territory should at least recognize rights to services of its internal minorities.

While sociolinguists provide valuable information about the dynamics of language planning and policy-making, nationalism scholars and political theorists debate the best politics of recognition for linguistic and national minorities. Political economists argue that the process of language planning and policy-making is not informed solely by the goal of accommodating languages.[6] Other power relations come into play. This chapter shows how the recognition of both English and French as official languages in Canada, and that of French in Quebec were informed by political debates that go back, at the very least, to the eighteenth century, when Britain conquered New France. Debates on the future of French in both Canada and Quebec are particularly lively in Quebec, where the French-speaking population constitutes the largest French national group in North America but remains a minority on the continent. As a result, Quebec and Canadian language debates are an important reference for any student of language politics, sociolinguistics, nationalism studies, or political theory.

The chapter is divided into three sections. First, it briefly surveys the status of English and French in Canada and Quebec, looking at the most recent language data published by Statistics Canada. Second, it proposes some milestones for understanding the dynamics of language planning and policy-making in Canada and their impact on Quebec. Third, it discusses language planning and policy-making in Quebec and its effect on the equilibrium between linguistic groups within the province. In conclusion, it identifies some of the most pressing language issues which could be addressed by both the Canadian and the Quebec states.

ENGLISH AND FRENCH IN CANADA AND QUEBEC

As in the United States and other parts of the world, numerous mother tongues are represented in Canada and Quebec. According to Statistics Canada, of the 1.1 million immigrants who arrived in Canada from 2001 to 2006, 81 per cent had a mother tongue other than English or French—notably Chinese languages, Italian, German, Punjabi, Spanish, Arabic, Tagalog, and Urdu (see Table 13.1). This growing linguistic diversity is felt in metropolitan areas especially: in Montreal 22 per cent of the population has a mother tongue other than French or English; in Toronto the figure is 44 per cent and in Vancouver, 41 per cent. Italian, Arabic, and Spanish are the leading languages among Montreal's allophones (those whose mother tongue is neither French nor English); Chinese languages, Italian, and Punjabi dominate allophones in Toronto; and Chinese languages, Punjabi, and Tagalog in Vancouver.

Despite the demographic importance of these communities, not all languages have official status in Canada. For historical, social, and political reasons that we will explore further, English and French are Canada's two official languages. French is the mother tongue of 22.1 per cent of the Canadian population (6,147,655 people), compared with 57.8 per cent (17,882,775 people) for whom English is their mother tongue (see Table 13.2). Most people whose mother

TABLE 13.1 The most common non-official mother tongues, 1971, 2001, and 2006

Mother tongues	1971			2001			2006		
	number	Percentage of non-official mother tongues	Percentage of all mother tongues	number	Percentage of non-official mother tongues	Percentage of all mother tongues	number	Percentage of non-official mother tongues	Percentage of all mother tongues
Chinese languages	95,915	3.4	0.4	872,400	16.4	2.9	1,034,090	16.4	3.3
Italian	538,765	19.2	2.5	493,985	9.3	1.7	476,905	7.6	1.5
German	558,965	19.9	2.6	455,540	8.5	1.5	466,650	7.4	1.5
Punjabi	..	..	..	284,750	5.3	1.0	382,585	6.1	1.2
Spanish	23,950	0.9	0.1	260,785	4.9	0.9	362,120	5.8	1.2
Arabic	28,520	1.0	0.1	220,535	4.1	0.7	286,785	4.6	0.9
Tagalog	..	..	..	199,770	3.7	0.7	266,440	4.2	0.9
Portuguese	85,845	3.1	0.4	222,855	4.2	0.8	229,280	3.6	0.7
Polish	136,540	4.9	0.6	215,010	4.0	0.7	217,605	3.5	0.7
Urdu	..	..	..	86,810	1.6	0.3	156,415	2.5	0.5
Ukrainian	309,890	11.0	1.4	157,385	3.0	0.5	141,805	2.3	0.5

Sources: Statistics Canada, censuses of population, 1971, 2001, and 2006. www12.statcan.ca/english/census06/analysis/language/tables/table_17.htm (accessed 6 March 2009)

TABLE 13.2   Population by mother tongue, Canada, provinces and territories, 2006

	Total	English	French	Non-official language	English and French	English and non-official language	French and non-official language	English, French and non-official language
Canada	31,241,030	17,882,775	6,817,655	6,147,840	98,625	240,005	43,335	10,790
Newfoundland and Labrador	500,610	488,405	1,885	9,540	295	435	30	15
Prince Edward Island	134,205	125,265	5,345	2,960	495	105	25	10
Nova Scotia	903,090	832,105	32,540	34,620	2,100	1,440	140	140
New Brunswick	719,650	463,190	232,980	18,320	4,450	560	120	25
Quebec	7,435,900	575,560	5,877,660	886,280	43,335	16,200	31,350	5,520
Ontario	12,028,895	8,230,705	488,815	3,134,045	32,685	131,285	7,790	3,565
Manitoba	1,133,515	838,415	43,960	236,315	2,630	11,675	435	85
Saskatchewan	953,845	811,730	16,055	118,465	1,130	6,080	245	140
Alberta	3,256,360	2,576,665	61,225	583,525	5,405	27,725	1,325	480
British Columbia	4,074,385	2,875,775	54,740	1,091,530	5,920	43,785	1,840	790
Yukon Territory	30,195	25,655	1,105	3,180	110	130	10	0
Northwest Territories	41,055	31,545	970	8,160	40	320	10	0
Nunavut	29,325	7,765	370	20,885	20	260	25	0

Source: Statistics Canada. 2007. Population by mother tongue and age groups, 2006 counts, for Canada, provinces and territories – 20% sample data (table). Language Highlight Tables. 2006 Census. Statistics Canada Catalogue no. 97-555-XWE2006002. Ottawa. Released December 4, 2007. www12.statcan.ca/english/census06/data/highlights/Language/Table401.cfm?Lang=E&T=401&GH=4&SC=1&S=99&O=A (accessed 6 March, 2009)

tongue is French live in Quebec, where they make up 79 per cent of the population (5,877,660 people). Approximately one million people whose mother tongue is French live outside Quebec.

French in Quebec is protected by the provincial government's French language charter, Bill 101. Federal legislation on official languages protects French in the rest of Canada, and likewise promotes English in Quebec. Both French and English are official languages of New Brunswick, but elsewhere in English Canada, measures to promote French are limited. Ontario is unique; in 1986, it adopted a French Language Act which provides French language services in designated areas where French is the mother tongue of either 5,000 people or 10 per cent of the local population. But overall, it is difficult

to be optimistic about the future of French outside Quebec. Rates of assimilation in some parts of the country are as high as 70 per cent, when those who claim French as their mother tongue are subtracted from those who still use the language at home. For example, in Ontario and in New Brunswick, where there are still significant concentrations of people whose mother tongue is French, 41.8 per cent and 11.2 per cent of French speakers respectively spoke English most often at home. In British Columbia, the rate is 72 per cent and in Alberta 69 per cent.

Concerning francophones in Quebec, data reveal that for the first time since 1931, the proportion of Quebecers with French as their mother tongue has dropped below 80 per cent. While figures such as this play on the linguistic insecurity of French Canadians, the data also show that 24 per cent of allophones in Quebec use French at home, which is encouraging. In contrast, English is threatened neither in Quebec nor in Canada. As already mentioned, the language rights of the minority of people in Quebec whose mother tongue is English are protected by both the Quebec and federal governments.

An allophone may be able to receive some services in his or her mother tongue at the local level, but other languages are not promoted as intensely as English or French. This does not mean that non-official languages are not valued. Some Canadians and Quebecers do learn and speak three or four (or even more) languages. However, especially outside of Quebec, most speakers of non-official languages eventually adopt English as their home language. Similarly, French is adopted as the language spoken at home by many allophones in Quebec. In 2006, while 20 per cent of Canadians declared a non-official language as their mother tongue, there is considerable movement towards English; 67 per cent of Canadians (20,584,770) use English at home (compared to the 57.8 per cent [17,882,775] whose mother tongue is English—see Table 13.3).

In fact, since 1971, English has made net gains everywhere in Canada, and the situation is not about to change. Despite its multicultural and multilingual identity, the country appears to be heading toward linguistic uniformity. If we examine bilingualism in Canada, we find that in 1996, 17 per cent of Canadians could conduct a conversation in both

TABLE 13.3   Population by language spoken most often at home, Canada, provinces and territories, 2006

	Total	English	French	Non-official language	English and French	English and non-official language	French and non-official language	English, French and non-official language
Canada	31,241,030	20,584,770	6,608,125	3,472,130	94,055	406,455	58,885	16,600
Newfoundland and Labrador	500,610	494,345	650	4,905	180	525	0	0
Prince Edward Island	134,205	130,115	2,680	1,095	150	165	0	0
Nova Scotia	903,090	866,685	17,165	15,700	1,310	2,120	80	25
New Brunswick	719,650	494,215	211,665	8,350	4,295	965	130	30
Quebec	7,435,905	744,430	6,027,730	518,320	52,330	26,560	54,490	12,035
Ontario	12,028,895	9,655,830	289,035	1,811,620	26,050	239,890	3,065	3,405
Manitoba	1,133,515	989,215	19,515	107,875	1,825	14,870	110	105
Saskatchewan	953,845	897,130	3,860	46,605	860	5,335	50	10
Alberta	3,256,355	2,893,240	19,315	297,955	3,340	41,645	460	395
British Columbia	4,074,385	3,341,285	15,325	639,380	3,610	73,730	465	580
Yukon Territory	30,195	28,540	540	935	65	110	0	0
Northwest Territories	41,060	36,795	445	3,570	30	210	0	0
Nunavut	29,325	12,955	205	15,810	15	320	20	0

Sources: Statistics Canada. 2007. Population by language spoken most often at home and age groups, 2006 counts, for Canada, provinces and territories – 20% sample data (table). Language Highlight Tables. 2006 Census. Statistics Canada Catalogue no. 97-555-XWE2006002. Ottawa. Released December 4, 2007. www12.statcan.ca/english/census06/data/highlights/Language/Table402.cfm?Lang=E&T=402&GH=4&SC=1&S=99&O=A (accessed 6 March, 2009)

English and French; an increase from 12 per cent in 1951. But the data from the 2006 census shows that French–English bilingualism is stagnating, as Canadians fluent in both languages remains at 17 per cent (see Table 13.4). Only 9 per cent of English Canadians are able to conduct a conversation in both French and English. Outside of Quebec, 7.4 per cent of anglophones and 5.6 per cent of allophones consider themselves fluent in English and French. There is a big gap between the number of francophones (42.4 per cent) and the number of anglophones (7.4 per cent) who can use both official languages. But the rate of bilingualism among anglophones in Quebec is quite high, at 68.9 per cent. However, one may question if that number necessarily means that they can sustain a conversation in French. In fact, it has not been possible so far to evaluate adequately the proficiency level of French among English-speaking students in Quebec[7].

TABLE 13.4 English-French bilingualism among Anglophones and Allophones (single mother tongue), Canada, provinces, territories, and Canada less Quebec, 1996 to 2006

Regions	Anglophones			Allophones		
	1996	2001	2006	1996	2001	2006
	Percentage					
Canada	**8.8**	**9.0**	**9.4**	**11.2**	**11.8**	**12.1**
Newfoundland and Labrador	3.5	3.7	4.3	6.7	6.5	6.8
Prince Edward Island	7.2	8.3	9.2	11.6	9.7	9.1
Nova Scotia	5.7	6.4	7.1	9.0	10.6	9.9
New Brunswick	14.0	15.0	16.0	15.7	17.5	16.9
Quebec	61.7	66.1	68.9	46.7	50.4	50.2
Ontario	8.1	8.2	8.4	6.3	6.8	6.6
Manitoba	6.3	6.5	6.5	2.5	2.9	2.8
Saskatchewan	3.7	3.6	3.7	1.9	2.0	2.1
Alberta	5.1	5.3	5.4	3.9	4.1	4.1
British Columbia	5.7	6.0	6.6	4.3	4.4	4.5
Yukon Territory	7.3	7.3	8.0	6.2	8.0	9.7
Northwest Territories	6.2	7.0	7.7	2.5	3.1	3.7
Nunavut	8.5	7.2	7.9	0.6	0.7	0.9
Canada less Quebec	**6.9**	**7.1**	**7.4**	**5.3**	**5.7**	**5.6**

Source: Statistics Canada, censuses of population, 1996 to 2006. www12. statcan.ca/english/census06/analysis/language/tables/table_17.htm (accessed 6 March, 2009)

LANGUAGE PLANNING AND POLICY-MAKING IN CANADA: SOME MILESTONES

After the Conquest[8] of New France by Britain, the Quebec Act of 1774 guaranteed French Canadians the right to maintain their own legal system, the Civil Code; to practise their religion, Catholicism; and to keep the *seigneurial* system of land ownership. The French language was thus recognized indirectly, as it was entwined with all these institutions. Almost 20 years after the adoption of the Quebec Act, the status of French was first tested in 1791 when Loyalists fleeing the American Revolution pressured the British crown to partition the Province of Quebec into Lower Canada and Upper Canada. Loyalists were invited to immigrate to Upper Canada where land was more readily available and the landowners among them could control a legislative assembly—which they believed to be

their right—and form a political majority. In contrast, those who went to Lower Canada had to collaborate with French Canadians. French-Canadian landowners were not excluded from participating in politics and constituted the majority of elected officials in the Lower Canadian Assembly.[9]

Despite the French-Canadian majority, no Loyalists would have expected that language would be an issue at the very first meeting of Lower Canada's legislative assembly. After all, the English ruled the Empire, which now included Lower Canada. It was the prerogative of the conqueror to impose its language, as was seen in Ireland at the time. In contrast, French speakers, who formed the majority, took for granted that the new assembly belonged to them and that their language should prevail.[10] After fierce debates, French was imposed as the language of the assembly and has remained so until this day, despite the continuing presence of representatives of the English-speaking communities.

In 1867, Canada became a federation. Students of federalism agree that it is a form of government which allows the coexistence of different approaches to language planning and policy-making.[11] In Canada, this coexistence has both negatively and positively affected the development of language policies. In the nineteenth century, language planning and policy-making was limited and restrictive. Article 133 of the British North America Act (the Canadian constitution from 1867) recognizes that French or English can be used in parliamentary debates in both the federal and Quebec legislatures, that laws will be published in both languages federally and in Quebec, and that French and English are the languages of both federal and Quebec courts. Thus it guaranteed English speakers the constitutional right to use English in the new Quebec Parliament. However, there was no equivalent protection of the French-speaking populations living outside the province. Furthermore, French was prohibited in the legislatures of most English-speaking provinces and in their education systems. In these provinces the Orange Order and the Canada First movement, informed by a new nationalism advocating one language and one culture, were among the most popular and successful groups to influence language policies.[12] From 1840 to after the Second World War, language politics remained intense in Canada but it was in the 1960s that the country witnessed its most important debates on the future of French since the prohibitive movements of the nineteenth century.

Thus, following much political debate and study, in 1963 the Canadian government created the Royal Commission on Bilingualism and Biculturalism (better known as the B&B Commission) to examine the situation between the two founding peoples and make recommendations to improve it. Liberal leader and Canadian Prime Minister Lester B. Pearson appointed two co-chairs, André Laurendeau from Quebec and Davidson Dunton from Ontario, and ten commissioners.[13] The Commission published its first report in 1965 but concluded its work in 1970. It revealed important discrepancies between French- and English-speaking communities, especially in education and the workplace, where past discrimination against French

Canadians was discovered and acknowledged. The Commission made several important recommendations to redress the situation, some of which were accepted by the newly elected Liberal Prime Minister, Pierre Elliott Trudeau. It thus laid the foundation of Canada's contemporary linguistic regime.

More specifically, since the B&B Commission, it can be said that Canada has witnessed three generations of more positive language planning and policy-making derived from 1969, 1982, and 1988 initiatives. The 1969 Official Languages Act marked the first generation. It was the federal government's first major step towards bilingualism in federal institutions. Informed by the personality principle described above, the aim of the new legislation was for all federal departments and agencies to become fully bilingual; government services across the country were to be offered in both official languages and a fair share of public service employment was to be accessible to francophones. The Act also created the position of Commissioner of Official Languages whose role is to watch over the application of the Act and to investigate citizens' complaints of non-compliance with the Act. The Commissioner reports annually to Parliament.

A second generation of language planning and policy-making began in 1982, when Canada patriated its Constitution and adopted a Charter of Rights and Freedoms. It gave constitutional status to the French and English languages in bilingual institutions and education. Institutional bilingualism means ensuring that federal institutions can provide services in both official languages as indicated in articles 16 to 20 of the Charter. Article 23 states that 'parents belonging to a linguistic minority have the right to have their children educated in the minority language, in homogeneous schools which they can manage, where numbers warrant'. This article is particular important for French-speaking minorities outside Quebec, because it repairs nineteenth- and early twentieth-century injustices, wherein they lost their rights to education in their language. Likewise, English-speaking Quebecers benefit from article 23.

However, when the Charter was adopted, the Quebec government did not recognize the legitimacy of the new Constitution and refused to sign it. The Constitution was patriated two years after

The Royal Commission on Bilingualism and Biculturalism: A Meeting of the Two Solitudes[14]

In 1962, Social Credit MPs Réal Caouette and Gilles Grégoire, questioning the Diefenbaker government on bilingualism in Canada, underlined the fact that English and French didn't enjoy equal status. They demanded that a Royal Commission on bilingualism and on French-Canadian participation in the civil service be established.[15] The proposition was ignored until the newly elected Liberal government, under the leadership of Lester B. Pearson in 1963, appointed André Laurendeau, editor in chief of the newspaper *Le Devoir*, and Davidson Dunton, president of Carleton University, as co-chairs of a Royal Commission on Bilingualism and Biculturalism. Laurendeau was a committed French-Canadian nationalist. In 1942, his campaign against conscription led him to enter provincial politics under the Bloc populaire banner, but his career as a member of the Quebec legislature lasted only three years. He resigned his seat in 1947 to join *Le Devoir*, Quebec's nationalist newspaper. Dunton was an English-Quebecer. After working for the *Montreal Star*, he became editor of the *Montreal Standard* in 1938. By the end of the Second World War, he was appointed the first full-time chairman of the Canadian Broadcasting Corporation (CBC).[16] He left the CBC after 13 years to become president of Carleton University. Ten other members were appointed to the Commission, which held 23 regional public meetings across the country, attracting more than 10,000 people. The co-chairs also met with provincial premiers and received many written submissions.

The Royal Commission's mandate was an ambitious one:

> to inquire and report upon the existing state of bilingualism and biculturalism in Canada and to recommend what steps should be taken to develop the Canadian Confederation on the basis of an equal partnership between the two founding races, taking into account the contribution made by the other ethnic groups to the cultural enrichment of Canada.[17]

Three questions were raised at the beginning of each public meeting: 'Can English-speaking and French-speaking Canadians live together, and do they want to? Under what new conditions? And are they prepared to accept those conditions?'[18]

The preliminary report released on 1 February 1965 described a country that was undergoing the worst crisis in its history. French Canadians 'did not occupy in the economy, nor in the decision-making ranks of government, the place their numbers warranted'.[19] English Canadians did not understand what was going on in Quebec and expressed satisfaction with the status quo. The Royal Commission on Bilingualism and Biculturalism was published in six volumes from 1967 to 1970. Book I, *The Official Languages*, introduces the concept of the bilingual district, where services would be provided in both languages where an English- or French-speaking minority formed at least 10 per cent of the local population. It also recommended that the constitution be modified to recognize explicitly that English and French are Canada's two official languages.[20]

Book II, *Education*, recommends measures to give Canadians more opportunity to become bilingual. It suggests that the study of the second official language be mandatory for all students.[21] It also made recommendations for the extension of educational rights for official-language minorities. Book III, *The Work World*, made suggestions aimed at putting an end to the domination of English in the federal administration and in the Canadian Forces. The last three volumes were *The Cultural Contribution of Other Ethnic Groups* (1969), *The Federal Capital* (1970), and *Voluntary Organizations* (1970).

Four decades later, the Commission's effects are still felt in today's society. Some recommendations never materialized. Bilingual districts were abandoned as soon as Book I was released. But it did achieve some substantial results. The Official Languages Act was adopted in 1969, giving equal status to English and French. The Official Languages in Education Program was established in 1970 to encourage provinces to offer courses in the other official language. Thus it can be concluded that the Royal Commission on Bilingualism and Biculturalism made a significant contribution to the development of the contemporary Canadian language regime.

the first sovereignty referendum in Quebec. The governing Parti Québécois held a referendum asking Quebecers to give its government a mandate to negotiate the province's political independence from, while maintaining an economic association with, the rest of Canada. The majority of the population voted 'no', after Prime Minister Pierre Trudeau promised to reform the Constitution to meet Quebec's needs within the federation.

More than 25 years later successive Quebec governments of different parties have refused to sign the 1982 Constitution, and there are no indications that Quebec will do so any time soon. The Charter does not recognize Quebec's specific needs and demands for a special status within the federation. It also limits the legislative powers of Quebec's National Assembly, the province's legislature. For example, while article 23 of the Charter was welcomed by official language minorities, it was criticized severely by the Quebec government because it invalidated its own legislation toward English speakers.[22]

A third generation of language planning and policy-making began in 1988 with the adoption of a new Official Languages Act, in which the federal government added two new components to its approach. First, the Act now recognizes the right of civil servants to work in the official language of their choice (part IV). Second, and more importantly for our argument, the new Act states:

> The Government of Canada is committed to (a) enhancing the vitality of the English and French linguistic minority communities in Canada and supporting and assisting their development; and (b) fostering the full recognition and use of both English and French in Canadian society. (Section 41, part VII).

This section is another example of how legislation designed to benefit official language minorities can conflict with language policies adopted by the provinces. Section 41 allows the Canadian government to intervene in areas of provincial jurisdiction, which means that provinces lose some control over their programming. However, language rights in Canada are increasingly integrated in intergovernmental relations, where there is tentative recognition of the need to respect official language minorities in each province.

In 1998, the Supreme Court of Canada, in what is commonly called the 'Quebec Secession Reference', ruled on Quebec's right to a unilateral declaration of secession,[23] recognizing that the rights of minorities were one of the four unwritten principles of the Canadian Constitution, along with democracy, the rule of law, and federalism. It confirmed indirectly that the country was founded on a pact between the English- and French-speaking communities and made even more explicit the norms and values that have (or should have) shaped it since the nineteenth century. The Reference was thus important for official language minorities, but it also confirmed the legitimacy of Quebec's demand for sovereignty and recognized that any province could demand that negotiations for secession take place, provided its government had a clear mandate from a majority of the population in a referendum with a clear question. The Supreme Court did not specify what constitutes a clear majority and a clear question. The Reference was welcomed in Quebec, as it created a path toward sovereignty. It was followed by the federal Clarity Act, 2000,[24] which set out the conditions under which the Canadian government would recognize a clear question and a clear majority. The Act did not please the Parti Québécois Quebec government, because it constrained Quebec's capacity to hold a referendum on sovereignty.

Since the Conquest, any action on language has had an important effect in Quebec. In the 1867 constitution (The British North America Act), Article 133 determined the power relations surrounding language between the Canadian and Quebec governments, leaving French speakers outside Quebec without any linguistic protection. Federalism also gave the provinces the ability to set their own linguistic policy. Thus federalism has had both a negative and a positive impact on language recognition in Canada.

Language Planning and Policy-Making in Quebec: The Difficult Road to Linguistic Peace

Almost since its beginnings, Quebec, more than anywhere else in Canada, has been engaged in an important exercise in language planning and policy-making. It is a significant case study of how the personality principle (individual rights) interacts with the territoriality principle (collective rights) in a federal context.

While the Canadian approach is informed by the personality principle, the Quebec government takes a different course. Since 1969, one of the effects of the Official Languages Act in Quebec has been the promotion of English as a minority language in Quebec while guaranteeing the presence of French speakers in the federal civil service. The adoption of the personality principle has provoked many debates in Quebec, where it seems inadequate to protect French and transform power relations between French and English speakers in Quebec, which is considered the most pressing need.

Since 1867, most governments in Quebec have operated under the assumption that they represented a distinct nation within Canada, a notion that finally received symbolic recognition in a 2006 declaration by the Canadian Parliament. Quebecers do not think of themselves as immigrants. Their struggle remains that of a majority on a territory that they understand to be their own (despite tensions with Aboriginal nations

making the same claim).[25] In other words, majority and minority relations remain political despite the recognition of Quebec's right to self-determination.

Thus, in its continuing debate with the Canadian government, Quebec criticizes federal intervention in its provincial jurisdiction, such as the implementation of the Official Languages Act. It claimed that the new legislation did not promote French in the province and that it could not stop the assimilation of French speakers living outside the province. As a result, Quebec developed specific policies aimed at furthering its autonomy, including international affairs.

From the 1960s on, national liberation and civil rights ideals have been popular in Quebec. Many people were inspired by several African nations' demands for the right to self-determination in the 1960s and 1970s, while others believe that the province can pursue its own development within the federation.[26] However, certain causes rallied all parties: the control of the province's language regime, the end of discrimination towards French Canadians, the right to use French in the private sector, and the need to have immigrants attend French schools. Since the 1960s, the Quebec government has given considerable attention to developing a language regime that will provide the needed linguistic security for it to pursue its own development as a French-speaking nation, whether inside or outside the federation.

Bill 101 has been the cornerstone of Quebec's language policy since its adoption in 1977. In keeping with claims made since the eighteenth century, it recognizes that the majority of the Quebec population live in French and that the language is an expression of its identity. It thus provides a legislative basis for the collective dimension of language. Unlike the Canadian language regime, which grants linguistic rights to individuals, the Quebec approach is informed by the principle that links language to territory and grants the majority a collective right to use the language.

However, Bill 101 was not welcomed by many English speakers either inside or outside Quebec.[27] Many had to acknowledge that since the 1960s, the dominance of English in Quebec had waned, as the Quebec government gradually took steps to reverse power relations between English and French speakers.

Some saw Bill 101 as the first step in Quebec's secession from Canada. The language policies and the broader political and economic situation had a marked effect on the anglophone community in Quebec.[28] Between 1971 and 1981 approximately 225,600 anglophones left the province for other parts of Canada or the United States, and a further 124,400 left between 1981 and 1991. The anglophone population appears to have stabilized since 2001.

English-speaking Quebecers who stayed behind did not all support the movement for independence or Quebec's Bill 101, but most seemed willing to adapt to the new context.[29] Their identity was transformed as a result; they became Anglo-Quebecers. In 1982, following the re-election of the Parti Québécois as Quebec's government, the anglophone Alliance Quebec was formed with the goal of engaging in a constructive dialogue with the French speaking majority. However, it soon was fighting fierce legal battles against Bill 101. The anglophone-based Equality Party was formed in 1988 to run candidates in provincial elections. It radicalized the anglophone movement against Quebec's language laws and the independence movement; some dubbed it a party of 'angryphones'.[30] In the event of Quebec separation from Canada, the Equality Party supported partitioning the province. Prominent activists such as former Liberal Cabinet Minister Reed Scowen were adamant in promoting English in Quebec despite the fact that English speakers widely used French in obtaining public services.[31] In the 1989 election, four Equality Party candidates were elected to the Quebec National Assembly. The party is no longer active, but some of its members are still involved in public debates or court cases against Bill 101. It seems that most Anglo-Quebecers now support the Quebec Liberal Party.

Official-language minorities were encouraged to use the courts to fight for their language rights in Quebec. The federal government established and fully funded the Court Challenges Program in 1994; it is well known that, although this program addresses language and equality rights in general across Canada, it was established mainly to help the anglophone minority in Quebec fight Bill 101.[32] This strategy would allow the creation of a body of jurisprudence favourable to official-language minorities. It paid off handsomely.

Canada has developed a unique approach to minority or collective rights in language and education. But for anglophone activists in Quebec, the judicial process could lead to a reaffirmation of the individual rights of Anglo-Quebecers.

The Supreme Court of Canada played a key role in helping Quebecers and Canadians see the legitimacy of Bill 101 while addressing aspects that it deemed unconstitutional For example, the legislation's section on using only French in legal texts conflicted with article 133 of the British North America Act and was quickly amended by the Quebec government.[33]

In 1982, article 23 of the new Canadian Charter of Rights and Freedoms invalidated Bill 101's very restrictive provisions for the education of English speakers' children, and extended to all Canadian anglophones the right to have their children educated in English.[34] However, the Supreme Court confirmed the legitimacy of Bill 101's requirement that children of immigrants attend French schools. In a brief to UNESCO, the Canadian government recognized that this was a necessary measure because of the unique situation of French in Canada and in North America.[35] All Quebecers have freedom of choice in the language of postsecondary education.

Nevertheless, political and economic pressures on immigrants and francophone Quebecers to learn English has led some immigrant and francophone parents to challenge Bill 101 in the courts to obtain the right to send their children to English schools. Since 2005, the Supreme Court of Canada has addresses this issue in three cases, *Gosselin*, *Solski*, and *Nguyen*.[36] In *Gosselin*, it rejected the principle of freedom of choice in education for French speakers; Bill 101 legitimately restricts francophones to studying in the French school system. However, in *Solski* the Supreme Court determined that a child whose mother tongue was not English who had previously received the major part of his or her education in English had the right to attend an English school. It also established that the 'major part' of a child's previous education should be measured subjectively as well as quantitatively. Finally, in 2009, in *Nguyen*, the Supreme Court ruled unconstitutional a provision of Bill 101 added in 2002 to further regulate access to English schools for non-English speakers. This new section did not recognize time spent in a non–state-funded private school in quali-fying for an English school.[37] The Supreme Court gave Quebec one year to redraft this provision in keeping with its more subjective approach in assessing a child's previous education.

The debate over language in education is far from over. It clearly shows the tension between the per-sonality and the territoriality approach to language planning and policy-making. It also reveals how the Supreme Court of Canada is evolving from a trad-itionally 'objective' approach to a more 'subjective' one; it is suggesting that government policy in areas as sensitive as language need to take into account the individual's understanding of his or her identity and not only ready-made definitions.

With the adoption of Bill 101, French also became the exclusive language of public and commercial signs. The latter became another area of contention between French and English speakers. The measure was meant to transform corporate names and com-mercial signage in Montreal, which was almost exclu-sively in English.[38] However, in 1988, the Quebec government was once more summoned by the

Supreme Court to relax its restriction on other lan-guages on signs, because it was argued that it did not respect freedom of expression.[39] This judgement was not popular among the majority of Quebecers. Many mobilized and publicly protested, putting extra pres-sure on the Quebec government. As a result, the gov-ernment of Quebec did not comply with the Supreme Court judgment, and was denounced vigorously in English Canada while applauded at home. In 1993, a Liberal government under Robert Bourassa adopted Bill 86 which allowed signage in other languages, but required that French predominate.

These important court cases led to changes to Bill 101, but it remains a fundamental Charter that aims to reassert French-majority control over the province and to end discrimination against French speakers. It is still contested by some English-speaking activists who believe that it is illiberal legislation, especially in education. For them, freedom of choice should trump preservation of the French language. For others, living in Quebec as a linguistic minority involves important soul searching but they do recognize that English is not in the least threatened in the province.[40]

PORTRAIT OF A FRANCOPHILE: GRAHAM FRASER[41]

Graham Fraser, Canada's Commissioner of Official Languages, gestures after the release of his annual report during a news conference in Ottawa in May 2007.

The Canadian Press/Fred Chartrand

Graham Fraser was born in Ottawa in 1946. As a teenager, he moved to Toronto with his family. He attended the University of Toronto, where he earned a Bachelor of Arts and a Master of Arts in history. At age 19, a unilingual undergraduate student, he went to Quebec to work on an archaeological dig in Fort Lennox, south of Montreal. Fraser recalls that he joined 'less out of an interest in archaeology than out of a determination to learn French and something of

Quebec'.[42] Immersed in a French-speaking environ-ment, the young man felt like an immigrant in his own country. He experienced the frustration of being unable to communicate, but developed a fascination for Quebec. That deep interest has lasted ever since.

For the next two summers, Fraser worked as an orderly in a mental hospital in Montreal. His French improved and he witnessed the profound social change occurring in the province. In 1968, he became a journalist for *The Toronto Star*. One year later, he followed Premier René Lévesque 'as he toured English-Canadian universities, explaining his dream of sovereignty for Quebec and a new relationship with the rest of Canada'.[43] Interested in Quebec national-ism, Fraser made a radio documentary on the Parti Québécois (PQ) during the 1970 election campaign. In 1976, he moved to Montreal to write for *Maclean's*, a weekly current affairs magazine. This proved to be a turning point in his career, when he became English Canada's 'foremost interpreter of Quebec'.[44]

Fraser lived in Quebec for a decade, covering such crucial political events as the 1976 Parti Québécois election, the 1980 referendum on sovereignty-association, and the negotiations leading to the patriation of the Canadian Constitution. Meanwhile, he worked for various newspapers and periodicals, including *Maclean's*, *The Gazette*, and *The Globe and Mail*. After the PQ lost power, Fraser moved back to Ottawa. Between 1986 and 1997, he was successively parliamentary correspondent, Ottawa bureau chief, and Washington bureau chief for *The Globe and Mail*. In 1995, the Montreal-based newspaper *Le Devoir* asked him to write a weekly column in which he would share with Quebecers his thoughts on some of the main issues in the rest of Canada. Five years later, he left *Le Devoir* to join *The Toronto Star*. Finally, in 2005, he retired from journalism.

Fraser was Adjunct Research Professor at Carleton University from 2002 to 2006. He is the author of five books: *Fighting Back: Urban Renewal in Trefann Court* (1972), *René Lévesque and the Parti Québécois in Power* (1984, reissued in 2001), *Playing for Keeps: The Making of the Prime Minister* (1989), *Vous*

m'intéressez: chroniques (2001), and *Sorry, I Don't Speak French: Confronting the Canadian Crisis that Won't Go Away* (2006). This last book explains how Canada's language policy has evolved since the Royal Commission on Bilingualism and Biculturalism. The aim of the book is to remind anglophones that 'the language issue remains of the utmost importance for our country'.[45] He argues that it is time to build bridges between Quebec and the rest of Canada, and the best way to do that is to give all Canadians the opportunity to learn both official languages.

Graham Fraser's contribution to the language debate in Canada was recognized when he was appointed Commissioner of Official Languages on 17 October 2006. As Commissioner, he has expressed concerns about the situation of French immersion across the country, the elimination of the Court Challenges Program, and whether athletes and visitors at the 2010 Vancouver Olympics would be served in both official languages by public officials. Not surprisingly, his vision has not changed much since the publication of *Sorry, I Don't Speak French*; Fraser is still hoping he can convince his fellow citizens to appreciate both English and French, not as foreign languages, but as truly Canadian languages.[46]

CONCLUSION: THE FUTURE OF LANGUAGE DEBATES IN QUEBEC

This chapter has discussed briefly the politics of language planning and policy-making in Quebec and in Canada. It first commented on the most recent data on language in Canada with a particular focus on Quebec. It also discussed the status of both English and French in the federation. It then presented the context in which language planning and policy-making evolved in Canada. This was followed by a discussion of language planning and policy-making in Quebec and its impact on the equilibrium between anglophone and francophone groups in the province.

Overall, this socio-political and historical discussion of language planning and policy-making in both Canada and Quebec shows how principles such as personality and territoriality can guide the linguistic

policies of governments. It also helps understand the impact of federalism on the development of distinctive language regimes and the role of the courts in clarifying the legitimacy of language planning and policy-making processes, especially on how governments should treat their minorities.

The tensions between Canada's Charter of Rights and Freedoms and the Official Languages Act on one hand, and Bill 101 on the other, have framed the normative debate on how law relates to language and identity in Canada. This debate has influenced many internationally renowned authors such as Will Kymlicka and Charles Taylor (see Biography box in Chapter 10), whose works on the politics of recognition represent the main positions in the debate on the accommodation of linguistic and national minorities. Building on the contrast between the personality and territoriality principles, they have further contrasted individual and collective rights, the just and the good, and liberalism and communitarian theories, in order to address demands for minority recognition. While Kymlicka, for example, understands society as a context of choice in which individuals choose what they need in order to advance their conception of the good life,[47] Taylor argues that a conception of the good at the level of the state can also guide action.[48]

Applied to the Canadian and Quebec contexts, such debate leads to the question of whether it is just for the Quebec government to legislate in favour of French speakers.[49] While Taylor proposes a non-utilitarian approach to language and society, others have suggested that a state should legislate only to increase the salience of a language as a means of communication, not as a collective good. There is no ultimate resolution to such debate, except that any purely utilitarian attitude toward language seems to undermine its importance in one's identity, and that power relations will determine which principles might be the most appropriate for linguistic peace.[50]

One of the most pressing issues in Quebec is to better understand how the equilibrium between francophone and anglophone Quebecers is affected by the growing use of English as an international lingua franca. Will Quebec remain a predominantly French-speaking province? While knowledge of French is increasingly important for the anglophone population, there is also pressure to use English in the workplace and in the public sphere. Furthermore, in 2006, it was shown that French-speaking immigrants might face language discrimination, since they do not have access to jobs requiring bilingual skills.[51] Finally, in 2008, a study published by the Conseil supérieur de la langue française on the linguistic behaviour of young Quebecers revealed that many people whose first language is French did not feel the fight for French to be a priority.[52] This is a blow to older activists who remain convinced that the language is fragile and that its protection needs constant vigilance.

There is also some debate on the need for federal language legislation to acknowledge the predominance of Bill 101 in its dealings with Quebec. Conflicts between federal and provincial legislation need to be resolved; many suggest that Bill 101 be given constitutional status to confirm its importance and affirm its role as a fundamental tool for linguistic peace in Canada and in Quebec.[53]

Questions for Consideration

1. What is the status of English and French in Canada and in Quebec?

2. Explain why Canada has adopted both English and French as official languages.

3. What has been the impact of the Supreme Court of Canada on Bill 101?

4. Discuss possible impacts of globalization on the future of French in Canada and in Quebec.

Notes

1. I would like to thank the editors of the book for their suggestions and Simon Letendre from the School of Political Studies at the University of Ottawa for his assistance.

2. Jean-Claude Corbeil, *L'embarras des langues. Origine, conception et évolution de la politique linguistique québécoise* (Montreal: Québec Amérique 2007), 24, and J. Laponce, *Loi de Babel et autres régularités des rapports entre langue et politique* (Quebec: Presses de l'Université Laval, 2007).

3. Colin H. Williams, 'Language Policy and Planning Issues in Multicultural Societies', in P. Larrivée, ed., *Understanding the Québec Question* (Basingstoke: Palgrave, 2003), 1–56.

4. Kenneth McRae, 'The Principle of Territoriality and the Principle of Personality in Multilingual States', *International Journal of the Sociology of Language*, 1975, 4: 35–45.

5. Rainer Bauböck, 'Autonomie territoriale ou culturelle pour les minorités nationales?', in A. Dieckhoff, ed., *La constellation des appartenances. Nationalisme, libéralisme et pluralisme* (Paris: Presses de science po., 2004), 317–70.

6. Abram De Swaan, *Words of the World: The Global Language System* (Cambridge : Polity Press, 2001).

7. Patricia Lamarrre, 'L'enseignement du français dans le réseau anglophone' in A. Stefanescu and P. Georgeault, ed., *Le français au Québec. Les nouveaux défis* (Montreal: Fides, 2005), 553–68.

8. See Chapter 2 for an analysis of the impact of the Conquest.

9. Pierre Tousignant, 'Problématique pour une nouvelle approche de la constitution de 1791', *Revue d'histoire de l'Amérique française* 27 (1973): 181–234.

10. Ibid.

11. Linda Cardinal, 'Linguistic Peace: A Time to Take Stock', *Inroads* 2008, 23: 62–70.

12. Carl Berger, *The Sense of Power: Studies in the Ideas of Canadian Imperialism, 1867–1914* (Toronto: University of Toronto Press, 1970).

13. Graham Fraser, *Sorry, I Don't Speak French: Confronting the Canadian Crisis that Won't Go Away* (Toronto: McClelland & Stewart, 2006).

14. Prepared by Simon Letendre, School of Political Studies, University of Ottawa.

15. Fraser, *Sorry, I Don't Speak French*, 31.

16. J. H. Marsh, *Dunton, Arnold Davidson*, available at www.thecanadianencyclopedia.com/index.cfm?PgNm=TCE&Params=A1ARTA0002467, accessed 7 March 2009.

17. Royal Commission on Bilingualism and Biculturalism, *Report of the Royal Commission on Bilingualism and Biculturalism. Book I: The Official Languages* (Ottawa: The Commission, 1967), xxi.

18. Graham Fraser, *Sorry, I Don't Speak French*, 43.

19. G. Laing, *Bilingualism and Biculturalism, Royal Commission on*, available at www.thecanadianencyclopedia.com/index.cfm?PgNm=TCE&Params=A1SEC816888, accessed 7 March 2009.

20. Royal Commission on Bilingualism and Biculturalism. *Report, Book I: The Official Languages*, 147.

21. Royal Commission on Bilingualism and Biculturalism. *Report, Book 2: Education* (Ottawa: The Commission, 1968), 302.

22. Garth Stevenson, *Community Besieged: The Anglophone Minority and the Politics of Quebec* (Montreal and Kingston: McGill-Queen's University Press, 1999).

23. Reference re Secession of Quebec, [1998] available at http://csc.lexum.umontreal.ca/en/1998/1998rcs2-217/1998rcs2-217.pdf.

24. Available at: www.canlii.org/en/ca/laws/stat/sc-2000-c-26/latest/sc-2000-c-26.html.

25. See Chapter 8.

26. According to Corbeil (*L'embarras des langues*, 519), the publication in 1959 of Albert Memmi's *Portrait of the Colonized* had an important impact in Quebec.

27. Pierre Larrivée, 'Anglophones and Allophones in Quebec', in P. Larrivée, ed., *Understanding the Québec Question* (Basingstoke: Palgrave, 2003), 163–87 and Stevenson, *Community Besieged*.

28. Garth Stevenson, 'English-Speaking Québec: A Political History' in A.-G. Gagnon, ed., *Québec. State and Society* (Peterborough: Broadview Press, 2004), 329–44. See also G. Chambers, 'Les relations entre anglophones et francophones' in M. Plourde, ed., *Le Français au Québec. 400 ans d'histoire et de vie* (Quebec: Conseil supérieur de la langue française and Fides, 2000), 319–25.

29. Michael Stein, 'Changement dans la perception de soi des Anglo-Québécois', in G. Caldwell and É. Waddell, eds., *Les anglophones du Québec de majoritaires à minoritaires* (Québec: Institut québécois de recherche sur la culture, 1982), 125–6.

30. Pierre Larrivée, 'Anglophones and Allophones in Quebec', 177–8.

31. Ironically, for someone who wanted the expansion of English in Quebec, Scowen now lives in Toronto and has a chronicle in French on the Ottawa French national radio once a month. See also Garth Stevenson, *Community Besieged*, 206.

32. Linda Cardinal, 'Le pouvoir exécutif et la judiciarisation de la politique au Canada: une étude du programme de contestation judiciaire', *Politique et Sociétés*, 20, 2–3: 2000, 4–65.

33. See *Blaikie* (13 déc. 1979: (1979) 2 R.C.S. 1016, completed by: (1981) 1R.C.S. 312).

34. See *P.G. du Québec c. Quebec Protestant School Boards* (1984) 2 R.C.S. 66.

35. F. Cardinal, 'Ottawa défend la loi 101 devant l'UNESCO' *Le Devoir*, 1 July 2000.

36. *Gosselin (Tuteur de) c. Québec (Procureur général)* [2005] 1 R.C.S. 238 ; *Solski (Tuteur de)* c. *Québec* (Procureur général) [2005] 1 R.C.S. 201 ; *Nguyen c. Quebec* (Éducation, Loisir et Sport) [2009] CSC 47.

37. The concept of non-state-funded private school may read as a strange concept for non-Quebecers. One must understand that in Quebec private schools can either be partly state-funded or non-state-funded. When state funded, private schools make a commitment to teach state accredited programs and provide some teaching of French. Non-state-funded private schools do not have those requirements.

38. Marc V. Levine, *The Reconquest of Montreal: Language Policy and Social Change in a Bilingual City* (Philadelphia: Temple University Press,1990).

39. *Valerie Ford c. P.G. du Québec* (1988) 2 R.C.S. 712.

40. Leigh Oakes, and Jane Warren, *Language, Citizenship and Identity in Quebec* (Basingstoke: Palgrave, 2007).

41. Prepared by Simon Letendre, School of Political Studies, University of Ottawa.

42. Graham Fraser, *Sorry, I Don't Speak French*, 1.

43. Graham Fraser, *René Lévesque & the Parti Québécois in Power.* (Montreal and Kingston: McGill-Queen's University Press), 2001, viii.

44. University of Ottawa: Office of the President. *Honorary Doctorates: Graham Fraser, 2008*. See www.president.uottawa.ca/doctorate-details.html?var=748&more=citation, accessed 13 March 2009).

45. Graham Fraser, *Speech to the House of Commons Standing Committee on Official Languages*, 28 September 2006, available at www2.parl.gc.ca/HousePublications/Publication.aspx?DocId=2364029 &Language=E&Mode=1&Parl=39&Ses=1#Int-1658260.

46. Ibid.

47. Will Kymlicka. *Finding Our Way* (Toronto: Oxford University Press, 1998).
48. Charles Taylor, *Reconciling the Solitudes: Essays on Canadian Federalism and Nationalism* (Montreal and Kingston: McGill-Queen's University Press, 1994).
49. On this question, see Daniel Weinstock's chapter in this book.
50. Astrid von Busekis. 'Cannibales et gourmets: Quelques recettes d'équilibre linguistiques', in M. Werner (ed.), *Politiques et usages de la langue en Europe* (Paris: Éditions de la Maison des sciences de l'homme, 2007), 101–20; and

Linda Cardinal, 'Linguistic peace'.
51. Paul Morissette, 'Quand la politique officielle bute sur la réalité', *Le Devoir*, 24 August 2006.
52. Nathalie St-Laurent, *Le français et les jeunes* (Québec: Conseil supérieur de la langue française, 2008), 28.
53. John Richards, 'Breaking the "Vicious Cycle": A Retrospective and Prospective Examination of Quebec/Canada Relations', in M. Murphy, ed., *Quebec and Canada in the New Century: New Dynamics, New Opportunities* (Kingston, Institute of Intergovernmental Affairs, 2007), 233–56.

Relevant Websites

Centre de la Francophonie des Amériques: www.francophoniedesameriques.com/
Information about the situation of the French Language in the Americas.

French Language Charter: www.olf.gouv.qc.ca/english/charter/index.html
The English version of the French Language Charter (Bill 101)

Office de la langue française du Québec: www.oqlf.gouv.qc.ca/
Publications on the situation of the French language in Quebec and in Canada.

Office of the Commissioner of Official Languages: www.ocol-clo.gc.ca/
Annual Reports of the Commissioner of Official Languages—good documents to see trends in official languages policies in Canada.

Official Languages Act: http://laws.justice.gc.ca/en/O-3.01/

Select Bibliography

Bauböck, Rainer. 'Autonomie territoriale ou culturelle pour les minorités nationales?'. In A. Dieckhoff, ed. *La constellation des appartenances. Nationalisme, libéralisme et pluralisme* (Paris: Presses de science po., 2004), 317–70.

Berger, Carl. *The Sense of Power: Studies in the Ideas of Canadian Imperialism, 1867–1914* (Toronto: University of Toronto Press, 1970).

Cardinal, Linda. 'Le pouvoir exécutif et la judiciarisation de la politique au Canada: une étude du programme de contestation judiciaire', *Politique et Sociétés* 20, 2–3 (2000): 4–65.

———. 'Linguistic peace: a time to take stock', *Inroads* 23 (2008): 62–70.

Corbeil, Jean-Claude. *L'embarras des langues. Origine, conception et évolution de la politique linguistique québécoise* (Montreal: Québec Amérique, 2007).

De Swaan, Abram. *Words of the World: The Global Language System* (Cambridge, Polity Press, 2001).

Fraser, Graham. *Sorry, I Don't Speak French: Confronting the Canadian Crisis that Won't Go Away* (Toronto: McClelland & Stewart, 2006).

Kymlicka, Will. *Finding Our Way* (Toronto: Oxford University Press, 1998).

Laponce, Jean. *Loi de Babel et autres régularités des rapports entre langue et politique* (Quebec: Presses de l'Université Laval, 2007).

Larrivée, Pierre. 'Anglophones and Allophones in Quebec'. In P. Larrivée, ed. *Understanding the Québec Question* (Basingstoke: Palgrave, 2003), 163–87.

Levine, Marc V. *The Reconquest of Montreal: Language Policy and Social Change in a Bilingual City* (Philadelphia: Temple University Press, 1990).

McMillan, Michael. 'Federal Language Policy in Canada and the Quebec Challenge'. In P. Larrivée, ed. *Understanding the Québec Question* (Basingstoke: Palgrave, 2003), 87–117.

McRae, Kenneth. 'The Principle of Territoriality and the Principle of Personality in Multilingual States', *International Journal of the Sociology of Language* 4 (1975): 35–45.

Oakes, Leigh and Jane Warren. *Language, Citizenship and Identity in Quebec* (Basingstoke: Palgrave, 2007).

Richards, John. 'Breaking the "Vicious Cycle": A Retrospective and Prospective Examination of Quebec/Canada Relations'. In M. Murphy, ed. *Quebec and Canada in the New Century: New Dynamics, New Opportunities* (Kingston, Institute of Intergovernmental Affairs, 2007), 233–56.

Stein, Michael. 'Changement dans la perception de soi des Anglo-Québécois'. In G. Caldwell and É. Waddell, eds. *Les anglophones du Québec de majoritaires à minoritaires* (Québec: Institut québécois de recherche sur la culture, 1982).

Stevenson, Garth. *Community besieged: the anglophone minority and the politics of Quebec* (Montreal and Kingston: McGill-Queen's University Press, 1999).

Taylor, Charles. *Reconciling the Solitudes: Essays on Canadian Federalism and Nationalism* (Montreal and Kingston: McGill-Queen's University Press, 1994).

Tousignant, Pierre. 'Problématique pour une nouvelle approche de la constitution de 1791', *Revue d'histoire de l'Amérique française* 27 (1973): 181–234.

von Busekist, Astrid. 'Cannibales et gourmets: Quelques recettes d'équilibre linguistiques'. In M. Werner. *Politiques et usages de la langue en Europe* (Paris: Éditions de la Maison des sciences de l'homme, 2007), 101–20.

Williams, Colin. 'Language Policy and Planning Issues in Multicultural Societies'. In P. Larrivée, ed. *Understanding the Québec Question* (Basingstoke: Palgrave, 2003), 1–56.

CHAPTER 14

The Politics of Language: Philosophical Reflections on the Case of Quebec

Daniel Weinstock, Université de Montréal

INTRODUCTION

Language politics has been at the centre of political debate in Quebec for the past 40 years. The centrality of language politics is easy to understand. Quebec is home to a majority of the French speakers residing in Canada, and in North America. But francophones are a minority in the Canadian federation. Within North America and the Americas generally, they represent a very small fraction of the total population.[1] Furthermore, English within the Canadian federation is the language of the erstwhile conqueror, a fact that has been enshrined in many of the political institutions around which the Canadian federation was created.

Quebec's language debates have provided a very interesting and fertile laboratory for political philosophers. Most societies do not need to engage in language politics at all. That is, in most countries a majority language achieves institutional dominance without the need for any special policies. It is understood by everyone that when one moves, say, to France, French will be the language of instruction used in schools, the language in which one will be addressed in courts, and so on.

Things are different for societies such as Quebec, Catalonia, and a number of others. Catalan speakers and French-speaking Quebecers constitute a majority within a territory, but each of these territories is embedded within a larger political entity (Spain, Canada) in which the majority speaks another language. They therefore cannot simply expect that, as a matter of course, all those who come to their society will converge on their language. In the absence of deliberate policy, such as an official language policy,

it may seem just as natural for a new arrival to Quebec or to Catalonia to speak and transact business in English or in Spanish, since these are the majority languages of Canada and of Spain.

Quebecers and Catalans are thus faced with a dilemma. They could allow all inhabitants of their territories to speak whatever language they want, and risk seeing their own language eroded by the assimilative pressures of the broader society's language. Or they can enact mildly coercive legislation aimed at securing their language, and run the risk of being viewed as illiberal.

This chapter looks at the language debate within Quebec as a political philosopher might. The aim is not to provide readers with historical insight into the evolution of language policy in Quebec,[2] but rather to see whether a convincing liberal-democratic rationale can be provided for language policies such as Quebec's attempt to protect a vulnerable language without wholesale breaches of individual rights. The arguments canvassed and considered in what follows are therefore not necessarily the arguments that were actually presented at crucial junctures by the main protagonists on either side of Quebec's language saga. Rather, they are reconstructions aimed at couching those debates in the terms of the most prominent contemporary political philosophies.

LANGUAGE AND IDENTITY

Debates about language policy crystallize a number of broader political and philosophical debates that have been at the heart of Quebec's political and intellectual evolution over the past 40 years or so.

For most French-speaking Quebecers, the survival of the French language is central to the survival of Quebec as a distinct community within Canada and North America. The centrality of language for survival is due to the fact that French has become central to the *identity* of Quebecers.

For much of its history, French Canada was held together by the predominant place of the Catholic religion, and its accompanying values and institutions, within the lives of French Canadians both inside Quebec and in the rest of Canada. French-speaking Catholics were among the most devout people on the planet, a fact to which Quebec's architecture and place names still bear eloquent witness. Until the 1950s, the survival of French-Canadian identity was tied to the survival of a community bound together first and foremost by the values, symbols, and institutions of the Church. The refusal to allow non-Catholic immigrants into Catholic schools, which were most often de facto francophone, could be seen as part of this survival strategy. Though it might have meant that more children would have been integrated into the *French-speaking* community through the school system, it also would have carried the risk of watering down *Catholic* identity.

Things changed dramatically with the Quiet Revolution. Voices urging the liberalization and deconfessionalization of French-Canadian society had always been present in Quebec society, but in the course of one generation, they became dominant. Catholicism receded from the forefront of the identity of Quebecers. The self-understanding of Quebecers became much more pluralistic. The identity of Quebecers would from then on have to encompass a great many values and ways of life, rather than being tightly defined around a single religion.

As well, a French-speaking economic and political class emerged, intent upon using the levers of provincial power in Quebec to give institutional weight to the existence of a distinctive society within North America. A territorially concentrated identity was needed, one that might be shared by all people within Quebec, to replace the old, territorially dispersed French-Canadian identity, which spanned almost the entire breadth of the country, from the Atlantic provinces to Alberta. This identity would have to be one that all of Quebec inhabitants could adhere to, regardless of religion.

Language was well suited to replace Catholicism as a pillar of a new, territory-based Quebec identity. It unites a vast proportion of the society's inhabitants, regardless of religion or ethnic background. Further, it can more easily be used by the Quebec state as the focus for nation-building than religion ever could be. Indeed, a liberal democracy such as Quebec can insist on its citizens acquiring some competency in the French language without damaging its liberal-democratic status as a society that respects, protects, and promotes its citizens' individual civil and political rights. 'Thicker' aspects of identity, such as religion, are in this regard far more problematic. Today, and indeed since the 1960s, the survival of Quebec increasingly hangs upon the ability of its society and institutions to integrate immigrants, and it is much easier to have them share a linguistic identity than a religious one.

The growing centrality of language to Quebec identity explains the intensity of feeling that has surrounded rights-based challenges to the language law. '*Ne touchez pas à la loi 101*' has become a potent political rallying cry in Quebec, pointing to the fact that the legal tools that have been enacted to protect the French language, in addition to the language itself, have themselves become central to the way in which Quebecers have come to identify themselves.

LANGUAGE AND JUSTICE

Some evidence suggests that most French-speaking Quebecers think that language debates are an important stake in identity. English-speaking Quebecers and immigrants, as well as many outside observers, tend to view the language debates in Quebec from the point of view of *liberal justice*. They ask themselves how a liberal democracy committed to the protection of individual and minority rights should view the central issues in the formation of language policy. They have often been harsher in their judgment of Quebec's language laws than French-speaking Quebecers have been, because of the apparent conflict between measures intended to protect the French language and individual liberty.

The questions that the lens of liberal justice forces us to address concern the degree to which the state can use both incentives and coercion to alter the linguistic choices that citizens make for themselves and for their children. To what degree can a just society limit individual rights to achieve a collective end such as language protection? This question is at the heart of the debate about Quebec's language laws, which has been couched in terms of liberal justice.

Liberalism is perhaps above all else a theory of limited government. Liberals believe that the state should not interfere with the choices made by individuals unless there are weighty reasons to do so. There are debates among liberals about what those reasons might be. Some argue that the role of the state should be limited to securing physical safety and property rights. Others argue for a more expansive role for the state, because individuals interacting freely in their own self-interest cannot be relied upon to generate certain goods such as clean air and water, health-care institutions and the like. These are known as 'public goods', that is, goods that everyone wants but that people tend not to be sufficiently motivated to create on their own.

The default liberal view would therefore be that language choice should be left to individuals. Parents should be able to school children in the language of their choice, and all should be able to do business in whatever language they see fit. The very notion of a state having an 'official language' seems suspect, on a par with its having an established religion. The only acceptable posture for the state to adopt with respect to language would be 'benign neglect'.

Is anything wrong with this view? A complicating factor is that whereas the state does not have to privilege any one religion, it cannot avoid taking sides when it comes to language. It uses language to frame legislation. Courts and public schools must operate in a common language, and so on. It cannot hope to treat all the languages spoken on its territory equally. It must pick some subset of the languages that are spoken on its territory, and communicate with all its citizenry in those languages.

Many things follow from this. If the state chooses to communicate with its citizens in the language of the majority, fairness dictates that it provide members of linguistic minorities and immigrants with the means to achieve competency in that language. Linguistic ghettos make it difficult to achieve a shared linguistic identity across the state's territory. But they are also bad for those stuck within them, who are prevented from achieving the political and economic opportunities that competency in the dominant language affords.

So the state must make language training in the dominant language available and accessible. But must it make it mandatory? After all, if minority language speakers are provided with the opportunity to learn the dominant language, and are made aware of the disadvantages of not doing so, should they not be free to bear those disadvantages if they so choose?

Reflecting on the case of Quebec shows that we cannot answer this question in the abstract. As we have seen, Quebec is a province within Canada. Canada is a bilingual country within which French speakers are outnumbered in a ratio of approximately three to one. Quebec's French speakers represent a tiny fraction within largely English-speaking North America. What's more, though French is a 'global' language, in the sense that it is spoken throughout the current and former colonies of France, it is not, as English is, a 'language of globalization'.

The speakers of a majority language in other parts of the world can make their language dominant without making it mandatory, in the confidence that minority-language speakers and immigrants will see it as being in their interest to acquire proficiency in the dominant language. Their language does not have to compete with any other language for pre-eminent status within the same territory, nor does it have to withstand the pressure of a continent massively dominated by another language. True, no language in the world is completely immune from the prominence of English as the language of global commerce and science. But most often, English becomes the *de rigueur* second language, rather than replacing the other language.

French speakers in Quebec can have no such confidence. Choosing English rather than French, for example as the language of instruction for their children, does not consign immigrants or minority-language speakers to a linguistic ghetto from which it would be rational for them to want to escape. Rather, it locates them within the national and continental majority. Even if the Quebec state were to generously provide immigrants with the means to learn French, it might be more rational for them to integrate into the English-speaking community.

Given the context of French in Canada and North America, it is thus easy to see why French-speaking Quebecers intent upon making French a chief pillar of a shared post-religious, territory-based identity, would *want* to make French mandatory by enshrining it in an official language law such as Bill 101. But is it *just* for them to do so? After all, the linguistic map of the world is changing all the time as people respond to different incentives. Though the disappearance of a language may cause regret, it does not always call for state action. The disappearance of a language does not always constitute an *injustice*.

According to the renowned Canadian philosopher Charles Taylor, the decision by the Quebec state to make French mandatory as the language of education, public communication, and business does not represent the kind of major departure from the standards of liberal democracy that would require special justification. As long as it protects its citizens' fundamental civil and political rights and freedoms—the right to bodily integrity, the freedoms of religion and of conscience, the right to equal participation in the institutions of democratic self-government—Quebec, in Taylor's view, acts within an appropriate discretionary range by limiting its citizens' language rights.[3]

According to Will Kymlicka, whose theories of minority rights have attained global prominence, the value that liberal justice ascribes to individual choice makes sense only if value is also ascribed to the 'contexts of choice' which individuals require in order to exercise their capacity for choice. It is because they are members of 'societal cultures', that is, of societies affording them a full range of choices across the full range of fields of human endeavour, that individuals are capable of choosing one thing over another. Members of minority societal cultures need to be able to protect themselves against external pressures that would push them toward assimilation. For Quebecers, this means protecting themselves against the assimilative pressure of English by enacting legislation that makes linguistic integration mandatory.[4]

A third approach would view language as a kind of public good. On this view, French-speaking Quebecers have a problem of collective action with respect to their language. Each francophone would rather that business transactions and official state communications be in French. But this preference is not unconditional. People will act on this preference on condition that enough of their fellow citizens do so as well. If this condition is not significantly fulfilled, too few speakers of the language will remain to keep it viable. In the absence of their fellow citizens' assurance that they too will choose French, it will be rational for each French-speaker to 'defect' to English, with all of the advantages of that choice in Canada and North America.

By backing the use of French with the force of law, the state in effect provides the required assurance. In so doing, it provides a public good that is structurally analogous to clean air. Someone who owns a factory that emits toxic gases might choose to pay the costs of limiting the emissions only if assured that other factory owners were doing the same; otherwise he or she would incur an economic disadvantage relative to them. Most people would say it is the state's responsibility to ensure collective action among factory owners to limit emissions. Similarly, the state can also be seen as responsible to ensure a public good such as language.

So far, we have seen that the default presumption of a liberal theory of justice on language—benign neglect—is not so simple for a language that, like French in Quebec, is subject to assimilative pressures. First, the Quebec state can't simply assume that its minority-language population and immigrants will acquire French on their own; it must take steps to make language training available and accessible. Second, there are several arguments to the effect that justice permits making French mandatory.

But making French mandatory does not necessarily mean making it *exclusive*. The status of French as the official language in Quebec does, however, make it exclusive in several domains. For example, schooling is unilingual for French-speaking Quebecers and for immigrants, and many state institutions function in French only. But are there any reasons to prohibit institutional bilingualism? At first glance, the requirement that children receive their instruction in French, and that French be used in all commercial signs and in all government communication is not incompatible with bilingualism. Children could after all be educated in bilingual schools, and signage and official communication could be in both English and French.

According to many sociologists, economists, and linguists, such as Jean Laponce, the ensuing asymmetrical bilingualism would mean the disappearance of French over time. Bilingualism in Quebec would inevitably be asymmetrical by virtue of the dominance of English in Canada, and more largely in North America. Given this asymmetry, there would always be more reason for francophones to use English than for anglophones to use French. The natural tendency would therefore be for communication between anglophones and francophones to occur in English. Over time, this would lead to English dominance in all public interactions. French would become 'folklorized', that is, relegated to the private and cultural spheres. The lowly status to which French has fallen in places like Louisiana, and the struggle it faces merely to maintain viability in other parts of Canada, suggest that this understanding of asymmetrical bilingualism might very well be borne out by the facts.

In general, then, many researchers in the area of language believe that it is difficult for languages to coexist peacefully on the same territory. In situations of asymmetrical bilingualism, the dominance of the 'weaker' language can be assured only by being engineered through state action. In the absence of state action, the 'stronger' language will naturally achieve the dominant position. The intermediate position—institutional bilingualism—is in their view inherently unstable, and will in time enshrine the dominance of the stronger of the two languages.

All of the arguments that have been canvassed above have been subjected to vigorous scrutiny and debate. Clearly, however, their cumulative effect is to suggest that achieving justice in language policy is a more complicated matter than simply allowing people to make unconstrained linguistic choices for themselves and for their children.

WHO IS A QUEBECER?

In retrospect, many of the conflicts that arose in the years following the adoption of Bill 101 can be seen as pitting against each other the two perspectives developed above. French-speaking Quebecers tend to view the protection of the French language as a necessary condition for the survival of Quebec as a distinct society. Many anglophones and immigrants tend to view the laws enacted to achieve that protection as antithetical to liberal rights and freedoms.

Over time, the conflict has significantly abated. Successive legal challenges have somewhat softened the law. For example, whereas the law originally banished English entirely from commercial signs, in its present form it merely requires that French be clearly dominant.

But the 'linguistic peace' that has characterized Quebec since about 1995 may also be due to the fact that the opponents of Bill 101 and its effects have come to realize that they actually stand to significantly benefit from them. Through being required to attend French schools, immigrant children emerge from school fluently bilingual, as do the children of anglophone Quebecers who, though they are entitled to attend English schools, are increasingly being sent to French schools by their parents.

Paradoxically, francophone children arguably do less well than their anglophone and immigrant counterparts. They are required to attend French schools exclusively. But whereas the other children attending French schools acquire proficiency in at least one other language at home, French-speaking children have little access to languages other than French. The cost of protecting the French language in North America may ultimately be the limitation of the linguistic horizons of francophone children.

Challenges to the language law in years to come are therefore likely to emanate from within the francophone community, torn between its desire to protect the French language and the inevitable desire to prevent their children from being at a competitive disadvantage in a globalized economy, compared to their English and immigrant counterparts.

Some francophone commentators have sounded an alarm, claiming that the language law is not having its desired effect, and that the dominance of French is still fragile, especially on the Island of Montreal.

These challenges raise important questions. What indicators should be used to determine whether the language law has been effective? Is acceptable linguistic integration marked by an individual being proficient enough in French to use it in public? Or does it also require that he or she use French in private life? Has integration failed if English (or some other language) is spoken at home? Does successful integration require that first-generation immigrants achieve fluency in French, or does it suffice that children of the second generation do so?

Different answers to these questions yield dramatically different pictures of the linguistic situation of the province. Focusing on the private linguistic choices of recent arrivals, for example, produces a picture quite different from that which emerges from looking at how well they can function in French in public settings such as workplaces, courts, legislatures, and schools. Choices of indicators are moreover likely to be highly ideologically motivated.

How will Quebec's language laws evolve over the years to come? The focus of legislation will undoubtedly vary, depending on which picture of the linguistic situation holds sway among decision-makers. But as long as French remains as central a pillar of the Québécois identity as it presently is, there will always be policies designed to protect the language against the enormous pressures that it must withstand in North America and on the global stage.

CHILDREN OF BILL 101 (*LES ENFANTS DE LA LOI 101*)

Children of Bill 101 (Les enfants de la loi 101) refers to the children who began their education under the language regime instituted by the Parti Québécois government in 1977. Bill 101 required that all Quebecers, except those whose parents were educated in English in Quebec, be schooled in French. The first children who entered the Quebec school system under this law are in their late 30s today. They serve as an important barometer of the success of Quebec's language policies. Like many modern societies, Quebec depends significantly on immigration (Quebec takes in roughly 45,000 immigrants every year[5]). The degree to which the education provisions of Bill 101 succeed in protecting the existence of a French-speaking society in Quebec therefore depends in great measure on the Children of Bill 101.

It is therefore not surprising that they have been intensely studied by researchers attempting to chart the course of the future of Quebec society. The evidence so far provides cause both for optimism and for concern among those who seek to protect and promote French in Quebec.

On the one hand, it is quite clear that the vast majority of the Children of Bill 101 exit the Quebec school system fluent in French, and thus capable of functioning with ease in a French-speaking public environment. The sights and sounds of young Quebecers of various ethnic backgrounds speaking in perfect French in school grounds and parks, comfortable with the idiomatic particularities of Quebec French, are everywhere in areas where many immigrants live, especially in the Greater Montreal area. There is thus reason for optimism that the language law is succeeding in creating French speakers out of children of very different linguistic backgrounds.

On the other hand, the attitude of new Quebecers schooled under Bill 101 is quite different from that of 'old stock' French-speaking Quebecers. Studies show that while the latter identify with the French language, in the sense that they view it as a non-negotiable part of their identities, newer Quebecers have a more instrumental attitude not just toward French, but toward language in general. They often speak three (or more) languages: their heritage language, that of their parents; French, which they acquire in school; and English, which they pick up from the pervasive North American culture (evidence shows they do this more readily than their francophone Quebecer counterparts). Given the range of languages in their repertoire, it is thus not surprising that they identify less with any one language. It is also not surprising that the linguistic choices that they make outside the public sphere vary. For example, they may choose to speak their mother tongues in private, domestic contexts, but choose English when the time comes to select colleges and universities.

Thus, the Children of Bill 101 speak French fluently, but they have less of an identity stake in its survival than do the French speakers who trace their origins in Quebec back through the centuries.

For some, this is not a cause for concern. The goal of language policy is after all in their view to make French the language of the *public* sphere. And to the degree that the Children of Bill 101 can function comfortably in French in public and commercial contexts, they view this goal being amply achieved by the language law.

Others are less sanguine. They point out that if the proportion of Quebecers, especially in and around Montreal, who have a more instrumental attitude toward French increases, a tipping point may be reached where they will decide on instrumental grounds to use English more in public. They therefore find the present language laws insufficiently robust. Some believe that the education laws should apply not only to primary and secondary schools, but to Quebec's CEGEPs as well (CEGEPs are Quebec's equivalent of American junior colleges). Others think that preference should be given to immigrants to Quebec whose first language is French, or who speak a language that is sufficiently close to French to make it more likely that they will identify with the French language.

Does the linguistic and sociological study of the Children of Bill 101 foster optimism or pessimism about the success of Quebec's language laws? It all depends on what the ultimate goal of these laws is taken to be. There can be no doubt that the requirement that immigrants and francophones educate their children only in French within the public school system increases the likelihood that French will continue to thrive in the province. Some proponents of the language laws think that this is all that can reasonably be achieved. Others aspire to firmer guarantees, and hope to strengthen the language laws in order to come as close as possible to securing the future of the French language against all possible cultural and linguistic threats.

Which of these two views will prevail among the intellectual and political elites of Quebec? It is impossible to answer this question with any degree of certainty. What is certain is that the emergence of the Children of Bill 101 will not mark the final episode in Quebec's ongoing language saga.

SNAPSHOT

Important Legal Challenges to the Charter of the French Language

The Charter of the French Language, Bill 101, was adopted by the National Assembly of Quebec in 1977. It very quickly became the object of legal challenges, and the Supreme Court of Canada had to render on numerous occasions decisions on the constitutionality of its various provisions. These legal challenges were, and continue to be, fraught with political tensions.

Before the adoption of the Charter of Rights and Freedoms in 1982, the British North America Act provided only a fairly narrow basis on which to challenge Bill 101. The BNA Act requires that all legislation enacted in Quebec be published in both English and French. Accordingly, the first legal challenge to Bill 101 produced the Supreme Court of Canada's decision that the provision that all Quebec legislation be published only in French was unconstitutional.

The 1982 Charter, and in particular section 23 of the Charter, provided opponents of the language law with a broader basis upon which to challenge the language laws. Section 23 ensures the education rights of francophone minorities in English Canada and of anglophone minorities in Quebec. The educational provisions of Bill 101 restricted access to English schools to children of parents who had themselves been educated in English in Quebec. On the basis of Section 23, the Supreme Court decision in the case of *Attorney General of Quebec v. Quebec Protestant School Boards of Quebec* extended access to English schools to all children of parents educated in English anywhere in Canada.

In 1988, the Supreme Court issued a decision that Bill 101's requirement that outdoor commercial signs be exclusively in French was unconstitutional. It argued that a less stringent requirement, that French clearly predominate on commercial signs, would be acceptable. The Liberal provincial government of the time, headed by Robert Bourassa, invoked the 'notwithstanding clause' of the Canadian Constitution in order to keep the law unchanged. The notwithstanding clause allows legislatures to override Charter provisions for five years. The use of this clause of the Constitution sent shockwaves through the rest of Canada. It is widely credited with having caused the failure of the Meech Lake Accord, a set of constitutional amendments designed to secure Quebec's acceptance of the 1982 Constitution. (The Constitution had been adopted in 1982 without Quebec's consent). The use of the notwithstanding clause to uphold the linguistic privileges of the majority, contrary to Charter rights, was seen by many in the rest of Canada as unreasonable, and dampened the enthusiasm for constitutional reconciliation with Quebec.

An era of relative linguistic peace in Quebec followed the rendering of these decisions on commercial signage and on the language of instruction. Many parents, both immigrant and anglophone, began to see the benefits of their children being educated in French.

A spate of recent cases, however, may reignite political unrest around the language law. In *Solski (Tutor of) v. Quebec (Attorney General)*, decided in 2005, the Supreme Court ruled that the provision of Quebec's language law that grants eligibility to attend English schools to children whose parents had received the 'major part' of their education in English in Canada should not be read in a strict quantitative manner. According to the judgment, it might suffice to qualify

a child for English instruction that a 'significant' part of the parents' education had been in English. They would thus signal their commitment to minority language instruction, and be eligible for such instruction under section 23 of the Canadian Constitution.

In 2002, Quebec introduced legislation designed to close loopholes in the language law on access to English schools. That loophole allowed children to become eligible for English education by spending at least a year in an unsubsidized (i.e., private) English school. (Schools receiving no subsidies are not subject to the language law). Bill 104 sought to close that loophole. The Quebec Court of Appeal struck the Bill down as unconstitutional, and the case, *Nguyen v. Quebec*, was heard by the Supreme Court of Canada in 2008. The decision in 2009 decreed that the time that a child spent in a private English school should be taken into account in assessing his or her eligibility for admittance into a public English school.

Taken together, these two decisions broaden the category of children admissible for English instruction. However, the Supreme Court has rejected other appeals aimed at loosening the strictures on the language of instruction. In *Gosselin (tutor of) v. Quebec (Attorney General)*, the Supreme Court rejected the claim made by a group of francophone parents that under the Charter equality rights, they should be able to choose to send their children to English schools. The Supreme Court's decision rested on interpreting the language law as not excluding categories of children from English instruction, but rather protecting the rights of the anglophone community.

Given the growing awareness among francophone parents of the competitive disadvantage that their children's education gives them in a globalized economy that functions largely in English, this challenge is unlikely to be the last one to come from the francophone community. It may be that the 20 years or so of linguistic peace in Quebec is more fragile than previously thought.

QUESTIONS FOR CONSIDERATION

1. How much do you identify with your mother tongue? How much does it matter to you that your children and grandchildren speak it fluently?

2. Do you think it is fair for the government of Quebec to require its immigrants to send their children to French schools, when English schools are available?

3. Do you think that the French language would survive in North America in the absence of legislation such as Quebec's?

NOTES

1. Francophones represent around 2 per cent of the total population of the Americas. See C. Frechette, *Les enjeux et défis linguistiques de l'intégration des Amériques*, (Québec, Conseil de la Langue française, 2001), 8.

2. See Chapters 11, 12, and 13 for the history of language debates.

3. Charles Taylor, *Reconciling the Solitudes. Essays on Canadian Federalism and Nationalism* (Montreal and Kingston: McGill-Queen's University Press, 1993).

4. Will Kymlicka, *Finding our Way. Rethinking Ethnocultural Relations in Canada* (Oxford: Oxford University Press, 1998).

5. See the Quebec government website for recent numbers at www.micc.gouv.qc.ca/fr/recherches-statistiques/stats-immigration-recente.html.

RELEVANT WEBSITES

L'AMÉNAGEMENT LINGUISTIQUE DANS LE MONDE: www.tlfq.ulaval.ca/axl/
Contains information about official language regimes in multilingual societies around the globe.

CONSEIL SUPÉRIEUR DE LA LANGUE FRANÇAISE: www.cslf.gouv.qc.ca/
This provincial governmental body advises the Minister responsible for the application of the Language Charter on cases involving potential infractions to the law. The website contains an archive of the Conseil's opinions.

DAVID CRYSTAL: www.davidcrystal.com/
David Crystal is one of the world's leading chroniclers of the world's endangered languages. The part of his website on 'language death and diversity' contains references to his major works on the subject.

DIVERSCITÉ: www.teluq.uquebec.ca/diverscite/entree.htm
An academic journal based in Quebec that publishes scholarly work on language trends as they affect minority languages in a context of globalization.

ETHNOLOGUE: www.cslf.gouv.qc.ca/
This website is an indispensable clearing house of academic studies on the languages of the world. Its bibliography now runs to some 13,000 items.

OFFICE OF THE COMMISSIONER OF OFFICIAL LANGUAGES OF CANADA: www.ocol-clo.gc.ca/html/publications_e.php
This federal governmental body monitors the situation of Canada's two official languages, English and French. It is particularly concerned with the status of French outside Quebec, and of English inside Quebec. Its annual reports are available on the website, and give a good sense of trends as they develop over time.

OFFICE QUÉBÉCOIS DE LA LANGUE FRANÇAISE: www.olf.gouv.qc.ca/
This provincial governmental body monitors trends in the use of French in Quebec. The website regularly publishes reports on the province's linguistic situation, and contains many tools for the francization of businesses subject to the provisions of the Language Charter.

SELECT BIBLIOGRAPHY

Bouchard, Chantal. *Obsessed with Language: A Sociolinguistic History of Quebec*. Montreal: Guernica, 2008.

Carens, Joseph H. ed. *Is Quebec Nationalism Just? Perspectives from English Canada*. Montreal and Kingston: McGill-Queen's University Press, 1995.

Commission des États Généraux sur la situation et l'avenir de la langue française au Québec. *Le français, une langue pour tout le monde*. Quebec: Gouvernement du Québec, 2001.

Conseil supérieur de la langue française. *Le français et les jeunes*. Quebec: Gouvernement du Québec, 2008.

Fraser, Graham. *Sorry, I Don't Speak French: Confronting the Canadian Crisis that Won't go Away*. Toronto: McClelland & Stewart, 2006.

Georgeault, Pierre, and Michel Pagé, eds. *Le français, langue de la diversité québécoise*. Montreal: Éditions Québec-Amérique, 2006.

Handler, Richard. *Nationalism and the Politics of Culture in Quebec*. Madison: University of Wisconsin Press, 1988.

Kymlicka, Will *Finding our Way: Rethinking Ethnocultural Relations in Canada*. Oxford: Oxford University Press, 1998.

———, and Alan Patten eds. *Language and Political Theory*. Oxford: Oxford University Press, 2003.

Laponce, Jean. *Loi de Babel et autres régularités des rapports antre langue et politique*. Ste-Foy: Presses de l'Université Laval, 2006.

Levine, Marc V. *The Reconquest of Montreal: Language Policy and Social Change in a Bilingual City*. Philadelphia: Temple University Press, 1991.

Maclure, Jocelyn, and Alain G. Gagnon, eds. *Repères en mutation. Identité et citoyenneté dans le Québec contemporain*. Montreal: Éditions Québec-Amérique, 2001.

Taylor, Charles. *Reconciling the Solitudes: Essays on Canadian Federalism and Nationalism*. Montreal and Kingston: McGill-Queen's University Press, 1993.

CHAPTER 15

Popular Music in Quebec

Christopher Jones, Carnegie Mellon University

— TIMELINE —

1920s–1930s   Mary Travers ('La Bolduc') pens many popular songs.

1940   Roland 'Soldat' Lebrun evokes sacrifices of war.

late 1940s   Opening of clubs Au Faisan Doré in Montreal and Chez Gérard in Quebec City, showcasing French chansonniers.

1945   Country stars Willie Lamothe, Paul Brunelle, and Marcel Martel begin their careers.

1950   Félix Leclerc invited to Paris by Jacques Cannetti.

1956   Concours de la Chanson Canadienne ('Canadian Song Contest') showcases many new (French) Canadian songwriters.

1958   Cabaret Chez Bozo groups Jean-Pierre Ferland, Claude Léveillée, Clémence Desrocher, and Raymond Lévesques, all of whom would have sustained careers.

1962   *Yé-yé* magazine and *Jeunesse d'aujourd'hui* (Youth Today) TV show address new teen pop market.

1972   Beau Dommage, Les Séguin, Harmonium, and Octobre shift from folk and country to progressive rock.

1974   Superfrancofête—100,000 hear Leclerc, Vigneault, and Charlebois.

1976   Saint-Jean-Baptiste concerts on Mont-Royal—400,000 hear chansonniers and bands on the mountain.

1978   Luc Plamandon's rock opera *Starmania* a hit in France and Quebec.

1970s   Folk movement strengthens; blues/rock of Offenbach and Michel Pagliaro.

1980s   Punk, disco, and *retrenchement* during economic and spiritual crisis.

1988   First *Francofolies de Montréal* francophone song festival.

1993   Les Colocs first album exemplifies a certain Montreal Plateau existence.

1999   Dubmatique—hip hop makes the radio (briefly).

1990s   Western-themed festivals expand.

2001   *Spin* magazine tags Montreal as 'the next big scene' for international anglophone rock.

2003   First *Star Académie* TV talent competition.

2002   Pierre Lapointe and Arianne Moffat—new genre-bending stars.

2004   Loco Locass 'Amour oral': their second major rap success.

2007   Arcade Fire, Simple Plan—international success for Anglo bands.

INTRODUCTION

The production and consumption of popular music in Quebec expanded enormously during the second half of the twentieth century. This echoed a trend found elsewhere in the Western world, where—along with television—song came to prominence as a mass cultural phenomenon. Aspects of this development in Quebec were nevertheless unique, as the musical explosion paralleled closely the social, economic, and political transformations discussed elsewhere in this volume. In the process, the production of French-language popular music came increasingly under local control; also, many artists abandoned Parisian and American conventions in favour of language inflection and imagery of clearly local origin. A significant number of artists also identified closely with the movement through the Quiet Revolution toward sovereignty, up to the failed referendum of 1980.[1] The subsequent maturing of the Quebec music industry involved a conscious adoption of American production standards for mainstream pop, the refinement of pop and rock sensibilities and musical skills, and a diversification of marginal genres (punk, metal, hip-hop). Influences also expanded to include other francophone music and those emanating from immigrant communities in a burgeoning multicultural society and from world youth cultures increasingly available via electronic means.

This chapter is a brief history of the periods, genres, and major figures of popular music in Quebec since the Second World War, as well as of the development of the music industry and the organs, history, and importance of public policy. We address, among others, the following questions: What is unique about popular music in Quebec in the North American context? What are the major influences on the development of this music? What special challenges do musicians in Quebec face? How does popular music shape the way Quebecers think about themselves?

1945–1958: QUEBEC SONG EMERGING

Quebec in 1945, despite its growing industrialization and urbanization, remained under the moral authority of the Catholic Church and the economic control of a primarily English-speaking upper class, with a francophone political class unable or unwilling to effectively change the status quo. Culturally, the Catholic influence could be extremely constraining; Simone de Beauvoir's 1959 interview for Radio-Canada, for example, was pulled from the air under pressure from the Archbishop of Montreal, no doubt for its frank discussion of atheism and feminism. Intellectuals in Quebec were well aware that they were at a disadvantage in the repressively conservative environment of the Duplessis years, known as *la grande noirceur* ('the Great Darkness') in history books, with the *refus global* ('total rejection') manifesto of 1948 being a memorable indicator of the level of discontent with the status quo.

The music industry had relatively little local autonomy. Local affiliates of large American companies commissioned and promoted French versions of American hits, often in mainstream crooner or country styles. The market for songs authored in French by Canadians was almost non-existent, as the songwriter Fernand Robidoux emphasized: 'R.C.A. Victor . . . obstinately refused the songs from Quebec that I suggested. Anything that came from us, by us, for us, had no importance whatsoever'.[2] Change was on the way, however.

Country music was emerging as a viable genre with the original recordings of Willie Lamothe, Marcel Martel, and Paul Brunelle, building on the popular though rather musically limited wartime recordings of Roland 'Soldat' Lebrun, like 'L'Adieu du soldat' ('The Soldier's Goodbye') or 'Courageux canadiens' ('Courageous Canadians'): 'Dear Canadians keep your courage / If one day you are called / Come combat those savages / To keep our liberty'.[3] If Martel was a rather plain songwriter and singer, inspired more by the Appalachian tradition, he as well as Lamothe and Brunelle saw themselves as Western (country) entertainers and built careers based on quality recordings and live performances. Their writing had both humour and variety, and they made recordings using the latest techniques.[4] Lamothe's 'Je chante à cheval' ('I Sing on Horseback') became the title of a documentary on his life and presaged the continuing fascination in Quebec with the myth of the West and its culture.

Folk music, descended from its Celtic origins in the west of France and from the British Isles, had many active practitioners, especially in the Gaspé and Acadian peninsulas to the east. Oscar Thiffaut was a prolific writer in the folk tradition, primarily by writing new words for traditional melodies. Several of his songs entered into cultural history, like 'Le rapide blanc' ('The White Express'), which tells an amusingly risqué story of a train-man's wife receiving a visitor while the train-man is at work. The *violoneux* ('fiddler') had long been a part of the folk tradition, and Jean Carignan's exceptional career was getting underway during this period.

Roger Chamberland dates the beginnings of Quebec chanson[5] to the extensive creations and popular success of Mary Travers, known as 'La Bolduc', in the 1920s and 1930s.[6] It was in postwar Quebec that chanson saw its first full flowering, though two of its important practitioners took a detour through Paris. Both Félix Leclerc (see Biography box) and Raymond Lévesque spent the early 1950s in France, returning to Quebec only after attaining success on the other side of the Atlantic. In Montreal, the cabarets Le Faisan doré and Le Saint-Germain-des-Prés, after having welcomed Parisian chansonniers (singer-songwriters) like Charles Aznavour and Mouloudji, began to feature homegrown talent. The appearance of television and radio shows dedicated to Quebec song showcased the variety of songwriting and performing talent and encouraged others to begin. Perhaps of most importance for the latter was the Concours de la chanson canadienne ('Canadian Song Contest') on Radio-Canada in 1956. The culmination of this period occurred (or the next one began) when Clémence Desrochers, Jean-Pierre Ferland, and Claude Léveillée, among others, gathered around the club Chez Bozo in central Montreal in 1959, performing songs that combined a cabaret-derived French musical foundation with Quebec themes and images.

Richard Baillargeon sees the 1950s as the last period in which pop music (primarily crooners and early rock 'n' roll) was on an equal footing with folk, country, and the early cabaret-style chanson. In the 1960s, with its increasing openness to Anglo-Saxon–dominated pop and rock influences, folk and country—perceived as pre-modern in a rapidly modernizing Quebec—would be pushed to the margins.[7]

FÉLIX LECLERC

Félix Leclerc

National Film Board of Canada. Photothèque / Library and Archives Canada / PA-107872

Félix Leclerc (1914–1988) was a poet, novelist, playwright, actor, and singer-songwriter. He began work in radio and theatre as early as 1934, and wrote his first song that year.[8] His fame as a songwriter, however, came first during his sojourn in Paris beginning in 1950, where he had been invited to record and perform by the French impresario Jacques Canetti, based on a homemade demo of Leclerc's 'Le train du nord' ('The Northern Train'), a song about a conductor bored with his existence: 'On the train to Saint-Adèle/ Was a man who wanted to get off / But try getting off / When the train's going fifty miles an hour / and what's more you're the conductor'.[9]

These narrative songs with rural settings found few fans among Quebec city-dwellers. In Paris, however, he was billed as the 'The Canadian', and his rough-hewn persona and poetic songs were attractive both for their exoticism and their quality. That Canetti subsequently discovered Jacques Brel and nurtured Georges Brassens furnishes two points of comparison for the songs of Leclerc. In North America of 1950 the comparisons are fewer; some of Woody Guthrie's work is possibly relevant, or a decade later, Bob Dylan,

Phil Ochs, and other singer-songwriters of the 1960s folk revival.

The notion that life in Quebec could be the stuff of popular song was a key realization for Leclerc. He was not the only songwriter in Quebec creating in this way (Oscar Thiffaut and Willie Lamothe, for example, were also fruitful in folk and country at this time), but Leclerc was the only one touring Europe and recording in France. By 1953 his success began to grow in Quebec, and he began performing there regularly. He continued to write for the theatre and for television, and turned down offers (like the Ed Sullivan Show and Las Vegas) that could have made him more money, but these styles of show business were at odds with his personality and values. He naturally gravitated toward the chansonnier ('songwriter') group beginning to emerge in the late 1950s and 1960s, having little in common with the American teen pop–inspired *yé-yé* groups of that period. The chansonniers saw him as the godfather of Quebec song, as he is still considered today.

In 1970, after a period in Switzerland, he installed himself in Quebec again, building a house with his own hands on Île d'Orléans in the St Lawrence River near Quebec City and beginning to participate in the movement toward independence then gathering momentum. Songs like 'L'alouette en colère' ('The

Angry Lark') were poetic expressions that resonated with many Quebecers: 'I have a son stripped of everything / Like his father before him / Water-carrier, wood-cutter / Renter and unemployed / In his own country / He has nothing left / but the pretty view of the river / and his native language / which is not recognized'. In 1974 Leclerc appeared on stage with Gilles Vigneault and Robert Charlebois at the Superfrancofête before 100,000 people. This performance—and especially the rendering of Raymond Lévesque's 'Quand les hommes vivront d'amour' ('When Mankind Will Live On Love') represented a meeting of both minds and generations and a cathartic moment in the nationalist movement, a movement which appeared to be inexorable until its first defeat in the referendum of 1980. During the 1970s, Leclerc found himself in an almost continuous round of creation, recording, touring, collaborations, and official honours. After 1980, Leclerc worked primarily on writing projects in his Orleans Island home until his death in 1988.

Leclerc is remembered in both France and Quebec in many ways, not least in the annual music awards given out at the ADISQ gala (equivalent to the American Grammy awards) named after him in 1979. There is no higher honour in Quebec popular music than receiving a 'Félix'.

1959–1968: CHANSON AND *yé-yé*

Maurice Duplessis died in 1959. In the 1960s, Liberal Jean Lesage is credited with initiating many of the reforms that characterized the Quiet Revolution. Other chapters in this volume deal with aspects of this period in depth, but it is worth recalling the breadth and rapidity of the change. In 10 years, 49 new governmental institutions were created, nearly equalling the number in the previous century.[10] Virtually overnight the Catholic Church lost its hold on health, education, and local government. The drop in both the birth and marriage rates, and the rise in the divorce and abortion rates, foreshadowed profound demographic changes. The residents of Quebec ceased to consider themselves Canadiens ([French]

Canadians), and adopted the term *Québécois* to name themselves and to describe everything emanating from their territory, including songs.[11]

It was the continuation of the chanson tradition that was most closely associated with the Quiet Revolution, by both explicit reference to it and by association through participation in mass gatherings with national implications. Its primary institution was the *boîte à chanson* (song club), the successor to the 1950s Montreal and Quebec City cabarets like Chez Bozo where Jean-Pierre Ferland got his start. The *boîte à chanson* developed a counter-cultural mystique with improvised decors where song lyrics were sung over simple musical settings, usually on guitar or piano, for audiences of college students. The songs' imagery often drew on a real or imagined rusticity associated with *québécitude* ('Quebec-ness', the nature of being of Quebec). These associations carried within them the seeds of their own destruction, if we consider the modernizing drive of the Quiet Revolution, but had parallels elsewhere in North America, notably in the hippie and back-to-the-land movements in the American 1960s, which occurred simultaneously with the folk revival.

A generation of remarkable artists emerged during this period, notably Gilles Vigneault, Robert Charlebois, and Louise Forestier, while others, like Félix Leclerc and Jean-Pierre Ferland, continued to work and, especially in Ferland's case, evolve. Vigneault, close to the Jacques Brel–Léo Ferré model of creation and performance, nevertheless wrote a number of songs anchored in Quebec life that touched Quebecers deeply. The godfather of the winter leitmotif songs, his 'Mon pays' ('My Country') poetically mixed the imagery of the white north (including the immortal line 'My country isn't a country, it's winter') with a subtle evocation of the emerging solidarity and identity among the Quebecers involved in the nationalist thrust. For an in-depth analysis of the song's lyrics and its metaphoric character, visit the *Encyclopedia of Music in Canada*.[12]

The chanson evolution did not define popular music in Quebec during this period, however; simultaneously a pure pop movement known as *yé-yé* echoed the French equivalent and its imitations of the fluffier side of American and British hit parades. It was quite probably *yé-yé* that offered the richer training ground for all aspects of the music business, from promotion to electric guitar and drumming techniques.[13] In *yé-yé* many bands sang in English and covered American hits. In important cases—the band Les Gants Blancs becoming the blues/rock powerhouse Offenbach, for example—the *yé-yé* apprenticeship led to extended careers, with bilingual or exclusively French song creation and an attention to *québécitude* at the later stages. Although the nationalist movement was important to some, the children of the 1950s working-class were not nostalgic about Quebec, which for them connoted hunger and misery in a not-so-distant past.[14] Their modernizing heroes were Elvis Presley, James Dean,

and perhaps the French rocker Johnny Hallyday; the glamour and wealth seemed available only in English and American contexts.

Michel Louvain bridged the gap between crooners and bands, beginning in 1958, basing his career on television exposure and attracting crowds of screaming teenagers (a phenomenon unknown in the chanson tradition); Michèle Richard was his female equivalent. It is *yé-yé* as well that initiates the televised presentation of artists via lip-synching to their recordings, a practice associated with Dick Clark's *American Bandstand* in the United States. From 1962 to 1974 *Jeunesse d'aujourd'hui* (Youth Today) ran a half-hour *yé-yé* showcase, corresponding roughly to the Golden Age of *yé-yé*, though the latter portion of that period is most commonly described as the union of chanson and *yé-yé* into a Quebec rock movement where this division has lost most of its meaning.[15]

The bands had names like Les Classels, Les Sinners, César et les Romains, and Les Barronets and took their inspiration from the Beatles, the Mamas and Papas, the Shadows, and so on. Les Classels combined white suits with white wigs and songs like 'Ton amour a changé ma vie' ('Your Love Changed My Life') rendered in a classic Philadelphia doo-wop style. Les Barronets' rendering of the Beatles' 'Love Me Do' as 'C'est fou mais c'est tout' ('It's Crazy But It's Everything') involved harmony singing while prancing through some basic choreography in rose-coloured suits of the British mod style.

There were those in the *yé-yé* movement who had their 15 minutes of fame and moved quickly on to another life. A few, like Renée Martel, returned to her father Marcel's roots and began a long and successful career in country music. The Mississippian Nanette Workman managed to follow her unlikely success in *yé-yé* with stints in France and the UK before returning to Quebec in the late 1970s to make several disco recordings, including the local version of the international hit 'Lady Marmelade', remembered primarily for its line 'Voulez-vous coucher avec moi ce soir?' Others graduated into the Quebec rock movement taking shape in the 1970s as band members, leaders, songwriters, and impresarios.

1968–1980: ROCK AND NATIONALISM

Many use 'May 1968', the shorthand designation for the student revolt, as a historical breaking point in France. In Quebec it could have been October 1970, when the Front de libération du Québec took the British diplomat James Cross and Labour Minister Pierre Laporte hostage, eventually killing Laporte. During the crisis the federal government imposed martial law and military occupation in Quebec. Historically there appeared to be a crescendo of nationalist fervour developing through the crisis that culminated in the electoral victory of René Lévesque and the Parti Québécois in 1976, followed by the defeat of the referendum on negotiating sovereignty for Quebec in 1980. This defeat stopped the music, in several senses of that expression.

What are collectively known as the 'language laws' emerged during this period, culminating in the Charter of the French Language in 1977, which would radically change language use in Quebec, with French being the official language of Quebec and the language of the workplace and school for most residents and virtually all immigrants.[16] This ended more than 200 years of English dominance among workplace elites and free choice of language of education. Of equal importance to musicians was the setting of radio quotas for francophone and Canadian content (65 per cent and 35 per cent respectively) in Quebec, established at the federal level in 1973.

The musical equivalent of October 1970 (ignoring for the moment the progressive rock group Octobre which took its name from the political events) was Robert Charlebois' series of L'Osstidcho revues beginning in the fall of 1968, which announced (some even say caused) the merging of chanson and yé-yé genres into a North-American blues and country-rock mainstream (see Snapshot box). As musical foundations moved further from cabaret tendencies toward blues, rock, and country mixtures, the language of Quebec as well as English mixtures began to appear in the lyrics. Québécois (the French spoken in Quebec), and the Montreal street variant joual seemed to adapt themselves more readily to the rhythms of rock than European French. As Luc Plamondon—who became famous as a lyricist for

Diane Dufresne and for musicals—commented (without apparent regard for political correctness), 'We're like ten years ahead of them [the French] when it comes to the Americanization of French'.[17]

If Charlebois opened the door for a more North-Americanized popular music scene in Quebec, most artists did not follow his genre-bending Osstidcho example, but rather chose a primarily blues-rock or country-rock vein and stuck to it. Among the latter were Les Séguin and Beau Dommage, while Harmonium mixed chanson and progressive orchestral rock.

In the blues-rock vein, Michel Pagliaro and the bands Offenbach and Corbeau began productive careers during this period. Pagliaro, who is still active more than 40 years later, began his formal apprenticeship during the yé-yé period with Les Chanceliers. He turned toward American-style rock as he began his solo career in 1968, and managed to record successfully in both English and French, as well as working as a producer in Quebec and in France.

Offenbach, created in part from the yé-yé group Les Gants Blancs, had a long itinerary marked by failed efforts to reach an English market, some instability in band membership (though one of the faithful was Willie Lamothe's son Michel), and an early indifference to their blues orientation in Quebec, where folk and country rock dominated the early part of this period. Once Pierre Harel joined and began to write French lyrics, they found an audience and defined a certain sort of approach with songs like 'Câline de Blues' ('Calling the Blues') and 'Le blues me guette' ('The Blues is After Me').

This period is often called the Golden Age of Quebec song, and in terms of its mass appeal there is little question: market share for Quebec song jumped from 10 per cent in 1970 to 25 per cent, then returned to 10 per cent by the end of the decade.[24] The expansion was helped by public policy decisions like the Canadian and French-language broadcast quotas instituted in 1973 and the general movement toward self-governance and self-awareness epitomized by the Parti Québécois's ascendance.

Large outdoor events like the Superfrancofête in 1974 (featuring Charlebois, Leclerc, and Vigneault) were mass celebrations that consecrated chanson as

Snapshot

Osstidcho

If the logjam (to use a Quebec-appropriate metaphor) of 1960s popular music caused by the split between *yé-yé* and chanson was indeed as severe as Robert Giroux and others claim, Robert Charlebois acted as the stick of dynamite that opened the cultural flow again.[18] *Osstidcho*, his multi-performer, multimedia revue, first presented in 1968, presented new possibilities in popular music in Quebec.

Charlebois had training as both an actor and a musician, and combined appearances in film with album production during a mid-1960s *boîte à chanson* period. He also began collaborating on revues, including (somewhat ironically) *Yé-yés versus chansonniers* in 1965 and *Terre des bums* (Land of the Bums) in 1967.[19] Trips to the West Indies and especially to California (at the height of the 'flower power' period) changed him both philosophically and musically: *Osstidcho* was conceived of as a 'happening' in the California sense, with all that implies in terms of spontaneity and improvisation.[20] The revue had three separate runs beginning in May of 1968, continuing with *Osstidcho King Size* in September (which toured outside of Montreal) with *L'Osstidcho meurt* ('Osstidcho Dies') in January of 1969 being the necessary end before it ossified into something permanent and rehearsed.[21] *Osstidcho* is taken to be a short form of *hostie de show*. The name was full of significance in a Quebec that was in the process of losing its religion: *hostie* means 'host', in the sense of the 'body of Christ' used in communion, but is also a common blaspheme in Québécois (along with several other key words in Catholic ritual). Thus *hostie de show* would mean something like 'showbiz communion', with its blasphemous usage muddying the waters even further, or adding to its resonance, depending on your point of view.

The revue itself was a hybrid, but one Charlebois had been working up to, mixing songs sung with Louise Forestier and his companion Mouffe (Claudine Monfette), humorous monologues by Yvon Deschamps, and music by the group Free Jazz of Quebec. The participants made mistakes and joked about them on stage, and early on the shows were endearingly unpredictable. What made them electrifying were two things: the use of relaxed *québécois*, *joual*, and even English in the song lyrics, and the mixing of rock, psychedelia, jazz, and soul into a soup that defied the characterization of the previously segregated chanson and *yé-yé* production in the 1960s.

It is important to realize that Charlebois broke not only the stylistic music taboos separating chanson and *yé-yé* production, but also ridiculed the aura of near-holiness which surrounded some of the early chansonnier reverence for rural and traditional imagery. This reverence, while invigorating to some extent in its local orientation, unfortunately recalled the rural Catholic nationalism promoted by Maurice Duplessis when the majority of Quebec workers had long since migrated to the cities into a working class beginning to organize to exercise its power.[22]

Thus, in 'Demain l'hiver' ('Tomorrow it's winter'), Charlebois takes neither himself nor Gilles Vigneault's 'Mon pays' seriously (the latter certainly the more serious crime):

> Tomorrow it's winter, I could care less
> I'm heading south, to the sun
> To bathe in the sea
> I'll think of you
> While I'm planting my toes in the soft sand[23]

The songs 'California' and 'Lindberg' are more closely linked to the revue, however, with the latter becoming a somewhat unlikely hit, with its rather tenuous relationship to the famous pilot (note the different spelling of the name), an intro of free jazz and sound effects, trumpet and sax improvisations throughout, and lyrics by Claude Péloquin including a chorus whose primary component is a list of airline companies.

As his career progressed, he came to lean increasingly on collaborations with lyricists, including Mouffe, Marcel Sabourin, Réjean Ducharme, and even used poems by Gilles Vigneault and Arthur Rimbaud, but he has managed to maintain a freewheeling atmosphere that was still identifiably Charlebois, the Charlebois forever linked to *L'Osstidcho*.

the voice of the people, and defined its newfound reach. During Saint-Jean-Baptiste celebrations in 1976, the year that the Parti Québécois would come to power bearing hopes for progress toward independence, two concerts on Mont-Royal in the centre of Montreal grouped Vigneault, Charlebois, Léveillée, Ferland, and Yvon Deschamps on the first day, and the new generation including Raoul Duguay, Beau Dommage, Octobre, and Harmonium on the second. Over the two days 400,000 people attended. This event seemed to define for the foreseeable future that popular music was the primary expression of an emerging sovereign and francophone society.[25] The movement seemed unstoppable. It proved not to be, neither politically nor in the dominance of the chanson heritage within Quebec popular music.

1980–1999: Crisis and Recovery

If the Mont-Royal concerts of June 1976 represented an apotheosis, they were simultaneously a turning point. In November, when the Parti Québécois achieved electoral victory, the oppositional role played by the chansonniers and new rockers was no longer necessary: their party had won. It was less attractive for artists to be attached to the new establishment than to the rising opposition. The PQ in power necessarily began to make decisions that alienated some of its base, like freezing salaries in the public sector (in 1982) as the recession lingered from the late 1970s and presenting a question to referendum in 1980 that seemed fairly toothless to many: a Yes victory would merely allow the government to begin negotiations toward a sovereignty whose character had yet to be defined. When even this mild initiative was voted down, the ideological link of Quebec chanson to the nationalistic project went on indefinite hiatus, along with the project itself, which lost ground in the 'me-first' 1980s, when social goals were replaced by individual ones: a 'loft' downtown, a BMW, and a vacation house in Magog'.[26]

The primary reasons for the ensuing crisis in the music industry were not political, however, but economic. A worldwide energy crisis and ensuing recession, followed by a reorganization of the music industries with the advent of CDs and music videos, combined to cause a flight from regional markets

by the major record labels. It is into this void that a combination of public subsidies and local initiative gave rise to a local music industry that had not fully existed before, with Audiogram and its retail, distribution, and concert arms becoming the poster child for success.[27] Available funding was nevertheless limited, and the insularity of small markets meant that new artists had difficulty breaking in. A music-industry trade group—ADISQ—was founded in 1979 and increasingly made its influence felt on issues such as subsidies and regulation in the following decade, as well as organizing awards (the Félix awards) that filled a need for Quebec-specific recognition of musical accomplishment.[28]

Of the two genres that appeared during this decade—punk and disco—the latter proved to be ephemeral, while the punk anti-establishment ethos has not only endured, but turned up as an influence among contemporary artists as diverse as Mara Tremblay and les Cowboys Fringants. Neither genre (nor the various other 'waves' of the period) offered much continuity to either chanson or the first wave of Quebec rock practitioners, who in some cases went away quietly, while others (Michel Rivard, Pierre Flynn of Octobre, Diane Dufresne [doing Bowie-esque shows], and Claude Dubois) continued solo careers as established stars. Artists attaining new prominence in this period worked primarily in the rock vein; these included Paul Piché and Daniel Lavoie. The Manitoban Lavoie produced a remarkable album—*Tension, Attention*—in 1983, featuring one of the first successful integrations of synthesizers, electronica, and timely lyrics.

The 1980s also saw the consecration of Luc Plamondon as a creator of musicals in French, with the huge success in Paris of *Starmania*, in collaboration with the composer Michel Berger. The show became a launching pad for new and existing Québécois artists (including Dufresne, Fabienne Thibeault, and Nanette Workman) and continues to be performed in French and English to this day.[29]

By the 1990s, a brief flirtation with synth-bands like Lili Fatale gave way to a host of fresh new voices in rock/chanson (Jean Leloup), mainstream rock (Éric Lapointe, France D'Amour, Les Respectables), new country (Bourbon Gautier, Gildor Roy, Steve

Faulkner), folk (La Bottine Souriante), fledgling hip-hop recordings, and artists like the collective Les Colocs. Les Colocs represented a kind of urban vitality and stylistic eclecticism, including brass-driven swing and blues that set them apart from most everything that had come before, but somehow evoked life in the vibrant Plateau Mont-Royal neighbourhood where founder André 'Dédé' Fortin and several others lived.

Quebec popular song during the 1990s regained its pre-1980 vigour and managed to compete with imports in terms of quality while offering a diverse palette of genre and influence to local fans. Music grounded in folk origins found renewed life at the end of the decade. Following in the footsteps of the international success of La Bottine Souriante ('The Smiling Boot'), were groups like La Volée de Castors ('The Flock of Beavers'), the a cappella group Les Charbonniers de l'Enfer ('The Coalmen of Hell'), and especially Mes Aïeux ('My Ancestors'), whose song 'Dégénérations' manages to chronicle five generations of change in land ownership, work, family, and music in eight short verses.[30]

1999 TO TODAY: THE CHALLENGES OF PLURALISM

Pluralism is commonly applied to political discourse or to ethnic and cultural diversity. The latter sense certainly has relevance for the current discussion, but a diversity of genres and of distribution and support structures within the music industry also partly characterize the twenty-first century in popular music, with manifestations and consequences just beginning to be understood. This trend of course does not date from 1999, but traces its roots to the 1980s implosion and rebuilding of the Quebec music industry with diminished regard for the importance of chanson, and increased insertion into a global pop mainstream. Certain characteristics of the twenty-first century evolution, however, are indicative of a true pluralism, one which includes strong genre/fan identification and scenes with their own internal logic and continuity and lines of influence that owe little to the history of Quebec song. This pluralism is tending to escape from the confines of the local

music industry itself, including a diminishing role for the trade group ADISQ and the instruments and beneficiaries of public policy. Three examples of this are hip hop, country, and Anglo rock from Montreal.

Hip Hop

I chose 1999 as the jumping-off point for pluralism because it is the year of the first commercially successful hip hop release in Quebec, Dubmatique's 1999 album *La Force de Comprendre* ('The Strength to Understand'). Dubmatique combined the strengths of its French influences (IAM and MC Solaar among them) with accessible refrains and French lyrics (written by members OT mc and Disoul) that is comprehensible from Senegal to Paris.

Hip hop in Quebec was already 10 years old, but early practitioners of black Caribbean origin rapped primarily in English and recorded rarely, in a Canadian context where black musicians were virtually invisible to the music industry.[31] The passage from imitation of African-American musicians in English to self-expression in French was cathartic. SP (Sans Pression) describes the defining nature of that moment:

> 'When I did shows [in French], it was fire, man. After that I could never go back to English.'[32]

After Dubmatique's success, major recording labels signed several other acts, including Muzion and Sans Pression, who were much harder, mixed creole, the Montreal dialect *joual*, and French, and were commercially not what the major labels had hoped for. By 2004 major-label interest had all but evaporated, and acts were primarily self-promoting and recording, with the exception of Loco Locass, three white rappers from Quebec City, who signed to Audiogram for their second album and managed significant sales. Though there is currently a small uptick in hip hop–related activity, the scene suffers from the lack of radio exposure and support of the industrial infrastructure. There is nevertheless enormous energy, though sometimes rather unfocused, in the shows on community radio, the two active websites dedicated to Quebec hip hop, and the strong cultural identification through dress and speech.

Country

Country, or Western, in Quebec has prospered almost entirely without critical and media support, in a system of Western and agricultural festivals where country artists appear and often hawk their wares from suitcases on the street. The festival at Saint-Tite is the largest of these, drawing more than 500,000 fans, who mostly travel in RVs, to a village of 4,000 inhabitants. There are Félix awards for country music, but the winners never appear on the televised part of the ceremony—a symbolic illustration of the tenuous relationship between country and the popular music industry. Country repertoires may include American songs in English, but excellent writers (such as Paul Daraîche, Gildor Roy, Bourbon Gautier, and Steve Faulkner) continue to work in French in the tradition of the early, very popular pioneers like Willie Lamothe. Critics, when they mention country at all, point to excessive sentiment, simplistic structures, and outlandish cult apparel (cowboy hats and boots, and fringed clothing) as reasons to ignore the genre, though one or more of these characteristics could be applied to various other genres equally well. Although Quebec is an overwhelmingly urban and industrialized society, country music projects mythical, pre-industrial, rural values that resonate with a mostly white working-middle-class audience for whom the benefits of a modern multicultural social environment are not clear. The Saint-Tite organizers know exactly what they're doing: 'We are not simple organizers. Every autumn we become the creators of a fantasy world, the world of the Far West'.[33]

Anglo Rock

In 2005 a *Spin* magazine article, entitled 'The Next Big Scene: Montreal' detailed the bands and clubs in a vibrant and mostly English-language rock scene.[34] Two years later I picked up a copy of the *Observer Music Monthly* in London to see one of these bands on the front cover with the headline: 'Could The Arcade Fire be the best band in the world?' In the related story, band leader Win Butler described how he came to Montreal (via Houston and Philips Exeter): 'I felt like I discovered Montreal . . . I never even looked at this place on the f— map, there's this great weird city, and it's full of arts and culture, and I was so shocked'.[35] But the Montreal Anglo bands do not all involve Americans: Simple Plan is a five-piece band of all native Quebecers, including three born in Montreal; Sam Roberts is a West Island (of Montreal) native; The Stills met at art school in Montreal; and the Dears are a changing cast around black Montrealer Murray Lightburn, who says: 'We all have strong feelings for Montreal—I often feel I have to go back to my birthplace before I can give birth to new songs'.[36]

How these comments and occurrences fit into the history and future of Quebec popular music requires some background about population and language trends. Quebec is commonly divided into three components: the capital (Quebec City), the metropolis (Montreal), and the regions (essentially all the rest). Of a total population of 7.5 million, 50 per cent live in the Montreal area, the cultural and economic engine, with popular song being no exception. The Island of Montreal is also the only area where French is not the native language of the majority, and where bilingualism or multilingualism is the norm.[37] The practical effect for musicians is that they can live in Montreal bilingually (or even without French altogether) and participate in a globalized pop environment with a local club base as an incubator, but otherwise almost entirely without local industrial support or subsidy. The reach of the most successful of these bands, who are signed to multinational labels (Arcade Fire, Simple Plan) reaches the entire anglophone market (i.e., the whole world). Montreal thus becomes just another of the magnet North American cities—Austin, San Francisco, Vancouver, Boston—which are not music industry centres like New York, Los Angeles, and London, but which draw artists and musicians to their cultural diversity and thriving arts communities. Unfortunately, linking this status to the Quebec nationalistic project, which has always assumed the French language as a given, and to the increasing monolingual ROQ (rest of Quebec) is uncomfortable, since it diminishes Montreal's role as the Québécois cultural capital. The most friction may come from a critical establishment, coupled with government and industry figures, which have invested heavily in a certain version of the history of Quebec popular song, a version defined a priori as francophone, and in which the Montreal Anglos are difficult, if not impossible, to place.

Other Trends

An interesting sidelight is the rebirth of a pop-chanson split (recalling *yé-yé–chanson*) following the success of the *Star Académie* television talent shows (loosely based on the French *Star Academy* and *American Idol* shows), which have produced a series of young pop stars dependent on a market and an industry that struggles to find a second act for them. Among participants who have subsequently produced at least two albums (one is subsidized for winners) are Émily Bégin, Marie-Élaine Thibert, Marie-Mai Bouchard, Wilfred Le Bouthillier, Cornelieu Montano, and Martin Giroux.[38]

Its title notwithstanding, the Francofolies song festival in Montreal has long included a 'multicultural' stage, where artists of ethnic origin but local residence, as well as artists from la francophonie (the French-speaking world), have performed, singing often in languages other than French. The festival's only requirement is that performers speak French on stage, not that they sing in French.[39] This aspect of the festival is intended to reflect the multicultural nature of contemporary Quebec society, and has included Montrealers Bïa, who is Brazilian and sings in five languages, singer Eméline Michel from Haiti, the accordion player and *merengue* artist Joachim Diaz from the Dominican Republic, and many others.

In spite of the impact of pluralism beginning to manifest itself, the chanson tradition is alive and well, with new artists integrating a wide spectrum of influence from country (Vincent Vallières), French cabaret (Pierre Lapointe) or rock/electronica/rap (Arianne Moffat). The language used varies from Lapointe's near-Parisian to Vallières's relaxed Québécois (recalling Charlebois or Lucien Françoeur).

Quebec Identity

Those of us listening to English-language popular music may find the national origins of artists a curiosity (Bjork from Iceland, or the Sri Lankan/London background of M.I.A.) but we don't necessarily imagine

that such artists are important for the national self-image of their countries of origin. They cross national borders in the process of the consumption of music in a globalized, but primarily English-language, popular music industry. Quebec popular music in French, however, is principally consumed in Quebec, with a small additional penetration of certain artists into other francophone countries such as France or Belgium. The net effect of local consumption is that there is a strong component of cultural identification between Quebec popular musicians and their fans which has a nationalistic overtone, quite independent of whether a given song has an overtly political message.

Gilles Vigneault's song 'Mon pays c'est l'hiver' ('My Country is Winter'), often considered to be Quebec's unofficial national anthem, is a good example of this. There is no specific mention of Quebec in the song, but some of the imagery is so strongly related to Quebec cultural (and climatic!) experience that the song had an immediate emotional impact on Quebecers of the period of the Quiet Revolution and became a part of that social and political constellation.

There have always been, and continue to be, artists that both celebrate and critique Quebec explicitly, however. The rappers Loco Locass are the most vocal and visible defenders of the cause of sovereignty in Quebec today, while the alt-rock-folk-country Les Cowboys Fringants constantly turn a satirical, if affectionate, eye on things québécois, in songs like 'Québécois de souche', where they take on the contradiction between white Quebecers who clamour for ethnic purity while slaughtering the French language in daily life.

The use of French, in and of itself, is an affirmative act with political connotations in North America, and francophone Quebecers live this out every day. Songwriters are no exception; Michel Rivard's 'Le Cœur de ma vie' ('The Heart of My Life') is perhaps the most eloquent musical statement of that reality, with the central metaphor establishing his French language as both love interest and foundation for his very existence.

CONCLUSION

The sonic record of Quebec popular culture is vital and varied, a remarkable accomplishment when we consider that its total population in 1941 was 3.3 million,[40] and even today is only 7.7 million, with approximately 80 per cent of those being first-language French speakers.[41] As reference points, the population of the state of Massachusetts is 6.5 million, and Pennsylvania 12.5 million.[42] This smallness, and the struggles to define and maintain a separate identity in a great North American sea of primarily Anglo-Saxon culture, have given Quebec popular music a dynamism that it might not otherwise have had. If cultural historians tend to over-emphasize this separateness, however, the musicians themselves rarely do: most recognize that, along with their *québécitude*, comes a healthy dose of *américanité*. Songwriters from Willie Lamothe to Charlebois to Atach Tatuq's Egypto have acknowledged, even embraced, the triumvirate of primary cultural sources for their music: North America, France, and Quebec itself.

The increasing fluidity of music distribution systems abetted by the Internet has made even this expanded vision seem quaint, however. Young musicians have easy access to 'world music' *and* the music of the world, both live in concert, through sites like Myspace and YouTube, and even sites dedicated to local genre audiences such as 'Hip Hop Franco' and 'Découvertes Country' (Country Discoveries). It is unlikely that the music of Quebec will become *less* diverse any time soon: the genre-mixing and expansion of influences reflects not only the increased modes of access, but also the nature of Quebec society itself, especially in Montreal, where multilingualism and ethnic diversity is a fact of daily life. The culinary metaphor for Quebec music will never be a steak dinner, but rather a traditional dish like the *tourtière* (meat pie): you're never quite sure what went into it, but the combination tastes good, and you can't get it anywhere but Quebec.

Questions for Consideration

1. What historical factors influenced the flowering of Quebec music in the 1950s and 1960s?

2. Give specific examples to illustrate the impact of Quebec's geographical situation in North America on the development of country and rock music.

3. How is each of these languages important in the Quebec musical context: French, English, and Haitian creole? (Other languages can be added to this list, of course.)

4. Describe the cultural and demographic differences within Quebec and their influence on musical production.

5. What special challenges do musicians in Quebec face in developing careers within the music industry?

6. How has popular music shaped and reflected the way Quebecers think about themselves?

Notes

1. Christopher Jones, 'Song and Nationalism in Quebec', *Contemporary French Civilization* 34, 1 (2000).

2. Bruno Roy, *Panorama de la chanson au Québec* (Montreal: Leméac, 1977), 40.

3. Roland S. Lebrun, 'Héritage québécois', MCA, 1991.

4. Catherine Lefrançois, 'La chanson country-western au Québec : État de la question et pistes musicologiques', *Quebec Studies* 45 (2008): 29–42. Lefrançois does an interesting study of the use of reverb in several early country songs, as an illustration of the fact that country artists were not behind other popular artists of the day in adopting new technologies.

5. The word *chanson*, in French, is literally translated as *song* in English. The connotations in French, however, are different enough—a greater emphasis on lyrics, authorship,

an anti-pop penchant—that *chanson* is not used in the generic sense, but rather to describe a specific current within the larger history of popular song.

6. Roger Chamberland, and André Gaulin, *La chanson québécoise : de La Bolduc à aujourd'hui* (Montreal: Nuit blanche éditeur, 1994), 21.

7. Richard Baillargeon, and Christian Côté, *Destination Ragou : Une histoire de la musique populaire au Québec* (Montreal: Les Editions Triptyque, 1991), 48.

8. Robert Thérien, and Isabelle D'Amours, *Dictionnaire de la musique populaire au Québec, 1955–1992* (Quebec: Institut québécois de recherche sur la culture, 1992), 64.

9. This lyric translation and all other translations in this chapter are the responsibility of the author. French lyric

sources include album covers, Roger Chamberland and André Gaulin's anthology *La Chanson québécoise : De La Bolduc à aujourd'hui*, and online sources verified against the original recordings where possible.

10. M. Durand, *Histoire du Québec* (Paris: Éditions Imago, 1999), 124.

11. Claude Gautier's song about a lumberjack rebelling against his British boss 'Le grand six-pieds' (The Big Six-Footer) originally included the line *Je suis de nationalité / Canadienne-française* ('I'm of French-Canadian nationality') which by 1965 he was singing as *nationalité québécoise-française* and by 1970 simply as *nationalité québécoise* (R. Chamberland and André Gaulin, op. cit., 110).

12. Hélène Plouffe, Suzanne Thomas, Stephen Willis, "'Mon Pays'" (*The Encyclopedia of Music in Canada*), www.thecanadianencyclopedia.com/index.cfm?PgNm=TCE&Params=U1ARTU0002417.

13. Robert Léger, *La Chanson québécoise en question* (Montreal: Québec Amérique, 2003), 47.

14. Renée-Berthe Drapeau, 'Le yé-yé dans la marge du nationalisme québécois (1960-1974)' in R Giroux, ed., *La Chanson prend ses airs* (Montreal: Editions Triptyque, 1993), 135.

15. Renée-Berthe Drapeau, 'Le yé-yé dans la marge du nationalisme québécois (1960-1974)' in R Giroux, op. cit.,141.

16. For more details about The Charter of the French language please see Martin Lubin and Chantal Bouchard articles in this section.

17. *Pour une chanson* (television series), Productions SDA Ltée, 1985.

18. The subsection on page 58 begins with the title '*Chanson polarized : yé-yés against chansonniers.*' Robert Giroux, Constance Havard, and Roch Lapalme, *Le Guide de la chanson québécoise* (Montreal: Éditions Triptyque, 1996), 58.

19. *Terre des bums* is an ironic riff on *Terre des hommes* (Land of Men/ Man and His World) the theme for Expo '67, the world's fair of that year in Montreal.

20. Sylvain Cormier, 'Essai—Ce show que l'on qualifia d'ossti', *Le Devoir*, 7 June 2008.

21. Bruno Roy, *L'Osstidcho ou le désordre libérateur* (Montreal: XYZ Editeur, 2008), 88.

22. M. Durand, op. cit.,110.

23. Robert Charlebois, 'Robert Charlebois (collection Québec Love)', Gamma AGEK-2201, 1993.

24. Jacques Aubé, *Chanson et politique au Québec (1960–1980)* (Montreal: Triptyque, 1990), 58.

25. Robert Léger, *La Chanson québécoise en question* (Montreal: Québec Amérique, 2003), 94.

26. Robert Giroux, Constance Havard, and Roch Lapalme, op. cit., 129.

27. Line Grenier, 'Aftermath of a Crisis: Quebec Music Industries in the 1980s', *Popular Music* 12, 3 (1993): 211.

28. Ibid., 214.

29. Robert Giroux, Constance Havard, and Roch Lapalme, op. cit., 152.

30. In French this title represents the homonyms *dégéneration* ('degeneration') and *des générations* ('[several] generations').

31. Roger Chamberland, 'The Cultural Paradox of Rap Made in Quebec' in A Durand, ed., *Black, Blanc, Beur: Rap Music and Hip-Hop Culture in the Francophone World* (Lenham, Md: Scarecrow, 2002), 126.

32. SP, personal interview with author, 2007.

33. Saint-Tite, *Historique du Festival Western de Saint-Tite*, available at www.festivalwestern.com/historique/, accessed 8 December 2008.

34. Rodrigo Perez, 'The Next Big Scene: Montréal', *Spin* 21, 2 (2005): 61–5.

35. Paul Morley, 'Could the Arcade Fire be the Best Band in the World?', *The Observer Music Monthly* 43 (2007): 30.

36. T. Jonze, *The Dears*, available at timjonze.googlepages.com/dearsdazed, accessed 10 October 2008.

37. The Hull/Gatineau area opposite Ottawa, as well as a few pockets in the Eastern Townships, are the only other areas where bilingualism effectively persists as a daily fact of life.

38. Information on the current competition can be accessed at www.staracademie.ca/.

39. The exception to this rule is anglophone artists, who have been excluded since the beginning. French-speaking artists often perform songs in English, I saw the French artist Laurent Voulzy perform a medley of 1960s American pop to close his set in 2003.

40. 1941 statistics taken from Institut de la Statistique du Québec, available at www.stat.gouv.qc.ca/donstat/societe/demographie/struc_poplt/102.htm.

41. Quebec statistics taken from the Banque de données des statistiques officielles sur le Québec, available at www.bdso.gouv.qc.ca/pls/ken/iwae.proc_acce?p_temp_bran=ISQ, accessed 23 January 2009.

42. State populations taken from US Census Bureau statistics, available at www.census.gov/popest/states/NST-ann-est.html, accessed 23 January 2009.

RELEVANT WEBSITES

ENCYCLOPEDIA OF MUSIC IN CANADA:

www.thecanadianencyclopedia.com/index.cfm?PgNm=HomePage&Params=A1

A website that includes historical and current aspects of popular, folk, religious, concert, and other forms of music in Canada.

QUÉBEC INFO MUSIQUE: www.qim.com

A very useful website and database about different Quebec music artists.

LA CHANSON DU QUÉBEC ET SES COUSINES: www.chansonduquebec.com

Find articles of the history of the Quebec chanson

and other articleson this website created by Danielle Tremblay and Yves Laneville:

HIP HOP FRANCO: www.hiphopfranco.com
Find songs and information about hip hop bands in Quebec.

DÉCOUVERTES COUNTRY: www.decouvertescountry.com
Find out more about Quebec country music artists.

SELECT BIBLIOGRAPHY

Alix, Yves. 'Restructuration de l'industrie de la musique et transformation du produit musical. In R. Giroux, ed. *La Chanson en question(s)*. Montreal: Editions Triptyque, 1985, 55–65.

Aubé, J. *Chanson et politique au Québec (1960–1980)*. Montreal: Editions Triptyque, 1990.

Baillargeon, Robert, and C. Côté. *Destination Ragou : Une histoire de la musique populaire au Québec*. Montreal: Editions Triptyque, 1991.

Chamberland, Roger, and André Gaulin. *La chanson québécoise : de La Bolduc à aujourd'hui*. Montreal: Nuit blanche éditeur, 1994.

———. 'The Cultural Paradox of Rap Made in Quebec'. In A. Durand, ed. *Black, Blanc, Beur: Rap Music and Hip-Hop Culture in the Francophone World*. Lenham, Md: Scarecrow, 2002, 124–37.

Cormier, Sylvain. 'Essai—Ce show que l'on qualifia d'ossti', *Le Devoir*, 7 June 2008.

de Beauvoir, Simone. 'Simone de Beauvoir censurée'. Radio-Canada, 1959. Viewed August 2008. Available at: http://archives.radio-canada.ca/arts_culture/litterature/clips/2015/.

Drapeau, Renée-Berthe. 'Le yé-yé dans la marge du nationalisme québécois (1960–1974)'. In R. Giroux, ed. *La Chanson prend ses airs*. Montreal: Editions Triptyque, 1993, 115–30.

Durand, Marc. *Histoire du Québec*. Paris: Éditions Imago, 1999.

Giroux, Robert, Constance Havard, and Roch Lapalme. *Le Guide de la chanson québécoise*. Montreal: Editions Triptyque, 1996.

Grenier, Line. 'Aftermath of a Crisis: Quebec Music Industries in the 1980s', *Popular Music* 12, 3 (1993): 209–27.

Jones, Christopher. 'Song and Nationalism in Quebec', *Contemporary French Civilization* 24, 1 (2000): 21–36.

Jonze, T. *The Dears*. Available at: http://timjonze.googlepages.com/dearsdazed. Accessed 10 October 2008.

Lefrançois, Catherine. 'La chanson country-western au Québec : État de la question et pistes musicologiques', *Quebec Studies* 45 (2008): 29–42.

Léger, Robert. *La Chanson québécoise en question*. Montreal: Québec Amérique, 2003.

Morley, Paul. 'Could The Arcade Fire be the Best Band in the World?', *The Observer Music Monthly* 43 (March 2007): 30–9.

Perez, Rodrigo. 'The Next Big Scene: Montréal', *Spin* 21, 2 (2005): 61–5.

Pour une chanson.Television series. Productions SDA,1985.

Roy, Bruno. *L'Osstidcho ou le désordre libérateur*. Montreal: XYZ Editeur, 2008.

———. *Panorama de la chanson au Québec*. Montreal: Leméac, 1977.

Saint-Tite. *Historique du Festival Western de Saint-Tite*. Available at: www.festivalwestern.com/historique/. Accessed 8 December 2008.

Straw, Will. *L'industrie du disque au Québec*. Available at: www.arts.mcgill.ca/programs/ahcs/html/Straw/Traite.pdf.

Thérien, Robert, and Isabelle D'Amours. *Dictionnaire de la musique populaire au Québec, 1955–1992*. Quebec: Institut québécois de recherche sur la culture, 1992.

RECORDINGS

Atach Tatuq. 'Deluxx'. AT Music ANUCD001. 2005.

Beau Dommage. 'Beau Dommage'. EMI 724387523425, 1974.

Bel-Air (Les). 'Les grands succès country'. Disques mérite, 1970.

Charlebois, Robert. 'Robert Charlebois (collection Québec Love)'. Gamma AGEK-2201, 1993.

Colocs (Les). 'Les Années 1992–1995.' BMG, 2001.

Cowboys Fringants (Les). 'La Grand-Messe.' Disques La Tribu, TRIICD-7233, 2004.

Déry, Marc. 'Marc Déry.' Audiogram, ADCD-10121, 1999.

Harmonium. 'Si on Avait Besoin D'une Cinquième Saison.' Polygram, 8339902, 1975.

Lamothe, W. 'Les Grands du Country'. BMG Musique Québec, 1995.

Lapointe, Pierre. 'Pierre Lapointe.' Disques Audiogramme, 2004.

Lavoie, Daniel. 'Tension, attention'. Kébec-Disc KD-584, 1983.

Lebrun, Roland S. 'Héritage québécois'. MCA, 1991.

Lelièvre, Sylvain. 'Ses Plus Belles Chansons.' Kébec-Disques, KDC 672, 1991.

Loco Locass. 'Amour oral.' Disques Audiogramme, 2004.

Mes Aïeux. 'En Famille.' Disques Victoire VIC2-1871, 2004.

Moffat. Ariane, 'Aquanaute.' Disques Audiogramme, 2002.

Muzion. 'Mentalité Moune Morne.' BMG 74321-65673-2, 1999.

Offenbach. 'L'Ultime Offenbach'. Disques Helena, 2007.

Parent, Kevin. 'Pigeon D'argile.' Tacca, TACD 4507, 1995.

Rivard, Michel. 'Le Cœur de ma vie.'

Sans pression. '514-50 Dans Mon Réseau.' Les Disques Mont Real, MRLCD-5069, 1999.

Séguin (Les). 'Récolte de rêves'. Disques Musi-Art, 1995 (reissue).

Tremblay, Mara. 'Le Chihuahua.' Audiogram ADCD 10120, 1999.

Vallières, Vincent. 'Chacun dans son espace'. Productions BYC, BYCD 130, 2003.

Vigneault, Gilles. 'Gilles Vigneault (Collection Émergence)'. Sony Musique C2K 91053, 1995.

PART D
CITIZENSHIP

INTRODUCTION

Since the conclusion of the late war, we have been happy in considering you as fellow-subjects; and from the commencement of the present plan for subjugating the Continent, we have viewed you as fellow-sufferers with us.

—SECOND CONTINENTAL CONGRESS,
'LETTER TO THE INHABITANTS OF CANADA', 29 MAY 1775.[1]

First we must secure once and for all, in accordance with the complex and urgent necessities of our time, the safety of our collective 'personality'. This is the distinctive feature of the nation, of this majority that we constitute in Quebec—the only true fatherland left us by events, by our own possibilities, and by the incomprehension and frequent hostility of others.

—RENÉ LÉVESQUE, AN OPTION FOR QUEBEC.[2]

I have always opposed the notions of special status and distinct society. With the Quiet Revolution, Quebec became an adult and its inhabitants have no need of favours or privileges to face life's challenges and to take their rightful place within Canada and the world at large.

—PIERRE ELLIOTT TRUDEAU, THE ESSENTIAL TRUDEAU.[3]

Throughout their history, the people of Quebec have often questioned their allegiances. Political leaders and other elites have variously tried to convince Quebecers that they should express their nationality and citizenship within the United States of America, within Canada, or within an independent Quebec. So how have Quebecers have decided? How have they expressed their desires for citizenship over the years? What does it mean to be a Quebec citizen? How does the French language relate to citizenship in Quebec? Are there distinct civil, political, and social rights for women, immigrants, and Aboriginals? Does citizenship in Quebec accommodate differences?

The concept of citizenship is broad. Political scientist Jane Jenson writes, 'the word does define societal boundaries, distinguishing insiders from outsiders, "we" from "they"'.[4] T.H. Marshall[5] provides a classic definition of citizenship, defined through its civil, political, and social aspects, while others reflect on different understandings, such as those highlighted by Daniel Weinstock: status, rights, democracy, practices, and identity.[6]

Historian Denyse Baillargeon begins our exploration of citizenship in this section of *Quebec Questions* by examining women's civil, political, and social journey in twentieth-century Quebec. Baillargeon explores how the road travelled by Quebec women, especially French-Canadian women, is measured. How did women in early twentieth-century Quebec live under the yoke of the Church and the state? For example, Baillargeon examines the arguments of political leaders and the Catholic Church over female waged labour. While many of these arguments in Quebec echoed those in other Western societies, Baillargeon argues that disputes took on a 'distinct' and 'patriotic' form in Quebec; one concerned with the survival of French Canadians as a people and the preservation of their 'true' identity. Nationalist leaders and church representatives loudly and clearly proclaimed that women had a maternal vocation. As a minority within both Canada and North America, French-Canadians attributed great importance to this vocation and the fertility rate. Many French-Canadian women chose not to work for wages, choosing instead a religious life. Why? What role did these women play in pre–Quiet Revolution Quebec?

Consider that in Quebec in 1941 there were 18 nuns for every 1,000 women.[7] What was their impact on laywomen and on the state? How can we evaluate their contribution from a feminist perspective?

Baillargeon then addresses the legal status of married women in Quebec, examining the individuals and organizations that fought for universal suffrage, a right that was obtained at the provincial level in 1940. The female presence in the labour market is another good indicator of the citizenship status of women. Baillargeon provides excellent documentation and analysis from the end of the Second World War to 2000. We discover the issues and battles that feminists took to the public and private spheres to bring about legal, political, and social changes. She ends by exploring the recent relations between Quebec nationalists and Quebec feminists. Do nationalists and feminists share views on how citizenship practices in Quebec can be inclusive for all citizens? How does the Quebec state respond to these issues?

This question leads us to the contribution of Raffaele Iacovino and Charles-Antoine Sévigny, political scientists who focus their inquiry on Quebec policies on ethnocultural diversity. Since the 1960s, Quebec has established many regulations, policies, and laws framing citizenship practices. Iacovino and Sévigny examine the Quebec Ministry of Immigration, created in 1968, which sought to control the selection and integration of immigrants to Quebec. What pushed the Quebec state to fight for this power? Immigration is a shared jurisdiction within the BNA Act; how do Canada and Quebec share these powers? As this chapter shows us, Quebec challenged Canada on this issue. Some categorize this confrontation as minority versus majority nationalism. Quebec has struggled for the recognition of a 'differentiated citizenship'[8] for itself within the Canadian framework. By examining the laws and policies adopted to manage diversity, the authors explore whether this Quebec model conflicts with the broader Canadian model. What are the principal values of the Quebec model, known as *interculturalism*? How has the model of interculturalism evolved? In addressing these questions, the authors reveal rich insights into how Quebec frames citizenship. What are the rights and responsibilities of individuals within Quebec? The authors describe the notion of a common public culture in Quebec. What are its principles? What could unite all Quebecers in the interests of social harmony and cultural preservation?

These questions bring us to Maryse Potvin's chapter on interethnic and race relations in Quebec. How do Quebecers of all origins live together? How can we characterize the state of interethnic relations in Quebec? From a sociological perspective, Potvin examines changes in intercultural and race relations in Quebec since the 1960s. How could we assess the Quebec state's performance in promoting equality for all Quebecers? Beyond the official Quebec state discourse, can we discern socioeconomic gaps between different minority and racialized groups and francophone Quebecers? Potvin appraises Quebec's public policies that attempt to end discrimination, racism, and ethnic inequalities. In Quebec, societal tensions have recently shifted from linguistic to religious ones, and religious diversity in public spaces has become a central issue. Potvin's chapter forces us to contemplate freedom within multinational democracies, amid significant issues and challenges that evolve and change. As Canadian philosopher James Tully argues:

> The primary question is thus not recognition, identity or difference, but freedom: the freedom of the members of an open society to change the constitutional rules of mutual recognition and association from time to time as their identities change.[9]

Next is Marie McAndrew's chapter on immigration and diversity in Quebec's schools. Schools contribute greatly to the formation of citizenship. How does the school system participate in managing diversity in Quebec? Can Quebec find a balance between its collective goals, such as preserving French as a common public language, and its desire to promote immigration, respect for diversity, and individual rights? McAndrew

looks at the effect of immigration policies since the 1960s on French-language schools in Quebec. Through analyzing policy statements she explores how interculturalism is enacted within the education system.

McAndrew examines how the linguistic debate affects the integration of immigrants in the school system. How did the 1977 Charter of the French Language affect the numbers of allophone students in French-language schools? McAndrew illustrates how the debate over diversity in Quebec schools has recently polarized around two competing concepts: secularization and preserving a traditional identity. How can we assess linguistic integration in Quebec schools? What do recent data tell us about the equality of opportunity and the academic success of students from all ethnic backgrounds? How are intergroup inequities, such as the disparity in secondary school graduation rates, fought? McAndrew closes by suggesting that full recognition of pluralism in Quebec's schools is a work in progress. Quebec teachers and school administrators have much in common with their Canadian colleagues in the challenges of successfully integrating intercultural perspectives into the curriculum. Nevertheless, McAndrew states that the identity issue of 'majority fragility' is specific to Quebec society.[10]

The chapters in this section reveal how challenges surrounding citizenship in Quebec are important to all Quebecers. As in most Western societies, Quebec is a pluralistic society striving to find a balance between common collective characteristics and respect for the diversity of individuals and cultural groups. Tensions, conflicts, and disagreements are all part of the decision-making process in a community. The notion of citizenship has been, is being, and will be re-examined. One can only hope that the Quebec democracy will encourage this debate, allowing all Quebecers to collectively determine a uniquely Quebec way of life.

NOTES

1. The full text of this letter can be found at http://lincoln.lib.niu.edu/cgi-bin/amarch/getdoc.pl?/var/lib/philologic/databases/amarch/.5722.

2. René Lévesque, *An Option for Quebec* (Toronto: McClelland & Stewart, 1968), 21.

3. Pierre Elliott Trudeau, *The Essential Trudeau.* Ron Graham, ed. (Toronto: McClelland & Stewart, 1998), 161.

4. Jane Jenson, 'Recognizing Difference: Distinct Societies, Citizenship Regimes and Partnership', in R. Gibbins and Guy Laforest, eds., *Beyond the Impasse: Toward Reconciliation* (Montreal: IRPP, 1998), 215–39.

5. Thomas H. Marshall, *Class, Citizenship, and Social Development: Essays* (Garden City, NY: Doubleday, 1964).

6. Daniel Weinstock, 'Citizenship and Pluralism', in R.L. Simon, ed., *Blackwell Guide to Social and Political Philosophy* (Malden, MA: Blackwell, 2002), 239–70.

7. Danielle Juteau, and Nicole Laurin, *Un métier et une vocation. Le travail des religieuses au Québec de 1901 à 1971* (Montreal: Les Presses de l'Université de Montréal, 1997), 2.

8. This term is attributed to Iris Marion Young.

9. James Tully, 'Introduction', in A-G. Gagnon and J. Tully, eds., *Multinational Democracies* (Cambridge: Cambridge University Press, 2001), 1–37.

10. Between 2004 and 2008, Quebec admitted an average of approximately 45,000 immigrants per year, most of whom (86.9 per cent) chose to live in the metropolitan area of Montreal. For comparison, Toronto is the home of 68.3 per cent of foreign-born Ontarians.

CHAPTER 16

Quebec Women of the Twentieth Century: Milestones in an Unfinished Journey

Denyse Baillargeon, Université de Montréal

— TIMELINE —

1893   Montreal Local Council of Women founded, consisting mainly of English Montreal's charitable or educational women's organizations. It also has individual members, including some francophones.

1897   National Council of Jewish Women of Canada founded, consisting mainly of Quebec Jewish women's organizations, much like its largely anglophone counterpart (see above).

1902   Coloured Women's Club founded by Anne Greenup and six other Black American women to aid Black population of Montreal.

1907   Fédération nationale Saint-Jean-Baptiste, an umbrella group for francophone women's associations, founded.

1908   École d'enseignement supérieur pour jeunes filles, first classical college for francophone women, opens its doors (later to become Collège Marguerite-Bourgeois in 1926).

1913   Montreal Suffrage Association founded by Carrie Derick, a professor of Genetics at McGill University.

1915   Cercles de Fermières organization founded by Quebec's Minister of Agriculture to educate rural women about agricultural production methods.

1917   Mothers of soldiers and military nurses are granted right to vote at federal level.

1918   Federal Act to confer the Electoral Franchise upon Women passed.

1919   An Act to Provide for Fixing a Minimum Wage for Women passed in Quebec.

1922   Provincial Franchise Committee founded by Marie Lacoste Gérin-Lajoie, Thérèse Casgrain, and Mrs. Walter Lyman.

1924   Matchwomen at E.B. Eddy Match Company in Hull walk out in wildcat strike.

1927   Alliance canadienne pour le vote des femmes du Québec founded by Idola Saint-Jean.

1928   Supreme Court of Canada denies women right to be senators, ruling that whereas British North America Act states that Senate seats are open to all 'persons', women are not 'persons' in the eyes of the law.

1929   Privy Council in London overturns Supreme Court's decision, recognizing that women are indeed 'persons' and may therefore sit as senators.

Commission on the Civil Rights of Women (called the 'Dorion Commission', after its president, Charles-Édouard Dorion) struck.

Provincial Franchise Committee becomes League for Women's Rights and is presided over by Thérèse Casgrain.

1930 Cairine Wilson of Montreal becomes first woman appointed to Senate in Ottawa.

1931 Further to Dorion Commission's recommendations, married women receive legal right to keep wages they earn.

1932 Married women who are separating property and are owners or signatories to a lease are granted the right to vote in municipal elections in Quebec.

1934 Married women can open their own bank accounts in Quebec.

1937 Some 5,000 female French-Canadian, Jewish, and immigrant garment-industry workers unite to strike in Montreal.

Fédération catholique des institutrices rurales de la province de Québec, first rural school-mistresses' organization, founded by Laure Gaudreault.

An Act respecting Assistance to Needy Mothers adopted in Quebec to assist single mothers, most of them widows.

1940 Quebec grants women right to vote and run in provincial elections.

1941 Quebec women law graduates are admitted to provincial Bar and thus permitted to practise law in the province.

Quebec women permitted to vote in municipal elections, provided they meet voter eligibility criteria.

1942 Quebec women granted right to become school board commissioners.

1943 Federal government opens daycare centres in Montreal to encourage mothers to join war effort.

1945 Federal Family Allowance program introduced, leading to conflict with Quebec over cheques being issued to mothers instead of fathers.

1952 Men and many women employees go on strike at French-Canadian department store Dupuis Frères.

1954 A double standard in Civil Code of Quebec abolished. Previously, a husband could obtain a legal separation if his wife committed adultery, but a wife could not separate from an adulterous husband unless he kept his mistress in the family dwelling.

1961 Bérengère Gaudet becomes first woman notary in Quebec.

Marie-Claire Kirkland-Casgrain becomes first woman to sit in Quebec Legislative Assembly.

1962 Married women are granted right to become teachers with Montreal Catholic School Commission.

1964 Bill 16 abolishes married women's legal incapacity and mitigates principles of paternal authority and of marital powers of husbands.

1965 Conference called 'La femme du Québec : hier et aujourd'hui' held and concludes with vote to found Fédération des femmes du Québec.

1966 Fédération des femmes du Québec (FFQ) founded.

Association féminine d'éducation et d'action sociale founded, comprising Cercles d'économie domestique and Union catholique des femmes rurales. Both organizations were created in 1945 following rift within Cercles de Fermières.

1967 Royal Commission on the Status of Women in Canada established, chaired by Florence Bird.

Indian Rights for Indian Women founded by Mary Two-Axe Early, a Mohawk woman from Kahnawake.

1968   Act respecting Divorce adopted in Quebec, authorizing civil marriage and divorce in the province.

1969   Providing information on contraceptives decriminalized in Canada. Hospitals authorized to provide abortions sanctioned by therapeutic abortion committee comprising at least three physicians.

Montreal Women's Liberation Movement founded.

All Aboriginal citizens are granted right to vote in Quebec.

'Partnership of acquests' replaces 'community of property' as legal matrimonial property regime.

Front de libération des femmes du Québec (FLF) founded and its *Manifeste des femmes québécoises* disseminated.

1970   Demonstration organized by FLF on 10 May (Mother's Day) to demand free and accessible abortion.

1971   Federal legislation on unemployment insurance amended to provide 17 weeks of maternity leave, granting new mothers 60 per cent of their salary for 15 weeks.

1972   Centre des femmes founded in Montreal, offering abortion services and publishing its *Manifeste pour une politique de planification des naissances* to advocate for family planning policy in Quebec.

1973   Government of Quebec creates the Conseil du Statut de la femme.

Claire L'Heureux-Dubé becomes first woman to be appointed judge to Superior Court of Quebec. She later becomes first woman to sit on Quebec Court of Appeal (1979) and Supreme Court of Canada (1987).

1974   Lise Bacon, Quebec Liberal cabinet minister, tables plan to introduce government daycare, mainly for low-income families.

Quebec Native Women's Association founded (later to become Quebec Native Women Inc.).

1975   Québec Charter of Human Rights and Freedoms adopted, prohibiting all forms of discrimination.

1977   Principle of 'parental authority' replaces 'paternal authority' in Civil Code of Quebec.

1978   Conseil du statut de la femme publishes comprehensive policy entitled 'Pour les Québécoises; égalité et indépendance'.

Quebec's Minimum Wage Act guarantees women right to take 18 weeks of maternity leave and prohibits firing women who take it.

First family-planning clinics with abortion services, called 'Lazure clinics', founded.

Regroupement des femmes québécoises founded.

Government of Quebec adopts maternity allowance program to cover two-week waiting period not covered by federal program.

CALACS network (Centres d'aide et de lutte contre les agressions à caractère sexuel) established to address issues around sexual assault.

Provincial Act respecting Child Day Care passed and the Office des services de garde created to implement and fund daycare services in homes, schools, and daycare centres.

1979   Regroupement provincial des maisons d'hébergement et de transition pour femmes victimes de violence conjugale founded to help women victims of domestic violence.

1980   Quebec's Bill 89 establishes equality between spouses in administration of assets and in children's education.

1982   Québec Charter of Human Rights and Freedoms amended to accommodate affirmative action programs. Charter requires future legislation to comply with principle of equality between sexes, prohibiting discrimination against pregnant women and sexual harassment.

1988 Supreme Court decriminalizes voluntary interruption of pregnancy, declaring section 251 of Criminal Code of Canada unconstitutional. Therapeutic abortion committees no longer legal in Canada.

1989 Quebec's Act respecting Economic Equality of the Spouses is proclaimed, providing for equal sharing of family patrimony between spouses after marriage is dissolved, whatever matrimonial regime a couple chooses.

In *Daigle v. Tremblay*, Supreme Court of Canada rules that a fetus is not a legal person and that third persons cannot prevent a woman from having an abortion.

On 6 December, 14 young women are gunned down at École Polytechnique de Montréal by a deranged man who accuses them of being feminists.

1990 A conference called 'Femmes en tête' celebrates 50th anniversary of Act Granting Women the Right to Vote in Quebec.

Unpaid parental leave of 34 weeks introduced in Quebec for parents of newborns or adopted children.

1992 Conference called 'Un Québec féminin pluriel' organized by FFQ to discuss and develop an inclusive feminist social project.

1995 FFQ organizes Bread and Roses march in Quebec.

Government of Quebec authorizes automatic collection of alimony payments.

1996 Quebec's Pay Equity Act adopted.

1997 New family policy measures include $5-a-day daycare program, network of early childhood centres, and parental insurance program to replace income during parental leaves.

Parental leave increased from 34 to 52 weeks.

1998 Midwifery legalized in Quebec.

1999 Juanita Westmoreland-Traoré becomes first Black woman judge appointed to Court of Quebec.

2000 First World March of Women against poverty and violence against women held.

2004 Quebec Court of Appeal rules that same-sex couples have right to marry in Quebec.

Like the children, women in Quebec seem never to have been just persons. They are pawns in the game, ornaments or slaves, means to pleasure, temptations to sin, instruments for the production of children, members of a labour force, but not quite people. Now that they are becoming recognized as people they are making a revolution in Quebec.

—MIRIAM CHAPIN[1]

This telling quote shows how for many years women in Quebec, particularly those of French Canadian origin, were perceived as creatures entirely subjugated by the Church and confined to their families. According to Miriam Chapin, it was not until the mid-1950s that women were recognized as persons and began effecting radical social change that would herald the Quiet Revolution of the 1960s. Today, women in Quebec, and particularly francophone women, have something of a reputation for their self-assurance, their independence from men, and the breadth of their egalitarian aspirations. According to many observers, Quebec women are more militant than their counterparts in other parts of North America, Europe, and particularly France. Indeed, Quebec's 'masculinist' movement, which agrees with this view, has virulently denounced the 'excesses' of feminism.[2] It is true that Quebec feminism appears very dynamic, compared to that of other Western societies. Clearly, women in Quebec enjoy more advanced and generous social legislation and family policies (e.g., daycare and parental leaves) than do other Canadian women, and that some rights (such as the right to abortion, for which feminists fought fiercely in the 1970s) are less violently challenged in Quebec than elsewhere in North America. So it is no wonder that the very women who used to be disparaged as the least emancipated of their kind in North America are now seen as the wave of the future.

But this straightforward black-and-white portrayal of Quebec women is ripe for a nuanced critique and even more, for a re-examination in light of its historical complexities. How should we measure the road travelled by Quebec women, especially French-Canadian women, during the twentieth century? What meandering turns did it take? How did their journey relate to the changes taking place in Quebec society? This chapter attempts to address these and other questions. While focusing on the place and role of women in the private and public spheres before and after the Second World War, we also pay particular attention to the 'national question' in Quebec, which strongly influenced gender relations and explains much about why the province's women came to win their freedom.

1900–1940: WOMEN UNDER THE YOKE OF CHURCH AND STATE?

Waged Labour

In the early twentieth century, Quebec was well on its way to becoming an industrialized society. In fact, from 1921 onward, most of the population would live in the cities, notably in Montreal, the province's

cosmopolitan hub, industrial heartland, and largest urban centre. At the turn of the century, attracted by urban job opportunities (particularly in domestic and unskilled factory work), single female city-dwellers between the ages of 15 and 30 outnumbered their male counterparts. Generally speaking, single young female workers of that era would leave the workforce as soon as they married, as the notion of a married woman holding down a salaried job was heartily condemned in Quebec. Estimates indicate that before the 1940s less than 5 per cent of married women held down jobs outside of the home. However, many housewives did odd jobs at home, a strategy that reconciled their domestic responsibilities with the need to supplement the family purse. As the railway system expanded, the 'sweating system' that flourished in the garment industry also recruited women in rural regions, where specialization and commercialization in agriculture had created more free time for farm women. As shown in Table 16.1, 1910 marked the beginning of an era in which a growing proportion of single young women also found work in offices, businesses, and in the professions available to them at the time: teaching and nursing.

TABLE 16.1   Distribution of the female workforce by professional sector and proportion of women in the workforce in Quebec as a whole, 1911–1941 (%)

Sectors of activity	1911	1921	1931	1941
Professions and administration	11.1	19.3	14.7	13.9
Business	4.1	4.9	5.3	5.4
Employees	58.1	51.8	61.7	60.2
Offices	4.2	10.6	10.5	10.5
Services	53.0	39.3	49.7	48.7
Transportation and communications	0.9	1.9	1.5	1.0
Workers	24.5	21.3	16.5	19.1
Others	2.2	2.7	1.8	1.4
% of women in the work force	16.9	18.4	21.0	24.4

Source: Bernier, G., and R. Boily, eds., *Le Québec en chiffres de 1850 à nos jours* (Montreal: ACFAS, Collection by GRÉTSÉ, 1986), 204.

Light industries and offices in early twentieth-century Quebec were quick to take advantage of women's cheap labour, but the presence of single young women in these contexts was perceived as a 'social problem' or a threat to women's moral integrity until the 1920s. In fact, although women were working under truly deplorable conditions, reformers, intellectuals, clerics, and even male labour organizers were more inclined to question the legitimacy of the female workforce than to denounce its low wages and shameless exploitation. After the First World War, waged labour for single young women became more widely accepted, but that of married women (while a very marginal phenomenon) continued to be met with staunch opposition, with some workers' organizations going so far as demanding their dismissal. Tolerated rather than truly accepted, women's waged labour was the subject of renewed attacks during the Depression of the 1930s, when thousands of men became unemployed. It was against this backdrop that Joseph-Napoléon Francoeur, a member of the provincial legislature, tabled a bill (which never became law) calling for 'women and young girls asking for work to prove that they really needed to do so'.[3]

Opposition to waged labour for women, particularly married women, resonated powerfully throughout the Western world. Everywhere, women's integration into the workforce was perceived as a threat both to men's privilege and to their patriarchal authority within the family. In Quebec, however, this opposition was magnified by fears about the survival of French Canadians as a people. At a time when thousands of francophone Quebecers had left for the United States and when the constitutional rights of francophones (especially those concerning education) were habitually violated in anglophone-majority provinces, traditional nationalists (including a large proportion of Catholic clergymen) believed that the continued existence of the French-Canadian nation was in jeopardy. As a minority in anglophone Canada's inhospitable political landscape, francophone Quebecers had great difficulty influencing any major decisions in Ottawa—decisions that would determine the future of the country. Even in Quebec, where francophones constituted the majority, they were economically dominated by the anglophone elite, which used its capital holdings to lord over the province's economic development. Traditional nationalists therefore held that industrialization was not only tangible proof of francophone subordination, but was also an Anglo-Saxon importation that was sapping the roots of French-Canadian society. They contended that industrial work and the urban way of life ran contrary to the fundamental values and the very identity of French Canadians, as represented in the triptych of Language, Faith, and Rural Vocation. So, as the countryside emptied to fill factories in the city, traditional nationalists looked on with great trepidation—especially when it came to women workers.

Motherhood First

Far from being a homogeneous or monolithic political block, Quebec nationalists of this era had various opinions about how French Canadians ought to assert their nationhood. Opinions sometimes differed over what measures might best safeguard the people's future, but they were unanimous on one point: French-Canadian mothers were the cornerstone of francophone survival in America and anything that might divert them from that mission had to be vigorously denounced. As the purveyors of language and tradition, it behooved women to ensure the reproduction of the 'race' (the French Canadian people), both biologically and culturally. Nationalists, and clerics in particular, were constantly reminding women of their overriding duty to be fruitful and multiply. Troubled equally by industrialization and the shrinking proportion of francophones in Canada, both the Catholic Church and the nationalists believed they could count on the proverbial high francophone fertility rate that had supposedly existed since the era of New France to maintain the proportion and standing of French Canadians within the Canadian political landscape and even gain back some ground—the better to propagate their high spiritual values.

Studies have shown that the so-called 'Revenge of the Cradle',[4] to borrow the title of the famous natalist speech given by Father Louis Lalande in 1918, never actually took place. For while Father Lalande and other nationalists were extolling the virtues of large families, these were already a minority, as only 20 per cent of married women born in 1887 gave birth to more than 10 children. In reality, fertility rates for Quebec women had been constantly decreasing since the latter third of the nineteenth century, and dropped off even more sharply during the 1920s, as shown in Table 16.2.

But compared to the rest of Canada, to Ontario, or to anglophone Quebec, French-Canadian families in Quebec were in fact bigger. Quebec francophone women born in 1903 had an average of 5.1 children, versus 4.4 children for Quebec women as a whole and 3.4 for Canadian women. Despite the Catholic Church's firm condemnation of contraception, the data show that its use was nonetheless becoming more widespread, especially in the cities, where difficult economic conditions were leading more couples to restrict the size of their families. The same trend continued during the Depression, as revealed in numerous testimonies from women who tried (though not always successfully) to limit their number of pregnancies.

While the ideal of the large family was far from being realized, it nonetheless epitomized the traditional nationalist concept of the place and role of women in society: maternity—'holy and fruitful maternity',[5] to quote Henri Bourassa (who founded the nationalist daily, *Le Devoir*)—represented the primary if not the sole legitimate function women could perform. Wanting to escape procreation, or simply wanting to pursue other interests, defied the grand design of Providence, which had crafted 'Woman's nature' for this purpose. This discourse on the maternal vocation of women was certainly not exclusive to Quebec nationalists: it was widespread in the Western world and was even endorsed by feminists to back their political demands. But in Quebec, where the national question had become an obsession, confining women to the domestic sphere where they would devote themselves exclusively to motherhood was undoubtedly expressed much more fervently; the repercussions were seen in the small proportion of married women in the workforce and a relatively slow decline in the fertility rate.

Nuns and Feminists

The predominance of the Catholic Church is often cited to explain Quebec's comparatively high fertility rate. But was the Church alone also responsible for Quebec women's remarkable number of religious vocations? The number of religious communities swelled from 15 in 1850 to 80 in 1941, and the exceptionally high proportion of nuns among single women over the age of 20, 9 per cent in 1921, set a record for its time in the Western world. Clearly, entering the cloister was a path that many young women in Quebec chose during this period. Often from large families, where Catholic precepts about reproduction were strictly obeyed and where religious practices were intense, these women (many of them very young) undoubtedly entered this life to answer God's calling. At the same time, for many, the religious life was also likely a vehicle for upward social and intellectual mobility, or a way to escape poverty and the physical travails of maternity. Quebec nuns could work in a variety of administrative capacities within their communities and were among the first women to gain access to higher education (often studying in American Catholic universities) and to professions that were difficult for laywomen to practise.

TABLE 16.2 General and total fertility rates* for Quebec and Ontario, 1901–1941

Year	General fertility rate,[†] Quebec	General fertility rate,[†] Ontario	Total fertility rate,[‡] Quebec	Total fertility rate,[‡] Ontario
1901	160	108	N/A	N/A
1911	161	112	5.4	3.6
1921	155	98	5.3	3.2
1931	116	79	4.0	2.6
1941	102	73	3.4	2.4

* Fertility rates measure live births to women aged 15 to 49.
[†] Fertility rate per 1000 women in a given year.
[‡] Average number of children that may be born to a woman over her lifetime (based on the fertility rates from that year).

Sources: Henripin, J. *Tendances et facteurs de la fécondité au Canada* (Quebec: IQRC, 1989), 21; Henripin, J. *Naître ou ne pas naître* (Quebec: IQRC, 1989), 35.

The role played by nuns in Quebec was considerable. Under the cover of their habits, they commanded a legitimacy that was denied to laywomen. Nuns founded and directed countless convent schools for girls, established and ran most of Quebec's major hospitals and, by the mid-nineteenth century, were attempting to minister to the needs of poor urban populations by significantly multiplying their works of assistance. It may be said without exaggeration that women's religious communities established (sometimes with little or no government funding) the first health-care, social assistance, and education network for girls in Quebec,[6] a network that they ran until the mid-1960s.

The impressive magnitude of the nuns' activities was a direct consequence of the Quebec government's reluctance to intervene in education and social welfare, areas regarded by the Catholic Church as its exclusive preserve. In the Church's view, dispensing charity within a religious framework was the best way to help the destitute while preserving the Christian family and social order—the foundations of the French Canadian nation. It was just as crucial to the Church to keep the upper hand in education, a highly sensitive social nerve centre in which young minds could be shaped according to Catholic ideals. Since any state incursion into these areas was deemed by the Church to be an attack on the Catholic character of francophones, it resolutely opposed mandatory school attendance until it was finally introduced in 1943. This said, Quebec state liberalism was very much at home with the Church's ambitions to expand the domain of its ministry and, although the government continued to increase funding to health and social assistance institutions run by the Church until the 1960s, the state took great care not to dispense any services directly to the public.

Nuns were both the spearhead and linchpin of the Church's front-line operations; the institutions founded by the nuns allowed the Church to reach Quebec's entire Catholic population and provide free health care, relief, succour, and education in environments that honoured its doctrine. The position of nuns in relation to the ecclesiastic authorities was therefore somewhat ambiguous. On one hand, these communities of women enjoyed considerable autonomy in directing their congregations and institutions, and many nuns occupied positions and assumed functions and responsibilities that would have been inaccessible to them as laywomen. On the other hand, their range of power was limited by that of the prevailing male clerical authorities, which they had to obey. Their social and educational activities were performed under the banner of 'spiritual maternity' and at least partly served to strengthen the Church's control over souls. So donning the habit may have opened many doors to these women, but whether it paved the way to their emancipation is less certain, given that these opportunities were available to them only if they abided by the decrees of the bishopric and assumed an eminently feminine and maternal identity.

The vibrancy of religious communities also had negative repercussions on the lives of francophone laywomen. Nuns, owing to their quasi-monopoly over social and educational services for girls, reserved administrative positions for each other within their institutions, thereby blocking the way for their 'worldly' lay sisters. For a time, nuns also represented a large proportion of nurses and teachers in Quebec, thereby further restricting laywomen's access to these female professions as well. Moreover, by working for free, in the name of their apostolic mission, nuns reinforced the idea that nursing and education were women's 'vocations', for which wages could be justifiably very low. Consequently, francophone women in these professions earned comparably less than did anglophone women. By multiplying their charitable social work, women's religious communities similarly limited the spheres in which middle- and upper-class women could practise philanthropy, a form of social engagement which, among Quebec anglophones, as elsewhere in the Western world, was a hotbed for feminism. The founding of Hôpital Sainte-Justine in 1907 by a group of upper-class French-Canadian women and of Assistance maternelle in 1912, a French-Canadian charity that provided succour to poor mothers in Montreal, were therefore exceptional feats.

Historian Micheline Dumont contends that, during the first decades of the twentieth century, entering a religious order was the only way in which French-Canadian women could challenge traditional roles without confronting Quebec's patriarchal society. But feminist historians have also recognized that the prevalence of the nuns probably delayed the formation of francophone feminist organizations. As early as 1893, anglophone women from Montreal had founded the Montreal Local Council of Women (MLCW), a local branch of the National Council of Women of Canada (NCWC), which was established the same year. The MLCW brought together anglophone women's organizations and individuals of all religious affiliations and attracted some francophone members, who were active for some time and even held administrative positions. But the ethnic tensions that were exacerbated around the beginning of the twentieth century and the hostility of the Catholic clergy (which disapproved of Catholic women's membership in groups dominated by Protestants) contributed in equal parts to the departure of francophone women from the MLCW. In 1907, these women went on to found their own organization, the Fédération nationale St-Jean-Baptiste (FNSJB).

The ethnic and religious schisms in Montreal's feminist forces did not prevent the two (francophone and anglophone) majority groups from working together on a number of social issues. In 1922, the Provincial Franchise Committee (directed by Marie Lacoste Gérin-Lajoie, president of the FNSJB) united francophone and anglophone women to campaign for the right to vote at the provincial level, a right that had been granted to women at the federal level in 1918. In this case, however, these feminists' requests were rejected by male politicians, secure in the conviction that they were acting with the Church's sanction. The Catholic clergy and the nationalists, who already regarded the FNSJB with great suspicion, opposed women's suffrage with all their might and even alleged that it violated Catholic doctrine. These men believed that giving women the vote would divert them from their primary mission in life—the reproduction of the 'race'—and would give them a power that could undermine patriarchal relationships within the family. It was not until 1940 (despite vehement opposition from the clergy) that the newly elected Liberal Party of Quebec, prompted by lobbying from Thérèse Casgrain, made good on a campaign promise to grant women citizens the vote.[7]

THÉRÈSE FORGET CASGRAIN (1896–1981)

Mme Marie Thérèse (Forget) Casgrain

Library and Archives Canada/PA-126768

Thérèse Forget Casgrain was the daughter of Lady Blanche MacDonald and Sir Rodolphe Forget, a Montreal lawyer, wealthy financier, and a Conservative Member of the House of Commons from 1904 to 1917. She was also the mother of four children and the wife of Pierre Casgrain, a Liberal Member of Parliament in Ottawa (1917–1941) before he was appointed to the Superior Court of Quebec. But, more importantly, she was one of the most tireless activists of her day.

As a member of Montreal's elite bourgeoisie who had been immersed in the world of politics since childhood, Thérèse Casgrain undoubtedly possessed the credentials required for a lengthy career as an activist, a role she fulfilled in every sense of the word. In the early 1920s, she took up the struggle for women's suffrage, working with the Provincial Franchise Committee. She was part of the first delegation of feminists to travel to Quebec City to attempt to convince Premier Alexandre Taschereau to grant women the right to vote. In 1929, following her presidency with the Provincial Franchise Committee, she founded the League for Women's Rights, which continued to lobby the provincial government, shoulder-to-shoulder with Alliance canadienne pour le vote des femmes (founded by Idola Saint-Jean) until 1940, when the franchise was won. Representing another cause championed by the League, Thérèse Casgrain appeared before the Dorion

Commission in 1929, demanding that the Civil Code of Quebec be changed to remedy the unequal legal status of married women. In 1926, she founded the Young Women's League, a non-denominational organization that encouraged engagement in social causes among young women. Throughout the 1930s, while continuing to lobby for the vote, Thérèse Casgrain hosted *Fémina*, a radio program for women. In 1937, she publicly sided with striking Montreal garment workers and later went on to publicize the plight of rural schoolmistresses, whose working conditions were particularly appalling.

Thérèse Casgrain played a pivotal role in the battle for women's suffrage. Through her position as vice-president of the National Federation of Liberal Women of Canada and supported by some 40 delegates, she succeeded in having women's suffrage incorporated into the Liberal party platform at its 1938 provincial convention. Once elected in 1939, the new provincial Liberal government, led by Adélard Godbout, made good on its platform promises, despite the Catholic Church's protestations. Thérèse Casgrain waged a war on two fronts when the lobby to have family allowance cheques issued to mothers was launched. She led a campaign on the issue in Quebec, while bringing a rain of protest to bear in Ottawa on Canadian Liberal Prime Minister William Lyon Mackenzie King, who ultimately reversed his decision and issued the family allowance benefits to mothers instead of fathers in Quebec.

During the Second World War, Thérèse Casgrain helped to launch the Wartime Prices and Trade Board, an organization that aimed to stem inflation through price and wage controls, and went on to establish the Board's Consumer Branch, which organized rationing across Canada. Driven by the conviction that women should exercise not only their right to vote but also their eligibility to hold public office, she ran in a 1942 by-election as an independent Liberal candidate for Charlevoix–Saguenay, a riding which both her father and husband had represented. Although defeated, she remained undaunted; during the 1940s and 1950s Thérèse Casgrain stood as a candidate in nine elections, both federal and provincial, without

ever being elected. As of 1946, she ran as a candidate under the banner of the Cooperative Commonwealth Federation (CCF), a social democratic party founded in the 1930s, which she felt was more deeply committed to pursuing the common good than were the conventional parties. In 1948, she became a CCF vice-president and, in 1951 she became the Leader of the party's Quebec wing, making her the first Canadian woman to hold such a position.

In the early 1960s, Thérèse Casgrain helped found the Civil Liberties Union, over which she presided for a number of years. As the founder of the Quebec chapter of the Voice of Women (1961), a women's organization that works for world peace, she took part in many international conferences. Her peace activism even led to her arrest and detention for several hours during a demonstration against nuclear arms, held in front of the NATO offices in Paris in 1964. The following year, to celebrate the twenty-fifth anniversary of women's suffrage legislation in Quebec, she initiated the organization of a two-day conference, entitled 'La femme du Québec : hier et aujourd'hui'. The conference was the catalyst for the foundation of the Fédération des femmes du Québec, an umbrella organization that comprised some 30 groups from the francophone and anglophone communities at its inception. In 1970, Thérèse Casgrain was appointed to the Canadian Senate by the Liberal government of Pierre Elliott Trudeau, nine months before her seventy-fifth birthday—the mandatory age of retirement for a senator. To a journalist who questioned her ability to achieve very much in the Senate in the little time she would serve, she apparently replied, 'Young man, you might be surprised to learn what a woman can do in nine months!'[8]

Thérèse Casgrain's spirited candour was an integral part of her personality: 'I was always picking fights with everyone. I suppose that's what kept me in form', she wrote in her autobiography. Indeed, even after retiring from the Senate, she continued to advocate for the rights of consumers (a cause she had supported as President of the Quebec branch of the Consumers' Association of Canada in 1969) and she lobbied for the abolition of mandatory retirement. In 1970, she publicly endorsed the application of the War Measures Act during the October Crisis, and in 1980 backed the 'No' camp in the referendum on sovereignty, stances which some Quebecers had difficulty forgiving.

Throughout the twentieth century, Thérèse Casgrain took on many a battle, not only for women, but also for the underprivileged, for human rights, and for world peace. Defining herself as a humanist, she actively fought against all forms of injustice, receiving scores of honours for her work. The contribution she made to the advancement of women and social causes likely makes her one of the most famous and highly respected feminists of her time. 'A woman in a man's world', she was committed and tenacious to the very end.

Among its other initiatives, the FNSJB, allied with other francophone and anglophone organizations, succeeded in lobbying the government for a commission of inquiry, the Dorion Commission, to examine the legal status of married women at the turn of the 1930s. The commissioners, a constellation of prominent legal experts and ardent nationalists, rejected most of their requests to change legislation, arguing that the Civil Code of Quebec, inherited from France, was one of the cornerstones on which the nation had been built and that most of its provisions (especially those entrenching the legal incapacity of married women and the marital powers of fathers) were emanations of Divine Law. Therefore, the provincial government only amended legislation to recognize married women's ownership of their wages, essentially preserving the spirit and the letter of the Civil Code, and with it, the nationalist notion of French Canadian women's place and duties to nation and family.

FROM 1940 TO 2000: A 'QUIET REVOLUTION' FOR QUEBEC WOMEN

Mothers and Workers

Although 1960–70 is the decade generally associated with deep structural transformations and the state takeover of strategic sectors (like education and health) in Quebec, many socio-cultural changes occurred as early as the Second World War. The labour shortfall during the war ushered in an era radically different from the Depression, as married women were called upon to join the workforce to support the war effort. This federal appeal to women angered traditional nationalists, who were convinced it would jeopardize the very existence of the family and believed society's morals were being eroded by married women who were deserting hearth and home. In truth, Quebec nationalists and the federal authorities were equally committed to the traditional provider–homemaker family model. The federal government saw the presence of married women in factories as a strictly temporary measure and expected that gender roles would return to 'normal' once the war was over. Indeed, many women did lose their jobs when munitions factories closed after the war, but their return to the home front proved to be just as temporary. By the late 1940s, more and more mothers were returning to work after they had raised their families. As the trend continued in the following decades, the percentage of employed married women soared from 17 per cent in 1951, to nearly 49 per cent in 1971, and shot up again to 62 per cent in 1981.[9] By the 1970s, even mothers of young children were working outside of the home—as 80 per cent of them do in Quebec today.

Also during the Second World War, the federal family allowance program began. Introduced in 1945, the program was designed to boost postwar consumer spending and coax married women back to full-time homemaking. But when family allowance cheques were issued to mothers rather than to the male 'head' of the household, Quebec nationalists protested; they viewed the program as a sacrilegious attack on the principle of paternal power, as established in the Civil Code of Quebec. Swayed by political pressure from the nationalists, the federal government agreed to make an exception for Quebec and pay benefits to fathers. But this time, the nationalists would not carry the day. Thérèse Casgrain led a coalition of women's groups and unions that successfully argued that an article of the Civil Code gave married women a tacit mandate to manage the everyday affairs of the family, and that paying family allowance benefits to mothers was consistent with this mandate.

Fewer Children, Fewer Parishioners

As in the rest of North America, postwar Quebec experienced a baby boom, but did not see higher fertility rates; more couples got married at this time, and thus more had children during this period, with the average number of children per family remaining at approximately four between 1946 and 1960. From the beginning of the 1960s, fertility rates continued to drop sharply and, by 1966, Quebec women had the lowest fertility rates in Canada, a statistical distinction they have maintained ever since.[10] Until the contraceptive pill was introduced, most Catholic couples in Quebec relied on the Knaus-Ogino Rhythm Method, widely taught in marriage preparation courses organized by the Jeunesse ouvrière catholique féminine (JOCF), or on the Sympto-Thermal Method, taught by the Service de régulation des naissances (Seréna), an organization founded in 1955 by a couple seeking to reconcile Church precepts with a humanist perspective on reproduction. Since these two groups were offshoots of the Catholic Church, the Church was indirectly contributing to lowering fertility rates, although it also expressed many reservations about the wide dissemination of these methods. The pill was strictly prohibited by the papal encyclical *Humanae vitae* in 1968, but this prohibition went unheeded and, by the end of the 1960s, the pill had become Quebec's most popular means of contraception.

Significantly destabilized by the shock of postwar socio-cultural changes (and particularly by the rise of consumerism), the Church's authoritarianism met with more and more overt challenges. Its ascetic, moralistic position on reproduction accelerated the spiritual defections that had been taking place since the 1950s. The downturn in religious fervour was evident in waning attendance at Sunday mass and in women's declining interest in joining religious communities. In fact, although the absolute numbers of nuns continued to increase until the mid-1960s, from the 1940s onward their growth rate declined relative to that of laywomen. In the latter half of the 1960s, membership in women's religious communities dropped by 14 per cent, owing to numerous departures.

Workers and Feminists

While the decline in the numbers of nuns and parishioners was another manifestation of the Church's unpopularity, it also reflected the new opportunities available to women in civil society at a time when big capital and the state were clamouring more loudly than ever for an abundant female workforce. After the Second World War, Quebec's economic development required more women to fill positions in the service sector and doing office work. The creation of a host of social programs caused both the provincial and especially the federal public service sectors to grow at an unprecedented rate, attracting an ever-increasing proportion of women workers. Moreover, during the 1960s, the government of Quebec became much more interventionist, amplifying trends from previous decades and effectively eliminating some vocations. From state intervention in the economy and culture to state-run health care, social welfare, and education, the 'social project' of the Quiet Revolution (fuelled by a new nationalism that had been gestating for a decade or more) took over several sectors that previously had been the purview of the Church. Under the welfare state, French Canadians began to redefine themselves as a secular Québécois nation. Looking back, Quebecers began to regard the charity-driven religious management of the Church's institutions as the amateur bunglings of a bygone era in which the state had recused itself of its putative social responsibilities. Government intervention, by contrast, seemed to bear the hallmark of competency and expanded social justice. The Quebec government changed the rules of the game accordingly, placing health care and schools under the authority of male administrators, while laywomen gradually replaced religious staff, whose numbers were dwindling dramatically.

The increased presence of laywomen in service-related jobs, facilitated by greater access to schools and universities for girls and single young women, fostered a feminist consciousness that would come into its own in the latter half of the 1960s. During the 1960s, as the secular nationalism of the Quiet Revolution emerged, a new kind of women's movement also clearly entered the public arena. After they had won the vote in 1940, women's social and political activism certainly did not disappear, as evidenced by the dynamic family movements they led, the consumer advocacy and anti-nuclear groups they founded, and the unions that a few women labour organizers fought to establish. Nearing the end of the 1950s (as Miriam Chapin observed) Quebec women had set the scene for yet another radical departure. In the 1960s, many new feminist organizations were created with the primary goal of denouncing sexist oppression and discrimination and promoting women's independence in all aspects of social, economic, and political life. As feminists struggled for greater sexual freedom during this period, the decriminalization of abortion became their predominant demand.

The fight for abortion rights figured prominently in Quebec throughout the 1970s, but was not championed by all feminists and their organizations, as opinions were divided. Two organizations that represented the reformist fringe of the new feminist movement (both founded in 1966) did not take up the cause immediately: the Fédération des femmes du Québec (FFQ) and the Association féminine d'éducation et d'action sociale (AFÉAS). The FFQ was an umbrella organization that brought together anglophones and francophones, and its activities typically focused on lobbying for legislation to guarantee equality between men and women in all areas. The AFÉAS, whose membership mainly consisted of rural women, concentrated its efforts on social and political activism and training for women. Neither group questioned liberal capitalist society nor believed that patriarchy perpetuated sexist discrimination and subordination. At the opposite end of the political spectrum, the Montreal Women's Liberation Movement (1968), the Front de libération des femmes du Québec (FLF—1969), Centre des femmes (1972), and a myriad of smaller feminist groups that emerged in the early 1970s believed that patriarchy was the root cause of women's oppression, and that women's liberation hinged on the eradication of men's control over women's bodies—meaning their maternity and their sexuality.[11] These groups and their members would go on to lead the struggle for decriminalized, free, and accessible abortion in the years to come.

Feminists set their sights on a wide range of other major issues during the 1970s, including ending physical and sexual violence against women and systemic discrimination against women in the workplace, establishing daycare and parental leave, the recognition of women's work within the family, and the equality of spouses in marriage.[12] Some feminist analyses partly attributed the advances made in these areas to the institutionalization of feminism that occurred with the birth of the Conseil du statut de la femme du Québec (CSF), created by the government of Quebec in 1973 as an advisory body on the status of women. With this institutionalization came the fear that feminism would be politically co-opted. At the same time, as grassroots feminist organizers were obtaining government funding to establish a growing multitude of women's groups and shelters, a number of feminists said that these social responsibilities, which should have been shouldered by all of society, had been unloaded onto the backs of 'feminist cheap labour'.[13] This kind of statement clearly shows the complexity of the dialogue between feminists and the state. Later, feminists would see that more women delegates in political parties, women members of the legislature, or even women ministers did not always facilitate this dialogue, as those who declared themselves feminists were frequently torn between personal convictions and party allegiances.[14]

The relationships that have developed between feminism and nationalism over the past decades in Quebec have proved to be just as complex. Broadly speaking, many francophone feminist activists have been drawn to the promise of the nationalist movement, seeing in its promotion of a more assertive, modern Quebec a reflection of their own hoped-for emancipation. The new Quebec nationalist movement certainly had everything to gain by winning over feminists (a growing social force) and in fact showed a degree of openness towards them.[15] But at times, the notion of a woman's place and role espoused by the nationalist social project was at odds with the feminist vision and caused considerable tensions between the two groups. Very frequently in the 1980s and 1990s, spokespeople for the Parti Québécois (the province's main sovereignist party) and nationalist conservatives alike voiced their concern that Quebec francophones were a shrinking minority within Canada and North America, denouncing the low fertility rates in Quebec, and proposing natalist policies, some of which even aimed to get women back into the home. During the 1995 referendum campaign, Quebec Premier Lucien Bouchard himself publicly expressed his dismay that 'White women' in Quebec were not producing enough children.

While contemporary nationalists can no longer use the moral authority of the Catholic Church to force women to have larger families, they nonetheless continue to be deeply concerned about the issue of reproducing the 'race'. While nationalist feminists have railed against the nationalist-natalist discourse, some of their own nationalist positions have created new rifts within feminist ranks and been roundly condemned by minority women's organizations.[16] Since the 1980s, the ethno-cultural reconfiguration of the population and the dismantling of the welfare state have presented major challenges for Quebec feminists. How can the movement sustain itself in the absence of an interventionist government? How will it bring all Quebec women together? Nationalists are asking themselves similar questions. Recently, spokespersons from both nationalist and feminist movements declared that equality between men and women was one of the most 'fundamental values' in Quebec. Will this unifying idea bring the two movements closer together? The answer may lie in the context that elicited their declarations—a highly publicized provincial Consultation Commission, known as the Bouchard-Taylor Commission.

The Consultation Commission, created to clarify Quebecers' views on the government's cultural policies, fostered fervent debate. During and after the commission's hearings, both nationalist and feminist discourses conveyed deep-seated apprehensions about the potential for religious fanaticism and sexist oppression among new Quebecers. After years of struggle against Church and patriarchy, devout religion and gender-specific traditions are seen by many in Quebec as inherently oppressive anachronisms that continue to haunt their collective memory. Therefore, taken in context, when feminists and nationalists agree on Quebec's 'fundamental values' it does not so much indicate a newfound unity but more likely a shared malaise about the new cultural and social landscape both must face in the future. Today, as before, feminists and nationalists will have to grapple with issues that are as likely to unite them as they are to tear them apart.

SNAPSHOT

The Yvette Affair

The Yvette affair provoked a flood of commentary from the moment it began, during the campaign for the 1980 Quebec referendum on sovereignty. Portrayed by the media either as a backlash against feminists or as a federalist strategy to secure the victory of the 'No' camp, it was one of the most remarkable events of the campaign—a genuine turning point, according to many observers. The quantity of ink that flowed in the press over the Yvette affair at the time, and the number of occasions on which it has been revisited for some 30 years now, clearly show that issues about the status of women are eminently political. The Yvette affair also shows how women's issues can be exploited for a wide variety of partisan purposes.

On 6 March 1980, Lise Payette, then Minister responsible for the Status of Women in the Parti Québécois government of René Lévesque, called a press conference to report on the progress of women's issues under her government. During the press conference, the Minister read an excerpt from a story in an elementary schoolbook. The story depicted a sweet, docile, and dutiful little girl named Yvette, who was always keen to help her mother. Yvette's brother, Guy, on the other hand, was an ambitious, daring young boy, who played a variety of sports. The Minister concluded by announcing: 'I am here to tell you that the days of Yvette are over!' By this, she meant that the days of being docile and submissive were over for Quebec women, who were on the road to equality. A few days later, at a rally for the 'Yes' camp (in favour of Quebec sovereignty), she asserted that women and anglophones were the two groups most resistant to Quebec sovereignty. To drive home her point—that women's fears about Quebec's future were based in their conditioning as subordinates—she reread the passage about Yvette and her brother, and then said, 'Let us have the courage to leave our prisons of fear behind.' For Payette, the feminist and nationalist causes had become one, and women had to emancipate themselves both as women and as Quebecers. Later, responding to a question from the audience, she quipped that Claude Ryan, the leader of the Liberal Party, and head of the 'No' camp, was very fond of 'Yvettes', since they were opposed to sovereignty, adding that Ryan was married to an 'Yvette'.

Payette had just committed a monumental political gaffe, particularly since Madeleine Ryan, who was indeed a housewife, was also deeply committed to a number of social causes. Naturally, the newspapers had a field day with the gaffe: in Le Devoir, Editor Lise Bissonnette berated Payette, contending that the Minister's words were an attack on all housewives.

But the Yvette affair did not end there. Toward the end of March, at a brunch in Quebec City for the female members of the Liberal Party, participants wore buttons marked 'Yvette', clearly embracing the moniker that Lise Payette had considered to be an insult. Some journalists noted that Payette's blunder had revitalized the federalist 'No' camp, which had been somewhat apathetic and lacklustre up until that point, and had given it ammunition which it very ably exploited.

Journalists continued to run stories about the federalists using the Yvette affair as a campaign strategy to win over a segment of voters (especially women). At the beginning of April, the affair took another turn, as over 14,000 women attended a rally held at the Montreal Forum. In the media, particularly in Le Devoir, the rally was depicted not as a political event orchestrated by the 'No' camp against sovereignty, but rather as an impromptu gathering of 'everyday' women, housewives, who felt targeted by Minister Payette's words and were showing how fed up they had become with feminists. Above all, contended Lise Bissonnette, the event's social significance lay in the fact that 'thousands of women . . . did not identify with the discourse of "liberation", and even felt slighted and ridiculed by the [feminist] movement, which was telling them their everyday lives were a dreary monotony from which they had to either escape at all costs—or amount to nothing'.[17] Bissonnette believed that these women had flocked to the Forum not to hear 'No' camp speeches, but rather to express their discontent with feminists. She went on to rebuke the Liberal Party and the 'No' camp for exploiting the anti-feminist backlash and manipulating women by inviting one and all to attend a mass event at the Forum that night.

The fact that, like Bissonnette, many journalists emphasized the anti-feminist angle of this story is most certainly symptomatic of the exasperation and anxiety that 10 years of feminist demands had elicited in some segments of Quebec—and among some members of the media. In the Yvette affair, the 'national question' was once again inextricably linked to women's issues, creating activist amalgams—feminist sovereignists; anti-feminist federalists—which surely ran contrary to the convictions of some female Liberal leaders, who were every bit as feminist as Minister Lise Payette, but which served the 'No' camp very well. Indeed, Payette's gaffe has often been cited as a major reason that the bid for Quebec sovereignty was lost in the 20 May 1980 referendum. With the help of massive media coverage, her few words put wind in the sails of the Liberal 'No' camp and turned the tide against a very strong 'Yes' camp that had seemed bound to sail on to victory.

Questions for Consideration

1. Why were there many nuns in Quebec during the first half of the twentieth century, and what was their impact on laywomen's involvement in social causes and feminism?

2. How did the 'national question' in Quebec influence the paths feminists took in the twentieth century?

3. How is the road travelled by French-Canadian women similar to and different from that travelled by other North American women?

Notes

1. Miriam Chapin, *Quebec Now* (Toronto: Ryerson Press, 1955), 96.

2. Mélissa Blais and Francis Dupuis-Déri, eds, *Le mouvement masculiniste au Québec* (Montreal: Les Éditions du remue-ménage, 2008).

3. Marie Lavigne and Jennifer Stoddart, 'Ouvrières et travailleuses montréalaises,1900–1940', in Marie Lavigne and Yolande Pinard, eds, *Les femmes dans la société québécoise* (Montreal: Boréal Express, 1977), 111.

4. In Quebec, the expression 'Revenge of the Cradle' conveyed the conviction that only a high fertility rate had allowed French Canadians to survive as a people, despite the British Conquest and the massive arrival of immigrants from England that began in the nineteenth century.

5. In Henri Bourassa's words, 'la sainte et féconde maternité' in his editorial 'Le suffrage féminin', *Le Devoir*, 30 March 1918, 1.

6. Boys were taken care of separately by male religious communities.

7. Given that at this point in history, federal law did not extend Canadian citizenship to persons of Asian descent and that Aboriginal people were treated as perpetual minors under the Indian Act, women and men in these groups as well as incarcerated individuals had to wait longer to obtain this right.

8. Quoted in the 'Biographie' page of the Fondation Thérèse F. Casgrain website, www.fondationtheresecasgrain.org/bio.html, our translation.

9. Francine Barry, *Le travail de la femme au Québec : L'évolution de 1940 à 1970* (Montreal: PUQ, 1977), 20; The Clio Collective, *Quebec Women: A History* (Toronto: Canadian Scholars Press, 1990), 482.

10. Since the early 1980s, the synthetic fertility index has remained between 1.4 and 1.6. Michel Venne, ed., *L'annuaire du Québec 2004* (Montreal: Fides, 2003), 148.

11. Louise Toupin, 'Les courants de pensée féministe', *Version revue du texte Qu'est-ce que le féminisme? Trousse d'information sur le féminisme québécois des 25 dernières années*, 1997, accessed 21 October 2008 at http://net-femmes.cdeacf.ca/documents/courants0.html.

12. Bill 16, passed in 1964 on the initiative of Marie-Claire Kirkland-Casgrain (the first woman MLA), had already abolished the legal incapacity of married women, but fell short of ensuring full equality between spouses within the family.

13. See Chapter 20.

14. Marie-Claire Kirkland-Casgrain was elected in 1961 in a by-election, becoming the first female member of the provincial legislature. In the general election of 1976, five women were elected. By 1985, this figure had climbed to 15 and by 2003 it stood at 38—the highest number of women members of the legislature ever elected in Quebec. In the general election of December 2008, 37 women won seats, occupying 30 per cent of the legislature. Marie-Claire Kirkland-Casgrain was also the first woman to head a provincial ministry. It was not until 1981 that two women occupied positions as ministers. Current figures are the highest ever, with 13 women occupying positions, in a cabinet comprising 27 members (almost half of all members). See the National Assembly of Quebec's website: www.assnat.qc.ca, accessed on 2 February 2009. Another noteworthy fact: Since June 2007, a woman, Pauline Marois, has been the Leader of the Parti Québécois.

15. In the 1960s, radical nationalists could be sexist and even misogynist. Women were perceived by many of the men in these movements as obstacles to the Quebec liberation movement. Moreover, their speeches and writing often referred to 'conquering' and 'taking' Quebec as a man would a woman—and this included raping her. S. Lanthier, *L'impossible réciprocité des rapports politiques et idéologiques entre le nationalisme radical et le féminisme radical au Québec: 1962–1972*, MA thesis (History), Université de Sherbrooke, 1998.

16. Women from a variety of minority communities have struggled to have a voice in Quebec's mainstream feminist movements. Although it is beyond the scope of this article to retrace the history and name all of the groups that have made major contributions to the advancement of feminism in Quebec, we would like to mention the

Quebec Native Women's Association (founded in 1974), the Montreal Regional Committee of the National Congress of Black Women of Canada (1974), the South Asian Women's Centre (1981), Collectif des femmes immigrantes du Québec (1983), Association de défense

des droits du personnel domestique de Montréal (1976), and its daughter organization, the Centre des femmes d'ici et d'ailleurs (1984).

17. Lise Bisonnette, 'L'appel aux femmes' in *Le Devoir*, 9 April 1980, 8, our translation.

RELEVANT WEBSITES

FÉDÉRATION DES FEMMES DU QUÉBEC:
www.ffq.qc.ca/

CONSEIL DU STATUT DE LA FEMME: www.csf.gouv.
qc.ca/fr/accueil/

LA GAZETTE DES FEMMES:
www.gazettedesfemmes.com/accueil/

NET FEMMES: http://netfemmes.cdeacf.ca/

CHRONOLOGIE HISTORIQUE DES FEMME DU QUÉBEC:
http://pages.infinit.net/histoire/femindex.html

SELECT BIBLIOGRAPHY

Auger, Geneviève, and Raymonde Lamothe. *De la poêle à frire à la ligne de feu. La vie quotidienne des québécoises pendant la guerre 39-45*. Montreal: Boréal Express, 1981.

Baillargeon, Denyse. *Babies for the Nation: The Medicalization of Maternity in Quebec, 1910-1970*. Waterloo: Wilfrid Laurier University Press, 2009.

———. *Making Do. Women, Family and Home in Montreal during the Great Depression*, Waterloo: Wilfrid Laurier University Press, 1999.

Barry, Francine. *Le travail de la femme au Québec. L'évolution de 1940 à 1970*. Montreal: PUQ, 1977.

Boyer, Kate. 'Re-Working Respectability. The Feminization of Clerical Work and the Politics of Public Virtue in Early Twentieth-Century Montreal'. In T. Myers et al., eds. *Power, Place and Identity. Historical Studies of Social and Legal Regulation in Quebec*. Montreal: GHM/MHG, 1998, 151–68.

Charles, Aline. *Travail d'ombre et de lumière. Le bénévolat féminin à l'hôpital Sainte-Justine 1907-1960*. Edmond-de-Nevers Collection no 9. Quebec City: IQRC, 1990.

Clio Collective. *Quebec Women: A History*. Toronto: Canadian Scholars Press, 1990.

Dandurand, Renée. *Le mariage en question. Essai socio-historique*. Quebec City: IQRC, 1988

Danylewycz, Marta. *Taking the Veil: An Alternative to Marriage, Motherhood, and Spinsterhood in Quebec, 1840–1920*. Toronto: McClelland & Stewart, 1987.

Dufour, Andrée, and Micheline Dumont. *Brève histoire des institutrices au Québec de la Nouvelle-France à nos jours*. Montreal: Boréal, 2004.

Dumont, Micheline. *Le féminisme québécois raconté à Camille*. Montreal: Les Éditions du remue-ménage, 2008.

———. *Les religieuses sont-elles féministes?* St-Laurent: Bellarmin, 1995.

———. 'The Origins of the Women's Movement in Quebec'. In Backhouse, Constance and David H. Flaherty, eds. *Challenging Times: The Women's Movement in Canada and the United States*. Montreal and Kingston: McGill-Queens University Press, 1992, 72–89.

———, and Nadia Fahmy-Eid. *Les couventines. L'éducation des filles au Québec dans les congrégations religieuses enseignantes, 1840–1960*. Montreal: Boréal, 1986.

———, and Louise Toupin. *La pensée féministe au Québec*. Montreal: Les Éditions du remue-ménage, 2003.

Fahmy-Eid, Nadia, and Micheline Dumont, eds. *Maîtresses de maison, maîtresses d'école. Femmes, famille et éducation dans l'histoire du Québec*. Montreal: Boréal Express, 1983.

Fahrni, Magda. *Household Politics: Montreal Families and Postwar Reconstruction*. Toronto: University of Toronto Press, 2005.

Gauvreau, Danielle, Peter Gossage, and Diane Gervais. *La fécondité des Québécoises, 1870–1970. D'une exception à l'autre*. Montreal: Boréal, 2007.

Gauvreau, Michael. 'The Emergence of Personalist Feminism: Catholicism and the Marriage preparation Movement in Québec'. In Nancy Christie, ed. *Household of Faith. Family, Gender and Community in Canada, 1760–1969*. Montreal and Kingston: McGill-Queen's University Press, 2002, 319–47.

Lacelle, Nicole. *Entretiens avec Madeleine Parent et Léa Roback*. Montreal: Les Éditions du remue-ménage, 1988.

Lamoureux, Diane. *Citoyennes? Femmes, droit de vote et démocratie*. Montreal: Les Éditions du remue-ménage, 1989.

———. *Fragments et collage. Essai sur le féminisme québécois des années 1970.* Montreal: Les Éditions du remue-ménage, 1986.

———. *L'amère patrie. Féminisme et nationalisme dans le Québec contemporain.* Montreal: Les Éditions du remue-ménage, 2001.

Lamoureux, Jocelyne, Michèle Gélinas, and Katy Tari. *Femmes en mouvement: Trajectoires de l'Association féminine d'éducation et d'action sociale, AFÉAS, 1966–1991.* Montreal: Boréal, 1993.

Laurin, Nicole, Danielle Juteau, and Lorraine Duchêsne. *À la recherche d'un monde oublié. Les communautés religieuses de femmes au Québec de 1900 à 1970.* Montreal: Le Jour Éditeur, 1991.

Lavigne, Marie and Yolande Pinard, eds. *Travailleuses et féministes, Les femmes dans la société québécoise.* Montreal: Boréal, 1983.

Lévesque, Andrée. *Making and Breaking the Rules. Women in Quebec, 1919–1939.* Toronto: McClelland & Stewart, 1994.

———, ed. *Madeleine Parent, Activist.* Toronto: Sumach Press, 2005.

Malouin, Marie-Paule. *Le mouvement familial au Québec. Les débuts: 1937–1965.* Montreal: Boréal, 1998.

Marshall, Dominique. *The Social Origins of the Welfare State, Quebec Families, Compulsory Education, and Family Allowances, 1940–1955.* Waterloo: Wilfrid Laurier University Press, 2006.

Myers, Tamara. *Caught:Montreal's Modern Girls and the Law, 1869–1945.* Toronto: University of Toronto Press, 2006.

Piché, Lucie. *Femmes et changement social au Québec .L'apport de la Jeunesse ouvrière catholique féminine 1931–1966.* Quebec City: Presses de l'Université Laval, 2003.

Sineau, Mariette, and Évelyne Tardy. *Droits des femmes en France et au Québec, 1940–1990.* Montreal: Les Éditions du remue-ménage, 1993.

Tardy, Évelyne, Manon Tremblay, and Ginette Legault. *Maires et mairesses. Les femmes et la politique municipale.* Montreal: Liber, 1997.

———, and André Bernard. *Militer au féminin dans la Fédération des femmes du Québec et dans ses groupes affiliés.* Montreal: Les Éditions du remue-ménage, 1995.

Tremblay, Manon. *Québécoises et représentation parlementaire.* Ste-Foy: Presses de l'Université Laval, 2005.

———. 'Quebec Women in Politics. A Reappraisal'. In Veronica Strong-Boag, Mona Gleason, and Adele Perry, *Rethinking Canada. The Promise of Women's History,* Toronto: Oxford University Press, 2002, 377–93.

CHAPTER 17

Between Unity and Diversity: Examining the 'Quebec Model' of Integration

—Raffaele Iacovino, Carleton University/Charles-Antoine Sévigny, Université du Québec à Montréal

---

— TIMELINE —

1968   Quebec's Union Nationale government creates Ministry of Immigration. A Quebec Immigration Service had been housed in Ministry of Cultural Affairs since 1965.

1971   Lang-Cloutier Agreement, first federal–provincial agreement on immigration, allows representatives of Quebec to work in Canadian embassies and to advise Canadian immigration officers stationed abroad about Quebec's unique social conditions.

1973   Andras-Bienvenue Agreement slightly expands role of Quebec agents abroad, allowing them to direct interviews with immigration candidates. Agents would be more active in selection process and in making recommendations to visa officers.

1975   Quebec enacts statutory Bill of Rights entitled Charter of Human Rights and Freedoms, which takes precedence over all provincial legislation. While most Bills of Rights in North America cover civil and political rights, Quebec Charter is unique in that it offers some important social and economic protections.

1977   Quebec enacts Charter of the French Language, also known as Bill 101. In its preamble, it resolves 'to make of French the language of Government and the Law, as well as the normal and everyday language of work, instruction, communication, commerce and business'.

1978   Cullen-Couture Agreement (The Quebec–Canada Accord in Matters of Immigration and Selection of Foreigners) granted Quebec greater role in selecting immigrants. Quebec could select desirable candidates from its own network of offices abroad, and could control temporary worker and student immigration. Federal government retained control over borders and admitting and selecting refugee claimants. Quebec had to still abide by categories of immigrants defined by federal legislation—independent immigrants, family class immigrants, and individuals in distress.

1981   Parti Québécois government of René Lévesque releases first major policy statement on Quebec's approach to integration, entitled *Autant de façons d'être Québécois : Plan d'action à l'intention des communautés culturelles*, developing and building on idea of 'cultural convergence' as compromise between cultural pluralism and protection of French language and culture in Quebec.

1990   Quebec Liberal Party of Robert Bourassa releases most comprehensive policy guide in immigrant integration to date, entitled *Au Quebec pour bâtir ensemble : Énoncé de politique en matière d'immigration et d'intégration.* Most closely associated with model of interculturalism, policy statement introduced two key concepts—'moral contract' and 'common public culture'—in shifting towards more culturally pluralist approach.

1991 Gagnon-Tremblay–McDougall Accord (Canada–Quebec Accord Relating to Immigration and Temporary Admission of Aliens). This Accord is most recent and remains in force. Quebec received exclusive responsibility in three areas of permanent immigration: total volume for its territory; selection of candidates that seek settlement in Quebec (except for refugee and family reunification claimants); and management and follow-up of sponsorship arrangements and their duration, according to criteria established by federal legislation.

2000 Le forum national sur la citoyenneté et l'intégration, an attempt to explore questions around citizenship and diversity in Quebec, launched by Parti Québécois. It was heavily criticized for what was perceived to be foregone conclusions in the consultation document. It left very little trace of integration discourse in Quebec, other than the idea of internal citizenship for Quebec in order to facilitate its integration efforts.

2001 Estates General on the Situation and Future of the French Language in Quebec (Larose Commission) recommends the establishment of formal internal citizenship for Quebec, in order to clearly indicate that it is a society with distinct social needs centred around primacy of French language.

2004 *Des valeurs partagées, des intérêts communs,* latest policy blueprint, released by Quebec Liberal Party government of Jean Charest, returns to principles established in 1990 document. It comments on new importance of security interests and adds more specific anti-discrimination measures.

2008 Commission de Consultation sur les pratiques d'accommodement reliées aux différences culturelles (Bouchard-Taylor Commission). Established to study the legal practice of reasonable accommodation in Quebec, Commission widened its mandate to examine cultural diversity. Among its conclusions, Commission recommends more formal definition of interculturalism by state, and generally advocates return to synthesis and reciprocity to regulate cultural interactions.

Introduction: Diversity and Cultural Pluralism

Diversity

Like most contemporary societies, Quebec must reconcile its past with its future to form an identity that will define public life and anchor its integration policies. Francophone Quebecers have a minority collective identity in Canada as a whole, but a majority in Quebec, which includes a bounded territory, democratic institutions, its own internal diversity claims, and policy levers that qualify it as a host society. Quebec is at once responsible for the flourishing of its uniqueness, which draws upon its French-Canadian heritage, while debating the limits and possibilities of various other cultural influences and accepting cultural pluralism in defining the terms of belonging. As such, Quebec is both an *object* of diversity-management while making accommodation claims as a national minority; and a site of diversity, a *host society* that is responsible for managing socio-cultural difference. This is the socio-political context for managing diversity in Quebec.

While almost fully responsible for selecting and integrating immigrants, Quebec frames the norms of collective life through a set of policies meant to integrate newcomers and bolster democratic partici- pation. However, in attempting to carve out a 'citizen- ship space' in the larger Canadian context, Quebec has not left to chance the protection and flourish- ing of its francophone collective identity; certain collective goals cannot coexist with an unqualified commitment to cultural pluralism, on one end, and a neutral, civic, or universal conception of liberal citizenship, on the other.[1] The limits and constraints of such an environment have led to a distinct model called 'interculturalism', which is distinguished from the Canadian policy of multiculturalism. This chap- ter examines how diversity has been addressed in Quebec in particular.

The concept of diversity requires further clarifica- tion. As Daniel Weinstock[2] has highlighted, contem- porary liberal societies must first address *axiological pluralism,* which consists in the diversity inherent in a free and democratic society, the result of the mul- titude of differences produced by the freedoms of association, thought, and expression—essentially, identities that emerge out of life choices. Second, *cul- tural pluralism* refers to groups that seek recognition by the larger society on the basis of their cultural, linguistic, ethnic, religious, or national differences. While axiological pluralism explores the extent to which the state may justifiably intervene in shaping these life-affirming choices, a commitment to cul- tural pluralism involves finding a balance between the identity-based claims of groups, the terms of integration with the wider political community, and bases of social cohesion. The latter manifestation of diversity is explored here.

More specifically, we focus on an even smaller slice of this complex tapestry and limit ourselves to Quebec's response to *ethnocultural diversity.* Indeed, cultural differences are not the only manifestation of politically salient diversity in Quebec. National minorities such as Aboriginal peoples or the anglo- phone minority in Quebec enjoy some recognition by the state as historical collectives rather than as the result of recent immigration.[3] Moreover, other forms of pluralism in which groups make accommodation demands on the larger society include identities of gender, sexual orientation, urban versus rural life- style, class, and so on.

Quebec is a particularly interesting case because it has charged itself with these questions as a sub-state national minority. It has devised its own model of interculturalism as a somewhat alternative approach to Canadian multiculturalism and the traditional American melting pot. As such, it is a case worthy of assessment on its own terms, particularly since it has acquired many of the powers for recruiting, selecting, and integrating immigrants; has committed significant resources to a wide network of immigration offices abroad; and has consistently shown a desire to craft its own boundaries of belonging to Quebec society.

Citizenship and Cultural Pluralism

Responses to diversity range from outright cultural assimilation to the complete exclusion of culture from the public sphere; most states have attempted to strike a balance between unity and recognizing difference. Most liberal democracies have dismissed cultural assimilation as morally excessive and instead seek to re-think the terms of integration for minor- ity cultures with two broad objectives. First, they foster and promote cultural diversity as important in itself, drawing upon both the norms of tolerance and the benefits of intercultural exchange as the basis for social cohesion. Second, members of minority cultural groups are deemed more likely to integrate effectively if they can be recognized by the larger community without a wholesale shedding of their particular identities. A commitment to equal condi- tions of membership requires some acknowledgment that such groups need to maintain the integrity of their cultural attachments, since imposing a majority culture would require a much more difficult transi- tion. The basic thrust here is to avoid the shock of cultural distance and the possibility of such groups closing themselves off to the wider society. As such, public institutions ought to recognize this fact and not be heavily slanted towards sustaining the collec- tive integrity of the majority culture at the expense of minority contributions, as a matter of equality.[4]

A commitment to cultural pluralism implies that citizenship—the rights, responsibilities, terms of membership, and nature of entitlements, as well as expectations of democratic participation—should not simply recognize people as undifferentiated individuals, where culture is merely a private concern and not a matter for state intervention. As we illustrate below, the spectrum of policy options for integration in Quebec have generally fallen within these parameters since the Quiet Revolution. A commitment to cultural pluralism has ranged from moderate to more robust versions, determined by the need to maintain the integrity of the minority nation in the face of evolving challenges. Prior to exploring these debates, we provide a brief overview of immigration and integration in Quebec.

ETHNOCULTURAL DIVERSITY AND QUEBEC

Following the Second World War, an increase of immigrants from Southern and Eastern Europe made Quebecers begin to think about how their francophone culture could survive and flourish in North America.[5] As the birth rate declined among francophones, most immigrants adopted English,[6] threatening the demographic weight of francophones in both Quebec and Canada. This renewed interest in the social and political consequences of immigration coincided with the onset of a more positive and open attitude toward the role and contributions of cultural minorities in Quebec.

Several events precipitated this shift in thinking. First, the horrors of the Second World War caused the Catholic hierarchy in Rome, and subsequently the clergy in Quebec, to re-evaluate its social doctrine on relations between ethno-religious groups. Second, French-Canadian nationalists began to view new arrivals as potential allies in developing an identity that would willingly disengage from the British Empire. Third, more liberal thinkers associated with the Quebec Liberal Party began to explore and develop ideas about the economic benefits of immigration.[7] New international human rights standards, coupled with Quebec's specific demographic, economic, and identity-related concerns fostered growing interest in immigration policy.

Quebec gradually accepted that it required policy instruments appropriate to its status as a French-speaking host society, and it could no longer leave these matters to Ottawa. In 1968, a Ministry of Immigration was created,[8] and between the 1970s and the 1990s, the Quebec state secured increasing powers of selection and integration in a series of bilateral agreements with the federal government.

In 1991, the two parties signed the Canada-Quebec Accord Relating to Immigration and Temporary Admission of Aliens (Gagnon-Tremblay–McDougall Accord), the most comprehensive agreement to date. The Accord stipulates that the federal government is responsible for annual volume to Canada, criteria of residency, categories of immigrants, criteria for family sponsorship and assisted relative cases, and asylum claims. Quebec has exclusive responsibility in three domains relative to permanent immigration:

- Total volume for its territory;
- The selection of candidates that seek settlement in Quebec (except refugee and family reunification claimants); and
- The management and follow-up of sponsorship arrangements and their duration, according to the criteria established by federal legislation.

In terms of temporary immigration, Canada must receive Quebec's consent in issuing work permits; issuing student permits and admitting international students (except those participating in a Canadian assistance program with developing states); and the authorization for a visitor to Quebec to receive medical treatment. In short, while Canada sets the broad guidelines, including selection criteria, Quebec enjoys much latitude in how it chooses to meet its own needs, including altering the relative weight of priorities.[9] Moreover, Quebec immigration officials review files of applicants, interview them, and ultimately grant approval for entrance, clearly demonstrating that it is the government of Quebec that admits applicants, in order to help alleviate potential confusion among immigrants about the society to which they are being admitted.

Immigration is intimately linked with controlling and developing the boundaries of identity in any democratic political community; thus the state expects to be able to develop and enact what Michael Sandel has termed 'formative projects'[10] without the added burden of having to constantly justify them within a larger political association. Quebec has largely achieved this, although without formal constitutional recognition as a host society. The Canadian Constitution recognizes Quebec as a province equal in status to the others, and its Charter of Rights and Freedoms is meant to apply from coast to coast. Canada is officially a multicultural country within a framework of bilingualism. Belonging in Canada is thus formally defined through the choice of language (French or English) and the capacity to maintain one's particular cultural attachments. The idea of a different set of rights and responsibilities for citizens of Quebec, therefore, is developing outside of the formal structures of Canadian citizenship. There is no recognition of Quebec as a distinct host society, or a provision acknowledging its particular model of integration. The next section looks more closely at the extent to which Quebec, notwithstanding its greater institutional leverage, still faces distinct challenges in the Canadian context.

IMMIGRATION AND POLITICAL COMMUNITY IN QUEBEC

Assessing the immigration and integration policies of particular societies serves somewhat as a lens into the priorities, principles, and norms in its framing of citizenship—the bases of belonging and the obligations expected of its members. In a minority nation such as Quebec, where immigration is a shared jurisdiction, control over these policies carries a dual purpose.

First, immigration addresses various social and economic needs; thus it is a function common to most advanced capitalist political economies. Second, control over selecting and integrating immigrants reflects a desire, unique to minority nations, for a measure of self-determination, or more minimally, autonomy, in order that it may maintain and develop its society for future generations, according to its collective needs. Joseph Carens states this feature of immigration succinctly:

> The degree of openness to immigrants, the criteria of selection and exclusion, the kinds of adaptation, and the degree of conformity to the dominant population expected of new arrivals

and their descendants—all these factors indicate something about who belongs, what is valued, and what membership and citizenship mean.[11]

Indeed, Quebec has always seen itself as a constituted political community, a 'societal culture'[12] within Canadian federalism—a vision often pitted against a pan-Canadian project based on provincial equality, bilingualism, and multiculturalism as the foundations for citizenship. Quebec must thus constantly justify its role as a primary host society, since this can never simply be assumed as long as the minority nation is within an alternative host society that simultaneously frames the boundaries of citizenship.

In the 1960s, a new era of rapid modernization through increased state intervention resulted in a profound transformation of politically salient identity in Quebec. Quebec moved to structure its national identity along civic and territorial lines. Previously, the nation of French Canadians had been defined along ethnic lines, based largely on Catholicism and the French language and culture.[13] Indeed, in what is characteristic of most ethnically based collective movements, immigrants were viewed as somewhat threatening to the integrity of the nation and a challenge to French-Canadian culture and institutions; thus foreign influences were shunned in a defensive posture of survival. With a more open, inclusive, and territorial conception of belonging, however, Quebec defined itself not only as a society open to immigration for instrumental reasons, but as one that began to embrace the contributions of immigrants. A policy document from 1990 nicely captures this point:

> The social and cultural impact of immigration is certainly more difficult to determine when demographic, economic and linguistic indicators, on their own more easily quantifiable, are called into question. Nevertheless, the number of examples of Quebecers that have come from abroad and have enriched Quebec's culture and institutions; have allowed this society to be appreciated abroad and, inversely, have sensitized this society to important if sometimes misunderstood realities, speaks largely to the significance that immigration can represent with regards to sociocultural dynamism and openness to the world.[14] (our translation)

The next section traces the various attempts to address the terms of integration since the early 1980s.

The Evolution of the 'Quebec Model' of Cultural Pluralism

The Canadian Context: Competing Projects and Ambiguous Citizenship

A persistent problem for Quebec is that despite its efforts to implement a coherent integration policy and to frame Canadian citizenship in differentiated terms, many newly arrived immigrants and even established ethnocultural groups continue to identify primarily with the markers of Canadian citizenship. Competing interpretations of political community create both a sense of ambiguity for new arrivals and a challenge for public policy that most nation-states do not face.[15]

Canada is responsible for granting formal citizenship status, which is broadly based on multiculturalism within a bilingual framework, a Charter of Rights and Freedoms, and provincial equality.[16] Apart from administrative agreements with Quebec, Canada does not formally endorse constitutional asymmetry.[17] Many initiatives of the Quebec government that bear upon citizenship continue to be viewed with suspicion by ethnocultural community leaders.[18] They see the initiatives either as hidden projects for assimilation contrary to Canadian pluralism, or as nationalist ploys to further sever ties with Canada, rather than as genuine efforts to integrate immigrants into a distinct democratic space.[19] The Charter of the French Language, for example, seeks social cohesion and integration; but for a time it was rejected and viewed as the imposition of a majority language in what is formally a bilingual country, as an illegitimate instrument of linguistic peace, or as the means of doing away with the use of English altogether.[20]

Indeed, the basic idea behind Canadian multiculturalism is that all cultural identities could participate equally in social and political spheres. Culture is constitutionally recognized and protected, and no official culture forms the basis of citizenship. The key element in this discussion is multiculturalism's inherent centralizing effect. By not differentiating between various forms and manifestations of politically salient collective identities—historical national minorities, the majority nationalist identity, and ethnocultural groups—all 'cultural claims' are treated equally, and their primary reference is the bundle of rights granted by the central government.[21]

Multiculturalism as one of the pillars of Canadian citizenship is thus not merely a commitment to a model of cultural pluralism that embraces cultural rights. Successive Quebec governments, however, have viewed the policy as a nation-building device meant to undermine the primacy of any particular collective grouping that claims the right to govern a separate democratic political community, or host society, as part of the federal framework.

With the larger context established, we now turn to the ways in which Quebec has grappled with these internal challenges over time. Indeed, the obstacles confronting Quebec have not prevented governments from engaging in much soul-searching about the terms of belonging to Quebec society, as illustrated in the series of policy statements and formal consultative commissions devoted to this issue. Rather than muddling through specific policy programs on ethnocultural diversity management, we have selected documents that provide a lens into the broad framework through which Quebec has addressed these questions, and that illustrate the evolution of a model that is specific to Quebec.

Managing Diversity in Quebec

While integration involves many policy areas, including education, training and employment, and poverty alleviation, this section looks at the broad orientations of the terms of integration developed in a series of policy statements and official commissions. While tangible results and policy applications are valid concerns, the aim here is to highlight the general contours of citizenship in official discourse, as a window into the values, identities, and norms that guide integration policies.

Before examining the ideas that have shaped the Quebec model, however, we must highlight the two foundations of the larger framework within which interculturalism has been developed. First, in 1975

Quebec enacted its own Charter of Human Rights and Freedoms, the guarantor of fundamental rights that was not undermined by subsequent Quebec governments. A second foundational background instrument is the Charter of the French Language (1977), which explicitly links integration with the public use of French. This Charter powerfully makes it clear that protecting the French language and allowing it to flourish are not merely the responsibility of the francophone majority, but are fundamental to the rights and responsibilities of belonging in Quebec.

In 1981 the Quebec government published *Autant de façons d'être Québécois*,[22] which is a founding document of the Quebec interculturalism. Recall that an actual law outlining the model of interculturalism was never formulated. In 1990, the government produced a more comprehensive policy statement on immigration and cultural pluralism, *Au Québec pour bâtir ensemble*.[23] Subsequently, two other less successful attempts to structure Quebec citizenship are examined: *Le forum national sur la citoyenneté et l'intégration*, in 2000, and the final report of the Larose Commission (2001)[24] on the future of the French language in Quebec. Finally, the most recent policy statement, *Des valeurs partagées, des intérêts communs*, in 2004, and the final report of the Consultation Commission on Accommodation Practices Related to Cultural Differences(2008), (Bouchard-Taylor Commission) round out the overview.

Autant de façons d'être québécois : Énoncé de politique en matière d'immigration et d'intégration (1980)

In 1981, following a series of consultations with representatives of cultural communities, which recognized them as interlocutors in defining the Quebec democratic space, the first policy blueprint emerged. The plan highlights three objectives:

- ensuring the preservation, specificity, and development of cultural communities;
- sensitizing francophone Quebecers to the place of cultural communities in developing a common heritage; and
- promoting the integration of the cultural communities in Quebec society, especially in the

sectors where they were under-represented, particularly in the public service.

The document explicitly acknowledges the salience of framing integration such that minority cultures are protected, and refers to the various measures undertaken previously to ensure their integrity, including programs such as Centre d'orientation et de formation des immigrants and Programme d'enseignement des langues d'origines.[25] Moreover, it encourages cultural exchanges with countries of origin and minority language instruction, and even proposed subsidizing such programs.

As an overarching blueprint, the theme of the document is *convergence*, emphasizing the promotion of markers of belonging around the majority group. Integration is thus defined as a process where newcomers are expected to eventually converge toward Quebec's francophone culture. While it does not advocate outright cultural assimilation, since the contribution of minority cultures is explicitly valued, the overriding theme is that belonging in Quebec means proceeding toward the identity markers of the established majority culture. As such, it does not limit integration to language acquisition merely in an instrumental sense, or in strictly public terms.

This approach rests on a hierarchy of cultures in Quebec, with an established majority culture as the basis for integration. It nevertheless represents a watershed in diversity management in Quebec, particularly in inter-community relations. The document is replete with references to the past and expected future contributions of minority cultural groups to Quebec's development. Quebec identity is thus to become open to much more influence by minority cultural groups integrating into its society; the document includes concrete recommendations for increasing allophones' accessibility to public service jobs, for services better adapted to immigrants' specific needs, and for financial assistance to minority cultural community associations. The Ministry of Immigration was renamed the Ministry of Cultural Communities and Immigration, which signalled a greater awareness of the specific needs of newcomers.

While explicit references to meeting the particular needs of members of minority cultures represent a modest pluralist turn, the strong language of cultural convergence resulted in a model that placed most of the responsibility to integrate and adapt onto the minority groups themselves—to integrate into a Quebec identity still defined largely as an expression of francophone culture. The majority was thus limited to demonstrating a greater sensitivity to the difficulties encountered by newcomers, and that this would contribute to more effective efforts at integration. While the government demonstrated a firm intention of establishing a propitious environment for accommodating minority cultures, the expectation of unity around an established core dampened the pluralist intentions of the approach.

Finally, the policy statement clearly demarcates Quebec as a host society, embedded in but distinct from the Canadian policy of multiculturalism, and states its divergence from the American melting pot. In 1990, Quebec would once again tackle these questions in a more comprehensive model.

Au Quebec pour bâtir ensemble: Énoncé de politique en matière d'immigration et d'intégration (1990)

This document outlines three fundamental principles of Quebec's approach to integration. Quebec is to be:

- a society in which French is the common language of public life;
- a democratic society where the participation and the contribution of everyone is expected and encouraged; and
- a pluralist society open to multiple contributions within the limits imposed by the respect for fundamental democratic values, and the necessity of inter-community exchange.

The policy statement remains to this day the one most closely associated with the Quebec model of interculturalism. The basic thrust is that the integration of immigrants or minority cultures into the larger society is to be a reciprocal endeavour—a *moral contract* between majority and minority groups, with the aim of establishing a *common public culture*. It emphasizes that the responsibility for integration belongs to all Quebecers, not merely immigrants.

The first principle reaffirms the primacy of French as the common public language in Quebec. Language is described not merely in its instrumental function, but as a symbolic identity marker. New arrivals and minority cultures signal their willingness to belong to the Quebec political community by embracing French and engaging with its flourishing collective. However, the document insists that linguistic assimilation is not the aim, and individual choice of language in private life is encouraged. The mutual recognition inherent in the notion of a moral contract also requires that the host society provide the necessary resources for French language instruction and adoption throughout Quebec.

Second, regarding democratic participation, the model invokes the importance of social justice and equality of opportunity laid out in the Quebec Charter of Human Rights and Freedoms. The host society is also called upon here to help alleviate socio-economic and cultural barriers, to strengthen the avenues of participation for neo-Quebecers. Integration into democratic life is thus a two-way street and involves more than an expectation that immigrants make an effort to learn about the values and institutions of the larger society.

Third, the principle of intercultural dialogue indicates a willingness to move towards greater pluralism. An intercultural turn is evident here, since the model shifts toward cultural exchange that would transform both the minority and majority cultures in a synthesis of a common public culture. Without denying the importance of the francophone heritage in fostering this common identity space, the model nevertheless turns away from the language of convergence and stresses reciprocal exchange. Cultural contact becomes the basis for new common references and a new identity for the larger community—a 'fusion of horizons' through open dialogue and participation. Thus, a main pillar of the model discourages cultural enclosure and isolation. There is no cultural recognition outside of a democratic imperative—it is an outcome of participation and deliberation, the result of contributing to a common public culture that is open to change.

Much like its predecessor, this approach explicitly maintains a strong distinction from Canadian multiculturalism. Despite its many similarities to multiculturalism, interculturalism differs in that it links cultural recognition to the act of participation and deliberation. It is this emphasis on a responsibility to participate in public life, contributing through the lens of one's particular culture in a reciprocal exchange with other minority groups as well as the majority, that most fully characterizes the model.

Forum national sur la citoyenneté et l'intégration (2000)

While the 1990 policy statement attracted much attention, several events resulted in a shift in the government's discourse. The Parti Québécois took power in 1994 and launched a sovereignty referendum that resulted in a very close loss, leaving ethnocultural groups with a sense of resentment. At the same time, integration and diversity under this government shifted towards a discourse centred on citizenship, universal markers of identity, and essentially, a more civic conception of belonging. The immigration and integration portfolio dropped references to cultural communities, and was renamed the Ministry of Citizen Relations and Immigration. The idea was to establish more inclusive criteria for membership, stressing formal equality rather than the recognition of cultural differences.[26] In short, this period was characterized by a retreat from interculturalism. One concrete measure in applying this approach was the cancellation of the COFI program, which was seen as promoting cultural enclaves rather than facilitating integration.

In this context the Quebec government launched the *Forum national sur la citoyenneté et l'intégration* in 2000. The forum's rationale is outlined in the first section, where the challenges, principles, and issues surrounding Quebec citizenship and integration are highlighted. Challenges included rapid technological change, population movements, intensification of negotiations with Aboriginal peoples, and increased urbanization and cosmopolitanism. Moreover, it examines the fundamental tension and resulting ambivalence in a situation where Canada and Quebec engage in overlapping efforts at integrating newcomers. Indeed, this is taken as a clear obstacle to the host society effectively integrating newly arrived citizens. Generally, the report makes little mention of a commitment to cultural pluralism, proposing a new civic contract in place of cultural reciprocity:

Whether it involves the promotion and the protection of rights, establishing one's civil status, or even the framework for information exchanges that touch individuals and their private lives, the mission of the different branches of the Ministry of Immigration and Citizen Relations converge towards an appreciation of the value of Quebec's civic heritage.

Moving away from an approach that categorizes citizens according to their ethnic origins or their migratory paths, the Government of Quebec chooses to adopt an inclusive approach that ties together the various ministries and public institutions. A person that has arrived as an immigrant is thus no longer considered through the status of his/her origin, but rather through his/her status as a citizen in relations with the state.[27] (Our translation)

The consultation document was heavily criticized for its slant toward a Quebec citizenship that would reinforce common identity references and cohesion. Citizenship is thus defined in its transcendental function, as an institution meant to overcome, rather than to accommodate, particular identities. As it was conceived, citizenship was not open to diverse contributions in determining the orientations of Quebec society. Jocelyn Maclure, for example, criticized the exercise as a veiled promotion of sovereignty rather than a serious debate about integration and the markers of belonging in Quebec.[28] In other words, this was an exercise in large-scale consultation and deliberation about the boundaries of Quebec citizenship in which some of the conclusions were pre-determined. In the end, the forum was generally viewed as a missed opportunity, and it never quite achieved guidepost status for meeting the challenges of managing diversity.

Report of the Larose Commission on the Future of the French Language in Quebec (2000)

The idea of a public consultation that would contribute to formalizing Quebec citizenship was not abandoned. Indeed, in the Estates General on the Situation and Future of the French language in Quebec, the Larose Commission, language was explicitly linked with citizenship. The French language was seen as the bond that holds public life together—a condition of democratic participation and a necessary vehicle for attaining equality—and thus the primary marker of Quebec citizenship. In this light, the Commission described the foundations of an active citizenship in Quebec, expressed through a common language and a set of democratic values and institutions, as well as a common heritage. Moreover, it identified the cultural contributions of all Quebec's constituent groups as integral to Quebec identity. It also suggested a move away from multiculturalism towards interculturalism, signalling somewhat of a return to the discourse of a distinct approach. This passage from the report nicely captures the concerns and conclusions of the Commission:

> Bringing together the values, knowledge, and institutions of the Quebec people, channelling artistic, intellectual, material activities and production, as well as original symbols, Quebec culture lies naturally at the heart of its identity, and consequently, at the heart of Quebec citizenship. In effect, citizenship can be seen as the recognition of belonging to a nation, to a community of people that make the choice to live together within a common culture.
>
> The concept of citizenship is not well served by a demographic discourse that slices society into three ethnolinguistic categories: francophones, anglophones, and allophones, with the latter having become the group upon which the weight of safeguarding the French language has been placed. These categories, which give the image of a fragmented and polarized society, ought to be denounced when they move beyond the realm of statistical categories. Leaving behind the defensive attitude of minorities and rejecting the divisive and ethnic character of multiculturalism, the Quebec nation rests increasingly on the binding potential of a common culture, as the fruition of the creativity of all its members, to raise the level of consciousness with regards to sharing a single citizenship.[29] (Our translation)

All citizens of Quebec are expected to contribute to the flourishing of the French language, particularly in the face of constant pressures from expanding globalization. The Commission recommended the formalization of an internal citizenship for Quebec as the most effective way to address growing concerns over language.

While not insignificant, the Commission's recommendations said very little about relations with minority cultural communities and the role of minority languages in building Quebec identity. It continued along a civic path, where language was to trump all differences and serve as both a condition for participation and the basis for social cohesion. Most critics decried the overly stringent association of language and Quebec citizenship, as though Quebec did not contain historically protected minority languages on its territory. Also, the report failed to rally a consensus. Its recommendations, like the forum preceding it, never quite caught on, and most observers continued to point to the Quebec Charter of Human Rights and Freedoms, the Charter of the French Language, and the 1990 policy statement as the main structuring principles of Quebec's approach to diversity management.

Des valeurs partagées, des intérêts communs (2004)

The return to power of the Quebec Liberal Party in 2003 marked another shift in emphasis. Most notably, the government dropped references to citizenship and returned to 'cultural communities' as its preferred designation. The name of the Ministry was again changed, to 'Immigration and Cultural Communities'.

A return to the 'moral contract' was one of many elements borrowed from the 1990 statement, and few innovations were included, except for a note on the prominence of national security in a post–9/11 context. Moreover, the statement rejected the Parti Québécois's use of the language of citizenship, strong insistence on unity, and the development of a primary allegiance and loyalty towards Quebec.

Nevertheless, there are some indications of some refinement in Axis 4 of Section 2, 'Un Québec fier de sa diversité'. Here we find a strong appeal to encourage intercultural dialogue and promote openness to diversity among members of the host society and to combat discrimination and inter-community tensions. More concretely, to raise awareness of the importance of intercultural communication, the statement suggests targeting specific areas in which such tensions might emerge, including schools, workplaces, civil society, government institutions, relations between landlords and tenants, and finally, in situations particularly conducive to racial profiling. Overall, however, the policy statement is largely a return to the principles outlined in 1990, and does not build upon any suggestions for internal citizenship that arose in the intervening years.

Consultation Commission on Accommodation Practices Related to Cultural Differences (Bouchard-Taylor Commission, 2008)

While it does not enjoy the force of a governmental policy statement, the recent recommendations of the Bouchard-Taylor Commission represent the most comprehensive account of Quebec interculturalism to date:

> Often mentioned in academic papers, interculturalism as an integration policy has never been fully, officially defined by the Quebec government, although its underlying principles were formulated long ago. This shortcoming should be overcome, all the more so as the Canadian multiculturalism model does not appear to be well adapted to conditions in Quebec. . . . According to the descriptions provided in scientific documentation, interculturalism seeks to reconcile ethno-cultural diversity with the continuity of the French-speaking core and the preservation of the social link. It thus affords security to Québecers of French-Canadian origin and to ethnocultural minorities and protects the rights of all in keeping with the liberal tradition. By instituting French as the common public language, it establishes a framework in society for communication and exchanges. It has the virtue of being flexible and receptive to negotiation, adaptation and innovation.[30]

The report refines and provides coherence to many of the established principles around which the preceding debates had evolved. Several distinctive normative and descriptive features merit further discussion.

First, the Commission clearly stipulates that the nation of Quebec constitutes the operational framework for interculturalism. This is an essential attribute of the model—it is meant for this political community in its particular set of circumstances. The framework is clearly distinct from Canadian multiculturalism, even though the model of multiculturalism has itself changed in the direction of social cohesion and unity in the past 30 years.[31] The authors note four particularly salient conditions: a much stronger language-related anxiety in Quebec; existential anguish over its minority status; the fact that there is no longer a dominant majority ethnic group in Canada; and finally, that there is much less concern in Canada for maintaining a founding culture and more for promoting national unity. The authors conclude, without delving deeply into the politics of multiculturalism as it relates to Quebec, that the models represent distinct attempts to apply a pluralist philosophy.

Second, the model is lauded for its ability to adapt to a variety of influences on Quebec identity, due to the principle of intercultural reciprocity. As such, a static conception of an existing culture as a centre of convergence, and of a civic space situated above the reach of cultural influence, is not in keeping with a model of interculturalism. A commitment to cultural pluralism does not confine cultural differences to the private sphere.

Finally, and most significantly, the Commissioners proposed that to alleviate ambiguity, the National Assembly of Quebec should adopt an official text on interculturalism, whether a statute, statement, or declaration. Following extensive public consultations, this would serve as a social blueprint to provide continuity and overarching identity to Quebec in its capacity as a host society—an effective reference point and coherent guide for public and community interveners. Moreover, it could promote awareness and teaching about the value of cultural pluralism, which might help reduce racism and other forms of ethnocultural discrimination. Like Canadian multiculturalism, interculturalism could eventually become a national symbol and a core value.

GÉRALD GODIN: FATHER OF QUEBEC INTERCULTURALISM

Gérald Godin

© Office du film du Quebec;
Photographer: Gabor Szilasi

I have learned to understand (immigrants) through my profession, to appreciate more profoundly who they were here in Quebec, thus to increasingly love them. In this sense, it's a new phase of Quebec nationalism, a much more open nationalism that is more conducive to respecting others that are here and to ensure that every one of them can contribute to the construction of the country. In the beginning, we believed that we would build the country practically alone; now, we believe we must do it with others.[32]

While Gérald Godin's influence on the intellectual life of Quebec is difficult to capture in a brief synopsis—he was an accomplished politician, poet, essayist, novelist, songwriter, painter, and journalist—it is his enduring mark on Quebec's early debates on immigration and integration policy that would have a profound and lasting impact. Godin was a pioneer in Quebec's continuing social and political debates on cultural pluralism. For Godin the humanist, culture was paramount in building a forward-looking and confident Quebec society. Ever the artist, Godin infused political life with an open affirmation of difference, justice, and knowledge as universal and human values, injecting the strategic and rational world of politics with a gentle and serene sensibility. In his view, the affirmation of Quebec as a confident and strong nation went hand in hand with the promotion, recognition, and respect of the plurality of cultures on Quebec soil.

Godin's quest began with his elegant appeal for a Quebec literature to replace traditional French-Canadian literature, which he believed stifled creativity, belonged to the past, and failed to reflect the artistic expression inherent in a modern, flourishing, and new Quebec society open to the world. It was a call for liberation in Quebec—a sense of 'artistic decolonization' away from dogma of the past.

His entrance into politics was marked by a bold initiative. Against most strategic and calculated advice, he ran in the 1976 provincial election for the Parti Québécois in a multi-ethnic neighbourhood—against the leader of the opposition, Robert Bourassa—rather than in one of the 'safe' ridings usually reserved for high-profile candidates such as himself. He diligently met the people of the riding, learned about their interests and identities, and extolled a vision of a new, exciting future for Quebec—and surprisingly defeated Robert Bourassa as part of the Parti Québécois victory. He would go on to win three more elections for the PQ.

In 1980–1 he served as Minister of Immigration, and at his insistence, as the newly named Minister of Immigration and Cultural Communities from 1981–5. Here his legacy is felt to this day. Godin viewed building a new Quebec as inextricably linked to welcoming and fully integrating the diverse contributions of newly arrived citizens. He became the strongest advocate of the value of difference in his government and party, often at odds with factions that promoted ethnic allegiance in pursuing independence, particularly his colleague Jacques Parizeau, who at times openly speculated that sovereignty might be legitimately determined by francophones alone. Godin thought Quebec culture and society would inevitably benefit from the contribution of a diversity of cultures, and that this should be embraced rather than rejected as a threat to the sovereignty movement. This was the birth of Quebec interculturalism. It is through Godin's vision for Quebec that the seeds of a 'common public culture' approach to immigration were sown—the value of cultural exchange and the capacity to respect and recognize others. From literature characterized by an independence of spirit, to Quebec national affirmation, to the politics of embracing difference, Godin's vision for Quebec was nourished by a common element, a quiet collective confidence that signalled a coming of age for Quebec, a new beginning and a thorough and genuine curiosity about the needs and aspirations of people from all walks of life.

The questions of integration and ethnocultural relations lie deep in the heart of Quebec identity, as they ask citizens to understand their place in the political project that is under construction, constantly changing, challenged at many turns, and always the subject of passionate debates. Godin found it particularly difficult to make a case for cultural pluralism as a member of a political party that has traditionally elicited strong negative reactions from new Quebecers, the ethnocultural and linguistic minorities. Moreover, he took control of the dossier of immigration and integration soon after the referendum, which had caused many rifts and persisting tensions between the francophone majority and ethnocultural minorities. Godin's deft touch was all the more remarkable in those circumstances.

Indeed, until the Quiet Revolution, Quebec was not always the most hospitable place for immigrants: Montreal was for the most part a divided city, linguistically and culturally; very few immigrants lived in Quebec's regions; and socio-economic and cultural forces fostered strong xenophobic tendencies. Moreover, federal policies were assimilationist and did not address Canadian dualism. By the end of the 1960s, francophone Quebec would reject its minority status and begin to affirm itself as a majority nation that could be a host society in its own right, with inclusive citizenship practices that would no longer threaten the existence of the nation. Integration became a key aspect of this project, encompassing concerns about Quebec's demographic weight in Canada, social and economic integration, and the place of religious and ethnic minorities in Quebec.

From 1968–81, much effort of the Quebec state was devoted to concluding bilateral agreements with the federal government to transfer some authority to Quebec. When Godin became Minister of Immigration and Cultural Communities in 1981, he made full use of Quebec's new powers, and launched a series of programs aimed at fostering cultural convergence. The ministry's name change was accompanied by three fundamental objectives under Godin's leadership: maintaining and developing cultures of origin, promoting integration and the full participation of cultural communities in the wider society, and encouraging exchange between minorities and the larger francophone majority. The list of initiatives was long: financing cultural community organizations that provided services and activities for members, subsidizing the construction or renovation of cultural centres, funding the media development for cultural groups, providing heritage language retention programs, and so on.

In 1983 Godin was asked by Premier René Lévesque to review the Charter of the French Language, a difficult task that could alienate both nationalists, who saw it as an untouchable text, and the anglophone and allophone minorities, who were increasingly mobilizing against the perceived bureaucratic and unreasonable rigidities of the law. This was soon after Canada had patriated its Constitution without Quebec's consent, an act seen by many nationalists as a betrayal. Godin the nationalist and pluralist again struggled to reconcile seemingly clashing ideals. Throughout 1983 Godin held tension-filled public consultations on the future of the Charter.

The status of the anglophone minority was particularly challenging—a minority, yet historically dominant, which was linked to the wider Canadian political community. Godin's vision was to grant the anglophone minority a particular status as a co-founding people of Quebec—a historical national group and not an ethnocultural group among others. He made the case that the anglophone community in Quebec, unlike wider North American and global structural forces, should not in itself be considered threatening to a vibrant francophone Quebec. Its institutions should not be held responsible for the fears of linguistic assimilation that precipitated language legislation in the first place. This vision represented a new course that was never publicly stated in Quebec, much less by the PQ.

Godin once again laid the foundation of new basis for rapprochement between the linguistic communities in Quebec. Some concrete results of his intervention include a measure of institutional bilingualism for anglophone schools, hospitals, and social service agencies, while ensuring the continuation and improvements of francization in the workplace. Godin also proposed reciprocal arrangements on minority language education with other provinces that provided it for their French-speaking minorities, which ended the impasse between Quebec and other provinces on this matter.

In 1984 Godin co-organized the Breakthrough Conference with the Jewish community, which an unprecedented 20 PQ ministers attended. It addressed many issues that concerned the Jewish community, including health, education, senior citizens, employment, youth, and the like. One result was a generous program of subsidies for not only Jewish schools, but Greek, Armenian, and Chinese as well. In his five or so years at the helm of what can be called Quebec's 'identity portfolio', his capacity to apply the deft touch of a humanist in addressing political challenges is evident in the myriad testimonials on his behalf from all parts of Quebec society—and most would agree that Gérald Godin can indeed be called a prominent founder of contemporary Quebec.

Source: Lucille Beaudry, Robert Comeau, and Guy Lachapelle, *Gérald Godin: Un poète en politique*, (Montréal: Éditions de L'Hexagone, 2000).

Snapshot

Au Quebec Pour Bâtir Ensemble : Énoncé de politique en matière d'immigration et d'intégration/Building Quebec Together: Policy Statement on Immigration and Integration (1991)

Until the 1960s, francophone Quebec society was not perceived as open to immigrant integration, and francophone Quebecers were considered either as a majority group within Quebec or as part of a larger ethnocultural group that spanned Canada. The larger Canadian community was responsible for citizenship, and immigrants to Quebec were for the most part integrated into the anglophone community, particularly in Montreal. Following the Quiet Revolution, the Quebec state assumed a more activist role in constructing the boundaries of belonging and membership in Quebec society, and made it clear that immigration and integration were significant to the future of francophone Quebec.

In 1991, the Quebec government published an unprecedented and comprehensive policy statement of its fundamental motivations, justifications, and visions regarding immigration, including selection and integration. For the first time, the government clearly linked immigration to the challenges inherent in the development of Quebec. The importance of this document cannot be overstated—it was an exercise in systematic and coherent introspection that we rarely get from governments, and it lays bare all of the challenges confronting a minority nation that does not fully control the policy levers of citizenship. It is a statement about what a society stands for, where it came from, and where it wants to go. Essentially, the way a society frames immigrant integration is a lens into its fundamental notions of justice—the rights of, and the responsibilities expected of, all citizens. After having negotiated with the federal government extensive powers in selecting and integrating immigrants, Quebec suddenly began to act like, and become, a host society. This is still a work in progress and social debates still rage in Quebec, but this was the first formal attempt to outline the main orientations of the state in a policy area that is unlike most others, in that it explicitly and quite self-consciously seeks to answer questions about belonging.

For inter-community relations specifically, the document spells out three broad objectives. First, it aims to develop the tools to ensure that newcomers and their cultural communities better know and understand Quebec society. Second, it promotes pluralism as an integral aspect of Quebec society. Third, it seeks to provide the foundations for a rapprochement between members of the cultural communities and the majority community. These rather ambitious issues would set the tone of the approach established by the policy statement, in the sense that integration was everybody's business, not an unwarranted burden placed exclusively in the hands of newcomers.

Quebec's position on immigration included a commitment to a flourishing francophone society, with an emphasis on economic prosperity accompanied by values such as family re-unification and international solidarity. Quebec thus concerned itself with establishing the admission criteria for both independent and temporary immigration. Moreover, Quebec made a commitment to be more involved in political asylum claims, particular in reception services. Quebec would also determine levels of immigration appropriate to its needs and capacities as a host society, an issue that has been firmly entrenched in political debates to this day.

For integration, Quebec's primary goal is to develop resources for newcomers and members of ethnocultural minorities to learn French, and to promote its use. Moreover, the policy statement called for the host society to be more open to the full participation of such groups in the economic, cultural, political, and institutional life of Quebec. Finally, the state would intervene directly in ensuring harmonious relations among ethnocultural groups of all origins.

Perhaps more importantly, the statement explicitly links Quebec's particular development challenges as a 'distinct society' (the common terminology at the time) with immigration, and links it with four major challenges in its future: demographic concerns, economic prosperity, the perpetuation of French as a majority language, and an opening to the world. The Quebec state for the first time laid out a framework for belonging that would form the backbone of debates about Quebec identity for years to come—even the recent Bouchard-Taylor Commission refers to this statement in outlining its model of Quebec interculturalism. The policy statement produced a new area of comparative inquiry as well, loosely labelled 'integration within a minority nation', and examination of its similarities to, and compatibilities and competition with, Canadian multiculturalism has blossomed into a full-blown interdisciplinary field of research. Suddenly, questions about immigration and integration came to be centred on Quebec society as a point of reference.

It is in this document that Quebec introduces the notion of a 'moral contract', —a reciprocal obligation between minority groups and the majority group. The moral contract comprises three main orientations for Quebec's model of integration:

- a society in which French is the common language of public life;
- a democratic society where all members are expected and encouraged to participate and contribute ; and
- a pluralist society that is open to multiple contributions within the limits of a respect for fundamental democratic values and the necessity of inter-community exchange.

The model goes on to stress that the three themes of this moral contract involve rights and responsibilities for both immigrants and the host society—again, successful integration involves society as a whole. The state is responsible for making available to all the tools needed for successful integration according to the moral contract. Immigrants would thus understand this distinct society into which they were integrating, and Quebecers would accommodate efforts at integration, including committing resources for them, and would be aware of the rights and responsibilities which they freely and proudly took upon themselves as fundamental values and principles. Through such a framework, the objective was to foster an evolving and plural 'common public culture' distinct from past attempts to define a national culture as a site of integration and as a dominant pole of cultural convergence.

Source: Government of Quebec, *Au Quebec Pour Bâtir Ensemble : Énoncé de politique en matière d'immigration et d'intégration*, (Quebec: Direction des communications du ministère des Communautés culturelles et de l'Immigration du Quebec, 1991).

Conclusion

We have outlined the main tenets of a 'Quebec model' of diversity management and how it has evolved. On a unity–diversity continuum, Quebec has for the most part leaned towards unity. This is not surprising, since the goal has primarily been to carve out a citizenship space within Canadian federalism. Over the years and due to the shifting priorities of successive governments, the model has been slightly altered in emphasis, vacillating between social cohesion and unified citizenship, and more pluralistic notions of belonging that allow for much more public recognition of the distinctiveness of ethnocultural groups. These shifts in emphasis, however, have been rather narrow, and the model's main premises have stood the test of time as a uniquely Quebec approach to the question of cultural diversity.

Quebec governments have consistently rejected the Canadian policy of multiculturalism as inadequate for protecting the collective goals of Quebec and its ability to manage its unique socio-cultural characteristics. Indeed, one of the forgotten yet salient points in the persistent debate about the differences between interculturalism and multiculturalism is the fact that

Quebec has consistently and forcefully attempted to develop its own model to fit its particular sociological challenges. While the policies may overlap to some extent, particularly since they are both committed to cultural pluralism, interculturalism is a unique approach that is meant to serve as an alternative to multiculturalism—a reference of sorts that delineates Quebec citizenship.

At the very least, it follows from Quebec's activities in selection and integration that there is a distinct normative framework for diversity management, and perhaps it will be formally recognized as a constitutive aspect of Quebec society. For students interested in the management of ethnocultural diversity, the Quebec case offers a unique lens into an alternative approach, a genuine national model of diversity management emerging from a rich body of policy statements, commissions of inquiry, and public policies. The traditional American melting-pot model, inspired by republican principles, and the Canadian policy of multiculturalism have been explicitly rejected in what can be considered Quebec's own interpretation of the rights and responsibilities that follow in the complex entanglement of culture and citizenship. This is an achievement that cannot be ignored.

Questions for Consideration

1. Provide a brief overview of Quebec's approach to the management of cultural diversity. In what ways is it distinct or similar to Canadian multiculturalism? What explains the fact that Quebec has adopted its own approach to cultural diversity?

2. Explain the difference between the concepts of cultural synthesis and cultural convergence in

the elaboration of the Quebec model over the past 30 years.

3. Why is the idea of citizenship invoked in discussions about immigrant integration and ethnocultural diversity management? How would you justify or reject the case for internal Quebec citizenship?

Notes

1. A commitment to cultural pluralism implies that the state makes special provisions or allows certain legal accommodations for cultural groups as constitutive socio-political entities that are recognized as such in public institutions. Traditional liberal citizenship, on the other hand, recognizes individuals as the primary units of public recognition, through a set of rights, entitlements and responsibilities.

2. Daniel Weinstock, 'La citoyenneté comme réponse aux problèmes du pluralisme des sociétés modernes', in Les enjeux de la citoyenneté. Un bilan interdisciplinaire, Laboratoire de recherche, Immigration et métropole, June 1998, 75.

3. See Leigh Oakes and Jane Warren, Language, Citizenship and Identity in Quebec (London: Palgrave Macmillan, 2007).

4. See Will Kymlicka for a groundbreaking theoretical contribution on the importance of recognizing culture(s) as

integral to the liberal project, *Multicultural Citizenship* (Oxford: Oxford University Press, 1995).

5. See Chapter 18.

6. See Chapter 19.

7. Fernand Harvey, 'L'Ouverture du Quebec au multiculturalisme (1900–1981)', *Études Canadiennes/Canadian Studies* 21, 2 (1986): 222.

8. See Martin Pâquet, *Toward a Quebec Ministry of Immigration, 1945 to 1968*, Canada's Ethnic Groups Series, Booklet 23 (Canadian Historical Association, 1997).

9. J. Carens, 'Immigration, Political Community and the Transformation of Identity', in J. Carens, ed., *Is Quebec nationalism Just* (Montreal and Kingston: McGill-Queen's University Press, 1995), 26.

10. M. Sandel, *Democracy's Discontent* (Cambridge, Mass.: Harvard University Press, 1996), 6.

11. Joseph Carens, 'Immigration, Political Community and the Transformation of Identity', 20.

12. Will Kymlicka defines 'societal culture' as 'a culture which provides its members with meaningful ways of life across the full range of human activities'. Kymlicka, *Multicultural Citizenship*, 76.

13. See Fernand Harvey, 'La question de l'immigration au Quebec. Genèse historique', in *Conseil de la langue française, Le Quebec français et l'école à clientèle pluriethnique. Contributions à une réflexion*, Coll. Documentation du Conseil de la langue française, 29 (Quebec: Éditeur officiel du Quebec), 1–55. See also Chapter 5 in this volume.

14. Gouvernement du Quebec, *Au Quebec pour bâtir ensemble. Énoncé de politique en matière d'immigration et d'intégration* (Ministère des communautés culturelles et de l'immigration du Quebec, Direction des communications, 1990), 15.

15. Jean-François Lisée, *Sortie de secours* (Montreal: Boréal, 2000). Lisée argues that among allophones (citizens whose mother tongue is neither French nor English), 51 per cent identified themselves as Canadian in 1979, while that number rose to 70 per cent in 1999. Lisée attributes this to an aggressive symbolic initiative by the federal government to tout the merits of Canadian citizenship in relation to the sovereignty movement in Quebec. See also Micheline Labelle and Daniel Salée, 'Immigrant and minority representations of citizenship in Quebec', in T. A. Aleinikoff and D. Klusmeyer, eds, *Citizenship Today: Global Perspectives and Practices* (Washington: Carnegie Endowment for International Peace, 2001).

16. See Alain-G. Gagnon and Raffael Iacovino, *Federalism, Citizenship and Quebec: Debating Multinationalism* (Toronto: University of Toronto Press, 2007), for elaboration on these principles.

17. Constitutional asymmetry refers to a legal framework in which some member-states enjoy different sets of jurisdictions vis-à-vis the others in the federal division of powers between the central government and the provinces.

18. Micheline Labelle, and Joseph J. Lévy, *Ethnicité et enjeux sociaux. Le Quebec vu par les leaders de groupes ethnoculturels* (Montréal, Liber, 1995).

19. For more on the phenomenon in which minority nations seek to create a separate democratic space vis-à-vis the majority nation, through concurrent and evolving nation-building processes, see G. Bourque, 'Between Nations and Society', in M. Venne, ed., *Vive Quebec: New Thinking and New Approaches to the Quebec Nation* (Toronto: James Lorimer and Company, 2001).

20. Micheline Labelle, and Daniel Salée, 'Immigrant and minority representations of citizenship in Quebec'.

21. For an excellent overview of the Canadian policy of multiculturalism, see the *Citizenship and Immigration Canada Ministry's* website devoted to the topic at www.cic.gc.ca/multi/index-eng.asp.

22. Marcel Gilbert, *Autant de façons d'être Québécois. Plan d'action à l'intention des communautés culturelles* (Quebec: Ministry of Communications, Direction générale des publications gouvernementales, 1981).

23. Gouvernement du Quebec, *Au Quebec pour bâtir ensemble.*

24. Gouvernement du Quebec, *Le français, une langue pour tout le monde*, Rapport de la Commission des États généraux sur la situation et l'avenir de la langue française au Quebec (Quebec: Gouvernement du Quebec, 2001).

25. Centres d'Orientation et de Formation des Immigrants; Programme d'étude des langues d'origine. The first was meant to provide French language instruction as well as to provide basic transitional services for newcomers, while the second was a program devoted to the maintenance of languages of origin, through educational programs specific to particular cultural groups and generally targeted to children.

26. Micheline Labelle, 'La politique de la citoyenneté et de l'interculturalisme au Quebec', in H. Greven-Borde and J. Tournon, eds, *Les identités en débat, intégration ou multiculturalisme?* (Paris: L'Harmattan, 2000), 269–94.

27. *Forum national sur la citoyenneté et l'intégration, Document de Consultation* (Quebec: Ministère des Relations avec les citoyens et de l'immigration, September, 2000), 20.

28. Jocelyn Maclure, 'Commission nationale sur la citoyenneté: pour une politique des relations civiques', *Le Devoir*, Montreal, Wednesday, 8 August 2001, A7.

29. *Le français, une langue pout tout le monde : une nouvelle approche stratégique et citoyenne* (Quebec: Commission des États généraux sur la situation et l'avenir de la langue française au Quebec, 2001), 14.

30. Gerard Bouchard, and Charles Taylor, 'Building the Future: A Time for Reconciliation', *Commission de Consultation sur les pratiques d'accommodement reliées aux différences culturelles* (Gouvernement du Quebec, 2008), 21.

31. See Will Kymlicka, *Finding Our Way: Rethinking Ethnocultural Relations in Canada* (New York: Oxford University Press, 1998); and Y. Abu-Laban and Christina Gabriel, *Selling Diversity: Immigration, Multiculturalism, Employment Equity and Globalization* (Peterborough, Ont.: Broadview Press, 2002).

32. Lucille Beaudry, Robert Comeau, and Guy Lachapelle, *Gérald Godin: Un Poète en Politique* (Montreal: Éditions de L'Hexagone, 2000), 106.

Relevant Websites

Government of Quebec. Immigration et Communautés culturelles: www.immigration-quebec.gouv.qc.ca/en/index.html
Useful website to find statistics on Quebec immigration.

Citizenship and Immigration Canada: www.cic.gc.ca/english/index.asp
Find more about statistics and Federal policies on Immigration.

Quebec Charter of Human Rights and Freedoms: www.cdpdj.qc.ca/en/commun/docs/charter.pdf
Complete English version of the Quebec Charter.

Quebec Charter of the French language: www.oqlf.gouv.qc.ca/english/charter/index.html
English version of the Quebec Charter of French Language.

Gagnon-Tremblay–McDougall Accord: www.parl.gc.ca/information/library/PRBpubs/bp252-e.htm#provincial
An English version of the Accord.

Au Quebec pour bâtir ensemble. Énoncé de politique en matière d'immigration et d'intégration: www.micc.gouv.qc.ca/publications/fr/ministere/Enonce-politique-immigration-integration-Quebec1991.pdf
The complete French version of this important Quebec State policy.

Larose Commission final report (French): www.spl.gouv.qc.ca/etatsrapport_pdf/COM1-021_Rapport_final.pdf
Final report of the Larose Commission.

Des Valeurs partagées, des intérêts communs: www.micc.gouv.qc.ca/publications/fr/planification/PlanAction20042007-integral.pdf
French version of this public policy on Immigration in Quebec.

Bouchard-Taylor Commission: www.accommodements.qc.ca/index-en.html
Final Report of the Commission.

Metropolis: http://canada.metropolis.net/index_e.html
Canadian research network on migration, diversity, and immigrant integration.

Select Bibliography

Blad, Cory, and Phillipe Couton. 'The Rise of an Intercultural Nation: Immigration, Diversity and Nationhood in Quebec', in *Journal of Ethnic and Migration Studies*, 35, 4 (2009): 645–77.

Carens, Joseph H. 'Cultural Adaptation and the Integration of Immigrants: The Case of Quebec'. Chapter 5 in *Culture, Citizenship and Community: A Contextual Exploration of Justice as Evenhandedness*. Oxford: Oxford University Press, 2000.

Gagnon, Alain-G. and Raffaele Iacovino. *Federalism, Citizenship and Quebec: Debating Multinationalism*. Toronto: University of Toronto Press, 2007.

Joppke, Christian, and Ewa Morawska. 'Integrating Immigrants in Liberal Nation-States: Policies and Practices'. In Joppke and Morawska, eds. *Toward Assimilation and Citizenship*. New York: Palgrave Macmillan, 2003.

Juteau, Danielle. 'The Citizen Makes and Entrée: Redefining the National Community in Quebec'. *Citizenship Studies* 6, 4 (2002): 377–94.

Karmis, Dimitrios. 'Pluralism and national Identity(ies) in Contemporary Quebec: Conceptual Clarifications, Typology, and Discourse Analysis'. In Alain-G. Gagnon, ed. *Quebec: State and Society*. 3rd edn. Peterborough, Ont.: Broadview, 2004, 69–96.

Kymlicka, Will. 'The Unhappy Marriage of Federalism and Nationalism'. Part Two in *Finding Our Way: Rethinking Ethnocultural Relations in Canada*. (Oxford: Oxford University Press, 1998), 127–81.

Labelle, Micheline, and Francois Rocher. 'Debating Citizenship in Canada: The Collide of Two Nation-Building Projects'. In P. Boyer, L. Cardinal, and D. Headon, eds. *From Subjects to Citizens: A Hundred Years of Citizenship in Australia and Canada*. Ottawa: University of Ottawa Press, 2004, 263–86.

McAndrew, Marie. 'Quebec's Interculturalism Policy: An Alternative Vision'. In Keith Banting, Thomas J. Courchene, and F. Leslie Seidle, eds. *Belonging? Diversity, Recognition and Shared Citizenship in Canada*. Montreal: IRPP, 2007,143–54.

Oakes, Leigh. 'French: A Language for Everyone in Quebec?' *Nations and Nationalism* 10, 4 (2004): 539–58.

Salée, Daniel. 'The Quebec State and the Management of Ethnocultural Diversity: Perspectives on an Ambiguous Record'. in Keith Banting, Thomas J. Courchene, and F. Leslie Seidle, eds. *Belonging? Diversity, Recognition and Shared Citizenship in Canada*. Montreal: IRPP, 2007,105–42.

CHAPTER 18

Interethnic Relations and Racism in Quebec

—Maryse Potvin, Université du Québec à Montréal

1701 The Great Peace of Montreal signed between France and 39 Aboriginal nations to end their conflicts.

1709 New France legalizes slavery through ordinance from Intendant Raudot. Practised since beginning of seventeenth century under Code Noir (adopted by France in 1685), slavery would continue under British regime in Quebec until it was abolished in 1833.

1759 Conquest of Quebec results in British dominance over French population, which is five times more numerous.

1816–51 Canada's first wave of massive immigration brings nearly one million British, Scottish, and Irish immigrants to Quebec City, Montreal, and other Atlantic ports.

1839 Lord Durham's *Report on the Affairs of British North America* recommends that British immigration be increased in Canada to speed cultural and linguistic assimilation of French Canadians.

1879–1914 Dominions Land Act (free land grants, 1872), John A. Macdonald's National Policy (1879), and the Sifton Plan (1896) are part of largest push in Canada's history to increase immigration. Immigrants are sought to colonize the West, set up farms, provide cheap labour force in industrial Ontario and Quebec, build Canada's national railway, and establish nation's infrastructure.

1880–5 Immigration policy restricts and excludes Asians (especially Chinese and Japanese) through quotas and taxation, and subsequently prohibits their entry into Canada outright (through legislation affecting Japanese immigration applicants in 1908 and Chinese Immigration Act of 1923).

1874–9 Deep recession causes massive exodus of French Canadians to United States. Between 1880 and 1890, nearly 150,000 (or 11.3 per cent of Quebec's population) leave the country. Between 1840 and 1930, one million emigrate southward.

1923 After First World War, Canada's federal government passes Empire Settlement Act to pursue its development of West through immigration.

1939–45 During Second World War, thousands of Jewish refugees, seeking refuge from Nazism, turned away from Canada. When Japan joins war, Canadians of Japanese ancestry interned in work camps or deported, and their property confiscated.

1946–61 Many Italian and British immigrants settle in Quebec, followed in numeric importance by Germans, Austrians, French, Greeks, and Jews from various countries (including numerous Holocaust survivors).

1947 First federal Citizenship Act creates legal status of 'Canadian Citizen', but is still based on an ethnic conception of 'nation' and the importance of preserving cultural homogeneity.

1952 Immigration Act establishes framework for managing immigration and grants major discretionary powers to immigration officers in selection of candidates. Eligibility and exclusion criteria remain unclear.

1956 Federal regulation clearly establishes hierarchy of ethnic preferences for Canadian immigration policy. Canada decides to prioritize immigrants from Commonwealth and northern Europe; then eastern Europe; southern Europe, Middle East, and Latin America; and Asian and Africa.

1962 New regulations abrogate preferential provisions for British, French, or American immigration candidates and replace them with 'objective' selection criteria, based on applicants' education level, employability, and professional and technical qualifications.

1967 Abolition of all preferential (or discriminatory) immigration provisions.

1968 'St Leonard School Crisis' triggered when a suburban Montreal school board decides to do away with bilingual classes and replace them with classes taught in French.

Creation of Quebec's first Ministry of Immigration (MIQ).

1971 Multiculturalism Policy of Canada passed.

1975 Quebec's Charter of Human Rights and Freedoms adopted, establishing fundamental rights of citizens as inalienable principles that take legal precedence over all other legislation.

1977 Charter of the French Language (Bill 101) passed, establishing links between integration

of immigrants and province's common public language.

1982 Canadian Charter of Rights and Freedoms entrenched in Canadian Constitution. Multiculturalism integrated into Charter.

1986 Federal Employment Equity Act adopted, introducing term *visible minority* and forcing companies under federal jurisdiction to adopt an equity plan for some target groups, including women, visible minorities, and Aboriginal peoples.

1988 Canadian Multiculturalism Act passed.

1990 Gagnon-Tremblay–McDougall Accord gives Quebec exclusive jurisdiction over integration and selection of 'independent' immigrants.

Policy Statement on Immigration and Integration adopted. It is subsequently updated in government's 2004 Action Plan, which best describes the Quebec model of interculturalism.

Oka standoff becomes a political crisis over Aboriginal land claims that lasts three months, pitting Mohawk nation and its allies against governments of Quebec and Canada.

2005 Canadian government passes *Canada's Action Plan Against Racism*, presented as pan-governmental effort against racism.

2006–8 Reasonable accommodation crisis. On 8 February 2007, Consultation Commission on Accommodation Practices Related to Cultural Differences (also known as the Bouchard-Taylor Commission) struck. It files its final report on 19 May 2008.

October 2008 The Quebec government unveils *Diversity: An Added Value: Government policy to promote participation of all in Québec's development*, which focuses on fighting discrimination based on sex, age, disability, social condition, sexual orientation, colour, and ethnic or national origin.

September 2009 Bill 16, 'An Act to promote action by the Administration with respect to cultural diversity' tabled, immediately contested, and indefinitely shelved.

Contrary to some received wisdom, Quebec has never been a homogeneous society. It is true that Quebecers of French-Canadian origin currently account for 78 per cent of the population, that 81.6 per cent of Quebecers speak French at home, and 83 per cent claim to be Catholic.[1] But historically, Quebec (and Canadian) society has been shaped by successive waves of population settlement, beginning with the Aboriginal peoples, followed by French and then British colonizers, and sustained by an increasingly diversified combination of newcomers.

Although Quebec's population has grown increasingly diverse and recent governments have adopted an inclusive public discourse, (backed by a substantial battery of measures to promote equality), there are still major gaps between this 'official' normative discourse on one hand and the reality of inter-group relations and their mutual representations on the other hand. Persistent instances of social malaise and racializing discursive 'slips' have been observed vis-à-vis immigration and the integration of newcomers to Quebec. Our hypothesis is that these instances of malaise seem to be linked to the fragile status of francophone Quebecers as a majority group and their attachment to the gains of 'modernity' in Quebec—the secularization of institutions, movements toward gender equality, and the entrenchment of French as the common public language.

This chapter sets forth some explanatory hypotheses about the gaps between official normative discourses and popular/media discourses in Quebec. It provides a snapshot of diversity and ethnic relations in the province, and more specifically examines racism in its shifts, empirical forms, and manifestations in social practices and discourses,[2] particularly in public debates (as we will show with the 'reasonable accommodation' debate). It also resituates the influence of Quebec–Canada relations within the problematics of racism in Quebec and the dual majority/minority identity status of francophone Quebecers of French-Canadian origin which permeates the province's social discourse on ethnic relations. It concludes with an appeal to bring broad-based civic education to a variety of settings in Quebec.

ETHNIC DIVERSITY AND INTER-GROUP RELATIONS

Ethnic pluralism, or pluriethnicity, is inherent to the history of Quebec and Canada. This land of Aboriginal peoples and French and British colonizers has also been a land of hope and sanctuary for many subsequent waves of immigrants, including the United Empire Loyalists, Black Americans using the Underground Railroad to escape slavery, the Irish fleeing the Great Potato Famine of 1847, the Chinese seeking work, and the Jewish people escaping pogroms and political problems in eastern Europe. Other more recent waves of immigration have followed.

However, many groups of immigrant origin were victims of classic racism, 'nativism',[3] and open, systemic discrimination until the 1960s. Black and Aboriginal peoples could be legally enslaved between 1709 and 1834, an episode of history that was long hidden by historians.[4] Canadian immigration policy was openly discriminatory until 1967, as its entry criteria effectively excluded or restricted the migration of many individuals of what we now call 'visible minority' groups. The policy specified that British and American immigrants were to be sought first, followed by northern Europeans. Southern Europeans were only somewhat tolerated and citizens from other continents, entirely undesirable. This institutionalized hierarchy of ethnic preferences led to the exclusion of non-Whites, to selective recruitment measures, and to quotas on applicants from Asia and the Indian sub-continent from the early twentieth century until the 1950s.

In 1967, the federal government abrogated all preferential and discriminatory provisions based on race, religion, culture, language, and national origin and replaced them with 'objective' selection criteria (e.g., education, occupational qualifications), which were to be applied to all prospective newcomers. The face of Quebec and the rest of Canada would quickly diversify as a result.[5] The number of immigrants of European origin decreased, whereas those from the 'Third World' increased. At the time of the 2006 census, 11.5 per cent of the population of Quebec was of immigrant origin (foreign-born) and 8.8 per cent belonged to 'visible minorities'.[6] The Montreal region was the place of elected residence for 89.6 per cent of Quebecers of immigrant origin and 90.2 per cent of those from visible minority groups. In Montreal, immigrant denizens made up 20.6 per cent of the population and 16.5 per cent were in the visible minority, a group that had grown by 28.8 per cent since 2001.[7] Of all the visible minority groups, 60 per cent were immigrants. Black Quebecers represented the largest visible minority in the province (189,000, or 2.5 per cent of the population): most lived in Montreal and 4 out of 10 were born in Canada. Most Quebec citizens of Arab and Latin American origin (numbering 109,000 and 89,500 respectively) also lived in Montreal and registered the fastest growth of any communities, with their numbers soaring by 48.6 per cent and 50.4 per cent between 2001 and 2006.[8]

NORMATIVE DISCOURSE AND SOCIAL REALITIES

Following the Second World War, immigration and the development of human rights at an international level forced democratic countries to adopt legislation and other measures to combat discrimination and inequalities. In the same spirit, since the 1970s, Quebec has been developing an inclusive 'official' normative discourse on diversity, and implementing a series of measures to defend the rights and facilitate the integration of newcomers to the province.[9] Despite this systemic and inclusive adaptation to diversity, a significant gap remains between normative discourse and the reality of inter-group relations and mutual representations. Three factors partly explain this gap: the shifts that have taken place in contemporary racism, the paradoxical situation of racism in Quebec, and the dual majority/minority status of francophone Quebecers.

Racism: Shifts, Mechanisms, and Processes

Today, racism is a paradoxical reality. While 'classic racism', based on biological materialism (peoples' physical attributes), has been discredited, there has been a resurgence in racism since the 1980s, notably in societies where anti-racist movements have progressively weakened[10] (as was the case with the labour movement in Europe). While these social and political struggles ran out of steam, a retreat into identity and the rise of populist figures took place. These elements came to typify a global shift in racism.[11]

But shifts in racism have also been attributable to its illegality and its illegitimacy in this era of human rights. Since the Second World War, systematized racism in the form of ideas, theories, and doctrines, based on the presumption that 'races' were unequal, has been replaced by a more implicit neo-racism of human rights, recentred around the dual theme of identity and difference, and founded on ostensibly more legitimate differentiation criteria.[12] Neo-racism's ideological terms changed (*culture* replaced *race*) along with its manifestations and discursive modes, which were implicit, indirect, and symbolic. The targets of neo-racism (those in the minority) were no longer constructed as biologically inferior, but as 'unassimilable', irreducible, or natural carriers of pathological differences, much as the presumed 'races' of yesteryear were.

Neo-racism continues to combine two processes: the differentiation and the 'inferiorization' of the Other, with difference (e.g., mores and beliefs) being constructed as a marker of social inferiority.[13] These indissociable processes, combined with socio-historical realities, have allowed racism to adapt to modernity.[14] Today, the process of domination-differentiation-inferiorization is no longer used to justify colonization[15] or the economic exploitation of immigrant workers, but serves instead to establish the inferiority of certain cultural practices as 'medieval' or 'barbaric' in order to preserve 'historically acquired rights', democratic values, or national unity. It is founded on the presumption that peoples or 'nations' exist rather than on the presumption that 'races' exist. Its manifestations in popular discourses clearly illustrate these shifts. The processes of neo-racism often appear to be natural reactions, coming from citizens who are 'legitimately' defending themselves against the 'imposition' by minorities from 'unassimilable' cultures that would erode 'historically acquired rights,' the order of things, a national identity, or the presumed unity of a people.

Contemporary neo-racism presents itself as being egalitarian, democratic, and respectable. It condemns flagrant forms of racism, deemed to be socially unacceptable from a human rights perspective, finding its justifications in irreproachable arguments, drawn from universalist and liberal concepts.[16] Therefore, neo-racism is not simply a reaction to migrations and demographic changes, but much more a result of cultural shifts and of global issues. In an age of mass media and new communications technologies, neo-racism is appearing as a by-product of the mediatization of power relations between groups in a context of globalization (neo-colonialism), and therefore of North–South relations and the prejudices and inequalities that these relations generate. Neo-racism tends to spread in symbolic and imagination-based modes, divorced from any real contact with members of different groups. Thus, neo-racism cannot be eliminated using institutional correctives alone. The subjective elements of constructing the Other will always escape state control, but contribute just as much to making racism a 'social fact,' acting upon inter-group relations in many forms (e.g., prejudices, discrimination) and drawing upon many sources (e.g., economic and historical differences).

While the manifestations and victims of racism have changed over the course of history, its structure, function, and *mechanisms* have stayed the same. Racism remains a process: the construction of irreducible differences prompted by power relations and serving to justify inferiorizing the Other to legitimate domination.[17] The underlying justifications are often emotional—based on feelings that privileges, prestige, property, security, or identity are being threatened. These feelings lead to the desire to destroy, inferiorize, or exclude the threat in order to defend a real or potential personal 'entitlement'. Differentiation and inferiorization operate based on sociocognitive mechanisms,[18] which we have defined and systematized in our discourse analyses as:

- *negative dichotomization* (Us–Them);
- *inferiorization* of the Other;
- *generalization* about an entire group;

- *self-victimization*;
- *catastrophism*;
- *demonization* of the Other;
- the *desire to expel* the Other ('Go back to where you came from'); and
- *political legitimation* (one of the upper echelons of neo-racism).[19]

These discursive mechanisms may be understood as echelons of racism, which are often linked to one another.

The effects of discrimination on society and its manifestations in society are many and may be fraught with ambiguity. For example, spatial segregation, which may be a strategy of social mobility among some groups, may not always be attributed to discrimination, but may result from it. Likewise, 'ethnic businesses', school failure, or socio-economic disparities may fuel racism or veer towards its production without being clearly attributable to it. Affirmative action programs or the obligation to make reasonable accommodation for various groups may correct the effects of discrimination or feed the ills that they are claiming to combat. Racism (or neo-racism) may be an instrumental cause or effect in many social phenomena. Its visibility and intensity fluctuate according to economic times, political events, everyday relationships, social sectors of life, and public debates.

A Paradoxical Situation in Quebec

The changes that have taken place in Quebec make it difficult to paint a clear picture of the state of racism in the province.[20] Overall, the situation is paradoxical. Viewed from one perspective, there is no racist political party in Quebec and racist violence is relatively rare. The extremist or neo-Nazi groups who kept police busy between 1989 and 1996 have almost all disappeared, as have most of the anti-racist groups that fought against them. Racism and xenophobia are less present in Quebec's public debates than they are in Europe, where extreme-right-wing parties are part of the political scene. Human rights jurisprudence has developed exponentially, but cases of violations cited by the Commission des droits de la personne et des droits de la jeunesse (CDPDJ) are relatively rare and few appear before the courts. Similarly, only rarely are major racist incidents the subject of public inquiries (as was the case in Montréal-Nord in 2008).[21] The number of Quebecers who openly call themselves racists has decreased and, in the aggregate, data on social mobility among some Quebecers of immigrant origin has been relatively positive.[22]

But viewed from another perspective, the situation has revealed itself as more complex. Public opinion polls or complaints filed with the CDPDJ do not paint an accurate picture of what racism and discrimination entail. Mutual representations between groups and everyday relationships in different sectors of society are difficult to measure. From the 1970s until the debate around 'reasonable accommodation' (2006–8), polls indicated that the public's attitudes towards immigration and diversity were increasingly favourable, but public behaviour did not reflect this trend. Hate-mongering websites were proliferating, cultural conflicts within institutions flared, racist conduct was taking place in the job and housing markets and in schools, and inequalities persisted for some minorities at the same time these opinion polls were conducted. And no indicators seemed to allow us to predict the inter-group perceptions and racializing discursive 'slips' in recent public debates about religion, territory, culture, and political opinions, which have morphed into 'social crises'.[23]

As in other egalitarian societies, the paradox in Quebec lies in the conflict between a system of democratic values and a system of complex interrelating historical oppressions and expressions of racism (in forms that are analytically interrelated but empirically scattered). This conflictual coexistence of systems affects some groups (e.g., Jewish, Black, Muslim, youth, women) differently than it does others.[24]

By and large, social practices in the media and in the housing and job markets have been escaping state control. In the job market, for example, unequal (often systemic) gaps between groups have usually been measured in terms of differential market access and integration experienced by foreign-born Quebecers, but also in terms of the differential distribution of status and of unequal opportunities between "White" and "non-White" Canadians. A segmentation and a double (ethnic and social) stratification of the job market have long been observed:[25] since 1971, census data has

shown a persistent trend towards an overrepresentation of visible minorities in both reduced- or high-qualification level jobs. This polarized job market profile reflects the bimodal nature of immigration in Canada (the effect of selection policies) and the dual bilinguistic job market (posing problems for those who are not linguistically qualified) in Quebec, both of which are difficult to separate from the phenomenon of racial discrimination.

Statistical analyses show enduring disparities between groups, which have been apparent in income gaps between foreign-born and native-born Canadians for two decades, in the declining economic well-being of newcomers, and in increased inequalities for some visible minorities.[26] The *Ethnic Diversity Survey* (EDS) conducted in 2002 by Statistics Canada revealed that incomes among visible minorities (notably Black Canadians) were substantially lower and their poverty levels higher than those among Canadians of "White" European ancestry. Employment rates and incomes among visible minorities have tended to increase with the duration of their residency in Canada, but gaps in relation to other Canadians have widened over time.[27] People from visible minorities were better educated on average than the population as a whole, but given the same level of education, had higher rates of unemployment and lower rates of representation in senior positions and in the public service. The quantitative studies in Quebec that have set forth a hypothesis of discrimination have, by adopting a residual approach, observed 'unexplained gaps' in income, unemployment, and employment among Black Quebecers.[28]

Similarly, second-generation Quebec youth from visible minorities have difficulties getting and keeping jobs—difficulties that are not attributable to insufficient academic qualifications or occupational skills. Since these youth were not foreign-born, they were fluent in French and familiar with job market practices, and their credentials were recognized.[29] Objectively speaking, their employment profiles were similar to or better than those of other young Quebecers: on average, their academic records, graduation rates, and levels of bilingualism or trilingualism were equal or superior to those of young Quebecers as a whole.[30] Nevertheless, their unemployment rates were markedly higher and they found they had to contend with prejudices from prospective employers.

Racism and Dual Majority/Minority Status among Francophones

Racism has also been the product of the historical Quebec–Canada relations surrounding the recent transition of francophones in Quebec from a minority status (French Canadians) to a majority status (Quebecers or Québécois). The age-old rivalry between francophones and anglophones in Canada has regulated relations between ethnic groups, still defined and stratified within a 'vertical mosaic'.[31] Power relations and competition between the two 'founding peoples', tinged with neo-racism,[32] have had some notable repercussions on the way that both majorities have addressed immigration and Aboriginal issues.

We may recall that in 1960s Quebec, when ethnic and class boundaries separated francophones and anglophones, some French Canadians took a dim view of immigrants, who tended to integrate into the anglophone community in hopes of boosting their social mobility. At that time, anglophones controlled the economy and job market in Montreal, lived in the best neighbourhoods, and enjoyed a level of prestige unequalled in the rest Canada. They also had well-developed and attractive institutions for integrating immigrants into their community.[33] French Canadians, who defined themselves as a dominated and exploited 'minority', therefore perceived immigration as a threat that the government of Quebec was not controlling. For these reasons, with a view to planning its own development, Quebec decided to involve itself in the process of selecting and integrating immigrants *into the francophone majority*. Immigration thereby became a major political issue and was perceived as a means of countering the demographic and linguistic decline of francophones in North America.

From that point forward, the sociological transition of francophones to the status of a 'majority people' oriented a civic, intercultural, and inclusive dominant normative discourse vis-à-vis the integration of immigrants *into the majority population*.[34] With this change of status and with the Parti Québécois taking office in 1976, normative discourse progressively dissociated itself from its former militant, anti-colonial rhetoric. Critical perspectives on relations of oppression and power essentially disappeared from social discourse by the end of the 1980s, in the wake of rising neo-liberalism. The focus shifted from denouncing the 'oppressive relationships' suffered by minority groups (including francophones of French-Canadian origin, who felt historically victimized) to integrating minorities into the new francophone-majority society. The discourse of national liberation as a minority people made way for a discourse of national assertion as a majority.

From the 1980s until 2006, the subject of racism in Quebec would fade from normative discourse, appearing as a marginal matter in official government policies, one that a more voluntarist integration policy would surely resolve. Successive governments would become increasingly reticent and guarded about taking action when accusations of racism were periodically directed at Quebec by the rest of Canada. In fact, for a long time, in the various halls of government, recognizing the existence of racism through public policy seemed tantamount to admitting that the Quebec model of integration had failed.

In a social and political context that had profoundly changed over the course of the 1990s, racism took on new forms in public debates. Owing to the successive failures that had marked the constitutional debate for 30 years, and to the many racializing discursive 'slips' in Quebec–Canada relations since 1995,[35] Quebec nationalism was no longer driven by the same social aspirations or the project of modernization that began in the Quiet Revolution. The spectre of 'referendum repeats' and the fear that integrating immigrants or meeting their demands for accommodation would cause the francophone Quebecers to disappear as a people seemed to foster a return to conservative nationalism.[36] At the same time, the referenda and constitutional failures that periodically exacerbated tensions between Canada's two majority groups had consequences for ethnic minorities in Quebec, who often found themselves stuck in the middle of debates and conflicts between the two 'founding peoples', much as Canada's Aboriginal peoples had been. Gone unchecked, this 'sandwiching' of Others sometimes made them easy targets for venting or scapegoating.[37]

This tendency surfaced near the end of the 1980s in the xenophobic overtones of the documentary film *Disparaître*. Similarly, when the 'No' side narrowly won the 1995 referendum, Quebec Premier Jacques Parizeau publicly declared that 'some ethnic votes' had helped vote down the sovereignty option.

The 'reasonable accommodation' debate (2006–8) would further illustrate how Quebec–Canada power relations negatively influenced the treatment of ethnic minorities.

The 'Reasonable Accommodation' Debate

The gap between 'official' normative discourse and other social discourses was palpable in the debate around reasonable accommodation, which lasted over two years in the Quebec media. This 'crisis' highlighted the state of ethnic relations, mutual intergroup perceptions, and specific sensitivities related to the still-recent transition of francophones to a majority status in Quebec. It brought to the fore the perception gap between Montreal Quebecers and those in other regions, along with the dearth of knowledge among some of the public about the realities of immigration and the measures and infrastructure devoted to integration and human rights. It also opened a forum for populist and racist discourses, which were often used unconsciously in public and journalistic opinion.[38]

The debate began to crystallize in the media in March 2006,[39] and morphed into a 'crisis' by January 2007. In a context of media one-upmanship and proliferating racializing discourses, on 8 February 2007, as a matter of apparent urgency and at the beginning of his election campaign, Premier Jean Charest struck the Consultation Commission on Accommodation Practices Related to Cultural Differences (also known as the Bouchard-Taylor Commission). Many Quebecers said they had the impression that they had been transported back in time 'to Quebec pre-1977,

JUANITA WESTMORELAND-TRAORÉ: BLAZING A TRAIL FOR HUMAN RIGHTS

Juanita Westmoreland-Traoré, Officer of the Ordre national du Québec

Source: CP PHOTO/ Windsor Star-Scott Webster

In Quebec, Juanita Westmoreland-Traoré is known mainly as the province's first judge of African-Canadian descent. In the rest of Canada, she is known for being the first—and, to date, the only—Black dean of a Canadian law faculty. But these achievements are only a small part of her career path and social activism, which have been guided by a deep devotion to defending the rights and dignity of her fellow citizens.

Quebec-based lawyer Juanita Westmoreland-Traoré was born in Verdun (on the Island of Montreal), a second-generation Quebecer whose English-speaking parents originated from Guyana, South America. As a teenager, young Juanita was steeped in the excitement of the anti-discrimination and civil rights movements of the 1950s, working as the secretary of her high school's Negro Citizenship Association. These were the awe-inspiring days of America's Black civil rights movements. Hopeful Black students were risking their lives to enrol in White schools and universities. Martin Luther King and his Southern Christian Leadership Conference were taking unprecedented stands to demand civil rights, like the year-long bus boycott in 1955, after Rosa Parks was arrested for refusing to give up her bus seat to a White person. These courageous movements made a lasting impression on the girl from Verdun. She was particularly influenced by Thurgood Marshall, lead counsel for the National Association for the Advancement of Colored People, who in 1967 became the first Black person to be appointed as a US Supreme Court judge. Westmoreland-Traoré resolved to follow in Marshall's footsteps, aspiring to use the law as a tool for social action in the cause of underprivileged and defenceless people. After earning a law degree at Université de Montréal and a Doctorate of State in Public Law at Université de Paris II, she was called to the Quebec Bar in 1969, specializing in immigration and citizenship, human rights, and family law.

Within the first months of her career as a newly minted lawyer, Maître Westmoreland-Traoré's skills were put to the test. It was 1969 and she was one of two Black lawyers practising in Quebec (the other was her uncle). Some Concordia University students had been charged with illegally occupying and ransacking the university computer centre. They had occupied the premises to protest against the trivializing approach that Concordia University administration had taken regarding some allegations of racism. As part of a team of defence attorneys, Westmoreland-Traoré helped have these students acquitted of 11 of the 12 charges filed against them in what would become a landmark case.

Not surprisingly, the determined lawyer's pursuits quickly diversified. In addition to her private practice, she was an assistant professor at the Université de Montréal's Faculty of Law and then a half-time professor in the Department of Legal Science at Université du Québec à Montréal. It was around this time that she became a member of the Office de protection des consommateurs du Québec and served as a Commissioner on the Canadian Human Rights Commission.

Westmoreland-Traoré also found time to write several significant articles in the *Revue du Barreau* and for the Presses de l'Université de Montréal. She collaborated on the *Rapport sur les attentes de la Communauté noire relatives au système d'éducation publique* for the Conseil supérieur de l'Éducation du Québec and worked with the implementation committee for the *Plan d'action en faveur des communautés culturelles*. In 1985, Westmoreland-Traoré played a major role in establishing the Conseil des communautés culturelles

et de l'immigration, which she chaired for five years. During her term of office at the Conseil, she was active in the development of the 1986 *Declaration on by the Government of Quebec on Ethnic and Race Relations*, which committed the government of Quebec to recognize and promote the right to non-discrimination for minorities in fulfillment of its responsibilities under international conventions.

In the 1990s, her career rose to new heights within Canada and abroad as she became the Ontario Employment Equity Commissioner for five years and subsequently worked in Haiti as an advisor to United Nations' Truth and Justice Committee. Becoming Dean of the University of Windsor's Faculty of Law, and Quebec Court judge, in the Criminal and Penal Division and the Youth Division, she also marked two more firsts for African-Canadians in Quebec.

As a judge, the Honourable Justice Westmoreland-Traoré has made noteworthy rulings, which have set pioneering precedents in the area of discrimination. For instance, in a 2005 ruling, she acquitted a young Black man charged with drug possession for the purposes of trafficking on the grounds that the city of Montreal's police department had used an illegal method of racial profiling. Before this case, no Quebec tribunal had ruled in this way on this kind of case.

The list of honours bestowed upon Westmoreland-Traoré is long and substantial. She has been appointed as an officer of the Ordre national du Québec and received honorary doctoral degrees from both the University of Ottawa and Université du Québec à Montréal. She holds a medal from Université de Montréal for her extraordinary contribution to human rights; the Alan Rose Award for human rights; the Jackie Robinson Achievement Award, conferred on Black individuals who are models of success and contribute to their community; the Canadian Bar Association's Touchstone Award, for her outstanding contribution to the promotion of equality in Canada's legal community; the Mérite Christine-Tourigny, awarded by the Quebec Bar for her social involvement and contribution to the advancement of women in the legal profession; and the Droits et Libertés award from Quebec's Commission des droits de la personne et des droits de la jeunesse, for her unflagging commitment to the fight against discrimination, on the occasion of the sixtieth anniversary of the Universal Declaration of Human Rights.

Behind all of these honours lies the public's appreciation for Juanita Westmoreland-Traoré's resolute devotion to fighting discrimination on many fronts, from community to institutional settings. At the community level, she has served as legal counsel to the Congress of Black Women of Canada, the Black Community Centre and the Association québécoise des organismes de Coopération internationale. She has travelled to observe trials and elections for the international missions organized by Ligue des droits et libertés, Centre d'information et de documentation sur l'Afrique australe, and the South Africa Education Fund. She has worked with Centraide of Greater Montreal, sat on the Canadian Civil Liberties Association Board of Directors, served on the Canadian Human Rights Foundation executive, acted as a panellist with the Canadian Council on Social Development Court Challenges Program, presided over the Montreal Regional Committee of the National Congress of Black Women, been a member of the Consultative Committee on Education of the National Judicial Institute and of the Board of Directors of the Canadian Institute for the Administration of Justice,

and chaired the Canadian Association of Provincial Court Judges' Equality and Diversity Committee.

Throughout her long career, Juanita Westmoreland-Traoré was often struck by the dearth of resources for judges in cases that involved diversity and equality. With this in mind, during her tenure on the Board of Directors of the Canadian Chapter of the International Association of Women Judges, she co-coordinated the publication of a judicial guide to these issues that encourages judges to carefully consider social context as a matter of course when interpreting the law—a practice that Westmoreland-Traoré holds to be crucial to the balanced evolution of Canada's jurisprudence. The guide contains dozens of articles on doctrine and jurisprudence. It addresses grounds for discrimination, such as race, age, disability, and impoverishment (drawn from human rights legislation) as factors that intersect within a social context to produce social inequality between citizens of the same country.

Juanita Westmoreland-Traoré has used her renown and resources to raise awareness about the unstable living conditions faced by poor and vulnerable citizens (especially women and children) in Quebec, Canada, and abroad. Having seen the ravages of poverty, war, genocide, and crimes against humanity, she has worked ardently to make her voice heard in some of the world's most respected organizations.

when the French Canadian nation saw itself as being homogeneous and experienced its relationship to the Other in terms of an identity-based threat'.[40]

In this debate, the juridical-political apparatus and normative discourse were called into question and virulently criticized by a host of citizens and journalists. Quebec's Charter of Human Rights and Freedoms, Canada's Charter of Rights and Freedoms, and the obligation of making reasonable accommodation were presented as unidirectional legal instruments in human rights jurisprudence that forced public institutions to always accept requests for accommodation from minority groups, and even to grant them privileges. Journalists set about scrutinizing public policies on immigration and integration and their application, looking for a fight. During the debate, media confusion

over the concept of reasonable accommodation, its objectives, limitations, and application led some citizens and municipal politicians to request that governments change the Charters, or even abolish them, in response to this 'state of emergency'[41] and to the 'injustice' done to Quebec's majority group.

The role of the media was central in turning this debate into a social crisis, through its strategies and selective coverage of social discourses.[42] Some of the media's processes, framing, and staging around 'reasonable accommodations' allowed it to set the political agenda and generate a state of 'Moral Panic'.[43] Some journalists contributed to fuelling the pervasive confusion by conflating 'reasonable accommodation' (which is an obligation and a remedial measure used to address a discriminatory situation) with voluntary adjustments or private agreements, which did not result from the violation of a fundamental freedom. Indeed, over 75 per cent of the 'incidents' reported by journalists regarding 'reasonable accommodations' between March 2006 and April 2007 were private agreements or anecdotal current events that they blew out of all proportion.

Some newspapers went out of their way to break one news story after another, thereby elevating a collection of anecdotal events to the rank of a 'social crisis'. Using a sweeping array of public opinion polls about 'racism among Quebecers', daily spot polls and 'exclusive news investigations', these newspapers began constructing issues, 'storytelling', and 'agenda setting'[44] for public debate, forcing politicians and citizens alike to take a stand on a number of questions. Their over-the-top magnification of events had a huge influence on the public and the political agenda during this period.

The way journalists framed their stories (their 'angle') and the importance they attributed to some points of view allowed them to influence the public's understanding of the issues. Two ways of framing stories were unmistakably used by the media: a legal-juridical frame and a dramatic-conflictual frame. The legal-juridical frame, which was the starting point for most 'breaking' news stories, misled the public or, at the very least, fed public confusion by erroneously associating private agreements with reasonable accommodations. Requests for accommodation were often presented from the angle of 'privileges' or 'abuses'[45] rather than presenting a citizen's right to equality or to negotiated agreements. The dramatic-conflictual frame was used in polarized interpretations of events and in the race for fresh content, be it real or imagined. The angle of polarization between minority and majority groups intimated that some minorities enjoyed privileges and threatened common values, thereby engaging readers of the majority group in a victimizing reading of events.

Media Coverage: Factual Treatment and Opinion Discourses

Our analysis of the factual media coverage of events revealed that the media contributed to exacerbating popular prejudices towards certain minorities by covering events in the following ways:

- Publishing images of the minority members of religious minority groups—Muslim women wearing nikabs or burkas; Ultra-Orthodox Jews (Hasidim)
- Running headlines and leads that featured populist quotes from the Action démocratique du Québec (ADQ) party (a populist right-wing party)
- Conducting daily spot polls, often from a victimizing point of view—'Are you fed up with . . . ?'
- Mainly quoting people who viewed themselves as victims
- Participating in herd behaviour (in print, television, radio, and Web), in which media responded to each other
- Producing copious amounts of 'exclusives' and 'breaking news' in competition with other newspapers, upping the ante in front-page headline news and media hype
- Passing off hypothetical, fictitious events[46] as examples of social deviancy, anti-social behaviour, or non-conformity to majority-group norms, thereby building momentum for what is called a 'deviancy amplification spiral' in Moral Panic theory
- Providing disproportionately extensive coverage of a small-scale phenomenon (there were only a handful of bona fide cases of reasonable accommodations at the time)
- Staging the defining issue of the election campaign

Indeed, the debate was used as a 'hot-button' issue and a decorative prop in staging the 2007 February–March provincial election campaign. Constantly solicited to comment on 'breaking news,' obliging politicians helped to artificially prolong the media-driven debate. Politicians hazarded opinions without investigating the veracity of the facts related by journalists or distinguishing anecdotal information from real cases of accommodation. 'Breaking news' could therefore be used as a kind of litmus test to judge the competency of public figures.

At this time, numerous journalists attributed the rise in popularity of ADQ to the populist positions taken in the debate by its leader, Mario Dumont. Claiming to speak on behalf of the majority, daring to 'say out loud what everyone is thinking', Dumont politically legitimated populist discourse by constantly accusing his political adversaries of being 'lax' on the issue of reasonable accommodation, by favouring a 'hard-line' approach, and by making striking declarations such as 'We cannot defend our identity with one knee [already] on the ground'.[47] This type of legitimation became commonplace and even banal in the media, whereas one year earlier, the issue would not have found a public tribune. Letters to the editor made ample use of Dumont's populist expressions—'wear the pants', 'one knee [already] on the ground', and 'bending to the demands of minorities'—which were reprised in scores of articles on current events.

Our analysis of opinion discourses—based on a corpus of 654 editorials, columns, and letters to the editor from intellectuals and readers published in Quebec's five major newspapers—revealed that populist and (neo-)racist discursive mechanisms were explicitly and implicitly present in half of the texts. Any of the eight discursive mechanisms specified in our analytical grid could be found in 14 per cent of the editorials/columns and 52 per cent of letters from readers.[48] Some opinion discourses combined a range of discursive mechanisms from our grid:

1. Us–Them *negative dichotomization* ('They come to our country to impose their ways on us')
2. *Generalization* about all immigrants or all members of a minority ('They're not integrating into society'; 'They're all fundamentalists')
3. *Inferiorization* of the Other ('They're still living in the Middle Ages')
4. *Self-victimization* ('one knee [already] on the ground'; loss of power and identity; 'They come along and impose their customs on us/get privileges')
5. *Catastrophism* (state of emergency; conspiracy theories; 'Things will only get worse')
6. *Demonization* (invasion; the Other being 'unassimilable' to democratic values; 'They are strange, unpredictable, and worrisome')
7. Justification for the *desire to expel* the Other ('Go back where you came from')
8. Appeals for *political legitimation* (through elected ADQ politicians or municipal representatives, like those in Hérouxville, who proposed that a 'code of conduct' for immigrants be adopted)

The momentum of these discursive mechanisms drove the issue into an upward spiral, from one echelon to the next between March 2006 and April 2007, as though their almost banal presence in the media had legitimated taking a harder line.

Among the opinion discourses of newspaper editors, columnists, and intellectuals, these mechanisms were most often found in articles about Hassidic Jews. Negative dichotomization tended to be used to contrast majority values (defined as those of Quebec's 'citizens' or 'society') with those of the Jewish Hassidic community, notably in the area of gender equality (which was posited as irreducible and non-negotiable) to demonstrate that the community had not adapted to a 'modern' way of life. Derision was frequently used by these journalists and intellectuals, along with absurd humour and extreme examples, to denounce the potential escalation of 'hare-brained' requests and to weigh up the 'limits' that had been breached. Many associated making 'reasonable accommodations' with 'fundamentalism', contrasting the progression of religious fundamentalisms in the public sphere with the 'laxity' of Quebecers regarding requests made by minorities. For some, this contrast implicitly expressed victimhood or catastrophism.

More readers than journalists wrote about feeling their values and cultural points of reference were being threatened and that they, as members of the majority, had been wronged by minorities, who would 'abuse' the 'laxity' of 'Quebecers', or by judges, politicians, or institutions that would 'unduly' grant 'privileges' to the minorities, whom these readers perceived to be 'fundamentalist'. We observed a sense of distance and powerlessness in relation to the political and juridical authorities that were purportedly making disembodied decisions contrary to 'popular will'. The federal and provincial Charters and the power of judges were sharply criticized in two contradictory tendencies of popular discourse: the Charters seemed to be allowing what they forbade by granting rights to people whose collective religious beliefs ran contrary to individual rights and the choices of the 'majority'. Many blamed judges, the Supreme Court, or the Charters for this situation and questioned their ability to serve the population. Whereas some argued in favour of amending the Charters, others questioned the soundness of their principles and their adequacy for dealing with present-day realities.

Dominant representations of the Other in this racializing discourse saw a major Us–Them dichotomization. Among readers, 'Them' generally referred to recent immigrants and foreigners, often amalgamated as Sikh–Muslims and even Islamicist–fundamentalists. A number of opinion discourses about religious minorities also depicted 'Them' as 'fundamentalists', and singled them out as causing various kinds of social unrest around identity, in a context of destabilizing international events. The rigidity of the 'precepts' in these communities was often contrasted with the hard-fought 'rights and freedoms' historically acquired by native-born civil society and social movements. Some made the distinction between 'good immigrants' who 'wanted' to integrate into society (by becoming 'just like Us') and 'bad immigrants' (who demanded accommodation, and were therefore seen to be refusing Quebec's 'common values'). Those who wished to continue to live 'as they did in their own country' were not part of 'Us'.

There was also a perception that the Charters had violated the rights of some (the majority) to create privileges for others (the minority), rather than protecting rights (equality) as the central value of Quebec's collective identity. In some discourses, we observed an inversion of the Charters' values for the purposes of 'delegitimating' and inferiorizing the 'Other'. The refusal to accept divergence and the demand for 'loyalism' (or for a presumably consensual social conformity) therefore displaced respect for rights and freedoms. The equality of individuals was replaced by the conviction that favouritism was being shown to certain groups and an injustice done to other citizens; the 'inclusive Us' became a drive for homogeneity. Racializing discursive mechanisms were based on the conviction that they represented the 'universal' and on a stereotypical and even mythical representation of those who stood accused of opposing it.

SNAPSHOT

A Policy to Fight Racism in Quebec

Until recently, the issues of racism and discrimination were practically absent from 'official' normative discourse in Quebec. The government's *Policy Statement on Immigration and Integration* in 1990 and its *Policy on Educational Integration and Intercultural Education* in 1998 devoted only a few lines to racism and framed the issue as a potential individual transgression rather than a systemic phenomenon. Portions of Quebec's anti-poverty legislation (Bill 112) and its *National Strategy to Combat Poverty and Social Exclusion,* targeted 'immigrants' and 'visible minorities' as 'vulnerable groups', but did not discuss the sociological mechanisms that interlink racism, discrimination, social inequalities, and exclusion. There has been a reticence or guarded attitude in Quebec toward dealing directly with racism, naming it, and introducing it into public policies as an issue to combat. There has also been a fragmentation of provincial initiatives, instead of a systemic, coherently applied approach, based on the effectiveness of human rights regarding equity, equality, diversity, and anti-poverty issues.[49]

Institutional responses regarding these issues have remained ambivalent and often circumstantial or sporadic. Generally speaking, racism elicits a reaction from Quebec's public authorities when it leads to excessive racializing discursive 'slips' (as occurred in public debates around reasonable accommodation) or to violence, but it is often treated as a marginal, individual loss of control, as though it was not an issue that plays out every day as the cause or effect of social inequalities. Consequently, the struggle against racism and discrimination has been left to the field of law and to the legal apparatus, but has not become part of public discourse or of a coherent overall policy to more comprehensively address the mechanisms that perpetuate discriminations and unequal power relations.

During the summer of 2006, the Quebec government struck a parliamentary commission to address racism and discrimination. The commission launched public consultations based on a document entitled *Towards a government policy to fight against racism and discrimination*, the provincial follow-up document to the federal government's 2005 *Canada's Action Plan Against Racism* (itself much awaited and called for by numerous groups and observers after the World Conference on Racism, Racial Discrimination, Xenophobia and Related Intolerance in Durban, South Africa in 2001). Nevertheless, because of the media crisis and the populist political 'slips' on 'reasonable accommodation', which shook Quebec from 2006 until 2008, it was not until after the Consultation Commission on Accommodation Practices Related to Cultural Differences (also known as the Bouchard-Taylor Commission) that a government policy was adopted in this area. Indeed, in November of 2008, a few days before a provincial election was called, the Liberal government of Quebec launched *Diversity: An Added Value: Government policy to promote participation of all in Québec's development*. This policy was met with total indifference by the media and public opinion alike. It promoted equal opportunity and supported anti-racist and anti-discriminatory initiatives, which had been neglected in the 1990 *Policy Statement* and in government actions during the intervening years. The new policy proposed a comprehensive approach, covering education and awareness-raising, prevention, redress of injury to rights, mobilization of institutions and diversity management, victim support, and the suppression of racist violence. It was built around three main orientations:

Recognizing and combatting prejudices and discrimination by ensuring that all citizens are educated about their rights;

Renewing practices through real equality and the full participation of all citizens in Quebec's economic, social, and cultural development, by promoting access to and advancement in employment; and

Coordinating efforts to ensure coherence and complementarity in government programs.

The action plan, which includes 21 measures, collectively targets all provincial government bodies and ministries.

In order to implement some specific aspects of the action plan, Minister of Immigration Yolande James tabled Bill 16, *An Act to promote action by the Administration with respect to cultural diversity* on 22 September 2009, which quickly rekindled the controversy around 'reasonable accommodation'. The bill was meant to ensure that government bodies would establish and follow accountability directives and rules on 'diversity management' to set a good example by integrating Quebecers of all origins and providing high-quality services to an increasingly diversified clientele.

Some, such as the Conseil du statut de la femme, viewed this bill as an unlimited obligation imposed by the state to adapt to diversity. The Conseil pointedly remarked that the government had not placed any demands on new Quebecers to respond in kind by adapting to Quebec society. Others even viewed the bill as a setback or a reversal of the 'moral contract' between minority and majority groups, as described in the 1990 *Policy Statement*. The Conseil du statut de la femme proposed a number of amendments, asserting that the principles of secularism, gender equality, and the promotion of the French fact should guide the interpretation of this bill.

In the end, this initiative was shelved indefinitely and did not follow the usual path of bills in the National Assembly. With this bill, the explosive question of reasonable accommodation came back to haunt the Charest government, which was accused of placing religious freedom above gender equality. Still unsettled and unsettling, the actions proposed in this bill and the recommendations of the Bouchard-Taylor Commission have also been shelved.

The problem of 'racial profiling' that has affected relations between police and some racialized groups, a problem that requires a broader government response, has also not yet been addressed with concrete action. Indeed, following events in the summer of 2008 in Montréal Nord, when an altercation with police led to the shooting death of a Latino youth, and a spectacular riot ensued in this underprivileged, stigmatized neighbourhood, still grappling with its criminal gang problems, the Commission des droits de la personne et des droits de la jeunesse (CDPDJ) held public consultations on racial profiling. It put out a call to hear from youth aged 14 to 25 originating from racialized communities, along with groups and individuals who might offer solutions to this problem. According to the CDPDJ, it has received approximately 60 complaints regarding racial profiling from all over Quebec and has presented about 10 profiling cases before the Tribunal des droits de la personne. The report on the CDPDJ's consultations, slated for release in the fall of 2010, could pressure the government to accelerate the implementation of a new bill and a policy better designed to fight racism.

Conclusion

This chapter has shown that there is a major gap between the development of Quebec's inclusive and pluralistic official discourse on one hand, and the persistence of exclusion and discrimination (in addition to public debates tinged with fears over identity and racializing discourses) on the other hand. We have also seen that because racism is constantly shifting, it is difficult to measure progress in ethnic relations.

The debate around 'reasonable accommodation' revealed that inclusive, egalitarian discourse does not seem to have entirely penetrated the fabric of Quebec society. On the contrary, this debate led to something of a backlash against 'official' normative discourse, leaving the floor wide open for racializing discourses whose mechanisms inverted the values entrenched in both federal and provincial Charters. Major 'Us–Them' boundaries and guarded conceptualizations about Quebec identity persist to this day in some sectors of public opinion and among certain politicians. The controversy was first engaged through one-upmanship in the media, then in the political arena with the ADQ leader's declarations and the racializing 'slips' from some elected municipal officials (e.g., Hérouxville's code of conduct), reaching a state of 'crisis'. Within a few weeks, the crisis had spiralled past several echelons of racism and affected social cohesion in Quebec.

This crisis was not just a sudden expression of exasperation and scapegoating that involved religious minorities. It was, and is, a *symptom* of the fragility of Quebec's identity as a national entity (as a people). This fragility has been caused by social and economic upheaval in a context of globalization, and draws upon the historical malaise created by competitive relations between Quebec and the rest of Canada over the allegiance of immigrants, in matters both linguistic and symbolic. Social malaise (linked to the fragility of the majority status of francophones) was manifested in discourses that were strongly opposed to the Charters, Canadian multiculturalism, and the 'power of judges'. They took the form of a series of insecurities in opinion discourses: fears of losing the recent gains of Quebec's modernity (e.g., gender equality, francization); fears regarding the majority's ability to conceptualize itself as a bigger, more inclusive 'Us' ('Nous') that could successfully integrate immigrants; fears of being called 'racist' by the rest of Canada[50] and the world; and, in sum, fears about the success or failure of the Quebec model of integration.

According to many front-line workers in education and social services, reasonable accommodation is generally well managed day-to-day in communities. The large gap between reality and perceptions in this debate shows us how valuable education in human rights, diversity, citizenship, critical media analysis, and the management of reasonable accommodation and conflicts can be.

Questions for Consideration

1. What is contemporary neo-racism?
2. What kinds of neo-racist discursive mechanisms have we seen manifested in social discourses?

3. In what way did the dual majority/minority status of Quebec francophones permeate the debate around 'reasonable accommodation'?

Notes

1. *The Evolving Linguistic Portrait*, 2006 Census, Catalogue no. 97-555-XWE2006001; Ministère des Relations avec les citoyens et de l'Immigration, *Données sur la population recensée en 2001 portant sur la religion. Analyse sommaire*. Direction de la population et de la recherche, 27 May 2003.
2. Marc Angenot defines social discourse as 'the aggregate of all that is said and written in a state of society, to the extent that this aggregate does not appear to be composed of *random* statements, but of [statements] governed by conventions, held within ideological configurations.' Our translation of (*Glossaire pratique de la critique contemporaine*. La Salle: Hurtubise HMH, 1979: 63) M. Angenot, 'Théorie du discours social,' *COnTEXTES*, numéro 1, Discours en contexte (September 2006). http://contextes. revues.org/document51.html, accessed 15 August 2008.
3. 'Nativism' was an ideology that aimed to favour those born in Canada and exclude foreigners.
4. Marcel Trudel, *Deux siècles d'esclavage au Québec*. Montreal: Hurtubise HMH, 2004; Brett Rushforth, 'A Little Flesh We Offer You': The Origins of Indian Slavery in New France. *The William and Mary Quarterly*, Third Series 60, 4 (October 2003): 777–808.
5. Ethnic diversity is measured in three (self-declared) categories in the Canadian Census: foreign-born (immigrant), visible minority, and ethnic origins (ancestry). Second-generation Canadians are counted through a question about their parents' country of origin.
6. *Visible minority* is an official term in the Employment Equity Act (1986). It refers to 'persons, other than Aboriginal peoples, who are non-Caucasian in race or non-white in colour'. In the 2006 census, this category included persons of Chinese, South Asian, Black, Filipino, Latin American, Southeast Asian, Arab, West Asian, Korean, and Japanese origin.
7. The 2006 census showed that 851,600 people living in Quebec were foreign-born, an increase of 20.5 per cent compared with 2001. Statistics Canada, 2007, Immigration and Citizenship Highlight Tables, 2006 Census, Statistics Canada, Catalogue no. 97-557-XWE2006002. Ottawa. Released 4 December 2007. Statistics Canada. 2008. Topic-Based calculations. Ethnic Origin and Visible Minorities. Catalogue no. 97-562-XCB2006011.
8. Haiti was the place of birth for 52.5 per cent of Quebec's Black immigrants. Among Quebecers of Arab origin, 71.9 per cent were foreign-born, mainly in Morocco (26.4 per cent), Lebanon (22.1 per cent) and Algeria (20.1 per cent), and most (100,000) lived in Montreal. There were 75,400 Latin Americans in Quebec in 2006, representing 2.1 per cent of the population of Montreal.
9. Quebec's Charter of Human Rights and Freedoms (1975) and Charter of the French Language (1977), which established links between the integration of immigrants and the recognition of minorities and Quebec's common public language; the Commission des droits de la personne et des droits de la jeunesse, and the Tribunal des droits de la personne; the Affirmative Action Program; major developments in legislation and jurisprudence in this area and the adoption of official policies, including the recent policy to fight against racism and discrimination (2008) (see 'A Policy to Fight Racism in Quebec' in this chapter).
10. Michel Wieviorka, *L'espace du racisme* (Paris: Le Seuil, 1991).
11. Pierre-A. Taguieff, *La force du préjugé* (Paris: La Découverte, 1987); Martin Barker, *The New Racism* (London: Junction Books, 1981), and many others.
12. Étienne Balibar, 'Y-a-t-il un 'néo-racisme'?' in E. Balibar and I. Wallerstein, *Race, Nation, Classe. Les identités ambiguës* (Paris, La Découverte, 1988); Pierre-André Taguieff, *Face au racisme 2. Analyses, hypothèses, perspectives* (Paris, La Découverte, 1991); Taguieff, *La force du préjugé*.
13. Colette Guillaumin, *L'idéologie raciste. Genèse et langage actuel* (Paris: Mouton, 1972).
14. Alain Touraine, 'Le racisme aujourd'hui' in M. Wieviorka, ed., *Racisme et modernité* (Paris: La Découverte, 1993).
15. John Rex and David Mason, eds., *Theories of Race and Ethnic Relations* (Cambridge: Cambridge University Press, 1986); Balibar and Wallerstein, *Race, Nation, Classe*.
16. In fact, democratic and universalist values, as entrenched in the charters of Canada and Quebec, were inverted for the purpose of inferiorizing the Other (perceived as being barbaric, particularistic, or communitaristic). Maryse Potvin, 'Les dérapages racistes à l'égard du Québec au Canada-anglais depuis 1995', *Politique et Sociétés* 18, 2 (1999): 101–32; Maryse Potvin, 'Some Racist "Slips" About Quebec in English Canada between 1995 and 1998', *Canadian Ethnic Studies* 32, 2 (2000): 1–26.

17. Albert Memmi, *Le racisme* (Paris: Gallimard, 1982, 1994).

18. These are sociocognitive (social and cognitive) mechanisms because they appeal simultaneously to people's personal reasoning abilities and draw upon the political, ideological, historic, social, economic, or cultural determinants that are specific to a given context.

19. See Potvin, 'Les dérapages racistes', 'Some Racist "Slips" About Quebec'; Maryse Potvin, *Crise des accommodements raisonnables. Une fiction médiatique?* (Montreal: Athéna Éditions, 2008); Maryse Potvin et al., *Les médias écrits et les accommodements raisonnables. L'invention d'un débat* (Montreal, January 2008), available at www.accommodements.qc.ca/documentation/rapports/rapport-8-potvin-maryse.pdf.

20. Marie McAndrew and Maryse Potvin, *Le racisme au Québec : éléments d'un diagnostic*, Collection Études et Recherches N°13, Ministère de l'Immigration et des Communautés Culturelles (Quebec: Éditeur officiel du Québec,1996); Maryse Potvin, 'Racisme et discrimination au Québec : réflexion critique et prospective sur la recherche,' in Jean Renaud, Annick Germain, and Xavier Leloup, eds., *Racisme et discrimination : permanence et résurgence d'un phénomène inavouable*. (Quebec: Presses de l'Université Laval, 2004), 172–96.

21. A number of investigations were conducted in 1980–90. Most notably, the Commission des droits de la personne et des droits de la jeunesse has investigated racial discrimination experienced by Haitian nurses (1992–3) and by Black taxi drivers (1982–5), along with some blunders committed by police (Bellemare and Yarovski Reports, 1987 and 1992).

22. Jean Renaud et al, *Ils sont maintenant d'ici. Les dix premières années au Québec des immigrants admis en 1989*. Études, Recherche et Statistiques No. 4 (Quebec: Ministère des Relations avec les citoyens et de l'Immigration, 2000).

23. Racializing 'slips' occurred in dealings with Aboriginals during the 'Oka standoff' of 1990, between Quebecers and citizens in the rest of Canada after Quebec's referendum in 1995 (Potvin, 'Les dérapages racistes', 'Some Racist "Slips" About Quebec'; Maryse Potvin et al. 'Du racisme dans les rapports entre groupes nationaux au Canada et en Belgique?,' *Revue canadienne des études ethniques* 36, 3 (2004): 25–60), and with religious minorities during the debate around 'reasonable accommodations' between 2006 and 2008 (Potvin, *Crise des accommodements raisonnables*).

24. Often, many forms of discrimination are present at the same time, their patterns intersect, and it is difficult for researchers or judges to pinpoint whether racism, sexism, or classic discrimination may be involved in some situations.

25. John Porter, *The Vertical Mosaic* (Toronto: Toronto University Press,1965).

26. Statistics Canada, *The Deteriorating Economic Welfare of Immigrants and Possible Causes: Update 2005*. Research document by G. Picot and A. Sweetman, Analytical Studies Branch Papers Series, Catalogue no. 11F0019MIE, Issue no. 262. Business and Labour Market Analysis Division, Statistics Canada, and School of Policy Studies, Queen's University. Ottawa: Industry Canada, June 2005.

27. Jeffrey G. Reitz and Rupa Banerjee, 'Racial Inequality, Social Cohesion and Policy Issues in Canada,' in Institute for Research on Public Policy, *Belonging? Diversity, Recognition and Shared Citizenship in Canada* (Montreal: IRPP, 2007).

28. Renaud et al., *Racisme et discrimination*; Victor Piché, and Jean Renaud, 'Immigration et intégration économique : peut-on mesurer la discrimination?' in Roch Côté and Michel Venne, eds, *Annuaire du Québec 2003* (Montreal: Fidès, 2002), 146–51. In connection with the theory of human capital, investigations of this type provide clues about the existence of 'probable' discriminations, observed when discrepancies between groups cannot be explained based on differences in controlled variables (e.g., age, gender, education, professional credentials, language proficiency, qualifications). These studies take into account indicators such as income, unemployment, type of employment, and education to explain discrimination, which is presented as an 'unexplained discrepancy' between groups.

29. Monica Boyd, 'Variations in Socioeconomic Outcomes of Second Generation Young Adults,' *Canadian Diversity*, Thematic issue: *The Experiences of Second Generation Canadians* 6, 2 (Spring 2008): 20–4; Maryse Potvin, Nancy Venel, and Paul Eid, eds, *La 2e génération issue de l'immigration. Une comparaison France-Québec* (Montreal: Athéna Éditions, 2007); Marie McAndrew et al., *La réussite scolaire des jeunes des communautés noires au secondaire*. Research report (Montreal: Immigration et métropoles, 2005).

30. James L. Torczyner et al., *L'évolution de la communauté noire montréalaise : mutations et défis* (Montreal: Consortium de McGill pour l'ethnicité et la planification sociale stratégique, 2001).

31. Porter, *The Vertical Mosaic*.

32. Potvin, 'Les dérapages racistes', 'Some Racist "Slips" About Quebec'; Potvin et al., 'Racisme et discrimination au Québec'.

33. Marc V. Levine, ed., *The Reconquest of Montreal: Language Policy and Social Change in a Bilingual City* (Philadelphia: Temple University Press, 1990).

34. Maryse Potvin, 'Discours publics et discriminations au Québec', *Les Cahiers du 27 juin* 2, 2 (Hiver-Printemps 2005): 47–52; Maryse Potvin, 'Racisme et discours public commun au Québec', in Stéphan Gervais, Dimitrios Karmis, and Diane Lamoureux, eds, *Du tricoté serré au métissé serré ? La culture publique commune au Québec en débats* (Quebec: Les Presses de l'Université Laval, 2008), 227–48.

35. Potvin, 'Les dérapages racistes', 'Some Racist "Slips" About Quebec', and 'Racisme et discrimination au Québec'.

36. Notable articles include those by Mathieu Bock-Côté and by some young conservatives in the nationalist review *L'Action Nationale* since about 2005.

37. Some of the racist 'slips' regarding the constitutional crisis are described in Potvin, 'Les dérapages racistes', 'Some Racist "Slips" About Quebec', and 'Racisme et discrimination au Québec'.

38. Potvin, *Crise des accommodements*; Potvin et al., *Les médias écrits*.

39. The debate had reappeared every so often since 1985, but generally concerned bona fide cases of reasonable accommodation (in the legal sense of the term). From 2006 onward, following the Supreme Court judgement that allowed a baptized Sikh student to wear a kirpan to a Quebec public school, media headlines were flooded with 'breaking news,' incorrectly categorized as cases of 'reasonable accommodation', thereby creating confusion and intolerance in public opinion (Potvin, *Crise des accommodements raisonnables*; Gérard Bouchard and Charles Taylor, *Building the Future A Time for Reconciliation Final Report* (Quebec: Government of Quebec, 2008), 15–17.

40. The reference to 1977 pertains to the year that the Charter of the French Language (Bill 101) was implemented. Marie McAndrew, 'Pour un débat inclusif sur l'accommodement raisonnable', Revue *Éthique publique* (2007).

41. In January of 2007, the municipal council of Hérouxville (a small municipality—population 1,300) adopted a 'code of conduct', designed for potential immigrants to the town. The code prohibited public stoning, female excision, and the wearing of burkas. Drafted by André Drouin (a municipal councillor who became a major media figure), the 'code of conduct' drew comments from around the globe and on 5 February 2007, Drouin asked the Premier of Quebec to declare a state of emergency. Five neighbouring towns asked their municipal and provincial governments to review the Canadian and Quebec charters.

42. We conducted a study that constructed two analytical grids to examine factual media coverage on one hand (451 articles) and opinion discourses on the other hand (654 editorials, columns, and letters from intellectuals and readers) in Quebec's five major newspapers: *Le Devoir, La Presse, Le Journal de Montréal, The Gazette,* and *Le Soleil.* In addition, 734 commentaries on two blogs were analyzed, for a total of 1,839 texts (Potvin, *Crise des accommodements raisonnables*; Potvin et al., *Les médias écrits*).

43. Stanley Cohen, *Folk Devils and Moral Panics* (London: MacGibbon and Kee, 1972).

44. Ibid., xvii.

45. At least six times, *Le Journal de Montréal* used the angle of 'privileges' accorded to Jews in breaking news. For example, on 17 May 2006, its headline read: 'Special Privilege for Jews—Charest Government is Accommodating' (news story about a Jewish day care centre—a 'CPE'). On 18 May 2006, it read: 'Quebec City Ignores the Charter', (to open the Jewish daycare centre).

On 25 May 2006, page 2 read 'Quebec City Keeps Code of Silence about Two CPEs,' with the subtitle: 'Jewish Community *Favoured* by Process'. On 19 November 2006, page 9 read: 'Laval CLSC. Preferential Treatment for a Jew'. This article recounted an incident from the day before in which a Jewish man jumped a queue in a health-care centre so that he could keep Shabbat. On 15 December 2006, *Le Journal* set off the 'CLSC de Ste-Thérèse de Blainville affair' (p. 3) with the headline: 'Reasonable Accommodations—Special Privileges for Jews'. The subtitle underscored the fact that: 'Nurses Must Bend to Their Demands to Provide Care to Patients from the Community'. Here we see a mechanism of victimization among the majority group as well as a generalization of the so-called demands of 'all Jews'. In many instances, persons belonging to the minority groups being discussed have little or no voice. Our translations.

46. Some anecdotes were presented as 'abusive' demands on institutions, when no such demands had actually been made by the minorities concerned. Such was the case for the 'directive' handed down by Montreal's police service and by Quebec's chief electoral officer on the issue of whether Muslim women wearing nikabs could vote with their faces covered.

47. Another example: 17 November 2007, *Le Journal de Montréal* quoted Mario Dumont in a lead headline: 'Reasonable Accommodations—'We are slipping into abuses of the Charter', with the subtitle, 'Leader of the ADQ judges some concessions to minorities to be worrisome'. The lead caption in the article reinforced this generalizing and negative angle: 'Accommodations made for ethnic and religious minorities defy common sense, according to Mario Dumont'. The article began with a quote from Dumont, who played up the victimization of the majority group: 'While a young Sikh is walking around with his dagger at school, the majority of Quebecers can no longer use the word "Christmas"'. The linkage of these kinds of quotes clearly oriented public debate: 'If a majority of citizens defends values that are its own, that does not constitute a racist attitude or a singular phenomenon in the modern world.' Quebec society was defined as being 'generous' in this article, reinforcing the notion that minorities were receiving 'privileges' and that in exchange they had to respect 'our values': 'The police haven't gone and kidnapped anyone in the world to force them to come and live in Quebec,' Dumont contended. Our translations.

48. Opponents of reasonable accommodation did not all use racializing discursive mechanisms. For example, 79 per cent of the 391 letters from readers we analyzed expressed opposition, but 202 letters (52 per cent of the corpus) contained racializing discursive mechanisms. For more detailed data and numerous excerpts illustrating these mechanisms, see Potvin, *Crise des accommodements raisonnables.*

49. Potvin, 'Discours publics et discriminations au Québec'; Potvin, 'Racisme et discours public commun au Québec'.

50. The rest of Canada has a long history of accusing Quebec (and the sovereignty movement) of racism. These accusations are perceived by many Quebecers as a denigration of the national character of francophones in Quebec (initiated by the dominant anglophone group in Canada) and an attempt to reduce francophones to the status of 'just another minority'.

RELEVANT WEBSITES

COMMISSION DES DROITS DE LA PERSONNE ET DES DROITS DE LA JEUNESSE (CDPDJ):www.cdpdj.qc.ca/en/home.asp?noeud1=0&noeud2=0&cle=0

THE QUEBEC CHARTER OF HUMAN RIGHTS AND FREEDOMS: www.cdpdj.qc.ca/en/commun/docs/charter.pdf

THE CONSULTATION COMMISSION ON ACCOMMODATION PRACTICES RELATED TO CULTURAL DIFFERENCES (CCAPRCD): www.accommodements.qc.ca

MINISTÈRE DE L'IMMIGRATION ET DES COMMUNAUTÉS CULTURELLES: www.micc.gouv.qc.ca

LIBRARY AND ARCHIVES CANADA: www.collectionscanada.gc.ca/

SOME MISSING PAGES: The Black Community in the History of Québec and Canada: www.learnquebec.ca/en/content/curriculum/social_sciences/features/missingpages/

SLAVERY: www.champlain2004.org/html/07/03_e.html
Part of the *New France, New Horizons* website produced by Library and Archives Canada.

TORTURE AND THE TRUTH: www.canadianmysteries.ca/sites/angelique/accueil/indexen.html
The story of Angelique (a Black slave) and the Burning of Montreal in 1734.

SELECT BIBLIOGRAPHY

Abella, Irving, and Harold Troper. *None is Too Many: Canada and the Jews of Europe, 1933–1948*. Toronto: Lester & Orpen Dennys, 1982.

Abu-Ladan, Yasmeen, and Daiva Stasiulis. 'Ethnic Pluralism Under Siege: Popular and Partisan Opposition to Multiculturalism', *Canadian Public Policy* 18, 4 (1992): 365–86.

Anctil, Pierre, Norma Ravvin, and Sherry Simon. *New Readings of Montreal Yiddish*. Toronto: University of Toronto Press, 2007.

Balthazar, Louis. *Bilan du nationalisme au Québec*. Montreal: Éditions l'Hexagone, 1986.

Berthelot, Jocelyn. *Apprendre à vivre ensemble. Immigration, société et éducation*, 2nd edn. Montreal: Éditions Saint-Martin, 1991.

Bissoondath, Neil. *Selling Illusions: The Cult of Multiculturalism*. Toronto: Penguin, 1994.

Bouchard, Gérard, and Charles Taylor (Commission de consultation sur les pratiques d'accommodement reliées aux différences culturelles). *Fonder L'avenir. Le temps de la réconciliation*. Abridged report. Quebec: Gouvernement du Québec, 2008.

Commission Gendron. *Rapport de la commission d'enquête sur la situation de la langue française et sur les droits linguistiques au Québec*, Vol III. Québec: Éditeur officiel, 1972.

Coutu, Michel, and Pierre Bosset. 'La Charte des droits et libertés de la personne et culture publique commune au Québec : une quasi absence?' In Stéphan Gervais, Dimitrios Karmis, and Diane Lamoureux, eds. *De tissé serré à métissé serré? La culture publique commune en débats*. Quebec: Les Presses de l'Université Laval, 2008, 183–206.

Drouilly, Pierre. 'Le référendum du 30 octobre 1995 : une analyse des résultats'. In Robert Boily, ed., *L'année politique au Québec, 1995–1996*. Montreal: Presses de l'Université de Montréal, 1996.

Juteau, Danielle. 'L'État et les immigrés : de l'immigration aux communautés culturelles'. In P.Guillaume, J.M. Lacroix, J. Zylberberg, and R. Pelletier, eds. *Minorités et État*. Bordeaux, France and Quebec: Presses universitaires de Bordeaux and Presses de l'Université Laval, 1986, 35–50.

———, and Marie McAndrew. 'Le multiculturalisme canadien et l'intégration "à la québécoise" : est-il possible de dépasser leurs limites?' Unpublished paper, 1998.

LaFerrière, Michel. 'Les idéologies ethniques de la société canadienne: du conformisme au multiculturalisme'. In Monique Lecomte and Claudine Thomas, eds. *Le facteur ethnique aux États-Unis et au Canada*. Lille, France: Presses universitaires de Lille, 1983, 203–12.

Levine, Marc V., ed. *The Reconquest of Montreal: Language Policy and Social Change in a Bilingual City.* Philadelphia: Temple University Press, 1990.

McRoberts, Kenneth. *Misconceiving Canada: The Struggle for National Unity.* Oxford: Oxford University Press, 1997.

Meisel, John, Guy Rocher, and Arthur Silver. *As I Recall—Je me souviens bien.* Montreal: Institut de recherche en Politiques publiques, 2000.

Ministère des communautés culturelles et de l'immigration. *La politique québécoise du développement culturel.* 2 vols. Quebec: Éditeur officiel, 1978.

———, *Au Québec pour bâtir ensemble. Énoncé de politique en matière d'immigration et d'intégration.* Quebec: MCCI, 1990.

Palmer, Howard, ed. *Immigration and the Rise of Multiculturalism.* Toronto: Copp Clark, 1975.

Piché, Victor, and Danièle Laliberté. *Portrait statistique de la nouvelle immigration à Montréal.* Working document of the Société des transports de la Communauté urbaine de Montréal (STCUM). Montreal: STCUM, 1987.

Porter, John. *The Vertical Mosaic.* Toronto: University of Toronto Press, 1965.

Potvin, Maryse. *Crise des accommodements raisonnables. Une fiction médiatique?* Montreal: Athéna Éditions, 2008.

———. 'Les dérapages racistes à l'égard du Québec au Canada-anglais depuis 1995'. *Politique et Sociétés* 18, 2 (1999): 101–32.

———. *Les médias écrits et les accommodements raisonnables. L'invention d'un débat. Analyse du traitement médiatique et des discours d'opinion dans les grands médias québécois sur les situations reliées aux accommodements raisonnables, du 1er mars 2006 au 30 avril 2007.* Report submitted to Commission de consultation sur les pratiques d'accommodement reliées aux différences culturelles. Montreal, 7 January 2008. Available at: www.accommodements.qc.ca/documentation/rapports/rapport-8-potvin-maryse.pdf.

———. 'Racisme et discours public commun au Québec'. In Stéphan Gervais, Dimitrios Karmis, and Diane Lamoureux, eds. *De tissé serré à métissé serré? La culture publique commune en débats.* Quebec: Les Presses de l'Université Laval, 2008, 227–48.

———. 'Racisme et discrimination au Québec : réflexion critique et prospective sur la recherche'. In J. Renaud, A. Germain, and X. Leloup, eds. *Racisme et discrimination : permanence et résurgence d'un phénomène inavouable.* Quebec: Presses de l'Université Laval, 2004, 172–96.

———. 'Some Racist "Slips" About Quebec in English Canada between 1995 and 1998'. *Canadian Ethnic Studies/ Revue canadienne des études ethniques* 32, 2 (2000): 1–26.

———, Anne Morelli, and Laurence Mettewie. 'Du racisme dans les rapports entre groupes nationaux au Canada et en Belgique?', *Revue canadienne des études ethniques/ Canadian Ethnic Studies* 36, 3 (2004): 25–60.

Rioux, Marcel. *La Question du Québec.* Montreal: L'Hexagone, 1974, 1987.

Royal Commission on Bilingualism and Biculturalism (B&B Commission). *Preliminary Report* (1965); *The Official Languages* (1967); *Education* (1968); *The Work World* (1969); *The Cultural Contribution of the Other Ethnic Groups* (1969); *The Federal Capital* (1970); *Voluntary Associations* (1970). Ottawa: Queen's Printer.

Stein, Michael. 'Changement dans la perception de soi des Anglo-Québécois'. In Gary Caldwell and Eric Waddell, eds. *Les anglophones du Québec. De majoritaires à minoritaires.* Quebec: Institut québécois de recherche sur la culture, 1982, 111–30.

Taylor, Charles. 'The Politics of Recognition'. In A. Guttman, ed. *Multiculturalism and the 'Politics of Recognition'.* Princeton: Princeton University Press, 1992, 25–73.

Thériault, J. Yvon. 'L'individualisme démocratique et le projet souverainiste', *Sociologie et sociétés* XXVI, 2 (automne 1994): 19–32.

Trudel, Marcel. *L'esclavage au Canada français : histoire et condition.* Quebec: Presses de l'Université Laval, 1960.

Waddell, Eric. 'L'État, la langue et la société : les vicissitudes du français au Québec et au Canada'. In Alan C. Cairns and Cynthia Williams, eds. *Les dimensions politiques du sexe, de l'ethnie et de la langue au Canada.* Ottawa: Commission Royale sur l'avenir économique et les perspectives de développement du Canada, 1986.

Williams, Dorothy W. *The Road to Now: A History of Blacks in Montreal.* Montreal: Vehicule Press, 1997.

CHAPTER 19

Immigration and Diversity in Quebec's Schools: An Assessment

Marie McAndrew, Université de Montréal

— TIMELINE —

1969 First welcoming classes for students of immigrant origin introduced through the Commission scolaire de Montréal.

1977 Bill 101 adopted, requiring newcomers to attend French-language schools.

1978 Heritage language program (Programme d'enseignement des langues d'origine à l'école publique—PELO) established.

1978 Couture-Cullen Agreement gives Quebec increased jurisdiction in immigration.

1981 *Quebecers, Each and Everyone*, Quebec's first action plan in intercultural relations, released.

1982 Grid for the elimination of discriminatory stereotypes included in teaching material across Quebec.

1985 Report by Committee on Québec Schools and Cultural Communities introduces term *intercultural education*.

1990 *Let's Build Quebec Together: Vision: A Policy Statement on Immigration and Integration* outlines Quebec government's immigration policy orientation and Quebec model of integration and diversity relations.

Gagnon-Tremblay–McDougall Accord on immigration gives Quebec exclusive jurisdiction in selection of independent immigrants and in linguistic and economic integration of all newcomers to Quebec.

1994–5 Muslim girl wearing hijab expelled from public school in Montreal, generating wide public debate.

1995 Intercultural awareness enters into approval criteria for teacher education programs in universities.

1996 *Learning from the Past: Report of the Task Force on the Teaching of History* (the Lacoursière Report) recommends fostering openness to teaching international history and improving students' knowledge about contribution of Aboriginal peoples and cultural communities to Quebec's history.

1998 Major educational reform takes place in Quebec's education system, introducing new program for inclusion that is more open to diversity.

Confessional school boards become linguistic school boards (although individual schools may remain confessional).

A School for the Future: Policy Statement on Educational Integration and Intercultural Education adopted, introducing diversification in reception services, providing guidelines for reasonable accommodation, and bringing intercultural education to all regions of Quebec.

1999 *Religion in Secular Schools: a New Perspective for Quebec* (also known as the Proulx Report) on place of religion in school forms basis of courses in ethics and religious culture, but its recommendations are not immediately ratified by Quebec government.

2002 Multani conflict over Sikh student Gurbaj Singh Multani wearing a kirpan in a Montreal public school.

2006 Supreme Court of Canada rules in Multani case, granting Sikh student right to wear his kirpan according to specific guidelines to ensure safety of his fellow students.

2007 Advisory Committee on Integration and Reasonable Accommodation in the Schools tables its report, *Inclusive Québec Schools: Dialogue, Values and Common Reference Points*

in November 2007, providing an overview of situation, defining guidelines for action, and instituting conflict resolution process.

Commission on Accommodation Practices Related to Cultural Differences (the Bouchard-Taylor Commission) created and public hearings held. There is much controversy between proponents of pluralism and integral secularism, and those favouring a return to a 'traditional' definition of Quebec identity.

2008 Bouchard-Taylor Commission presents its report.

INTRODUCTION

Regardless of the complexity of their ethnic relations, all immigrant-receiving societies share common challenges. Quebec is no exception. It must ensure the linguistic, social, and economic integration of newly arrived Quebecers while effecting major change in the host society itself. For the past 30 years in Canada (and in the United States), these two objectives have given rise to numerous, recurring debates in education milieus. For students of immigrant origin and their families, school is often the primary vehicle of social mobility; recognizing ethno-cultural diversity (in both schools and society) has become a crucial tool for ensuring equal opportunity. But the culture of tomorrow is being shaped and the identities and attitudes of our future citizens defined in the modern public school. It must therefore perform a delicate balancing act, determining the respective positions of various languages and cultural heritages, while emphasizing the common values of citizenship. Achieving this equilibrium is a difficult task that needs constant redefining.

The case of schools in Quebec is particularly revealing. For while Quebec society resolutely strives to be modern in its active commitment to immigration and in its search for a conciliatory middle path between assimilation and multiculturalism, it remains somewhat fragile. This fragility lends complexity to the challenges in the linguistic, academic, and social integration of newcomers. Indeed, exposure to diversity

is a more recent phenomenon in Quebec, at least for much of the francophone community, than in other North American contexts. All these factors make for remarkably dynamic policy formulation, program design, and social action, but they have also generated numerous tensions.

English-language schools are also characterized by cultural diversity in Quebec; however our focus here is on French-language schools, attended by 90 per cent of Quebec's students, including the vast majority of allophone students[1] and students of immigrant origin.[2]

MAJOR POLICY FRAMEWORKS

Immigration Policy and its Impact on Schools

Since the late 1960s, Quebec, more than any other Canadian province, has sought to play a major role in immigration, a shared jurisdiction between the federal and provincial governments under the Canadian Constitution. In essence, Quebec's interest in this area was motivated by the same factors that guided the development of its language policy: the assimilation of most immigrants into the anglophone community and the impact of this assimilation on the demolinguistic equilibrium in Montreal.[3] But from the first, this early involvement was part of a nation-building process, which often manifested itself in competition with that of the Canadian government and became more obvious over time. Gradually, a series of agreements culminated in the Canada–Quebec Accord Relating to Immigration and Temporary Admission of Aliens (the Gagnon-Tremblay–McDougall Accord), which enshrined Quebec's exclusive jurisdiction in selecting 'independent' immigrants (who account for 60 per cent of total movement) and over the linguistic and economic integration of all newcomers to Quebec.

Quebec's involvement in immigration follows principles fairly similar to those in Canadian immigration policy and is currently characterized by three goals.[4] First, given the feared economic consequences of a demographic deficit and an aging population, Quebec is targeting a gradual increase in intake so that it will ultimately receive 25 per cent of total immigration to Canada. Currently, Quebec falls well short of that mark: in 2008, it received only 19 per cent of Canada's immigrants. However, with an average intake of some 40,000 immigrants over five years, for its population of 7 million, Quebec has a significant immigration rate compared with other jurisdictions (see Table 19.1).

Second, Quebec's selection policy attempts to balance competing selection criteria: the recruitment of French-speaking immigrants, the contribution of immigration to economic development, the promotion of family reunification, and the commitment to international solidarity. The combined complexity of these criteria has led to a highly diversified

immigrant population both in language skills and national origin. Indeed, within the selection grid, prior knowledge of French is not an eliminatory criterion, although currently over 60 per cent of admitted immigrants already speak some French. In addition, over 80 per cent of immigrants now come from regions other than North America or Europe. The five largest immigrant groups (from Algeria, France, Morocco, China, and Colombia) account for less than 35 per cent of all entrants, which explains the heterogeneity of most multi-ethnic classrooms.

Third, the primary goal of both the federal government's and Quebec's immigration policy is permanent settlement. Citizenship may be acquired very quickly (after three years), which contributes to the significant political influence of minorities in society generally, and in the education system in particular.

Successive waves of immigration have shaped the school population,[5] which now comprises some 116,500 students (10.7 per cent of the total school population) whose first language is not English, French, or an Aboriginal language. Students of immigrant origin (i.e., those born abroad or with at least one parent born abroad), now number 206,125 (19.1 per cent) of Quebec's total school population.

While most immigrants typically settle in Montreal, Montreal-born francophones tend to move to the suburbs and often enrol their children in private schools. Consequently, in Montreal's public French-language schools, 46 per cent of students do not speak French as their first language and 51 per cent are of immigrant origin. In this respect, Montreal is on par with averages for large cities in Canada and the United States (see Table 19.2). In over one-third of Montreal schools, students of immigrant origin account for the majority of the population, and just under one in ten schools have an immigrant population of over 75 per cent.

Interculturalism and Intercultural Education: A Longstanding Normative Commitment

Once Quebec's francophone community had successfully reasserted its majority status and committed to increasing immigration, it was faced with the

TABLE 19.1: Gross immigration rates in six jurisdictions* (2007)

Country	Immigration as a Percentage of the Total Population
Canada	0.72
Quebec	0.59
United States	0.35
California	0.63
New York	0.70
Australia	0.67

*Measured solely on the basis of permanent admissions as a percentage of the total population.

TABLE 19.2: Percentage of students whose first language or language spoken at home is neither French (Quebec) nor English (rest of Canada and the United States) in five major North American cities*

Montreal French-language schools (2008)	Toronto English-language schools (2008)	Vancouver English-language schools (2008)	New York English-language schools (2008)	Los Angeles English-language schools (2006)
46.0%	52.2%	37.0%	41.8%	59%

*First language: Montreal, Toronto, Vancouver; Language most often spoken at home: New York; Students enrolled in the English Learners program during their schooling: Los Angeles.

challenge of defining a normative position vis-à-vis the growing pluralism in its public institutions and in civil society. Quebec interculturalism may be described as the quest for a middle path between Canadian multiculturalism and French Jacobinism. Canadian multiculturalism has been criticized for essentializing cultures and for isolating them from each other. Conversely, French Jacobinism, by relegating diversity to the private sphere, is not entirely compatible with the recognition of pluralism, an ideal widely embraced in Quebec.[6]

In the 1980s, following the publication of *A Cultural Development Policy for Quebec* and *Quebecers, Each and Everyone*, the government adopted an approach of intercultural rapprochement between individuals whose membership in clearly distinguishable groups was taken for granted. The idea was to create a culture of convergence, centred around a traditional but modern francophone culture, and enriched by the province's various ethnic groups, which are called 'cultural communities' in Quebec.

With *Let's Build Quebec Together: Vision: Policy Statement on Immigration and Integration,* adopted in 1990 (and still in effect), expanded recognition of cultural hybridity began to emerge. This document acknowledged both plurality as a fundamental aspect of Quebec culture, and the right of Quebecers of all origins to express their cultures 'within the limitations imposed by the respect for fundamental democratic values and the need for intergroup exchanges'. The policy statement expressly identified gender equality, respect for children's rights, non-violence, and Quebec's societal choices (including language rights) among the democratic values to be promoted. It also called for the

full participation and the equal contribution of all citizens, specifically those of immigrant origin.[7]

The *Policy Statement on Educational Integration and Intercultural Education,* published in 1998 by the Ministère de l'Éducation, du Loisir et du Sport (MELS) followed a similar path.[8] Intercultural education was defined as learning how to live together in a democratic, pluralist, French-speaking society. Ways to promote the normative recognition of diversity made up a significant part of the statement and were essentially governed by the same parameters set forth in 1990; protecting individual rights and Quebec's linguistic choices, and ensuring that institutions can operation smoothly. This document stands out for its complex treatment of the concept of culture. It urges that instead of essentializing differences, teachers should regard ethnic identity as only one among many factors influencing integration and academic success.

The 1998 policy statement specifically highlighted three key challenges in intercultural education: the first, integrating people of various ethno-cultural origins at all levels of employment in the education system; the second, providing training and professional development of teaching staff; and the third, implementing a pluralist transformation of the formal and real curriculum. This last objective was at the crux of most debates regarding the policy statement. Indeed, the tension between common values and the recognition of diversity is evident throughout the document, which underwent a mostly cosmetic rewrite in French, aimed at addressing the sensitivities of more nationalist segments of Quebec society.

Although the 1998 policy statement was adopted over a decade ago, the official discourse it promoted has been neither questioned nor updated. Its principles still form the basis of MELS initiatives and have significantly influenced statements formulated by school boards with the highest concentration of students of immigrant origin. However, while the policy statement was meant to extend the recognition of diversity to milieus that do not experience diversity daily, progress has been limited. Over the past decade, only six school boards outside of Montreal have adopted a policy on intercultural education. These boards are generally in areas becoming increasingly multi-ethnic due to urban sprawl or to the regionalization of immigration.

PUBLIC DEBATE

Language and the Educational Integration of Immigrants

Before the enactment of Bill 101 in 1977, over 80 per cent of newly arrived immigrants chose English-language schooling, since English was the dominant language of business and French-language institutions were not especially open to cultural diversity. Thus, immigrant schooling profiles became the central focus of the language debate in the 1970s, which pitted proponents of mandatory French-language education for immigrants against supporters of free choice. Support for mandatory French-language schooling came massively but not exclusively from nationalist milieus, based on the rationale that fluency in French (the common language of Quebec), and a shared educational experience were vital to integration. Support for free choice in schooling came from practically all of the anglophone community and much of the immigrant population, based on objections to the coercive nature of the proposed legislation and on the argument that French could be learned just as well in the English-language school system or in bilingual schools.[9]

This round of Quebec's language debates was settled with the enactment of Bill 101, the Charter of the French Language. The bill's main purpose was to make French the common language of public life. It also made attendance at French-language schools mandatory for all francophone and allophone students, while preserving the historical right of the anglophone community and anglicized immigrant

communities to attend English-language institutions. As a result, over 80 per cent of allophone students and over 90 per cent of students of immigrant origin now attend French-language schools. In fact, today the French school system in Montreal is more multi-ethnic than the English school system.[10]

In public debates over the integration of students of immigrant origin, the prominence of language issues, although still significant, has faded steadily since 1977.[11] From 1977 to the end of the 1980s, public concern focused more specifically on whether immigrant students were learning French and whether their families were actively or passively resisting attendance at French-language schools. Nonetheless, a growing consensus (corroborated by ministerial exam results) emerged during this period that young immigrant students were in fact becoming reasonably fluent in French. Moreover, changes in immigration, newly dominated by more francophile groups, such as Haitians, Vietnamese, and Latin Americans, helped to reduce resistance to attending French-language schools.

In the early 1990s, the focus of public debate shifted to the use of French and attitudes towards the language. Three issues were central to this debate: how concentrations of ethnic groups affected the linguistic environment in schools; whether students of immigrant origin were choosing to attend English- or French-language CEGEPs[12] (not governed by Bill 101 and therefore subject to individual choice) and the extent to which using French in schools would affect longer-term linguistic practices among allophones. Although numerous research studies and reports yielded mainly positive findings regarding these issues, attendant controversies remained heated until the late 1990s. During this time, a relatively large wave of young anglophone or anglophile immigrants arrived from South Asia and Hong Kong (following political changes in that region). Moreover, several prominent nationalist figures in Quebec continued to cite substantive indicators, such as which language was used in private life or whether CEGEP-level studies were pursued in French, as the only reliable predictors of future linguistic behaviour among newcomers.

In the 2000s, under the combined effect of an unprecedented wave of francophone immigration from North Africa and an international malaise spawned by the events of 11 September 2001, the language debate faded in prominence. Issues around the culture and, especially, the religion of newcomers, captured media attention and generated public concern. Indeed, public apprehensions have not yet disappeared, particularly on the ground.

Cultural and Religious Diversity in Schools

For over three years now, Quebec has been involved in another heated controversy, this time over 'reasonable accommodation'.[13] The debate has centred around the place of ethno-cultural diversity within Quebec identity. The controversy was set in motion by a Supreme Court of Canada decision in April 2006 regarding a student who wore a Sikh kirpan to his public school (see Snapshot box). This incident spiralled into a crisis that encompassed a raft of other identity-related issues, many of which were expressed at the fall 2008 hearings of the Consultation Commission on Accommodation Practices Related to Cultural Differences (the Bouchard-Taylor Commission), set up by the Quebec government to manage the crisis.[14]

As the process of adapting schools to diversity continued, two issues were broadly debated in public by two distinct groups: one championing strict secularism (inspired by France) and the other a return to a 'traditional' Quebec identity. The pro-secularist group strongly opposed students and teachers wearing the hijab (the Muslim headscarf). After the major controversy in Quebec in 1994–5, (when a girl was expelled from her school for wearing a hijab), the consensus seemed to be that the hijab would be tolerated, within the guidelines defined by the Commission des droits de la personne et de la jeunesse, that equal access to school activities would not be compromised and that freedom of choice for students and their parents would be preserved. Indeed, at the Bouchard-Taylor Commission hearings in 2008, these guidelines were reiterated by official educational bodies, but were still largely absent from the briefs of ordinary citizens, who often drew direct connections between wearing the hijab and Muslim women's putative oppression. Moreover, given the relative success in recruiting teachers and student teachers of all origins and religious persuasions, the question of whether teaching staff should be allowed to wear religious symbols was now central to current public debate. The Commission's report, which expressed some openness to this position, attracted many negative comments.

SNAPSHOT

The Right to Wear the Kirpan

One of the events fuelling the debate around 'reasonable accommodation' was the Supreme Court's decision of 2 March 2006 that authorized a Sikh student to wear his kirpan[15] to a Quebec public school. The Multani decision was widely misunderstood and in some cases condemned outright. The events that triggered this controversy, the court decisions it generated and the subsequent place of religious diversity in schools that was envisioned thereafter had a profound impact on stakeholders in education and the public alike.

Gurbaj Singh Multani is a baptized orthodox Sikh (about 10 per cent of Sikhs in Canada are orthodox). As such, he strictly adheres to the tenets of the Sikh religion and wears a ritual dagger, the kirpan, which symbolizes the purity of the faith and his commitment to defend it. Multani, 12 years old at the time of the incident, belonged to a predominantly anglophone community, but under Bill 101 attended a French-language school. Ethno-cultural diversity in this school, attended mostly by francophone students, was a relatively recent phenomenon. On 19 February 2001, the kirpan that Multani was wearing inside his clothes slipped out accidentally in the schoolyard. On 21 December 2001, as a reasonable accommodation of Multani's religious convictions, the Commission scolaire Marguerite-Bourgeoys (CSMB) sent a letter to his parents stating that he could wear the kirpan at school, provided it was sealed inside his clothing. This solution, widely applied across Canada, had been previously adopted following an Ontario Superior Court decision in the early 1990s. Multani and his parents accepted these terms. However, on 12 February 2002, the governing board of the school (wielding considerable decision-making power in Quebec), comprising predominantly francophone school parents, refused to approve the accommodation. The board deemed that wearing a kirpan violated the school's code of conduct, which prohibited carrying weapons and dangerous objects. On 19 March 2002, after much equivocation and internal tension, the CSMB's elected Council of Commissioners concurred with the governing board and rejected the initial accommodation for the kirpan. The family was asked to have their son wear a symbolic pendant or a non-metallic kirpan. On 25 March 2002, Multani's father filed a motion with the Superior Court of Quebec, requesting that this decision be declared void and of no effect. On 17 May 2002, the motion was granted and Gurbaj Singh Multani was allowed to wear his kirpan. However, in a dramatic turn of events two years later (in 2004), the Quebec Court of Appeal overturned the Superior Court's judgement, citing security issues and the importance of following common rules, such as reasonable limits on the right to express religious beliefs. Some considered this ruling to be an indicator of an emerging culture in Quebec courts in which the values of good citizenship were taking precedence over the culture of personal rights that (it was claimed) epitomized Canadian jurisprudence. In 2006, the Supreme Court of Canada reversed the Court of Appeal decision, upholding the original 2001 proposal that the student be allowed to wear his kirpan securely fastened inside his clothes, provided that Multani not surrender it at any time, that its loss be immediately reported to school authorities, and that school staff be authorized to verify that all of these conditions were being followed.

The Supreme Court decision belongs to a vast body of jurisprudence on reasonable accommodation that has been building since 1985. It is now recognized that when an apparently neutral standard or practice is applied to all the people within an institution, it may, in some instances, infringe on equality or fundamental rights or freedoms of some individuals, including religious freedoms. In such cases, the courts have consistently sought compromises negotiated in good faith between the parties, called 'reasonable accommodations'. While such compromises may exempt a person from certain standards or practices, they must still ensure the smooth operation of institutions. It was not the concept of reasonable accommodation in itself that made the ruling in the Multani case significant, but rather that for the first time this concept was applied to a school as a service provider for students and their families. The judges of Canada's highest court were asked to reflect upon this accommodation's compatibility with the school's complex mandate of preparing future citizens for life within society. The Supreme Court rejected the CSMB board's argument that the kirpan was a symbol of violence, based both on a lack of proof and because it showed a lack of consideration for Canadian multicultural values and a disrespect for the Sikh faith. The Court reminded Canadians that schools are a place for meeting and dialogue and must be founded on principles of tolerance and impartiality. Since leading by example is the best way to promote respect for constitutional rights within a democratic society, the Court reiterated that institutions and teachers are therefore bound to respect students' rights and provide an education that is free of prejudice, bias, and intolerance.

While some politicians and editorial writers welcomed the nuanced reasoning of the Supreme Court ruling, it was nonetheless misunderstood and in some cases very poorly received by a vocal segment of the population in Quebec. Negative public opinion was divided into three camps. One camp recognized the legitimacy of reasonable accommodations in general, but disagreed with the Court's opinion that kirpans pose little danger. A second camp attacked the ruling as a classic example of the impasse created by the federal multiculturalism policy and its negative impact on Quebec. They noted that while in principle the Court recognized the importance of common civic values, in practice reasonable accommodation consistently favoured the rights of individuals or specific cultural communities, thereby factionalizing society, even within schools, where, of all places, developing social cohesion should be paramount. A third camp took advantage of the decision to make overtly anti-immigration or discriminatory remarks, primarily in blogs and open online letters not published in newspapers, against some religious groups. The fact that the family of the Sikh student and the spokesperson of his community spoke only English also fuelled tensions by linking language issues to religious issues.

The shockwave created by the Multani decision led the Ministère de l'Éducation, du Loisir et du Sport to relaunch a series of measures aimed at recognizing diversity. These measures had been most intensely implemented during the 1995 'hijab crisis' (in which a girl was expelled from a public school for wearing a hijab), but were less actively implemented by the end of the decade. Two measures were particularly noteworthy. First, a training unit for school principals on consideration for cultural and religious diversity was updated and a training campaign, led by a team of educational instructors has been implemented since 2008. Second, in the fall of 2006, the Ministère struck the Advisory Committee on Integration and Reasonable Accommodation in the Schools, comprising representatives from various areas of the education system, including school boards, parents' committees, professional associations, and unions. The Advisory Committee's report, submitted in November 2007, included an update that set the record straight on the frequency and nature of requests for accommodation. It also reiterated and strengthened existing guidelines for recognizing diversity, proposing some practical ways of fostering harmonious negotiations between schools and parents.

The chief focus for those championing a return to Quebec's 'traditional' identity was the threat they perceived in the new Ethics and Religious Culture Program. This program was the culmination of a secularization process initiated in 1998 that transformed confessional school boards into English- and French-language school boards. In the fall of 2008, it replaced the Catholic Religious and Moral Instruction Program, the Protestant Moral and Religious Education Program, and the Moral Education Program (the latter choice being the only alternative for non-Christian students up to that point). The new Ethics and Religious Culture Program was criticized for placing all religions on an equal footing and ignoring both the central role that the Catholic religion had played in the development of Quebec and its contemporary demographic weight. Traditionalist supporters also argued that teaching religion from a cultural perspective could constitute an infringement on the religious freedom of young children, who would be unable to distinguish the facts presented on various religions from the beliefs that their parents wished to instill in them.

On the whole, the briefs submitted and the positions taken publicly at the Commission's hearings cast the role of the education system in transforming Quebec's identity in a positive light. Even the most apprehensive or negative participants at the Commission's hearings often mentioned that the 'children of Bill 101' bore little resemblance to them, since this new generation has lived and breathed diversity. Indeed, a number of young people spoke out at the hearings to remind their elders to practise more moderation in their assertions about other cultures.

PROGRAMS AND MEASURES

Reception Services for Newly Arrived Immigrants

In contrast to the model prevailing in the rest of Canada, which places students lacking host language proficiency directly into regular classes but provides ESL (English as a Second Language) support, Quebec has opted for a closed 'welcoming class' model. The first welcoming classes, introduced in 1969, reflected the view that the best way for allophone students to learn French was through a systematic and structured approach, not by merely exposing them to the language in regular classes (an approach that often suffices when the target language is clearly dominant in society). Welcoming classes enjoy a reduced student/teacher ratio. The language learning program is well developed and includes a component on the life and culture of the host society. In outlying regions, if there are too few allophone students to warrant a separate class, they attend regular classes but receive FSL (French as Second Language) support. In 2008, some 18,000 students, over 85 per cent of them residing in Montreal, attended welcoming classes or were provided with linguistic support.[16]

Until very recently, heritage languages were not recognized as having any role in the various measures adopted for teaching French to newly arrived immigrants.[17] However, since 1977, Quebec has been offering a heritage languages program, known by its French acronym, PELO (Programme d'enseignement des langues d'origine), for allophone students who have mastered French. The program was originally designed to reassure Quebec's older, established cultural communities that multilingualism was a valued complement to efforts in promoting the French language. Today, 14 heritage languages are taught to some 7,000 students, but the program is less popular than might be expected, owing to the resistance of public school teachers and to the schooling choices of highly committed allophone parents, who would rather enrol their children in private trilingual schools, partially funded by the government of Quebec. The program also suffers from a lack of focus. While research indicates that this approach is most effective when the host language is learned simultaneously with the heritage language, the PELO program is not available to new arrivals still attending welcoming classes, and it targets elementary school students, whereas problems in mastering French arise mainly at the secondary school level.

Further to the publication of the Quebec government's *Policy Statement on Educational Integration and Intercultural Education* in 1998, welcoming programs and other measures evolved significantly. Observers had noted that the 10 months that students were to spend in a welcoming class tended to be extended, which caused some concern regarding the social integration of newcomers into schools. Therefore, various innovative models have been explored in recent years to help immigrant students make the transition from welcoming classes into regular classes. These models may involve partial immersion in regular classes tackling less linguistically demanding subjects, team teaching between teachers from welcoming classes and heritage language classes, or placing allophone students in regular classes with linguistic support. Experiments with developing students' linguistic heritages within regular classes are also being attempted, based on similar experiments by the European Language Awareness movement.

Adapting to Pluralism

In Quebec's elementary and secondary school programs, there are many points of entry for promoting intercultural, anti-racist, or citizenship education. These points may be found both in the general aims of the curriculum and in the detailed descriptions of targeted student competencies, of broad areas of learning, and of various academic subjects.[18] The learning area entitled Citizenship and Community Life, which comprises the teaching of Geography, History, and Citizenship Education, has the greatest number of stated commitments to providing education on diversity. Moreover, all three of these subjects involve a common educational aim: 'openness to the world and respect for diversity'. Other broad areas of learning like Media Literacy, and Environmental Awareness and Consumer Rights and Responsibilities include elements related to intercultural education, such as awareness of the interdependence of all peoples and the consequences of globalization on the distribution of wealth, as well as the ability to recognize stereotyped media messages. There are also three targeted student competencies that contribute to intercultural education which must be taught in all programs: 'To exercise critical judgment', which teaches the recognition of prejudices and the importance of putting opinions in perspective; 'To construct his or her identity', which requires students to recognize their cultural roots and acknowledge those of others; and 'To cooperate with others', which encourages respect for differences, developing openness to others, and constructively embracing pluralism and non-violence.

Through the new Ethics and Religious Culture Program, students will also learn about major world religions such as Islam, Buddhism, Hinduism, and Sikhism, although the primary emphasis is on Christian and Aboriginal traditions. The program targets two complementary aims: acknowledging each student's sense of belonging or not belonging to a religious tradition; and promoting the sharing of values and involvement in co-operative projects in a pluralist society. Students learn to weigh ethical questions, demonstrate their understanding of religious phenomena, and discuss these topics with people who do not necessarily share their own beliefs.

For these ambitious programs to succeed, bias-free teaching material had to be produced to properly reflect diversity. Quebec's track record in this regard, though not without its flaws, has been improving.[19] Beginning in 1982, an approval process for teaching materials was implemented to ensure that designs and depictions of ethno-cultural minorities were not discriminatory. By the late 1980s, minorities were included more in the materials' content and overt stereotypes had been eliminated. At that point, the qualitative treatment of diversity required that omissions and more subtle ethnocentric biases be addressed. Several studies conducted in the 1990s showed that although textbooks during this period generally promoted cultural diversity, they often folklorized various cultures and portrayed 'them' as outsiders to the target readership. In addition to underplaying the contribution of minority groups to Quebec society, the presentation of non-Western civilizations (especially the Muslim world) was stereotypical. Further to the implementation of the educational reform in 1998, no studies on the evolution of the treatment of cultural, religious, and ethnic diversity in teaching materials have been conducted. However, an examination of some of the history books in current use indicates that there are increased international perspectives on non-Western societies and cultures, and Quebec-based perspectives on Aboriginal cultures and groups of immigrant origin. A recent study also noted significant progress in depictions of Islam and the Muslim world, although the contribution of the Muslim community in Canada and Quebec is still insufficiently recognized.

Teachers also need training to be able to adapt fully to the new diversity in schools. In this area, reviews are more mixed.[20] Since 1995, MELS has made intercultural awareness activities an early requirement for teacher training programs and its framework of competencies for educators contains at least three activities that incorporate an intercultural or anti-racist perspective. The faculties of education at Montreal's two French-language universities have introduced several mandatory courses on ethnic diversity, inequality and discrimination, and developing adapted approaches to teaching. Other courses on teaching History or French to allophone students address these issues, although they are not the main focus. But there is a widespread consensus that current efforts are insufficient or, at least, that their impact on future teachers is not always conclusive. Some student teachers see no connection between these 'theme' courses and their other courses, which are focused on psycho-pedagogical or academic subject-related skills that they consider to be more important. Also, teaching competencies in intercultural matters may not always be adequately reinforced during internships within regular schools.

The MELS, school boards, various government bodies like the Commission des droits de la personne et de la jeunesse, and some community organizations also offer in-service training for teaching staff on topics such as intercultural communication, intervention in multi-ethnic schools, prevention of racism, relations with parents, and reasonable accommodation. However, none of this training is mandatory and it has been criticized for preaching to the converted, that is, to teachers already making major efforts to adapt to cultural diversity.

Other initiatives, aimed at increasing the representation of minority students in teacher training through university education faculties and later among future school teaching staff, are beginning to bear fruit.[21] This positive development is partly due to the efforts of these bodies to update equal opportunity plans in recruitment and employment. It is also due to the retirement of many teachers and the growing presence of qualified francophones in recent waves of immigration, many of whom take up teaching when they encounter obstacles to practising the professions for which they were initially trained.

Outcomes

Linguistic Integration

Overall, three decades of concerted efforts in linguistic integration in Quebec schools have borne positive results.[22]

In terms of students' command of the French language, a cohort study of youths who started secondary school between 1994 and 1996 found that students of immigrant origin had a success rate of 85.1 per cent in French, while the Quebec student body had an overall success rate of 89.6 per cent. Average marks were within the same range, at 73.4 per cent for youths born abroad and 76.2 per cent for Quebec students overall. But these findings should be considered with two caveats in mind. First, because this exam is administered at the end of secondary school, the participation rate for students of immigrant origin was 10 points lower than that of the student population as a whole. Second, success on the exam does not reliably indicate that students have mastered French at the level of complexity required for scholastic success, as indicated by other research on students' linguistic competencies and by the perceptions of teachers, who have identified many of these students' shortcomings.

As for language use in school, the impact of mandatory French-language schooling seems to be well established. A 1999 study conducted in 20 Montreal multi-ethnic elementary and secondary schools confirmed this fact, at a time when the socio-linguistic context was clearly less favourable than it is today. In the 10 elementary schools, observations of informal conversations indicated that French was used between 67.5 per cent and 99.7 per cent of the time (in six of these schools, it was used more than 90 per cent of the time). In the 10 secondary schools, despite the more complex linguistic situation, speaking French also ranked first, with use rates varying from 53.1 per cent to 98.4 per cent. Languages of origin aside, the relative strength of French over English also confirmed an overall trend towards the adoption of French. In elementary schools, the relative strength of French over English varied from 70 per cent to 100 per cent. For secondary schools, the respective rates were 59.9 per cent to 99.3 per cent. Overall, the level of French-language use observed among students was much higher than expected, that is, higher than their parents' recorded linguistic behaviour (as reported in the Canadian census). Interviews with students also revealed that the most successful approaches to promoting French were those that complemented (and did not oppose) the competencies that students already possessed in other languages.

The choice of language of instruction at the CEGEP level has also been closely studied over the years, since some view it as an important predictor of future behaviour among young people. The statistics indicate a stepwise progression. In the late 1980s, the first allophone student cohorts educated entirely in French chose French-language CEGEPs in over 70 per cent of cases. In the years that followed, that percentage decreased each year, reaching 53.6 per cent in 1999. Since then, the percentage of allophone students choosing French-language CEGEPs has steadily increased, and by 2007 this figure had reached over 63 per cent. Currently, there is no consensus as to why students choose English-language CEGEPs. While some see cause for concern in this choice, viewing it as long-term predictor of language habits, others argue that it is chiefly strategic; young allophones who have acquired a command of French simply wish to acquire English-language skills in CEGEP, something they likely have not been able to do at secondary French-language schools, which are known for their under-performance in this subject.

As for the longer-term impact of French-language schooling, a study conducted by the Conseil de la langue française among a large sampling of anglophones and allophones aged 20 to 35 showed that French was used by 65 per cent of those who had attended French-language schools as the predominant language of their public lives, but by only 36.5 per cent of those educated in English-language schools. Moreover, these positive results did not include young immigrants whose first language was French and whose numbers are increasing. Census data from 2006 on the language most frequently spoken in the home indicate that French is more popular among foreign-born allophone youth in the 15–25 age bracket than it is in older age brackets.

Still, for those who believe that multilingualism will eventually lead to the dominance of English,[23] statistics on the substantial maintenance of languages of origin and the significant ongoing use of English may be read more pessimistically.

Equal Opportunities and Academic Success

The issues of equality of opportunity and of academic success have long been the poor cousins of the debate on the educational integration of youth of immigrant origin in Quebec. But after 2000, these issues gained prominence in public debates. At that point data became much more accurate, thereby qualifying formerly predominantly positive findings. Schools and communities became more aware of problems as many among the immigrant population (even those initially selected as highly employable) experienced downward social mobility. Indeed, 60 per cent of disadvantaged schools on the Island of Montreal are now multi-ethnic schools.

A recent study[24] indicated that, in relation to the school population as a whole, students born abroad or whose parents were born abroad entered secondary school with greater academic delay, which continued to accumulate, even when they started at the usual age of entry. They were less likely to obtain a Secondary School Diploma after five years (45.5 per cent versus 57.8 per cent) or even after seven years of schooling (57.4 per cent versus 69 per cent). Fewer of these students took ministerial exams and, as noted above, they had slightly lower success rates and averages in French, but their marks in History and the Physical Sciences were similar to those of the general student population and they had slightly higher marks in English. However, students in this group did seem to show greater resilience since they pursued CEGEP-level studies in proportions similar to that of the student population as a whole (52.8 per cent versus 54.8 per cent). Among the many factors influencing academic success, five were especially important: gender, whether a student was born in Canada or abroad, entry level in the school system, cumulative delay during schooling, and socio-economic status. As regards intergroup differences, the study also documented an especially dramatic situation among students from Black communities. After seven years of secondary school (which should last five years in Quebec), their graduation rate was 17 percentage points lower than that of the overall population and, among students of West Indian origin whose first language was English or Creole, only four out of ten students graduated from secondary school. These data provide some insight into the prevalent feeling of alienation among this segment of the population, a feeling that found its expression in the 2008 riots that broke out in Montréal-Nord after a police blunder resulted in the death of a local youth.

After the publication of the aforementioned study and its wide dissemination within educational milieus and the communities concerned, a number of measures specifically targeting the Black community were implemented under the aegis of a MELS follow-up committee. Moreover, the government bodies responsible for implementing intervention strategies in underprivileged milieus are now analyzing the specific needs of ethnic communities and developing interventions that are adapted to their situations.

Intercultural Relations at School: Teachers, Parents, and Students

Promoting the recognition of diversity in Quebec schools has been challenging[25] and remains a work in progress. But noteworthy progress has been made, including the many initiatives designed to better adapt schools to their communities. In a survey of all Quebec's school principals, over 25 per cent stated that they had implemented various measures on their own initiative and reported over 1,000 successful examples of 'best practices'. The survey also showed that requests for accommodations have remained stable for the past three years and that schools are not as ill-equipped as previously reported, having acquired the necessary tools to cope with community and parental pressures. Thus, on average, 50 per cent of these requests were accepted, slightly less than 25 per cent refused, and alternative solutions were found in just over 25 per cent of cases. Significantly, despite widespread stereotypes, requests for accommodation do not come exclusively from newly arrived immigrants or Muslims. Two-thirds of these requests come from Christians and Jehovah Witnesses (many of whom are long-established Quebecers) and one-third come from Muslims.

Nevertheless, a number of stakeholders in education still harbour reservations about the impact of adapting to diversity. In the short term, they are worried about the potential conflicts between some of the accommodation measures taken and the requirements of the Education Act regarding school attendance, academic programs, or student safety. They are also questioning whether providing 'too much' accommodation could have longer-term consequences on sharing common values, creating social cohesion, or ensuring a broader inclusion of minority youth. In recent years, in Quebec as elsewhere, Muslims have become emblematic figures for many people's fears surrounding cultural and societal identity. The adaptability of Muslim families and students to sharing the common values promoted by the school system is therefore perceived by some as being problematic.

Meanwhile, although many teachers do address human rights and intercultural relations issues in their classrooms on an ad hoc basis, some research indicates that many others still resist introducing a full-scale intercultural perspective into the curriculum.[26] For example, according to a survey conducted across a large sample of francophone teachers in Montreal, Vancouver, and Toronto, their overriding objectives were to integrate students into the host and school cultures and to ensure their academic success. Thus, differences were often implicitly recognized by teachers, who adapted their teaching strategies to their students. But expressly acknowledging differences by making changes to programs and instructional content was a rarer occurrence. Anti-racist interventions mainly consisted of crisis management and ad hoc conflict resolution. Course material on racism tended to focus on events elsewhere in the world rather than the dynamics experienced within the province or within schools. It is true that many of these findings could be applied to any multi-ethnic society. But other research, analyzing the discourse of Quebec teachers of French-Canadian origin shows varying degrees of defensiveness related to their minority status in Canada and within North America and/or their concerns as a fragile majority (one that has fought long, hard battles to achieve linguistic and economic recognition, even within Quebec). Thus, adapting to diversity is seen by some teachers as a threat to 'traditional' Quebec identity. Their discourse also conveys civic concerns and stresses the need to defend values such as gender equality and democracy.

Research among youth generally confirms this glass half-empty/half-full assessment. A 1995 survey, conducted among some 2,800 Montreal secondary school students, showed that they generally shared the values of 'liberal individualism' and 'democratic egalitarianism'. Primarily, these students identified as youth and maintained a critical distance from the values of their parents, notably in inter-ethnic relations. The students of immigrant origin felt strongly about being part of Quebec society, albeit less so than third-generation students. Similarly, a more recent study found that both groups converged more than they diverged in their opinions on priority social problems and their definition of citizenship. Where differences did exist, they were more likely linked to socio-economic status than to ethnic identity.[27]

These positive trends do not mean that the blueprint (implicit among many proponents of Bill 101) to turn the children of immigrants into *Québécois d'abord et avant tout* ('Quebecers first and foremost') has actually come to fruition. Actually, many studies show that identifying as a Quebecer still ranks lower than identifying as a Canadian for most of these allophone 'children of Bill 101'. Some nationalist public figures believe that this trend reflects Quebec's ambiguous political status within Canada and can only be rectified if Quebec achieves its independence. Others view this situation differently. They contend that Canadian identity is positively linked with cultural and linguistic diversity, whereas a Quebec identity continues to be associated more exclusively with a French-Canadian heritage. Thus, many youth of immigrant origin who conduct their public lives in French, enthusiastically embrace many aspects of Quebec culture, and possess little knowledge of other Canadian provinces still tend to identify as Canadians first and foremost, an identity which they view as being more open and civic-minded and hence more apt to include them.[28] Whatever the case, any attempt to assess the impact of schooling on identity-formation processes would be presumptuous, given the multiplicity of influences on young people's identities and the fact that institutional change is still relatively new in Quebec.

LISE COUPAL: JUST AN ORDINARY TEACHER?

Lise Coupal in her classroom

Photographer: Michel La Veaux.
Les Films du 3 Mars.

Born in 1953 to a middle-class family, Lise Coupal grew up in Villeray, a working-class francophone neighbourhood in Montreal. From as far back as she can remember, she dreamed of becoming a teacher. Following her studies at CÉGEP Ahuntsic, she attended the Faculty of Education at Université du Québec à Montréal, where she earned her bachelor's degree in 1980. After working for a few years as a preschool teacher for 4-year-olds in a community setting, she joined the Protestant School Board of Greater Montreal as a welcoming class teacher for immigrant children in 1988. When Quebec's confessional school boards became linguistic school boards, she began teaching regular classes with the Commission scolaire de Montréal.

Since 2000, Lise Coupal has taught Grade One at École Barthélemy-Vimont, one of Montreal's most multi-ethnic schools, where she plans to spend the remainder of her teaching career. Every year, Coupal says she relives the special magic of Grade One, the year when she believes the metamorphosis in students is most remarkable. She also feels that teaching in a multi-ethnic setting is easier than in a more homogeneous student population. Coupal particularly appreciates the respect that parents and children show the teachers, and the importance they ascribe to education.

Transforming a public institution like a school into a welcoming, pluralistic learning environment does not just happen from the top down. It requires patience and persistency from a host of front-line participants. Lise Coupal, also known as 'Madame

Lise' is a teacher who possesses both of these qualities, in abundance. In fact, when she and her 20 students starred in a film called *La classe de Madame Lise*, it won the 2006 award for best documentary at the Jutras (Quebec's modest equivalent of the Oscars). Here is our adaptation of what *La Presse* (North America's foremost French-language daily) had to say about Madame Lise's classroom:

The Incredible Madame Lise

In Lise Coupal's classroom, you won't find many Carolines or Jean-Mathieus. The desks in her class are occupied by students with names like Adnan, Noura, Furkans, Tajinder, Sumbbal, and Hatyum. Documentary filmmaker Sylvie Groulx followed this École Barthélemy-Vimont elementary school teacher and her class of about 20 first grade students throughout the school year in Montreal's Parc-Extension neighbourhood. In her film, *La Classe de Madame Lise*, she showed that when you learn your ABCs with Madame Lise, you also learn a great deal about different cultures.

'I've never had a White Catholic class with names like Bouchard or Tremblay,' says Lise Coupal. Seated in her classroom in front of some Lilliputian desks, this devoted teacher speaks with pride about her school, where cultures mix like the multicoloured lines on the students' little rulers.

'When Sylvie Groulx walked into the school yard she was impressed by the number of nationalities she found, all together in one place,' says Lise Coupal. She reaches into the closet and takes out an imposing calendar of the cultural and religious holidays celebrated by her students. École Barthélemy-Vimont brings together students of almost 80 different ethnic origins, who speak in 30 different languages.

The small film crew came to visit Lise Coupal's class about 30 times between September and June. 'After a while, the students and I forgot about the camera completely,' says Coupal. A very discreet cameraperson succeeded in capturing some precious private moments between the teacher and her students, who were experiencing difficulties.

'I knew when I came here that people would see my method and criticize it,' she says. 'But I decided to take the plunge just the same.' Although, as she says, she plays the role of nurse, psychologist, and mother for her students, her real challenge remains teaching French and reading. 'The biggest challenge comes when parents don't speak French,' she explains. 'In those kinds of cases, I ask their older brothers or sisters to be my interpreters.' Some of Lise Coupal's students go to school on Saturdays to learn their parents' languages, like Chinese. Others study Arabic, Vietnamese, or Spanish at noon hour.

'What I like about first grade is discovering reading. I have the privilege of being part of this important moment in their lives,' says Coupal.

It has been said that École Barthélemy-Vimont is one of the most underprivileged schools in one of Montreal's most violent neighbourhoods. 'I don't believe that there is any more violence here than there is elsewhere,' says Coupal. 'That would be a distorted image of the neighbourhood.'

Coupal once turned down an offer to go teach elsewhere. After 18 years of teaching, she has difficulty understanding why young people become violent. 'When children come to my class they aren't violent. Why does it change when they turn 14 or 15? I often ask myself that question.'

When you meet her, it is easy to guess why Lise Coupal was chosen for a documentary film. Madame Lise is the ideal school teacher. Smiling, affectionate, strict but not disagreeable. With her, anyone would want to get an 'A' in every subject.

'Today' says Coupal, 'I have a great deal of difficulty hearing close-minded ideas about immigrants.'

Conclusion

Quebec's traditionally homogeneous French-language education system has undergone some radical changes over the past 30 years and continues to be shaped by public policies geared toward promoting French and openness to ethno-cultural diversity. The province has come a long way and now compares favourably with other immigrant-receiving societies. Nevertheless, many challenges lie ahead. Among other things, the marginalization of some ethnic groups, and most especially that of the Black community, must be better understood and actively prevented. Adapting to religious diversity, still a source of tension for some, will also have to be further addressed. Quebec's educational system is relatively well positioned to meet these challenges, now that it can draw upon the major policy frameworks developed by the government and upon the expertise developed by many front-line participants. Still, given the current context, in which intercultural conflict is growing in many areas around the globe and in which globalization could jeopardize some gains (notably regarding language rights), only time will tell to what extent the theories of the optimists or of the pessimists will prevail.

Questions for Consideration

1. To what extent should diversity be taken into consideration in schools?

2. What do you think are the main strengths and weaknesses of the measures taken in the integration of immigrant students and in intercultural education?

3. What results have been achieved in the integration of immigrant students and in intercultural education?

4. Do you think that Quebec's experience in adapting to ethno-cultural diversity is specific to the context and challenges of its society? How are Quebec's experiences similar or different to those in the United States or the rest of Canada?

NOTES

1. Students whose first language is neither French nor English.
2. Under Bill 101, in addition to the traditional anglophone community, English-language schools are also attended by students from Quebec's established communities of immigrant origin, the majority of whom are at least third-generation denizens. However, the transformation of English-language institutions (among other things, through the introduction of French-immersion schools), which took place in the wake of the new linguistic dynamics in Quebec, would clearly warrant further attention as a case study unto itself.
3. See chapters 12, 13, and 14.
4. Ministère de l'Immigration et des Communautés Culturelle, *Let's Build Quebec Together: Vision: A Policy Statement on Immigration and Integration* (Montreal: Direction des communications, 1990); Marie McAndrew, 'Quebec Immigration, Integration and Intercultural Policy: A Critical Assessment', *Indian Journal of Federal Studies* 15, 1 (2007): 1–18; Ministère de l'Immigration et des Communautés culturelles, *Tableaux sur l'immigration au Quebec 2003–2007* (2008).
5. Ministère de l'Éducation, du Loisir et du Sport, *Portrait scolaire des élèves issus de l'immigration: de 1994–1995 à 2003–2004* (Quebec: Government of Quebec, 2006); Marie McAndrew, *Immigration et diversité à l'école. Le débat québécois dans une perspective comparative* (Montreal: Presses de l'Université de Montréal, 2001).
6. Danielle Juteau, Marie McAndrew, and Linda Pietrantonio, 'Multiculturalism à la Canadian et intégration à la Québécoise: Transcending their limits', in Rainer Bauboeck and John Rundell, eds, *Blurred Boundaries: Migration, Ethnicity and Citizenship* (Aldershot: Ashgate / European Centre Vienna, 1998) 95–110; Daniel Salée, 'The Quebec State and the Management of Ethnocultural Diversity: Perspectives on an Ambiguous Record', in K. Banting, T.J. Courchesne, and F.L. Seidle, eds, *Belonging? Diversity, Recognition and Shared Citizenship in Canada* (Montreal: IRPP, 2007), 105–42.
7. For an overview of policy development and the surrounding debates, see Chapter 17.
8. Ministère de l'Éducation du Quebec, *A School for the Future: Policy Statement on Educational Integration and Intercultural Education—A New Direction for Success* (Quebec: Government of Quebec, 1998); McAndrew, *Immigration et diversité*.
9. J. Mallea, *Quebec's Language Policy: Background and Responses* (Quebec: CIRB, 1977); Marc V. Levine, *The Reconquest of Montreal: Language Policy and Social Change in a Bilingual City* (Philadelphia: Temple University Press, 1990).
10. Ministère de l'Éducation, du Loisir et du Sport, *L'effectif scolaire à temps plein et à temps partiel du secteur des jeunes (2003–2004 à 2007–2008) selon la langue maternelle (regroupée) et la langue d'enseignement, par région administrative et sexe* (Table 8) (Quebec: Government of Quebec, 2008).
11. Marie McAndrew, 'La loi 101 en milieu scolaire : impacts et résultats', *Revue d'aménagement linguistique*, numéro hors-série, (2002): 69–83; G. Larose, *Le français, une langue pour tout le monde* (Montreal: Commission des États généraux sur la langue française, 2001); Marie McAndrew, 'Le remplacement du marqueur linguistique par le marqueur religieux en milieu scolaire', in Jean Renaud, Linda Pietrantonio, and Guy Bourgeault, eds, *Ce qui a changé depuis le 11 septembre 2001 : les relations ethniques en question* (Montreal: Les Presses de l'Université de Montréal, 2002) 131–48.
12. Between secondary school (which ends at about age 16) and university, Quebec's school system provides an intermediate academic institution commonly referred to as CEGEP (collège d'enseignement général et professionnel) where most students study between the ages of 16 to 18. CEGEPs are somewhat akin to US community colleges, although according to international standards, they do not constitute a form of post-secondary education.
13. It is through this concept (now tainted by its overuse in the media) that Canadian jurisprudence has designated exceptions to be granted by public and private institutions to handicapped persons or members of minority groups, for whom apparently neutral or universal standards and practices effectively constitute a form of indirect discrimination.
14. Gérard Bouchard and Charles Taylor, *Building the Future: A Time for Reconciliation* (Quebec: The Consultation Commission on Accommodation Practices Related to Cultural Differences [CCAPRCD] 2008), final report available at www.accommodements.qc.ca/documentation/rapports/rapport-final-integral-en.pdf; Jocelyn McClure, 'Le malaise relatif aux pratiques d'accommodement de la diversité religieuse: une thèse interprétative' in Marie McAndrew et al., eds, *L'accommodement raisonnable et la diversité religieuse à l'école publique. Normes et pratiques* (Montreal: Fides, 2008), 215–42.
15. A kirpan is a metal dagger with a curved blade. Kirpans vary in length, but may be several centimetres long and are carried in a scabbard attached to a belt worn over the shoulder.
16. Marie McAndrew, *Immigration et diversité*; Ministère de l'Éducation, du Loisir et du Sport, *Statistiques de l'éducation : Enseignement primaire, secondaire, collégial et universitaire* (Quebec: Government of Quebec, 2007).
17. Marie McAndrew, 'Ensuring Proper Competency in the Host Language: Contrasting Formula and the Place of Heritage Languages', *Teacher College Review* 111, 6 (2009): 1528–54; Françoise Armand and Diane Dagenais 'Languages and Immigration: Raising Awareness of Language and Linguistic Diversity in Schools', *Journal of the Canadian Studies Association* Special Issue (2005): 99–102.

18. Ministère de l'Éducation, *Quebec Schools on Course: Educational Policy Statement* (Quebec: Government of Quebec, 1997); Ministère de l'Éducation, *Quebec Education Program: Preschool Education—Elementary Education* (Quebec: Government of Quebec, 2001); Ministère de l'Éducation, *Quebec Education Program: Secondary School Education, Cycle One* (Quebec: Government of Quebec, 2004); Ministère de l'Éducation, du Loisir et du Sport, *Establishment of an Ethics and Religious Culture Program: Providing Future Direction for all Quebec Youth* (Quebec: Government of Quebec, 2005).

19. Marie McAndrew, *Immigration et diversité*; B. Oueslati, 'The Evolution of the Coverage of Islam and Muslim Cultures in Quebec French-language Textbooks since the 1980s', in M. McAndrew, P. Brodeur, and A. Triki-Yamani, eds, *Islam and Education in Pluralistic Societies: Integration and Transformations* (forthcoming).

20. Maryse Potvin, Marie McAndrew, and Fasal Kanouté, *L'éducation antiraciste en milieu francophone montréalais : bilan critique*, Rapport de la Chaire en relations ethniques (Montreal: Université de Montréal, 2006); F. Kanouté, A. Lavoie, and L. Duong, 'L'interculturel et la formation des enseignants', *Éducation Canada* 44, 2 (2004): 8–10, 54.

21. Fasal Kanouté, J. Hohl, and N. Chamlian, 'Les étudiants allophones dans les programmes de premier cycle de la Faculté des sciences de l'éducation de l'Université de Montréal', in D. Mujawamariya, ed, *L'intégration des minorités visibles et ethnoculturelles dans la profession enseignante* (Outremont: Les Éditions Logiques, 2002), 183–201.

22. Marie McAndrew, 'La réussite éducative des élèves issus de l'immigration: enfin au cœur du débat sur l'intégration?', *Options CSQ* (2006):109–28; McAndrew, 'La loi 101 en milieu scolaire'; Marie McAndrew, Mathieu Jodoin, Michel Pagé, and J. Rossell, 'L'aptitude au français des élèves montréalais d'origine immigrée: impact de la densité ethnique de l'école, du taux de francisation associé à la langue maternelle et de l'ancienneté d'implantation', *Cahiers québécois de démographie* 29,1 (2000): 89–118; M. McAndrew, 'Cégeps: des nuances s'imposent. Avant de conclure à l'échec de la loi 101, il y a tout un pas à ne pas franchir', *La Presse*, 25 January 2008.

23. Catherine Girard-Lamoureux, *La langue d'usage public des allophones scolarisés au Quebec* (Quebec: Conseil supérieur de la langue française, 2004); Statistics Canada, *Le portrait linguistique en évolution, Recensement de 2006: Évolution de la situation linguistique au Quebec*, 'Analyses' series, 2007.

24. Marie McAndrew, B. Garnett, J. Ledent, C. Ungerleider, M. Adumati-Trache, and R. Ait-Said, 'La réussite scolaire des élèves issus de l'immigration : une question de classe sociale, de langue ou de culture?', *Éducation et Francophonie* XXXVI, 1 (2008): 177–96; McAndrew, 'La réussite éducative des élèves issus de l'immigration'.

25. Advisory Committee on Integration and Reasonable Accommodation in the Schools, *Inclusive Québec Schools: Dialogue, Values and Common Reference Points*, Report submitted to Minister of Education, Recreation and Sports (Quebec: Government of Québec, 2007); Marie McAndrew 'The Muslim Community and Education in Quebec: Controversies and Mutual Adaptation', in McAndrew, Brodeur, and Triki-Yamani, eds, *Islam and Education in Pluralistic Societies.*

26. Potvin, McAndrew, and Kanouté, *L'éducation antiraciste*; J. Hohl and M. Normand (2000), 'Enseigner en milieu pluriethnique dans une société divisée' in M. McAndrew and F. Gagnon, eds, *Relations ethniques et éducation dans les sociétés divisée: Quebec, Irlande du Nord, Catalogne et Belgique* (Montreal/Paris: L'Harmattan, 2000), 169–81; D. Gérin-Lajoie, *Le discours du personnel des écoles sur la diversité de la clientèle scolaire.* Paper presented at the 60th ACELF Congress, 2007.

27. Michel Pagé, Marie McAndrew, and Mathieu Jodoin, *Vécu scolaire et social des élèves scolarisés dans les écoles secondaires de langue française de l'île de Montréal*, Research report (Montreal: Ministère des Relations avec les citoyens et de l'Immigration du Quebec, 1997); A. Laperrière and P. Dumont, *La citoyenneté chez de jeunes Montréalais: vécu scolaire et représentations de la société*, Research report (Montreal: GREAPE, Université de Montréal, 2000).

28. Marie-H. Chastenay and Michel Pagé, 'Le rapport à la citoyenneté et à la diversité chez les jeunes collégiens québécois: comment se distinguent les deuxièmes générations d'origine immigrée?' in Nancy Venel, Paul Eid, and Maryse Potvin, eds, *Les deuxième générations en France et au Quebec* (Montreal: Éditions Athéna, 2007); Maryse Potvin, 'Second Generation Haitian Youth in Quebec: Between the "Real" Community and the "Represented" Community', *Canadian Ethnic Studies* 31,1 (1999): 43–73.

RELEVANT WEBSITES

CANADA RESEARCH CHAIR IN EDUCATION AND ETHNIC RELATIONS: www.chereum.umontreal.ca/

MONTREAL SCHOOL BOARD: www.csdm.qc.ca/csdm/index.asp

MINISTÈRE DE L'ÉDUCATION, DU LOISIR ET DU SPORT DU QUÉBEC (MELS): www.mels.gouv.qc.ca/

METROPLIS WEBSITE: http://im.metropolis.net/frameset_e.html

An international network for comparative research and public policy development on migration, diversity, and immigrant integration in cities in Canada and around the world.

SELECT BIBLIOGRAPHY

Advisory Committee on Integration and Reasonable Accommodation in the Schools. *Inclusive Québec Schools: Dialogue, Values and Common Reference Points.* Report submitted to Minister of Education, Recreation and Sports. Quebec: Government of Québec, 2007.

Bouchard, Gérard, and Charles Taylor. *Building the Future: A Time for Reconciliation.* Quebec: The Consultation Commission on Accommodation Practices Related to Cultural Differences (CCAPRCD), 2008.

McAndrew, Marie. 'Ensuring Proper Competency in the Host Language: Contrasting Formula and the Place of Heritage Languages'. *Teacher College Review* 111, 6 (2009): 1528–54.

McAndrew, Marie. 'The Education of Immigrant Students in a Globalized World: Policy Debates in a Comparative Perspective'. In M. Suarez-Orozco, ed. *Global Understandings: Learning and Education in Troubled Times.* Berkeley/London/New York: University of California Press/Ross Institute, 2006, 232–55.

Ministère de l'Éducation du Québec. *A School for the Future: Policy Statement on Educational Integration and Intercultural Education—A New Direction for Success.* Quebec: Government of Québec, 1998.

Ministère de l'Immigration et des Communautés Culturelles. *Diversity: An Added Value: Government Policy to Promote Participation of all in Québec's Development.* Quebec: Direction des politiques et programmes d'intégration, de régionalisation et de relations interculturelles, 2008.

Ministère de l'Immigration et des Communautés Culturelles. *Let's Build Quebec Together: Vision: A Policy Statement on Immigration and Integration.* Montreal: Direction des communications, 1990.

Part E
Quebec Models

Introduction

Part 5 of *Quebec Questions* speaks directly to Quebec's distinctive style and form. Titled 'Quebec Models', this section presents contributions on how Quebec has successfully developed unique approaches and policies to a variety of significant social and economic matters. The central questions that permeate each of these essays, designed to lead readers into analytical inquiry, are: Why has Quebec chosen to carefully craft a distinctively unique, context-specific approach?; What factors and personalities have shaped the agenda?; Has this pursuit of an identifiably Quebec-style model benefitted Quebecers?

Diane Lamoureux's examination of feminism in Quebec makes it clear that the Quebec feminist movement is, from the outset, and for a variety of reasons, 'exceptional within North America'. This movement is indeed most strikingly still foremost a movement. It has not, unlike the United States, been reconceptualized and institutionalized in the framework of higher education nor has it undergone pervasive fragmentation. It has changed over time, Lamoureux writes, most notably in the expanding agenda of Quebec

feminism, increased majority representation of francophone women, and the increasing success of feminist-sponsored legislation and corresponding policies. This contribution sketches a rich history of feminism *à la Québécoise*, underscoring the much needed and pivotal roles that women have played in advancing Quebec society.

Health care in Quebec is the focus of the second chapter in this section. It has been driven and shaped, author Antonia Maioni reminds us, by political, social, economic, and medical factors that have combined to produce a distinctively Quebec approach to health-care policy and services. The historical development of health care in Quebec is explained against a backdrop of federal and provincial personalities, policies, and institutions. This overview effectively demonstrates that the planning and delivery of health care in Quebec is decidedly different, from that in the rest of Canada and in the United States. The negotiation of physicians' fees, the implementation of medical insurance, and the general relationship between the state and the medical community all illustrate this point. Maioni does point out, however, that private health care has recently made inroads in Quebec—the lasting impact of which, given Quebec's particular approach to health care, largely remains to be determined.

Hydroelectricity—its development and use—is yet another seminal issue that further distinguishes Quebec. Author David Massell walks us through the history of hydroelectric power in Quebec throughout the twentieth century, stressing first the role of private enterprise, and then examining the establishment of the colossus public corporation Hydro-Québec, and the eventual nationalization of the industry. Driven by 'practical and ideological' considerations, Quebec's hydroelectric footprint has not, Massell informs us, been without controversy. As that footprint has sought to grow ever larger since the 1970s, with varying degrees of success, voices of concern—notably those of Quebec's First Nations communities—have repeatedly arisen. The story of hydroelectricity in Quebec has been and will continue to be, this chapter tells us, one of fundamental 'human struggle to contest and control the province's hydro sector'.

Peter Graefe, in his examination of social and economic development in Quebec, provides compelling evidence that politics—as fashioned and championed by the push and pull of political parties and leaders, the business community, labour, and various interest groups—is pivotal to any understanding of Quebec's development model. The principal model of development for Quebec, we learn, emerged in the Quiet Revolution of the 1960s and to this day, maintains significant resonance. Yet as Graefe importantly

underscores, since the government of Robert Bourassa, and most notably today under the leadership of Jean Charest, Quebec has undergone a movement toward neo-liberalism, and its social consensus is thereby challenged. The Quebec model nonetheless remains 'distinct in North America in its adoption of shareholder partnerships and community development'.

The final contribution in this section, focused on the regional dynamics of Quebec, is provided by Gilbert Gagné. The author seeks to place and measure Quebec's regional economic relationships in a North American context, with a focus on the notable impacts of the 1989 Canada–United States Free Trade Agreement and the subsequent 1994 North American Free Trade Agreement between Canada, the United States, and Mexico. We learn that the Quebec–US economic relationship before these agreements was indeed significant, with Quebec exporting nearly 80 per cent of its goods and resources to the United States and having an excellent track record for attracting American foreign direct investment. The north–south dynamic of Quebec's substantial economic engagement with the United States thus pre-dates the arrival of free trade. Yet what did the two far-reaching international agreements do to this dynamic? The answer, as Gagne illustrates, has been a discernible deepening of the dynamic, especially that with the United States. The author provides a rich variety of statistical economic indicators that demonstrate a robust level of integration between these actors. The regional dynamics of Quebec's economic relationships clearly suggest, Gagne notes, a distinctive Quebec approach.

CHAPTER 20

The Paradoxes of Quebec Feminism

Diane Lamoureux, Université Laval

— TIMELINE —

1966   Fédération des femmes du Québec formed.

1969   Montreal Women's Liberation Movement founded.

Front de libération des femmes founded.

1970   First pro-choice demonstration in Quebec takes place on Mother's Day.

1972   Centre des femmes established.

Teach-In on feminism held at Université du Québec à Montréal, bringing together academics and activists.

1974   *Nous aurons les enfants que nous voulons* manifesto published.

1975   Centre de santé des femmes established.

First battered women's shelter opens, managed by feminists.

1975   Bookstore Librairie des femmes d'ici opens.

1976   Publishing house Les Éditions du remue-ménage created.

Play *La nef des sorcières* performed at Théâtre du Nouveau Monde.

First issue of radical feminist newsletter *Les Têtes de pioche* released.

Debates held and speakers featured at the first anniversary of Librairie des femmes d'ici.

1977   First issue of *Pluri-elles*, a liaison newsletter for women's groups, released, and later becomes *Des luttes et des rires de femmes*, (also a feminist collective).

Play *Les fées ont soif* performed, leading to general protest and mobilization of Catholic groups.

Coop-femmes, Quebec's first francophone lesbian group, founded.

1978   Coordination nationale pour l'avortement libre et gratuit founded and mobilizes a large pro-choice movement.

Parti Québécois releases its *Pour les Québécoises : Égalité et Indépendance* report on improving the status of women in an independent Quebec.

1980   *La Vie en rose*, a high-circulation feminist magazine, launches its first issue (1987).

1982   *Amazones d'hier, lesbiennes d'aujourd'hui*, a radical lesbian magazine, launches its first issue (1992).

First annual Journées de visibilité lesbienne held (and continues).

1984   Quebec feminist magazine *Marie-Géographie* publishes its first issue (1987).

Projet Gilford, a multidisciplinary feminist and lesbian activity centre, established.

1985 Network of women's centres L'R des centres de femmes du Québec founded.

1988 Book fair La Foire internationale du livre féministe held in Montreal.

1989 Record-breaking number of pro-choice demonstrations held in support of Chantal Daigle.

Fourteen women gunned down in anti-feminist Montreal Massacre at École Polytechnique.

Association canadienne-française pour l'avancement des sciences (ACFAS) creates Feminist Studies section.

1990 Conference Les 50 heures du féminisme held to celebrate fiftieth anniversary of women's suffrage legislation in Quebec.

1992 Pour un Québec féminin pluriel conference held.

1995 Bread and Roses March takes place.

1998 Némésis, a feminist alter-globalization group, formed.

2000 FFQ organizes the year 2000 World March for Women.

Radical feminist magazine *Les sorcières* launches its first issue.

2003 Penser enfin une démocratie avec les femmes conference held, linking women's equal political representation with electoral reform.

FFQ's young feminists hold the Colloque des jeunes féministes.

2005 *La Vie en rose* publishes a special issue.

2008 Toujours RebELLES—Waves of Resistance Pan-Canadian Young Feminist Gathering held.

Feminism shows every sign of being alive and well to this day, throughout Quebec. With its thousands of groups, a solid capacity to mobilize its forces and attract a new generation of feminists, and an impressive ability to influence public debate, the Quebec feminist movement is often the envy of women from other countries and sometimes the bane of masculinists in its own back yard[1] (who see in it a [post]modern resurgence of matriarchy). It has even succeeded in motivating Quebec's political elites to declare, in a rare show of unanimity, that equality between women and men is now an integral part of 'Quebec's values'.[2]

Quebec's situation is exceptional within North America, in that elsewhere on the continent feminist ideas and practices had their heyday in the 1970s, only to see the resultant poles of reflection move into university subjects such as Women's Studies and Gender Studies thereafter. Today, in much of North America, there is little connection between the ideas expressed in academic discussions and the practices developed in women's groups. Perhaps in this respect the comparatively small-scale institutionalization of feminist studies in Quebec universities represents an advantage for the feminist cause, in that it remains well connected to movements on the ground. The other element that distinguishes the feminist movement in Quebec is its sustained ability to rally a united front, whereas in the rest of Canada and the United States, feminist movements have been forced to contend with attacks from (neo-)conservative and religious fundamentalist currents and consequently suffered widespread fragmentation over the past 15 years or so.

The robust constitution of feminism in Quebec has been the fruit of long, hard work and dedication. For more than 40 years, the demands made by women's groups for gender equality and women's liberation not only have changed the course of women's and men's lives in Quebec, but also have succeeded in legislating change to eradicate legal discrimination against women (by reforming family law, the legal status of women, and labour legislation) and in instituting new wide-ranging public policies (such as daycare, parental leaves, pay equity, family planning services, and battered women's shelters). It is because of feminism that Quebec women have broken through glass ceilings to establish themselves in a variety of professional fields, dramatically transforming both public and private life in the process.

Regrettably, for years the movement has mainly involved women from Quebec's 'majority group', often called 'les Québécoises de souche'.[3] But, little by little, Quebec's 'minority' women have come to play a larger part in the mainstream movement. Feminist Aboriginal women, who have developed a movement unto themselves with their own distinctive dynamics, have also carved out a place for themselves within the movement, signing a solidarity declaration with Quebec's largest feminist umbrella organization, the Fédération des femmes du Québec (FFQ). Anglophone women have been active in promoting feminism since its inception in Quebec but, as a group, no longer play the predominant role they once did in the early twentieth century.

More recently, we have seen successful Quebec-wide meetings, like that organized by the FFQ's young feminist committee in 2003, or the Quebec-initiated Toujours RebELLES—Waves of Resistance Pan-Canadian Young Feminists Gathering, held in 2008. These kinds of events, along with steady enrolment in feminist studies programs, are clearly demonstrating that feminism was not just a cause taken up by one or two generations, but is quite naturally being championed by the next— if only because gender inequalities and patriarchy have continued to feed revolt and anger among younger and older women alike.[4]

In this look back at the recent history of Quebec feminism, I will highlight the fascinating paradoxes it presents: the importance of the reformist pole and the concurrent presence of a radical pole; the provision of services and the work to politicize and mobilize; the cultural homogeneity of the movement and its openness to pluralism; the collective public movement and the individual lifestyle transformations it has introduced into women's private lives. Through each of these paradoxes, it will become apparent that Quebec feminism not a uniform, monolithic movement but one that continues to be enriched by unsuspected resources and undercurrents.

MICHÈLE ASSELIN

Michèle Asselin (left) receives the Prix québécois de la citoyenneté 2008 (Quebec's 2008 citizenship award) from the provincial Minister of Immigration and Cultural Communities, Yolande James. Asselin's award acknowledged her work as president of the Fédération des Femmes du Québec in the fight against racism.

© MICC

Michèle Asselin's activism exemplifies that of thousands of feminists like her, working in women's groups throughout Quebec. You could say she has made Quebec women's groups her career, as they have formed the backdrop to her entire professional life. In contrast to the ideologically entrenched feminist approaches of the 1970s, Asselin built up her understanding of feminism through her own careful circumspection about the issues she tackled in her activism.

After studying community organizing at Université du Québec à Montréal, Michèle Asselin worked as the Coordinator of the Centre d'éducation et d'action des femmes de Montréal (CEAF). Founded in 1972, this centre in the Ste-Marie–St-Jacques riding of Montreal is a good example of how local roots and networking have served the Quebec women's movement. Although mainly concerned with popular education, CEAF also offers a range of services for women in this underprivileged neighbourhood (such as Internet access and a drop-in daycare service). It was instrumental in developing a local community health service centre (CLSC), introducing social housing resources for single mothers, and setting up a popular local daycare centre, which was then integrated into the CPE (Centres de la petite enfance or early-childhood agency) network. The centre has a reputation for promoting grassroots politicization as part of its mandate of popular education, organizing, for example, workshops on such topics as the impact of neo-liberal globalization on women and the Déclaration citoyenne, in which women envisioned the kind of city they wished to live in. Moreover, it was CEAF that established a structure for coordinating women's centres across Quebec: L'R des centres de femmes du Québec (R stands for 'regroupement' or 'grouping').

Not surprisingly, after working for several years as the coordinator at CEAF, Michèle Asselin went on to become the coordinator of L'R des centres de femmes du Québec, a position she held for some 15 years. It was during her tenure as CEAF coordinator that Asselin sat on the Coalition des femmes pour l'accès à l'égalité, on the advisory board for women's programs at the Commission de la formation professionnelle de Montréal, and on the board of directors at Relais-femmes (an organization that links feminist researchers and women's groups). Her work was a reflection of the areas in which women's groups played an active role in Quebec at the time: group-to-group networking, advocacy for equality rights policies (with government and paragovernmental organizations), and linkages between feminist researchers at universities and women's groups.

When Asselin was the coordinator of L'R des centres de femmes du Québec (1988–2003), the group was very active on several fronts: ensuring that women were participating in regional development structures; establishing the Equal Access to Decision Making program to increase the number of women holding key positions in local and municipal governing bodies; and mobilizing to fight both neo-liberal globalization and poverty. Again, Asselin's work embodied the ever-expanding gamut of the feminist movement's priorities of the times, including participating in government consultations on women's equality, and rallying wider forces for new civil rights and public policies. While she was coordinating

L'R des centres de femmes du Québec, she was also involved in organizing Les 50 heures du féminisme (a conference to celebrate the 50th anniversary of legislation on women's suffrage in Quebec).

This was a pivotal period in the relationship between women's groups and the Quebec government. From the outset, the women's movement had a polemical relationship with the state apparatus: while it was well aware of the government's shortcomings when it came to promoting gender equality, it intended to take full advantage of favourable 'structures of political opportunity' to influence these policies in a positive manner. However, by 1996 the neo-liberal watershed established by successive 'cost-cutting' government administrations (irrespective of the party in power) progressively closed political opportunities for grass-roots organizations and radicalized the women's movement.

An early example of this radicalization was the Bread and Roses March, which promoted the movement's anti-poverty agenda, with a specific (but not exclusive) focus on poverty affecting women. The march inaugurated two crucial linkage initiatives within the women's movement. The first was the link women made between their struggles with the fight against neo-liberal globalization. This led the movement to establish an enduring association with the Collective for a Law on the Elimination of Poverty (comprising community and union organizations), then with the Réseau de vigilance (an umbrella group of feminist, union, community, and environmental organizations that were taking a stand against neo-liberal policies and against the Charest government itself), and to participate in the 2001 People's Summit and the 2007 Forum social québécois. The second linkage initiative made connections between local, national, and international feminist struggles during the NGO Forum at the UN World Conference on Women in Beijing; the organization of the year 2000 World March of Women; the various editions of the World Social Forum; and the adoption of the Women's Global Charter for Humanity in 2005.

Throughout Michèle Asselin's presidency at the FFQ from 2003 to 2009, she was confronted with a multitude of challenging issues: carving out a place in the movement for Aboriginal and minority-culture women; creating a cohesive local, national, and international approach to the movement's activities; repositioning the FFQ politically on local and global issues; and combating the united forces of neo-liberalism and neo-conservatism, along with the rise of masculinism.

Under her tenure, Asselin initiated a major reorganization of the FFQ. Among other achievements, a committee of immigrant and racialized women was struck and a collaborative agreement signed with Quebec Native Women. She took a pro-active role in the FFQ political platform review at home, maintained a dynamic presence abroad, and ensured much greater autonomy for the World March of Women (as an independent but affiliated entity), both within francophone spaces and at the World Social Forum. Michèle Asselin also distinguished herself as a vocal defender of free access to abortion and an expert builder of coalitions to maintain and expand women's rights.

THE 1970S: SEPARATE PATHS

The 1970s have been lauded by some as the golden age of feminism in Quebec, as in many other parts of the Western world.[5] Three major elements set this decade apart: the drive of some governments to 'modernize' by updating family law to suit new social realities; the new cohort of reformist feminists who were willing to work with their respective governments; and the emergence of a more radical feminist fringe that raised new issues and developed terms of engagement in the struggle.

This remarkable generalized trend in North America and Western Europe was accompanied in Quebec by the dynamics of the Quiet Revolution—a vast state-engineered modernization of Quebec society through a movement that had been building for two decades. The Quiet Revolution began with the election of the provincial Liberal Party under Jean Lesage in 1960 and continued until the Quebec referendum of 1980. Although women were not the first to be invited to the table during the Quiet Revolution, their influence was undeniable. Using the Quiet Revolution as a jumping off point, this chapter focuses on the reconfiguration of the reformist feminist current and the emergence of radical feminism in Quebec. But first, let us revisit one vital event in feminist history.

Quebec passed legislation granting eligible women citizens the right to vote in 1940 (the last province in Canada to do so). As in many other parts of the world, this landmark victory led to a relative post-suffrage lull among Quebec's feminist groups. But while activity waned in these groups, scores of women continued putting feminism into practice in labour organizations, pacifist movements, university communities, and professional groups. So in demonstrable ways the feminist movement did continue, building expertise in various areas, but was less visible for many years.

Fast-forward to the effervescent years of the Quiet Revolution. In 1965, women decided to rally together to celebrate the twenty-fifth anniversary of suffrage legislation. It was an occasion for feminists to stand together once again and boost the movement's visibility. It was also a chance to make the most out of having a newly elected female provincial cabinet minister and of the Quebec government's new openness to significantly change the legal status of married women[6] and guarantee equal scholastic opportunities for girls and boys.[7]

Former suffragettes like Thérèse Casgrain, labour organizers like Madeleine Parent, young academics like sociologist Monique Bégin, committed pacifists like Simone Monet-Chartrand and Laurette Sloane, and a host of other women (mostly from the greater Montreal area) came together for the twenty-fifth anniversary celebrations. They would all take part in founding a new feminist lobby group, the Fédération des femmes du Québec (FFQ), that would take advantage of the winds of change at both federal and provincial levels to promote women's rights.[8] The FFQ was similar to some of Quebec's past feminist organizations in that it set out to bring anglophones and francophones together and to provide a coordinating structure for the political representation of Quebec women to public authorities. For this reason, the FFQ was predominantly constituted by organizations, though individual women could also hold membership.

Being the last women in Canada to receive the vote in provincial elections, these women had learned valuable lessons from the suffrage movement. They had also seen how particularly reactionary the Quebec provincial government had been compared with the Canadian government, which had been engaged in the process of building the welfare state since the end of the Second World War. This process gained momentum and integrity at the end of the 1960s, when Prime Minister Pierre Elliott Trudeau's Liberal Party government presented its 'just society' political platform. As the Liberal Party's progressive policies continued to win favour with feminists, it was not surprising, during the 1980 referendum campaign on sovereignty, to see the (officially non-partisan) FFQ discreetly support the Liberal-backed 'Yvettes' movement.[9] Moreover, the sitting FFQ president, Sheila Finestone, would later go on to become a Liberal Member of Parliament.

The Quiet Revolution also brought major transformations to rural areas, leading women in these communities to feel that their organizations were due for some major change as well. In 1966, the same year that the FFQ was founded, the Association féminine d'éducation et d'action sociale (AFÉAS)[10] was established. AFÉAS was the product of a merger between the Union catholique des femmes rurales and the Cercles d'économie domestique. In the beginning, AFÉAS was more conservative than the FFQ and defended 'feminine specificity', an approach predicated on the role of rural women within the family. However, AFÉAS quickly shifted its political orientation to suit the changing needs of its members. Many of the Association's members were de facto partners or 'co-operating spouses' in their husbands' family businesses (farms, professional occupations, or small businesses), often receiving no financial consideration. During the 1970s, after access to separation and divorce was expanded and the influence of the Catholic Church on social mores had broken down, some of these former 'homemakers' were getting separated and divorced—and losing everything they had worked for in the process. AFÉAS vigorously lobbied

to have the legal status of 'co-operating spouses' recognized and fought for them to receive a more equitable share of the family patrimony.[11]

Soon enough, the separate political lobbying of the FFQ and AFÉAS became so similar that their efforts fell 'into sync', and their combined impetus prompted the Quebec government to take a comprehensive look at the 'status of women', close on the heels of an identical initiative taken by the federal government. Consultation on Carrefour 75 process (the Quebec government's initiative to celebrate International Women's Year declared by the UN) was subsequently launched, along with the consultations that culminated in the *Pour les Québécoises : Égalité et Indépendance* report. It was these consultations that would later serve as the basis for substantive legislative reform to improve the status of women in Quebec.

As this reformist pole of feminism established itself, another more radical current was also developing, demanding women's 'liberation'.

> What was obvious for the women's liberation movement at the end of the 1960s was the radical will to break with everything it found in the present: there was no acknowledgement of the legitimacy of earlier feminist currents. On the contrary, feminists now considered it a priority to mark a break with earlier women's movements.[12]

This radical new kind of feminism included the belief that women-only organizations were needed if feminist struggles were to succeed. Furthermore, since there was a perception that women's legal equality had been achieved but that de facto equality had yet to be realized, 'women's liberation' came to trump 'equality' as the radical movement's chief imperative. 'Liberation' was the only demand deemed to be truly radical, as it marked a dramatic departure from past feminist movements, like that of the suffragettes, which were indiscriminately labelled as 'bourgeois' or 'reformist'—supreme insults in the radical feminist political epithets of the times.[13]

Into this era of radicalism, two major radical feminist organizations were born. The Montreal Women's Liberation Movement (MWLM) was founded mainly by anglophone women students from McGill University, and the Front de Libération des femmes (FLF) was founded mainly by francophone women, and most members of both groups subscribed to the tenets of radical Quebec nationalist currents.[14] Instead of addressing the issues of discrimination against women and equal opportunity as past groups did, these two groups drew their inspiration from radical American feminism, which held that women's exploitation and oppression were caused by a sexist, materialist, male-dominated social system, the patriarchy. Since these radical groups distrusted capitalist, patriarchal governments, they placed no faith in legislative change but introduced consciousness-raising activities for women and staged direct action events to unmask the various manifestations of women's oppression. Some of these actions included occupying taverns (to condemn their longstanding men-only rule), occupying the jury bench during the court case of Lise Balcer[15] (to protest the fact that women could not legally serve as jurors),[16] and disrupting proceedings at the Salon de la femme, a women's trade show (to denounce the diktats of the fashion and beauty industries).

It was not long before the MWLM and the FLF added their voices to those calling for the decriminalization of abortion, which was already included in the recommendations of the federal government's Royal Commission on the Status of Women (the Bird Commission).[17] But this was only the beginning of their involvement in the struggle for abortion rights. Both organizations operated referral and transportation services for women to get safe abortions in New York state, where legislation was more liberal at the time, and worked with qualified physicians in Montreal who were willing to provide clandestine abortions. These services became part of their shared tradition of direct action.

Quebec's radical feminist current was also committed to linking women's liberation with the drive for Quebec sovereignty. This commitment was clearly expressed in one slogan from that era:

No women's liberation without the liberation of Quebec, no liberation of Quebec without women's liberation![18]

As with most social movements during the Quiet Revolution (including community, student, and union movements), the scope of this feminist current's actions was resolutely Québécois[19] and not Canadian. A particularly striking example of this tendency was the FLF's refusal to join a radical Canadian feminist initiative in its pan-Canadian feminist caravan to promote abortion rights in 1971.

When the FLF was dissolved in 1972, the Centre des femmes was quick to take up the mantle of its pro-choice activities, particularly through its abortion referral services. Some Centre activists began organizing homemakers in low-income neighbourhoods and set up daycare facilities so that mothers of young children could pursue their professional aspirations,[20] while others worked in solidarity with labour struggles or defended the rights of social assistance recipients—more often than not, women. One of the most important activities of the Centre des femmes was publishing its radical feminist newsletter, *Québécoises deboutte!*

The Centre des femmes ceased operations in 1975 and was replaced by more specialized organizations loosely connected by an inter-group structure.[21] Taking advantage of a window of opportunity afforded by Carrefour 75, women's groups established a wide array of organizations throughout Quebec, setting up bookstores, publishing houses, newspapers, battered women's shelters, women's health centres, community women's centres, non-union women's labour groups, labour-union status of women committees, and lesbian organizations. Most of these organizations identified with radical feminism and their early combined physiognomy remains intact in Quebec to this day: together, they form a highly decentralized movement, stretched out in a capillary fashion across the province, often dispensing services to a population larger than the membership of its collectives, each of which use consensus decision-making on an independent basis but still have a remarkable ability to rally their numbers to organize common-front initiatives.[22] It has been through this physiognomy that a wide spectrum of ideological currents have grown and blossomed in Quebec over the years.

Certainly, no survey of Quebec radical feminism would be complete without mentioning two influential newsletters that drew attention to the ideological currents of the late 1970s and early 1980s: *Les Têtes de pioche*,[23] which aimed to be the standard-bearer of radical feminist thinking, and *Amazones d'hier, lesbiennes d'aujourd'hui* (AHLA), which defended the ideas of radical lesbianism. *Les Têtes de pioche* was created as a reaction to a tendency it perceived in part of the Quebec feminist movement to dilute women's struggles among other social struggles. Its goal was to disseminate the ideas developed by radical American feminists and to promote the full independence of the women's movement from patriarchal institutions, be they left-wing political groups, governmental organizations, or unions. As for AHLA,[24] it defended lesbian autonomy from the feminist movement and the idea that the constructed social nomenclatures of 'men' and 'women' only hold meaning within a heterosexual political, economic, ideological, and social matrix.

FEMINIST CONFLUENCES: 1980–1995

By reconfiguring as a vast network of small collectives, working on specialized issues (linked by type and region), the Quebec women's movement not only laid solid foundations for feminist ideas but also effectively ensured the wide dissemination of these ideas throughout Quebec society. This reconfiguration transformed mindsets, but that was not all. It also meant that the 'feminist' movement became the 'women's' movement, it allowed for the development of service provision, and it ensured greater social visibility for feminist ideas. The ideological boundaries between the radical current and the reformist current, which had structured much of 1970s feminism, were significantly blurred in the process.

The transition from a 'feminist' movement to a 'women's' movement took place gradually and almost imperceptibly, through the provision of services and the dissemination of the movement across Quebec.[25] In a way, women's groups had become women's 'unions', representing the interests of women as a social category, but women's groups were also charged with the responsibility of 'managing' women. These roles were constructed on two levels: at a first level, women's groups were essentially constituted to represent women's interests, but within the government's established parameters of interest-group policy

management; at a second level, the government would use the expertise of women's groups to translate feminist demands into public policies. These dynamics explain why some feminists ended up working in government offices or (through political parties) entered government itself.

The struggle for abortion rights was a case in point, as the Comité de lutte pour l'avortement libre et gratuit and some women's centres that provided abortion services agreed to work with civil servants from the Ministère de la Santé and the Ministère des Affaires sociales[26] to set up services in some CLSCs[27] and to partner with the Centre de santé des femmes de Montréal as an accredited abortion facility.[28] Groups for the prevention of violence against women also organized workshops designed for civil servants from the Ministère de la Justice and various police forces to formulate intervention protocols for partner violence. Yet other women's groups contributed to drafting the Quebec government's policy on pay equity.

The drive to provide services to women was congruent with a desire not to await the downfall of the patriarchal system to improve women's lives in the here-and-now. Still, ambivalence about choosing this path was evident, and surfaced in three core points of tension: program funding and political activism; the transition from activism to employment; and the subordinate integration of women's groups within the state apparatus. Underlying all of these tensions was the fact that these services were often bogged down in their everyday concerns and had little capacity to innovate.

This brings us to the first point of tension: funding and political activism. Simply securing government funds (often piecemeal, short-term, and in competition with other groups) for the survival of these services was an exhausting exercise in itself, leaving little time or energy for mobilization. So base groups attempted to remedy this situation by forming non-competitive Quebec-wide coordinating structures (according to type of service) to establish leverage through collective bargaining with the government rather than undergo case-by-case evaluations.

The second point of tension—concerning the transition from activism to employment—was twofold. First, the relative distance between 'permanent' employees and 'clients' could undermine democracy within women's groups.[29] Second, their political logic was partially replaced by therapeutic logic. Instead of using a political analysis of the patriarchal social structures causing women's problems, groups began to focus on finding solutions for individual women within the framework of existing social systems, reducing their broader focus to a case-by-case therapeutic analysis (with all of its inherent political limitations).

The third point of tension was that these services, which were primarily state-funded, served as smokescreens for public-sector inaction, allowing the government to buy social services at a discount. This type of transaction was the epitome of neo-liberal logic: the state had ensured that civil society would shoulder the burden of social solidarity. Thus feminist-initiated social service provision and its ambivalent position—between direct action activism and subordinate integration into public policy initiatives—effectively contributed to blurring the boundaries between the radical and reformist currents discussed earlier.

From 1980 to 1995, the visibility of feminism increased considerably in the public space. The many factors that contributed to this visibility included legal gains (which demonstrated feminists' ability to influence public policy) and a widespread media presence. This media presence was enhanced by the dissemination of 'writing in the feminine'[30] as a new generation of female authors emerged, adopted feminism to varying degrees, and managed to have their work published. All of this was made possible because feminist publishers like Les Éditions du remue-ménage and La pleine lune led the way, but also because many publishers had decided to produce 'women's collections' to keep up with the new competition(!). The same pattern was seen throughout the creative arts. Not only were more women gaining prominence in theatre, dance, and visual arts, but the venues dedicated to women's creation were also growing and developing (such as Powerhouse Gallery, now called La Centrale, and Théâtre expérimental des femmes, which later became L'Espace Go). In print, *La Vie en rose,* a high-circulation feminist magazine, not only influenced the mass media, which began covering feminist issues, but also influenced mainstream women's magazines, which began to venture beyond the subjects of fashion,

beauty, and cooking to maintain their readerships. Landmarks that promoted and generated creation, such as Maisons de femmes, feminist bookstores, and women's cafés, dotted the urban landscape.

In 1989, the Quebec feminist movement was thrust more squarely into the media spotlight both at home and abroad by two incidents. The first occurred when the abortion rights[31] of a Quebec woman named Chantal Daigle were violated.[32] For weeks on end, the media focused on Daigle's harrowing (and highly saleable) personal narrative with rapt attention as pro-choice forces rallied feminist lawyers, health-care advocates, performers, artists, and activists, setting records for the number and breadth of demonstrations they held. The second incident occurred a few months later, when 14 female engineering students were gunned down at École Polytechnique by a man who 'accused' them of being feminists. Of course, the media provided extensive coverage of the incident and of the plethora of feminist events held in Quebec[33] and around the globe that denounced the anti-feminist, misogynist nature of the 'Montreal Massacre'.[34] But in an effort to 'balance' coverage, feminist expertise on male violence was ignored.

Clearly, reporting on feminist issues did not make the Quebec media pro-feminist. In fact, the recurring message during this period was that feminism had lost its relevance. According to this distilled post-feminist reasoning, the feminist movement had been necessary in the 1960s and 1970s when discrimination against women was blatant and prevalent in almost all aspects of society; but since the proper laws had been put in place and society had changed for the better, feminism was no longer necessary; therefore, anyone who still believed feminism to be necessary was just going to drag society into a messy war of the sexes that would be a lose–lose proposition for men and women alike.[35]

Against this backdrop of neo-liberal politics and 'post-feminist' media messages, the 1990 Les 50 heures du féminisme conference (organized by Relais-Femmes to celebrate the fiftieth anniversary of suffrage legislation), was planned as an opportunity for the feminist movement to take stock of past struggles and practices, and look to the future. However, history would take an unexpected turn when relations between the 'majority'

'Québécoises de souche' feminist groups and those from 'minority' cultures became a central concern. In this case, the object of concern was not past struggles between the two groups,[36] but the very controversial Lise Payette, who had been chosen as a figurehead for the event. Payette was a media celebrity who polarized opinion on several fronts. Certainly, no one questioned her feminist convictions. She had denounced injustices against women and taken action to effect change both during her career as a radio and television host and as a provincial cabinet minister. Controversy had swirled around Payette over her role in the Quebec nationalist movement and the Yvettes affair in 1980, but that was of relatively little concern in 1990. It was her prominent role as a writer and narrator of the documentary film *Disparaître* that exposed her to more damning criticism. The premise of the documentary was that the French-Canadian nation was losing ground in Canada (demographically, socially, and politically) to the anglophone majority, due to Quebec's low birthrate and insufficient measures to ensure that immigrants to Quebec would learn French. A number of women's groups who regarded the film as being xenophobic vigorously protested Payette's presence at the conference and promised to boycott it if the organizing committee did not reverse its decision to reserve a place of honour for Payette. The decision was not reversed, Payette continued as a figurehead of the event, and the boycott was carried out.

The Payette controversy brought about a major paradigm shift in relations between majority-group and minority-group women in the Quebec feminist movement. Fortunately, the matter was not completely swept under the rug. In fact, it formed the basis of another meeting to adopt the Québec féminin pluriel[37] platform, an attempt (years after the *Manifeste des femmes québécoises*[38] was drafted to address the issue of the intersectionality of oppressions[39]) to pave the way for a new kind of feminism in Quebec, one that would actively welcome a diversity of women. These kinds of ideas opened a new chapter in the development of Quebec feminism, although they did not heal all wounds. Only a few months later, when the Meech Lake Accord was rejected by some Canadian provinces,[40] the wounds were reopened as discussions about the Accord between feminists

in Quebec and feminists from 'Canada-outside-of-Quebec',[41] and also among feminists within Quebec, caused major rifts once again. During the 1995 sovereignty referendum campaign, relations fared no better when the FFQ decided to support the 'Yes' camp (in favour of Quebec sovereignty) despite an embarrassing public declaration from Lucien Bouchard, leader of the federal Bloc Québécois, that Quebecers constituted: 'one of the White races [in the world] that [was] producing the fewest number of children'. Even greater damage was done on the evening of the referendum when the results were known, and Quebec nationalist Premier Jacques Parizeau made an infamous speech blaming the defeat of his sovereignist forces on 'money and some ethnic votes'.

SINCE 1995: SOCIAL JUSTICE FOR ALL

The most recent period of Quebec feminism began with the Bread and Roses March in 1995. Organized on the initiative of the FFQ, this march allowed feminist forces to remobilize women at a crucial juncture in the history of Quebec and of Quebec feminism. Indeed, the repercussions of this march and especially the defeat of the sovereignty movement in the Quebec referendum a few months later marked important turning points in Quebec politics. Moreover, the Quebec government was progressively relinquishing its long-held vision of the welfare state (an ideal championed by the Quebec nationalist movement since the Quiet Revolution), and adopting the prevailing North American neo-liberal approach. The repercussions of the government's actions were acutely felt in the women's movement as political opportunity structures were shutting down and the possibilities of influencing the political agenda were growing slim. Consequently, the terms of polemic engagement between the state and the women's movement changed, and unlike the preceding period, polemics started to overshadow co-operation.

Oddly enough, things seemed to have started well in 1995. The anti-poverty measures proposed by women at the Bread and Roses March were warmly received by the public and by some female cabinet ministers in the Quebec government. Not only were the women who participated in the march greeted at the Quebec National Assembly in 1995 by a number of members of the assembly, but their demands were partially met.[42] However one year later, in 1996, the winds of politics had shifted. The government flatly refused to add the notion of 'zero poverty'[43] to its 'zero-deficit' policy and this refusal led to a major rift between the government and women's groups. With divisions in the air on a number of fronts, some Quebec feminists started to explore (and revisit) the rudiments of 'intersectionality'.

SNAPSHOT

We need roses
A breather, a break
We need bread
Take our hand
We now stand taller
Than we seem to you
We want peace
For the world that we have made.[44]

The Bread and Roses March

The Bread and Roses March played a major role in constructing the physiognomy of Quebec's present-day feminist movement. The organizers chose the name of the March very consciously. By borrowing the early twentieth-century American socialist feminist slogan, 'Bread and Roses', they aimed to underscore a new orientation within the Quebec women's movement towards broader social issues. In fact, the march was a vehicle for linking issues beyond gender and class, including ethno-cultural diversity. In this way, it was designed to mend some of the wounds left by the 1990 Les 50 heures du féminisme conference and was an extension of the remedial Pour un Québec féminin pluriel conference. This event subsequently empowered the vision behind the World March of Women, and generally made it easier for broad sectors of the women's movement to join alter-globalization struggles and the fight against neo-liberalism.

The beauty of this form of mobilization was that it not only allowed many people to participate, but also offered the possibility of getting involved in different ways at different levels. A substantial proportion of the marchers were employees from women's groups or belonged to labour union status-of-women committees, and some were retired. Grassroots women's groups were extensively mobilized to prepare the event and greet the marchers.

From 26 May to 4 June 1995, 850 women marched across Quebec and on to Quebec City to deliver nine main demands on various issues. Over those 10 days, the marchers not only received support from women's groups but were resoundingly cheered on by the general public. The day they converged on Quebec City, over 20,000 people were waiting to join them in delivering their demands to the government. With a referendum on sovereignty just a few months in the offing, the marchers reaped the benefits of a vibrant political atmosphere and made some positive gains. The demands they presented covered a variety of issues.

The first proposed the introduction of 'a system for automatically collecting support payments through source deductions'. Women's groups had been making this demand for over a decade because separation or divorce (situations affecting a good half of married women) often led to marked impoverishment for women, partly owing to the lax administration and application of court rulings on the collection of child support. On 11 May 1995, shortly before the march began, the Quebec government adopted a bill addressing this problem.

The second demand, 'a tuition freeze and larger bursaries for students', had been a recurring issue in student struggles since 1968 in Quebec, as the government had never been willing to apply the Parent Commission's recommendations on educational reform, which called for a gradual phase-out of tuition fees. It took a wave of student strikes in 1996 for the government to commit to a tuition freeze, which was maintained until 2007. But the fact remained that since the 1970s, the bursary portion of the loans-and-bursaries pie had been shrinking, creating correspondingly bigger student loans. This trend became the central issue in the 2005 general strike by students, who opposed even more restricted access to higher education for lower-middle-income and low-income Quebecers and burdensome debt for many students upon graduation.

The third demand called for 'the creation of at least 1,500 units of social housing annually', a recurring appeal made by women's groups and the housing rights movement. During this period, the rental vacancy rate in cities was low, causing rents to increase. Indeed, one year before the march, the government had promised to build 1,200 social housing units, then failed to fulfill its promises. The marchers wanted immediate action, but in the end reached an agreement that 60 of the planned units would be reserved, with community support, for women with specific challenges such as drug addiction or psychiatric disorders.

The fourth demand sought to establish 'access for all women to general and vocational training programs and services, accompanied by adequate financial support, with a view to helping them join or return to the labour market'. This demand was in keeping with the 'workfare' philosophy promoted by the Quebec government, which aimed to reduce the number of people on social assistance. Here again, the gains were minimal: in every non-traditional vocational training program, the government simply reserved one-third of the positions to women.

The fifth demand, 'a social infrastructure programme, with jobs open to women', was inspired by a federal government infrastructure program that had created employment by investing in built environments and roadways. The women's movement wanted a similar program to be set up, but in the social sector, so that women would be more likely to be hired for the jobs that were created. The government responded to this demand by effectively hijacking it. Although most of the members on the advisory committee it set up to study social infrastructures were representatives from women's groups, the committee's work was partially short-circuited when the 1996 Socio-Economic Summit established a social economy committee, into which the bulk of relevant budget allocations were subsequently channelled.

The sixth demand called for 'a retroactive reduction of the length of sponsorship from 10 to 3 years for immigrants sponsored by their husbands, and access to social programmes for immigrant women subjected to spousal or family violence'. This demand forced Quebec to use the full measure of its immigration powers. It also highlighted the fundamentally sexist nature of Canadian immigration legislation: there is a heavy bias in the criteria used to determine an immigrant's category ('independent' or 'sponsored'), which results in men obtaining 'independent immigrant' status over women. Many women therefore have no choice but to be sponsored by their husbands. During the sponsorship period, this means they have no access to social programs or French-language proficiency training. It follows that sponsored women become increasingly dependent on their husbands, which reinforces patriarchal structures and makes it practically impossible for them to escape from situations of partner and family violence. In this matter, the government met the marchers' demand and shortened the sponsorship period from ten years to three.

The seventh demand also involved a longstanding issue for the women's movement: 'a proactive Pay Equity Act'. The net impact of the march was to spur on the movement for pay equity itself, since the mechanisms for introducing such legislation and labour committees were already in place but had been stalled since 1992. In the fall of 1996, the Pay Equity Act was finally adopted, thanks to sustained activist pressure. It took the June 1996 vigil in Quebec City, in which women formed a human chain around the National Assembly, to finally force the government to pass its legislation.

The eighth demand for the 'application of the Labour Standards Act for all participants in employability measures' was similar to the fourth demand in that the women's movement was not challenging the philosophy of workfare, but merely seeking to adjust it. At first the government committed in principle to meet the demand, but in practice, subsequent amendments to the Act respecting income security made this commitment meaningless. The living conditions of people on social assistance deteriorated substantially as a result.

The ninth demand, a 'raise in the minimum wage above the poverty line ($8.15 an hour)' met with partial success. Although the government did not accept the underlying principle of the demand (that full-time paid employment enabled people to overcome poverty), it did raise the minimum wage to $6.45 per hour—the largest increase that had been seen in many years.

The Bread and Roses March breathed new life into the struggle for women's rights and helped to establish the women's movement as a key proponent in the fight against poverty. The fight would continue in the years that followed, as neo-liberalism made the rich richer and the poorest in society, among whom women were overrepresented, poorer still. Buoyed by the success of the march, the Quebec delegation at the NGO meeting of the UN World Conference on Women in Beijing launched the idea of a World March of Women, a dream that would become a reality in 2000.

The concept of the intersectionality (or the integrative nature) of issues of class, race, and gender implicitly informed the development of Quebec feminism's radical currents in the 1970s, as mentioned earlier, and was more explicitly present in the issues raised by the Québec féminin pluriel conference, which recognized the need to take the diversity of women's situations into account to develop a truly inclusive feminism.[45] But it was not until after 1995, through its growing involvement in the struggle against neo-liberal policies, that the Quebec women's movement could take in the magnitude of what intersectionality would demand and see the limitations intrinsic to a brand of feminism that focused solely on gender issues.

In 2000, the World March of Women (WMW) was launched with the goal of uniting the women's movement around two issues: violence against women and poverty. Mobilizing the entire women's movement in Quebec over a period of almost three years, the WMW was an opportunity to create a new form of activism for the movement while extending the increasingly intersectional register of its concerns. The WMW not only provided an opportunity to develop internationalism within the Quebec feminist movement, but also raised awareness about the need to integrate issues of race, class, and gender into strategies of struggle against social inequalities. This lesson was valuable as the WMW was immediately followed by the first World Social Forum, held in Porto Alegre, Brazil, to which the FFQ was invited, having established an international presence through its organization of the WMW and especially through its significant presence and mobilization activities for the massive demonstrations in Quebec City around the 2001 Summit of the Americas (convened by politicians for the purpose of making North and South America Free Trade Areas).

In Quebec City, the women's movement held a full day of panels the day before the opening of the People's Summit (an alternative to the Summit of the Americas) organized by a coalition of unions, community and feminist groups, and international solidarity organizations. The anti-FTAA (Free Trade Area of the Americas) struggle was presented in information sessions in many local women's groups. New feminist collectives linked with the alter-globalization current, such as Némésis[46] or the group publishers of the magazine Sorcières, also participated, developing women-only activities and an explicitly feminist alter-globalization perspective.

At this juncture, many women saw a logical link between their own struggles and the struggle against neo-liberalism and were inspired to participate in anti-poverty coalitions like the Réseau de vigilance. Some even went on to found a new political movement called Option citoyenne, which would later become the provincial Québec solidaire party.[47] These feminists, who had worked to build a women's movement that would include all women, went on to constitute a 'social justice project' that would include all members of society. This project would emphasize the integral links between the issues of gender, race, and class.

The struggle against neo-liberalism also stimulated the emergence of new collectives of young women who identified as radical feminists and had various ties with anarchism.[48] In addition to these currents, more radical feminists joined the movement through meetings like Rencontres des féministes radicales (2003, 2008), the conference held for young feminists by the young women's committee of the FFQ (2003),[49] and the Canada-wide RebELLEs conference (2008).

Conclusion

Feminism in Quebec has developed in a protean fashion in environments and communities so diverse that it would be impossible to draw up an exhaustive list of them all. In studying Quebec feminism, we could single out specific ideological currents, detail issues, or conduct a survey of women's groups. In so doing, however, we would be overlooking one essential point: it was through feminism that women began to trust each other and initiate a mutually inclusive dialogue. Be they scholars or drop-outs, rich or poor, city or country dwellers, 'Québécoises de souche' or more recent citizens, through feminism women recognized in each other their positions as active participants in a shared 'herstory'. Women also attained

the status of 'speaking beings', a status previously denied them, because so many people claimed not to understand what they were talking about. 'What on earth could they still want?' had become the familiar dismissive refrain. Women began to speak out and speak to each other, even though this new speech act fell on the deaf ears of those who dominated them. 'Feminism' is the name of this act and of the diverse movements that it empowered, movements to establish gender equality, to subvert the place that society had assigned to women, and to position the disputes between the sexes at the very heart of the body politic. Using the word in the plural, 'feminisms', would more faithfully represent the diversity of the practices and reflections within these movements of resistance and of critical thought.

Epilogue: Quebec and the United States

The Quebec women's movement developed its own distinctive traits and, hearkening back to the 1960s, developed dynamics that were different from those that prevailed in the United States. Indeed, in the 1980s Quebec feminists were not forced to confront any major hostilities, in sharp contrast to the situation in the United States, where the defeat of the Equal Rights Amendment and the concurrent rise of the conservative and religious right (fighting abortion and gay rights) impeded feminist mobilization and meant that the women's movement was constantly on the defensive. The 'sex wars' of the 1980s (debating issues around pornography) further split the US movement. The fact that in Quebec the feminist movement's confrontation with the combined forces of neo-liberalism and neo-conservatism occurred only after 1995 has afforded feminists the opportunity of becoming better equipped to resist and organize against these highly anti-feminist trends in contemporary politics.

Questions for Consideration

1. What were the differences between reformist feminists and radical feminists in the 1970s?
2. To what can we attribute the ability of the Quebec women's movement to mobilize its forces?

3. What kinds of issues reshaped the Quebec women's movement in the 1990s?

NOTES

1. Masculinist thought differs from other currents of thought regarding masculinity in that masculinists believe that men in Western societies are dominated by women. Consequently, they contend that they must organize, as women have, to struggle against the discrimination to which men are purportedly being subjected. This current is particularly active in Quebec and its key points of contention are high rates of suicide among young men, drop-out rates among male youth, violence against men and the experiences of separated or divorced fathers who have lost custody of their children. Their lobby is particularly insistent on this last point and has had some success with public authorities. For more information, see the collective work edited by Mélissa Blais and Francis Dupuis-Déri, *Le masculinisme au Québec. L'antiféminisme démasqué* (Montreal: Les Éditions du remue-ménage, 2008).

2. See my chapter 'Comment l'égalité entre les femmes et les hommes est devenue une "valeur fondamentale" de la société québécoise' in Robert Laliberté, *À la recherche d'un Québec qui bouge* (Paris: Centre des travaux historiques et scientifiques, 2009).

3. A colloquial name for women from Quebec's majority group of French-Canadian ancestry. This expression denotes the concepts of 'founding people' or 'old-stock Quebecers' and is not universally embraced.

4. Although Denyse Baillargeon, in Chapter 16, documents major gains in the women's movement, there is still significant social inequality between men and women in employment, wages, violence, reconciling work–family commitments, and domestic work, to name but a few examples.

5. I have discussed this question in a much more detailed fashion in *Fragments et collages* (Montreal: Les Éditions du remue-ménage, 1986).

6. The legal equality of married women, a demand that the Quebec feminist movement began making at the beginning of the twentieth century, was incorporated into the Fédération nationale Saint-Jean-Baptiste's platform by Marie Gérin-Lajoie. Although in 1964 Bill 16 was the first step to achieving equality of legal status between men and women in Quebec, it would not be until the Civil Code of Quebec was reformed in 1980 that gender equality came into effect.

7. Educational reform was one of the major initiatives of the Quiet Revolution. The Parent Commission, established to examine this issue, included a common school curriculum for female and male students among its recommendations.

8. Around the mid-1960s, when Pierre Elliott Trudeau, Jean Marchand, and Gérard Pelletier (who were associated with opposition to the Duplessis regime in Quebec) became part of the federal Lester B. Pearson government, far-reaching changes were effected in this area. Under pressure from many women's groups, the Pearson government established a Royal Commission on the Status of Women, chaired by journalist Florence Bird, with research services headed by the Commission's Executive Secretary, Monique Bégin. Established in 1967, the Commission submitted its report in 1970 and drafted a set of recommendations for the equal treatment of women in law, education, pay, and employment opportunities, calling for improved access to abortion and many other services and programs. The recommendations were much the same as the demands of the reformist feminist component of the movement, which was lobbying for equal opportunities between women and men within the existing social system.

9. During the 1980 referendum campaign on sovereignty in Quebec, the federalist 'No' camp mobilized thousands of women under the moniker of 'Yvettes' to oppose sovereignty in Quebec. (See 'The Yvette Affair' in Chapter 16).

10. For a history of AFÉAS, see Jocelyne Lamoureux, Michèle Gélinas, and Katy Tari, *Femmes en mouvements: trajectoires de l'Association féminine d'éducation et d'action sociale* (Montreal: Boréal, 1993).

11. The legal term used in Quebec for the total family assets acquired or used during a marriage or civil union.

12. Dominique Fougeyrollas-Schwebel, 'Feminism in the 1970s', in Christine Fauré, ed., *Political and Historical Encyclopedia of Women* (New York: Routledge, 2003), 426.

13. See for example Zillah Eisenstein, *The Radical Future of Liberal Feminism* (Boston: Northeastern, 1981). Ironically, since large sections of radical feminism were heavily influenced by liberalism, it would be more appropriate to acknowledge the 'Liberal Future of Radical Feminism'.

14. The history of the FLF and that of the Centre des femmes, as well as the reproduction of the magazine *Québécoises deboutte!* are addressed in Véronique O'Leary and Louise Toupin, *Québécoises Deboutte!,* 2 vols.(Montreal: Les Éditions du remue-ménage 1982–3).

15. Lise Balcer was infamous for her indictment as a member of the FLQ (Front de libération du Québec) in trials arising from the kidnapping and death of Pierre Laporte.

16. This direct action event is analyzed in detail in Marjolaine Péloquin, *En prison pour la cause des femmes* (Montreal: Les Éditions du remue-ménage, 2007).

17. A recommendation that was not adopted by the federal government, which opted to authorize abortion in hospitals (conditional on the sanction of a therapeutic abortion committee) if the life or health of a mother or fetus were in jeopardy.

18. Our translation of the original French slogan: 'Pas de liberation des femmes sans Québec libre, pas de Québec libre sans la liberation des femmes !'

19. During the Quiet Revolution, French Canadians in Quebec began to call themselves 'Québécois', a name that referred to the territory of the province of Quebec, the

only province in which francophones made up the majority of the population. Today this word has come to include any resident of Quebec, regardless of language group.

20. These popular community daycare centres, managed by staff and parents, were the precursors to Quebec's current Centres de la petite enfance (CPES) (early-childhood centres).

21. Member organizations of this 'intergroupe' included Centre de santé des femmes du Plateau–Mont-Royal, Comité de lutte pour l'avortement libre et gratuit, Théâtre des cuisines, and Les Éditions du remue-ménage. The proliferation of women's groups during this period soon made the 'intergroupe' obsolete as a coordinating structure, and its operations were therefore partly transferred to *Pluri-elles*, a liaison newsletter for independent women's groups that would in turn become an independent feminist newsletter and collective under the name of *Des luttes et des rires de femmes*.

22. This impressive capacity for mobilization has been demonstrated in the fight for abortion rights, feminist counteractions to the Montreal Massacre at École Polytechnique, the organization of the fiftieth anniversary of suffrage legislation (*Les 50 heures du féminisme*), the *Pour un Québec féminin pluriel* conference, and the Bread and Roses March and the World March of Women in 2000.

23. The complete collection of this magazine may be found in *Les Têtes de Pioche* (Montreal: Les Éditions du remue-ménage, 1980).

24. An excellent analysis of this collective may be found in Louise Turcotte's article 'Itinéraire d'un courant politique : le lesbianisme radical au Québec', in Irène Demczuk and Frank W. Remiggi, eds., *Sortir de l'ombre, Histoires des communautés lesbienne et gaie de Montreal* (Montreal: VLB éditeur, 1998).

25. I discuss these issues in chapter 7 of *L'Amère patrie* (Montreal: Les Éditions du remue-ménage, 2001).

26. This process began in 1977 and results were apparent during the 1980s and beyond.

27. Centre local de services communautaires (CLSC) ('Local Community Service Centres' in English) were established in the 1970s within the framework of universal and public health care insurance coverage. These individual clinics brought together medical, social and community services and developed the preventive and curative concept of health care of the period.

28. See Louise Desmarais, *Mémoires d'une bataille inachevée* (Montreal: Trait-d'Union, 1994).

29. See Nancy Guberman et al., *Les défis des pratiques démocratiques dans les groupes de femmes* (Montreal: Saint-Martin, 2001).

30. '*L'écriture au féminin*' is based on the important locution '*au féminin*', used to indicate a woman-centred cultural perspective which gained currency in Quebec's feminist discourse in the late 1970s and early 1980s. In 1980 it appeared in a text by lesbian feminist writer

Nicole Brossard and was incorporated into the name of an important Montreal conference in 1982, 'Emergence d'une culture au féminin'.

31. In a landmark decision in January 1988, the Supreme Court of Canada permanently struck down criminal prohibitions on abortions on the basis that they were unconstitutional.

32. A pregnant Quebec woman whose violent ex-boyfriend temporarily prevented her from getting an abortion by serving her with a civil injunction, which was overturned by the Supreme Court of Canada, thereby setting a vital precedent in Canadian law. See Desmarais, *Mémoires d'une bataille inachevée*.

33. Most of the feminist reactions to this event in Quebec were compiled in a publication edited by Marie Chalouh and Louise Malette, *Polytechnique, 6 décembre* (Montreal: Les Éditions du remue-ménage, 1990).

34. December 6, the date of the Montreal Massacre, continues to be commemorated every year by feminists in Quebec.

35. This was the message conveyed by Roch Côté in *Manifeste d'un salaud* (Terrebonne: Le portique, 1990); and by Denise Bombardier in *La déroute des sexes* (Paris: Seuil, 1993).

36. This retrospective analysis was compiled in Femmes en tête, *De travail et d'espoir* (Montreal: Les Éditions du remue-ménage, 1990).

37. The minutes from this meeting are published in *Pour un Québec féminin pluriel* (Montreal: Les Éditions Écosociété, 1994).

38. The *Manifeste des Femmes québécoises* was written by Quebec nationalist feminists.

39. This notion was developed in the United States to better problematize the overlapping or 'integrative' oppressions that women experience. See Kimberle Creenshaw, 'Mapping the Margins: Intersectionality, Identity Politics and Violence against Women of Color', *Stanford Law Review* 43 (1991): 12–41.

40. According to the overriding formula stipulated in the Canadian Constitution Act of 1982, the Meech Lake Accord, which was drawn up in 1987, had to be ratified by all provinces and territories by 1990. Such was not the case, as Newfoundland retracted its ratification and Manitoba refused to ratify the Accord.

41. Although most authors take a Canada-centric view with expressions like 'Quebec and the *rest* of Canada', in this case I am mirroring this expression to underscore an opposite perspective.

42. There was a marked contrast between the situation in 1995, when the march was positively received by the government and that of 1996 (the referendum and the zero-deficit Socio-Economic Summit had been held in the interim). In 1995, the government established an advisory committee on social infrastructure whose members included some of the march's founding organizers, whereas in 1996 it raised minimum wage by a meager $0.10 per hour.

43. This policy demand was originally championed by the Collective for a Law on the Elimination of Poverty and was delivered during the 1996 Socio-Economic Summit, where the notion 'zero-poverty' was adopted by the FFQ and Front d'action populaire pour le réaménagement urbain (FRAPRU).

44. Our free translation of an excerpt from the chorus of the march's theme song, 'Du pain et des roses', lyrics by Hélène Pedneault. The slogan 'Bread and Roses' was originally part of an English-language poem (which also became a song), inspired by the 1912 Lawrence Textile strike in Lawrence, Massachusetts. Printed with Permission from Fondation Léa-Roback.

45. To the notion of intersectionality we could add that of seriality, developed by Iris Marion Young 'Gender as Seriality', *Intersecting Voices* (Princeton, N.J.: Princeton University Press, 1997).

46. For a history of this group, see Anna Kruzynski, 'De l'opération SalAMI à *Némésis*', *Recherches féministes* 17,

2 (2004): 227–62. For an overview of the ideas behind the magazine, *Sorcières*, see Mélissa Blais, Laurence Fortin-Pellerin, Éve Marie Lampron, and Geneviève Pagé, 'Pour éviter de se noyer dans la (troisième) vague : réflexion sur l'histoire et l'actualité du féminisme radical', *Recherches féministes* 20, 2 (2007): 141–62.

47. Françoise David, long-time president of the FFQ helped found the Option citoyenne movement and would become the female spokesperson (there is also a male spokesperson) of the provincial party, Québec solidaire, in 2006. See Chapter 23 in this volume.

48. See Émilie Breton, Julie Grolleau, Anna Kruzynski, and Catherine Saint-Arnaud Babin, 'Mon/notre/leur corps est toujours un champ de bataille', *Recherches féministes* 20, 2 (2007): 113–39.

49. See Elsa Beaulieu and Barbara Legault, 'The Making of' in Maria Nengeh Mensah, ed., *Dialogues autour de la troisième vague* (Montreal: Les Éditions du remue-ménage, 2005).

Relevant Websites

Association féminine d'éducation et d'action sociale: www.afeas.qc.ca

La Fédération des femmes du Québec: www.ffq.qc.ca

L'R des centres de femmes du Québec: www.rcentres.qc.ca

Le Regroupement des maisons pour femmes victimes de violence conjugale: www.maisons-femmes.qc.ca

Au bas de l'échelle: www.aubasdelechelle.ca

La Centrale Galerie Powerhouse: www.lacentrale.org

Regroupement québécois des calacs: http://rcalacs.qc.ca

Treize revue lesbienne: www.revuetreize.org/

RebELLEs: www.rebelles.org

Select Bibliography

Beauchamp, Colette, ed. *Pour un Québec féminin pluriel*. Montreal: Les Éditions Écosociété, 1994.

Dumont, Micheline. *Le féminisme raconté à Camille*. Montreal: Les Éditions du remue-ménage, 2008.

———, and Louise Toupin, eds. *La pensée féministe au Québec*. Montreal: Les Éditions du remue-ménage, 2003.

Femmes en tête. *De travail et d'espoir*. Montreal: Les Éditions du remue-ménage, 1990.

Lamoureux, Diane. *Fragments et collages. Essai sur le féminisme québécois des années 1970*. Montreal: Les Éditions du remue-ménage, 1986.

———. *L'Amère patrie*. Montreal: Les Éditions du remue-ménage, 2001.

Mensah, Maria-Nengeh. *Dialogues autour de la troisième vague féministe*. Montreal: Les Éditions du remue-ménage, 2005.

O'Leary, Véronique, and Louise Toupin. *Québécoises deboutte!*, Vol. 1. Montreal: Les Éditions du remue-ménage, 1982.

CHAPTER 21

Health Care in Quebec

Antonia Maioni, McGill University

— TIMELINE —

1932   Public health law adopted.

1941   Creation of Ministère de la santé et du bien-être.

1961   Loi sur l'assurance-hospitalisation adoptée.

1963   Fédération des médecins omnipraticiens (FMOQ) chartered in Quebec.

1965   Fédération des médecins spécialistes du Québec (FMSQ) chartered in Quebec.

1966   Castonguay Commission launched.

1970   Loi sur l'assurance-maladie (Bill 8) adopted.
Quebec institutes separate payment schedules for generalists and specialists.
Quebec specialist doctors strike.

1971   Loi sur la santé et les services sociaux (Bill 65) adopted.

1972   Final report of Castonguay-Nepveu Commission.

1985   Rochon Commission launched.

1988   Publication of Rochon Report.

1990   New government initiative: *Une réforme axée sur le citoyen*.

1991   Loi sur les services de santé et les services sociaux adopted.

1992   Bill 9 (de-insuring certain services) adopted.

1993   Regional boards (Régies régionales) set up adopted.

2001   Clair Commission Report released.

When Canadians are asked what sets them apart from Americans, many invariably mention the health-care system. In every province, including Quebec, health care is regulated as a 'public good' and each provincial government plays a crucial role in ensuring that this good is available to all citizens. The design of health-care policy reflects a commitment to collective responsibility, in which access is universal, coverage is comprehensive, and funding is primarily assumed by the public sector through general revenues from taxpayers. Although health care remains a very popular social program, Canadians are concerned about the overall sustainability of the health-care system.

This is especially true in Quebec, where health reform has been fraught with political struggle. In addition to ideological divisions about the role of the state in society, in Quebec the debate over health reform has always been subject to the larger debate about the role of Quebec in Canada, and the complexities of the federal–provincial relationship. In fact, health care has served both as a lightning rod for the tension in this relationship and as a model of how Quebec has been able to develop a unique system within the contours of the federal arrangements.

The development of hospital and medical insurance in Quebec is above all a history of federal–provincial relations superimposed against a landscape of profound socio-economic and political change. The stories of that relationship and of the period of social change have been well-documented and dissected. Yet, the place of health reform remains an incomplete picture. The Quebec experience offers not only insights into the health-care dossier per se; it also reveals how health policy-making is bounded within specific institutional and ideological environments.

Today in Quebec, as in other Canadian provinces and territories, health care is universally provided—in contrast to the United States—to all its official residents. This system, despite recent, albeit selective, accommodation of private health-care insurance, remains enormously popular. This chapter examines health policy in Quebec. Why and how has health care in Quebec developed as it has? What key factors have and continue to shape the features and current direction of Quebec health-care policy?

THE HISTORICAL ANTECEDENTS OF HEALTH INSURANCE IN QUEBEC

Prior to 1960, Quebec's health-care system was largely in the hands of the Catholic Church, charitable organizations, and the private sector. With the division of linguistic and religious communities in British North America, and more importantly, that between Quebec and the rest of the colonies, a 'marriage of convenience' emerged between the colonial administration and Catholic Church leaders in Quebec, which gave religious authorities substantial power in shaping local poor relief, including hospital care.[1]

Because religious communities were so important in providing social and health-care services, other religious groups did likewise. In the early nineteenth century, the influx of new settlers led to the founding

of Protestant hospitals, with the help of merchant benefactors and benevolent societies. Later, the Jewish community developed voluntary relief dispensaries for new immigrants in Montreal.

Confederation reinforced this situation, transferring the responsibility for hospitals to provincial governments, which in turn subsidized local public health initiatives and charity cases in voluntary hospitals. In Quebec, most of these remained church-affiliated, and many relied at least in part on municipal funding derived from provincial subsidies. In 1921, the Quebec government formally adopted its first health-care law, la Loi de l'assistance publique (Public Assistance Law) which allowed for the direct reimbursement of care provided to 'indigents' in Quebec hospitals recognized as charitable institutions. This emphasis on public subsidies of private (religious) charity became the key in maintaining the Catholic Church's autonomous role in social provision within French-Canadian society.[2] The creation of a ministry of health in 1936 did little to change this dynamic, since the new ministry was mainly responsible for the coordination of public health departments in the municipalities.

During the 1940s, a new momentum was emerging in Ottawa around health and other social policy matters. The Report of the Rowell-Sirois Commission (the Royal Commission on Dominion–Provincial Relations) in 1940 underscored the idea that federal involvement in health insurance was feasible even within the constraints of the British North America Act. The Marsh report, published in 1943, reinforced the notion of federal leadership in social programs, although it was careful to suggest that medical care would be an exception under provincial administration (with federal co-financing).

In Quebec, a similar momentum was in play. The Liberal government there, led by Prime Minister Mackenzie King's protégé, Adélard Godbout, was already interested in moving forward on health insurance. Premier Godbout commissioned a provincial inquiry into hospital care, and the Lessard Commission recommendations, released in 1943, became the centrepiece of the Liberal legislative agenda, receiving the support of union groups and the firm opposition of the clergy in Quebec.[3] When Union Nationale's Maurice Duplessis returned to power in 1944, his government quickly scuttled plans for such legislation.

Duplessis was likewise less than enthralled with the ideas of public financing and any attempts to relinquish religious control of the health sector. Like his influential ally, Ontario's Conservative Premier George Drew, Duplessis was openly critical of the Liberal government in Ottawa and the spectre of increasing burdens on provincial coffers.[4] Together, the two fiscal conservatives were largely responsible for scuttling the social policy promise of the Dominion–provincial conference on reconstruction in 1945 through their refusal to relinquish taxation control. Since health insurance was tied to the plan's fiscal arrangements, the proposals for health insurance expired along with the conference.

Hospital Insurance: La Réforme malgré tout

During the 1950s, there were nevertheless changes that would have an important influence on the development of Quebec's health-care system. A program of National Health Grants, federal grants-in-aid for the provinces to assist public health measures, medical research, and hospital construction, had an impact in Quebec, despite Duplessis' bitter condemnation of federal intrusion in provincial jurisdiction. As hospital construction expanded in Quebec, so too did health insurance, particularly private or 'voluntary' initiatives supported by the medical profession.[5] The Liberal Prime Minister, Louis St Laurent, also emphasized provincial responsibility in health insurance. During the 1953 election campaign, he framed the issue by insisting it was the provinces that 'have to take the initiative' in health insurance 'which should, as far as possible, be left to Provincial administration'.[6] A special commission on federalism in Quebec, the Tremblay Commission, was set up in 1954.[7] In its final report, the Commission recognized that health, welfare, and education were matters of provincial jurisdiction, and that the federal government's role was to ensure that provinces, in particular Quebec, had the fiscal means to fulfill their responsibilities in this regard.[8]

By this time, given the inauguration of hospital insurance in Saskatchewan, there was considerable discussion of federal involvement through federal grants-in-aid.[9] But the Prime Minister was reticent, as was Maurice Duplessis, not to mention the Canadian Hospital Council and the Catholic Hospital Conference.[10]

Nevertheless, political pressure led St Laurent to reluctantly address the issue and in 1957, the House of Commons passed the Hospital and Diagnostic Services Act. Although other provinces soon signed on to this cost-sharing arrangement, the Union Nationale government in Quebec refused to be swayed.[11] Duplessis' last throne speech in November 1958 invoked his 'faith' in private health insurance; after his death the following year, his successor Paul Sauvé reiterated the same sentiment.[12]

Quebec's resistance to hospital insurance had been based on the Union Nationale government's aversion to secular, state, and federal intervention in societal issues. This bolstered influential interest groups—such as insurers and the medical profession—in resisting health reform. Nevertheless, Quebec society was rapidly changing in the postwar era. The labour movement, for example, had championed such reform, as did the new middle class emerging from Quebec's universities.[13] The arrival in power of the Liberal party in 1960, led by former federal minister Jean Lesage, and transformed by its association with the labour struggle and the new technocratic elites in its ranks, signalled an important shift in political thinking about autonomy, society, and the state in Quebec.

During the 1960s, the discourse of federalism in Quebec changed, just as the discourse about the role of the state in society changed: the division of powers was no longer a firewall against social reform emanating from the Canadian state; instead, reformers in Quebec would argue that the division of powers gave Quebec the necessary levers to effect social change.[14]

The new premier, Jean Lesage, was under intense popular pressure to introduce hospital insurance. In 1961, in one of its first legislative actions, the Liberal government signed on to the federal–provincial cost-sharing agreement and in 1962, the Loi sur les hôpitaux (the Hospital Act) effectively shut out religious communities from the administration of health services in Quebec.[15] Hospitals remained voluntary institutions, and as elsewhere in Canada they would become 'public' institutions as well, in the sense that they would henceforth rely entirely on public funds.[16]

MEDICAL INSURANCE: THE NOT-SO-QUIET REVOLUTION

As the *Révolution tranquille* (Quiet Revolution) began to re-arrange the relationship between state and society in Quebec, medical insurance became the next battleground elsewhere in Canada. This same period was marked by events unfolding in Saskatchewan, as the CCF–NDP (social democratic) government attempted to implement universal government-run medical insurance against the resistance of the medical lobby there.[17]

In 1964, a Royal Commission studying the issue (the Hall Commission) recommended that 'the Federal Government enter into agreement with the provinces to provide grants on a fiscal need formula to assist the provinces to introduce and operate comprehensive, universal, provincial programs of personal health services'.[18] These sweeping recommendations were seen by many observers in Quebec to have ignored constitutional impediments to federal action in this area; nevertheless, public opinion in favour of medical insurance soon intensified in Quebec.[19]

At the 1965 Federal–Provincial Conference, Liberal Prime Minister Lester Pearson outlined a medical insurance program in collaboration with the provinces, based on principles rather than conditions. Premier Lesage refused the bait, emphasizing that any Quebec plan would be outside the federal government's reach, preferably through opting-out in return for sufficient tax points to underwrite the province's own program.[20]

Fiscally speaking, much had changed in Quebec–Canada relations since the advent of hospital insurance. Premier Lesage had demonstrated a vigorous defence of Quebec's desire for opting-out of federal initiatives with financial compensation to develop a Quebec pension plan.[21] Lesage's second-guessing of federal initiatives in social policy, however, was not based on the same resistance as that of the Union Nationale: the question was not the interference of the *state*, but rather of the *federal* state in these matters. Inside Quebec, the nationalization of hydro-electricity, the swift movement in education reform, and the rise of nationalist sentiment, all contributed to an effervescent but volatile situation.[22]

In the fall of 1965, Lesage appointed Claude Castonguay (the actuary who had been a central player in negotiations with the federal government over pension reform), to head a research committee to develop a medical insurance plan for Quebec. Lesage wanted above all to avoid the kind of 'improvised' program he had felt compelled to implement with hospital insurance in 1961. Castonguay's 1966 report stressed that any medical insurance plan should above all respond to the particular context and needs of Quebec.[23]

CLAUDE CASTONGUAY: THE QUIET REVOLUTIONARY

Claude Castonguay in 1970, as leader of the Quebec Ministry of Social Affairs

THE CANADIAN PRESS/
Jacques Boissinot

Claude Castonguay is the person responsible for introducing Quebec's first health insurance plan. An actuary by training, he was the epitome of the new generation of technocrats responsible for the rapid modernization of the Quebec state during the Quiet Revolution. For example, Castonguay was part of the team that hammered out the Quebec Pension Plan of 1965, alongside the Canadian Pension Plan, a remarkable feat of co-operative federalism.

In the fall of 1965, Premier Jean Lesage appointed Castonguay to head a research committee to develop a medical insurance plan for Quebec. The following year, Premier Daniel Johnson appointed Castonguay to head a public commission of inquiry on health and social services. By the time he reported, Castonguay had become convinced of two essential points: the best way to improve access and to find a more equitable way to finance health care in Quebec would be through the collective pooling of risk and financing through public health insurance; and any new medical insurance plan had to be developed with Quebec's particular context and needs in mind. Castonguay believed that asymmetry was both necessary and desirable when it came to social programs for Quebec.

In 1970, Castonguay was tapped by Robert Bourassa to develop and implement his own recommendations, as the new Minister of Health and Social Services. Quebec health-care legislation created a distinctive health-care system in Quebec, based on the integration of health and social services, the creation of CLSCs (local community service centres), public health departments, and regional health boards.

Having accomplished what he set out to do, Castonguay left politics in 1973 to take up a successful career as an insurance executive in Quebec. He was not forgotten, however, as for years Quebecers would fondly refer to their health-care card as *la castonguette*. He re-emerged on the political scene in 1990 when he was appointed to the Senate of Canada by Prime Minister Brian Mulroney. Following the failure of the Meech Lake Accord, he left the Senate in 1992.

More recently, Castonguay was coaxed out of retirement to once again study the Quebec health-care system and make recommendations for a reform agenda. In his *Memoirs of a Quiet Revolutionary*, Castonguay had sharply criticized the inefficiency of Quebec's health-care system, and underlined the need for increased private investment in infrastructure and technology. In the May 2007 budget, Quebec Finance Minister Monique Jérôme-Forget announced that Castonguay would lead a task force to find new ways to finance health care and reassess the role of the private sector. He was to be joined

by two other members appointed by the opposition parties, well-known journalist Michel Venne for the Parti Québécois, and Joanne Marcotte for the Action democratique du Québec.

The report of the task force, *Getting Our Money's Worth*, was released in early 2008, and covered both organization and financial challenges in the Quebec health-care system. For example, Castonguay's group suggested that the system needed better continuity of care and more investment in primary care and home care, particularly in the context of an aging population. Even though Castonguay's original vision of the Quebec health-care system in the 1970s was based on a vision of integrated care, in practice, Quebecers have come to rely on specialists, walk-in clinics, and emergency rooms for the kind of care that could be provided much more cost effectively in other settings.

The report also tackled matters of governance and the allocation of resources in the health-care system, criticizing the top-down and overly bureaucratized approach to health-care organization. As for the allocation of resources, Castonguay suggested that money should flow where the patient goes instead of being allocated to health-care establishments on the basis of automatic budgeting. This would mean that even hospitals could be financed according to performance criteria, and have more leeway in purchasing services as a way of injecting more competitiveness into the health-care system.

The recommendations on health-care financing proved, however, to be more controversial. Castonguay's main preoccupation was how to control what he considered to be the unsustainable growth in public health expenditures. His remedy was to slow the rate of spending and reduce pressure on public finances by finding alternative sources of financing. The report also suggested that the public system cannot cover all the demand for health-care services, and emphasized that individuals have to adopt more healthy lifestyles. The report also recommended dedicated stabilizing funding and diversifying the financing of health care through an increase in the provincial sales tax, and allowing for deductibles that would encourage individuals to be more responsible in their use of medical services. Finally, the report recommends a widening of the private insurance industry and more flexibility in allowing physicians the ability to practise both in the public system and in the private market.

Although Castonguay's 2008 report stands in sharp contrast to the one he delivered in 1970, in both cases one can see the legacy of a blunt and straightforward technocrat making the case for bold and innovative change. Nevertheless, the political stakes around health reform are still apparent. Quebecers are still not yet ready to swallow such drastic medicine. While public opinion polls show that some Quebecers are in theory open to the idea of private markets, user fees, and the like, when faced with the actual recommendations—and price tags—for such initiatives, they have been less enthusiastic.

Still, Castonguay's diagnosis and prescription are unlikely to fade from public debate. Quebec's health-care reform dilemma is one that resonates in every province. Not only does it provide artillery to proponents of privatization, it also challenges the federal government over the worthiness of the Canada Health Act.

The defeat of the Liberal party in the provincial elections in the following June did not end the debate over medical insurance, but it slowed the pace of change. Union Nationale leader Daniel Johnson remained wary of the state, both federal and provincial. But he was above all a practical politician and he faced immediate problems in the health sector, including a general strike that was paralyzing hospital care in Quebec. He was also aware that, in December 1966, the House of Commons passed federal medical insurance legislation.

Premier Johnson asked Castonguay to head another commission, broadening the mandate to cover not only health but all social services.[24] Castonguay's 1967 report was unveiled to general praise from the media, opinion leaders, general practitioners, the union movement, and the Liberal opposition.[25] Still, the recommendation for universal, public medical insurance did not sit well with Premier Johnson, who preferred a system of medical assistance for the indigent. But Quebec's delay could not last for long once the federal government implemented the medical insurance program in 1968 and imposed a 2 per cent tax hike on Canadian taxpayers to finance it. The new Union Nationale premier (Johnson had died suddenly earlier that year), Jean-Jacques Bertrand, well known in Quebec as an outspoken social and fiscal conservative, vehemently opposed both the tax and the federal intrusion into Quebec's jurisdiction.[26] Still, public opinion in Quebec was reacting favourably to the prospect of medical insurance, and the Quebec government could not sustain its opposition while its taxpayers were being forced to subsidize the program.[27]

Ironically, given its long-standing suspicion of the state and social policy, one of the Union Nationale's last political gestures in office (for it would never return to power) was the introduction of the Loi sur l'assurance-maladie in 1969, which essentially outlined a universal, publicly funded medical insurance plan for Quebec incorporating the conditions outlined by federal government.

With the return to power of the Liberal party—under the new leadership of Robert Bourassa—health reform returned to the care of Claude Castonguay, now the new Minister of Health and Social Services. As minister, Castonguay was able to quickly reformulate the legislation: a significant difference was that it limited the *droit au désengagement* (opting out), and it was the first medical insurance legislation in Canada that prohibited *la surfacturation* (extra-billing) for physicians. While the Bourassa government was able to negotiate with general practitioners, dentists, and dental surgeons on the basis of this legislation, the specialists remained intractable.[28] The Loi sur l'assurance-maladie was duly adopted in July 1970 but it soon became clear implementation would be difficult. By the first week of October, the specialists' federation went on a generalized strike. Even as the sudden and tragic events of the October Crisis began to unfold at the end of that week, the specialists held their position. As the press, the college of physicians and surgeons, and the public turned against the specialists' federation, the Quebec government was able to pass emergency measures that put into place the medical insurance law—and forced the specialists back to work.[29] Overshadowed by the grim events of that autumn, it was a bitter victory.

One of the other distinctive features of the Quebec health-care system would be the enduring relationship between physicians and the Quebec state. Historically, Quebec had represented an important centre for medical research and the training of the medical profession. Indeed, until 1954, the Canadian Medical Association had its headquarters in Montreal before moving to Ottawa and subsequently Toronto.

In other provinces, the provincial division of the CMA negotiates with public agencies. This has not been the case in Quebec, where a public agency, the Régie de l'assurance-maladie du Québec, negotiates fee schedules with two professional 'unions', the Fédération des médecins omnipraticiens du Québec (FMOQ—a federation of regional associations of general practitioners) and the Fédération des médecins spécialistes du Québec (FMSQ—a federation of specialist associations), as well as with other federations representing residents and medical students. The FMOQ and the FMSQ were formed in the 1960s in anticipation of the development of public medical insurance in Quebec.

The implementation of medical insurance in Quebec also happened differently than in other provinces. In 1970, general practitioners in the FMOQ agreed to negotiate with the provincial government over Bill 8 (for medical services in Quebec), but it was specialists in the FMSQ who objected to certain provisions of the bill (namely, the bans on extra-billing and opting out) and declared the strike that would coincide with the October Crisis. Although medical associations in other provinces would also go on strike (notably, the Saskatchewan Medical Association in 1962 and specialists in Ontario in 1986), 'divide and conquer' has been a recurring theme in Quebec, where the provincial government can negotiate separately with two medical federations. In addition, the province can offer a salary option to physicians willing to work within the CLSC (local community service centres) network, as opposed to the fee-for-service model that was the default mode of payment for physicians. Thus, through the late 1970s and early 1980s, the Parti Québécois government was able to implement financial controls on doctors (such as salary caps on specialists) before any of the other provinces.

THE UNFINISHED BUSINESS OF HEALTH REFORM IN QUEBEC

Although the medical insurance battle was won, health-care reform in Quebec was just beginning, on two fronts. The first had to do with the organization of health and health-care services; the second with the financing of these services.

Organization and Re-organization of the Health-care System

The unfinished business in the reorganization of the health-care system had dogged Castonguay since he began his commission work, underscoring the structural problems in the delivery and financing of health services in Quebec. The work of the Castonguay Commission continued after Castonguay became a cabinet minister, with Gérard Nepveu being named the new chair. A scathing portrait indeed was emerging.[30] Essentially, the commission's research found that compared to the rest of Canada, Quebec had the lowest rate of hospital use and the highest per capita cost of hospital care; in addition, they found a growing shortage of general practitioners, a hodgepodge distribution of medical specialties, conflict among doctors, hospitals, and administrators, and little coordination or integration of care. In addition, the health-care system in Quebec tended to focus on specific diseases, with scant attention to the complexity of conditions or the social determinants of health.[31]

The 1971 Loi sur les services de santé et les services sociaux was intended to address these serious deficiencies and to put into place a distinctive health-care system which included 'holistic medicine' as part of an integrated system of health and social services, and the creation of CLSCs, public health departments, and regional health boards.[32] After considerable legislative debate and amendments, some inspired by Nepveu's final report, the legislation passed in 1972. It was to be Castonguay's crowning achievement (for years Quebecers would refer to their health-care card as *la castonguette*), and one of the lasting legacies of both Lesage's Quiet Revolution and Bourassa's grand designs for the Quebec state.

The law put into place hospital insurance (Régime d'assurance-hospitalisation du Québec, administered by the ministry of health and social services) and health-care insurance (Régime d'assurance-maladie, administered by the Régie de l'assurance-maladie du Québec [RAMQ], a public agency responsible to the ministry). While most hospitals in Quebec are operated as voluntary, non-profit institutions (rather than being owned and operated by the government), they are financed by global budgets negotiated with the provincial government. This dependence on public funds means that hospitals are subject to political decisions (either directly by government or through the intermediary of regional boards) about their operation, including closure. As for medical insurance, physicians are paid for their services through a fee schedule negotiated between the RAMQ and the provincial medical federations. Thus, the provision of medical services remains 'private' in the sense of an exchange between doctor and patient, but the payment of services is handled through the public purse. The principle of public administration is taken one step further than most provinces by allowing for alternative methods of health-care delivery and physician payment through the CLSCs. Quebec was also the first province to impose limits on physicians by capping the salary of specialists; placing limits on how much physicians can bill the RAMQ; and encouraging new physicians to move to under-serviced areas in the province for their first few years of practice, or face limits on the reimbursement of their fees.

Quebec's health-care law was unique in Canada in that it emphasized primary care, made room for the integration of health and social services based on community-centred access, and organized services by region in an explicit attempt to decentralize decision-making.[33] Nevertheless, the implementation of this Quebec health-care model proved politically difficult.[34] Physicians retained their 'special status' as autonomous professionals in the health sector and remained wary of the network of community health and social service clinics. Although the CLSC network covered the entire territory and population of Quebec, these clinics were not as successful in reaching out to people in urban areas, where residents had many health-care options to choose from. In fact, many physicians initially boycotted the CLSCs and set up alternative general-practice clinics.

In 1988, the Rochon Commission report reminded Quebecers of the gap between the promise of initial reform and the actual progress in the system. Dr Jean Rochon (who would later become Minister of Health in the Parti Québécois government) called for a *virage ambulatoire* (move toward ambulatory care) that again emphasized regionalization and integration, but the hurdles to such reform remained apparent.[35]

The attempts to 'move' health care away from the medicalized model was pre-empted by the fiscal crises of the 1990s. Like most provinces, Quebec cut enrolments in medical schools in 1993, as a response to fiscal concerns. And, in 1995, the Quebec government announced the closure of several hospitals in an attempt to rein in soaring health-care costs. Despite intense public protest, five acute-care hospitals were closed in the Montreal area, while several others became long-term care facilities. It also became apparent that access to care was being affected by capacity problems, as emergency rooms became overcrowded, and waiting times for certain elective procedures increased.

One of the most important innovations of this era was Quebec's drug insurance plan. Coverage for prescription drugs is not widespread in provincial health care systems, despite the increase in drug-based therapies and the aging of the population. In 1997, Quebec introduced the first universal drug insurance plan; it allows Quebecers to choose between a private group insurance (through their employers) and a public plan administered through the RAMQ.

Since 1999, as the fiscal crisis eased, Quebec's governments turned again to the organizational lacunae of the health-care system. The Clair Commission report of 2001 (Michel Clair had also previously served as a PQ health minister) concentrated on the reorganization of front-line services, and the creation of new networks of family physician practices. The first projects for these Family Medicine Groups (Groupes de médecine familiale) have been underway since, in tandem with the setting up of a new network of Health and Social Services Centres (Centres de service de santé et des services sociaux). Part of the challenge of this initiative has been the perception of a shortage of general practitioners in Quebec, as more and more medical students choose more lucrative specialization.

Quebec Health Care and Fiscal Federalism

One of the key issues in the development of health care in Quebec has been the tension over *chevauchement* (overlapping jurisdiction) between the federal and provincial governments in the financing and orientation of health services. In hospital and medical insurance, Quebec was concerned also with the conditions imposed by Ottawa in return for federal transfers. Already, as early as 1971, Quebec was sensing its isolation vis-à-vis the other provinces and the federal government in this regard.[36]

The original financing formula was a series of conditional federal grants to the provinces for hospital and medical care insurance. Quebec's health-care plan had to meet certain conditions to qualify for federal funding, but this cost-sharing was relatively open-ended in that the federal government covered almost half of provincial expenditures in health. By the mid-1970s, however, a series of fiscal crises almost immediately placed the two levels of government at loggerheads over health-care financing. In 1977, the Established Programs Financing (EPF) formula was introduced, which covered both health care and post-secondary education transfers to the provinces on a per capita basis. Through the 1980s, the Progressive Conservative government would reduce and eventually freeze EPF transfers.[37]

Even as the share of its health-care transfers was being reduced, the federal government moved toward the formalization of conditions on the money through the passage of the Canada Health Act (CHA) in 1984. The CHA explicitly listed the five conditions that provincial health plans had to meet in order to receive federal monies: public administration (the health-care system must be publicly financed and accountable); universality (every legal resident must be eligible for health insurance); comprehensiveness (all 'medically necessary' services must be covered); portability (Canadians travelling or moving from one province to another must be covered); and equal access (access to health care must be on 'equal terms and conditions' for everyone). To the Quebec government, the imposition of these central norms represented a serious violation of provincial sovereignty. The CHA was considered especially intrusive because Quebec already subscribed to such norms (for example, the equal access provision and the ban on extra-billing) within the Loi sur les services de santé et les services sociaux.

By the 1990s, the reductions in federal transfers, along with worsening economic conditions, forced the Quebec government to react. In 1995, health care transfers were consolidated within a larger Canada Health and Social Transfer (CHST), which substantially reduced the cash portion of federal transfers to the provinces. Overall, Quebec governments found themselves in an unpopular political dilemma: reduced federal transfers, increasing deficits, and making cuts to health-care services.

By 1999, the worst seemed to be over, as the federal budget earmarked additional funds to the CHST. In 2000, a health-care funding agreement further increased transfers to the provinces, and in 2003 the Canada Health Transfer (CHT) came into effect, with increased funding provided through a Health Reform Fund which intended to fund targeted initiatives (primary health care, home care, catastrophic drugs, and diagnostic/medical equipment). While Quebec governments engaged in these federal–provincial arrangements, they remained wary of federal attempts to set the direction of specific health reforms. After extensive negotiations at a high-profile First Ministers' meeting in 2004, the premiers reached another agreement that included significant side deals (such as Quebec's non-acceptance of certain conditions and its refusal to participate the newly-formed Health Council of Canada). This agreement raised eyebrows about asymmetry in the federation. The federal government committed to a 10-year plan for increased health-care transfers and a special fund to reduce waiting times, which had become a thorny political issue.

Although per capita health-care spending has increased since then, Quebec remains the lowest per capita spender of all the provinces ($4,653, compared to the Canadian average of $5,170).[38] Costs are lower due in part to the distinct organizational features of the system.

The Push for Private Health Care in Quebec

One of the most important events in recent Canadian health-care history was an important court case in Quebec, which emerged during the most difficult years of cutbacks to the provincial health-care system. The case involved an elderly patient, George Zeliotis, who waited over a year for hip-replacement surgery, and a maverick physician, Jacques Chaoulli, who had been trying for over a decade to pressure the Quebec government to allow more private medicine in the health-care system. In 1997, Zeliotis and Chaoulli claimed that Article 15 of the Quebec Health Insurance Act, which proscribes private insurers from covering publicly funded services, and Article 11 of the Quebec Hospital Insurance Act, which prevents non-participating physicians from contracting for services in publicly funded hospitals, were unconstitutional under the Canadian Charter of Rights and Freedoms and the Quebec Charter of Human Rights and Freedoms. The initial ruling of the Quebec Superior Court rejected their claims in 2000, as did a subsequent hearing before the Quebec Court of Appeal in 2002.

But the plaintiffs pursued their case to the Supreme Court of Canada, and in 2005, the Court invalidated prohibitions against private insurance for core medical services provided through Quebec's public health-care system.[39] The decision, known as *Chaoulli v. Quebec*, was a divided and controversial one involving three separate judgments. The majority decision overturned rulings by provincial courts, and found Quebec's hospital and health insurance legislation to be in violation of the Quebec Charter of Human Rights and Freedoms (the right to life and inviolability of the person).

After requesting a stay of one year, the Quebec government finally drafted a legislative response in June 2006. Bill 33 opened the provision of core services in the Quebec health-care system to private insurance, but only in three specific areas: hip, knee, and cataract surgery. It also goes further and opens the door to the eventual extension of private insurance to other procedures, and introduces a new instrument for the provision of services through the establishment of 'affiliated medical clinics' through public–private partnerships, a central theme of the Liberal government's attempts to 're-engineer' the Quebec state. At the same time, however, the proposal retains the 'wall' between physicians who remain in the public system and those who opt out of it, and introduces a wait-time guarantee akin to what the federal government had been trying to persuade provincial governments to do.

The impact of the *Chaoulli* case has been felt beyond even this new legislation. Two subsequent reports commissioned by the Liberal government in Quebec—a report by Bank of Montreal executive Jacques Ménard in 2005 and a working group under the direction of Claude Castonguay in 2008—have both used the *Chaoulli* decision as a basis to argue for more private delivery and the creation of supplemental funding instruments to ensure the sustainability of the health-care system.

CONCLUSION

If Quebec's economic policy since the 1960s is an example of what Jean Lesage's Liberal slogan meant for Quebecers to be *maîtres chez nous* ('masters in our own house'), health policy in Quebec can be characterized by Robert Bourassa's idea of *un Québec maître de ses choix* ('master of its choices'). The issue at stake is that Quebec be free to choose the direction of its health reform, based on societal choices and economic realities, rather than change imposed from Ottawa or elsewhere.

Scholars of Canadian federalism tend to describe the early postwar era of the 1950s and 1960s as an era of 'co-operative' or 'collaborative' federalism.[40] The historical record reveals that the relationship between Quebec and Ottawa, at least on the health care, remained fraught with tension and disaccord during that period.

This tension still characterizes the political fault lines in Quebec. The first fault line is the relationship between state and society, and the ideological differences about the delineation between private and public spheres in areas such as health care. The insistence on provincial autonomy brandished by the Union Nationale under Duplessis had more to do with resistance against state intrusion and public spending than with federalism. Essentially, the federal government was used as a proxy for state intrusion and secular control. Although that resistance was overlaid by a more specific concern with religious and cultural preservation in Quebec, it was essentially a fundamental struggle about the role of the state in social matters.

While the role of the state characterized this ideological debate, the second enduring fault line is the demarcation of responsibilities between the federal and provincial states. Here, the fault lines become more complex. Quebec during and after the Quiet Revolution found itself at odds not so much with the federal government's characterization of the role of the state in health and other social matters, but rather with the location of that state power. Successive Quebec governments since the 1960s have wanted the provincial state to wield that power.

In the decades since these pivotal moments in health policy development, both tensions have persisted.

Today, reformers such as Claude Castonguay have become outspoken critics of the public system in Quebec and have laid much of the blame for its shortcomings on the absence of private funding and on the rigidity of the Canada Health Act.[41] Federalism is once again being portrayed as an imposition of external values about the role of the state. And, the controversy over the landmark *Chaoulli v. Québec* case and its aftermath indicate the profound societal debate on these matters.

At the same time, the fiscal battles over the share of public financing between federal and provincial governments in the *déséquilibre fiscal* debate evoke the more practical problems of the division of responsibilities within jurisdictional purviews. Rather than trivial actuarial details, the minutiae of fiscal federalism have been from the outset the symbolic sticking point of the relationship between Quebec and Ottawa, and of the place of Quebec in the federation.

SNAPSHOT

The Doctors' Strike in Quebec

The 1970 strike by specialist physicians in Quebec would be one of the most bitter labour disputes in Quebec, and it would coincide with one of the darkest periods in Quebec history, known as the October Crisis.

In anticipation of the development of public medical insurance in Quebec, two organizations were founded in the 1960s: a federation of general practitioners known as the FMOQ (Fédération des médecins omnipraticiens du Québec) and a federation of specialists known as the FMSQ (Fédération des médecins spécialistes du Québec). They were recognized by government and by professionals as the collective bargaining agent for physicians in Quebec.

This arrangement offers another example of Quebec's distinctiveness vis-à-vis the other provinces. The Association des médecins de langue française du Canada was founded in 1902, as a language-based association of francophone doctors in Quebec and across Canada. This association represented more than the economic and professional interests of their

members; it was seen as a vital marker of the identity of its cultural group in Canada and Quebec. As the politics of identity changed, so did the role of traditional professions, such as physicians. By the 1960s, the Canadian Medical Association had emerged as the most powerful lobby of physicians in Canada, with federated associations in every province, but its representative group in Quebec, the Quebec Medical Association, remained a relatively weak professional association, particularly among francophone doctors. In addition, as the Quebec state began to extend its reach into social and economic life, physicians would become 'syndicalized' in a different way than their counterparts in other provinces.

When medical insurance legislation was tabled in Quebec in June 1970 as Bill 8, it soon became apparent that not all physicians relished this new initiative. While the generalists in the FMOQ agreed to negotiate with the provincial government, the specialists' federation refused to sign on to the agreement. The

Quebec legislation differed significantly from other provincial initiatives in that it limited the opting-out provisions for physicians and prohibited extra-billing altogether.

The FMSQ leaders likened the bill to 'conscription', forcing specialists to practise in the public system. The most controversial aspects for specialists were two-fold: they wanted a guarantee that they could opt out of the public system and practise on their own, and they wanted to retain the right to bill over and above the fee schedule ('extra-billing'). The specialists argued that this would allow more experienced physicians to charge a differential fee that would reflect their expertise.

Despite the efforts of the Quebec government—including the Minister of Health, Claude Castonguay—to negotiate with physicians, by the autumn of 1970 Quebec specialists were moving toward strike action. They were widely supported by colleagues throughout Canada. A precedent had been set in Saskatchewan, where in 1962 physicians had gone on strike to protest the implementation of the Saskatchewan medical insurance plan. Although the strike proved to be very unpopular, the Saskatchewan government had in effect agreed to allow extra-billing by physicians. Note that the two cases were not identical; in Saskatchewan the entire medical community went on strike, as opposed to only specialists in Quebec.

With the entry date for the new medical insurance system announced for 1 November 1970, the FMSQ voted for strike action on 8 October. As specialists pulled back their services, leaving patients and medical students without recourse, Quebec was already plunged in an unprecedented political crisis. Just days before, on 5 October, British diplomat James Cross had been kidnapped by members of the Front de libération du Québec (FLQ) and only days later, on 10 October, another FLQ cell would kidnap Quebec Labour minister Pierre Laporte. As the War Measures Act came into effect and Mr Laporte's murdered body was found, it became clear that the specialists had no hope of winning any public relations battle or labour conflict with the Quebec government. The National Assembly held a special session to pass legislation that forced the specialists to return to work, and on 18 October, the strike was officially over. On 11 November, the FMSQ formally signed an agreement with the provincial government that would allow its members to be reimbursed for their services through the Régie de l'Assurance-maladie. Although some concessions were made over fee schedules and paid leave, the ban on extra-billing remained in place.

Although the strike was unpopular and coincided with an extraordinary political crisis, the debate over extra-billing was not really resolved. Many Quebec specialists voted with their feet and moved out of the province as a consequence. Extra-billing remained the Achilles heel for many provincial governments trying to regulate their health-care systems. In 1984, the passage of the Canada Health Act explicitly prohibited extra-billing by physicians, forcing several provinces to change their health-care legislation to comply with the new federal statute. A strike by the Ontario Medical Association in 1986 was inspired by the Quebec example, as a protest against the new ban on extra-billing. It proved just as unpopular, not only among the public but also within parts of the medical community, and ended within a month.

Portions of this chapter appeared in *Parting at the Crossroads: The Emergence of Health Insurance in the United States and Canada*, by Antonia Maioni, published by Princeton University Press, 1998.

QUESTIONS FOR CONSIDERATION

1. How have recent events changed the debate around health care reform in Quebec?

2. Why is health care a central feature of Quebec's Quiet Revolution?

3. What makes federalism so important in the study of health care in Quebec?

NOTES

1. Terry Boychuck, *The Making and Meaning of Hospital Policy in the United States and Canada* (Ann Arbor, Mich.: The University of Michigan Press, 1999), 47.

2. Joseph Facal, *Volonté politique et pouvoir médical* (Montreal: Boréal, 2006), 32.

3. See Yves Vaillancourt, *L'évolution des politiques sociales au Québec, 1940–1960* (Montreal: Presses de l'Université de Montréal, 1988), 176–7.

4. Ibid., 177–9.

5. House of Commons *Debates*, 20 June 1951, 4349.

6. Statement by St Laurent, broadcast on the **CBC** on 9 July 1953; reprinted in House of Commons *Debates*, 19 June 1954, 6302.

7. The official title was *La Commission royale d'enquête sur les problèmes constitutionnels* (Royal Commission on Constitutional Problems).

8. See Guy Lachapelle, Gérald Bernier, Daniel Salée, and Luc Bernier , *The Québec Democracy: Structures, Processes and Policies* (Toronto: McGraw-Hill Ryerson, 1993), 380.

9. PAC; RG 29; Vol. 1061; 500-3-4 Pt. 1 ('Confidential'); 'Working Committee on Health Insurance of the Interdepartmental Committee on Social Security: Final Draft of Report', 14 February 1950.

10. Malcolm G. Taylor, *Health Insurance and Canadian Public Policy: The Seven Decisions that Created the Canadian Health Insurance System and Their Outcomes*, 2nd edn (Montreal and Kingston: McGill-Queen's University Press, 1987), 193–4. This group had substantial political influence given its regional and linguistic concentration.

11. The other four were Saskatchewan, British Columbia, Alberta, and Newfoundland. On this legislative adventure, see Taylor, *Health Insurance and Canadian Public Policy*, ch. 4; Paul Martin, *A Very Public Life*, Volume 2, *So Many Worlds* (Ottawa: Deneau, 1983), ch. 7.

12. Vaillancourt, *L'évolution des politiques sociales au Québec*, 198–9.

13. Ibid., 200. For a sociological portrait of this changing society, see Marcel Rioux and Yves Martin, eds, *French-Canadian Society*, vol. 1 (Toronto: McClelland & Stewart, 1964).

14. Christopher P. Manfredi and Antonia Maioni, 'The Last Line of Defence for Citizens: Litigating Private Health Insurance in *Chaoulli v. Québec*', *Osgoode Hall Law Journal* 44, 2 (Fall 2006): 249–71.

15. Facal, *Volonté politique et pouvoir médical*.

16. Boychuk, *The Making and Meaning of Hospital Policy*, 98 (emphasis in the original).

17. This story is well told in Edwin A. Tollefson, 'The Medicare Dispute', in N. Ward and D. Spafford, eds., *Politics in Saskatchewan* (Don Mills, Ont.: Longmans Canada, 1968); and Robin F. Badgley and Samuel Wolfe, *Doctors' Strike: Medical Care and Conflict in Saskatchewan* (Toronto: Macmillan, 1967).

18. *Report of the Royal Commission on Health Services*, vol. 1, 1964, 19. These services included medical, drug, prosthetic, and home care for all, and dental and optical services for specific groups.

19. Taylor, *Health Insurance and Canadian Public Policy*, 387.

20. Ibid., 386. The four principles were: comprehensiveness, universality, portability, and public administration; the fifth, equal access, was eventually added via the 1984 Canada Health Act. For an overview of the birth of Quebec Medicare, see ibid., chapter 7.

21. Richard Simeon, *Federal–Provincial Diplomacy: The Making of Recent Policy in Canada*, new edn (Toronto: University of Toronto Press, 2006), 59, Claude Morin, *Mes premiers ministres* (Montreal: Boréal, 1991), 140–2.

22. Réjean Pelletier, 'La Révolution tranquille', in G. Daigle and G. Rocher, *Le Québec en jeu: comprendre les grands défis* (Montreal: Presses de l'Université de Montréal, 1992).

23. Claude Castonguay, *Mémoires d'un révolutionnaire tranquille* (Montreal: Boréal, 2006), 48–50.

24. Ibid., 54–6. The extension of the commission's reach to social welfare was apparently a surprise for Castonguay, but it would have far-reaching consequences in the future organization of Quebec's health and social services.

25. Ibid., 59.

26. Taylor, *Health Insurance and Canadian Public Policy*, 391; Facal, *Volonté politique et pouvoir médical*, 42.

27. John Meisel, Guy Rocher, and Arthur Silver, *As I Recall/ Si je me souviens bien: Historical Perspectives* (Montreal: Institute for Research on Public Policy, 1999), 149; Taylor, *Health Insurance and Canadian Public Policy*, 392–3.

28. On the left, meanwhile, union leaders pressed for coverage of prescription drugs and other non-insured services; Bill 69 passed the following year would guarantee prescription drug coverage of the elderly and social welfare recipients, as well as dental care for children (Facal, *Volonté politique et pouvoir médical*, 53).

29. Facal, *Volonté politique et pouvoir médical*, 50–1.

30. See Marc Renaud, 'Réforme ou illusion ? Une analyse des interventions de l'État québécois dans le domaine de la santé', *Sociologie et sociétés* 9, 1 (1977): 127–52.

31. Facal, *Volonté politique et pouvoir médical*, 44–5.

32. See Raynald Pineault, Andre-Pierre Contandriopoulos, and Richard Lessard, 'The Quebec Health System: Care Objectives of Health Objectives?', *Journal of Public Health Policy* 6, 3 (September 1985): 394–409.

33. Jean Turgeon and Vincent Lemieux, 'La décentralisation : panacée ou boîte de Pandore?', in Clermont Bégin et al., *Le système de santé québécois : un modèle en transformation* (Montreal: Presses de l'Université de Montréal, 1999),173–94.

34. Renaud, 'Réforme ou illusion ?'

35. Pierre Bergeron, 'La commission Rochon reproduit les solutions de Castonguay-Nepveu', *Recherches sociographiques* 31, 3, (1990): 359–80.
36. Morin, *Mes premiers ministres*, 407–8.
37. Miriam Smith, and Antonia Maioni, 'Health Care and Canadian Federalism', in Francois Rocher and Miriam Smith, eds, *New Trends in Canadian Federalism* (Peterborough, Ont., Broadview Press, 2003).
38. Canadian Institute for Health Information, National Health Expenditure Trends 1975–2008 (Ottawa: CIHI, 2009).
39. Christopher P. Manfredi and Antonia Maioni, 'The Last Line of Defence for Citizens: Litigating Private Health Insurance in *Chaoulli v. Québec*', *Osgoode Hall Law Journal* 44, 2 (Fall 2006): 249–71.
40. Ian Robinson and Richard Simeon, *State, Society, and the Development of Canadian Federalism* (Toronto: University of Toronto Press, 1990).
41. The latest example: Castonguay, 'Santé : pour des changements en profondeur', *La Presse*, 16 mai 2007, available at www.cyberpresse.ca/article/20070516/CPOPINIONS/70514064/6732/CPOPINIONS.

Relevant Websites

Quebec Ministry of Health and Social Services/ Ministère de la Santé et des services sociaux du Québec: www.msss.gouv.qc.ca

A description of Quebec's current heath care system, in both French and English.

Québec Commissaire à la santé et au bien-être: www.csbe.gouv.qc.ca/index.php?id=60

Background information and monitors the public debate on health and social policies.

CBC and Radio-Canada: http://archives.radio-canada.ca/sante/sante_publique/dossiers/213/ http://archives.cbc.ca/health/health_care_system/clips/430/

A fascinating historical journey through the conflicts that led to health insurance in Quebec and Canada.

Canadian Health Services Research Foundation/Fondation canadienne de la recherche sur les services de santé: www.chsrf.ca/

Current information on research into the health care system.

Canadian Institute for Health Information/ L'Institut canadien d'information sur la santé: http://secure.cihi.ca/cihiweb/splash.html

The most up-to-date health data for Canada and Quebec.

Institut national de santé publique au Quebec: www.inspq.qc.ca/

Information related to public health and population health in Quebec.

Select Bibliography

Boychuck, Terry. *The Making and Meaning of Hospital Policy in the United States and Canada.* Ann Arbor: The University of Michigan Press, 1999.

Castonguay, Claude. *Mémoires d'un révolutionnaire tranquille.* Montreal: Boréal, 2006.

Facal, J. *Volonté politique et pouvoir médical.* Montreal: Boréal, 2006.

Lee, Sidney S. *Quebec's Health System: A decade of Change, 1967–77.* Ottawa: Institute of Public Administration of Canada, 1979.

Maioni, Antonia. *Parting at the Crossroads: The Emergence of Health Insurance in the United States and Canada.* Princeton: Princeton University Press, 1998.

Manfredi, Christopher P., and Antonia Maioni. 'The Last Line of Defence for Citizens: Litigating Private Health Insurance in *Chaoulli v. Québec*'. *Osgoode Hall Law Journal* 44, 2 (Fall 2006): 249–71.

Smith, Miriam, and Antonia Maioni. 'Health Care and Canadian Federalism'. In Francois Rocher and Miriam Smith, eds. *New Trends in Canadian Federalism.* Peterborough, Ont., Broadview Press, 2003.

Taylor, Malcolm G. *Health Insurance and Canadian Public Policy: The Seven Decisions that Created the Canadian Health Insurance System and Their Outcomes*, 2nd edn. Montreal and Kingston, McGill-Queen's University Press, 1987.

Vaillancourt, Yves. *L'évolution des politiques sociales au Québec, 1940–1960.* Montreal: Presses de l'Université de Montréal, 1988.

Chapter 22

A Question of Power:
A Brief History of Hydroelectricity in Quebec

David Massell, University of Vermont

— Timeline —

1895 Entrepreneurs harness water-powers of Niagara Falls, New York, inaugurating era of large-scale hydroelectric energy development in North America.

1898 Quebec enters age of hydroelectricity when Shawinigan Water and Power Corporation launches construction of dam at Shawinigan Falls on Saint-Maurice River.

1910 With organization of Hydraulic Service, government of Quebec definitively abandons outright sales of waterpowers in favour of leases and royalty taxes, and thus begins serious regulatory effort in hydro sector.

1934 Under intense political pressure to better regulate 'electrical trust', Liberal administration of Louis-Alexandre Taschereau agrees to formation of Electricity Commission to study province-wide nationalization.

1944 Government of Quebec under Liberal Adélard Godbout expropriates assets of Montreal Light, Heat and Power Consolidated, which become property of newly formed Quebec Hydro-Electric Commission or 'Hydro-Québec'.

1960 Jean Lesage's Liberal Party defeats Union Nationale and launches reforms of Quiet Revolution.

1962 Just two years into mandate, Lesage calls snap-election on full-scale nationalization of remaining private electric utilities. In campaign of *maîtres chez nous* Liberals are victorious.

1963 On 1 May, Hydro-Québec takes possession of Quebec's remaining private electrical utilities at a cost of some $600 million.

1969 'Manic 5' is completed, a multiple-arched dam on Manicouagan River that stirs pride and joy in French Quebecers.

1971 Liberal Premier Robert Bourassa launches 'project of the century', James Bay Hydroelectric Project.

1975 By James Bay and Northern Quebec Agreement (JBNQA), Quebec's Cree and Inuit attempt to settle traditional land claims covering two-thirds of province of Quebec while allowing construction of James Bay Project to proceed.

2002 Cree Grand Chief Ted Moses and Parti Québécois Premier Bernard Landry sign La Paix des Braves, which resolves Cree court litigation over JBNQA and permits development of Rupert and Eastmain rivers, while assuring joint Cree–Quebec management and shared profits from mining, forestry, and hydroelectricity on traditional Cree territory.

INTRODUCTION

Turbines and transmission lines, volts and kilovolts, kilowatts and megawatts. These are but some of the technical terms used to describe and measure the production and flow of electrical energy—from distant waterfall to home refrigerator, air conditioner, or personal computer. And such technical terms speak correctly to the fact that the history of hydroelectricity is, to some extent, a story of science and technology applied to the natural world, ever since Thomas Edison patented a practical incandescent light bulb in 1880 and industrialists pioneered large-scale electrical generation at Niagara Falls in the following decade. Still, technophobes may relax, and humanists rejoice. For the central term in our chronology is neither tailrace nor kilowatt-hour; it is simply *power*. One needn't master the difference between volts and watts to grasp the human history of electricity in Quebec. *Power* means more than energy; it denotes a source of authority and strength and the capacity to act. In French, the noun *pouvoir* doubles as the crucial verb 'to be able'. In English, similarly, the term connotes not only a means of supplying energy, but also, to quote Webster's New Collegiate Dictionary: 'possession of control, authority, or influence over others . . . physical might . . . political control or influence'.[1]

The story of power in Quebec is not merely one of technological achievement, but of a century's power struggle over the most crucial and contested of Quebec's natural resources. At the dawn of the hydro age, English-speakers, especially Americans, dominated this industry in their scramble for hydro sites and corporate profits on the northern resource frontier. By the middle of the twentieth century, French Canadians contested Anglo control of hydroelectric energy production, both as a practical means of meeting rising consumer demand for electricity at reasonable rates

and as a proud symbol of surging francophone influence, instrumental (as René Lévesque put it) in 'the economic re-conquest of Quebec'. As the century turned, Aboriginal people—Crees, Inuit, and Innu—had themselves challenged the status quo.

THE IMPORTANCE OF HYDROELECTRICITY TO QUEBEC

That our focus should be *hydro*electricity (power generated by falling water, as opposed to oil-fired or coal-fired 'thermal' energy or nuclear energy) is due to the geographic makeup of Quebec. Ninety percent of the province's territory is the rocky, granitic Canadian Shield. As historians Albert Faucher and Maurice Lamontagne point out, this terrain made Quebec a coal-starved province, whose late-nineteenth-century industrial development was long hampered by (among other things) the lack of this essential fossil fuel of the Industrial Revolution.[2] Through the 1920s, industry lagged behind neighbouring Ontario, and Quebec's populace outside Montreal remained largely rural and poor, and tempted to migrate southward to the burgeoning mill towns of New England.

Meanwhile, the province's abundant falling waters, or 'white coal', made hydroelectricity Quebec's major energy substitute and industrial saving grace. Humans had long used waterpower to mill grain into flour or saw wood into boards with water wheels and pulleys. As hydro*electric* technology emerged in the 1890s —dams, power houses, transmission lines— and was demonstrated at Niagara Falls (deemed 'the great modern experiment in hydro-electric engineering'),[3] it promised to correct this provincial imbalance, bolster urban industry, and slow

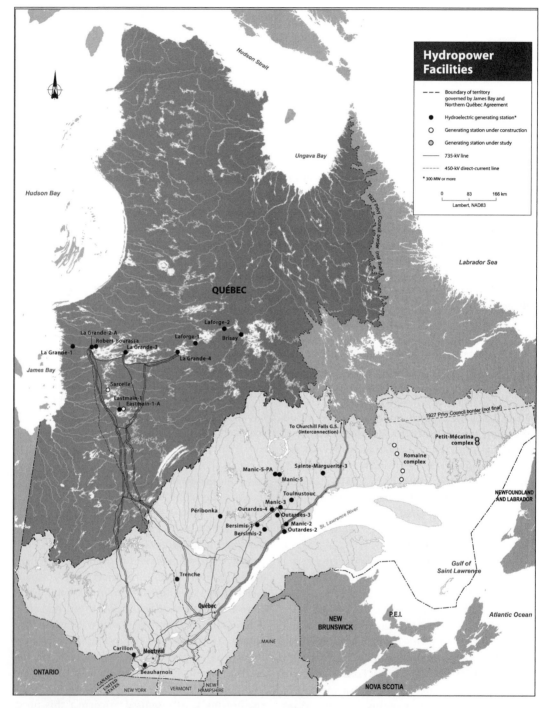

FIGURE 22.1 Map of Quebec and surrounding regions.

Source: Hydro-Québec

the hemorrhage of French Canadians to the United States. A full 10 per cent of Quebec's surface area is water; the province holds 3 per cent of the planet's fresh water reserves. Moreover, many of Quebec's best, high-volume waterpower sites are situated along the southern fall line of the Canadian Shield (along the Ottawa, St Maurice, and Saguenay rivers, as well as the St Lawrence River itself) within transmission distance of the fertile and populous St Lawrence Valley as well as New England and Ontario markets. This lends a natural advantage to the development of this resource. The Shield also offers natural storage of water in its myriad lakes (which regulates the flow of a river across the seasons) as well as excellent and secure footing for the construction of dams.

Quebec's hydro-rich landscape has proved an extraordinary gift to the province. By the end of the 1920s, Quebec was already the leading hydroelectric producer in Canada, ahead of Ontario; by mid-century, Quebec accounted for over one-half the hydroelectric output of the nation (itself among the world's most hydro-rich countries) and could be safely dubbed by Hydro-Québec as 'the power province': 'the world's most richly endowed region in hydro-electric resources'.[4] By 2008, Quebec's Crown corporation Hydro-Québec, with assets of some $64 billion and 23,000 employees, can claim the honour of being Canada's largest electric utility, as well as the planet's largest producer of hydroelectric power. With the capacity to generate over 35,000 megawatts (a megawatt is one million watts; a light bulb burns in a range of 40–100 watts), Hydro-Québec can serve nearly four cities the size of New York, or six the size of Toronto. Producing far more energy than its population can use, Quebec has been able to export power for significant profit since the 1970s to consumers in New York, New England, Ontario, and New Brunswick (some 20 per cent of Quebec's power is exported). Large quantities of inexpensive hydro power have also allowed Quebec to manufacture the power-intensive metals aluminum and magnesium for export. Hydro-Québec's move to purchase the assets of New Brunswick Power late in 2009 appeared as a sign to some observers that Quebec's 'energy behemoth' had mastered its own territory and was moving to colonize that of its neighbours.[5] Hydroelectricity constitutes some 96 per cent of the electricity produced in

Quebec (in the United States the figure is 10 per cent); 3 per cent is derived from nuclear power and 1 per cent from thermal plants and wind power (the latter likely to grow in importance in coming years). Thus electrical development and hydroelectric development are practically synonymous in the province. In sum, the 'generosity of Nature' according to Laval University economist Jean-Thomas Bernard, has produced in Quebec a set of circumstances 'unique in the world'. The result, as Hydro-Québec's current President and CEO Thierry Vandal has put it, is that Quebec is 'the land of large dams'.[6]

ANGLO DOMINANCE OF THE HYDRO SECTOR

That hydroelectric production was dominated early on by an English-speaking elite should not surprise students of Quebec history. This was a province of Canada whose majority French-speaking populace owned and controlled but a small fraction of its factories, wealth, and resources well into the twentieth century. In the hydro sector, moreover, such were the fixed or overhead costs of dams, power stations, and transmission lines, that Canada's anglophone bourgeoisie was itself largely displaced by wealthier American capitalists who were hustling to first acquire and develop, and then profit from, the continent's most promising hydro sites. Quebec's provincial government, meanwhile, dominated by French Canadians and certainly the constitutional owner of provincial lands, lacked the funds to engage in large-scale dam building and was content to leave the task to private enterprise. 'I'd rather import American dollars,' said Premier Louis-Alexandre Taschereau repeatedly in the 1920s, 'than export Canadians to the United States'.

A case in point is the Saguenay River, which was dominated by America's tobacco baron, James 'Buck' Duke. Invited by Canadian entrepreneurs to take an interest in damming the massive Saguenay on the eve of the First World War, Duke quickly seized control of the enterprise for himself, working through local agents to buy up water powers and farm lands, and selecting a political ally in Quebec City–based paper producer William Price. Through Price, Duke secured generous concessions from the Quebec government of Louis-Alexandre Taschereau to impound Lac Saint-Jean as a holding reservoir. Duke's chief engineer, William States Lee, hailed from the Carolinas like Duke himself. The price tag of Duke-Price's Isle Maligne dam—touted by Lee as 'the largest single installation in water-power development ever undertaken', and dubbed by local residents an awesome 'eighth wonder of the world'—exceeded the entire provincial revenue for the year of its completion, 1926. Duke eventually drew to the region the power-intensive aluminum industry in the form of a subsidiary of Alcoa (the Aluminum Company of America, now Rio Tinto Alcan). Alcoa would spawn Alcan, which would in turn complete the Saguenay's hydroelectric development during the Second World War by constructing the similarly enormous Shipshaw dam downstream near Chicoutimi. This electricity was intended to make aluminum ingot, and to a lesser extent newsprint, both for export to the United States.[7]

Alcan is unusual in Quebec in that it was exempted from the large-scale nationalization of hydro resources in the 1960s; but its origins are otherwise typical of the province's major electricity producers. The neighbouring Saint-Maurice valley's hydro–industrial development was begun by two Bostonians: brewer John Joyce and banker John Aldred. Its dams were built by a New York construction firm under the guidance of engineer Wallace Johnson of Massachusetts. At the head of the Montreal Light, Heat and Power Company was the self-made Irish-Canadian railway engineer and business genius Herbert Holt. The Ottawa Valley became the purview of US-based International Paper's Gatineau Power Company. The Southern Canada Power Company, led by Montreal financiers C.J. McCuaig and A.J. Nesbitt, among others, developed the relatively small rivers of the Eastern Townships.

Thus the hydroelectric industry conformed to the other major twentieth-century industries of the Canadian Shield, the so-called 'new staples' of hydro, pulpwood, and minerals. All three were exploitable due to new technologies of the late nineteenth century, which, in turn, granted great new value to this frontier region; and all three were so costly and speculative to develop that new enterprises gravitated to the most capable and powerful American-controlled firms.[8] As

historian Jose Igartua puts it, 'the resource regions of Canada were simple pawns on the continental, even global chessboard of American corporate capitalism.'[9] 'By multiplying and accentuating lines of continental force,' historian H.V. Nelles writes, such investments in pulpwood for paper and hard-rock minerals, as well as hydroelectric dams, 'drew Canada irresistibly into an ascendant American empire'.[10] For its part, the Quebec government acted as a seller of waterfalls to the highest bidder until 1910, and then, stung by nationalist criticism of foreign ownership, as a long-term lessor of water-power sites; or, through the Quebec Streams Commission (founded in 1910) as the builder of several dams which created holding reservoirs—including the Gouin Reservoir of the upper Saint-Maurice and the Kenogami Reservoir of the Saguenay—which powered the turbines of private corporations.[11]

What did this arrangement between the provincial government and private enterprise yield in the decades before the Second World War? It certainly attracted foreign capital, which helped Quebec to escape its *retard* (delay) in industrialization. As hydroelectricity was a leading agent of industrial change, it dictated the location of factories and factory towns, as industries set up shop in outlying areas near water power, such as Jonquière and Shawinigan Falls and, along the Saint-François River, the Eastern Townships. Thus urban factory life, with its attendant benefits and miseries, began to spread beyond Montreal to the hinterlands. It also dictated the type of industry, since hydroelectricity (unlike coal, the basis of the iron and steel industries) creates power rather than heat; thus Quebec became and remains an important world centre for electricity-intensive industrial processes such as aluminum and magnesium smelting, some chemical production, and pulp and paper manufacturing.

Regional, watershed-based monopolies also grew to dominate Quebec industry according to their control of hydraulic resources; and this pattern of 'one river, one company' (as historian John Dales has described it) meant low wholesale electrical rates to large industrial customers and very high retail rates to individual (largely French-Canadian) consumers in need of power and light for households and small businesses. In turn, private power companies may well have helped repress living standards among the

French-Canadian majority and fuel growing discontent. To quote Dales: 'Through their rate structures, the power companies . . . favored the imposition of twentieth-century big business on a *habitant* culture—with all that that implies in terms of social and cultural friction.'[12] Indeed, the combined circumstances of foreign/Anglo ownership, and their excessively high retail profits, inspired a nationalist outcry by French Canadians alarmed by the perceived exploitation of their race.

The 'Economic Re-conquest' of Quebec

The nationalization of hydroelectricity in Quebec has its roots in the post–First World War unease about urbanization and industrialization among Quebec's French-Canadian petite bourgeoisie, including growing anxiety about foreign and American investments.[13] Such Progressive Era concerns gained popularity and traction during the hard times of the Great Depression. Quebec City dentist Philippe Hamel, an unlikely leader for Quebec's public power movement, denounced the city monopoly held by the Quebec Power Company (a subsidiary of Shawinigan Water and Power) and indeed the entire interconnected 'electricity trust'—both in Quebec and beyond—which had already come under attack in the United States. Although Hamel's 1930 fight to municipalize electrical services failed, the cause of public power was embraced by French-Canadian nationalists such as journalist Ernest Robitaille, university professor J.-E. Grégoire, politician René Chaloult, and Mayor Télesphore-Damien Bouchard who had successfully municipalized electricity in the town of St-Hyacinthe. Political pressure mounted on the long-ruling Liberal Party already tainted by the hydropower-related Beauharnois Scandal. Premier Louis-Alexandre Taschereau, accused of turning French Canadians into an economic underclass by overly generous concessions in hydro, forestry, and mining, finally sanctioned an Electricity Commission in 1934 to study province-wide nationalization. Still, real reform came to naught. Maurice Duplessis, posing as a progressive nationalist, craftily co-opted the public power

movement to seize the premiership in 1936, before adopting the lax and pro-business policies of his predecessor and fully frustrating those who sought more radical intervention.

Only in the brief and enlightened tenure of agronomist turned Liberal politician Premier Adélard Godbout (1939–44) did enduring electricity reform begin in the provincial government's creation of the Hydroelectric Commission of Quebec (Hydro-Québec) to expropriate and operate the energy assets of the Montreal Light, Heat and Power Company (MLHP). Godbout's public statements suggest that this far-reaching decision was made to take control of a corporation that was earning exorbitant profits and charging its Montreal customers unjustifiably high rates.[14] Behind the scenes, the action was also likely embedded in wartime politics as well, as the Godbout administration attempted to fend off criticism of generous concessions to Alcan and court the support of nationalists in an upcoming election.[15] And, of course, the takeover of MLHP was rooted in decades of discontent: French-Canadian nationalist demands to wrest control of the development of crucial hydraulic resources from an anglophone economic elite. Whatever the motives and triggers, Godbout's expropriation of a major Quebec power company (at a cost of $112 million to the province and including the Beauharnois power plant on the St Lawrence River) certainly sealed his reputation as a progressive reformer, whose legislative record comprises universal education, rural electrification, and women's suffrage, in addition to partial nationalization of the electrical industry.[16]

Hydro-Québec! A political lightning rod since the Quiet Revolution, the electrical behemoth has drawn lavish praise for promoting the economic interests of French Canadians and also ferocious criticism for overlooking the interests of Aboriginal people and/or the environment, or for assuming the arrogant demeanour and behaviour of 'a state within a state'.

Amid the hype, it is useful to recall the original and prosaic charge by the Quebec legislature of its Crown corporation in 1944: 'to furnish energy to municipalities, industrial or commercial enterprises and to citizens of this province at the lowest possible rates compatible with sound financial administration'.[17] Reporting annually to the National Assembly,

Hydro-Québec's president and four commissioners had the authority to hire and manage its personnel. With the approval of cabinet (via the minister in charge[18]) the corporation could construct dams, power stations, and transmission lines to generate and transport energy; raise capital in financial markets beyond Quebec; and purchase stock in other energy-related companies (which would pave the way for the second nationalization of the 1960s). Thus was Hydro-Québec fashioned as a public corporation, holding a measure of autonomy from the government, to do the will of the provincial electorate.

In the post–Second World War economic boom, with energy demand roughly doubling every decade, Quebec's immediate need was to expand electrical production. Through the 1950s, Hydro-Québec twice enlarged the Beauharnois power station just upstream from Montreal on the St Lawrence, built additional dams on the upper Ottawa River, undertook a new project along the Bersimis River of the North Shore, expanded the provincial transmission network to the Gaspé region and elsewhere, and launched the construction of the Carillon dam on the lower Ottawa. French Canadians had been the primary labour force in provincial dam construction across the century, and only with the establishment of Hydro-Québec did they also become managers and engineers. Carillon was notable in this regard. As Hydro-Québec's official history records with pride, this was 'the first grand project for which the direction was given over to French-Canadian engineers'; and despite their youthfulness, as well as the particular technical challenges of the Ottawa River site, they 'directed the execution of the works with great dexterity'.[19] Hydro-Québec's engineers also surveyed and made plans to build a massive hydroelectric complex along the North Shore's Manicouagan and Outardes rivers. The expansion of power and transmission facilities since 1944 multiplied by six the utility's capacity to generate electricity, keeping pace with consumer demand, and lowering rates by as much as one-half in the Montreal area.[20]

In 1960 other watersheds were crossed. In a historic election, Jean Lesage and the Liberal Party defeated the long-reigning Union Nationale (following Duplessis's death in 1959) and were poised to usher in the reforms of the Quiet Revolution. Hydro-Québec would play a major role in this tumultuous period as an instrument of Québécois economic liberation. The man to shape and wield that instrument was the future premier and founder of the Parti-Québécois, René Lévesque. Charismatic journalist, spirited and bilingual communicator, independent thinker, and political leftist-nationalist determined to use the power of the state to undo the 'economic subordination' of the French-Canadian majority, Lévesque entered politics by accepting a cabinet post in the Lesage government as Minister of both Public Works and, at his insistence, Hydraulic Resources. Within weeks of taking office, the Lesage government followed through on the Liberal promise to 'assure Hydro-Québec the ownership and right to exploit all hydroelectric energy not yet conceded'. In this way was the corporation endowed with a rich source of renewable energy for generations hence.

More radically, Lévesque and his economic advisors[21] planned a second and final stage of nationalization. Once again, its purpose was both practical and ideological: to integrate and rationalize what these men deemed 'the mess' of multiple power companies and distribution systems, thereby lowering and/or equalizing electrical rates across regions; to create white-collar managerial jobs in the hydroelectric industry for the rising francophone middle class; and also, as Lévesque explained, to 'decolonize the hydro sector' by removing it from the control of 'a dozen different principalities' ruled by 'feudal barons'—'a clutch of bigwigs, mainly from the West Island and Ontario, who were happy to accept money from our shareholders and consumers but who hewed to the line that outside the "family compact" there was no chance of promotion by merit, and even less of anyone having a say in running the shop'.[22] As this was a momentous and contentious issue, and an expensive proposition, Lesage called an election in the autumn of 1962 to renew his mandate to carry it forward. Its rhetoric was borrowed from a half-century's nationalist critique of Anglo control of the hydro industry. Its campaign slogan *Maîtres chez nous!* ('Masters in our own house!') evoked perfectly a half-century's yearning by French-speaking Quebecers to seize control of their own rocky, river-strewn, northern

RENÉ LÉVESQUE: A LITTLE GIANT

René Lévesque, photographed by Yousuf Karsh

Yousuf Karsh/Library and Archives Canada, e010752248/
© Estate of Yousuf Karsh

In a chapter focused on electrical power, it is tempting enough to cast René Lévesque (1922–1987) in the role of 'Mr Hydro': the political champion and mobilizing force behind the full-scale nationalization of the electricity industry, principally responsible for the transformation of Hydro-Québec from a Montreal-based public utility to a province-wide engine and instrument of economic development and French-Canadian liberation. True enough. But the moniker hardly does justice to the richness of Lévesque's biography or the full range of his influence. A short, balding man from the Gaspé Peninsula with the husky voice of a lifelong chain smoker, Lévesque was in fact a political giant of twentieth-century Quebec. Any discussion of the Quiet Revolution, or of the political independence movement that followed, must account for his dynamic presence.

Lévesque spent his youth in the village of New Carlisle, Quebec, in a region originally settled by American Loyalists. Although he later described it as a 'prison for my parents . . . on the margin of history'.[23] Growing up in this English-speaking pocket of the province gave him a fluent, nearly accent-free English that would open doors to the wider world. The oldest of four children in a middle-class family (Dominic Lévesque was a country lawyer), René obtained a classical education at the Séminaire de Gaspé and then, in Quebec City, at the Collège des Jésuites. From a young age, his nationalism was strong and certain: 'Never forget that you are French Canadians,' he wrote as a student, 'that your own people have been stagnating for generations, and that if they, the people, *your* people, do not act, they are lost!'[24]

This passionate young man set out to be a lawyer like his father, but it wouldn't stick. In 1943, at the height of the Second World War, Lévesque abandoned his legal studies at Laval University to pursue full-time work as a journalist and see the world. He served as a radio war correspondent, reporting from London during the last bombardments by the German Luftwaffe and then with the advancing Allied troops on the continent. Accompanying the first group of American soldiers to liberate the Dachau concentration camp, Lévesque witnessed firsthand one of the darkest images of the war. 'We stood there stunned,' he recalled, 'staring at these phantoms in striped pyjamas who were staggering out of the huts.'[25] After war's end, he reported on politics for the Canadian Broadcasting Corporation's French-language counterpart, Radio-Canada, covering the Korean War of the early 1950s and stories from across Canada and the United States.

Lévesque's journalism career reached its peak between 1956 and 1959 as he hosted a weekly television program for Radio-Canada. *Point de Mire* ('On Target'), a critically acclaimed and hugely popular news program, put the charismatic and cosmopolitan Lévesque in Quebecers' living rooms to explain, using maps, charts, and film footage, such international issues of the day as the Algerian Crisis. A bitter producers' strike at Radio-Canada in the winter of 1959 brought an end to several popular programs including *Point de Mire*; but Lévesque's leadership role in the union battle gave him a taste for politics. His broad familiarity as a public figure encouraged him to run for political office.

With Jean Lesage's invitation to join the Liberal cabinet in 1960, Lévesque entered the political arena. When Lesage offered the Ministry of Public Works, Lévesque apparently rather casually asked for and received the additional file of Hydraulic Resources (later Natural

Resources). 'I was soon to discover,' wrote Lévesque in his memoirs, 'that under that afterthought hid the goose that laid the golden eggs.'[26] Inspired by the calls of Hydro-Québec's commissioners to expand the state's authority over waterpower development, Lévesque assembled the requisite financial feasibility studies. From early in 1962, his strong public advocacy for nationalization split the Lesage cabinet and then forced the Premier to stand with him. With the Liberals' election victory in November, Hydro-Québec took possession of Quebec's remaining private utilities.

Lévesque's evolution from Liberal nationalist to committed separatist was gradual. 'Slowly and at first subconsciously,' Lévesque himself explained, 'I became convinced that Quebec should safeguard its identity and develop into an independent political entity.'[27] His advocacy of hydro's nationalization already made him the government's most radical spokesman for French-Canadian autonomy. By 1964, Lévesque's positions in several other policy realms (including greater provincial control over taxation, health and social welfare, and international relations) put him at odds with the majority of the Liberal Party. When the Liberals lost power in 1966, and then refused to discuss a sovereign Quebec at the 1967 party convention, Lévesque leapt and formed a new Movement for Sovereignty-Association (Mouvement Souveraineté-Association, MSA) to advocate a fully pro-independent Quebec that maintained economic ties to the rest of Canada. The MSA was one of several pro-independence factions in Quebec society of the 1960s.

It was in the tumultuous year of 1968 (with violent student protests and political confrontations worldwide) that Lévesque united most of these factions as the Parti Québécois. His political success stemmed from well-crafted policy, in addition to his charismatic personality. Faithful to democratic process, Lévesque rejected violence (and violent fringe groups such as the FLQ) as a means of change; and sovereignty-association posed the least possible threat to the economic well-being of the growing French-Canadian middle class. The Parti Québécois steadily gained voter support in the general elections of 1970 (23 per cent) and 1973 (30 per cent). Then in

November 1976, taking 41 per cent of the popular vote in a three-way contest with the ruling Liberals and the Union Nationale, in an event that stunned the rest of Canada and suggested to many that the nation itself was splitting apart, the Parti Québécois swept to power.

As Premier, Lévesque experienced the soaring highs and disappointing lows of governance. In his victory speech, an ebullient and emotional Lévesque told the party faithful 'I never thought that I could be so proud to be a Quebecer.' In the summer of 1977, his government passed Bill 101, the Charter of the French Language, cementing the place of French in provincial education and commercial life. The law remains the centrepiece of Quebec language policy. Achieving independence was more difficult. Lévesque's government called a province-wide referendum on secession from Canada that took place in May of 1980. The question was sufficiently vague in an effort to garner a majority, asking citizens to allow its government 'to negotiate a new agreement with the rest of Canada' that would result in 'sovereignty' as well as 'economic association including a common currency'. Still, 60 per cent of the electorate rejected it. Conceding defeat, an emotional Lévesque told Quebecers: 'If I have understood you well, you are telling me: until the next time.'

There would be no 'next time' for Lévesque. He won a second mandate in 1981, with the PQ taking 49 per cent of the popular vote. But the deep recession of the 1980s reduced support for the Parti Québécois. In failing health, Lévesque resigned as party leader in 1985. He died of a heart attack two years later at the age of 65.

What is Lévesque's legacy? To many Canadians outside Quebec, Lévesque represents the fracturing force of Quebec separatism and the misguided belief that Quebecers require their own country to enjoy the full rights of citizenship. Within Quebec, understandably, far more positive impressions linger: a learned and worldly journalist who in midlife turned to politics to defend the rights of French Quebecers; a charismatic visionary who gave spirited voice to a people coming into their own power; a major force of the Quiet Revolution; the father of the Quebec sovereignty movement. Two grand boulevards, one in Quebec City and the other in Montreal, were renamed in his honour. Appropriately, on Montreal's Boulevard René Lévesque stands the headquarters of Hydro-Québec.

landscape and its economic potential.

Victorious by a wide margin, the Liberal government authorized Hydro-Québec to purchase the stock of 11 private power companies (all but Alcan) for just over $600 million. Roughly half of this amount was borrowed on US financial markets. With expropriation successfully completed in May 1963, Hydro-Québec had doubled its power-generating capacity and begun to rationalize electricity rates and power transmission province-wide. By the mid-1960s, this *colosse en marche* (as *La Presse* journalist Renaude Lapointe dubbed Hydro-Québec) was forging ahead with grand construction projects on the Manicouagan and Outardes rivers, negotiating the joint development of Labrador's Churchill Falls (which would enable the corporation to export huge quantities of power for profit), and had captured the imagination, admiration, and pride of French Canadians by proving that *après tout, on est capable* ('after all, we can do it'). Hydro-Québec's engineers pioneered the world's highest voltage transmission lines (735 kilovolts, or 735,000 volts) in order to conduct electricity from the Manic-Outardes complex to urban markets without excessive power loss; and the research laboratory l'Institut de recherche d'Hydro-Québec was founded shortly thereafter to experiment and innovate in long-distance transmission. Visitors to a film theatre at Montreal's Expo '67 could follow construction progress of the beautiful and massive, multiple-arched dam at 'Manic 5'; more than one French Canadian emerged shedding tears of joy (a striking image to this author, then a seven-year-old boy on his first visit to Canada from the United States). Songwriter Georges Dor struck a chord with 'La Manic', its lyrics a love letter from a lonely construction worker, which proved the most successful record ever by a Quebec songwriter. Revived in the 1990s by Quebec pop singer/heartthrob Bruno Pelletier, the plaintive words and melody still stirred audiences. Si tu savais comme on s'ennuie / A la Manic / Tu m'écrirais bien plus souvent / A la

Manicouagan . . . ('If you knew how lonely we were, / at the Manic, / You would write me much more often, / At the Manicouagan . . .')

As Hydro-Québec grew ever larger and more visible as a symbol of francophone accomplishment, it also grew more politicized. Robert Boyd has pointed out that when the Manic-Outardes project was publicly launched in 1960, it was announced by Hydro-Québec's commissioners and engineers, as was the custom, who spoke to a group of journalists about rising energy needs, in terms of megawatts and kilowatt-hours. By 1971, it was Quebec Premier Robert Bourassa who launched the mammoth James Bay Hydroelectric Project as an instrument of job creation and francophone pride, in a speech to several thousand Liberal supporters in a Quebec City hockey arena.[28] What Bourassa dubbed 'the project of the century', involving world-class dams and power stations, and river diversions hundreds of miles north of Montreal, would be celebrated by French Quebecers as an 'epic' and 'pioneering' achievement by which the North was 'conquered and opened to civilization'.[29] But it would also be the first major project since Hydro-Québec's creation to be seriously contested within Quebec society.

There were disagreements between the Liberal government and Hydro-Québec's commissioners as to whether the James Bay Project should go forward at that time or perhaps later, followed by an internal struggle over which institution was to manage the project: Hydro-Québec or the Bourassa government's Société de développement de la Baie James (James Bay Development Corporation). Members of the opposition Parti Québécois, who preferred to pursue nuclear energy, raised more public objections. 'Just because a river is French-Canadian and Catholic,' economist (and later premier) Jacques Parizeau said famously, 'it isn't absolutely necessary to put a dam on it.'[30] And why, they asked, should Quebec pay an American firm, Bechtel International, to supervise the project when Quebec engineers themselves were capable of it? Another problem concerned organized labour. Nationalization in 1963 had created multiple labour unions, 33 originally, a number of which sought primacy to win Hydro-Québec construction contracts, including for the La Grande River work sites. The simmering tensions erupted in 1974 as members of the Fédération des travailleurs du Québec (Quebec Workers Federation) rioted, vandalizing a work camp and halting construction for seven weeks at a cost of some $35 million.[31]

THE RISE OF FIRST NATIONS

Far more costly to Hydro-Québec was the rise of First Nations activism, beginning with that of the James Bay Crees.

Well before the 1970s, of course, hydroelectric dams had damaged northern Aboriginals' lands and lifeways. As the Shield's resources gained economic value at the end of the 1800s, entrepreneurs and provincial governments alike pushed northward to harvest minerals, forest resources, and hydroelectric energy. And every one of these projects, across the breadth of Canada, disturbed millennia-old societies of hunter-trappers such as the Dene, Crees, Algonquin, and Innu. As hydroelectric projects were often in the vanguard of resource exploitation, they did particular harm. Reservoirs flooded the habitat of beaver and muskrat. Dams cut off salmon (or inland salmon, *ouananiche*) from their spawning grounds, and blocked and altered the flow of rivers, long the natural arteries for canoe transport and the essential corridors for harvesting fish and game. Perhaps most importantly, access roads built to distant hydro sites opened hitherto inaccessible lands to forest companies as well as non-Aboriginal trappers, and sport fishers and hunters. Forestry operations rolled northward from the beginning of the twentieth century; hunting and fishing clubs proliferated after the Second World War. Most of these clubs barred Aboriginals from hunting and trapping on their properties and reduced animal and fish populations nearby. 'When the White Man touches something, he destroys it,' a Montagnais/Innu hunter of the Saguenay watershed put it bitterly. 'It's only the rocks that the White Man cannot destroy.'[32] From the 1950s, it became

increasingly difficult, and eventually impossible, to sustain a family from the bounty of the fragile boreal ecosystem. As hydroelectricity also fostered northern industry—whether paper mills or mines—such spinoff projects drew Aboriginals out of the bush to wage labour, permanent settlement on reserves, and dependency on government welfare.

Hydroelectricity is known as a renewable and clean energy, with some justification. Once the dams, powerhouses, and transmission lines are constructed, fossil fuels are no longer required to generate power; with proper maintenance, and with adequate rain and snowfall, power production can proceed indefinitely. Thus, 'Québec hydropower helps avoid the substantial greenhouse gas emissions resulting from thermal generation.'[33] Hydro-Québec has stated on its website that it is 'clean and green . . . in harmony with nature.' It is ironic then that hydroelectricity has been a particularly potent catalyst for social change in the North. The hydro sector has in fact been instrumental in what anthropologist Paul Charest describes as the 'sedentarization' of Aboriginal peoples—the quiet Canadian tragedy by which autonomous migratory hunter-trappers were caught in the encroaching industrial frontier and rendered childlike wards of the state.[34]

Aboriginals played no part in the decisions to dam Quebec's rivers at least until the 1970s. During the Second World War, for example, the Alcan Corporation constructed large reservoirs high in the Saguenay watershed to feed power plants downstream and smelt aluminum for Allied aircraft; and so-called lakes Manouan and Peribonka were fashioned squarely in the middle of the hunting-trapping terrain of the Lac Saint-Jean and Bersimis Montagnais/Innu who were engaged in the fur trade. In granting its permission to Alcan, the provincial government consulted with forest and paper companies, and carefully examined the consequences for French-Canadian farmers and factory workers. Yet Aboriginals, still disenfranchised and powerless in the affairs of the province, were wholly excluded from the political dialogue. Nor were they offered any form of financial compensation.[35] In the 1960s Manicouagan project of Hydro-Québec, similarly, the Montagnais/Innu of the North Shore were neither informed nor compensated. In a moving documentary on this subject by

French-born filmmaker Arthur Lamothe, four Innu hunters are interviewed in front of the giant Manic 5 dam. Here, before the pre-eminent symbol of French-Canadian arrival as masters of the provincial house, the camera records the sad and angry hunters and their tales of flooded trapping grounds and cemeteries, of lost livelihoods.[36] In effect, as one Quebec cohort rose to power, others not yet liberated were suffering the consequences. A once-downtrodden francophone majority, ironically, rode roughshod over the rights of those weaker than themselves.

But 'Red Power' was rising. North American Aboriginal populations rose rapidly in the postwar era due to permanent reserve and village settlement and access to health care. Formal classroom education could be a psychologically dislocating experience, especially in the off-reserve residential schools, but it also groomed the first generation of northern Canadian Aboriginals (who some called 'briefcase Indians', for example James Bay Cree leaders Philip Awashish, Billy Diamond, Matthew Coon Come, Ted Moses, and Matthew Mukash) able to deal with the legalistic and bureaucratic language of government and business on its own terms. Rising political strength among Aboriginals was matched by growing North American middle-class sensitivity toward them. Worldwide decolonization and the US civil rights movements led thoughtful citizens to examine their own society's practices of racism or internal colonialism. The American environmental movement beginning in the late 1960s romantically cast Indians in the role of 'first ecologists' and increased sympathy for their cause. Environmental consciousness seeped north to Canada. The 'Red Power' or American Indian Movement also spread northward, challenging Canadian First Nations to seize the rights of self-government and the tools of economic development. Canadian politics helped trigger Aboriginal activism in Canada as well: Prime Minister Trudeau's 'Just Society' slogan of 1968 raised expectations, but his government's notorious White Paper of 1969—deemed by Aboriginals to be a blueprint for their assimilation into the dominant culture—galvanized Aboriginal political organization and resistance.[37]

The Crees' resistance to the James Bay Project is by now a well-known story of Quebec and Canadian history, widely disseminated by journalists, academics, activists, and the Cree themselves.[38] Bourassa's government moved to dam the rivers of the James Bay region without consulting or even considering the 5,000 Crees and 3,500 Inuit who occupied that vast terrain. Young Cree leaders sought the advice of their elders and decided to oppose the project. As Ottawa (with jurisdiction over Indian affairs) would do nothing to intervene with Quebecers (fearing the antagonism of the separatist movement), the Crees went to court in Montreal seeking an injunction to halt construction. Aiding them was a batch of sympathetic English-speaking Canadians (the second language of Quebec's Crees and Inuit was English, rather than French, as they had long done business with the British-chartered Hudson's Bay Company) including lawyer James O'Reilly and McGill University–affiliated biologists and anthropologists. They were initially victorious, but the decision of Quebec's Superior Court was overturned on appeal within a week. Still, the court's favourable consideration of the Crees' case, including validation of their title to the land by virtue of continuous occupation and use, forced the government of Quebec to negotiate a settlement.

The resulting James Bay and Northern Quebec Agreement (JBNQA) of 1975, often described as Canada's first modern land-claim settlement, set important precedents in Quebec and Canada. The Crees and Inuit won cash, in investment funds for all communities ($20,000–$30,000 per person), additional subsidies for trappers, exclusive hunting, fishing, and trapping rights in a portion of the territory, and significant recognition of Aboriginal self-governance in political, social, and economic affairs: school boards, health and social services, and municipal services, for example, all would continue to be subsidized by Canada but would now be directed by the Crees and Inuit themselves. Moreover, the negotiation process had forged region-wide political institutions (the Grand Council of the Crees, the Northern Quebec Inuit Association) to represent what had been distinct, isolated, and far-flung communities, while other organizations (the Cree Regional Authority, the Makivik Corporation) were fashioned to manage the investment funds deriving from the agreement. Quebec, for its part, had finally met its obligation (dating from the extensions of Quebec's territory northward in 1898 and 1912) to formally recognize the Aboriginal rights of the inhabitants of the North. No longer could any private corporation or government body attempt to develop resources without first resolving Aboriginal claims. And having done so, Hydro-Québec could now legally proceed with its gargantuan hydroelectric complex along the La Grande River.

The struggle was hardly over, however. Government subsidies do not create a self-supporting revenue base or a sense of accomplishment. It remains unclear whether Crees or Inuit or any other traditional hunting culture, largely dispossessed of their original livelihood and inundated by the material comfort and gadgetry of industrial civilization, can retain or refashion a sense of identity and rootedness. More immediately and practically, the Crees successfully fought Hydro-Québec's second phase of development in the Great Whale River hydro project, claiming that they had only sanctioned the La Grande River complex. They raised objections about the slow pace by which Ottawa and Quebec City met their financial obligations to the 1975 treaty, including job training and employment contracts. Following decades of legal wrangling, Cree Grand Chief Ted Moses and Premier Bernard Landry agreed to the so-called Peace of the Brave (Paix des braves) of 2002, by which the Crees withdrew their lawsuits and relinquished development rights to the mighty Rupert and Eastmain rivers. In exchange they won a lot more money for economic development (at least $70 million annually for 50 years) and the opportunity to become business partners in the logging and mining of their ancestral lands. The Paix des braves broke new ground in recognizing a partnership between a First Nation and a provincial government. Moreover, as the Crees may now benefit from the economic development of the entire traditional territory, the accord moves ever further away from the treaties of old by which an Aboriginal nation parted with the vast portion of its land in return for fixed financial compensation. Thus did the Crees become 'major participants in resource management', Cree Director of Government Relations Romeo Saganash has written, and in fact 'the major players with regard to how, when

and if development takes place'.[39]

The Crees' success in bargaining with Quebec was made possible by excellent historical timing: in an era when non-Aboriginals were forced to pay attention to Aboriginal interests, the Crees still held a trump card of resource-rich land. The Montagnais (or Innu) to the east, whose population slightly exceeds the Crees, were initially less fortunate. Large-scale hydroelectric development invaded their ancestral watersheds—from the Saguenay's Peribonka tributary, northeastward to the Bersimis (Betsiamites), Outardes, and Manicouagan rivers—before the recent era of environmentalism and Aboriginal claims. Still, in the wake of the JBNQA, new agreements were possible for new hydro projects; such negotiations inevitably involved broader Aboriginal settlements as redress for grievances over flooded lands dating back several decades. Thus through the 1990s, at the Peribonka, Sainte-Marguerite, and Toulnustouc rivers, Hydro-Québec negotiated separate multi-million-dollar compensation claims with each of the different Innu bands to be affected by hydroelectric projects along with 'partnership' guarantees of jobs and work contracts. Future projects slated farther up the North Shore, on the Romaine, Little-Mecatina, and Labrador's Lower Churchill rivers, must similarly entail Innu partnership and profit sharing. Since the 1970s, the Innu have also sought broader title and rights to their ancestral lands (so-called 'comprehensive claims') similar to the JBNQA. Quebec's strong desire to build new dams in the Innu homeland have motivated the province to accelerate negotiations with Innu tribal councils on these broader accords. Several comprehensive claims are nearing completion as this chapter is written.[40]

From the perspective of the dam-builder, 'the aboriginal cause' emerged in the 1980s as one of Hydro-Québec's 'thorniest problems'.[41] But one party's problem has proved to be another's opportunity. Quebec's Aboriginals, no longer dismissed, today possess an influence over the northern resource economy that they have perhaps not leveraged since the early part of the Canadian fur trade. In the election of 2008, Jean Charest's Liberal Government pushed its *Plan Nord* (Plan North), promising resource development in a declining economy via 8,000 new megawatts of electricity by 2035 and accelerated mining and forestry operations in the 'last great frontier of Quebec'. 'We absolutely must occupy our territory,' stated Charest. 'It's ours. It's our future.' But now, the government vows consultation with Aboriginal people, who, in turn, promise to hold the premier to his word. 'Jean Charest now has a chance to make a difference,' said Chief of the Assembly of First Nations of Quebec and Labrador Ghislain Picard, 'to turn talk into action, to put an end to the colonialist attitude which still prevails in the relationship with the First Nations. We will no longer be ignored.'[42]

CONCLUSION

This brief history of hydroelectricity in Quebec illustrates a human struggle to contest and control the province's hydro sector, whether motivated by profit, pride, or homeland, or a combination thereof. In fact, the power industry is itself a marvellous bellwether for the socio-political history of the province. From the advent of Anglo-directed industrialization, to the rise of French power, to the dawn of Aboriginal claims, harnessing the energy of Quebec's rivers has reflected the aspirations of distinct constituencies. Similarly, it has reflected collective or national self-assertion in other parts of the world: in Soviet Russia and the United States in the 1930s, and in China today with the construction of the gargantuan Three Gorges dam on the Yangtze River. To the thoughtful reader, however, this sketch of hydroelectric development might reveal more than just politics or 'power'. 'Power struggle' is but one of several themes we might identify at this complex intersection of human and environmental history. There are, of course, other ways to trace this story.

Consider *government regulation*. From waterfalls' outright sale or lease, to the creation and growth of the Crown corporation Hydro-Québec, hydro's regulation and management parallels the growth of state bureaucracy and strength in a province that has been dubbed 'Quebec Inc.' in the last generation. *Technology*, largely overlooked in this chapter,

has indeed been an essential strand of hydroelectric history: from the inception of hydro technology to serve urbanizing societies, to the scaling up and refinement of turbine design, dam construction, and long-distance transmission. Along the way, an industry that began by harnessing individual waterfalls grew to amass whole stretches of river and ultimately burst the bounds of individual watersheds—as in the James Bay Project—to generate electricity in ever-larger quantities. In turn, technology to transmit lots of power over long distances permitted Quebec to profitably export its growing surpluses to the United States, beginning in earnest from the completion of the Churchill Falls and James Bay projects in the 1970s, and increasing with the deregulation of US energy markets in the 1990s.

And so, to *technology*, we should add *economy*. Anglo-Americans dominated the earliest third of our chronology before being displaced by French Canadians, yet the influence of American capital or markets never dwindled. Wall Street's reach has been expressed contemporarily by its role in helping to fund the second stage of nationalization in the 1960s as well as the greater part of the James Bay Project. Whether it pursues export contracts with New York or New England, similarly, Quebec hydro traces the history of continental finance. With high fixed costs and a dependence on future markets for their return, among hydro's greatest challenges is finding the money to build and sustain its projects.

Hydro's history also takes in the history of the boreal *landscape and environment*. As industrializing human societies reached ever northward for the raw materials deemed necessary for their comfort or survival, they reshaped river valleys and aquatic ecosystems along with the lives and livelihoods of indigenous peoples. Similarly, hydro's low-priced power (Quebecers pay some of the lowest rates in North America), by limiting the consumer's incentive to conserve energy, poses an environmental-ethical dilemma in an era of rapid, human-induced climate change. In all, turbines and transmission lines form a marvellous, and multifaceted, lens through which the historian may view the past. Quebec's power history reveals an entire panoply of human phenomena and events.

SNAPSHOT

Quebec's Election of 1962, A Referendum on Hydro's Nationalization

Interpreting the Sources

Background

The long and conservative reign of Maurice Duplessis's Union Nationale came to an end in 1960. With the election of the Liberals under Jean Lesage, the stage was set for the multiple and modernizing reforms of the Quiet Revolution, in education, democratic governance, and organized labour. Still, the Liberals' rise to power in no way guaranteed that the Quebec government would proceed with the radical and controversial step of full-scale nationalization of the hydro sector.

René Lévesque, Lesage's Minister of Public Works as well as Hydraulic Resources (later Natural Resources), certainly intended to 'tackle this aspect of our economic subordination'—to seize 'the goose that laid the golden egg' (as he wrote in his memoir). Gathering support and economic advice from André Marier, Michel Bélanger, Jacques Parizeau, and others, Lévesque assessed the cost and viability of buying up the remaining 11 private power companies. With the information in hand by January 1962, Lévesque began publicly to call for nationalization, which split the members of Lesage's cabinet and angered the Premier himself. In September of 1962, at a Laurentian cabinet retreat at Lac-à-l'épaule, Lévesque finally won Lesage's support for the nationalization project.

Yet Lesage would proceed only with a specific mandate from Quebec voters. So although the Liberals had been in power for only two years, Lesage called for the dissolution of the Assembly and for an election to take place on 14 November 1962. 'It is for the people of Quebec to decide, freely and proudly,' the Premier stated, 'whether they wish to take into their hands the most important of all the keys to a progressive economy.' The specific origins of the campaign slogan are not clear. What is clear, in retrospect, is that *Maîtres chez nous!* ('Masters in our own house!') struck a powerful chord with the electorate. The Liberals increased their majority in the Assembly substantially, from 51 to 63 seats of the total 95. On 1 May 1963,

Hydro-Québec took possession of the remaining electrical utilities of the province at a cost of $604 million.

Questions

The sources below (both visual and written) should permit you to assess the debate between the two major political parties over nationalization that culminated in the election of 1962.

1. What arguments or symbols did the Lesage government employ to coax Quebec voters to vote Liberal?
2. What was the Union Nationale Party's position on nationalization?
3. Ultimately, what can we reasonably infer about the mood of Quebec society from a close reading of these historical documents?

Sources

1. Liberal Election Poster: 'Maintenant ou jamais! Maîtres chez nous'.

2. '1962: Manifeste du parti liberal du Québec' (our translation)

> 'The era of economic colonialism is over in Quebec. Now or never, Maître chez nous.'
>
> —Jean Lesage

On June 22, 1960, the electorate approved the platform of the Liberal Party of Quebec by granting to it a mandate to organize national and economic life in such a manner that would favor the well being of Quebec citizens. Jean Lesage and his team set out resolutely to this task, determined to endow Quebec with social and cultural legislation without precedent. They are doing the same in the domains of education and the economy; and they are cleaning up governance. At the same time, they have established the *Conseil d'orientation économique* charged with studying the means to bring to reality our economic expansion, which is the essential factor of our social and cultural blossoming. Following serious study, it has become clear that the unification of the electricity network—key to the industrialization of all Quebec regions—is the primary condition for our economic liberation and a policy of full employment . . . . It is up to the Legislative Assembly and the Cabinet to adopt the necessary legislation to bring this task to a conclusion, the largest and most fruitful ever proposed by a government in Quebec since Confederation.... We won't replace 30,000 stockholders by more than 5,300,000 without consulting the latter. Jean Lesage and his team calls on the entire population to give them a clear and precise mandate which will permit them to pursue, with renewed vigor, the realization of the Liberal platform of 1960. Now or never 'maîtres chez nous.' Such is the goal of the Liberal Party of Quebec . . . . [Note: the entire Liberal pamphlet is devoted to the issue of nationalization.]

3. '1962: Programme de l'Union nationale' (our translation)

The Union Nationale presents to the people a platform based on the following principles: a sense of responsibility . . . social justice . . . [and] regional development . . . For the human being and the family [the U.N. promises tax reductions, adjustments in health insurance, etc.]; for the farmer [the U.N. promises aid regarding credit, rural roads, etc.]; for the workers [the U.N. promises a $1 hour minimum wage, a pension system, etc.] . . . . [Note: roughly two-fifths of the pamphlet is devoted to these issues.]

For progress and economic emancipation . . . immediate nationalization of the Lower St. Lawrence Power Company and of Northern Quebec Power in order to reduce rates and improve service in the regions served by these two companies. Conversion form 25 to 60 cycles in Northwest Quebec; and a referendum, no later than June 30, 1963, on the nationalization of the other private electric companies, in order to permit the population to express itself freely, outside of any partisan consideration and in complete knowledge of the issue . . . . [Note: roughly one-fifth of the pamphlet is devoted to 'economic emancipation' of which nationalization forms a part.]

For the municipalities [better collaboration between the province and its towns, more help maintaining winter roads, etc.]; for education and culture [maintain the province's sovereignty in education, maintain the religious character of schools, etc.]; for financial independence and political sovereignty [reestablish financial independence of the province, etc]." [Note: roughly two-fifths of the pamphlet is devoted to these issues.]

QUESTIONS FOR CONSIDERATION

1. Hydro-Québec: What is it, exactly? When was it formed, and why? What would you say have been the milestones of its growth and development? Most broadly, what does this institution suggest or reveal about Quebec history or society?

2. Massell employs the phrase *power struggle* to describe a century of hydroelectric

development in Quebec. Does his evidence support this claim throughout the essay? Would *national struggle* or *tribal struggle* be more, or perhaps less, appropriate descriptors? Explain.

3. This story of power takes place not in a vacuum, but in a particular place: the province of Quebec. What larger issues or themes of Quebec history and the Quebec experience do you recognize in this chapter?

4. The history of power production in Quebec is but one way to slice the modern history of Quebec. What other subjects does this chapter suggest for further research?

Notes

1. *Webster's New Collegiate Dictionary* (Springfield, Mass.: Merriam, 1975), 902.
2. Albert Faucher and Maurice Lamontagne, 'History of Industrial Development', *Essais sur le Québec contemporain,* Jean-Claude Falardeau, ed. (Quebec: Les Presses Universitaires Laval, 1953).
3. Blodwen Davies, *The Story of Hydro: White Thunder* (Toronto: Ryerson Press, 1931), 12.
4. Quebec Hydro-Electric Commission, *Quebec, The Power Province*, brochure dated circa 1957.
5. Andy Blatchford, 'Hydro-Québec's transformation into energy behemoth has rivals quaking in U.S., Canada', *The Canadian Press*, 29 October 2009.
6. Quebec Hydro-Electric Commission, *Quebec, The Power Province*; personal communication with Bernard, Nov. 2008; Louis-Gilles Francoeur, 'Rencontre avec Thierry Vandal: La terre des grands barrages', *Le Devoir*, 14–15 juin 2003, G5.
7. David Massell, *Amassing Power: J.B. Duke and the Saguenay River, 1897–1927* (Montreal and Kingston: McGill-Queen's University Press, 2000).
8. Morris Zaslow, *The Opening of the Canadian North, 1870–1914. (Toronto:* McClelland & Stewart 1971); and *The Northward Expansion of Canada, 1914–1967 (*Toronto: McClelland & Stewart 1988).
9. José Igartua, '"Corporate" Strategy and Locational Decision-Making: the Duke-Price Alcoa Merger, 1925', *Journal of Canadian Studies* 20 (1985–6): 97.
10. H.V. Nelles, *The Politics of Development* (Toronto: Macmillan, 1974), 307.
11. Claude Bellavance. 'L'état, la "houille blanche" et le grand capital: L'aliénation des ressources hydrauliques du domaine public québécois au début du XXe siècle', *Revue d'histoire de l'Amérique française* 51, 4 (1998): 487–520; and Massell, *Amassing Power.*
12. John H. Dales, *Hydroelectricity and Industrial Development: Quebec, 1898–1940* (Cambridge, MA: Harvard University Press, 1957), 180.
13. Yves Roby, *Les Québécois et les investissements Américains (1918–1929)* (Quebec: Les Presses de l'Université Laval, 1976); Susan Mann Trofimenkoff, *The Dream of Nation: A Social and Intellectual History of Quebec* (Toronto: Gage, 1983), ch. 15; Yvan Lamonde, *Histoire sociale des idées au Québec 1896–1929,* vol. 2 (Montreal: Éditions Fides, 2004), ch. 7.
14. On the formation of Hydro-Québec, see Clarence Hogue, André Bolduc, and Daniel Larouche, *Québec: un siècle d'électricité* (Montreal: Libre Expression 1979), ch. 7. See also in Yves Bélanger and Robert Comeau, *Hydro-Québec: Autres temps, autres défis* (Quebec: Presses de l'Université du Québec, 1995): Gilles Gallichan, 'De la Montreal, Light, Heat and Power à Hydro-Québec', 64–70; Claude Bellavance, 'Un long mouvement d'appropriation de la première à la seconde nationalisation', 71–8; and Robert Boyd, 'Cinquante ans au service du consommateur', 97–103.
15. David Massell, *Quebec Hydropolitics: The Peribonka Concessions of the Second World War* (Montreal and Kingston: McGill-Queen's University Press, forthcoming 2010), ch. 5.
16. Jean-Guy Genest, *Godbout* (Sillery: Les editions du Septentrion, 1996).
17. Hydro-Québec Act, 17 April 1944.
18. The cabinet minister responsible for Hydro-Québec changed over the years as the ministries themselves were reorganized, from Terres et Forêts (1944–5), to Ressources hydrauliques (1945–61), to Richesses naturelles (1961–76), to Énergie.
19. Hogue et al., *Québec: un siècle*, 250.
20. Robert Boyd, 'Cinquante ans', in *Hydro-Québec: Autres temps, autres défis*, 97–103.
21. Principal among Lévesque's advisors regarding nationalization were Michel Bélanger, Jacques Parizeau, Roland Giroux, and André Marier.
22. René Lévesque, *Memoirs* (Toronto: McClelland & Stewart, 1986), 169–72.
23. Lévesque, *Memoirs,* 9.
24. René Lévesque, *My Quebec,* trans. Gaynor Fitzpatrick (Toronto: Methuen, 1979), 4.
25. Lévesque, *Memoirs,* 102.
26. Lévesque, *Memoirs,* 167.
27. Lévesque, *My Quebec,* 6.
28. Boyd was an engineer (from 1945), commissioner (from 1969) and eventually president of Hydro-Québec

(1977–82). See his 'Cinquante ans', in *Hydro-Québec: Autres temps, autres défis.*

29. Roger Lacasse, *Baie James, une épopée: L'extraordinaire aventure des derniers des pionniers* (Montreal: Libre Expression, 1983), 28–9.

30. Ibid.

31. Ibid., 129, ch. 7, ch. 11.

32. Quoted/translated by Massell, *Quebec Hydropolitics.*

33. Hydro-Québec *Moving Forward* Sustainability Report (Montreal: Hydro-Québec, 2004), 6.

34. Paul Charest, 'Les barrages hydro-électriques en territoire Montagnais et leurs effets sur les communautés amérindiennes', *Recherches amérindiennes au Québec* IX, 4 (1980): 323–37; or Charest's 'Hydroelectric dam construction and the foraging activities of eastern Quebec Montagnais' in Eleanor Leacock and Richard Lee, eds, *Politics and History in Band Societies* (Cambridge: Cambridge University Press 1982), 413–26.

35. Massell, *Hydropolitics.*

36. Arthur Lamothe, *Manicouagan*, Les Ateliers Audio-Visuels du Québec, 1973.

37. Olive Dickason, *Canada's First Nations: A History of Founding Peoples from Earliest Times* (Toronto: McClelland & Stewart, 1992), and J.R. Miller, *Skyscrapers Hide the Heavens: A History of Indian-White Relations in Canada*, 3rd edn (Toronto: University of Toronto Press, 2000).

38. An accessible and balanced summary of the James Bay Project through the 1980s is Sean McCutcheon's *Electric Rivers: The Story of the James Bay Project* (Montreal: Black Rose Books, 1991). More scholarly is Richard Salisbury's *A Homeland for the Cree: Regional Development in James Bay, 1971–1981* (Montreal and Kingston: McGill-Queen's University Press, 1986). More partisan is Boyce Richardson's *Strangers Devour the Land* (Toronto: MacMillan, 1975).

39. Romeo Saganash, 'The "Paix des Braves": An Attempt to Renew Relations with the Cree', in Thibault Martin and Steven M. Hoffman, eds, *Power Struggles: Hydro Development and First Nations in Manitoba and Quebec* (Winnipeg: University of Manitoba Press, 2008), 205–13.

40. Paul Charest, 'The Land Claims Negotiations of the Montagnais, or Innu, of the Province of Quebec and the Management of Natural Resources', in Colin H. Scott, ed., *Aboriginal Autonomy and Development in Northern Quebec and Labrador* (Vancouver: University of British Columbia Press, 2001), 255–73; and Charest, 'More Dams for Nitassinan: New Business Partnerships Between Hydro-Québec and Innu Communities', in Martin and Hoffman, *Power Struggles*, 255–79.

41. Boyd, 'Cinquante ans', 102.

42. 'Charest unveils plan for northern Quebec', *The Gazette*, 28 September 2008; Liberal video 'Le Plan Nord', available at www.plq.org/en/PlanNord_energies.php; 'Charest's Plan Nord troublesome news for First Nations', *Montreal Environment*, 8 December 2008.

RELEVANT WEBSITES

RADIO-CANADA ARCHIVES: http://archives.radio-canada.ca/
Search *hydro*; *hydroélectricité*; *électricité*.

GRAND COUNCIL OF THE CREES: www.gcc.ca/

HYDRO-QUÉBEC: www.hydroquebec.com/en/index.html

SELECT BIBLIOGRAPHY

Bélanger, Yves, and Robert Comeau, eds. *Hydro-Québec: Autres temps, autres defies.* Quebec: Presses de l'Université du Québec, 1995.

Bellavance, Claude. "L'état, la 'houille blanche' et le grand capital: L'aliénation des ressources hydrauliques du domaine public québécois au début du XXe siècle," *Revue d'histoire de l'Amérique française* 51, 4 (1998): 487–520.

———. *Shawinigan Water and Power, 1898–1963, Formation et déclin d'un groupe industriel au Québec.* Montreal: Les Éditions du Boréal, 1994.

Bourassa, Robert. *Power from the North.* Scarborough: Prentice-Hall, 1985.

Charest, Paul. 'Les barrages hydro-électriques en territoire Montagnais et leurs effets sur les communautés amérindiennes'. *Recherches amérindiennes au Québec* IX, 4 (1980): 323–37.

———. 'Hydroelectric dam construction and the foraging activities of eastern Quebec Montagnais'. In Eleanor Leacock and Richard Lee, eds., *Politics and History in Band Societies.* Cambridge: Cambridge University Press, 1982, 413–26.

———. 'The Land Claims Negotiations of the Montagnais, or Innu, of the Province of Quebec and the Management of Natural Resources'. In Colin H. Scott, ed., *Aboriginal Autonomy and Development in Northern Quebec and Labrador.* Vancouver: University of British Columbia Press, 2001.

Dales, John H. *Hydroelectricity and Industrial Development: Quebec, 1898–1940.* Cambridge, MA: Harvard University Press, 1957.

Dickason, Olive. *Canada's First Nations: A History of Founding Peoples from Earliest Times.* Toronto: McClelland & Stewart, 1992.

Dirks, Patricia. 'Dr. Philippe Hamel and the Public Power Movement in Quebec City, 1929-1934: The Failure of a Crusade'. *Urban History Review* 10, 1 (June 1981): 17–29.

Gagnon, Alain-G., and Guy Rocher, eds. *Reflections on the James Bay and Northern Quebec Agreement.* Montreal: Québec-Amérique, 2002.

Genest, Jean-Guy. *Godbout.* Sillery: Les editions du Septentrion, 1996.

Hogue, Clarence, André Bolduc, and Daniel Larouche. *Québec: un siècle d'électricité.* Montreal: Libre Expression, 1979.

Hydro-Québec. *Des premiers defies à l'aube de l'an 2000.* Montreal: Libre Expression/Forces, 1984.

Igartua, José '"Corporate" Strategy and Locational Decision-Making: the Duke-Price Alcoa Merger, 1925'. *Journal of Canadian Studies* 20 (1985–6): 82–101.

Lacasse, Roger. *Baie James, une épopée: L'extraordinaire aventure des derniers des pionniers.* Montreal: Libre Expression, 1983.

Lévesque, René. *Memoirs*, trans. Philip Stratford. Toronto: McClelland & Stewart, 1986.

———. *My Quebec*, trans Gaynor Fitzpatrick. Toronto: Methuen, 1979.

Martin, Thibault, and Steven M. Hoffman, eds. *Power Struggles: Hydro Development and First Nations in Manitoba and Quebec.* Winnipeg: University of Manitoba Press, 2008.

Massell, David. *Amassing Power: J.B. Duke and the Saguenay River, 1897–1927.* Montreal and Kingston: McGill-Queen's University Press, 2000.

McCutcheon, Sean. *Electric Rivers: The Story of the James Bay Project.* Montreal: Black Rose Books, 1991.

Miller, J.R. *Skyscrapers Hide the Heavens: A History of Indian-White Relations in Canada*, 3rd edn. Toronto: University of Toronto Press, 2000.

Niezen. Ronald. *Power and Dignity: The Social Consequences of Hydroelectric Development for the James Bay Cree.* Toronto: University of Toronto Press, 1993.

Provencher, Jean. *René Lévesque: Portrait of a Québécois*, trans. David Ellis. Toronto: Gage, 1975.

Regehr, T.D. *The Beauharnois Scandal: A Story of Canadian Entrepreneurship and Politics.* Toronto: University of Toronto Press, 1990.

Richardson, Boyce. *Strangers Devour the Land.* Toronto: MacMillan, 1975.

Salisbury, Richard. *A Homeland for the Cree: Regional Development in James Bay, 1971–1981.* Kingston and Montreal: McGill-Queen's University Press, 1986.

Zaslow, Morris. *The Opening of the Canadian North, 1870–1914. Toronto:* McClelland & Stewart, 1971.

———. *The Northward Expansion of Canada, 1914–1967.* Toronto: McClelland & Stewart, 1988.

CHAPTER 23

The Politics of Social and Economic Development in Quebec

Peter Graefe, McMaster University

— TIMELINE —

1960   Quebec election on 22 June, felt to mark launch of Quiet Revolution.

1976   Parti Québécois wins election and forms government on 15 November.

1981–2   Major recession pushes PQ government to rein in public spending, sparks conflict with public sector unions.

1985   Quebec Liberal Party wins provincial election on 2 December, on promises of significant economic liberalization.

1995   Marche du Pain et des Roses (Bread and Roses March Against Poverty and Violence), 26 May–4 June.

1996   Conférence sur le devenir social et économique du Québec, 18–20 March.

1996   Sommet sur l'économie et l'emploi, 30 October–1 November.

2003   Election of Quebec Liberal Party on 14 April, felt to mark a shift to more neo-liberal style of governing.

In 2005, a group of prominent thinkers, including former Quebec premier Lucien Bouchard, published a manifesto for a 'clear-eyed vision of Quebec'.[1] They argued that Quebec's standard of living was threatened by the costs of dealing with an aging population, as well as economic competition from China and India. They made the case for experimenting with public–private partnerships in public services, increasing tuition fees for post-secondary education, and reducing taxes. Within weeks, this manifesto was joined by one for a 'solidaristic Quebec' that questioned a number of the 'clear-eyed' assessments, and that proposed collective solutions to Quebec's challenges to be delivered through state institutions.[2] The debate between the 'clear-eyed' and the 'solidaristic' continued in the newspapers' opinion pages and in university colloquia for the ensuing year, and many politicians and opinion leaders felt compelled to reveal which manifesto they backed.

All democratic societies debate how they will organize economic and social policy so as to secure growth and equity, although not always as openly as in this case. This particular debate was the latest of a long series in Quebec about how to reform the institutions inherited from the Quiet Revolution of the 1960s, pitting supporters of economic liberalism[3] (the 'clear eyed') against supporters of social democracy (the 'solidaristic'). Yet to look at this as simply a running debate is problematic on two fronts. First, the fact that the debate recurs, and is thus in a sense unresolved, does not mean that important changes in the development model have not occurred over the past quarter century. Second, while a debate nominally occurs between equals each trying to convince others that their position is strongest, the setting of a development model comes not only from rational argument, but also through social power and the contest of different social actors (business, unions, social movements, interest groups).

This chapter seeks to describe the major features of Quebec's development model since 1960, with particular emphasis on the competing programs to transform it in the last quarter century. After a very brief background on Quebec's economy and a discussion of development models, it considers the development model that came out of the Quiet Revolution of the 1960s, the model that continues to serve as the backdrop for contemporary debates. Since the 1980s, the strongest challenge to the model has come from employers' associations, who have advanced a neo-liberal model. While this latter model was in part resisted in the 1990s by counter-proposals of 'progressive competitiveness' and partnership, it has gained traction since the election of a Liberal provincial government in 2003. While the future remains open, it would appear that the actors who had successfully championed alternatives to neo-liberalism have been weakened and are now less able to develop imaginative counter-proposals for Quebec's development.

BACKGROUND

There is not space here to give a comprehensive survey of economic and social indicators (but see Table 23.1, and also Chapter 28), but suffice it to say that Quebec boasts a modern and diversified economy. If Quebec were a country, its economy would rank roughly fortieth in size in the world, and its per capita GDP would rank it as the twenty-eighth richest country in the world.

Quebec's economy has traditionally relied on natural resource extraction and primary processing, particularly in forestry and mining. More recently,

it has used its significant hydroelectric resources to promote energy-intensive primary metal manufacturing (aluminum and magnesium). These resource-based activities have been grafted onto the more diverse economy of Montreal, which was the major financial hub in British North America and Canada into the mid-twentieth century, as well as the cradle of Canada's industrial revolution in the nineteenth century. The reliance on primary exports has given a boom-bust character to Quebec's economy, while declining manufacturing has contributed to a pattern of lower wages and higher unemployment than the Canadian average. Successes in higher-end manufacturing and services have not had sufficient employment effects to erase this disadvantage, although unemployment and poverty have fallen in recent years toward the Canadian average after being structurally higher through most of the 1970s to the 1990s.

How one characterizes Quebec's performance is heavily politicized. Some have pointed out that Quebec is falling behind, with its per capita GDP

TABLE 23.1   Quebec–United States Comparison of Selected Indicators (adjusted, after-tax 2007 figures)

Economic Indicators	Quebec	United States
Poverty rate	9.0%	12.5%
Labour force participation rate	67.7%	67.8%
Annual hours of work	1,607	1,953
Wages (weekly) average	Can$774	US$690
Women's wages as a percentage of men's wages	0.81	0.78
Union density		
Total	39.7%	12.4%
Public sector	81.5%	36.8%
Private sector	26.3%	7.6%
Distribution of total income (by household)		
Lowest quintile	5.4%	3.4%
Second quintile	11.1%	8.7%
Third quintile	16.7%	14.8%
Fourth quintile	24.1%	23.4%
Highest quintile	42.8%	49.7%

Sources: US Census Bureau Current Population Reports, 'Income, Poverty, and Health Insurance Coverage in the United States: 2008'; US Bureau of Labor Statistics; Institut de la Statistique Québec, 2008; Statistics Canada, 2008; Survey of Labour and Income Dynamics 2008.

being lower than every state in the United States. Others point out that this reflects the presence of more wealthy individuals in the United States, but that the standard of living of the bottom 50 per cent of Quebec's population is in fact higher than the bottom 50 per cent in the US, and that a good portion of the overall income gap reflects Quebecers' choosing to work fewer hours.[4] From this perspective, Quebecers have a high standard of living. For our purposes, it is enough to note that Quebec has developed an advanced capitalism that is slightly more redistributive and egalitarian than the American variant, and which has delivered relatively high standards of living despite levels of poverty and unemployment that reflect the difficulties of transforming a resource-based economy.

WHAT ARE DEVELOPMENT MODELS?

To speak of development models is to argue that capitalism has a geography and a history. While capitalism now spans the globe and disciplines economic activity with the rigours of competition and profit, the manner in which capitalist economies are organized differs across countries and over time. Many things vary, even among the advanced industrial countries, such as labour markets (degree of unionization, extent of regulation of working conditions), financial institutions (type of banking system, design of central bank), taxation (levels and structure), and social provision (size of welfare state, design of programs). There are many ways to put together a capitalist economy, and this has led to attempts to differentiate national capitalisms and to periodize changes within capitalism (e.g., Keynesianism, neo-liberalism).

The distinction between capitalist models is not an abstract academic exercise. Differences in the organization of capitalism have real and tangible impacts on how people live. They affect who gets what, through such things as wage rates, degrees of job stability, ability to take time to care for young children or elderly relatives, access to income when injured or unemployed, and ability to have a voice in the workplace. The definition of development models is therefore

bound up in power relations between political actors, each vying to advance forms of economic organization that advance their own interests. And the play of power is very complex, as part of it involves convincing others that a given form in fact represents the common interest, or of making partial compromises and concessions to bring others to accept a particular form of development.

In a capitalist system, society relies heavily on the owners of large pools of capital (i.e., capitalists) for major decisions about investment and production. Where firms invest, and how they produce, will affect things like the number and quality of jobs or the amount of pollution in a community. Capitalists therefore have great power in shaping development models, since they can invest elsewhere if wage levels or regulations are making them unprofitable. Nevertheless, there is room for negotiation, in part since different capitalists may have different interests,[5] and in part since other interests in society can organize to extract concessions over aspects of the development model, or to propose positive-sum compromises.[6] Capitalist societies are not just about capitalism, however. A series of other cultural understandings, for instance about the appropriate roles of men and women, about what forms of sexuality are deemed acceptable, or about who is deemed to be a full citizen or a second-class citizen, are also the subject of ongoing negotiation and struggle, and affect the economic and social policies that are adopted.

DEVELOPMENT MODELS IN QUEBEC

The Quiet Revolution[7]

Current debates about Quebec's development model invariably refer back to the economic nationalism and welfare-state building of the Quiet Revolution of the 1960s. In the 1940s and 1950s, a number of sectors of Quebec society, including francophone capitalists, the labour movement, intellectuals, and the middle classes, came to criticize the Quebec government's liberal economic policies on several grounds. First, while the economy grew strongly over the period, this growth was weaker than in neighbouring Ontario, and was insufficient to prevent unemployment from increasing. The province's rapid urbanization and industrialization also created social problems as the provincial government hesitated in regulating the labour market or in developing a modern welfare state. Second, control of the economy rested largely in the hands of anglophones, leaving the francophone majority without much say over private investment decisions affecting their society's development. This lack of control was worsening as the concentration of economic activity into larger corporations made it difficult for francophone capitalists, who were most present in smaller-scale economic activities, to get into the game. Third, the pattern of ownership translated into a labour market where francophones were excluded from higher-order management jobs (see Chapter 12).

This coalition of business, labour, intellectuals, and the middle class managed to replace the Union Nationale government with a Liberal one in the 1960 election. The new administration embarked on an aggressive strategy of state building to respond to the three concerns discussed above. To respond to the first challenge, the government adopted labour legislation and social policies to bring Quebec into line with those across the industrialized West in those years. It also invested heavily in public infrastructure to maintain high employment levels. To meet the challenge of economic control, it developed a series of investment vehicles and sector-specific state corporations (in forestry, petroleum, aluminum, and so on) to consolidate francophone holdings, upgrade the industrial structure, and create pools of capital to aid francophone capitalists to succeed in mergers and acquisitions. These tools helped to overturn some of the under-representation of francophones at the commanding heights of the economy, and the expansion of the state as a whole provided high quality professional jobs for francophones. However, real incursions into the world of work to overcome the linguistic inequality in the labour market would have to wait until the 1970s with Bill 22 in 1974 and Bill 101 in 1977, and their measures to 'francize' the workplace by making French the language of work, with exceptions for head offices, research centres, and small firms (see Chapter 12).

Already by the early 1970s, this development model was under criticism from various quarters. Quebec nationalists in the Parti Québécois (PQ) felt that the reforms had not gone far enough in transferring economic control to the francophones and in ensuring that foreign investment served national interests. They therefore looked to France's postwar planning institutions and called for greater control over investment, and a larger state presence through public enterprises. The labour unions, influenced by the radicalism of the late 1960s, developed socialist critiques of the existing model. These emphasized how the state intervention of the 1960s served the interests of capitalists and strengthened American imperialism rather than leading to balanced economic development that reduced inequalities between the rich and poor and between anglophones and francophones. Meanwhile, community organizations and women's groups criticized the bureaucratic nature of the new welfare state, its failure to adequately address continued poverty and exclusion, as well as its silence on key questions such as violence against women.

Faced with these calls for greater state regulation, as well as an overall uneasiness with the growth of state intervention post-1960, the business community responded by creating its own peak association, the Conseil du Patronat du Québec (CPQ). The CPQ proposed a counter-strategy of increased economic liberalism extolling the contribution of capitalist competition to the spread of mass consumption (such as having a car in every driveway), and dismissing the idea that economic control was largely out of the hands of francophone Quebecers.

Faced with these divergent views, the Liberal government of 1970–6 and the government elected in 1976 largely followed the course of the Quiet Revolution, with the Liberals giving more space to economic liberalism, and the PQ implementing more moderate demands of the unions, community organizations, and women's groups in terms of greater union rights and labour market regulations, some recognition of the role of co-operatives and community organizations in regional development, and a modest extension of women's rights. By the time it took office, the PQ no longer wished to emulate France's economic planning, but it did believe that economic competitiveness required government policies to aid firms in acquiring new technologies, undertaking research and development, or developing export markets.

The decision of the US Federal Reserve in 1979 to break inflation by dramatically increasing interest rates, and its effect of creating a hard recession across the Western industrialized countries, was very strongly felt in Quebec. Given that Quebec embarked on building its welfare state a decade later than elsewhere, it was left holding a significantly greater debt that would have to be financed at a significantly higher interest rate. This, coupled with significant job losses in the manufacturing sector, depressed state revenues, and increased costs, ultimately produced a budgetary crisis. This allowed the employers' associations to make a plausible case that the interventionist strategy of the Quiet Revolution had run its course. They felt that the public had unrealistic expectations about what sort of public services the state could afford, and that an in-depth reworking of the state–economy relationship was required. The CPQ argued that taxes and spending needed to be cut, particularly through aggressive cuts in government programs and through imposing user fees for public services.

On the other hand, the union federations proposed *concertation* ('concerted action') as a way out of the impasse: having the state bring together economic stakeholders to find collective and positive-sum solutions to problems of industrial or regional decline. This was particularly the strategy of the largest union federation, the Fédération des travailleurs et travailleuses du Québec (FTQ). It had moved from its radical discourse of the early 1970s to embrace the Swedish idea of peak-level bargaining between employers, unions, and the state to set economic and social policy.

The PQ government wavered between these two options up to its defeat in the 1985 election. On the one hand, it took on its public employees' union, and unilaterally re-opened contracts to cut wages and strip out benefits. It also adopted punitive features targeted at young people on social assistance. On the other hand, it experimented with concertation, for instance by creating the Table national de l'emploi. But the overall impression was one of muddling through rather than of bold departures.

New Directions Under the Bourassa Liberal Government, 1985–1994

The election of a Liberal government headed by Robert Bourassa in 1985 at first appeared to signal a clear choice. The party's platform, *Mastering the Future*, was sympathetic to the CPQ's outlook, and the party's caucus in the National Assembly included a clutch of high-profile business people. Bourassa set up three working groups, on privatization, deregulation, and state finances, whose recommendations rehearsed the mantras of significantly reducing state expenditures, privatizing most state-owned corporations, and significantly reducing the regulatory burden. While these were perhaps close to his preferences, Bourassa was too cautious to adopt such radical proposals; program cuts would draw the opposition of those who relied on those programs, while early attempts at privatization ran into concerted union campaigns to ensure that unionized jobs were not replaced by non-unionized ones in the process.

If Bourassa's government was not radical, it nevertheless set a course of restraining the growth of public expenditure and of reducing state ownership. Faced with a worsening balance sheet in the early 1990s as a result of a North American economic downturn and the Bank of Canada's high interest rate policy, restraint in public spending became more severe. At the same time, the social assistance (or welfare) program was restructured to reduce benefits but increase the number of subsidized work placements in the private and community sectors, a move that drew strong opposition from welfare rights organizations.

This overall shift, which could be described as 'neo-liberal', nevertheless developed some unusual trappings at the turn of the 1990s.[8] Across fields, the government experimented with new forms of partnership and concerted action. Recognizing that market mechanisms alone could not be counted on to ensure a smooth restructuring of the Quebec economy into advanced manufacturing and service activities, the government launched a cluster strategy and a provincial training board (the Société québécoise de développement de la main d'oeuvre—SQDM). The cluster strategy adopted the premise that firms working in similar industries might increase their competitiveness from sharing information or developing partnerships to overcome common problems (e.g. training, research and development, relationships between firms and suppliers), and thus created roundtables of key firms in various industrial sectors. The idea behind the training boards was that employers and employees shared an interest in creating a skilled labour force, and that giving employers and unions responsibility for governing training initiatives would both lead to better training, and force these 'social partners' to overcome their differences about the best approaches to training.

The impetus for supporting partnerships is difficult to pin down. Partly it reflected bureaucratic learning about industrial strategies being used elsewhere, and in particular the work of management guru Michael Porter, and their applicability to smooth economic adjustment in Quebec. They could also build on certain partnership initiatives outside of the state, such as union-business-community alliances in the Partenaires pour l'emploi (Partners for Jobs), an attempt to bring stakeholders together to fight unemployment. Finally, the failure of the Meech Lake constitutional amendment in 1990, and the resurgence of Quebec nationalism that followed from this, forced the Bourassa government to develop a broader national consensus in order to maintain legitimacy in its ongoing negotiations with the federal government. This too favoured initiatives that married a commitment to economic liberalism with the development of institutions of social partnership.

These programs certainly reached out to the union federations, who were proposing a more robust series of union–management partnerships as part of a program of 'progressive competitiveness'. In their view, Quebec could continue to be competitive in industries that paid high wages and offered good working conditions, provided employers were required to consult and work in partnership with unions, both at the level of the plant and at the level of industry sectors. These partnerships would pay off, as they would allow firms and workers to identify positive-sum compromises that would increase productivity while maintaining employment levels in well-paid jobs. Similar positive-sum compromises were envisioned in other areas, such

as community economic development efforts in impoverished neighbourhoods.

The government's experiments with partnerships went beyond the economic realm to influence social policy. This reflected the strength of the women's movement and community organizations. These groups recognized that the Bourassa government wished to save money by cutting health and social services, and by downloading responsibility for social programs onto community organizations, which could ostensibly provide the services at lower cost. But rather than simply opposing this move, they applauded the idea of removing bureaucracy in order to empower service users and better respond to their needs. However, they argued that for community organizations to play such a role in democratizing state services, they needed stable, recurrent funding to be able to allow service users and providers to identify priorities and innovative solutions. They also argued that the community sector and women's organizations needed to be formally represented in decision-making structures so that they would be true partners in the governance of health and social services, rather than simply sub-contractors.

The Parti Québécois in Power 1994–2003: The Referendum and After[9]

The election of a PQ government in 1994 opened the possibility of a further shift from economic liberalism. Having promised a referendum on sovereignty within a year of taking office, the PQ had an interest in assembling as broad a coalition as possible in order to ensure the sovereignty option won. This meant presenting a vision of an independent Quebec that was highly inclusive. An important part of the PQ's referendum strategy was to portray Quebec as a beacon of social democracy, at risk of being swamped by a Canadian neo-liberalism unless it gained its independence. This was a tricky game for the PQ, since they also needed to reassure the business community that its position would be protected in an independent Quebec, and that trade and investment liberalization agreements with the United States (such as the North American Free Trade Agreement) would continue to apply. It managed to square the circle, at least for the referendum campaign, by drawing on the unions' progressive competitiveness—making the case that national economic competitiveness under globalization required the nation to mobilize all of its resources, thereby necessitating both labour–business partnership and compensatory measures to ensure no one was left behind.

Following the loss of the 1995 referendum, the PQ government was forced to regroup and develop solutions to the persistence of double-digit unemployment and of large budget deficits. This was necessary both to ensure its electoral viability, but also to put Quebec on a sound economic footing for a future

referendum. In addition, the business community made it clear that it would not invest in Quebec, given the unresolved nature of Quebec's national status, unless the deficit was tamed through spending cuts. A straightforward strategy of making broad and deep cuts to government programs, as undertaken at the time in neighbouring Ontario, was not open to the PQ as it would impose too many costs on its political base (unions, community organizations, women's groups). Instead, it convened a summit of economic stakeholders in an attempt to tackle the twin problems of unemployment and deficit spending (see Snapshot box).

SNAPSHOT

The 1996 Social and Economic Summits

In calling major social actors together for an economic summit in March 1996, the Quebec government was hardly modest in its ambitions: 'The pact at the base of our society is broken: we must reinvent it.' Faced with recurrent budget deficits and high rates of unemployment and poverty, the government called on social partners to develop new solutions. These reached beyond the employers and unions to include representatives of student, women's, and community organizations. The summits were called in part in response to union demands for concerted action, but the participation of business came with a bottom line, namely balancing the budget in two years without increasing taxes. The union federations were not particularly opposed to this approach, although they wanted meaningful job-creation commitments from the government and the private sector. Their modest bargaining position reflected the sense that many of their members favoured reducing the deficit. In addition, the summits represented an example of the social partnership that they wished to see repeated, and so the very fact of holding one was a victory.

The process of balancing demands nevertheless was more tricky than simply bringing the employers and unions to agreement, as the women's and community groups had their own demands. The

women's movement had held a widely covered Bread and Roses March against violence and poverty in 1995. The March built on several years of organizing and popular education around a different model of development. Rather than leaving development to the private decisions of capitalists, as in the business associations' view, or of emphasizing partnerships enabling Quebec firms to compete without downgrading wages and working conditions, as in the unions' plan, the March proposed development on the basis of meeting the basic needs of all Quebecers. The March's first demand was to create and solidify 'social infrastructures' that created jobs and met needs. The idea was to take women's often precarious, unpaid, or underpaid work in community organizations, and to properly recognize it by providing stable funding to the organizations. Since many community organizations relied on social assistance recipients and on subsidized work placements to keep their programs running, there was an existing funding stream which could be converted into support for permanent and sustainable work. Alongside the social infrastructures, the March also emphasized anti-poverty strategies, including higher minimum wages and the stronger enforcement of minimum labour standards.

The women's movement's call for *social infrastructures* is often confused with a parallel call for investment in the *social economy* (economic ventures that prioritize social goals over profit) that came from other parts of the community sector. Partisans of the social economy argued that both economic and social development could be advanced by experimenting with new forms of non-profit organization that mixed social goals with market activity. An example would be a community restaurant in a poor neighbourhood serving very inexpensive meals. The restaurant could simultaneously provide people in poverty with access to food and sociability; provide food preparation and service training to the unemployed; and create a small number of jobs for the managers of the enterprise. In addition, such enterprises could democratize their activity by providing worker and user input through a community board of directors and participatory forms of management.

The Summit in March 1996 gave rise to agreement on deficit reduction, albeit on a four-year timeline rather than the proposed two years. It also set up working groups to explore avenues of job creation, which were to report back to the October summit. One of these groups was on the social economy, and provided an opportunity for more entrepreneurial parts of the community sector to advance a series of community economic development projects, although in the process, the program of social infrastructures proposed by the women's movement was marginalized.

The October Summit was less harmonious. The unions and employers were again ready to pay tribute to joint action, and parts of the community sector were overjoyed with the prominence given to the social economy as an example of how to bring different social actors together around job creation. Women's and anti-poverty groups nevertheless felt that their concerns were ignored, and made a show of leaving the table before the summit ended. This dissent was nevertheless somewhat deflected by agreement at the summit to set up a $250 million anti-poverty fund to support community initiatives to help the jobless find work. The veneer of consensus hid the fact that the plan for job creation was long on good intentions but short on firm commitments. This meant that eliminating the deficit would ultimately rely on program cuts rather than on increased tax revenue from the newly employed. As that logic led to the downsizing of the public sector workforce, the union leadership came under strong criticism from their members.

The 1996 Summits therefore can be seen in two different ways. In one reading, they confirm Quebec's exceptionalism (at least in North America), in that difficult economic decisions about public finances and employment were made by consensus between social actors. In the process, actors discovered new approaches to social and economic development, such as those represented by the social economy. As part of the behind-the-scenes negotiations, Quebec's family policy, including universal low-cost childcare, an enriched child tax credit, and improved parental leaves, was also given the green light. In another reading, however, the Summits represent the conversion of the Parti Québécois to a neo-liberal platform of cuts to state programs and regulations, and highlight its ability to co-opt the unions and other social democratic actors by appealing to their nationalism with the argument that getting state finances in order will ensure a winning referendum. In this second reading, the Summits are a first step in breaking links between the PQ and social democratic actors, preparing the way for the former's loss in the 2003 elections and the schism in the nationalist movement between the PQ and Québec solidaire.

The 1996 Summits set the tone for the remainder of the PQ's term in office. It was attentive to the business community, yet invested strategically in the social economy and progressive competitiveness. This mix of supporting business while experimenting with partnerships and social innovation was marketed by the PQ as 'the Quebec model'—a model that set Quebec apart. While academics debated how distinct and effective Quebec's development model truly was, this model was only partially successful politically. While the PQ was attentive to business demands, the employers' federations preferred to support the Liberals. And while the PQ argued that Quebec had a more progressive model than the neo-liberal one found elsewhere in Canada or the United States, an increasing number of activists in the unions and in the women's and community movements found the government closed to their demands when they might offend the business community. For example, many feminists lost faith in the PQ when the latter responded to a demand for higher minimum wages with a paltry hike of 10 cents an hour. As with the 1996 Summits, critics on the left argued that the PQ's compromises and trade-offs systematically favoured the demands of business actors.

In its later years in office, the PQ increasingly looked to European debates about the knowledge-based economy to navigate this tension. This involved pairing market liberalization through reduced regulation and rates of taxation with social policies favouring social cohesion. The latter included an anti-poverty law binding current and future governments to develop poverty-reduction plans, but also enriched child benefits, core funding for community-based advocacy organizations, and continued support for experiments with social entrepreneurship. In the process, there was less use of concertation, and indeed the PQ wound down the SQDM in favour of a less powerful roundtable of economic partners. The government also revamped the regional health boards, reducing the seats available to the community and women's movements. For the most part, the PQ did not roll back these bodies but neither did it move them forward, causing the project of concertation to lose steam.

The Charest Liberals and the Attack on 'Corporatism'[10]

Although the PQ government eliminated the deficit, cut taxes and regulation, and started to experiment with public-private partnerships in delivering state services, it was not embraced by business interests. The employers' federations were unhappy that the government did not use all of its fiscal room to cut taxes, but also spent on initiatives like a universal low-cost child-care program, and that it reformed the labour code to protect a larger number of workers. This impatience led them to undertake new initiatives, including creating a free-market think tank, the Montreal Economic Institute, to foster public

acceptance of market solutions to public problems, and flirting with the Action démocratique du Québec (ADQ) party, which was offering a far more neo-liberal platform of policy reform than the usual party of business, the Quebec Liberal Party.

The Liberals nevertheless won a majority in the 2003 provincial election, positioning themselves as more moderate than the ADQ, yet fresher than a tired PQ government worn down by a decade in power. Once elected, the Liberals introduced neo-liberal reforms that challenged the ethos of social consensus that stretched back to the later Bourassa period, and in some ways back to the Quiet Revolution. These included diminishing stakeholder involvement in a series of institutions of concertation such as local and regional health boards and local development boards. This was premised on the idea that concertation did not promote positive-sum compromises, but instead created a 'corporatism' that prevented necessary changes by allowing groups to protect their narrow self-interests. The government also changed a key section of labour legislation to make it easier for firms to get rid of existing unions in cases where work was subcontracted, and it unilaterally re-arranged union representation in the health sector. The Liberals also tried to roll back the highly popular $5 per day daycare program, by proposing measures to significantly increase the daily rate for those with higher incomes. This was beaten back by a wave of protests (although the daily rate increased to $7), but the government allowed the private sector to increase its share of the daycare market relative to non-profit providers, and it reduced community involvement in service planning. Another controversial aspect of the government's agenda was to engage in public-private partnerships to deliver public services, despite concerns about their cost effectiveness.

These initiatives provoked large-scale mobilizations led by the labour movement, as well as a student strike (over cuts in student loans and bursaries) that shut down parts of several universities in February and March 2005. The leaders of these mobilizations argued that the Liberals had run on a fairly innocuous platform, and that they therefore lacked a popular mandate for such controversial reforms. These mobilizations damaged the government's popularity, and indicated that the appetite for a large-scale replacement of existing institutions with neo-liberal ones was limited. The government thereafter decided to pursue a less radical course of reform, premised on incremental changes, such as increasing the role of the private sector in the management of public infrastructure via public–private partnerships, and slowly opening the door to for-profit providers of medical services. The language about uprooting the corporatist interests inhibiting change largely disappeared. Re-elected as a minority government in 2007 and as a majority in 2008, the Liberal government continues to slowly advance neo-liberal reform.

The loss of momentum in the Liberals' reform agenda frustrated the employers' federations, and helps explain how the 'clear-eyed manifesto', discussed in the introduction, saw the light of day. The manifesto writers were clearly upset by the Liberals' inability to uproot 'corporatism', and by the capacity of groups to block a more substantial adoption of market liberalism. Thus, while the business community was pleased with the direction of change, they remained frustrated by its slow speed.

While the union federations and various social movements (women, students) were relatively successful in slowing the Liberal Party's reform agenda, they have proven relatively weak in either reversing it or proposing an alternative. A group of high-profile union leaders and some progressive activists formed a group within the PQ called the SPQ libre (unionists and progressives for a free Quebec) in the hope of pulling the PQ to the left. Meanwhile, those on the political left who had been dissatisfied with the PQ government crystallized into a new political party, Québec solidaire (QS). While Québec solidaire has been the most successful left-wing alternative yet to the PQ, it drew fewer than 4 per cent of the votes in the 2007 and 2008 elections, electing its first member, Amir Khadir, in 2008. The originality and creativity that marked the alternative development strategies in the 1990s (progressive competitiveness, partnership, social infrastructures, social economy) were also largely absent from both the PQ and QS platforms. Neither party promised much to rebuild concertation, nor did they emphasize community action or the social economy.

This loss of creativity results from the demobilization of the labour and women's movements. Twenty years have passed since the crafting of progressive competitiveness strategies, but the union movement has not updated them or replaced them with a new approach. As a result, it remains on the defensive, trying to wring concessions from the government of the day or gains from concertation in the partnership forums in which it has a seat. For the women's movement, which does not have a base of dues payers like the unions and which has a harder time maintaining its autonomy from the state given its reliance on government money, the task of maintaining mobilization has been challenging (see Chapter 20). After the success of the 1995 March, and the central role in organizing the inaugural World March of Women in 2000, there has been some burnout as well as internal disagreements over strategy (e.g., was the 2000 March worth the effort expended?) and program (e.g., Does the focus on women's poverty address the needs of middle-class women? Does it disempower women in poverty by portraying them as victims?). In this context, the slow but steady progress of economic liberalism, started under Bourassa, continued under the PQ government, and now followed by the Charest Liberals, seems set to continue. It faces constant opposition, but no well-organized and well-articulated counter-propositions.

CONCLUSION

As this chapter has demonstrated, however, the future remains open. Over time, social actors change their strategies about how to achieve development, and their relative influence waxes and wanes. Quebec adopted a particular set of institutions in the 1960s, and these have been reworked over time. Sometimes this reform has followed the liberal blueprint of reducing state social provision and strengthening state protection of private property rights. Other times, this reform has had a more social democratic cast in fostering the participation of a wider set of interests through concertation or in supporting social provision via social infrastructures and the social economy. Organized interests have been crucial players in generating and publicizing ideas for reform, but elections have also been significant as switching points for choosing some ideas over others. The push-and-pull of conflict in setting the development model has created a Quebec model that is distinct in North America in its adoption of stakeholder partnerships and community development (although this distinction is eroding with time), but that remains distinctively North American from a European perspective in its economic liberalism.

Returning to the future challenges identified by the 'clear-eyed manifesto', namely global economic competition (especially from China and India) and an aging population, Quebecers have important choices to make in the coming years. It would be presumptuous and arrogant to claim that there is only one path to choose. Quebec could follow the 'clear-eyed' path in adopting a market liberalism that allows the decisions of capitalists, responding to the whip of market competition, to set the course for competitiveness, and that relies on individuals to look after their own welfare. Or it could supplement private decision-making with economic policies favouring a wider participation of stakeholders, empowering community-based development, and expanding public policies that enable people to adapt by protecting them against emerging social risks. Academics can certainly debate the trade-offs involved in any model, but ultimately it will be the Quebec people who will decide through the demands and negotiations of their collective actors (employer's associations, unions, community groups, social movements, and so on), and through the ballot box.

FRANÇOISE DAVID

Québec solidaire co-leader Françoise David takes part in an anti-poverty protest in front of the Congress Centre in Quebec City on 15 June 2009.

Francis Vachon/TCPI/The Canadian Press

Françoise David is a fascinating figure for a discussion of Quebec's development, as the public associates her with a feminist and social democratic vision of Quebec's future. Through her trajectory, we see both how the women's and community movements have shaped development, and how they are currently at a political impasse.[11]

Ms David was born in 1948 into an upper middle-class family. She enjoyed a privileged childhood, but grew up with a sense of responsibility for those less fortunate. This desire to help others led to the decision to study social work and community organizing at university. This was in the late 1960s when there was a radicalization of the community sector, which was innovating in developing new services, such as community health clinics or child care, that were not being offered by the public sector. As these services matured, the community sector and the state entered into tense negotiations over their funding and governance—the state wanting to bring them into the public sector, and community organizations wishing to preserve their more responsive and democratic character while receiving state support.

Ms David's experience of this period is somewhat singular, as she belonged to the Marxist-Leninist group En Lutte ('In Struggle') until its implosion in 1982. Like other Maoist parties of the time, it demanded intense loyalty to the organization and its line of analysis, as well as the dedication of several hours a day (above and beyond full-time work) to popular education, outreach, and recruitment. When the group imploded, many members disappeared for several years into wrenching self-questioning: How did their search for social justice lead to blind commitment to an anti-democratic and hierarchical organization? This was the case for Ms David, who faced the additional challenges of a marital breakdown and caring for a young child.

She emerged from this period of introspection in 1987 to become coordinator of L'R des centres des femmes du Québec, the provincial network of women's centres. Women's centres vary from place to place depending on the priorities of local women, but offer a mix of support services, education, and collective action (demonstrating, lobbying, participating in governance structures). They tend to work with poor and isolated women, and thus to focus on poverty and violence. L'R brought together 53 of these at its founding in 1985 (its membership now surpasses 100), so as to strengthen the centres in negotiating with the state (by speaking with a common voice, and sharing strategies between localities) and to allow them to pool resources by acting as a clearinghouse for expertise and education.

In the late 1980s and early 1990s, L'R broadened the Quebec women's movement's thinking, pushing the idea that women's centres were not just about meeting *social* needs, but also about *economic* activity. The centres employed people, produced goods and services (such as meals in a collective kitchen, or the repair of damaged clothes for resale), and provided support and training for those in crisis, enabling them to return to employment more quickly or with better skills.

In 1992, Ms David became a vice-president of the Fédération des femmes du Québec (FFQ), the umbrella organization of women's organizations, which was at a low point as many women's organizations felt it did little for them. The FFQ nevertheless renewed itself at its 1993 Convention by positioning itself as the voice of women who were poor, excluded, or faced discrimination, and in 1994 elected Ms David as president. She oversaw the organization of the Bread and Roses March against violence and poverty in the summer of 1995 which imported much of L'R's thinking about the economic contributions of meeting social needs, particularly in its headline demand to invest in 'social infrastructures' that aimed to meet the needs of people in poverty by addressing unpaid or underpaid work.

The March was a high point for the FFQ's program, but its voice became increasingly marginal given demands for cutting state spending and lowering taxes. Ms David continued to lead the FFQ until 2001; under her leadership it organized the World March of Women in 2000. On the one hand, this March was a success, allowing the Quebec women's movement to work with women from around the world, and to bring out over 40,000 people for its local March. On the other hand, the March demonstrated the near-complete closure of the PQ government to the FFQ's demands. Many feminist activists grew disillusioned with the PQ government to the point of looking for a political alternative, but there were also tensions within the FFQ: women across the province had burned themselves out to organize the 2000 March, and for what?

Upon leaving the FFQ, Ms David nevertheless continued to advocate for development to fight poverty, and briefly headed the group Au bas de l'échelle, which was pressuring the state to protect vulnerable workers by improving labour standards. Here she had more success than with the World March, with the PQ government agreeing to extend the application of standards to more workers, and to improve standards to remedy a number of abuses.

Nevertheless, her disappointment with the PQ led her to explore the creation of a left-wing alternative to it, starting with the publication of a personal manifesto,[12] followed by the creation of the Option Citoyenne (Citizen's Option) and its merger with another left-wing party to form Québec solidaire, of which she is co-spokesperson. This party has proven more responsive than the PQ to the demands of the women's and community movements, but has had limited electoral success (garnering roughly 4 per cent of the vote in the 2007 and 2008 elections) beyond electing Amir Khadir to the National Assembly in 2008. It remains to be seen whether building an alternative to the PQ strengthens the place of feminist and social democratic ideas in Quebec, or whether it weakens the incentive of the PQ to respond to them.

Questions for Consideration

1. This chapter portrays social and economic development in Quebec as a debate between social democracy and liberalism, but claims that similar debates are common to most societies. How does the debate in Quebec, both in its evolution over time and in its current form, compare to the debate in your society?

2. The development plans of various social actors (women's movement, labour movement, employer's associations) were discussed in this

   chapter. How do these plans differ or overlap? What are their respective primary goals? Are there collective actors holding similar ideas in your society?

3. Looking across the half-century covered in this chapter, how important were elections and political parties in setting the Quebec development model, and how important was social pressure brought to bear by collective actors such as employers' associations, the women's movement, and unions?

Notes

1. Manifesto for a Clear-Eyed Vision of Quebec available at www.pourunquebeclucide.com/.

2. Manifeste pour un Québec solidaire available at www.ccmm-csn.qc.ca/MGACMS-Client/Protected/File/J764Y66955UG45B7Z43BP3G6F9MW88.pdf.

3. *Economic liberalism* refers here to a policy of leaving economic decision-making to individual property owners, and limiting state intervention to the protection of property rights and the enforcement of contracts. This can be confusing for American audiences, where the use of liberalism is often used in the opposite sense of state interventions to counter market inequality. Where economic liberalism is most concerned with the freedom of individuals to enjoy their property, social democrats are more concerned with creating a basis of equality so that all citizens can effectively enjoy their rights and fulfill their duties, and in extending the realm of decisions over which citizens exercise democratic choice.

4. See Pierre Paquette, 'Relever les vrais défis', in Luc Godbout, ed., *Agir maintenant pour le Québec de demain* (Lévis: Presses de l'Université Laval, 2006), 49–66.

5. Low-wage employers are more concerned about the minimum wage than high-wage ones. Firms who rely solely on the domestic market will be less in favour of free trade than firms who are large exporters. The insurance industry will be less opposed to anti-pollution measures than the automotive and oil and gas industry.

6. For instance, workers may agree to actively help increase productivity on the assembly line, in return for better wages.

7. This section draws on Kenneth McRoberts, *Quebec: Social Change and Political Crisis*, 3rd edn (Toronto: McClelland & Stewart, 1988); William D. Coleman, *The Independence Movement in Quebec, 1945–1980* (Toronto: University of Toronto Press, 1984); and Alain-G. Gagnon, and Mary Beth Montcalm, *Quebec: Beyond the Quiet*

   Revolution (Scarborough, Ont.: Nelson, 1990).

8. See Dorval Brunelle and Benoît Lévesque, 'Free Trade and Quebec Models of Development', in Ricardo Grinspun and Yasmine Shamsie, eds., *Whose Canada? Continental Integration, Fortress North America and the Corporate Agenda* (Montreal and Kingston: McGill-Queen's University Press, 2007), 391–406.

9. For a fuller treatment, see Daniel Salée, 'Transformative Politics, the State, and the Politics of Social Change in Quebec', in Wallace Clement and Leah Vosko, eds., *Changing Canada: Political Economy as Transformation* (Montreal and Kingston: McGill-Queen's University Press, 2003), 25–50; and Peter Graefe, 'The Dynamics of the Parti Québécois in Power: Social Democracy and Competitive Nationalism', in William K. Carroll and R.S. Ratner, eds., *Challenges and Perils: Social Democracy in Neoliberal Times* (Halifax: Fernwood, 2005), 46–66.

10. For fuller treatments, see Jane Jenson, 'Rolling Out or Back Tracking on Quebec's Child Care System? Ideology Matters', paper presented to the 2006 Annual Meeting of the Canadian Political Science Association, York University, June 2006, available at www.cpsa-acsp.ca/papers-2006/Jenson.pdf; Rachel Laforest, 'The Politics of State/Civil Society Relations in Quebec', in Michael Murphy, ed., *Quebec and Canada in the New Century* (Kingston: Institute of Intergovernmental Relations, 2005), 177–98; and Christian Rouillard, Éric Montpetit, Isabelle Fortier, and Alain-G. Gagnon, *Reengineering the State: Toward an Impoverishment of Quebec Governance* (Ottawa: University of Ottawa Press, 2006).

11. See also Françoise David, 'Life of Solidarity: Reflections on a Life in Politics', *Canadian Dimension* 41, 2 (2007): 31–7.

12. See Françoise David, *Bien commun recherché : Une option citoyenne* (Montreal: Écosocieté, 2004).

RELEVANT WEBSITES

Background Information

GOVERNMENT OF QUEBEC'S 'PORTRAITS OF QUEBEC' WEBSITE: www.gouv.qc.ca/portail/quebec/pgs/commun/portrait/?lang=en

INSTITUT DE LA STATISTIQUE DU QUÉBEC: www.stat.gouv.qc.ca/default_an.htm

Manifestos

MANIFESTO FOR A CLEAR-EYED VISION OF QUEBEC: www.pourunquebeclucide.com/

MANIFESTE POUR UN QUÉBEC SOLIDAIRE: www.ccmm-csn.qc.ca/MGACMS-Client/Protected/File/J764Y66955UG45B7Z43BP3G6F9MW88.pdf

Think Tanks

INSTITUT DE RECHERCHE EN ÉCONOMIE CONTEMPORAINE: www.irec.net/en_index.php3

INSTITUT ÉCONOMIQUE DE MONTRÉAL: www.iedm.org

INSTITUT DE RECHERCHE ET D'INFORMATIONS SOCIO-ÉCONOMIQUES: www.iris-recherche.qc.ca/

Major Collective Actors

CONSEIL DU PATRONAT DU QUÉBEC: www.cpq.qc.ca/

FÉDÉRATION DES TRAVAILLEURS ET TRAVAILLEUSES DU QUÉBEC: www.ftq.qc.ca/

CONFÉDÉRATION DES SYNDICATS NATIONAUX: www.csn.qc.ca/

FÉDÉRATION DES FEMMES DU QUÉBEC: www.ffq.qc.ca/

CHANTIER DE L'ÉCONOMIE SOCIALE: www.chantier.qc.ca/

SELECT BIBLIOGRAPHY

Brunelle, Dorval, and Benoît Lévesque. 'Free Trade and Quebec Models of Development'. In Ricardo Grinspun and Yasmine Shamsie, eds. *Whose Canada? Continental Integration, Fortress North America and the Corporate Agenda*. Montreal and Kingston: McGill-Queen's University Press, 2007, 391–406.

Coleman, William D. *The Independence Movement in Quebec, 1945–1980*. Toronto: University of Toronto Press, 1984.

David, Françoise. *Bien commun recherché : Une option citoyenne*. Montreal: Écosocieté, 2004.

———. 'Life of Solidarity: Reflections on a Life in Politics', *Canadian Dimension* 41, 2 (2007): 31–7.

Gagnon, Alain-G., and Mary Beth Montcalm. *Quebec: Beyond the Quiet Revolution*. Scarborough, Ont.: Nelson, 1990.

Graefe, Peter. 'The Dynamics of the Parti Québécois in Power: Social Democracy and Competitive Nationalism'. In William K. Carroll and R.S. Ratner, eds. *Challenges and Perils: Social Democracy in Neoliberal Times*. Halifax: Fernwood, 2005, 46–66.

———. 'The Quebec *Patronat*: Proposing a Neo-Liberal Political Economy after All', *Canadian Review of Sociology and Anthropology* vol. 41, 2 (2004): 171–93.

Jenson, Jane. 'Rolling Out or Back Tracking on Quebec's Child Care System? Ideology Matters'. Paper presented to the 2006 Annual Meeting of the Canadian Political Science Association, York University, June 2006. Available at: www.cpsa-acsp.ca/papers-2006/Jenson.pdf.

Laforest, Rachel. 'The Politics of State/Civil Society Relations in Quebec'. In Michael Murphy, ed. *Quebec and Canada in the New Century*. Kingston: Institute of Intergovernmental Relations, 2005, 177–98.

McRoberts, Kenneth. *Quebec: Social Change and Political Crisis*, 3rd edn. Toronto: McClelland & Stewart, 1988.

Paquette, Pierre. 'Relever les vrais défis'. In Luc Godbout, ed. *Agir maintenant pour le Québec de demain*. Lévis: Presses de l'Université Laval, 2006, 49–66.

Rouillard, Christian, Éric Montpetit, Isabelle Fortier, and Alain-G. Gagnon. *Reengineering the State: Toward an Impoverishment of Quebec Governance*. Ottawa: University of Ottawa Press, 2006.

Salée, Daniel. 'Transformative Politics, the State, and the Politics of Social Change in Quebec'. In Wallace Clement and Leah Vosko, eds. *Changing Canada: Political Economy as Transformation*. Montreal and Kingston: McGill-Queen's University Press, 2003, 25–50.

CHAPTER 24

Regional Economic Dynamics

Gilbert Gagné, Bishop's University

— TIMELINE —

1854–66   Reciprocity Treaty.

1867   Confederation.

1879   National Economic Policy.

1911   Rejection of a Canada–US free trade agreement.

1930   United States supplants Britain as main source of foreign investment in Quebec.

1947   Rejection of another Canada–US trade agreement.

1985–7   Negotiations for free-trade agreement between Canada and United States; in Quebec, political and economic elites are favourable to free trade.

1988   In federal election, Quebec overwhelmingly supports Progressive Conservatives, proponents of free-trade agreement with United States.

1989   Canada–US Free Trade Agreement comes into force.

1994   North American Free Trade Agreement comes into force.

In Quebec's case, regional economic dynamics refers primarily to trade and investment trends within North America. More than any other province, Quebec has been an enthusiastic supporter of increasing economic ties beyond Canada's boundaries. Aside from economic benefits, Quebec's stance has been adopted as a means to gain leverage vis-à-vis the Canadian government. With the Canada–United States Free Trade Agreement (FTA) of 1989, followed by the North American Free Trade Agreement (NAFTA) of 1994, which includes Mexico, Quebec has entered a new regional economic dynamic. In the present context of economic globalization and regionalization, although such integration essentially rests on market forces, we will see that insofar as

Quebec has consented to and actively favoured such a dynamic, it is a process that Quebec has sought to manage to its advantage.

First, the chapter reviews some key concepts and sums up Quebec's and Canada's positions on the North American economic dynamic prior to the free-trade regime beginning in the late 1980s. Next, it contrasts the attitudes in Quebec and Canada vis-à-vis North American free trade. Then we turn to Quebec's trade since the FTA and NAFTA came into force, followed by Quebec's and Ontario's relative economic performances and evolution. Finally, the chapter discusses ongoing issues and debates over the means to reach further benefits from the North American economic dynamic. Some concluding remarks follow.

QUEBEC, CANADA, AND REGIONAL ECONOMIC DYNAMICS PRIOR TO FREE TRADE

The concept of integration refers to progressive fusions of national economies and states, usually starting on the economic level, and which can extend to the social and finally the political level. International economic integration entails removing trade impediments between participating countries and establishing certain elements of co-operation and coordination between them, the latter depending on the form that integration takes or proposes to take. As free-trade areas, the FTA and NAFTA consist of the first and least ambitious stage or form of international economic integration. Tariffs and quantitative restrictions on trade between participating states are abolished, but each country retains its freedom in its commercial policy vis-à-vis countries outside the agreements.

Economic globalization is generally understood as expanding international trade and reducing barriers to the flow of goods, services, capital, and finance across nations. The internationalization of production and increased flows of foreign direct investment (FDI) are also important aspects of globalization. The corporate strategies of transnational firms on trade, technology, and FDI propel this process of globalization. Regionalization is a similar process but within a specific region, usually between neighbouring countries. It refers to the growth of integration within a region and to the often undirected processes of social and economic interaction, the latter often taking place without any action or willingness on the part of governments. One must distinguish between economic regionalism as a conscious policy of states to co-operate together and economic regionalization as the unintended outcome of 'natural' or market forces.

World trade flows have become increasingly regional and less global. Intra-NAFTA trade went from 34 per cent of North American trade in 1980 to 56 per cent in 2000. Although Europe and Asia experienced a similar increase in their share of regional trade, Canada's and Quebec's trade flows became even more concentrated.[1] Between 1993 and 2006, NAFTA's merchandise trade rose almost threefold,

now exceeding US$800 billion annually.[2] Among the 23 main regional economic agreements listed by the United Nations Conference on Trade and Development, it is in North America that the volume of internal trade between partners is the most important. The significant increase of world trade following the Second World War also caused export revenues to constitute an increasingly essential part of domestic income for many countries.[3]

It is well known that Quebec and Canada have depended on international trade and investment from colonial times, and that both have developed and grown rich through exports.[4] Historically, as in Canada, Quebec's trade with the rest of the continent greatly depended on the alternating periods of liberalization and protectionism that marked the relationship between British North America and the United States. Between 1854 and 1866, when the Reciprocity Treaty with the United States was in place, reported Canadian exports grew by over 300 per cent, while the share of exports destined for the US reached 70 per cent.[5] It was only after three failed attempts to revive the Reciprocity Treaty that Ottawa resolved in 1879 to adopt the National Economic Policy, which favoured domestic economic development and trade along an east-west axis. In 1929, merchandise exports accounted for 22 per cent of Canada's gross national product (GNP), with over one-third to the United States and another third to the United Kingdom.[6] In 1947, 39 per cent of Canada's exports were destined for the United States and 27.5 per cent for Britain. The UK portion had fallen to 15 per cent by 1950, while the US share of exports increased to 65 per cent.[7] In 1985, the proportion of Canada's exports to the United States had risen to 75 per cent.

As in Canada as a whole, it was around 1930 that the United States supplanted Britain as Quebec's main investor.[8] This was largely a by-product of the National Policy's strategy of attracting foreign investment to overcome import tariffs. In response to concerns over the domination of US capital in the national economy, Quebec's Premier Elzéar-Alexandre Taschereau responded in 1927 'I'd rather import foreign capital than export our workers.'[9] Indeed, from the 1840s to the 1930s, harsh conditions in Quebec and better prospects south of the border had caused close to one million Quebecers to emigrate to the United States.[10]

Hence, economic interdependence between Canada (including Quebec) and the United States was already pronounced before a free-trade regime was established by the end of the 1980s. In Canada's case, regionalization had deepened in spite of opposite governmental views and policies. In the 1970s, alongside the remnants of the import-substituting strategy inherent in Prime Minister Trudeau's National Policy, the so-called Third Option policy sought to extend and diversify export markets and, thereby, reduce Canada's high dependence on the United States. On the other hand, Quebec actively sought US investments and tried to secure new commercial outlets south of its border. Over the years many in Quebec came to see Canada's National Policy as protectionist, contrary to economic logic, and harmful to the province's interests. In the meantime, intensifying economic regionalization or market-led integration and the ensuing lesser importance of intra-Canadian trade had made the idea of free trade with the United States even more attractive. The United States received 58.2 per cent of Quebec's exports in 1970, 60 per cent in 1975, and 76 per cent in 1985.[11] In the year following the election in 1976 of the first Parti Québécois government and after the first referendum on sovereignty in 1980, Quebec's exports to the United States increased,[12] suggesting that a regional economic dynamic existed, regardless of the hazards of political life. In the 1980s, Quebec's successive governments were eager to secure an economic arrangement with the United States to satisfy the province's productive needs.

QUEBEC AND CANADA ON CONTINENTAL FREE TRADE

In view of the seemingly inescapable character of economic regionalization or continentalization, the Canadian government resolved in the mid-1980s to conclude a free-trade agreement with the United States to better secure Canada's interests, notably against growing US protectionist pressures. As in many parts of the world, regionalism was seen and used as a means to better respond to the challenges of globalization. Anglophone Canadians, including English-speaking Quebecers, were generally opposed to the idea of regional or continental free trade. In view of the weight and influence of the United States, they considered such a venture as a threat to the very existence of Canada as a distinct nation on the North American continent. For Canadian economic nationalists, the FTA signalled the end of a certain model of economic development where the state had a key role to play. In Quebec, on the other hand, the population was mainly favourable to the FTA and did not share English Canada's fears of annexation and acculturation. The absence of any noticeable defensive reaction is essentially attributable to the language difference, which slows and lessens US influence, and gives Quebecers a feeling of security as far as their identity is concerned.

Canadians were cautious at first about the ramifications of free trade, particularly during the economic slowdown of the early 1990s that coincided with the inception of the FTA. A poll conducted in 1993 for the *Toronto Star* newspaper found that while 58 per cent of Canadians were opposed to NAFTA, compared with 39 per cent who favoured it, a slight majority, 51 per cent, of Quebecers favoured NAFTA and 43 per cent opposed it.[13] Quebec was actually the only Canadian province where a majority of its citizens approved of NAFTA.[14] Today, however, a solid majority of Canadians seemingly favours the trade arrangement with the United States and almost three-quarters are optimistic about future relations between the two neighbouring states, according to a 2007 survey by the Association for Canadian Studies.[15] English Canadians, thus, have 'caught up' with Quebecers in their support of continental free trade.[16] Americans, on the other hand, have been very lukewarm about NAFTA, with roughly half in favour and half opposed, although much of the opposition has centred on Mexico.[17]

There was near consensus among Quebec's political and economic elites, federalists and sovereignists alike, on the idea of a free-trade agreement with the United States.[18] Quebec saw economic benefits and a means to gain leverage vis-à-vis the federal government, especially to limit Ottawa's intervention in fields of provincial jurisdiction. Regional or continental economic integration allows a political community such as Quebec to emancipate itself from the state to which it belongs by interacting more with other partners and being subject to rules and practices adopted in a larger framework with which it more willingly identifies. Hence, Quebec's support of North American free trade follows from its efforts to increase its autonomy, to affirm its national identity, and to pursue its own interests. According to Jean-François Lisée, this stance results from a willingness expressed by Quebec's elites, with a significant popular support, to become a *region-state*. This was seen to allow Quebec not only to attain an optimal level of economic growth, but also to act as a specific entity, regardless of its political status as a province or country. As Michael Keating noted with regard to the behaviour of stateless nations in the context of globalization, nationalism conditions their actions and market openings give nationalism another venue to be deployed.[19]

Although Quebec was favourable to free trade with the United States, it also wanted to ensure that its specific concerns were properly taken into account in Canada's negotiations with the United States. In particular, Quebec was conscious that the free-trade negotiations were to involve areas under its competence. In 1995, Quebec's National Assembly enacted Bill 51: An Act Respecting the Implementation of International Trade Agreements. In this legislation, Quebec insists that it alone is competent to implement such agreements when they contain provisions falling within its constitutional jurisdiction. In 2002, the National Assembly unanimously adopted Bill 52: An Act Respecting the Ministère des Relations internationales and Other Legislative Provisions. This act gives legislators a role in ratifying important international accords that impact on issues falling within Quebec's jurisdiction and indicates the manner in which the Quebec government may be bound, or give its assent to the federal government's expressing its consent to be bound, by an international agreement. Hence, in 2005, Quebec's National Assembly was the first legislature to give its assent to the Convention on the Protection and Promotion of the Diversity of Cultural Expressions that had been adopted by the General Conference of the United Nations Educational, Scientific and Cultural Organization.

QUEBEC AND REGIONAL ECONOMIC DYNAMICS FOLLOWING FREE TRADE

From 1988 to 1993, Quebec's total exports and imports to and from the United States grew by 58.2 per cent and 17.1 per cent respectively.[20] In 1992, Quebec's GDP was 22.9 per cent of Canada's, while its exports and imports accounted for 17.7 per cent and 19.5 per cent respectively of their Canadian equivalents. Quebec's under-representation, especially in exports, is mainly attributable to automotive-related exports and imports, concentrated in Ontario, and oil and gas exports, concentrated in Alberta.[21] There has been, since, a further decline of Quebec's importance in Canadian external trade, representing 16.7 per cent of Canada's total exports in 2006, while Ontario accounted for 45 per cent (nearly half of which was automotive products), and Alberta for 18.8 per cent.[22]

In 1992, 76.3 per cent of Quebec's exports were destined for the United States, as opposed to 76.9 per cent of Canada's.[23] The US share of Quebec's overall exports was 77.6 per cent in 2006, which is slightly lower than for the whole of Canada with 81.2 per cent. This is partly attributable to increased exports destined for the rest of the world. Indeed, the geographical distribution of Quebec's exports differs from that of other provinces, mainly due to the place occupied by European markets, and, to a lesser extent, Latin American markets, a trend already noticeable at the FTA's inception. Similar trends can be noticed in imports.[24] With regard to Latin America, it is not Mexico that explains this difference, as Quebec's exports to this other NAFTA partner accounted for only 13 per cent of Canadian exports in 2006, far behind Ontario at 46.5 per cent and Alberta at 15.1 per cent. The difference rather owes to the importance of Brazil, where Quebec occupies the first rank with 27 per cent of Canada's exports, and the rest of Latin America, where it ranks second after Ontario. These other, non-US, markets, however, have proven unstable.[25] Quebec's exports to the United States have also evolved in terms of destination, from a concentration of neighbouring regions such as New England, the mid-Atlantic, and the Northeast in favour of states in the American south and west.[26]

From 1988 to 1992, bilateral trade increased very substantially in liberalized products between Quebec and the United States.[27] This increase in exports to the United States was even more important for Quebec than Canada as a whole, whereas the growth of imports of liberalized products was far weaker in Quebec's case. Thus, for 1992, the share of liberalized products in Quebec's exports to the United States was 77.9 per cent, compared with 69.3 per cent for Canada. Conversely, the corresponding figures for imports are 39.5 per cent and 63 per cent. The impact of liberalized bilateral exchanges with the United States has, therefore, been more favourable to Quebec than to the whole of Canada. Also, between 1988 and 1992, 90 per cent of the increase in exports to the United States involved high-value-added sectors in Quebec's case, as compared with 49 per cent for Canada.[28] From 1993, Quebec experienced trade surpluses, and for 10 years, this was mainly attributable to a spectacular increase of its exports to the United States.

Following the inception of the North American free-trade regime, Quebec's exchanges with the United States generally increased. There had been an upward trend from the mid-1980s, so that 79.7 per cent of Quebec's exports by 1993 were destined for the United States. Yet while the exports increased exponentially, imports continued to fluctuate, as was the case before free trade, and later became somewhat stable. Thus, after 1976, US exports to Quebec grew steadily to a high of 53.1 per cent of the latter's imports in 1983, but decreased thereafter. The figures of Quebec's imports from the United States are also significantly lower than Canada's, which ranged from 70.1 per cent in 1980 to 68.7 per cent in 1987. In 1992, the US share of Quebec's total imports stood at 44.5 per cent, still significantly lower than Canada's at 65.2 per cent. In fact, while Quebec increased its exports to the United States between 1976 and the early 1990s, its imports became more diversified, although the United States is still accounting for approximately half of them. Canada's imports from the United States have also remained relatively stable since the FTA's inception.[29]

Although all provinces have benefited from freer trade with the United States, Ontario and Quebec were the first provinces to benefit due to the importance of the manufacturing sector in their economies and their proximity to key US markets. Quebec's share of exports moved from about 13 per cent of its GDP in 1980 to 22 per cent in 2005, while for the same years it was 19 per cent and 34 per cent for Ontario. In the latter's case, the figures indicate 12 per cent in 1980 and 19 per cent in 2005 when automotive products are excluded.[30]

ECONOMIC INTEGRATION AND PERFORMANCE: QUEBEC, ONTARIO, AND CANADA

In the 1980s, most of Quebec's exports were destined for Canada, primarily Ontario. Domestic trade was also more important to Quebec than to other Canadian provinces.[31] A study by Canadian economist John Helliwell of OECD countries affirms that two countries sharing a language will conduct a bilateral trade that is 50 per cent more significant than that of two similar countries that do not share a language.[32] Moreover, based on a gravity model developed by John McCallum, Helliwell asserted that in 1990 Quebec's trade was more oriented to other Canadian provinces than to US states of comparable size and distance. While McCallum had shown that interprovincial trade was on average 21 times more important than Canada's trade with the United States, Helliwell calculated that for Quebec, interprovincial trade was 26 times more important, thereby concluding that international borders were more significant for Quebec than for the rest of Canada. At the beginning of the 1990s, Quebec's exports to the rest of Canada slightly exceeded its foreign exports. By the end of the decade, Quebec exported abroad almost twice as much as what it exported to the rest of Canada. In 2000, Quebec was the United States' sixth main trading partner, ahead of the United Kingdom, France, Germany, Brazil, and Russia. A similar trend is noticeable for the whole of Canada. For Quebec, from a near perfect equilibrium between interprovincial and international trade in 1989, foreign exports had become twice as important as interprovincial exchanges in 2000.[33]

Both Ontario's and Quebec's foreign exports increased considerably from 1989 to 2000, by 192 per cent and 190 per cent respectively, exceeding the Canadian average of 180 per cent. When these rates are adjusted to account for population growth, Quebec's performance surpasses Ontario's: 173 per cent compared with 153 per cent. Although Canada's ratio of foreign exports in terms of its GDP had increased by 74 per cent up to 2000, Quebec's and Ontario's ratios were 94 per cent and 90 per cent respectively. What is noteworthy is that Quebec overcame both the negative effect of the language barrier, as estimated by Helliwell, and its relative higher dependence on interprovincial trade. To measure the emergence of a region-state, Thomas Courchene looks at, among other variables, the relative importance of international exports compared with interprovincial exports. From 1989 to 2000, the ratio between international and interprovincial exports increased by 85 per cent for the whole of Canadian provinces, while for Ontario and Quebec this ratio increased by 128 per cent and 124 per cent. Thus, Quebec's position moved from below the Canadian average to above average.[34]

The content of Quebec's exports also changed significantly during the period. Aerospace and telecommunications products came to figure more prominently in Quebec's overall exports than did raw materials. While remaining a world leader in the export of pulp and paper and aluminum products, Quebec's economy became more diversified, notably producing half of the world's civil helicopters. In 2000, 40 per cent of Quebec's exports were electronic and transportation equipment. It is interesting to notice that the intra-industry trade structure also distinguishes Quebec from its Canadian neighbours. The economist Pierre-Paul Proulx showed that Canada's intra-industry trade with the United States surpasses the one conducted with the rest of the world, while it is the opposite for Quebec, owing in great part to its closer links with Europe.[35]

Hence, a key aspect of Quebec's regional economic dynamic, from the late 1980s until recently, has been the 'decanadianization' of its economy. If it has been evident in terms of the exchanges of goods and services, investment figures are also worth considering. In spite of some data limitations, it was shown that in the course of the second half of the 1990s, more than for the whole of Canada, the north–south investment flux that Quebec has known was greater than the east–west one. Although Quebec accounts for 22 per cent of Canada's GDP, its share of US acquisitions reached 33 per cent between 1994 and 1999. Concurrently, its share of Canadian acquisitions in the United States reached a striking 49 per cent, which might be attributable to the fact that among Quebec firms' acquisitions in Canada and the United States, which reached Can$63 billion, 82 per cent went to the latter. In real estate and portfolio investment, the Caisse de dépôt et placement du Québec was the most important Canadian investor abroad, with $37 billion at the end of 2000. Also, between 1994 and 1999, US acquisitions were nearly three times more important in Quebec than in the rest of Canada, $27 billion compared with $10 billion.[36] American investments have long been significant for Quebec's economy, particularly in areas of natural resources (mining) and manufacturing, in which US investors control the most productive sectors.[37]

Quebec and Canada on Continental Free Trade

In 1985, the Canadian government signalled its intention to conclude a free-trade agreement with the United States. In late 1987, the Canada–US Free Trade Agreement (FTA) was concluded and came into force in January 1989. By 1991, Mexico's desire to obtain a similar arrangement with the United States prompted

Canada to join the pair, leading to the conclusion of the North American Free Trade Agreement (NAFTA) in 1992. NAFTA, superseding the FTA, became effective in January 1994.

The idea of continental free trade provoked different reactions in Quebec and in the rest of Canada. Anglophone Canadians, including English-speaking Quebecers, were generally opposed to the idea of regional or continental free trade. In view of the US weight and influence, they saw such a venture as a threat to the very existence of the Canadian state and the end of Canada as a distinct culture and nation on the North American continent. For Canadian economic nationalists, the FTA also signalled the end of a certain state model of economic development. In Quebec, on the other hand, people were mainly favourable to the FTA and did not share English Canadians' fears of annexation and acculturation. Whereas English Quebecers perceived the FTA as a big step toward greater integration with the United States, owing to a 'spill-over' effect, French Quebecers found nothing reprehensible with continental integration. The absence of any noticeable defensive reaction is essentially attributable to the language difference, which slows and lessens US influence, and gives Quebecers a sense that their identity is secure.

The main proponents of the FTA included the business community and the economists. Among the Canadian political elites, free trade was advocated by the Conservatives, both federally and provincially, and by eight provincial governments, including Quebec's. On the other hand, the federal Liberal party and the government of Ontario opposed the initiative. There was near consensus among Quebec's political and economic elites, both federalists and sovereignists, on the idea of a free-trade agreement with the United States. The two main political parties, the Liberals and the Parti Québécois, rallied behind continental free trade. As did other provinces, Quebec saw economic benefits from free trade, notably an increase in and more secure access to North American markets. Moreover, along with other provincial governments, free trade was seen as a means to increase Quebec's autonomy vis-à-vis the federal government. Inasmuch as free trade primarily rests on market forces, it reduced the Canadian government's interventionism, notably in spheres of provincial jurisdiction. Quebec's support of North American free trade follows from its efforts to increase its autonomy, to affirm its national identity, and to pursue its own interests.

In Canada, the opposition to free trade with the United States was formed principally by trade unions, community-based organizations, and by some nationalist leaders. The opponents to the FTA were grouped from 1987 within the Pro-Canada Network coalition, later to be known as Action Canada Network. In Quebec, the Coalition québécoise d'opposition au libre-échange, formed in 1986, grouped together principally the trade unions (FTQ, CSN, CEQ, UPA) to oppose free trade. Whereas in English Canada, the opponents to free trade were greatly concerned about Canadian sovereignty and culture, the opposition in Quebec rested essentially on socio-economic arguments. This also explains that while the opposition to free trade in Canada was led by nationalists and trade unions, in Quebec it was led by unions only.

The debate which the FTA had unleashed became the central issue of the federal elections in the fall of 1988. The Senate, dominated by the Liberal party, had refused to ratify the FTA. As Canada's most important province after Ontario, Quebec's overwhelming support of the FTA was key to the Conservatives' victory. Interestingly, it also led to Quebec being criticized for having imposed the FTA on Canada.

During the negotiations leading to NAFTA, Quebec's three main trade unions, together with international cooperation organizations, set up the Coalition québécoise sur les négociations trilatérales (1991). Here again, perspectives and approaches differed between Quebec and Canada. Whereas the Canadian coalition insisted on the FTA's abrogation and NAFTA's rejection, Quebec's coalition resorted to a pro-active approach. Acknowledging that continental free trade was a given, it sought to elaborate and promote a model of economic integration that went beyond the removal of trade barriers to include arrangements on minimal standards, notably on labour.

The debate which NAFTA provoked was nothing in comparison with the one over the FTA a few years before. It also coincided with a general election, but, this time, NAFTA was only one among other issues and not the most salient. Although the Liberal party won the election after campaigning for the rejection of NAFTA, it quietly endorsed it once in office.

Canadians were cautious at first about the ramifications of free trade, particularly during the economic slowdown of the early 1990s that coincided with the inception of the FTA. A poll conducted in 1993 for the *Toronto Star* revealed that while 58 per cent of Canadians were opposed to NAFTA, compared with 39 per cent who favoured it, 51 per cent of Quebecers approved of NAFTA and 43 per cent opposed it.[38] Quebec was the only Canadian province where a majority of its population supported NAFTA.[39]

Today, however, a solid majority of Canadians seemingly supports the trade arrangement with the United States and almost three-quarters are optimistic about future relations between the two neighbouring states, according to a survey of 2007 by the Association for Canadian Studies.[40] Despite a sovereignty and identity debate that accompanied the inception of the FTA and NAFTA within English Canada, a certain regional economic dynamic is also noticeable. In fact, English Canadians have caught up with Quebecers in their support of continental free trade. Americans, on the other hand, have been very lukewarm about NAFTA, with roughly half in favour and half opposed, although much of the opposition has centred on Mexico.[41]

REGIONAL ECONOMIC DYNAMICS: SUGGESTED AND ONGOING COOPERATION/INTEGRATION

Trade figures in Quebec–US trade have ceased to grow and have actually stalled since the first few years of this century. Quebec's exports to the rest of Canada have again, since 2007, been more important than its exports to the United States. It is widely concluded that the benefits of the FTA and NAFTA have now been reaped. Since NAFTA is primarily a commercial agreement and as most of its objectives have been achieved, particularly in trade and investment, it would be time for additional economic and business harmonization and liberalization. Given that Mexico is still a developing country and that its tensions with the United States, such as that over illegal immigration, are essentially bilateral, many believe that a specific and more ambitious Canada–US economic agenda is warranted. Either in a trilateral or bilateral setting, there have been many suggestions to move beyond a free-trade area and to a further form of economic integration, especially a customs union, in order to increase the benefits of freer trade. Following the events of 11 September 2001, NAFTA

member states have opted for less ambitious, more flexible and pragmatic arrangements to accommodate US security concerns with deepening economic integration. The Security and Prosperity Partnership, launched in 2005, has sought to achieve a balance between the security imperative, to better monitor border flows, and the economic imperative, to maintain unfettered access to the US territory.

Another impediment to regional or continental economic dynamics is that the goods, services, capital, and labour do not move completely freely between Canadian provinces, owing to the limited scope of Canada's common market clause in the British North America Act of 1867. Canada's economy would remain fragmented insofar as it is often more difficult to move goods and services across provinces than over international boundaries. Negotiations began in 1987 to create an open domestic market, concluding in July 1995 with the Agreement on Internal Trade, strengthened in 2007 and 2009.[42] In September 2009, Quebec also concluded a Trade and Cooperation Agreement with Ontario.

CONCLUSION

The North American trading regime, based on the FTA and later NAFTA, has had a significant integrating effect. It paved the way for additional trade and investment among member countries, and the North American economy may now be seen as a continental one. Although the FTA and NAFTA appear to have very successfully increased the integration of the North American economy, history reveals that there is a great deal of persistence in trade patterns and that deep North American integration is part of a long and stable process.[43] What is certain is that a regional economic dynamic has long been at play and that, at most, the FTA and NAFTA have facilitated this process.

As a distinct society within Canada and North America, and, thus, feeling more secure vis-à-vis US economic and cultural influence, Quebec has been the province most supportive of free trade with the United States. Its consent for continental free trade has been associated with its efforts to increase its autonomy, to affirm its national identity, and to pursue its own interests. Evidence suggests that Quebec has coped well with the North American integration dynamic.

JACQUES PARIZEAU

Jacques Parizeau, as Quebec premier, gestures during a speech to supporters the night of the 1995 referendum on Quebec independence.

CP PHOTO/Ryan Remiorz

Jacques Parizeau was born in Montreal on 9 August 1930. Son of a bourgeois family, he has kept the traits of his background in his attire and demeanour. He was educated in Montreal at Collège Stanislas and the École des Hautes Études Commerciales (HEC), where he met his mentor François-Albert Angers. In 1950, hired as a professor at HEC Montreal, he was sent to Paris to complete his training. Although admiring the work of François Perroux, he preferred to study at the London School of Economics under the supervision of James Meade, later a Nobel laureate. In 1955, at 24, he obtained his PhD and returned to Quebec.

As a professor of economics, Parizeau also served as an important consultant and advisor, especially to the government of Quebec. In this capacity, he was one of the key architects of the Quiet Revolution. The many changes he was engaged in include his involvement in 1962, with René Lévesque, in the nationalization of hydroelectricity and, in 1965, the establishment of the Caisse de dépôt et placement. By the end of the 1960s, Parizeau became convinced that Quebec

should be a sovereign state and joined the ranks of the Parti Québécois.

With the electoral victory of his party on 15 November 1976, Parizeau was appointed Minister of Finance, and, until 1981, also assumed the function of President of the Treasury Board. He notably managed to secure funds for Quebec's economic projects outside North America. He was also the instigator in 1979 of the Quebec Stock Savings Plan, which offered tax reductions to favour the capitalization of Quebec's enterprises. Following the failure of the first referendum on Quebec's sovereignty in 1980, Premier Lévesque's policy of cooperation with the federal Conservatives to renew Canada's federalism, known as the *beau risque*, led Parizeau and six other ministers to resign in 1984.

From 1985, together with other figures of the Parti Québécois such as Bernard Landry, Parizeau gave his support to the idea of a free-trade accord with the United States. He believed that this would strengthen Quebec's position vis-à-vis the rest of Canada by guaranteeing its access to the American market. With the Liberals under Premier Bourassa in agreement, Parizeau's position had a significant impact in making North American free trade acceptable to a large number of Quebecers. Parizeau became leader of the Parti Québécois in 1988.

In 1994, the Parti Québécois was returned to power and Parizeau became the twenty-sixth Premier of Quebec. Most of his premiership was dedicated to preparing Quebec for a second referendum on sovereignty. Parizeau had made it clear that he was not interested in being at the head of a province. Despite numerous objections, he insisted on holding a referendum early in his mandate. On 30 October 1995, with 49.4 per cent of the vote, the sovereignists came very close to achieving their objective. Considering this result the failure of his life, Parizeau announced the following day his intention to resign. Lucien Bouchard replaced him as Premier in January 1996.

In his distinctive, unorthodox way, Jacques Parizeau has continued to intervene in Quebec's political life, making him a living symbol of the unwavering pursuit of Quebec's sovereignty.

QUESTIONS FOR CONSIDERATION

1. Among all Canadian provinces, why has Quebec been most favourable to regional free trade?

2. Could continental free trade make Quebec increasingly detached from Canada and closer to the United States—economically, socially, and culturally?

3. As it was with the establishment of a free-trade area with the United States in the late 1980s, would Quebec still be at the forefront if Canada were willing to move to a further stage of economic integration with its southern neighbour?

NOTES

1. Eugene Beaulieu, 'Has North American Integration Resulted in Canada Becoming Too Dependent on the United States?', *Policy Options/Options politiques* 28, 9 (2007), 101.
2. Jeffrey Schott and Gary Hufbauer, 'NAFTA Revisited', *Policy Options/Options politiques* 28, 9 (2007), 84.
3. Beaulieu, 'Has North American Integration Resulted in Canada Becoming Too Dependent on the United States?', 101.
4. Ibid.
5. Ibid, 98–9.
6. The Gross National Product (GNP) corresponds to the value of all final goods and services produced by the nationals of a jurisdiction in a given year. The Gross Domestic Product (GDP) corresponds to the value of all final goods and services produced within a jurisdiction in a given year. While GDP focuses on where the output is produced, GNP focuses on who owns the production.
7. Beaulieu, 'Has North American Integration Resulted in Canada Becoming Too Dependent on the United States?', 99.
8. Anne-Marie Cotter, 'Quebec in North America: Historical and Socio-Political Dimensions', in Guy Lachapelle, ed., *Quebec Under Free Trade: Making Public Policy in North America* (Sainte-Foy: Presses de l'Université du Québec, 1995), 35.
9. Quoted in Cotter, 'Quebec in North America', 34.
10. Ibid, 36–8.
11. Guy Lachapelle, 'Quebec under Free Trade: Between Interdependence and Transnationalism', in Lachapelle, *Quebec Under Free Trade*, 19; Marc-André Bergeron, 'Le Québec et l'Accord de libre-échange canado-américain 1985–1987', in Stéphane Paquin, ed., *Histoire des relations internationales du Québec* (Montreal: VLB Éditeur, 2006), 190.
12. Lachapelle, 'Quebec under Free Trade', 19.
13. Kenneth M. Holland, 'Quebec's Successful Role as Champion of North American Free Trade', *Québec Studies* 19 (1995): 71–84.
14. James Csipak and Lise Héroux, 'NAFTA, Quebecers and Fear (?) of Americanization: Some Empirical Evidence', *Québec Studies* 29 (2000): 30.
15. Earl H. Fry, 'The Long Road to Free Trade', *Policy Options/Options politiques* 28, 9 (2007): 76.
16. As such pan-Canadian studies tend to overlook the 'regional' dimension, it would have been interesting to know about results proper to Quebec.
17. Fry, 'The Long Road to Free Trade', 76–7.
18. One exception to this was organized labour in Quebec. See Chapter 26 for a discussion of this point.
19. Jean-François Lisée, 'Comment le Québec est devenu une région-État nord-américaine', in Paquin, *Histoire des relations internationales du Québec*, 239–40.
20. Pierre-Paul Proulx, 'Quebec International Trade: Trade with American Regions', in Lachapelle, *Quebec Under Free Trade*, 55.
21. Gilles Duruflé and Benoît Tétrault, 'The Impact of the Free Trade Agreement on Bilateral Trade between Quebec and the United States', in Lachapelle, *Quebec Under Free Trade*, 137.

22. Dorval Brunelle, 'Portrait des exportations du Mexique, du Canada et du Québec après 20 ans de libre-échange', *Policy Options/Options politiques* 28, 9 (2007): 95.
23. Duruflé and Tétrault, 'The Impact of the Free Trade Agreement', 137.
24. Proulx, 'Quebec International Trade', 52–3.
25. Brunelle, 'Portrait des exportations', 95–6.
26. Proulx, 'Quebec International Trade'; Pierre-Paul Proulx,'L'ALENA et l'intégration économique dans les Amériques: vers une union douanière et des régions spécialisées?', in Dorval Brunelle and Christian Deblock, eds., *L'alena: le libre-échange en défaut* (Montreal: Fides, 2004), 261.
27. Liberalized products refer to those for which the tariffs in force before FTA's inception were most important.
28. Duruflé and Tétrault, 'The Impact of the Free Trade Agreement'.
29. Ibid, 137; John M.Curtis and Aaron Sydor, 'L'ALENA et le changement structurel', in Brunelle and Deblock, *L'alena: le libre-échange en défaut,* 194.
30. Craig Wright and Derek Holt, 'Canada's Free Trade Lessons for the World', *Policy Options/Options politiques* 28, 9 (2007): 20.

31. See Maryse Robert, 'Quebec and Its Canadian Partners: Economic Relationships and Trade Barriers', in Lachapelle, *Quebec Under Free Trade,* 79–102.
32. The Organization for Economic Cooperation and Development (OECD) groups together 30 mostly industrialized countries.
33. Lisée, 'Comment le Québec est devenu une région-État nord-américaine', 240–2.
34. Ibid, 242–4.
35. Ibid, 244–5.
36. Ibid, 246.
37. Lachapelle, 'Quebec under Free Trade', 19.
38. Holland, 'Quebec's Successful Role'.
39. Csipak and Héroux, 'NAFTA, Quebecers and Fear (?) of Americanization', 30.
40. Fry, 'The Long Road to Free Trade', 76.
41. Ibid, 76–7.
42. See Robert, 'Quebec and Its Canadian Partners'.
43. Beaulieu, 'Has North American Integration Resulted in Canada Becoming Too Dependent on the United States?', 102.

RELEVANT WEBSITES

UQÀM GROUPE DE RECHERCHE SUR L'INTÉGRATION CONTINENTALE (FRENCH ONLY): www.gric.uqam.ca/

INSTITUTE FOR RESEARCH ON PUBLIC POLICY: www.irpp.org/

GOVERNMENT OF CANADA POLICY RESEARCH INITIATIVE: www.policyresearch.gc.ca/

SELECT BIBLIOGRAPHY

Beaulieu, Eugene. 'Has North American Integration Resulted in Canada Becoming Too Dependent on the United States?', *Policy Options/Options politiques* 28, 9 (2007): 97–102.

Bergeron, Marc-André. 'Le Québec et l'Accord de libre-échange canado-américain 1985-1987'. In Stéphane Paquin, ed. *Histoire des relations internationales du Québec.* Montreal: VLB Éditeur, 2006, 188–93.

Brunelle, Dorval. 'Portrait des exportations du Mexique, du Canada et du Québec après 20 ans de libre-échange', *Policy Options/Options politiques* 28, 9 (2007): 94–6.

Cotter, Anne-Marie. 'Quebec in North America: Historical and Socio-Political Dimensions'. In Guy Lachapelle, ed. *Quebec Under Free Trade: Making Public Policy in North America.* Sainte-Foy: Presses de l'Université du Québec, 1995, 25–47.

Csipak, James, and Lise Héroux. 'NAFTA, Quebecers and Fear (?) of Americanization: Some Empirical Evidence', *Québec Studies* 29 (2000): 25–42.

Curtis, John M., and Aaron Sydor. 'L'ALENA et le changement structurel'. In Dorval Brunelle and

Christian Deblock, eds. *L'alena: le libre-échange en défaut.* Montreal: Fides, 2004, 179–209.

Duruflé, Gilles, and Benoît Tétrault. 'The Impact of the Free Trade Agreement on Bilateral Trade between Quebec and the United States'. In Guy Lachapelle, ed. *Quebec Under Free Trade: Making Public Policy in North America.* Sainte-Foy: Presses de l'Université du Québec, 1995, 131–74.

Fry, Earl H. 'The Long Road to Free Trade', *Policy Options/ Options politiques* 28, 9 (2007): 76–82.

Holland, Kenneth M. 'Quebec's Successful Role as Champion of North American Free Trade', *Québec Studies* 19 (1995): 71–84.

Lachapelle, Guy. 'Quebec under Free Trade: Between Interdependence and Transnationalism'. In Guy Lachapelle, ed. *Quebec Under Free Trade: Making Public Policy in North America.* Sainte-Foy: Presses de l'Université du Québec, 1995, 3–23.

Lisée, Jean-François. 'Comment le Québec est devenu une région-État nord-américaine'. In Stéphane Paquin, ed. *Histoire des relations internationales du Québec.* Montreal: VLB Éditeur, 2006, 239–62.

Proulx, Pierre-Paul. 'Quebec International Trade: Trade with American Regions'. In Guy Lachapelle, ed. *Quebec Under Free Trade: Making Public Policy in North America.* Sainte-Foy: Presses de l'Université du Québec, 1995, 49–78.

———. 'L'ALENA et l'intégration économique dans les Amériques: vers une union douanière et des régions spécialisées?'. In Dorval Brunelle and Christian Deblock, eds. *L'alena: le libre-échange en défaut.* Montreal: Fides, 2004, 241–71.

Robert, Maryse. 'Quebec and Its Canadian Partners: Economic Relationships and Trade Barriers'. In Guy Lachapelle, ed. *Quebec Under Free Trade: Making Public Policy in North America.* Sainte-Foy: Presses de l'Université du Québec, 1995, 79–102.

Schott, Jeffrey, and Gary Hufbauer. 'NAFTA Revisited', *Policy Options/Options politiques* 28, 9 (2007): 83–8.

Wright, Craig, and Derek Holt. 'Canada's Free Trade Lessons for the World', *Policy Options/Options politiques* 28, 9 (2007): 14–22.

PART F
QUEBEC INTERNATIONAL

INTRODUCTION

This next section of essays, the sixth and final of *Quebec Questions: Quebec Studies for the Twenty-first Century*, seeks to interpret and understand the role and place of Quebec within the larger international community. As such, readers of this section are presented with a core of related inquiries regarding Quebec's 'international footprint'. How did Quebec become involved in international affairs and what forces explain Quebec's desire to do so? When did this engagement begin and how has it evolved? Who—which actors—and where—geographically—has Quebec focused attention? And what has Quebec gained from the pursuit of international activities? What emerges from these contributions is a portrait of an actor that is richly engaged, indeed increasingly so, in myriad significant relationships around the globe.

Nelson Michaud's article portrays an activist Quebec, deeply concerned with staking a meaningful presence in the world. Characterizing Quebec as a sub-national actor operating within the context of a larger political federation, Michaud deftly illustrates—through theory and empirical evidence—that Quebec's deep-seated international role has gone

through three distinct stages. We learn of the seminal importance of key players, most especially Paul Gérin-Lajoie, who worked to promote and secure an international voice for Quebec. At the same time, Michaud's narrative provides a compelling standard by which to measure the ever-growing role of Quebec's international relations, most especially through his discussion of Quebec's role vis-à-vis UNESCO.

Geographically, Quebec's most pervasive international role, as Jody Neathery-Castro and Mark Rousseau demonstrate, is in the international organization known as La Francophonie. La Francophonie is important to Quebec, the authors point out, not simply because of the rich history and global reach of the organization, but because it 'constitutes the sole international organization to which Quebec belongs where it enjoys full autonomous participation'. In examining the development of La Francophonie, Neathery-Castro and Rousseau raise and address related key questions; among other things, they examine how participation in the organization serves Quebec's international interests and how the organization as a whole works to preserve and promote Quebec's linguistic, cultural, and economic objectives. In so doing, they give us a full picture of La Francophonie, the political context in which it emerged, and its larger organizational structure and mission. The authors conclusively demonstrate that Quebec's participation in La Francophonie has served and will continue to serve the interests of all Quebecers.

For Louis Balthazar, long regarded as the preeminent academic observer of Quebec–United States political relations, no country—historically or currently—has been as fundamental a priority for Quebec as has the United States. Placing Quebec's political engagement with the United States against a backdrop of provincial and federal developments, Balthazar specifically explores the motivations and interests behind Quebec's profound desire to engage in and with the United States. The official diplomatic presence of Quebec in the United States is thoroughly reviewed, as are American embassy and consular postings, along with the official position of the United States vis-à-vis the province's expressed desire—under the Parti Québécois in 1980 and 1995—to pursue a new political arrangement with Canada.

If political relations with the United States have been central to political and bureaucratic decision makers in Quebec City, we learn from Earl Fry's contribution that the Quebec–United States economic relationship is equally pivotal to the health and well-being of Quebec. Fry gives readers compelling evidence of the range and depth of Quebec's economic linkages with the United States, detailing trade and investment. Precisely how strong and meaningful are these linkages to Quebec? Perhaps one fact above all else that Fry points to puts matters in perspective—Quebec exports more goods to the United States than to the whole of the rest of Canada! This essay reminds us, however, that important economic, linguistic, and political barriers have existed and will continue to exist as Quebec attempts to attract American investment. Fry underlines that the future of Quebec's economic relationship with the United States will result in growing commercial ties between the partners.

The concluding essay in this section, offered by Sylvain Schryburt, explores a key artistic dimension of Quebec's role and place in the international community. Quebec theatre, Schryburt writes, is only recently being promoted and staged internationally with the success of Quebec playwrights, directors and theatre companies including Michel Tremblay, Robert Lepage, and UBU. To understand Quebec theatre on the international stage, this essay explores the development and growth of theatrical productions squarely focused on identity, the various challenges that emerged as a result, and the movement since 1980 toward greater diversification in theatrical content, form, and presentation. Schryburt's contribution, above all else, provides a clear analytical framework for conceptualizing how best to approach and understand the world of Quebec theatre—a theatre without boundaries, regardless of performer, production, or venue.

CHAPTER 25

Quebec's International Relations: Past and Current Directions

Nelson Michaud, École nationale d'administration publique (ENAP)

— TIMELINE —

1816 Opening of Quebec bureau in London, UK.

1834 Opening of United States consulate in Quebec City.

1859 Opening of French Consulate in Quebec City.

1871 Immigration officers sent to United Kingdom, Europe, and the United States.

1872 Appointments of agents in Dublin (John O'Neill) and Glasgow (James Whyte).

1874 John O'Neill is posted in London, UK.

1882 Appointment of *Agent général* in Paris (Hector Fabre) in February; on July 12, the federal government retains the agent's services 'with the consent of the Government of Quebec'.

1911 Appointment of *Agent général* in London (Pantaléon Pelletier).

1915 Appointment of *Agent général* in Brussels (Godfroi Langlois).

1937 Judiciary Committee of Privy Council (highest Court having jurisdiction in Canada) ruled that section 132 of British North America Act was not valid regarding provinces. This section gave Parliament of Canada 'all Powers necessary or proper for performing the Obligations of Canada *or of any Province thereof*, as Part of the British

Empire, towards Foreign Countries, arising under Treaties between the Empire and such Foreign Countries'. Ruling recognizes provincial autonomy in its spheres of jurisdiction, including international treaties. This is the basis on which Quebec claims its right to be active on international scene.

1940 Opening of Trade and Tourism Bureau in New York City, which later becomes government office (1943); legislature adopts bill, Loi concernant les agents généraux de 1940, in which agents' mandate is defined: develop trade, promote new industries in the province, market tourism, and work on 'all other mandates relevant to provincial jurisdiction' (author's translation).

1960 Agreement between France and Quebec to operate Maison du Quebec in Paris, which will open in 1961, and will be designated as *Délégation générale* in 1964.

1963 Opening of *Agence générale* in London, UK; renamed *Délégation générale* in 1971, even though English name will remain 'General Agency', for legal and tradition reasons.

1965 Signing of first agreement (entente) between France and Quebec regarding educational exchange and cooperation program; Paul Gérin-Lajoie's speech before Diplomatic Corps in Montreal on 12 April: first enunciation of his doctrine; opening of office in Milan.

1967 Adoption of bill instituting the Ministry of Intergovernmental Affairs; General De Gaulle's speech at Montreal City Hall on 24 July.

1968 Conference on Education in Libreville (Gabon); first international presence for Quebec.

1969–70 Quebec confirms its international standing in multilateral forum by taking part at the conferences held in Niamey (Niger), which will give birth to the Agence de coopération culturelle et technique (ACCT), later the Organisation internationale de La Francophonie (OIF), where Quebec is recognized with the status of *gouvernement participant*; opening of bureaus in United States: Boston, Chicago, Lafayette, Dallas, Los Angeles; Düsseldorf and Abidjan.

1972 Opening of *Délégation générale* in Brussels.

1973 Quebec's international action extends to North America at first Conference of New England Governors and Eastern Canadian Premiers Association; opening of bureau in Tokyo.

1977 Opening of bureaus in Atlanta and Washington, DC, latter a 'tourism office'.

1980 Opening of *Délégation générale* in Mexico and of bureau in Caracas.

1982 Inauguration of Wallonie-Bruxelles Delegation in Quebec City.

1984 Creation of Ministère des Relations internationales; opening of new bureaus and delegations in Bogota, Hong Kong, Singapore, Stockholm.

1985 Signing of Great Lakes Charter with American states and Canadian provinces; publication of a first White Paper: *Le Quebec dans le Monde*.

1986 Opening of bureau in Rome.

1988 Responsibilities for trade are now given to department renamed Ministère des Affaires Internationales.

1989 Opening of UNESCO office in Quebec City.

1991 Opening of bureau in Seoul; publication of a second policy paper: *Le Quebec et l'interdépendance: le monde pour horizon*.

1992 Quebec takes part in Earth Summit in Rio de Janeiro.

1994 Ministère de l'Immigration et des Communautés culturelles is integrated into Ministère des Affaires internationales.

1996 Due to budgetary constraints, 13 Quebec offices abroad are closed; some will reopen in 1998–9, and in 2001.

2001 Third Summit of the Americas in Quebec City—Quebec government takes stance on Free Trade Area of the Americas project; publication of strategic plan/third policy paper.

2002 Adoption of bill that states that any international treaty of importance and involving Quebec's own responsibilities should be evaluated by provincial legislature before being enacted locally.

2003 Premier Charest meets with US Secretary of State Colin Powell in New York.

2004 In speech, Premier Charest reiterates the importance of the Gérin-Lajoie doctrine; Premier Charest and French Prime Minister Jean-Pierre Raffarin conduct joint bi-governmental trade delegation in Mexico.

2005 Publication of statement by Monique Gagnon-Tremblay, Quebec Minister of International Relations, outlining five conditions under which Quebec will be part of Canadian delegations at international forums; adoption by UNESCO of Convention on the Protection and Promotion of the Diversity of Cultural Expressions—Assemblée nationale unanimously approves Convention on November 10—Quebec is first government in the world to do so.

2006   Signing of agreement between Quebec and Ottawa that allows Quebec to have representative at UNESCO— agreement formally recognizes Quebec's legitimacy to act on international scene; publication of Quebec's international policy.

2007–8   Quebec opens new bureaus in India and Brazil and more resources allocated to representation in China.

2008   While in Europe, Premier Charest launches idea of free trade agreement between EU and Canada—negotiations start in Prague in May 2009; former Premier, Pierre-Marc Johnson, is appointed Quebec's chief negotiator; following negotiations by former minister Gil Rémillard, Premier Jean Charest and French President Nicolas Sarkozy sign agreement on mutual recognition of professional qualifications.

2008–10   Quebec plays important role in reconstruction in Haiti.

2009   Release of second action plan following 2006 international policy statement.

For close to 45 years, Quebec has been actively engaged in the international community. Although most often driven by factors related to economy and cultural identity, these actions varied in their nature and exercised different types of influences. Criticized by some and taken for granted by others, Quebec's international role is often perceived as arising from one of the very few policy fields on which Quebec political parties of all stripes have regularly agreed. This consistency, however, may very well mask important differences in the conduct of Quebec's international relations.

This chapter explores the different phases through which Quebec's international relations and policies have evolved. This analytical exploration is rooted in a decidedly political science–international relations perspective, and seeks to provide a fuller understanding of the process by which Quebec established itself on the world scene.

It is not very well known that both the United States and France had diplomatic representatives posted in Quebec City well before the province became part of contemporary Canada in 1867. What is better known, but almost forgotten, is that Quebec had representatives abroad before Canada was allowed by the United Kingdom to conduct its own foreign relations. More importantly, although Quebec may have led the way in foreign relations conducted by a non-sovereign state,[1] it is no longer alone in so doing. First, as major world trends, norms, and standards involve issues falling under provinces', states', or länder's jurisdictions, federated entities are increasingly becoming involved in international affairs.[2] As they attempt to exercise an 'upstream influence' on these international factors, the manner in which they individually respond varies, for example, through formal constitutional agreements—Belgium; institutionalized processes—Germany, Austria, and Switzerland; compromises imposed by constitutional constraints—United States and Mexico; and restrictions expressed in court rulings—Australia.[3] Second, and closer to Quebec, other Canadian provinces such as Manitoba[4] and New Brunswick[5] have recently been expanding their international involvement. Alberta plays an active and autonomous international role (in Washington, DC, for example), but it has not yet committed itself to a written white paper–type policy. This proliferation of sub-national actors on the international scene is part of the background that colours the evolution of Quebec's international relations.

Some questions regarding Quebec's participation in international affairs are difficult to answer: Why is Quebec interested in playing an international role? Why is it involved the way it is, at such a level? The answers are not easy to find. There is much more to be considered than merely that the Parti Québécois has long advocated sovereignty. This fact does not explain why all Quebec political parties agree on the need for an international role for the province, nor is it useful in explaining why other Canadian provinces also have varying levels of international presence. In sum, it is mainly at the domestic level that we will find the factors from which to build the historical explanation this chapter offers.

CLUES TO UNDERSTANDING
FOREIGN-POLICY MAKING

Very few foreign policy theoretical models are useful to analyze the role played by a non-sovereign actor on the world stage. For instance, the realist theory, which takes the quest of power—often hard, military power—as the rationale behind any foreign policy or international involvement is of no use. The day has not yet come when Western Austria, Tasmania, or British Columbia will compete to be among the world's superpowers. In fact, some classical neo-realists as well as some hardcore offensive realists simply deny the possibility that a country not seeking power may engage in foreign relations.

Liberal theorists who consider a wider spectrum of options that inspire a country to act internationally, including active involvement in the international political economy and support for and participation in multilateral institutions, still focus on variables found in external sources that may influence foreign relations' behaviour. This is useful to explain a country's foreign policy when that policy can be independent of internal factors, but is weaker in explaining the policy adopted by a state that must take into account internal elements, such as constitutional division of powers or taxation powers, as they weigh policy options.

To solve this methodological problem, the analyst must turn to less classical options. Among these, we might rely on theories that focus on the head of state or of government. In this realm, strongly inspired by the works of Margaret Hermann, we see that the head of government's willingness to act makes the difference. I suggest here that this willingness or, more generally, the leader's stance and behaviour, is only one element that must be taken into account. For instance, a Quebec premier may very well wish to get Quebec involved in an international project, yet if resources are scarce, chances are that the project will never materialize. Moreover, this willingness may very well be traced in speeches, but if there are no specific policy objects to which this willingness can be grounded, it will not drive any initiative.

I have demonstrated in a number of other studies that three factors can be considered when one wishes to explain any foreign policy initiative. First, I agree with realists when they say that foreign policy and foreign relations are motivated by interests (but I fall short from continuing on by stating 'as defined in terms of power', as Hans Morgenthau did). What we find, however, is a proportional relationship between these interests and a state's foreign policy actions. In other words, the higher the interests are, the more probable is international action. But interests alone cannot explain foreign policy behaviour. For instance, by considering foreign policy/relations interests only, how can one explain that the Parti Québécois government led by Lucien Bouchard in the 1990s closed several of Quebec's delegations around the world? Did Quebec's international interests lessen or suddenly evaporate? The answer to this puzzle can be found in the harsh battle Bouchard fought against the province's deficit. In the absence of sufficient funding, these delegations had to be closed.

The second factor is thus the level of constraints that create stumbling blocks on the road to foreign involvement. These constraints that prevent federated entities from being active internationally might be a lack of human or financial resources, political pressures (as it was the case for Quebec when Pierre Elliott Trudeau's government was in power in Ottawa), or constitutional barriers (as in the United States). Here, the relationship between the factor and the result is reversed: more constraints imply less action.

The third factor has been mentioned already: the personality of the leader (head of state or of government). For it is true that two leaders facing the same situation and experiencing similar levels of constraints may still act differently.

If, to get a better image, one wants to formalize these relationships in terms of a mathematical function, it would appear as follows:

$$\text{Foreign policy action (A)} = \left(\frac{\text{Interests (I)}}{\text{Constraints (C)}} \right) \times \text{Leader's Personality (P)}$$

With this model in hand, we may start our exploration of Quebec's foreign policy activities over time.

QUEBEC INTERNATIONAL RELATIONS: AN OVERVIEW

Most studies that have examined Quebec's international relations agree in highlighting the innovative character of these relations and, on many points, their uniqueness.[6] This subject is not discussed here, but remains in the background of the brief overview of Quebec's international policies I conduct. In this respect, it is useful to refer to three phases of Quebec's international action that I identify as a *stage setting era* (1965–85), a *consolidation period* (1985–2002), and a recent shift that has directed Quebec's international action towards the realm of *foreign policy* (since 2002).

Of course, one could go much farther back in time to examine Quebec's initial presence in the international arena. In the nineteenth century, 'commercial agents' were sent to London, Dublin, Paris, and later Brussels. In those days, Canada's foreign relations were the Empire's responsibility, and the Canadian government was required to operate from British legations around the world until the adoption of the Statute of Westminster in 1931. This condition, however, did not apply to the provinces. Canada sometimes chose to operate through Quebec's offices abroad, as it did in France as early as the 1880s. But more important to the present analysis, we must note that Quebec's agents posted abroad at the end of the nineteenth century were the precursors of the *délégués* and *délégués généraux* who today represent Quebec around the world.

In 1940, Quebec opened a trade office in New York City, an initiative of Adélard Godbout's Liberal government. The rationale largely rested on the need to help the province to get out of the Great Depression through direct access to US money markets. In spite of his reservations on any international action, Union Nationale[7] Premier Maurice Duplessis kept the office open. These meagre operations began to grow only years later, thanks to the winds of change brought by the Quiet Revolution under Liberal Premier Jean Lesage, elected in 1960. It is from this time that we can really refer to a continuous international engagement for the province.

The Stage-Setting Era (1965–1985)

February 1965 can be established as the precise date when the *stage was set* in Quebec international relations. The modernization of governance was at the very heart of the Quiet Revolution. This meant, first, the establishment of a professional public service. A successful and swift implementation of these sweeping changes could only be possible by learning from the experience of other governments. In our model of interests, constraints, and personality, we may say that the interests were high.

In order to facilitate these exchanges, Paul Gérin-Lajoie, Minister of Education and Deputy Premier, signed a series of initial agreements with the French government.[8] The initiative met strong opposition from Ottawa, raising significantly the level of constraints towards future initiatives. A federated entity was defying the centuries-old Westphalian rules, which since 1648 have defined sovereign states as the sole recognized international actors. By signing a convention with a sovereign state, Quebec was effectively bypassing the federal government's prerogative. Ottawa, taking offence at this action,[9] would be reluctant to see Quebec act autonomously on the international scene for some 40 years. Even the federal government's international policy statement, published in 2005, denied the right of provinces to speak for themselves in international forums.[10] It was only in May 2006, in an agreement between the Harper and the Charest governments, that the legitimacy of Quebec's international role was formally recognized.

Despite this late recognition, the rationale for Quebec's international involvement had been voiced by Gérin-Lajoie in an April 1965 speech to the Consular corps based in Montreal.[11] The immediate effect of the statement was to lower the constraints that ad hoc initiatives promoted by Quebec might have otherwise encountered. The rationale statement—known as the 'Gérin-Lajoie doctrine'—was an important resource in this regard. Gérin-Lajoie reiterated his doctrine a few weeks later in

Quebec City at a dinner hosting European scholars. And it was at the Legislative Assembly, in 1967, during the second reading of the bill establishing the Ministère des relations intergouvernementales,

that, alluding to provincial constitutional rights, he asserted that Quebec's international relations are defined as 'the external extension of its domestic fields of jurisdiction'.[12]

PAUL GÉRIN-LAJOIE

Former Education Minister Paul Gérin-Lajoie speaks during the 20 November 2002 ceremony at the consulate of France in Quebec City, where he was awarded the highest decoration of France: Chevalier de la Legion d'Honneur.

CP PHOTO/Jacques Boissinot

Paul Gérin-Lajoie gave his name to the doctrine that has been the basis of Quebec's dedicated commitment to international engagement for over 45 years. Gérin-Lajoie served as the Minister of Youth, the first Minster of Education, and Deputy Premier of Quebec. He was a member of Jean Lesage's government, elected as a member for the riding of Vaudreuil-Soulanges (southwest of Montreal) in 1960.

Gérin-Lajoie was born on 23 February 1920. After studies at the Université de Montréal and as a Rhodes Scholar at Oxford University, he was admitted to the Quebec Bar in 1943 and received his doctorate in constitutional law five years later. He acted as counsel for federal commissions of enquiry, the City of Montreal, and diverse organizations and institutions throughout Quebec. In his thirties, he was very active within his profession and in 1957, he founded a regional weekly newspaper, *L'Écho de Vaudreuil-Soulanges et Jacques-Cartier.*

He soon became involved in politics, chairing the political commission of the Quebec Liberal Party. He ran for the leadership of his party in 1958, but lost to Jean Lesage, the man he would later serve as minister. He ran twice in his home riding with no success before he was finally elected in June 1960. He was re-elected in

1962 and in 1966 and resigned his seat on 20 June 1969.

Gérin-Lajoie is noted for his contribution to the development of Quebec's international presence. His contribution as Minister of Education is, however, no less important. He was behind the Parent Commission that brought fundamental reform to the education system, promoting a complete public school system, from elementary schools to the university level.

Following his political career, Gérin-Lajoie held various significant posts. He taught law at the University of Ottawa and Université de Montréal from 1969 to 1975; chaired the OECD mission that studied research and development in education in the United States in 1969; was vice-president of the Federal Commission on Prices and Wages in 1969; served as chair of the newly founded Canadian International Development Agency from 1970 to 1977; was director of Projecto International from 1978 to 1986; and was Director General of the Société du Vieux-Port de Montréal from 1981 to 1985. He is a member of the Governing Council of the World Bank.

In 1977 his commitment to education led him to launch a foundation. The mission of the Fondation Paul-Gérin-Lajoie is to contribute to the basic education of children and to the eradication of adult illiteracy in the poorest countries of the world. It also aims at awakening Canadian primary-school children to international concerns.

Over the years, Paul Gérin-Lajoie has received numerous awards and recognitions in Canada, France, and Africa. He was made doctor *honoris causa* by at least 12 universities across the Americas.

Gérin-Lajoie's famous contribution to the role that federated entities play on the world scene has of course profoundly marked his own society, Quebec. This influence, however, goes far beyond Quebec; several federated states refer to it; the regions and communities of Belgium and the autonomous region of

Catalonia are among those that consider it a cornerstone of their international engagement.

At the heart of the doctrine is a dynamic reading of federalism. It is based on the judicial recognition that the federal government may very well sign treaties that address questions of provincial jurisdiction, but it has no power to force a province, as a member of a broader political federation, to implement them. The Gérin-Lajoie doctrine goes one step further as it encourages provincial governments to negotiate and put into law their own international agreements, instead of simply being reactive or passive to those championed by central governments.

Gérin-Lajoie's first speech, delivered on 12 April 1965 before the consular corps in Montreal, immediately prompted a reaction from Ottawa. Although Prime Minister Lester B. Pearson did not seem to be overly concerned with the declaration—he is reported to have said 'Paul does not mean it'—his Secretary of State for External Affairs, Paul Martin Sr, went on the offensive, heralding the 'one Canada' stance; the Canadian federal government is the sole official representative in foreign policy. Gérin-Lajoie took the opportunity in a second speech—this time in Quebec City before a group of European academics—to go one step further, signalling that Quebec

should develop its own international policy. In these two speeches Gérin-Lajoie laid the groundwork for Quebec's international actions for years to come.

Gérin-Lajoie's doctrine would find formal voice two years later when the Assemblée Nationale debated the bill that created the Ministère des Affaires intergouvernementales. Short speeches were made by Premier Daniel Johnson Sr, who sponsored the bill, by the Leader of the Opposition, Jean Lesage, and by Gérin-Lajoie himself. Referring to provincial constitutional rights, he stated that Quebec's international relations are defined as 'the external extension of its domestic fields of jurisdiction'.

Oddly enough, in his memoirs Gérin-Lajoie is decidedly shy to recall the formulation and official adoption of his doctrine. He recognizes the original writer of the speech, André Patry, he refers to Ottawa's reaction to his words, but he does not disclose the intent behind the speech nor the impact it had, and still has, on Quebec's international role and policy.

As this book is written, Paul Gérin-Lajoie is still steadily involved in the work of his foundation. In his public appearances, he is still the elder statesman with a message to deliver. There can be no doubt that his works and thoughts have deeply affected several generations.

For the next 20 years, notwithstanding the changing political colour of the government, Quebec kept a foothold in foreign relations, in spite of the federal government's cautionary and less-than-supportive position. From the 1960s on, each of Quebec's international initiatives has been a venture whose uncertainty was alleviated only by the support of countries like France and some African states, effectively lowering the level of constraints Quebec faced. As the first formal policy statement came only in late 1985, most of Quebec's international actions between 1965 and 1985 were initiated case by case and presented within the framework of the Gérin-Lajoie doctrine.

With the election of the Progressive Conservative government of Brian Mulroney in 1984, the federal–provincial relationship changed and directly affected Quebec's international role. In 1985, Following René Lévesque's *beau risque*,[13] Pierre-Marc Johnson (PQ)

was sworn in as Premier and soon, an agreement between Ottawa and Quebec allowed the province to act on its own at summits of an emerging multilateral forum called La Francophonie.[14] Luc Bernier called this period the 'Golden Age',[15] for Quebec now had achieved the external recognition needed to gain some autonomy in managing its international relations. Interests were high, and the level of constraints was significantly lowered. By then Quebec was ready to move towards consolidating its stance.

The Consolidation Period (1985–2002)

The consolidation period for Quebec's international role began with Bernard Landry's contribution in the last weeks of the Pierre-Marc Johnson PQ–led government. Landry's White Paper outlined the principles of Quebec global relations and the areas of their application; it directly aimed at consolidating Quebec's world presence. It was conceived as an answer to the need for both self-assertion and recognition by foreign actors of Quebec's legitimacy on the international scene. Interests and constraints faced by a federated state are therefore made explicit. Its frame of reference is 'the values that are proper to our society, the fruits of its history and its culture'.[16]

This policy statement broke ground for a new phase in Quebec's international action, while offering a report on the previous stage-setting period and a portrait of the evolution of Quebec's international role since 1960. With the election of Robert Bourassa's Liberal government in November 1985, this policy statement was not fully implemented. Important elements of continuity, however, remained: the Bourassa government centralized Quebec's international action and supported this policy by enacting in 1988 a major administrative reconfiguration and creating the Ministère des Affaires internationales.[17]

A second[18] and a third[19] policy statement became available during this period. First, in 1991, under the new framework brought by the 1988 Act, the minister was required to publish an international relations policy. Essentially, the statement that ensued carried forward several items from the 1985 White Paper. This clearly was an exercise of consolidation, putting the emphasis on the economy and the world's interdependence in that sector.

Due to the evolving international context and to the difference in the government's party allegiance, the 1991 paper differs in some respects from the one of 1985. For instance, in 1985, the federal framework (understood to be a constraining factor) and potential constitutional changes are discussed, but they do not appear in the 1991 document, as both federal and provincial governments now had mutual interests on these issues. The 1985 paper sees international action as a means to buttress its aspirations for a new constitutional status; this motivation is not present in the 1991 document. The existing institutional framework is even seen in 1991 as a unique 'opportunity' for Quebec to grow externally.[20] And while culture and immigration convey different meanings, both documents consider them to be a vital part of Quebec's international interests. We can clearly identify where

interests and constraints are located and how they are defined.

The third policy statement, somewhat different from the first two, was published in 2001. First, by its own nature, it does not belong to the same family of statements. This document has been published as a 'strategic plan' to meet the requirements of the recent Loi sur l'administration publique.[21] Nevertheless, the document clearly outlines the interests, stakes, and potential orientations of Quebec's international policy. The final chapter constitutes the strategic plan per se, which lists the main objectives and issues on which Quebec intends to focus. These are meant to meet the litmus test of organizational capabilities.

The 2001 statement produced by the Parti Québécois government also lists constraints such as constitutional loopholes, which, while more craftily described than they were in 1985, are nevertheless noticeable. For instance, we read that in the context of multilateral trade negotiations, 'the Quebec government must be very vigilant in order to preserve its capacity to act and maintain its leeway, particularly in domains as sensitive as identity and recognition.'[22] In this regard, the introduction to the 2001 statement speaks for itself—not only does it express the government's position, but it also shows the result of an operational and structural consolidation of the department resulting from the new legislation, which 'makes it compulsory to the minister to see that the Quebec constitutional jurisdiction be respected'.[23] In fact, the return of constitutional concerns in 2001 matches the slight retreat of the economy to backstage and brings forward a leadership—rather than an accompanying—role for the government.

A final significant point needs to be made regarding the 2001 statement. More than ever before, the use of the concept of 'foreign policy' is underscored and used in the policy statement. This can be explained in part by the more administrative nature of the document. It is important to note, however, that such a use reflects the Quebec government's willingness to not simply react to external pressures on its domestic policies, but to position itself to influence international standards and norms to its advantage. These trends were reaffirmed in the 2006 White Paper, as growing international pressures in areas falling specifically under the jurisdiction of federated entities motivated the government to reinvest in its delegations network, to provide adequate resources, and to consider a definite move towards a genuine foreign policy stance.

Toward Foreign Policy (2002–Present)

The last period, which began in 2002, has so far been characterized both by the desire to continue creating new international engagements and, more importantly, by establishing and meeting genuine foreign policy objectives, as announced in the 2001 policy statement. Foreign policy activities, as put forward by Michaud and Ramet,[24] are characterized not only by a doctrine of, and the commitment of resources to, international relations, but primarily by the will of a state to actively influence the international context to its advantage.

This new phase was launched by the Assemblée Nationale's unanimous adoption of a bill that states that any international treaty of importance and involving Quebec's own responsibilities should be evaluated by the provincial legislature before it being enacted locally.[25] More concretely, this means that Quebec's prior consent is practically a prerequisite to Canada entering into any treaty that bears on Quebec's jurisdiction. Without this consent, the said treaty would not be applicable in Quebec. This empowerment allows Quebec, under any governing party to influence certain aspects of international negotiated agreements. This constitutes a major breakthrough in the realm of foreign policy as it was defined above.

The Liberal government of Jean Charest, elected in 2003 and re-elected in 2007 and in 2008, held to this position. Not only did Charest support this bill while in opposition, but it also became clear from the outset that the Premier adheres wholeheartedly to the Gérin-Lajoie doctrine. In a speech delivered at the École nationale d'administration publique (ENAP) in February 2004, Premier Charest paraphrased Gérin-Lajoie in stating 'that which is Quebec's jurisdiction at home, is Quebec's jurisdiction at large' (our translation).[26] Since then, this new mantra has been used time and again by Charest himself, by Monique Gagnon-Tremblay, his former Minister of International Relations, and by Benoît Pelletier, former Minister responsible for Canadian Intergovernmental Affairs and their successors.

Moreover, this government reached an agreement with the federal government to ensure that Quebec will have, within the Canadian delegation, its own permanent representative at UNESCO, a forum where questions falling under the province's jurisdiction, such as culture and education, are discussed and where related universal standards and norms are defined. Not only does this agreement settle a long-time dispute, but also it recognizes Quebec's legitimacy as an international actor. Finally, in May 2006, the Charest government tabled a new White Paper intended to guide the government's international role.[27] Could this White Paper be considered as an *ex post facto* effort or will it have a structuring effect?

The Quebec–Ottawa Agreement on Quebec's Participation at UNESCO

When Premier Jean Charest and Prime Minister Stephen Harper met in the Red Chamber of the Assemblée Nationale in Quebec City on 5 May 2006 to sign an accord allowing Quebec to have a seat at UNESCO, an important page of history was written. The accord in itself was a definite departure from past Canadian foreign policy and practice, and formally recognized what the Gérin-Lajoie doctrine had

advocated for 40 years: the legitimacy of Quebec's role in the conduct of international affairs.

The End of a Dogma?

It is true that Quebec's international role was given mild recognition by Prime Minister Brian Mulroney at a state dinner honouring French Premier Laurent Fabius in November 1984, a year before Ottawa and Quebec agreed that Quebec should have a role in La Francophonie. In a speech written by Lucien Bouchard, Mulroney greeted Fabius by saying that Quebec's exchanges with France were 'normal and desirable', based on Quebec's cultural identity. The affirmation is narrowly defined, however; first, it addresses only the relationship with France, and second, this relationship is legitimate as long as it does not bear on subjects of federal jurisdiction, while 'the Canadian government intends to fully exercise its constitutional responsibilities in terms of international relations.' Moreover, this opening, although slight, was never understood by Ottawa's foreign affairs bureaucracy as a change of direction in overall policy.

Confronted with the status quo, upon taking office in 2003, the Charest government petitioned Ottawa to recognize an international role better suited to the province's needs. This advocacy campaign was conducted by Quebec's ministers Monique Gagnon-Tremblay (International Relations) and Benoît Pelletier (Intergovernmental Relations). They expressed opinions that were at variance with Ottawa's traditional credo, publicly and privately stating that Quebec should be more fully involved in crafting Canada's international policies on questions of provincial jurisdiction. Moreover, they defended Quebec's right to express itself in forums where matters such as culture, language, education, health care, and labour, which all come under the province's constitutional responsibility, were discussed.

To better define the Quebec government's demands, Minister Monique Gagnon-Tremblay issued, in mid-September 2005, a document that outlined what the government's five priorities for Quebec's participation in international forums:

1. having access to all information and ensuring an upstream participation in the development of the Canadian position;
2. having a representative chosen by Quebec recognized as a full member of the Canadian delegation;
3. being recognized as having the right to express itself and speak from its own voice within international forums when matters related to its constitutional responsibilities are discussed;
4. being recognized as having the right to grant its approval before Canada signs or declares itself part of a treaty or of an international agreement that relates to matters of Quebec's jurisdiction;
5. being recognized as having the right to speak for itself when Canada appears before international organizations' control authorities, if it is a party to the case or if its interests are at stake.

Specifically in reference to UNESCO, the document asked for a review of the Canadian Commission's mandate, to allow the government of Quebec to directly consult with Quebec civil society. According to Gagnon-Tremblay's own statement, the goal of all Quebec's requests is to reinforce Canada's international stance and role.

Following the publication of the document, Gagnon-Tremblay and Pelletier met with their federal counterparts, Pierre Pettigrew and Lucienne Robillard, in October 2005, but no immediate resolution to Quebec's position was identified. Change came in December 2005, when Conservative leader Stephen Harper presented his electoral platform in Quebec City. Sponsoring 'open federalism', Harper appealed to Quebec's autonomist voters—those who were not hard-core separatists, but were nevertheless uncomfortable with a centralist federal government, who believed in respecting the separation of powers as constitutionally defined. Harper's remarks included a major commitment towards Quebec's role in international affairs: Quebec would get a seat at UNESCO following the model of its relationship with La Francophonie. At the beginning of 2006, Harper was elected and it remained to be seen if this campaign promise would materialize.

An Innovative Avenue

To understand the possibilities, one must first take into account the constraints that UNESCO itself imposed, as the model offered by La Francophonie— where Quebec has its own seat—was not possible according to the terms and conditions that govern UNESCO membership. Unlike La Francophonie,

UNESCO recognizes only UN members, a condition that Quebec obviously does not fulfill. Some considered amending the UNESCO charter, but this represented a long, complex, and high risk solution that offered meagre hopes of reaching favourable results. There was also the possibility raised of securing Quebec an 'associate membership', but, to meet UNESCO's criteria for such membership, Quebec would have had to acknowledge that it had no control over its own foreign relations—a counterproductive outcome that would have erased 40 years of work toward establishing an international role of its own.

The solution offered by the agreement ultimately signed by Harper and Charest was administrative, allowing Quebec to exercise a direct influence, although from within the Canadian delegation. It is therefore an innovative, hybrid solution that answers all requests made by Quebec, while respecting the rules of UNESCO and operating within the federal Canadian government framework for the conduct of international affairs.

In Line with the Gérin-Lajoie Doctrine

By giving Quebec a new international voice, the agreement is no doubt in line with the Gérin-Lajoie doctrine. In fact, it even reaches the level Gérin-Lajoie hoped for—Quebec having the possibility of openly influencing international organizations in their consideration of new norms and standards on matters within the province's jurisdictional responsibilities.

Perhaps more importantly, the most crucial aspect of the agreement is not found in its articles, but in its preamble. There, for the first time, the federal government of Canada formally recognizes the legitimacy of Quebec's international role. Although this recognition is not enshrined in the Canadian Constitution, this is a major turn of events, a step that would be very difficult, if not impossible, to retreat from. It is in this sense that the agreement signed on 5 May 2006 is a key moment in the history of Quebec's international relations.

Most observers considered the statement to demonstrate continuity with the former policies, that it is predicated on the same basic doctrine and builds on the experience of the past. But at the same time, it includes several important innovations, directly characteristic of the new period the paper comes from.

One of the key elements that strikes the eye is that the paper is a genuine *government* policy that encompasses efforts undertaken by several departments—all those ministries that now have an international component. It aims at attending to the many needs which are now an intrinsic part of daily government business. The document and the concrete action plan that accompanies it go beyond the rhetoric of 'horizontality' and the need to 'break the silos', as they suggest ways to implement this new type of horizontal management in the realm of international relations. In fact, they concretely answer the need for a cohesive policy that was invoked in former policy statements, but was rarely achieved. The efforts invested to reach this type of coordination at the policy-making stage, not an easy task in itself, might very well be rewarded at the time of the policy's implementation.

Indeed, the action plan[28] that complements the policy is an important tool that also contributes largely to its innovative character. As research shows, a White Paper can be used by an incoming government to leave its imprint in the political landscape, but it is seldom translated into actual measures. In other words, policy actions do not always arise from goals outlined in well-intentioned speeches. With this action plan, however, the Quebec government clearly expresses its willingness to act, as it provides itself with the tangible tools needed to implement the policy.[29] These are important public administration innovations that are confirmed in the second action plan released in 2009.[30]

The prevailing approach in this new international policy constitutes another major innovation. It is decidedly pluralistic, and although the advocacy of Quebec's identity is far from being abandoned, it is no longer the sole objective. Identity is here part of a holistic approach accurately reflecting a contemporary international reality, largely influenced by globalization.[31] Consequently, Quebec recognizes the importance of matters related to the economy and to security, just as any modern state must deal with these most important issues in the world today. Finally, 'international solidarity'—Quebec's equivalent of official development assistance, directed to recipients and not governments, and based on the UN Millennium goals—is also addressed in the new policy statement.[32]

As we have mentioned, this latest period marks a turn toward the implementation and conduct of foreign policy by Quebec, and the publication of this latest document is one of its defining moment. For the first time, all components of a genuine foreign policy—diplomacy, security, economy, aid—are addressed according to the jurisdiction of the province. For instance, security cannot be understood here as a military challenge, but rather, as the document eloquently addresses, through Quebec's role in providing safe border crossings, providing basic identity documents that enable citizens to get passports, or preparing the province to face pandemics.[33] All these elements are essential security concerns in the post–9/11 context, and the province must be vigilant on all these fronts if it wishes to be a credible state in today's world. Environmental risks and natural catastrophes are also security threats that the Quebec government addresses.[34] These examples demonstrate very well how 'domestic' departments, such as Health, Transport, and Justice, must be full partners in implementing this international policy statement.

This new approach to international affairs definitely turns the page on the days when Quebec's mere international presence was the subject of debate. Quebec's international efforts are no longer limited to seeking informational resources from abroad to modernize the machinery of state or to promoting its specific culture. As a new world order is unfolding, and as international standards in all key areas under Quebec's own jurisdiction are determined in foreign or multilateral forums, Quebec has chosen to take an active role in the process—and not only react *ex post facto*— and to directly influence the outcomes based on its own interests and context.[35] It is this type of influence that characterizes the actual conduct of foreign policy and distinguishes it from international relations. By establishing as their first objective the need to provide the tools in order to ensure 'Quebec's capability to intervene and to influence',[36] the policy

and the action plan do not keep secret the context in which Quebec's international action plan will be put into play, one which, in the mind of the government, best serves the interests of a modern Quebec.[37]

In sum, one might say that this new policy was designed to answer the many new international challenges which a state like Quebec faces. The solutions proposed in the policy and its parallel action plans provide both continuity and innovation, and thus the means to meet new international challenges. It is too early to evaluate the overall impact of the policy, but it contains enough indicators to allow us to determine that the changes go beyond partisan positions and constitute a basis for Quebec's international action for some time to come.

CONCLUSION

Today, Quebec has a presence all over the world. It actively participates in international forums such as La Francophonie and UNESCO. It has also entered into over 550 international agreements, with more than 300 of them still in effect. All this was accomplished in little over 40 years. Based on a strong statement, the Gérin-Lajoie doctrine, to which all Quebec governments have adhered and from which other federated entities have taken inspiration, this international presence has evolved through several phases, as we have seen in this chapter.

In the first phase, the stage-setting era, most of the work was done by trial and error. Some have portrayed it as an 'organized anarchy'. Generally in Quebec, most government initiatives were pure innovations and, in this sense, international relations were not conducted in an exceptional manner. It was perhaps even more difficult to plan ahead since international relations are traditionally the purview of the federal government. Each matter was considered case by case, and each new venture was an exploration of the unknown. In this stage, interests took precedence over the constraints, since expertise was needed quickly to open to the world a society awakening to new realities. And the personalities of premiers Lesage, D. Johnson, Lévesque, and P.-M. Johnson no doubt improved the chances for the new vision to be implemented.

In the second phase, the consolidation period, interests did not diminish, but constraints rose perceptibly, especially the fewer resources available to Quebec. The time was appropriate for reflections, for the crafting of written policies, and for organizational realignments. This period witnessed several changes in the ministry's mandate, but always, the Gérin-Lajoie doctrine remained at the heart of the action. Premier Bourassa, who had a keen interest in economic matters and paid less attention to cultural identity than did his predecessors, nevertheless left an imprint on this period, as did Lucien Bouchard, whose strong temperament and resolute support for 'zero deficit' budgets reduced the resources available to diplomatic endeavours.

The third phase was ushered in by globalization, as Quebec entered the realm of foreign policy-making. Globalization created challenges for Quebec, which immediately were translated as interests to be defended. At the same time, globalization brought new actors onto the international stage—such as NGOs and civil society—and diminished the constraints on Quebec's pursuit of foreign policy initiatives.

Non-sovereign states thus found more room to manoeuvre in the international political system. As well, political constraints were lowered in Quebec City by the unanimous consent of all parties in supporting key initiatives. In addition, the federal government led by Prime Minister Stephen Harper broke long-standing federal dogma by recognizing the legitimacy of Quebec's international actions. The fact that for most of the period, Quebec was under the leadership of Jean Charest, one of the most activist premiers in terms of international policy (in the off-the-record judgment of officials in the Ministry of International Relations), helps to understand Quebec's activist commitment to international affairs.

What does the future hold for Quebec's commitment to international engagement? According to the model used in this chapter, a few elements can guide our forecast. First, it is likely that Quebec's interests will continue to be defended within the framework of the Gérin-Lajoie doctrine. Second, as globalization and the consistent regionalization of issues will increase—both in Europe and in the Americas—the interests to be defended by Quebec will grow. Third, even if institutional and political constraints may seem to be lowered, varying economic pressures may create constraints, as international relations will always take a lower priority than many other sectors the government of Quebec must attend to. Finally, the level of interest and of energy that future leaders will devote to international questions is probably the least certain factor in any prediction. It is doubtful, however, that the trend of Quebec as an active international actor would be reversed.

QUESTIONS FOR CONSIDERATION

1. It can be said, on the one hand, that federated entities are sovereign in their own fields of jurisdiction; that international norms affect sectors of provincial/state level responsibility, that these governments wish to influence the crafting of these norms; and, that economic multinational actors as well as civil society are significant actors in the international arena. On the other hand, former UN Secretary General Boutros Boutros-Ghali warned of the danger of the proliferation of too many international actors; others argue that allowing a voice to sub-national actors will erode the central state's power. Given this context, should non-sovereign states have an international voice?

2. Does international involvement nurture a secessionist movement?

3. Are there limits to the role a non-sovereign state can play on the international scene?

4. The Red Cross enjoys diplomatic status at the UN. Should Quebec, as a federated entity within Canada, receive similar attention?

NOTES

1. As one of the first federated entities to enter the realm of international relations, Quebec is considered as an innovator by many other federated entities, such as Belgian regions (the work of Françoise Massart-Piérard is eloquent on this aspect), Catalonia, etc.

2. Among studies on the topic, see Nelson Michaud, 'Quebec and North American Integration: Making Room for a Sub-National Actor?', in J. Peter Meekison, Hamish Telford, and Harvey Lazar, eds, *Canada: The State of the Federation 2002—Reconsidering the Institutions of Canadian Federalism* (Montreal and Kingston: McGill-Queen's University Press, 2004), 377–410; see also Stéphane Paquin, *La revanche des petites nations. Le Quebec, l'Écosse et la Catalogne face à la mondialisation* (Montreal: VLB éditeur, 2001).

3. Nelson Michaud, 'Canada and Quebec on the World Scene: defining New Rules?' in Andrew F. Cooper and Dane Rowlands, eds, *Canada Among Nations 2006* (Montreal and Kingston: McGill-Queen's University Press, 2006), 232–47.

4. Government of Manitoba, *Reaching Beyond Our Borders: The Framework For Manitoba's International Activities*, available at www.gov.mb.ca/international/index.html, consulted on 12 May 2007.

5. Raj Venugopal, 'The White Paper in New Brunswick's International Affairs: An Analysis', in Nelson Michaud, ed., *Foreign Policy White Papers in Context: A Comparative Study* (New York, Edwin Mellen Press, forthcoming).

6. An extensive literature review on this uniqueness is presented in Nelson Michaud 'Le Quebec dans le monde : faut-il redéfinir les fondements de son action?', in Robert Bernier, ed., *L'État québécois au XXIe siècle* (Sainte-Foy,Que.: Presses de l'Université du Quebec, 2004), 125–68.

7. Quebec's conservative party from the 1930s up until the 1980s.

8. Claude Morin, *L'art de l'impossible : la diplomatie québécoise depuis 1960* (Montreal: Boréal 1987), 170.

9. Paul Martin Sr, *A Very Public Life: So Many Worlds* (Toronto: Deneau, 1985), Chapter 18; Claude Morin, *L'Art de l'impossible* (Montreal: Boréal, 1987). From these readings, one can appreciate both sides of the coin from actors who were involved in the process.

10. Government of Canada, *Canada's International Policy Statement: A Role of Pride and Influence in the World—Diplomacy* (Ottawa: Government of Canada, 2005), 34.

11. To identify the source of this longstanding policy, we must reach the man behind the doctrine: André Patry, a constitutional lawyer and an artisan of the Quiet Revolution. (On this, see Robert Aird, *André Patry et la présence du Quebec dans le monde* [Montréal, VLB éditeur, 2005]). Patry anchored the policy postulate on decisions rendered by the Judicial Committee of the Privy Council in the 1930s. These rulings clearly established

that provinces have full responsibility in the application and implementation of international treaties and standards in their own fields of jurisdiction. This interpretation is based, first, on the quasi-total silence of the British North America Act on questions of international relations and foreign policy—the only Section that deals with international questions is s.132 and it addresses the obligation the Dominion has towards treaties signed by the Empire; however this section became obsolete with the Statute of Westminster in 1931—it also rests on unambiguous jurisprudence related to section 92 that defines which questions fall under the provincial legislative responsibilities. It is on these constitutional grounds that Quebec built its international action. For a thorough review of the Gérin-Lajoie doctrine, see Stéphane Paquin and Louise Beaudoin, eds., *Histoire des relations internationales du Quebec depuis la Révolution tranquille* (Montréal, VLB éditeur, 2006).

12. Quebec Legislative Assembly, *Débats de l'Assemblée législative du Quebec* 5, 49, 13 April 1967.

13. In 1984, the Parti Québécois was in power in Quebec City; it had lost its referendum on sovereignty in 1980, and had seen Pierre Elliott Trudeau patriate the Canadian constitution without Quebec government's support or approval, in 1981–2. Federal Progressive Conservative leader Brian Mulroney's electoral platform partly rested on the commitment to 'bring Quebec back [into the Constitutional agreement] with honour and enthusiasm'; he was elected, and PQ leader René Lévesque accepted this held-out hand, against the will of hard-core sovereigntists, and portrayed this avenue as a *beau risque*—an 'attractive risk'.

14. The project, in the pipeline for a while, was delayed due to the contentious question of the role Quebec was to play in the organization. The French government would not launch a forum without another major power on board—Canada—which was virtually impossible as long as Quebec was not recognized in some form of autonomous membership.

15. Luc Bernier, 'Mulroney's International Beau Risque: The Golden Age of Quebec's Foreign Policy', in Nelson Michaud and Kim Richard Nossal, eds, *Diplomatic Departures: The Conservative Era in Canadian Foreign Policy, 1984–1993.* (Vancouver: University of British Columbia Press, 2001), 128–41.

16. Government of Quebec, *Le Quebec dans le monde—Le défi de l'interdépendance : énoncé de politique de relations internationales*, Second quarter, 1985, 2.

17. Loi sur le ministère des Affaires internationales, LRQ, c. M-21.1.

18. Government of Quebec, (Ministère des affaires internationales), *Le Quebec et l'interdépendance, le monde pour horizon : Éléments d'une politique d'affaires internationales*, 1991.

19. Government of Quebec (Ministère des Relations inter-nationales), *Le Quebec dans un ensemble international en mutation: Plan stratégique 2001–2004*, 2001.
20. The federal government is no longer seen as a rival or an obstacle to Quebec's international activities, but as a 'partner' (p. 138). As such, Quebec 'has to take into account the orientations and the considerable means of actions of the federal government' (p. 51).
21. RSQ Chapter A-6.01, sanctioned on 30 May 2000. Along with the paradigm in managing by result, performance, transparency, and imputability, this act now requires that all ministers and organisms produce an annual report and a three-year strategic plan. See www.assnat.qc.ca/fra/Assemblee/reforme/loi-administration.pdf, consulted 2 May 2005.
22. Government of Quebec, *Le Quebec dans un ensemble international*, 30.
23. Ibid.
24. Nelson Michaud and Isabelle Ramet, 'Quebec and foreign policy: contradiction or reality?', *International Journal* 59 (Spring 2004): 303–24. The authors highlight three features of this policy: an oriented action, a sufficient allocation of resources, and an influence on the inter-national context.
25. Loi modifiant la loi sur le Ministère des Relations internationales et d'autres dispositions législatives. Adopted 9 May 2002, available at www2.

publicationsduquebec.gouv.qc.ca/dynamicSearch/telecharge.php?type=5&file=2002C8F.PDF.
26. See www.premier.gouv.qc.ca/general/discours/archives_discours/2004/fevrier/dis20040225.htm.
27. I have analyzed this policy in an op-ed article, 'Une politique innovante', *Le Soleil*, 25 May 2006, 27.
28. Government of Quebec, Ministère des Relations inter-nationales, *Plan d'action 2006–2009*, 2006, available at www.mri.gouv.qc.ca/en/pdf/plan_action.pdf.
29. Ibid., 7.
30. Government of Quebec, Ministère des Relations interna-tionales, *Plan d'action 2009–2014*, 2009, available at www.mri.gouv.qc.ca/fr/pdf/plan_action.pdf.
31. Gouvernement of Quebec, Ministère des Relations inter-nationales, *La politique internationale du Quebec : la force de l'action concertée*, 2006, 81, available at www.mri.gouv.qc.ca/fr/pdf/Politique.pdf.
32. Ibid. 94.
33. Ibid, 65–77. For a more complete analysis of this unusual aspect, see Nelson Michaud, 'La politique internationale du Quebec et les questions de sécurité: davantage qu'une réponse à la mode' *Policy Options* 22, 6 (July/August, 2006): 59–62.
34. Ibid., 67–75.
35. Ibid., 1.
36. Ibid., 27.
37. Ibid., 6.

RELEVANT WEBSITES

MINISTÈRE DES RELATIONS INTERNATIONALES DU QUEBEC: www.mri.gouv.qc.ca

MINISTÈRE DE L'ÉDUCATION DU QUEBEC: www.mels.gouv.qc.ca

MINISTÈRE DE LA CULTURE DU QUEBEC: www.mcccf.gouv.qc.ca

QUEBEC'S INTERNATIONAL RELATIONS: www.etatquebecois.enap.ca/docs/pp/relations-internationales.pdf
A comparative reading (in French).

DIVERSITY OF CULTURAL EXPRESSIONS: http://portal.unesco.org/culture/en/ev.php-URL_ID=11281&URL_DO=DO_TOPIC&URL_SECTION=201.html

AGREEMENT ON UNESCO: www.mri.gouv.qc.ca/fr/pdf/unesco.pdf

ORGANISATION INTERNATIONAL DE LA FRANCOPHONIE: www.francophonie.org

IMPACT OF GLOBALIZATION ON FEDERATED ENTITIES' PUBLIC POLICIES: www.leppm.enap.ca

SELECT BIBLIOGRAPHY

This bibliography is not exhaustive. It provides an overview of key texts to be read by someone who wishes to know more about Quebec's inter-national relations.

Government documents

Bergeron, Marcel. *Évaluation du réseau de représentations du Quebec à l'étranger. Rapport synthèse présenté au ministre des Affaires internationales.* Quebec: Ministère des Affaires internationales, 1989.

Gouvernement du Quebec. *La politique internationale du Quebec : la force de l'action concertée*. Quebec: Ministère des Relations internationales, 2006.

———. *La politique internationale du Quebec : plan d'action*. Quebec: Ministère des Relations internationales, 2006.

———. *Le Quebec dans le monde : le défi de l'interdépendance. Énoncé de relations internationales*. Quebec: Ministères des Affaires internationales, 1985.

———. *Le Quebec dans un ensemble international en mutation : Plan stratégique 2001–2004*. Quebec: Ministère des Relations internationales, 2001.

———. *Le Quebec et l'interdépendance : le monde pour horizon. Éléments d'une politique d'affaires internationales*. Quebec: Les Publications du Quebec, 1991.

———. *Plan d'action 2009–2014*. Quebec: Ministère des Relations internationales, 2009.

Biographies and Autobiographies of Some Key Actors

(does not include biographies of Quebec premiers, which can also be of interest)

Aird, Robert. *André Patry et la présence du Quebec dans le monde*. Montreal: VLB éditeur, 2005.

Cardinal, Mario. *Paul Gérin-Lajoie : L'homme qui voulait changer le monde*. Montreal: Libre expression, 2007.

Décary, Jean. *Dans l'œil du Sphinx : Claude Morin et les relations internationales du Quebec*. Montreal: VLB éditeur, 2005.

Gérin-Lajoie, Paul. *Combats d'un révolutionnaire tranquille*. Montreal: Centre éducatif et culturel, 1990.

Martin, Paul Sr. *A Very Public Life: So Many Worlds*. Toronto: Deneau, 1985, Chapter 18.

Morin, Claude. *L'art de l'impossible : la diplomatie québécoise depuis 1960*. Montreal: Boréal, 1987.

General Studies

Balthazar, Louis, and Alfred O. Hero Jr. *Le Quebec dans l'espace américain*. Montreal: Quebec-Amérique, 1999.

———, Louis Bélanger, and Gordon Mace. *Trente ans de politique extérieure du Quebec 1960–1990*. Sillery: Septentrion and CQRI, 1993.

Bastien, Frédéric. *Relations particulières : La France au Quebec après De Gaulle*. Montreal: Boréal, 1999.

Bélanger, Louis, Guy Gosselin, and Gérard Hervouet. 'Les relations internationales du Quebec : Efforts de définition d'un nouvel objet d'étude', *Revue québécoise de science politique* 23 (1993): 143–70.

Bernier, Luc. *De Paris à Washington : la politique internationale du Quebec*. Quebec: Presses de l'Université du Quebec, 1997.

———. 'Mulroney's International Beau Risque: The Golden Age of Quebec's Foreign Policy'. In Nelson Michaud and Kim Richard Nossal, ed. *Diplomatic Departures: The Conservative Era in Canadian Foreign Policy 1984–1993*. Vancouver: University of British Columbia Press, 2001, 128–41.

Bonin, Bernard. *Economic Factors in Quebec's Foreign Policy*. Research Paper 8201. Montreal: HEC-Cetai, 1982.

Cloutier, Jean. 'Le Quebec à l'étranger', *L'Action nationale* 85, 8 (1985): 187–237.

Comeau, Paul-André, and Jean-Pierre Fournier. *Le Lobby du Quebec à Paris : les précurseurs du général De Gaulle*. Montreal: Quebec-Amériques, 2002.

Dehousse, Renaud. 'Fédéralisme, asymétrie et interdépendance : Aux origines de l'action international des composantes de l'État', *Études internationales* 20, (1989): 283–309.

———. *Fédéralisme et relations internationales : une réflexion comparative*. Brussels: Bruylant, 1991.

Duchacek, Ivo D., Daniel Latouche, and Garth Stevenson, eds. *Perforated Sovereignties and International Relations*. New York: Greenwood, 1988.

Fry, Earl. 'Quebec Confronts Globalization: A Model for the Future?', *Quebec Studies* 30 (2000): 57–69.

———. 'Quebec's Relations with the United States', *The American Review of Canadian Studies* 32, 2 (2002): 323–42.

Gervais, Myriam. 'La politique africaine du Quebec de 1960 à 1984', *Politique*, 7 (1985): 53–66.

Hamelin, Jean. 'Quebec et le monde extérieur: 1867–1967'. In *Anuaire du Quebec*. Quebec: Bureau de la statistique du Quebec, 1969, 2–36.

Jockel, Joseph T. 'Quebec's External Relations', *The American Review of Canadian Studies* 32, 2 (2002 Special Issue).

LeDuc, François, and Marcel Cloutier. *Guide de la pratique des relations internationales du Quebec*. Quebec: Ministère des relations internationales, 2000.

Legaré, Anne. *Le Quebec otage de ses allies : les relations du Quebec avec la France et les États-Unis*. Montreal: VLB éditeur, 2003.

Lisée, Jean-François. *Dans l'œil de l'aigle : Washington face au Quebec*. Montreal: Boréal, 1990.

Malone, Christopher. 'La politique québécoise en matière de relations internationales : changements et continuité'. Master's thesis, Université d'Ottawa, 1974.

Michaud, Nelson. 'Canada and Quebec on the World Scene: Defining New Rules?' In Andrew F. Cooper and Dane Rowlands, eds. *Canada Among Nations 2006*. Montreal and Kingston: McGill-Queen's University Press, 2006, 232–47.

———. 'La politique internationale du Quebec et les questions de sécurité: davantage qu'une réponse à la mode' *Policy Options* 22, 6 (July/August, 2006): 59–62.

————. *Le Quebec et l'intégration continentale : les stratégies d'un acteur fédéré.* Working Paper 9. Kingston: Queen's University Institute of Intergovernmental Relations, 2003.

————. 'Quebec and North American Integration: Making Room for a Sub-National Actor?' In J. Peter Meekison, Hamish Telford, and Harvey Lazar, eds.*Canada: The State of the Federation 2002—Reconsidering the Institutions of Canadian Federalism.* Montreal and Kingston: McGill-Queen's University Press, 2004, 377–410.

————, and Isabelle Ramet. 'Quebec and Foreign Policy: Contradiction or Reality?' *International Journal* 59 (Spring 2004): 303–24.

Noda, Shiro. *Entre l'indépendance et le fédéralisme : la décennie marquante des relations internationales du Quebec (1970–1980).* Quebec : Presses de l'Université Laval, 2001.

Nossal, Kim Richard. 'An Ambassador by any Other Name? Provincial Representatives Abroad'. In Robert Wolfe, ed. *Diplomatic Missions: The Ambassador in Canadian Foreign Policy.* Kingston: Queen's University School of Policy Studies, 1998.

Observatoire de l'administration publique, Nelson Michaud, and Marc Boucher. 2006. *Les relations internationales du Quebec comparées.* Available at: www.etatquebecois.enap.ca/etatquebecois/docs/pp/relations-internationales/a-relations-internationales.pdf.

Painchaud, Paul, ed. *Le Canada et le Quebec sur la scène internationale.* Quebec: Presses de l'Université Laval, 1977.

————. 'L'État du Quebec et le système international'. In Gérard Bergeron and Réjean Pelletier, eds. *L'État du Quebec en devenir.* Montreal: Boréal, 1980.

Paquin, Stéphane. *La revanche des petites nations. Le Quebec, l'Écosse et la Catalogne face à la mondialisation.* Montreal: VLB éditeur, 2001.

————, ed. 'Les nouvelles relations internationales : le Quebec en comparaison'. *Bulletin d'histoire politique* 10, 1 (2001Special Issue).

————. *Les relations internationales du Quebec depuis la Doctrine Gérin-Lajoie 1965–2005.* Quebec: Presses de l'Université Laval, 2006.

————, and Louise Beaudoin, eds. *Histoire des relations internationales du Quebec depuis la Révolution tranquille.* Montreal: VLB éditeur, 2006.

Patry, André. *Le Quebec dans le monde. 1960–1980.* Montreal: Éditions Typo, 2006.

Sabourin, Louis. *Canadian Federalism and International Organizations: A Focus on Quebec.* PhD Dissertation. New York: Columbia University, 1971.

————. 'Les relations internationales du Canada et du Quebec par les textes'. In Marie-Françoise Labouz, ed. *Intégrations et identités nord-américaines vues de Montréal.* Brussels: Bruylant, 2001, 157–85.

Thompson, Dale C. *De Gaulle et le Quebec.* Saint-Laurent: Trécarré, 1990.

CHAPTER 26

Quebec and La Francophonie: Quebec between Provincialism and Globalization

Jody Neathery-Castro and Mark Rousseau, University of Nebraska-Omaha

— TIMELINE —

1880 French geographer Onésime Reclus coins *Francophonie* to denote all peoples and countries using French.

1950 UIJPLF (International Union of French-language Journalists and Press) initiated by Quebec journalist Émile-Dostaler O'Leary.

1961 AUPELF (Association of Partially or Wholly French-language Universities) founded in Montreal, on initiative of Quebec activist and journalist Jean-Marc Léger; now called AUF (University Agency of la Francophonie), it is headquartered in Montreal.

1970 During conference in Niamey, Niger, Canada helps found first intergovernmental body of Francophonie: ACCT (Agency for Cultural and Technical Cooperation). Jean-Marc Léger becomes its first Secretary-General, a title sub-sequently held by another Quebecer, Jean-Louis Roy, from 1990 to 1997.

1971 Governments of Canada and Quebec agree on terms and conditions for Quebec's participation in institutions, programs, and activities of ACCT and with New Brunswick in 1977. They are recognized as participating governments (along with Canadian government) within the OIF.

1979 AIMF (International Association of Francophone Mayors) created to serve as Francophonie's urban development wing.

1984 Europeans launch TV5, a global French-language television network. In 1986, CTQC (Consortium de télévision Québec-Canada) created in Canada to provide European channel with Canadian programming.

1987 Second Summit of la Francophonie held in Quebec City, institutionalizing perma-nent process of consultation on important international issues. Proposal for Francophonie Games launched at summit. The Games adopt an original formula, combining sports and cul-tural events.

1988 IEPF (Francophonie Energy and Environment Institute) founded. Based in Quebec City, this subsidiary body of OIF helps develop national capacities and partnerships in energy and environmental sectors.

1997 Quebec hosts the first Conference of Francophonie Ministers responsible for Information Highway. Ministers gather in Montreal to discuss future of French on the Internet; in 1998, Francophone Information Highway Fund created to finance French efforts.

1997 Seventh Francophonie Summit held in Hanoi, Vietnam; election of first Secretary-General, Boutros Boutros-Ghali, spokesperson and official representative of La Francophonie internationally. Decision made to focus efforts on peace and prevention of conflicts in member countries, and to co-operate with international community in protecting human rights.

1999 Eighth Francophonie Summit held in Moncton, New Brunswick. Its final declaration marks milestone in evolution of La Francophonie, as greater emphasis is placed on peace and security, protection of civilian populations, and human rights. Information highway theme, addressed at Cotonou Summit, becomes priority in Moncton.

2000 Bamako Declaration, policy document created at symposium in Bamako, Mali, enables Francophonie to respond to crisis situations, breakdowns in democracy, and human rights violations. This Declaration, a legacy of Moncton Summit, places Francophonie at forefront of international and regional organizations working in support of democracy, rights, and freedoms.

2002 Ninth Francophonie Summit held in Beirut, Lebanon. Abdou Diouf, former President of Senegal, succeeds Boutros Boutros-Ghali as Secretary General. Role of culture as instrument of peace, democracy, and human rights reaffirmed.

2004 Tenth Francophonie Summit held in Ouagadougou, Burkina Faso, with theme 'Francophonie, showing solidarity toward sustainable development'. Ten-year strategic framework adopted, defining La Francophonie's objectives and means to influence international affairs.

2008 Ministerial Conference of La Francophonie and Twelfth Francophonie Summit held in Quebec City focuses on four issues: democracy and rule of law, economic governance, environment, and French language.

Source: Adapted from Foreign Affairs and International Trade Canada, 'Canada in la Francophonie,' www.international.gc.ca/franco/evolution.aspx.

From the standpoint of a student in the United States, the number and degree of foreign policy activities carried out by the provincial government of Quebec are quite extraordinary. In fact, Quebec is one of the most politically powerful sub-national units of government in the world, having extensive and varied international relations.[1] L'Organisation Internationale de la Francophonie (abbreviated OIF, or La Francophonie), for example, is the sole international organization to which Quebec belongs where it enjoys full autonomous participation as if it were a sovereign state, as a result of a legal understanding between Quebec and Canada.[2] Within the OIF Quebec represents itself; in other international organizations it is merely a participant observer under Canadian representation. Quebec's autonomous standing in OIF helps it promote Quebec culture and identity internationally.

Quebec has long pursued two prime policy goals: vigorous participation in the global economy and the preservation and promotion of French as the national language within Quebec. Elsewhere in this volume, Gagné and Fry point out that, as for many small nations, Quebec's economy depends heavily on international exports, particularly to the United States. At the same time, Quebec (metaphorically) remains a small French-speaking island within English-speaking North America. Its future as a French-speaking society is critical for economic opportunity and advancement for the 80 per cent of Quebecers whose native tongue is French. Because economy and culture mutually influence one another in varied ways, Quebec faces the paradox that its active global economic participation can challenge the maintenance of French within Quebec. As we shall see, OIF participation helps Quebec achieve both of these policy goals by providing a forum and pooled funds for addressing common international policy goals while promoting the French language among the member countries and internationally.

This chapter addresses one central question: How does Francophonie serve Quebec's foreign policy interests, economic development goals, and the maintenance of the French language? To answer this question, we will examine how and why La Francophonie developed, how it helps Quebec preserve its language and culture, how it supports Quebec's economic goals, and how it promotes Quebec's interest in cultural diversity.

HOW AND WHY DID LA FRANCOPHONIE DEVELOP?

L'Organisation internationale de la Francophonie (OIF) is an international organization comprising francophone or French-speaking member states and governments, which aims to enhance the political, economic, and cultural standing of the French language internationally. Francophone meetings, conferences, and associations proliferated in the wake of the Second World War and global independence movements. France and Quebec were key instigators of the growing alliance among francophone countries. France had suffered traumatic defeat in 1940 and subsequent division and humiliation during the war; its prestige was further diminished in global independence movements (particularly the conflicts in Vietnam and Algeria). French elites feared that a decline in the instrumental value of their language would mean economic loss.[3] Similarly, the Quebec Quiet Revolution originated as Quebec nationalism led by francophones who 'sensed their relative powerlessness in English-speaking North America; they observed a relative decline in population; they feared an influx of immigrants preferring to learn English; and they realized Anglophones controlled the mass media of communication, thus setting the agenda for problem-solving'.[4] Ultimately, elites in French-speaking countries sensed their minority status within states and led the movement which would become Francophonie.[5]

The first francophone organizations evolved out of intergovernmental bodies promoted by the colonial

ties between France and Africa, but many elites from Quebec were prominent in their development. In 1950, Quebecer Émile-Dostaler O'Leary founded Union internationale des journalistes et de la presse de langue française (International Union of French-language Journalists and Press—UIJPLF) to advance co-operation among the francophone media of the world. In 2001 the organization was renamed Union internationale de la presse francophone (Union of the Francophone Press—UPF). O'Leary served as president of the UPF from 1950–5, which eventually morphed from a convention of French-speaking journalists into a professional union.

Association des universités partiellement ou entièrement de langue française (Association of Partially or Entirely French-Speaking Universities—AUPELF) was established at Université de Montréal in 1961 to develop co-operative programs to support international research and education at institutions using French (see Biography box). At the 1989 OIF Dakar summit it was renamed Agence universitaire de la Francophonie (University Agency of Francophonie—AUF), and today is responsible for linking 692 educational establishments in 81 countries. With an annual budget of more than US$56 million, every year it provides over 200 grants to qualifying projects.

In spite of increased international francophone co-operation, tensions between France and Canada flared in 1967 during French President Charles de Gaulle's triumphant visit to Quebec to pay a visit to Expo 67. In remarks to a crowd of Quebecers at Montreal's city hall de Gaulle shouted, '*Vive le Quebec libre*' ('long live an independent Quebec'), energizing Quebec's separatists. This direct challenge to Canadian sovereignty was ill-received by the Canadian government and most anglophone Canadians.

Tension between Canada and Quebec was heightened several years later in efforts to develop an international francophone organization, l'Agence de cooperation culturelle et technique (Agency for Cultural and Technical Cooperation—ACCT). In 1966 the descendant organization of the colonial French community, OCAM,[6] began to plan a 32-country meeting to take place in 1969 in Niamey, Niger, to establish a multilateral aid organization. At the initial organizing conferences in 1969 and 1970 the question immediately arose of Canadian and Quebec membership. France wanted to exclude Canada from the planned organization, reserving membership solely for Quebec. Canada naturally opposed this proposal, arguing that membership should be open only to countries, not to governments, and that Quebec would participate as a member of the Canadian delegation. France lobbied hard, directly and indirectly, during and after the Niamey conferences for independent membership for Quebec as a French-speaking government. Canada eventually agreed, much to the satisfaction of Quebec, which assumed membership in an international organization for the first time. The signatories thus included 23 countries plus two associated states and one 'participating government' (a special category created for Quebec). The 20 March 1970 official founding is now commemorated annually as the Journée internationale de la Francophonie (International Day of Francophonie).[7]

The issue of Quebec's standing in La Francophonie continued to fester for some years, with Canada insisting on a veto over Quebec's actions if necessary. Only with the departure of Canadian Prime Minister Pierre Trudeau from the political scene were Quebec's and New Brunswick's governmental standing in La Francophonie fully accepted and regularized by Ottawa. These early Canada–Quebec disagreements over Quebec's standing in ACCT presaged later battles over such matters as budget and competences in the new organization. In an interesting twist, France nominated Jean-Marc Léger, a Quebec nationalist and francophone internationalist, as the first head of ACCT, which would be headquartered in Paris. After some doubts Canada acceded, believing Léger to be an honest and trustworthy Canadian as well as a Quebecer.

The organizational structure of what is now known as the OIF or La Francophonie has continued to evolve to reflect its increasing interests. Currently the OIF comprises 56 member states and governments and 14 observer states all having in common the use of the French language. While Canada is an autonomous member, so are its provincial governments of Quebec and New Brunswick. Other members include industrial democracies like France and Belgium, as well as some of the world's poorest and most questionable democracies. In 1986, French President François Mitterrand

initiated the first summit of heads of member nations of the OIF and biennial summits have generally been held ever since. Policy goals and initiatives of the OIF are determined at these biennial summits. While the founding purpose of the OIF was to engage in actions supporting the development and spread of the French language and cultures, its scope of action has expanded in recent years. Under the active leadership of the first two Secretaries-General (Boutros Boutros-Ghali, 1997–2002, and Abdou Diouf, 2002–9), the OIF has developed an agenda to exercise influence in international affairs and tackle some of the challenges of globalization. In particular, the OIF has identified four objectives to pursue in areas where its experience and know-how have already proved their worth:

- promoting the French language and cultural and linguistic diversity;
- promoting peace, democracy, and human rights;
- supporting education, training, higher education, and research; and
- developing co-operation for sustainable development and solidarity.[8]

In supporting the efforts of the OIF and its components, Quebec favours the issues crucial for the development of member countries: the promotion of the French language, the international protection of cultural diversity, and the affirmation of democratic principles and human rights. The OIF plays an increasingly important role in defending French culture and language globally and in advancing the particular political and economic interests of francophone nations, particularly France and Canada. Quebec has been a major participant in the OIF from the beginning and benefits from OIF's strengthening of French language, culture, and economic interests globally. For Quebec, OIF is its most important and prominent world arena of participation.

How Does La Francophonie Help Quebec Preserve its Language and Culture?

As the unique French-speaking province in Canada, Quebec has long had two dominant, somewhat contradictory goals: participating actively in the global economy and protecting and deepening its French language and cultural heritage. Growing international trade in the global economy increases economic interdependence between nations. Thus, Quebec's active participation in and dependence on the global economy challenges its culture. English has become the primary second language in many nations around the world, diminishing the traditional role of French. Rules of the World Trade Organization (WTO), the regime that regulates international trade, hinder Quebec's ability to subsidize its cultural industries, a practice followed in nearly all non-English speaking nations, as well as a number of anglophone nations. As referenced by Lubin, Weinstock, and Cardinal in this volume, some 80 per cent of Quebec's citizens are native French speakers, and the Quebec government has long been committed to maintaining French as the official language of Quebec. The Quebec government plays an active and decisive role in preserving and promoting the use of French in Quebec as well as internationally. While francophones are a majority in Quebec, they make up only 2 per cent of the North American population. Thus Quebec is an island of French speakers surrounded by an English-language North America, challenging Quebec's ability to maintain French as its national language.

While the Quebec government fosters the maintenance of French within Quebec, it also acknowledges the fragility of the language's position. The government asserts that maintaining the French language is one of its fundamental preoccupations. Participation in the OIF gives Quebec significant support in its efforts to promote French within the province as well as internationally.

Quebec and its partners in the OIF have for many years led the demand for the 'cultural exception' in international trade. France, Quebec, and Canada, with the backing of the OIF, argue that culture and cultural goods are unique commodities, unlike steel, personal computers, or cellphones, and should not be subject to the rules of the WTO trade regime. OIF believes cultural goods represent an aspect of a nation's cultural identity and heritage and that various arts industries (such as publishing, film, and music,) need protection in the form of government subsidies to support them

from foreign invaders, especially the encroachment of Hollywood on the worldwide film industry.[9] While the cultural exception in trade has remained central to OIF, it has more recently addressed these concerns under the more inclusive concept 'cultural diversity', which espouses a state's right and need to promote and subsidize its own cultural industries. This right applies not only to French-speaking nations but also to other language nationalities such as Spanish, Portuguese, and Arabic. While withstanding the dominance of English is a daunting task, Francophonie's expansion of its pro-French stance to one of 'plurilingualism'[10] has boosted its international appeal to even non-French speakers.[11]

HOW DOES LA FRANCOPHONIE SUPPORT QUEBEC'S ECONOMIC GOALS?

While defending the French language and culture remains a fundamental preoccupation for Quebec, active participation in the global economy is both a major desire and a necessity. Uniquely the OIF enhances both of these goals. The OIF allows Quebec to develop its trade, particularly with developing countries in francophone Africa, while demanding pluralism in trade rules and the language of exchange. As Quebec's government acknowledges, 'International trade plays a vital role in Quebec's economy and in creating greater wealth for society as a whole.'[12] Like that of most small nations, Quebec's economy is highly dependent on exports. Today exports make up some 53 per cent of Quebec's gross domestic product (GDP). While raw materials (forest products, paper, mining, and the like) remain important, diversified advanced industries make an increasingly important contribution. Supported by a high level of research and development activity, Quebec enjoys growing economic production in such advanced sectors of the economy as information technologies, biotechnologies, pharmaceuticals, aerospace, and genomics.[13]

Quebec was an early and staunch supporter of the United States–Canada Free Trade Agreement (FTA) and its successor, the North American Free Trade Agreement (NAFTA).[14] The Quebec government, however, believes that when English serves as the exclusive language of international trade, English-speaking nations have an advantage over non-English-speaking nations. First, businesspeople of non-anglophone nations are obliged to negotiate in a language other than their own. Second, non-anglophone nations must support and finance English language training, expending funds that English-language nations can invest directly in endeavours like information technologies and science research. As a result, tangible economic advantage accrues to anglophones when English serves as the lingua franca of the WTO and related trade bodies. Quebec believes that non-anglophone nations should push for guaranteed official status in the WTO for all four major New World trade–area languages (Spanish, English, Portuguese, and French).

Louise Beaudoin, Quebec's Minister of International Relations (1991–2003), suggests that Quebec, like many modern nations, finds itself caught between two contrasting goals: 'The normal desire of a people to commit itself to globalization and to share in the prosperity of the world around it; the other is that same people's need to preserve an essential part of its personality, namely its cultural distinctiveness, its soul, its unique relationship to the world.'[15] While Quebec has been a strong supporter of trade liberalization, like many other non-English speaking nations it struggles to maintain its own language and culture. Beaudoin observes, 'Our support for trade liberalization is however, not blind and unconditional . . . . Essentially the Quebec government believes that, if care is not taken, the general process of globalization and trade liberalization can threaten the abilities of countries and governments to take measures to support culture and cultural diversity. We attach paramount importance to the protection and promotion of culture. Globalization must not deprive countries and governments of all flexibility.'[16] This stance is consistent with the Quebec government's position paper on international policy *Quebec's International Policy—Working in Concert* (2006), which seeks to reinforce and strengthen Quebec's international influence and action.

Within the OIF there exists a major divide between the well-developed, wealthy nations of France and Canada and the relatively undeveloped and poor nations of francophone Africa. The combined GDP of France and Canada equals about 80 per cent that of all the Southern Hemisphere nations in the OIF.[17] OIF's emphasis on economic development thus has strong appeal for the poorer, less-developed nations in the OIF. The OIF has taken an active role in providing technical assistance to its less-developed members, a task in which Canada, Quebec, and France particularly participate. Power in the OIF is heavily concentrated in France and Canada/Quebec, as they provide the bulk of finances for the organization.

With the exception of its participation in La Francophonie, the government of Quebec is not a major provider of developmental aid. It prioritizes its efforts in the areas of its expertise: human resources development and governance capacity-building programs. Quebec has signalled its intent to devote its energies to helping a limited number of countries, with those belonging to La Francophonie among its top priorities. Haiti provides an interesting case study, where most of Quebec's monetary aid is channelled through Francophonie, but the effort is multifaceted:[18]

- Some 75 Quebec police officers participate in the UN stabilization mission in Haiti.
- Hydro-Québec supplies technical support for the production, transportation, and transmission of electricity in certain regions.
- With the École nationale d'administration publique (ENAP), the government of Quebec is preparing a project to support the modernization of the Haitian government, in collaboration with the Canadian International Development Agency (CIDA).
- Since 1997, Quebec has contributed more than Can$11 million in humanitarian aid and in grants for development projects in Haiti.[19]

Language and cultural ties propel Quebec's active economic and cultural participation in the OIF. At the same time Quebec's participation in the global economy raises challenges for French language maintenance and cultural development within Quebec. For economic advancement and upward social mobility, Quebec's largely French-speaking working class needs a Quebec economy that functions in French. At the same time the French-speaking middle classes (including journalists, academics, writers, and the like) produce French-language cultural products that require a French-speaking audience. Thus the maintenance of French as the national language has broad support. Quebec's leadership across political parties remains committed to French language protection.[20] For example, Minister of International Relations Louise Beaudoin stated that, 'Support for Bill 101 is a bipartisan consensus—the PQ and PLQ agree French must be maintained as the national language. There is support for French as the language of the workplace and economic success.'[21] Quebec's membership in OIF adds legitimacy to these concerns.

During the Quiet Revolution and following, as Quebec built a modern urban, industrial economy, the standing of French in the workplace took on increasing importance for both the largely French-speaking working class and the middle-class culture producers; the language of business had been less important in Quebec's earlier rural, agricultural economy. Quebec enacted a series of policies to make French the sole official language of the province and ensure its dominance. These efforts culminated in 1977 in the adoption of the Charter of the French Language (Bill 101) requiring the use of French in commerce, the workplace, government, education, and other areas of public life. Quebec's current policies ensure that French remains the national language, helping to maintain economic opportunity for the French-speaking working class and culture-producing, French-speaking middle class.

While Quebec participates vigorously in international trade in the increasingly global economy, some negative consequences result. For example, organized labour in Quebec strongly opposed NAFTA, seeing it as an assault on the Canadian economy by US multinational corporations.[22] In opposing NAFTA, organized labour argued the treaty would diminish Quebec's ability to develop its own cultural policies on language, advertising, and education—such policies would elicit accusations of erecting barriers to bilateral commerce. As subsequent events have shown, these concerns were reasonable. Further, a number of contemporary social analysts have suggested that globalization might more appropriately be labelled 'Americanization'. George Ritzer argues, 'There is no question that exportation of

the American means of consumption to the rest of the world involves a process of Americanization.'[23] French sociologist Pierre Bourdieu (1930–2002) argued that globalization is essentially imperialism by wealthy countries. He suggests that the ideology of neo-liberal economics is propagated under a cloak of modernization and neutrality such that globalization seems inevitable. He believed that while the United States is not the only economically imperialist country, it is in a uniquely powerful position to impose its views on much of the world.[24]

These concerns propel Quebec's active participation in the OIF, where it finds support for its desire to protect and enhance French language and culture. For these reasons Quebec was among the OIF member nations pushing hard for the adoption of the UNESCO treaty on the Convention on the Protection and Promotion of the Diversity of Cultural Expressions. Quebec's strong support for the treaty and its activities in OIF helped to achieve the overwhelming adoption of the treaty by UNESCO member nations.

How Does La Francophonie Support Quebec's Interest in Cultural Diversity?

Quebec sees protection of the French language and support for cultural diversity as complementary. While globalization has been widely promoted in recent years, it has also been criticized. Many point to the economic and social costs of international trade policies (particularly those promoted by the WTO) on citizens in developed and developing countries alike. Scholars have pointed to Francophonie as an organization poised to challenge what is often deemed 'Americanization'.[25]

Along with the federal government, with the backing of the cultural sector in many countries and the concerted efforts of La Francophonie, Quebec encouraged the negotiation of the international Convention on the Protection and Promotion of the Diversity of Cultural Expressions under the auspices of UNESCO. The issue of cultural diversity was one where 'Quebec showed its capacity to exert influence on the international scene.'[26] By working with experts from civil society, academia, the OIF, and the federal government, Quebec was instrumental in UNESCO's 2005 adoption of the Convention.[27]

Countries had begun trying to minimize the WTO's impact on their policy options soon after the creation of the WTO in 1994. In June 1998, Canada's Minister of Heritage, Sheila Copps, invited culture ministers from 19 other countries to Ottawa to resume a dialogue begun two months earlier at the UNESCO Intergovernmental Conference on Cultural Policies for Development. The result was the International Network on Cultural Policy (INCP), an informal network of ministers of culture who agreed to establish a loose but ongoing association to pursue common concerns involving cultural policy.[28] The INCP has held annual meetings since 1998 and its membership has grown from fewer than 20 countries in 1998 to 69 in 2009 (over one-third of these are either members or observers of the Francophonie). Within the INCP, the Working Group on Cultural Diversity and Globalization, chaired by Canada, and comprising government ministers and advisors from member nations, share proposals and advice on policy to promote cultural diversity, both nationally and internationally. The INCP drafted a cultural diversity statement in 2001, which was endorsed by the member ministers of culture and passed on to UNESCO, which used it as the basis for its 2005 Convention.

Similarly, the International Network for Cultural Diversity (INCD) is an international NGO organized in 1998 by the Canadian Ministry of Heritage to 'complement the efforts of the INCP by acting as an umbrella group for individual artists, cultural activists, and cultural NGOs from different countries'.[29]

Conferences of OIF professionals were also convened between 1999 and 2001 to discuss and promote a New International Instrument on Cultural Diversity (NIICD). In the Final Declaration of its Beirut Summit in 2002, the OIF became the first international governmental organization to support the adoption of such an instrument. The contributions of Francophonie to the UNESCO Convention were one of the main achievements of the OIF and demonstrated the increasing political dimension of the organization.[30] Recent OIF Summits have regularly confirmed OIF's desire not to let cultural goods and services be reduced to the status of ordinary commodities. Member states affirm their sovereign rights to define freely their cultural policies and to wield the tools with which to do so.[31]

WHAT CAN WE CONCLUDE ABOUT QUEBEC AND LA FRANCOPHONIE?

Quebec's membership in L'Organisation internationale de la Francophonie has facilitated its seemingly contradictory goals: to be connected to the global economy and to preserve its cultural heritage and French language. It is through La Francophonie that Quebec most skilfully asserts its priorities in a multinational setting. Quebec enjoys multiple benefits of its OIF participation. These include:

- international prestige deriving from its governmental status that puts it on par with the member states in OIF;
- an important environment in which to consolidate Quebec's influence in multilateral forums like the UN and the Organization of African Unity (OAU);
- strengthened alliances with the other member countries and governments; and
- mutually beneficial cultural, economic, and commercial exchanges, including entrée to emerging markets that play to Quebec's economic strength in the pharmaceutical, telecommunications, energy, and transportation sectors[32]

The OIF, along with other international organizations and countries,[33] has faced the uncertainty of globalization with unease and even hostility, particularly as elements of culture and language are threatened. However, in its strong leadership role within the OIF, Quebec has been instrumental in shaping the organization's increasingly political agenda. In particular, on cultural diversity Quebec has shown its capacity to shape international affairs. Working closely with Francophonie, international groups, and cultural and trade allies, Quebec played a key role in initiating the debate and moving the issue forward to its culmination in the adoption in 2005 of the UNESCO Convention on the Protection and Promotion of the Diversity of Cultural Expressions.[34]

The chapter in this volume by Nelson Michaud illustrates Quebec's growing international ambitions. In some ways the cultural diversity process might be viewed as a 'critical test case' of Quebec's international aspirations. While constrained within the Canadian federal framework from pursuing fully its own international agenda, Quebec has leveraged its leadership role within the OIF to expand its international authority. A Quebec government publication lists the following means that it believes will help it attain its ambitions for participating in international organizations:

1. 'Access to all information and participation during the initial stages of negotiations toward establishing Canada's position;
2. 'Full member status in Canadian delegations and exclusive responsibility for designating its representative;
3. 'The right to speak for itself at international forums on matters related to its responsibilities;
4. 'Recognition of Quebec's right to give its approval before Canada signs or declares itself bound by a treaty or agreement; and
5. 'The right to express its position when Canada appears before supervisory bodies of international organizations for matters involving Quebec or affecting its interests.'[35]

In 2008, Quebec hosted both the biennial OIF Summit (see Snapshot box) and a Canada–European Union summit to explore integrating Canada's economy with the EU. Both events are indicative of the expanding role in international affairs that Quebec is carving out for itself. Further, with its international ambitions and keen interest in cultural diversity, Quebec negotiated a historic agreement with the Canadian government in 2006,[36] to allow Quebec an official representative on Canada's Permanent Delegation to UNESCO, not just to observe, but to fully participate in all proceedings, and to confer with Canada on matters falling under provincial jurisdiction. Quebec's representative has diplomatic authority to express the opinion of the government of Quebec as distinct from that of Canada's government. In the event of disagreement with Canada, 'the Quebec government has the right not to implement conventions, action plans, and other international instruments determined by UNESCO.'[37] These extensive successes at the international level illustrate the contention with which we began this chapter: among sub-national governments, Quebec enjoys multiple international relations that could not be imagined by any state in the United States. L'Organisation internationale de la Francophonie has made it possible for Quebec to leverage its tremendous ambitions and capacities as it stretches its international wings.

JEAN-MARC LÉGER

Jean-Marc Léger, officer of the National Order of Quebec

Jean-Marc Léger, born in Quebec in 1927, has had an engaged and varied career working variously as a social theorist, a journalist, and a political activist. After attending the Institute for Political Studies in Paris he worked as a journalist for the Montreal newspapers *La Presse* and *Le Devoir*, the latter the leading intellectual and political paper of Quebec.

At the University of Montreal he helped found the Social Research Team that examined social, political,

and economic problems in Quebec preceding the Quiet Revolution. The research group argued that the style of nationalist politics developed by Quebec Premier Duplessis primarily benefited anglophone Canadian corporations who located in Quebec to exploit Quebec's low-wage francophone working class, retarding Quebec's own economic modernization. Through his writing and speaking, Léger was a major contributor to the Quiet Revolution, which resulted in the Quebec economy being increasingly owned by francophones and the emergence both of a francophone professional and managerial class and of a consciousness among Quebecers of their unique identity as French-language speakers in anglophone North America.

Carrying his activism into the international arena, Léger became a principal founder and first Secretary-General of the Montreal-based Association des universités partiellement ou entièrement de langue française (Association of French Language Universities) in 1961, one of the first and most important non-governmental international organizations of the Francophonie. He also helped found the Union internationale des journalistes et de la presse de langue française (International Association of French Language Journalists) earlier, in 1950. Building on this work, Léger, long an advocate of francophone unity, became a major founder and contributor to the creation of l'Agence de cooperation culturelle et technique (Agency for Cultural and Technical Cooperation— ACCT), the precursor of l'Organisation internationale de la Francophonie, becoming its first Secretary-General in 1970. The efforts of France in support of Quebec's membership in ACCT eventually resulted in full Francophonie membership for Quebec, as a

government representing itself, giving it greater recognition and prominence on the international stage.

Léger was appointed as the first director of Quebec's Office of the French Language, serving from 1961–3. He has also held a number of other government posts in his long, distinguished career, including Associate Deputy Minister of Quebec's Ministry of Education and Minister of International Affairs.

Léger has received numerous recognitions for his many contributions to La Francophonie, to the French language internationally, and to Quebec's development as a modern French-speaking nation. Chief among these awards was his elevation to the rank of Commander in France's Legion of Honour, emblematic of his work for French and La Francophonie on the global stage.

Léger remains a forceful voice for the concerns of French speakers both in Quebec and internationally. During the meetings of Quebec's Estates General on Language in 2000, Jean-Marc Léger testified that the French language is in a crisis and he called for a complete reworking of Bill 101 to make French not just the official language of Quebec, but the common everyday language of Quebec.

SNAPSHOT

Two Francophonie Summits in Quebec—1987 and 2008

Quebec has hosted two international Francophonie Summits, in 1987 and 2008. The two events, 21 years apart, illustrate the gradual evolution of the OIF from a strictly cultural organization to an international political and economic entity. Both summits also illustrate enduring challenges like the ongoing quarrels between the governments of Canada and Quebec and the claim that the organization turns a blind eye to human-rights violators among its own membership.

Forty-one OIF states and governments were eligible to participate in the 1987 Francophonie Summit, with Canadian Prime Minister Brian Mulroney

and Quebec Premier Robert Bourassa sharing the host's spotlight. The transition in the office of Prime Minister from Pierre Trudeau to Brian Mulroney was pivotal to the creation of the summit. France had refused to hold a summit in which Quebec was not a full partner, while Canada's Trudeau objected to treating a province as a 'half-country' and refused to put Quebec on a level footing with sovereign nations. As part of Mulroney's 'national reconciliation' and insistence on Quebec's right to 'direct and privileged' relations with France, Quebec was given the position as 'interlocutor' between Canada as a whole and the

French-speaking countries of the world. The understanding was that Quebec could have full participation at the summit on topics under provincial jurisdiction, but would remain as an 'interested observer' on issues under federal jurisdiction. At both the 1986 inaugural Summit in Paris and at the 1987 Summit, Quebec Premier Bourassa tested this arrangement by speaking publicly on international issues without the explicit imprimatur of the Prime Minister. In 1986 Bourassa held a press conference on international aid without first clearing it with the Prime Minister, while in 1987 he proposed tying Third World debt to commodity prices—an economic issue clearly under federal, not provincial, jurisdiction (although apparently this proposal had been conveyed to Prime Minister Mulroney in advance).

The 1987 Quebec City Francophonie Summit claimed several successes, notably the announcement of a new energy institute (IEPF) in Quebec dedicated to utilizing hydro-electricity to help solve Third World energy problems, the creation of the Francophone Games sports competition to be held every four years, the forgiving of seven African states' debts to Canada, as well as a variety of co-operative communications and cultural programs. Despite the positive claims of the 1987 meeting, controversies were also highlighted, including human rights protestors angry over Vietnam's inclusion at the Summit, as well as some concerns over the future of the organization voiced by the spiritual father of La Francophonie, Senegal's former president, Leopold Sedar Senghor. Senghor expressed concern that in the rush to emulate the Commonwealth's economic and technical approach to international assistance, the French language was at risk of becoming a mere industrialized tool for doing business.

The 2008 Francophonie Summit in Quebec included representatives from 55 member countries and 13 observer nations. While some of the agenda was overshadowed by concerns about the growing global economic crisis, a milestone on climate change was established, with Francophonie countries pledging to reduce greenhouse-gas emissions by 50 per cent by 2050 (with poor countries eligible for some $100 million in Canadian government aid make the transition).

Once again the 2008 Summit was plagued by charges of hypocrisy in its stated commitment to democracy and human rights. Amnesty International issued a report on the eve of the Summit deploring the state of human rights in the majority of the developing countries that make up the Francophonie and blaming the organization for not doing enough to address problems ranging from arbitrary arrest to political violence and torture. In an interview with reporters, Béatrice Vaugrante, director general of the Francophone Canadian branch of Amnesty International claimed, 'They must condemn them, suspend them, simply be much more strict.' A spokesperson maintained that Prime Minister Harper believed that leaders of these nations should not be isolated from the rest of the world if they are to be influenced by the organization's norms.

Breaking with France's traditional neutrality on the issue of Quebec sovereignty, French President Nicolas Sarkozy vocalized firm support for Canadian unity. 'If anyone tries to tell me that the world today needs an additional division, then they don't have the same read of the world as me,' Sarkozy said, with Canadian Prime Minister Harper by his side. 'I don't know why a fraternal, familial love of Quebec would have to be nourished through defiance toward Canada.' Leaving no room for nuanced interpretation, Sarkozy reinforced his repudiation of Quebec nationalism a few months later in Paris. When it was pointed out that he had just rejected the cornerstone of the French principle toward Quebec nationalism, the policy of 'non-interference, and non-indifference,' Sarkozy replied, 'It's not my thing.'

Questions for Consideration

1. How do Quebec's goals of preserving/enhancing French and actively trading in the global economy conflict? Does OIF membership benefit Quebec's achievement of either or both goals?

2. If you were making the decision for the government of Canada, what advantages and/or disadvantages would you perceive in allowing Quebec to participate as a member government in the OIF?

3. Does the French language constitute enough of a shared bond to facilitate international organizing? If not, on what grounds should such international co-operation be based? In your view, has La Francophonie emerged beyond a language-based organization on the international stage?

Notes

1. Daniel Latouche, 'Quebec and Canada: Scenarios for the Future', *Business in the Contemporary World* 3, 1 (1990), 58–70.
2. New Brunswick is the only other Canadian province to have this unique independent standing.
3. Brian Weinstein, 'Francophonie: A Language-Based Movement in World Politics', *International Organization* 30, 3 (1976), 487–8.
4. Weinstein, 'Francophonie: A Language-Based Movement', 488.
5. Ibid., 491–3.
6. Organisation Commune Africaine et Malgache.
7. Weinstein, 'Francophonie: A Language-Based Movement', 496–7.
8. Jody Neathery-Castro and Mark O. Rousseau, 'Quebec, Francophonie and Globalization', *Québec Studies* 32, (2002), 20.
9. Adapted from www.francophonie.org/actions/index.cfm.
10. The notion behind plurilingualism is that a single language (English) is not sufficient for international relations.
11. Jean-Benoît Nadeau and Julie Barlow, *The Story of French* (New York: St Martin's Press, 2006), 349–50.
12. Quebec Ministry of International Relations, *Québec's International Policy: Working in Concert* (Government of Quebec, 2006), 54, available at www.mri.gouv.qc.ca/en/pdf/Politique.pdf.
13. Quebec Ministry of International Relations, *Québec's International Policy*.
14. Please see Chapter 24.
15. Neathery-Castro and Rousseau, 'Quebec, Francophonie and Globalization', 23.
16. Ibid., 23–4.
17. Ibid., 17.
18. Quebec Ministry of International Relations, *Québec's International Policy*, 95–6.
19. Ibid.
20. Neathery-Castro and Rousseau, 'Quebec, Francophonie and Globalization', 25.
21. Louise Beaudoin, Remarks at the Association for Canadian Studies in the United States meetings, Pittsburgh, 18 November 1999.
22. Mark O. Rousseau, 'Ethnic Mobilization in Quebec, Federalism in Canada, and the Global Economy', *Research in Social Movements, Conflicts and Change* 21 (1999): 205–23.
23. George Ritzer, *Enchanting a Disenchanted World: Revolutionizing the Means of Consumption* (Thousand Oaks, California: Pine Forge Press, 2005), 45.
24. Pierre Bourdieu, *Acts of Resistance against the Tyranny of the Market* (New York: The New Press, 1998); and 'Uniting to Better Dominate', *Items and Issues* 2, 3–4 (2001): 1–6.
25. Weinstein, 'Francophonie: A Language-Based Movement', 485; Ritzer, *Enchanting a Disenchanted World*, 51.
26. Quebec Ministry of International Relations, *Québec's International Policy*, 27.
27. Ibid.
28. P.S. Grant and C. Wood, *Blockbusters and Trade Wars: Popular Culture in a Globalized World* (Vancouver, Douglas & McIntyre, 2004), 383.
29. Keith Acheson, and Christopher Maule, 'Convention on Cultural Diversity', *Journal of Cultural Economics* 28, 4 (2004), 246.
30. Jody Neathery-Castro and Mark O. Rousseau, 'Does French Matter? France and Francophonie in the Age of

Globalization', *The French Review* 78, 4 (2005): 678–95; Anne-Marie Laulan, 'La Diversité Culturelle à L'UNESCO', in Anne-Marie Laulan and Didier Oillo, eds., *Francophonie et Mondialisation* (Paris, CNRS Editions, 2004).

31. Organisation Internationale de la Francophonie, 2002

32. The OIF member states and governments together comprise Canada's fifth-largest trading partner, responsible for US$18 billion in 1998 (Ron Duhamel, 'Africa Direct Natural Resources and the 21st Century Economy: The Case for Stronger Canadian-African Collaboration', speech given in Calgary, Alberta, 8 May 2000).

33. Robert W. McChesney, 'Global Media, Neoliberalism and Imperialism', *Monthly Review* 52,10 (2001), 16.

34. Quebec Ministry of International Relations, *Québec's International Policy*, 27–9.

35. Ibid, 28.

36. The Conservative government of Stephen Harper followed through on its 2005 election campaign promise to give Quebec an increased international role and a UNESCO representative.

37. Quebec Ministry of International Relations, *Québec's International Policy*, 28.

RELEVANT WEBSITES

INTERNATIONAL ORGANIZATION OF FRANCOPHONIE: www.francophonie.org

UNESCO CONVENTION ON THE PROTECTION AND PROMOTION OF THE DIVERSITY OF CULTURAL EXPRESSIONS: http://portal.unesco.org/culture/

GOVERNMENT OF QUEBEC'S WEBSITE ON CULTURAL DIVERSITY: www.diversite-culturelle.qc.ca/

QUEBEC MINISTRY OF INTERNATIONAL RELATIONS INFORMATION ON FRANCOPHONIE: www.mri.gouv. qc.ca/en/relations_quebec/francophonie/index.asp

QUEBEC 2008 FRANCOPHONIE SUMMIT: www. francophoniequebec2008.qc.ca/en/

CANADA IN FRANCOPHONIE: www.international.gc.ca/ franco/index.aspx

CANADIAN INTERNATIONAL DEVELOPMENT AGENCY: www.acdi-cida.gc.ca/cidaweb/acdicida.nsf/En/Home

SELECT BIBLIOGRAPHY

Acheson, Keith, and Christopher Maule. 'Convention on Cultural Diversity', *Journal of Cultural Economics* 28, 4 (2004): 243–56.

Beaudoin, Louise. Remarks at the Association for Canadian Studies in the United States meetings. Pittsburgh, 18 November 1999.

Bernier, Ivan, 2001. *La préservation de la diversité linguistique à l'heure de la mondialisation.* Available at www.mcc.gouv.qc.ca/diversite-culturelle/pdf/diversite-linguistique.pdf.

Bourdieu, Pierre. *Acts of Resistance against the Tyranny of the Market.* New York: The New Press, 1998.

———. 'Uniting to Better Dominate', *Items and Issues* 2, 3–4 (2001): 1–6.

Duhamel, Ron. 'Africa Direct Natural Resources and the 21st Century Economy: The Case for Stronger Canadian-African Collaboration'. Speech given in Calgary, Alberta, 8 May 2000.

Durand, C. 'Les Menace de l'Espéranglais'. In T. Bambridge et al., eds. *Francophonie et Mondialisation.* Paris: CNRS Editions, 2004.

Farchy, Joëlle, and Heritiana Ranaivoson. 'La Diversité Culturelle, Soubassements Économiques et Volonté

Politique'. In Anne-Marie Laulan and Didier Oillo, eds. *Francophonie et Mondialisation.* Paris: CNRS Editions, 2004.

Grant, P.S., and C. Wood. *Blockbusters and Trade Wars: Popular Culture in a Globalized World.* Vancouver, Douglas & McIntyre, 2004.

Groupe de travail franco-québécois sur la diversité culturelle. *Évaluation de la Faisabilité Juridique d'un Instrument International sur la Diversité Culturelle.* 2002. Available at www.diversite-culturelle.qc.ca/fileadmin/documents/pdf/106145_faisabilite.pdf.

Latouche, Daniel. 'Quebec and Canada: Scenarios for the Future', *Business in the Contemporary World* 3, 1 (1990): 58–70.

Laulan, Anne-Marie. 'La Diversité Culturelle à L'UNESCO'. In Anne-Marie Laulan and Didier Oillo, eds. *Francophonie et Mondialisation.* Paris, CNRS Editions, 2004.

Léger, Jean-Marc. *La Francophonie : Grand Dessein, Grande Ambiguïté.* Montreal: Hurtubise, 1987.

———. 'Le Quebec et la Francophonie'. In Michel Plourde, Hélène Duval, and Pierre Georgeault, eds. *Le Français au Quebec, 400 ans d'histoire et de vie.* Quebec: Conseil Supérieur de la langue Française, 2007, 335–42.

McChesney, Robert W. 'Global Media, Neoliberalism and Imperialism', *Monthly Review* 52,10 (2001): 1–19.

Nadeau, Jean-Benoît, and Julie Barlow. *The Story of French.* New York: St Martin's Press, 2006.

Neathery-Castro, Jody, and Mark O. Rousseau. 'Quebec, Francophonie and Globalization', *Québec Studies* 32, (2001): 15–35.

———. 'Does French Matter? France and Francophonie in the Age of Globalization', *The French Review* 78, 4 (2005): 678–95.

Organisation Internationale de la Francophonie 2001. *Trois Espaces Linguistiques Face aux Défis de la Mondialisation.* Actes du Colloque International. Paris, 20–21 March 2001.

Quebec Ministry of International Relations. *Québec's International Policy: Working in Concert.* Government of Quebec, 2006. Available at www.mri.gouv.qc.ca/en/pdf/Politique.pdf.

Ritzer, George. *Enchanting a Disenchanted World: Revolutionizing the Means of Consumption.* Thousand Oaks, Calif.: Pine Forge Press, 2005.

Rousseau, Mark O. 'Ethnic Mobilization in Quebec, Federalism in Canada, and the Global Economy', *Research in Social Movements, Conflicts and Change* 21 (1999): 205–23.

Thérien, Jean-Phillipe. 'Cooperation and Conflict in la Francophonie', *International Journal* 48, (1993): 492–526.

UNESCO. *Universal Declaration on Cultural Diversity.* Paris, 2001.

Weinstein, Brian. 'Francophonie: A Language-Based Movement in World Politics', *International Organization* 30, 3 (1976): 485–507.

CHAPTER 27

The Ottawa-Quebec-Washington Dance: The Political Presence of Quebec in the United States

Louis Balthazar, Université Laval

— TIMELINE —

1774 Continental Congress sends Address to inhabitants of Province of Quebec.

Quebec Act: recognition of Quebec's civil law and Catholic religion.

1775 American revolutionaries invade Quebec; Richard Montgomery from south through Montreal and Benedict Arnold from east through Chaudière River. Quebec City under siege.

1776 End of siege of Quebec. Benjamin Franklin comes to Montreal with Bishop John Carroll and printer Fleury de Mesplet to persuade Quebecers to join revolution, with no success.

1837–8 Rebellions in Lower Canada (Quebec). Leader Louis-Joseph Papineau flees to United States.

1849 Beginning of annexationist movement.

1867 Foundation of modern Canada. British Parliament votes British North America Act. United Canada's legislature approves; 60 per cent of Legislative Assembly of Lower Canada approves.

1911 Prime Minister Wilfrid Laurier and President Howard Taft sign free-trade agreement that never materializes after Laurier loses general election to protectionist Conservative Party.

1940 Creation of Quebec office in New York City.

1962 New York office becomes delegation general.

1963 Government of Quebec borrows from Wall Street firms to buy all private hydro power companies.

1969 Opening of Chicago delegation.

1970 Opening of delegations in Boston and Lafayette.

1971 Premier Robert Bourassa launches James Bay hydroelectric project.

1973 Founding of Conference of New England Governors and Eastern Canadian Premiers.

1976 In provincial general election, secessionist Parti Québécois takes majority of seats in Quebec's National Assembly.

1977 Premier René Lévesque presents his sovereignty-association project to Economic Club of New York; its reception is lukewarm. Quebec government launches public relations campaign in United States. President Jimmy Carter expresses American position ('mantra') on Quebec sovereignty.

1978 Opening of delegation in Atlanta, bureau in Washington.

1980 Sixty per cent of Quebecers reject proposition of giving mandate to government to negotiate sovereignty-association.

1982 Serious economic recession in Quebec.

1984 Brian Mulroney becomes Prime Minister of Canada.

1985 President Ronald Reagan and Brian Mulroney meet in Quebec City and launch negotiations for Free Trade Agreement (FTA).

1988 FTA concluded but not be ratified until after election in Canada on 21 November. Quebec votes overwhelmingly to return Mulroney to power and have FTA ratified.

1990 Rejection of Meech Lake Accord by Newfoundland and Manitoba, thus failing to obtain necessary unanimity of all provinces. Public opinion polls show that majority of Quebecers now support sovereignty.

1994 PQ regains power under Jacques Parizeau, who promises to conduct referendum.

1995 Referendum held on 30 October on proposed sovereignty-partnership.

Quebecers say 'No', in slim majority of 50.6 per cent. US Ambassador James Blanchard, Secretary of State Warren Christopher, and President Bill Clinton openly supported 'No' campaign.

2001 Quebec's National Assembly expresses sympathy for victims of September 11 attacks. Quebec commits to act on safeguarding the border.

2003 Quebecers protest in great numbers against invasion of Iraq.

2008 Quebecers applaud election of Barack Obama as President of United States. Never before has US electoral campaign been so thoroughly covered by Quebec media.

From the very beginning, Quebec has been inextricably linked to the American continent. Therefore, the French province's inhabitants and its rulers have always had a deep interest in its immediate neighbours to the south. Especially since the Second World War, the government of Quebec has maintained a presence in the United States. This presence was reinforced at the time of the Quiet Revolution in the 1960s in a variety of ways. Canada's central government has reacted to this political presence sometimes positively, sometimes negatively. Washington's response has been generally prudent and careful to maintain harmonious relations with Ottawa and support Canadian unity, while tacitly recognizing Quebec's distinct character.

In this chapter, we begin by examining the historical background of Quebec's involvement in the United States. Next we deal with the objectives and the instruments of Quebec's representation. Finally, Quebec's political presence in the United States will be considered within the triangle formed between it, the federal government of Canada, and the response from the US government.

HISTORICAL BACKGROUND

French colonials were driven by religious, economic, and imperial desires to expand their presence through the whole of North America (see Chapter 1). With the help of allied Amerindians, explorers travelled the Great Lakes, and journeyed south along the Mississippi River to the Gulf of Mexico, founding the large territory that would be called Louisiana. They also travelled west all the way to the Rocky Mountains. Indeed, the first frontiersmen of America were the French!

Permanent Attraction

After the British Conquest of 1760, this continental interest was revived by the insistence of American rebels that Quebec join their Revolution; but two addresses from the Continental Congress met with refusal from the Quebec clerical and feudal elites. Nonetheless, when Quebec was invaded by American militia, in the winter of 1775–6, many Quebecers showed some empathy with Yankee soldiers, offering them assistance, food, and shelter.

Later, in 1837, the leader of an aborted rebellion, Louis-Joseph Papineau, fled to the United States, looking for support in the Republic that he admired. He received some help and encouragement among New Englanders, but none in Washington. The government of the United States seemed to be more preoccupied with not offending the former metropolis than in assisting an uncertain revolutionary cause.

American attraction was kept alive in Quebec throughout the nineteenth century by an important minority that was fascinated by the Republic to the point of promoting annexation. Many Quebecers opposed to the 1867 British North America Act were associated with annexationism.[1]

Another important development from the mid-nineteenth century to the 1930s was the massive exodus of French Canadians from Quebec to the United States, mainly to the adjacent New England and North Atlantic states. Economic conditions were so harsh in Quebec that many had to leave their homeland to make a living. While the other Canadian provinces were not especially hospitable to Catholic French-speaking Quebecers, the United States was an appealing alternative. There, French Canadians could regroup, form a few parishes, and create for a while what were called 'little Quebec' enclaves. Almost one million Quebecers migrated to the south. During this period, several links were established between Quebec and the United States, especially by the Church, but also by Quebec officials who traveled across the border. Two key factors led to the end of this massive migration: first, a new wave of industrialization in Quebec, in great part due to American investment, beginning around 1910, providing jobs for those who otherwise would have left; and second, during the 1930s, jobs that had lured French Canadians to the United States disappeared during the Great Depression.

Yet the attraction of the neighbouring country did not recede. Industrialization was frequently coupled with American products and influence, and Quebec governments were generally quite favourable toward American investments. The Second World War brought Canada closer to the United States, due to co-operation in defence and defence production. In 1940, the Quebec Liberal government of Adélard Godbout (1939–45) created a Quebec bureau in New York to promote tourism and boost economic relations.

New Ties in Modern Times

In 1962, Quebec's New York mission was upgraded into a delegation general, a type of embassy. One of the main reasons for this was Quebec's need to find capital to finance its various projects, the most spectacular of which was the 1963 nationalization of all hydro-power companies. Since Canadian investors were lukewarm to this endeavour, Quebec officials turned to Wall Street. This was the beginning of a special relationship between several American brokerage firms and both the Quebec government and its public corporation of Hydro-Quebec (see Chapter 22).

Premier Jean Lesage (1960–6) traveled extensively to the United States. Besides his deep interest in promoting investment and trade, he fostered the renewal of old ties between Quebecers and French Canadians in New England and in Louisiana. In 1970, delegations were opened in Boston and in Lafayette. In Boston, the economic dimensions and the promotion of Quebec's modern culture (Quebec theatre, for example) soon took precedence over the cultural relations with traditional French-Canadian associations. In Lafayette, early on Quebec used its delegation to encourage programs for teaching French among the Cajuns (descended from the French Acadian settlers in what are now Nova Scotia and New Brunswick), but when Quebec policy became dominated by economic interests, the delegation was closed in 1986. Other delegations were opened in Chicago (1969), Los Angeles (1970), and Atlanta (1978).

In 1965, when Quebec called for the right to negotiate international treaties in matters under its jurisdiction, Ottawa asserted its claim to be solely responsible for external affairs. This did not prevent the government of Quebec from maintaining its position that on issues within its jurisdiction it had the right not only to implement policy, but also to be party to negotiations of international agreements. This was called the 'Gérin-Lajoie doctrine' named after Paul Gérin-Lajoie, Minister of Education in Lesage's cabinet, who first formulated the claim (see Chapter 25).

In 1970, Premier Robert Bourassa (1970–6; 1985–94) announced a gigantic project: the construction of huge dams in James Bay (northern Quebec). The James Bay project would substantially increase Hydro-Quebec's production of electricity both to satisfy the growing needs of Quebecers and eventually for export to adjacent American states. With this in mind, Bourassa called for massive investment, 60 per cent of which came from American investors, managed by the First Boston Corporation.[2] Thus relations with the United States were further enhanced.

In 1976, the Parti Québécois (PQ) came to power in Quebec City with the commitment to hold a referendum on its proposal of sovereignty-association. This produced a shock in the US milieus interested in Canada. In this context of possible political upheaval, one would expect difficult times for Quebec in its relationship with the United States and a downgrading of its political representation. On the contrary, even more than its Liberal predecessor, the PQ government remained open to American investment and sound economic relations. The PQ made it clear that

Quebec's proposed new relationship with Canada would occur democratically and peacefully. Several members of this government visited the United States to allay fears and clarify the situation. Quebec soon expanded its influence in Washington, where a bureau was opened in 1978 with the official objective of promoting tourism but also serving as a pied-à-terre for officials visiting the capital.

After the defeat of the referendum on sovereignty-association in 1980, the PQ government maintained and reinforced its presence in the United States to the end of its second mandate (1981–5). It was more aggressive than ever in calling for American investment, during a period of economic recession.

In 1986, under the Progressive Conservative government of Brian Mulroney in Ottawa, negotiations began for a new trade pact between the United States and Canada. An agreement was concluded in 1988 and was the main reason for the calling of a Canadian federal election in November of that year. Except in Alberta and Quebec, there was strong opposition to this free trade agreement (FTA) throughout Canada. In Quebec, both the Liberal government of Robert Bourassa and the PQ opposition were very favourable toward it, and Quebec provided strong popular support that allowed the re-election of the Conservatives and the advent of FTA.

SNAPSHOT

Fall 1988: Confrontation on Free Trade and Language Policy

In the fall of 1988, the US and Canadian governments had agreed on a comprehensive free trade agreement (FTA). In Canada, the Mulroney government (1984–93) met with strong opposition as it submitted this agreement to Parliament. The ratification bill gave rise to hot debate in the House of Commons where both the Liberal Party and the New Democratic Party (NDP) presented strong objections. This was expected from the NDP but less from the Liberals, known historically as champions of free trade. Since the 1960s under leader and Prime Minister Pierre Elliott Trudeau (1968–79; 1980–4), the Liberals had

become more nationalist and had promoted and implemented restrictive policies in the hope of diversifying the Canadian economy, which was considered to be too dependent on the United States. This orientation was still present when, in 1984, John Turner replaced Trudeau at the head of the party and as Prime Minister but was defeated soon after by the Progressive Conservatives (PC) in a general election. Yet the idea of a free trade agreement had made significant headway among the Liberals when a Royal Commission, appointed by the Trudeau government and chaired by a prominent Liberal former minister,

Donald Macdonald, tabled a report in 1985 favourable to a free trade pact with the United States. Times had changed in the atmosphere of a crumbled economy in the early 1980s and many in Canada were calling for increasing the flow of goods and capital across the southern border. Thus John Turner, as leader of the Opposition, did not squarely oppose FTA but claimed that the treaty that was negotiated and signed between Canada and the United States in 1988 was disadvantageous for Canada. His arguments against the agreement were well received by many Canadians, especially among the centre-left and left-wing, in the arts and cultural circles, and in the academic community (except for most economists). It was argued that under FTA, Canadian identity would be seriously eroded, its social policies jeopardized, and its cultural productions threatened by American competition.

The climate was quite different in Quebec (as it was in Alberta, a province that has always been very open to trade with the United States due to its profitable oil and gas exports). With some minor reservations, both major provincial political parties were favourable to FTA. It was argued that Quebec was left aside by the Auto Pact of 1965 that was so beneficial to southern Ontario. Quebec's growing economic and business elites were eager to penetrate the large American market. In fact, although it has always sought north–south ties with the United States, Quebec was much less integrated with the American economy than was that of its sister province of Ontario. While Toronto and the Niagara Peninsula are part of a dynamic international Great Lakes area and close to cities like Buffalo, Syracuse, and Rochester in northern New York, Quebec is separated from large American centres by mountains, and its closest neighbours across the border are very small urban centres like Plattsburgh, New York and Burlington, Vermont. Finally, Quebecers did not deem that their culture would be threatened by American connections, because of the language barrier and the strong attachment of its population to its local cultural productions, especially in television.

In spite of the outspoken opposition voiced by the Liberals and the NDP, the legislation to ratify the FTA was passed by the House of Commons, but it still had to be endorsed by the appointed Senate where the Liberals had a majority of seats. Normally, this unelected branch of Parliament may present objections or call for amendments to bills without ever directly opposing the Commons. But it has the formal power to delay the adoption of legislation and even recommend its rejection. With the approval of a large part of the population, the Liberal Senate engaged in this unusual procedure over the FTA bill to the point of forcing the Prime Minister to call a general election. FTA was, of course, the dominant issue of the campaign.

The election was held on 21 November and returned Mulroney's Progressive Conservatives to power with a substantial majority of 169 seats to 83 for the Liberals and 43 for the NDP. Quebec and Alberta were the only two provinces to vote overwhelmingly for the PC. In other parts of Canada, opposition to FTA and support for the Liberals and NDP prevailed, notably in all urban centres. Given that Quebec had almost half of the PC seats, one could say that the Quebec vote was responsible for the Conservative victory and the advent of FTA, which subsequently was implemented in January 1989.

The FTA produced bitter division among Canadians. In academic milieus in particular, some English-speaking intellectuals who had been sympathetic to Quebec's claims—such as those addressed in the Meech Lake Accord, which called for enhanced recognition of the French province and important amendments to the Canadian Constitution—became sour towards Quebecers, accusing them of betraying the cause of an independent Canada.

Thus while the whole of English-speaking Canada had shown concern for cultural and social protection against the United States, Quebec was more liberally inclined and open to a stronger connection.

A few weeks later, the Supreme Court of Canada pronounced an important judgment concerning Quebec's Charter of the French Language, commonly referred to as Bill 101. It declared sections of the law related to public signage unconstitutional. According to the Court's compulsory ruling, the practice that all visible signs be exclusively in French was contrary to both Canada's and Quebec's Charters of rights and freedoms. Public opinion in Quebec expressed outrage with this ruling, urging its provincial government not to comply, as the language Charter was seen as essential to maintaining distinct Quebec identity and culture. In response, the Quebec government used the 'notwithstanding clause' of the Constitution, which allowed for the suspension of the application of the Charter of Rights in certain special cases. This action was perfectly legal but was radical enough to again provoke bitter reactions in the rest of Canada. This time, it had been Quebec's turn to deem (perhaps wrongly) its language and culture in danger.

These important events of late 1988 show how Quebecers and other Canadians all wanted to protect their role, identity, and place in North America, while disagreeing on what exactly these were. All Canadians have reservations about their belonging to North America, but they express these in clearly different ways.

Quebec's political and economic leaders saw in the FTA an opportunity for significant growth. While Ontario was favoured by the 1965 Canada–United States Automobile Agreement (commonly called the Auto Pact) and Western Canada by massive exports of energy, Quebec was seeking a larger and freer access to the gigantic US market. Unlike other provinces, it did not feel that its identity was threatened by this economic agreement.

Throughout the 1990s, Quebec remained a champion of FTA and its successor deal, the North American Free Trade Agreement (NAFTA), which includes Mexico. A change of government, when the PQ was elected in 1994, did not alter this policy. It produced another climate of uncertainty however, as Quebec would go through another referendum on sovereignty in 1995. Yet economic relations were not substantially affected and Quebec support for NAFTA did not lessen either before or after the referendum (which the PQ lost by a very narrow margin).

For various reasons, the climate of relations would change in the new millennium. Most Quebecers were displeased with the Bush administration in the United States. They strongly opposed both the invasion of Iraq in 2003 and, by and large, the conservative tenets of the Republican government. Also at this time Quebec's trade with the United States became less profitable, due to the economic downturn in the United States and the strengthening of the Canadian dollar. Nonetheless, Premiers Bernard Landry (2001–3) and Jean Charest (2003–) were and are both ardent supporters of harmonious relations with American partners, especially with state governments. A new important concern has appeared due to the tightening of the border after 2001: agreements with the US on security and facilitation of transborder trade were concluded with both Canada and Quebec.

Through this historical review we see that Quebec governments, whatever their political orientation, were always favourable to a close political relationship with the United States, especially in the last 50 years. Why has it been so? What are the principal objectives of successive Quebec governments in seeking ties with the United States?

QUEBEC'S OBJECTIVES

Apart from the traditional purpose of maintaining a connection with descendants of French settlers in Louisiana and more recent former Quebecers in the Northeast, two main objectives have marked the political presence of Quebec in the United States in modern days: (1) the promotion of Quebec's economic interests; and (2) making known Quebec's distinctive character, language, and culture.

Promotion of Economic Interests

Promoting economic interests means having American capital invested in Quebec, thus creating jobs and technological expertise, and opening a large market for Quebec products. Yet, from time to time, nationalists have criticized provincial governments for 'selling out' to Americans and 'Americanizing' Quebec. Premiers have responded by pointing out the benefits of such investments.

Louis-Alexandre Taschereau (1920–36) famously stated: 'I prefer importing American dollars than exporting Canadian workers.'[3] Quebec leaders have often sought American investment despite attempts by the federal government to restrict it over worries that American investment gave the United States too much influence in Canada.[4]

Especially since the early days of the Quiet Revolution (as we have seen above) Quebec's governments have sought capital to finance its public debt and major semi-autonomous corporations like Hydro-Québec. It is therefore important for Quebec to be on the spot to negotiate with the firms that will float its bonds on the financial market. A presence in the United States is important as well to promote Quebec exports. Small- and medium-sized enterprises in particular appreciate the help of Quebec officials abroad. American markets are by far the most lucrative of all for Quebec producers. This Quebec presence is even more important in the context of the FTA and NAFTA. For example, when Quebec exporters are confronted with countervailing duties on account of public subsidies, or anti-dumping duties, Quebec officials and their lawyers can best defend the interests of these exporters in the very places where they are penalized.

To Make Quebec Better Known

The second objective of maintaining close relations with the United States is often referred to in the Ministry of International Relations as the 'public affairs mission'. The underlying assumption is that Quebec is not well known. If Canada has reasons to lament that, in spite of its proximity and its numerous ties with the United States, it is often ignored in the American public agenda and remains unknown except in the border regions, Quebec has even greater cause for concern. Not only are most Americans unaware of the importance of Quebec as a trade partner in the Northeast, few are well informed about the distinctiveness of the French province. In most of North America, where the English language is universal, it is difficult to believe that a whole society functions primarily in French. Given the importance of the United States as a trade partner, it is therefore necessary for Quebec to

make itself known as a province that is different from the other provinces in Canada.

Since the federal government does not tend to spread abroad an image of national heterogeneity[5] and decentralization, Quebec has to make its case and explain to its American partners why its constitutional autonomy is so dear to its population and why it is considered as a homeland and a 'nation' for its large majority. It may also, from time to time, have to explain to Americans why there is an important movement calling for the sovereignty of Quebec.

Quebec officials in the United States must also promote the province's cultural products. In the last 50 years, Quebec has been a cauldron of cultural products of all sorts, in literature, music, dance, theatre, and visual arts. It has become a vibrant part of the French-speaking world and an ardent member of the Organisation internationale de la Francophonie. It is important that Americans be aware that the French language used in Quebec, although it has its own peculiarities, is a species of international French. Quebec literature may therefore be used in teaching French in the United States, and Quebec universities are as well-equipped as their counterparts in France, if not better, for the learning of French. In fact the American Association of Teachers of French frequently holds its annual meetings in Quebec. The United States was also home to the first academic association outside of Canada devoted exclusively to Quebec: the American Council for Quebec Studies (ACQS), and the first university-based research and teaching centre—the Institute on Québec Studies—established at State University of New York College at Plattsburgh in 2004.

THE MEANS OF A POLITICAL PRESENCE

To attain its objectives in its relationship with the United States, Quebec has a limited number of means at its disposal. Although it may claim the right to conduct international activities, the state of Quebec is not a sovereign entity and does not enjoy diplomatic recognition in the United States. The Canadian state officially represents all Canadians and deploys an impressive arsenal of missions to several American cities as well as a large and well-staffed embassy in Washington.

The Quebec government has generally acknowledged that it is well served by Canadian diplomacy, but it seeks to play a role of its own to complement and improve this mission for its own interests. Ironically, Quebec representatives, while not being diplomatic agents as such, may at times deploy more diplomacy than Canadian officials; not only is their culture more foreign to Americans, but also they must play on the delicate balance of making the best of Canadian efforts using their own means.

Quebec is officially recognized by the Foreign Agents Registration Act, an American law that oversees the activities of foreign agents in the United States. In accordance with this law, the Quebec government must submit an annual report to the Justice Department. This is done by the New York delegation general, which acts as the voice for all the other delegations. Not surprisingly, it is Quebec's most important mission, in the financial centre and the industrial metropolis of the United States, located just 350 miles, or 563 kilometres, from the border.

Other delegations have equally distinct purposes. The New England delegation, situated in Boston, has its particular relevance. Of the six New England states, three share a border with Quebec, and the whole region receives around 20 per cent of Quebec exports. Boston is also an important centre for scientific and technological research, the home of prestigious universities, and a centre of transnational relations. This delegation also serves as a link to Americans of French-Canadian descent.

In Washington, even though Quebec does not have any official diplomatic contact, the capital is the location of numerous headquarters of national associations, and the delegation there is working to bring tourists to Quebec, mainly in the form of large conferences to be held in Montreal and Quebec City. Moreover, Quebec representatives are charged with the valuable mission of monitoring the various think tanks, institutions, and people present within the Beltway on behalf of the New York delegation and the Quebec government. Atlanta is the hub of the southeast, and the delegation there promotes Quebec's economy in the region.

Chicago is further away from Quebec, but it is the heart of the greater industrial region of the Midwest, located at the western end of the Great Lakes. Because of its role as a transportation network, and the deep interest of Quebec in aeronautics and railway materiel, having a delegation there is important. The Great Lakes area is also vital for Quebec concerns about water pollution and the environment in general.

Los Angeles is the city with the largest concentration of aeronautic firms with which Quebec makes contact to promote its own industry. California is also the largest market in the United States and, even if physically remote from Quebec, the state is important for its exports and its cultural relations with Quebec, especially in the film industry.

In a country as decentralized as the United States, relations at the state level are inescapable. For Quebec, which is itself autonomous in many jurisdictions, as a province in the Canadian federation, these relations are vital and have proved fruitful. Especially in the Northeast but also with other large industrial states, contacts have been fostered and intensified, notably during the 1990s. Quebec has been one of the most enthusiastic members of the Conference of New England Governors and Eastern Canadian Premiers since its inception in 1973. This organization deals with several issues concerning New England, the four Atlantic provinces, and Quebec; the environment, energy, trade, education, and cultural exchanges. This conference meets every year, rotating among the 11 capitals, and has permanent head offices in Boston and Halifax. Quebec also participates in the various activities of the National Conference of State Legislatures and of the Council of State Governments. The latter even held its annual convention in Quebec City in 1999. Finally, several agreements have been signed between Quebec and states as varied as California, Virginia, and Louisiana on transportation and educational exchange.

With the state of New York, Quebec has a special relationship. Every year, there is a summit meeting between the governor and the premier to discuss various topics such as the environment, sustainable development projects, taxation, transportation, and trade. This has led to numerous agreements on these various issues.

LIVING IN A TRIANGLE

We have seen that Quebec is connected in several ways with the United States. Yet Quebec belongs to Canada and cannot help but take the federal government into account. As a consequence, one can say that Quebec's relations with its American partners take place within a triangle, as of course do those of all Canadian provinces. Canadians are caught between the east–west dimension of their country's history, and the north–south orientation that seems inevitable, as most Canadians live within 150 kilometres of the US border.

Nonetheless the Canadian polity makes for special ties between all provinces. Significant research shows that 'borders matter'.[6] For example, Canadian cities are more relevant to each other than are American cities of a similar size and distance. Toronto is more important for Montreal than are Boston and New York. Yet on the whole, proximity and size often make the United States more vital for most provinces, notably for Quebec, than the rest of Canada. Thus Quebec may be bound to Ontario in several ways but it is also bound to the United States, as is well illustrated by the fact that during the 1990s Quebec trade with the United States surpassed its trade with other parts of Canada.

This phenomenon has become an argument for nationalists in Quebec, especially for those who advocate sovereignty. They contend that Quebec could bolster exports with the United States, and thus strong political ties with Canada would become less important. Trade with Ontario could continue across an international border.

A strong case can be made against this attitude. Isn't there a contradiction between Quebecers' concern for the protection of their identity, culture, and language and accepting American influence? There is no doubt that, in spite of English-speaking Canadians' reluctance to recognize Quebec's distinctive character, this character is much better protected in the Canadian federation than it would be in the United States. The example of the disappearance of the French language in Louisiana speaks for itself. Especially after the Civil War, the pull towards conformity and cultural and linguistic homogeneity has been much stronger in the United States than in

Canada. Quebecers are aware of this and generally no longer support annexation to the United States. Yet they tend to consider the United States, since it is a foreign country, as less intrusive than the Canadian government. They feel, rightly or wrongly, that their culture and language make them less susceptible to Americanization than other Canadians.

In fact, English-speaking Canadians have often felt more threatened by the United States than have French-speaking Quebecers.[7] Canadian nationalists have wished to include all Canadians (English, French, and multicultural) in the protection of the Canadian ethos and values against the challenge of Americanization. Quebecers, for their part, have tended to stress that duality and bilingualism make Canada distinct from the United States.

This divergence is somewhat reflected in relations with the southern neighbour. The government of Canada, devoted to reinforcing Canadian unity, does not always look favourably on the incursions of provincial governments into the United States. It maintains that it is well-equipped to represent the interests of all Canadians, including Quebecers. Especially in Washington, where politics are so complex and government is diversified by the separation of powers, Canadian representatives claim that Canada should speak with one voice in order to be efficient and to defend well all Canadians' interests. Indeed, the Canadian Embassy has proven to be an impressive organization with a capacity to deal with the various concerns of provinces as well as more general issues.

Yet since the development of the Gérin-Lajoie doctrine, all Quebec governments have emphasized the need for Quebec to defend its own interests and promote its own image. Their claim is that the official image projected by the Canadian government does not reflect Quebec's uniqueness. Especially in matters related to the constitutional debate, they argue that the Quebec point of view, its stand for greater respect of provincial jurisdictions, is not well explained or well defended even by French-speaking Canadian diplomats.

It may also frequently happen that typical English-Canadian views of Canada are presented in the United States as if they were American views, because English-speaking Canadians living in the United States are somewhat incognito, hardly recognizable as Canadians. Some journalists from Canada contribute to American media without being identified as Canadians: 'Canada is the only country in the world in which the United States networks frame reports by foreigners as if they had been done by United States network staffers.'[8]

In spite of Canadian opposition[9] or lukewarm acceptance, Quebec has maintained its presence in the United States, even to a modest extent in its national capital. Furthermore, Quebec representatives have sometimes proved to have enough subtlety and diplomacy to obtain the indispensable co-operation from the extensive network of Canadian missions in the United States to add to its own limited means. The Canadian government, however, has been successful enough to convey a faithful and friendly response from the American government to its claim of being a unique representative.

Response from the United States

For the US executive power, there is only one official interlocutor from Canada: the Canadian government. Canadian provinces are treated by American law as foreign agents on the same level as foreign corporations or institutions operating on US territory. This, however, does not prevent the US State Department and the intelligence community from following developments in Quebec, especially since the rise of the sovereignty movement. At the level of state governments, as mentioned above, Quebec's relations have usually been cordial and without any significant constraint from the central government of either country. Indeed, increasingly, governors and state legislators are interested in dealing with Canadian provinces, notably with Quebec.

The US government has found a way of tacitly recognizing Quebec's distinctiveness through its consulate general in Quebec City. This diplomatic mission has operated without interruption since 1855. In the contemporary era, its existence is not justified by consular affairs. The US consulate-general in Montreal is sufficient for that. In other Canadian provinces, the American government is not represented by more than one consulate. The only reason to keep a mission in Quebec City is Quebec's unique political stance

within Canada. It is well understood that the purpose of the US consulate general in Quebec City is to establish relations with officials of the Quebec government as well as with members of the Opposition and other political elites in the provincial capital. This does not imply in any way recognition of Quebec as a diplomatic partner. The US consul general in Quebec City is subordinated to the American Ambassador in Ottawa, to whom he or she regularly reports. His or her function, not unlike that of the Quebec delegate in Washington, is to monitor and report to the State Department. One US consul general in Quebec City summarized his role as follows:

> We are here to be the eyes and ears of Washington, to try to understand what is going on in Quebec and also to explain our policies to the Quebec government and to Quebec citizens.[10]

The post has been generally occupied by career diplomats of great quality, judgment, and personality who, in all likelihood, have produced fair and well-balanced reports on Quebec. Generally they have enjoyed their stays and the relationships they have developed. In most cases, they have remained friends of Quebec even after their departure.

In no way does this mean that these consulates general have empathized with all tenets of Quebec nationalism, especially with the sovereignty movement. In this respect, they have remained faithful to what has been called the Washington 'mantra', articulated for the first time by President Jimmy Carter in 1977, after the election of the PQ. It has been reiterated with very few modifications by all American administrations since then. It has three points:

1. The United States will not intervene in Canadian internal affairs; consequently it will not take a stand in the constitutional debate taking place in Canada.
2. The American government considers Canada as a special partner with which it entertains excellent relations. It favours whatever may reinforce Canadian unity and cohesion. It will always express therefore its preference for a united Canada as opposed to its fragmentation.
3. Only Canadians can take decisions concerning the future of their country. The United States will respect the popular will of Canadian citizens.

Most American administrations have been very discreet concerning Quebec. President Ronald Reagan, in a memorable visit in Quebec City in 1985, addressed the special character of the French province and President Bill Clinton gave a well-thought-out speech on the virtues of federalism at a Conference in Mont-Tremblant, Quebec, in 1999.

CONCLUSION

Quebecers have constantly striven to assert their identity within North America (as Yvan Lamonde has suggested in Chapter 6, having a certain Americanicity). This is why, throughout its history, Quebec has sought to establish, maintain, and intensify relations with its southern neighbour. All Quebec governments have sought to reinforce economic ties with the United States while trying to make Americans aware of the existence of a French province north of the border. Quebec has used various means to achieve these goals. In the last 40 years, it has pursued these goals by establishing a network of representatives across the United States and by meeting with state governments and participating in multilateral organizations.

In connecting to the United States, the rest of Canada has not always been on the same wavelength as Quebec. At times the Canadian government has been annoyed by Quebec efforts to stand on its own in the United States, but it has more or less tolerated a Quebec political presence there, provided it is maintained within the framework of Canada's own diplomacy. The US government has responded rather positively to Quebec efforts but would never officially consider the French province as a diplomatic partner.

Quebecers' interest in the United States was certainly reinforced with the election of Barack Obama as president. As of the beginning of 2009, the American president was much more popular in Quebec than Canadian Prime Minister Stephen Harper. This, however, does not change the nature of the issues at stake. Quebec's relations with the United States are still bound to be as complex as they are essential and vital.

CLAUDE MORIN

Claude Morin (right) waits with Saskatchewan's Roy Romanow (centre) and Justice Minister Jean Chrétien (left) in August 1980 for a final news conference in Ottawa at the end of official talks on the Constitution.

CP PHOTO/Rod MacIvor

Claude Morin has played a vital role in the development of Quebec's modern international relations, first as a public servant from 1961 to 1971, and second as a member of René Lévesque's Parti Québécois (PQ) government from 1976 to 1982. In this role, he constantly favoured strong ties with the United States.

Morin went to work with Jean Lesage soon after the latter became Quebec Premier in 1960. He directly participated, as a speech-writer, in launching the Quiet Revolution. He inspired most of Lesage's declarations, including his significant inroads in the United States. In 1963, he became deputy minister of the new Department of Federal–Provincial Relations. In this function he was at the heart of important negotiations and conflicts with the federal government, notably around Quebec's then-controversial international activities. He contributed substantially in giving a permanent legitimacy to Quebec's international relations and its prominence within La Francophonie. He worked under four successive Quebec premiers: Lesage, Johnson, Bertrand, and Bourassa.

In part because he had studied at Columbia University in New York, obtaining a master's degree in Social Welfare in 1956, he was always sensitive to the need for Quebec to maintain strong and meaningful ties with American partners. He was still in office when the Department of Federal–Provincial Relations became the Department of Intergovernmental Affairs in 1969 and when several delegations were opened in the United States, in Lafayette, Boston, Chicago, and Los Angeles.

When he left the government in 1971, he went to teach at École nationale d'administration publique (National School of Public Administration) on economic policies. He soon joined the Parti Québécois and was a candidate in the 1973 and 1976 elections in the riding of Louis-Hébert, in a Quebec City suburb. He was defeated in 1973, and then elected in 1976, the year the PQ formed the government. René Lévesque, predictably enough, chose him to become Minister of Intergovernmental Affairs with the responsibility for international relations.

Among other tasks, he worked to change his party's platform concerning a sovereign Quebec's participation in the organizations created in the context of the Cold War. He understood correctly that Quebec had a strong interest in participating in NATO and NORAD and, as a consequence, he fought to make this clear in his party's program. Along with Premier Lévesque and in contrast to some of his colleagues, he was persuaded that any policy that would prove to be confrontational to the American government would be totally misleading and counterproductive.

He also understood that there was no way his government could persuade American partners of the validity and pertinence of the sovereignty project. Thus he believed that the best Quebec could obtain from the United States government would be an attitude of respectful non-interference in the debate on the future status of Quebec. This translated into a campaign to persuade Americans that an independent Quebec would remain friendly to the United States and devoted to a market economy. Under the slogan of 'Operation America', his department and the government in general organized several visits of high-level officials in many American cities to broadcast this message.

At the same time, he made sure that Quebec's representatives adhered to their mission of fostering and deepening economic relations while making Quebec better known and its cultural products more widely available, and refraining from a militant advocacy of sovereignty. Indeed, he went so far as to maintain in office some delegates who did not support sovereignty for Quebec.

After the defeat in the 1980 referendum and the re-election of the PQ in 1981, Morin stayed in office and fought vigorously to maintain an autonomous status for Quebec in the Canadian Constitution. After his efforts proved unsuccessful, he resigned from the government.

Claude Morin was above all a pragmatist and always deeply conscious of the limits of political action and diplomacy. He could write a book with the daring title, *L'art de l'impossible* (*The Art of the Impossible*, Montreal, Boréal, 1987) to account for the hard-won breakthrough of Quebec on the international scene against all odds and against Ottawa's strong objections. Yet in all of his actions, as bold as he could be at times, he kept believing that politics is the art of the possible and that a half-way compromise was better than total failure.

He favoured strong ties with France, where Quebec always enjoyed a special status. Yet he was always deeply conscious that relations with the United States, although less spectacular, were as important, and much more so at the economic level. He always made sure his department would spend as much money and effort in strengthening relations with the United States as it did with France.

Perhaps because he was a pragmatist and a realist, Morin was never very popular in Quebec. Among federalists, he was seen as a promoter of sovereignty and among sovereignists as a lukewarm partisan. He must be counted nonetheless as one of the most valuable architects of the Quiet Revolution and especially as a champion of the development of international relations and meaningful ties with the United States.

QUESTIONS FOR CONSIDERATION

1. What are the main goals of the Quebec government in the United States?

2. Why does Canada object to Quebec's political presence in Washington?

3. In what sense could you possibly say the US government recognizes Quebec's specific character?

Notes

1. The BNA Act sanctioned the union of the three colonies: the Canadas (Upper and Lower Canada which geographically correspond with Southern Ontario and southern Quebec), Nova Scotia, and New Brunswick. The new colony was granted home rule, i.e. autonomy in domestic affairs. Canada did not become fully independent until the Statute of Westminster (1931) when it became autonomous in international relations. The Legislative Assembly of Lower Canada voted 60 per cent in favour of the union, called (incorrectly) Confederation.

2. 'To put these financial needs in perspective, 1973 estimates of the total cost of the project at Can$9 billion made it the largest project in history'. Alexander C. Tomlison, 'U.S. Perceptions of Investment Opportunities and Risks in Quebec', in Alfred O. Hero, Jr., and Marcel Daneau, eds., *Problems and Opportunities in U.S-Quebec Relations* (Boulder, CO, Westview Press, 1984), 39.

3. Quoted in Yves Roby, *Les Québécois et les investissements américains, 1918–1927* (Québec, Les Presses de l'Université Laval, 1976), 169 (our translation).

4. Here is how a Quebec Minister of Intergovernmental Affairs, Jacques-Yvan Morin, expressed Quebec's position in 1982: 'Quebec does not share Ottawa's viewpoint in foreign investment. We favour a much more open policy . . . we believe the future lies in the development of a strong north-south economic axis'. Lecture to the World Affairs Council of Northern California, San Francisco, 3 June 1982.

5. The image of a multicultural Canada may give the impression that the culture of French-speaking Quebecers is just one of the several subcultures in the Canadian mosaic.

6. John McCallum, 'National Borders Matter: Canadian–U.S. Regional Trade Patterns', *American Economic Review* 85, 3 (June 1995): 615–23; John F. Helliwell, 'Do National Borders Matter for Quebec Trade?', National Bureau of Economic Research Paper no 5215 (Cambridge, Mass.: National Bureau of Economic Research,1996), 5; John F. Helliwell and John McCallum, 'National Borders Still Matter for Trade', *Policy Options* 16 (July–August 1995): 45–8.

7. See Chapter 6 by Yvan Lamonde and especially his formula that Quebec is a mixture of a weakened French Tradition, British domination, growing American influence, and waning Catholic influence: $Q = -F + GB + US^2 - R$.

8. See Stephen Banker, 'How America Sees Quebec', in Alfred O. Hero, Jr and Marcel Daneau, eds., *Problems and Opportunities in U.S.-Quebec Relations* (Boulder, Colo.: Westview Press, 1984), 170–80.

9. In Washington, the federal government has often made life difficult for the Quebec representatives by ignoring them or denying residence to their personnel. Ottawa argued that it was better for all Canadians to be represented by a single institution.

10. From an interview done within the framework of a televised course by Louis Balthazar, *Les Américains, le monde et nous*, Université Laval, Direction de la formation continue, 1992.

Relevant Websites

Ministry of International Relations, Quebec Government: www.mri.gouv.qc.ca/en/relations_quebec/ameriques/amerique_du_nord/usa/relations.asp

United States–Quebec agreement on border security: www.ssa.gov/international/Agreement_Texts/quebec.html

Canadian–American Relations, Department of Foreign Affairs and International Trade, Government of Canada: http://geo.international.gc.ca/can-am/main/menu-en.asp?lang_update=1

American Council for Quebec Studies: www.acqs.org/

Select Bibliography

Balthazar, Louis. 'Les relations Québec-États-Unis'. In L.Balthazar, L. Bélanger, and G. Mace, *Trente ans de politique extérieure : 1960-1990*, Sillery, Que.: Les Éditions du Septentrion, 1993, 65–105.

———, and Alfred O.Hero Jr. *Le Québec dans l'espace américain*. Montreal, Québec-Amérique, 1999.

Bernier, Luc. *De Paris à Washington : la politique internationale du Québec*. Sainte-Foy, Que.: Les Presses de l'Université du Québec, 1996.

Bouchard, Gérard, and Yvan Lamonde, eds. *Québécois et Américains : la culture québécoise aux XIXe et XXe siècles*. Montreal: Fides, 1995.

Chartier, Armand. *Histoire des Franco-Américains de la Nouvelle-Angleterre : 1775–1990*. Sillery, Que.: Les Éditions du Septentrion, 1991.

Duchacek, Ivo, and Daniel Latouche, eds. *Perforated Sovereignties and International Relations:Trans-*

Sovereign Contacts of Subnational Governments. New York: Greenwood Press, 1988.

Hero, Alfred O., Jr. *Louisiana and Quebec: 1673–1993.* Tulane University Series in Political Science. Lanham, Md.: University Press of America, 1995.

———, and Marcel Daneau, eds. *Problems and Opportunities in U.S.–Quebec Relations.* Boulder, Colo.: Westview Press, 1984.

———, and Louis Balthazar. *Contemporary Quebec and the United States: 1960–1985.* Cambridge, Mass. and Lanham, Md.: Harvard University Center for International Affairs and University Press of America, 1988.

Lamonde, Yvan. *Ni avec eux ni sans eux : le Québec et les États-Unis*, Montreal: Nuit Blanche éditeur, 1996.

Lemco, Jonathan. *Turmoil in the Peaceable Kingdom: the Quebec Sovereignty Movement and its Implications for Canada and the United States.* Toronto: University of Toronto Press, 1994.

Lisée, Jean-François. *In the Eye of the Eagle.* Toronto: Harper Collins, 1990.

Roby, Yves. *Les Franco-Américains de la Nouvelle-Angleterre: rêve et réalité.* Sillery, Que.: Septentrion, 2001.

———. *The Franco-Americans of New England: Dreams and Reality,* trans. Mary Ricard. Quebec: Éditions du Septentrion, 2005.

Senécal, André and Robert Gill. *Plus ou Moins : the State of Quebec Studies in the United States.* Radford, Va.: ACQS, 1990.

CHAPTER 28

Quebec's Economic Relations with the United States: A Case Study of Multi-level Interdependence in an Era of Globalization

Earl Fry, Brigham Young University

— TIMELINE —

1940 Quebec government opens Trade and Tourism Bureau in New York City.

1965 Gérin-Lajoie doctrine regarding international relations proclaimed by Quebec government.

1967 Ministry of Intergovernmental Affairs created with responsibility for federal–provincial relations within Canada and Quebec's international affairs.

1977 Premier Réne Lévesque speaks at Economic Club of New York about his vision of future of Quebec and Quebec–US economic relations.

1984 Ministry of Intergovernmental Affairs renamed the Ministry of International Affairs.

1989 Canada–US Free Trade Agreement (FTA) put into effect. Quebec government is a key promoter of this agreement.

1994 North American Free Trade Agreement (NAFTA) begins to be implemented. Its members are Canada, the United States, and Mexico. Once again, the Quebec government is a key supporter of NAFTA.

1995 Ministry of International Affairs is renamed Ministry of International Relations (MRI).

2002 First Quebec–New York Economic Summit held in Plattsburgh, New York.

2006 MRI releases its 128-page *Quebec's International Policy: Working in Concert.* This document outlines major international priorities of Quebec. The United States and France identified as key international partners of Quebec government.

2008 NAFTA fully implemented. Quebec joins Western Climate Initiative to reduce greenhouse gas emissions in North America. Other members include several US states and Canadian provinces.

INTRODUCTION

If Quebec were a nation-state, it would have ranked as the world's seventh-largest exporter to the United States in 2007, a rather remarkable achievement for a province with only 7.7 million inhabitants. In this discussion of Quebec's economic relations with its neighbour, the United States, we should keep in mind that it is far more complicated than a casual observer would expect. For example, many would consider that exporting a good to another country simply involves growing, extracting, or fabricating a product and then shipping it to the foreign destination. However, in the very integrative economic setting which personifies the overall Canada–US relationship, perhaps a third of trade in goods involves cross-border units of the same company, and another one-third closely linked business networks and supply chains. For example, component parts for motor vehicles often cross the border a half-dozen times before the final product is ready to ship to the customer. Moreover, a company in Quebec might fabricate a product for shipment to the United States, but the company itself may be owned by American or other foreign investors.

In addition, Quebec's relationship with the United States exemplifies the complexities found within and between nation-states in a period of globalization. Globalization describes the growing interconnectedness and interdependence among nations and societies around the world. For example, over the past several decades, international economic exchanges such as trade and investment flows have been growing more rapidly than such exchanges within individual nation-states. Many jobs in Montreal or Quebec City

exist because consumers outside of Canada are willing to buy the products made in the province, or because foreign investors are willing to purchase companies within Quebec which produce these products. Figure 28.1 illustrates the evolving multi-level linkages not only between the international and national levels, but also between the international and the local levels within respective nation-states.

This chapter begins by examining the range of economic ties between Quebec and the United States, with special emphasis on trade, direct investment, and tourism. The next section places the issue in context by looking at the overall Canada–Quebec–United States economic relationship. The following section zeroes in on bilateral economic ties between Quebec and the United States, and the final section ponders the future of Quebec's economic relationship with the United States.

QUEBEC, CANADA, AND THE UNITED STATES

The United States and Canada maintain the world's largest bilateral trading relationship when measured

FIGURE 28.1 Quebec's Expansive Interactions with the United States

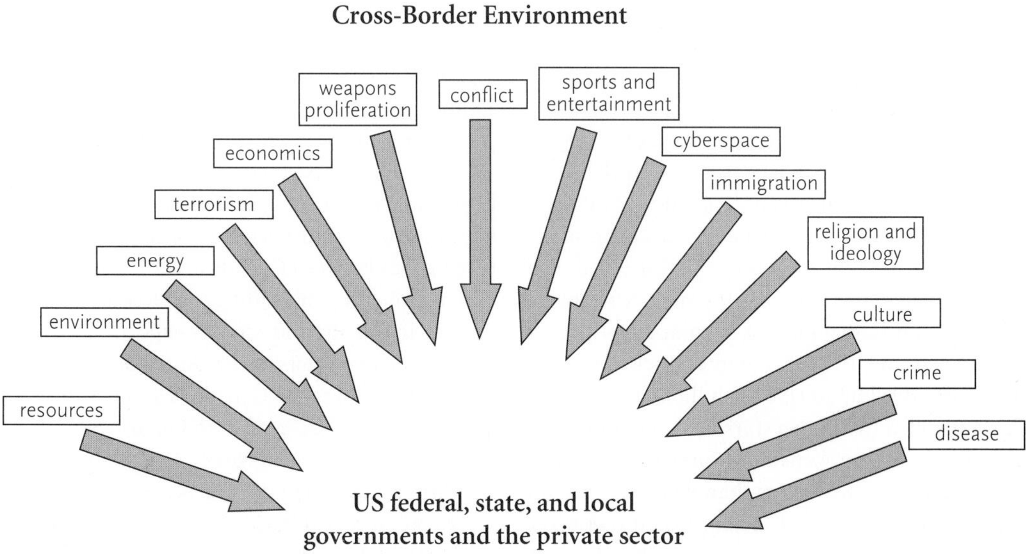

Cross-Border Environment

Source: to come

by the combined value of cross-border imports and exports of goods and services (totalling US$731 billion in 2007) and foreign direct investment (FDI) activity. In recent years, roughly 80 per cent of all Canadian exports have been destined for one foreign market, the United States. Until China became the largest exporter to the United States in 2007, Canada had held that position for each and every year since the end of the Second World War. This trading relationship between the two neighbouring North American countries has evolved into a very elaborate economic labyrinth. As Stephen Blank asserts, there now exists 'a deeply integrated continental system of supply chains structured by networks linking production centers and distribution hubs across the continent'. He adds that these supply chains 'depend on an efficient and secure physical infrastructure of rails, roads and bridges, pipelines and wires, and ports and border crossings, and on a coherent and consistent system of regulations that affect individuals, machines, firms, and goods'.[1]

From its inception as a nation in 1867 until the Second World War, Canada was closely linked economically to Great Britain and the British Empire. However, from 1945 onward, Canada's trans-Atlantic economic ties weakened noticeably while southward linkages to the United States strengthened dramatically. Today, no major nation in the world depends as much for its economic well-being on access to another nation's market and investors as Canada depends on the United States. In 2007, exports of goods and services accounted for roughly one-third of Canada's total gross domestic product (GDP), and the lion's share of these exports was purchased by American consumers. Investors in the United States are also the source for 58 per cent of total FDI in Canada, a type of investment which provides the American investor with a controlling interest in companies located on Canadian soil. In 2005, the total stock of US FDI in Canada added up to US$235 billion, and companies controlled by US investors accounted for over one million jobs for Canadian workers. Americans also account for slightly less than 90 per cent of all international visitors to Canada. When one takes into account Canadian exports to the United States, American FDI in Canada, and Americans visiting

Canada for business or tourism, more than a quarter of all private-sector jobs in Canada are attributable to economic linkages with the United States. A familiar adage is 'when the United States sneezes, Canada catches cold.' This adage may be somewhat exaggerated today, but Canada still gets the sniffles whenever the US economy stagnates.

For decades, Canada has also been very important to the American economy and has been the number one destination for US exports each and every year since the end of the Second World War. In 2007, the United States actually exported more to Canada (US$249 billion) with its 33 million people than to the 27 nations of the European Union (US$247 billion) with its combined 494 million people. That same year, businesses in 36 US states exported more to Canada than to any other country. Canadian investors were also responsible for a cumulative total of US$213 billion in FDI in the United States with this investment providing over 450,000 jobs for American workers. Canadians are also the leading source of international visitors to the United States, and in the vital energy sector, Canada ranks as the world's leading supplier to the United States of oil, natural gas, electricity, and uranium.

Quebec has the second-largest population among the provinces in Canada, but in 2007 ranked as the third-leading provincial exporter to the United States, behind Ontario and Alberta. Moreover, Ontario, with a population base two-thirds larger than Quebec's, shipped goods to the United States worth more than three times Quebec's exports. How does one explain these discrepancies? First, Ontario is the manufacturing hub of Canada and dominates the auto sector, which is the foremost category of trade in manufactured goods between Canada and the United States. Second, Alberta is the leading producer of oil and natural gas in Canada and actually exports more petroleum-related products to the United States than any nation-state other than Canada as a whole, including Saudi Arabia. In addition, both Ontario and Alberta shipped a larger percentage of their total exports to the United States than did Quebec.

As a province within Canada, Quebec is affected by national and international policies or trends that affect its economic ties to the United States. Quebec has certainly benefited substantially from the Canada–US Free Trade Agreement (FTA) which went into effect in 1989, and later by the North American Free Trade Agreement (NAFTA) which includes Canada, the United States, and Mexico and has superseded the FTA. Under both the FTA and NAFTA, Quebec's companies have been able to take full advantage of liberalized trade and investment arrangements with the United States. Exports to the United States and FDI in Quebec are up dramatically since these two regional agreements were implemented (see Chapter 24). For many years, the Canadian dollar also traded at a significant discount to the US dollar, reaching a low of 62 cents in 2002. This discount helped make Quebec goods more attractive to American buyers and spurred on increased export activity by Quebec firms. Recently, the Canadian dollar has strengthened in value, fluctuating between 75 cents and a little above par, thus making Quebec's exports somewhat more expensive for US consumers. Furthermore, the Canada–US border has been 'thickened' by policies implemented by Washington since the terrorist attacks of 11 September 2001. Fearful of another attack, the US government has made border inspections much more onerous and time-consuming. Washington is also requiring that Canadians and even Americans crossing the border carry passports or sophisticated identity cards. This emphasis on security has increased the costs for exporting products from Quebec and has prompted many individual travellers to think twice about planning trips to Quebec. Equally as important, American and other foreign investors might have second thoughts about starting or acquiring business enterprises in Quebec if the costs of shipping their products into the United States become too prohibitive.

The FTA and NAFTA were intended to bolster North American economic co-operation and integration. In particular, these regional accords were expected to assist the North American auto industry to compete more effectively against companies in Asia and Europe. As mentioned earlier, automobile parts assembled in US and Canadian plants for General Motors, Ford, or Chrysler cars or light trucks cross the border several times before the final product is ready to be purchased. However, because of these new post–9/11 policies resulting in major inspection delays at the Canada–US border, companies in Asia and Europe, which export their fully assembled cars or trucks to the United States and face only one inspection at the port of entry, now have a competitive advantage over North American–assembled vehicles.

Canada and the United States maintain the largest and most expansive bilateral economic relationship in the world, but the current decade has presented some major obstacles to further economic integration, especially for Canada. An index developed by Foreign Affairs and International Trade Canada, which measures Canada–US economic integration, nearly tripled from the time the FTA was implemented until 2000.[2] Since 2000, however, the index increased by only 12 per cent through 2006. This limited growth in economic ties represents a major challenge for Canada in general and Quebec in particular.

The current economic challenges include the following. First, the US Department of Homeland Security has established as its priority preventing any terrorists from entering the United States from Canada, regardless of the costs in terms of trade flows and the cross-border movement of people. The stationing of many more Border Patrol agents along the forty-ninth parallel and elaborate and time-consuming inspections of vehicles crossing the border have diminished some of the benefits of NAFTA and of Quebec's close physical proximity to the United States. Second, major fluctuations in the value of the Canadian dollar vis-à-vis the US dollar have complicated the efforts of Quebec's exporters to maintain their market shares within the United States. These fluctuations also prompt potential foreign investors to reconsider establishing plants in Quebec that would be intended to ship a good share of their production to the United States. Third, the recent downturn in the US economy has dampened US consumer demand for many Quebec-originated products, especially in the forestry and manufacturing sectors. Fourth, during periods of economic recession, Quebecers worry that, in spite of NAFTA provisions, the US federal and state governments will become more protectionist in their trade and investment policies and invoke 'Buy American' provisions which require government contractors to use US-made products exclusively.

The first decade of the twenty-first century has produced an unusual number of obstacles to the expansion of economic ties between Canada and the United States. Eventually, economic conditions in general will improve and border inspections will be streamlined. When this occurs, Quebec's business community will be in a much better position to take full advantage of the vast American marketplace with more than 305 million consumers.

Quebec's Expansive Economic Linkages with the United States

Economic Overview

Quebec's territorial expanse covers over 1.5 million square kilometres, making it three times larger than France. Its GDP of Can$298 billion in 2007 was only somewhat smaller than Denmark's, and it would have ranked as the twenty-eighth–largest 'national' economy in the world. Its population base is 7.7 million, almost identical to that of Virginia or Switzerland, and placing it as the fourteenth-most populous unit among the 60 states and provinces in the United States and Canada. However, its international outreach compares more favourably with that of Switzerland than Virginia.

There are two major countries that are clearly priority areas for Quebec's international relations: France and the United States. In the commercial and economic realms, however, the contest is not even close. The United States is Quebec's predominant partner in trade, investment, and tourism. Furthermore, even though governments in Quebec have often been viewed in Washington as far to the left on the political spectrum (as discussed in Chapter 27), they have actually been among the staunchest supporters in Canada of open commercial relations with the United States. The 1974 Foreign Investment Review Act (FIRA) of the national government of Pierre Trudeau in Ottawa was intended to slow down FDI in Canada, with most of that investment coming from the United States. The Parti Québécois (PQ) provincial government in Quebec City later opposed Trudeau's action and openly supported more US FDI within the province. Quebec governments were also a major force in pushing for the creation of the FTA and NAFTA. Former PQ Premier Bernard Landry even voiced strong support for going beyond NAFTA and establishing a North American customs and monetary union which would use the US dollar as its official currency.[3]

In 2007, Quebec's merchandise shipments to the United States totalled Can$52.2 billion, representing

---

Bernard Landry and North American Economic Integration

Bernard Landry smiles after being sworn in as Premier of Quebec in March 2001.

CP PHOTO/Ryan Remiorz

Bernard Landry has been a major figure in the Parti Québécois since he was first elected to Quebec's National Assembly in 1976. During a career spanning more than three decades, he would serve in PQ-led governments as Minister of State for Economic Development, Minister of International Relations, Minister of Finance, Deputy Premier, and finally in 2001 as Premier.

Landry was one of the first and most enthusiastic supporters of greater economic integration with the United States and later, through NAFTA, with Mexico. His vision of continental economic integration went well beyond NAFTA, because he believed that Quebec would benefit from the establishment of a North American customs and monetary union using the US dollar as its official currency. This perspective would transform North America from a simple free trade area into a much more complex and integrative economic entity.

In part, Landry's vision was intended to convince Quebec's voters that opting for political sovereignty would not jeopardize their economic well-being, because they would maintain strong commercial linkages with the rest of Canada and the United States and continue to do business in the world's strongest and most stable currency, the US dollar.

During the campaign leading up to Quebec's 1995 referendum on sovereignty, Landry had been bitterly disappointed that President Bill Clinton and Secretary of State Warren Christopher had interjected themselves into the campaign and warned that Quebec would not be given automatic membership into NAFTA if voters decided to support the sovereignty option. These statements from south of the border made some voters fearful that support for sovereignty might result in an economic downturn in Quebec. This uncertainty may have caused the ultimate defeat of the hotly contested referendum issue with 50.6 per cent opposed to the sovereignty option and 49.4 per cent in favour. Based on this turn of events, Landry was even more resolute in his assertion that Quebec should become a key part of a much more integrated North American economic community. He insisted that if this could be achieved, there would no longer be any question about Quebec's prosperity, even if a future referendum on sovereignty was successful.

He also believed that the challenges presented by globalization and complex interdependence would ultimately require Quebec to exercise greater political control over its own affairs. In an article appearing in *L'Action nationale* in March 1999, Landry argued that 'in the new global context, sovereignty is no longer a question of survival, prosperity or international influence of its people, it is the very quality of their democratic life that is challenged by this new realignment caused by globalization'[4] (our translation).

Landry had received his degree in law from the University of Montreal, but he had also obtained a degree in economics and finance from the Institut d'Études Politiques in Paris. He had been a keen observer of events in Europe and felt that European economic integration had presented a special opportunity for certain regions in Europe, such as Catalonia in Spain, Scotland in the United Kingdom, Flanders in Belgium, and Bavaria in Germany, to push for greater political autonomy, which would protect their linguistic and cultural distinctiveness within their own nation-states and still afford open access to the much larger EU marketplace. He surmised that the same scenario could unfold in an integrated North American marketplace and Quebec would be able to assume full control over its own political destiny and ultimately protect its French language and distinctive Québécois culture, even though it would still be vastly outnumbered by English speakers in the rest of Canada and the United States.

Thus far, Quebec voters have rejected in the 1980 and 1995 referendums Landry's vision of a politically sovereign Quebec nation-state prospering within an economically integrated North American community. However, many Quebec voters do support their province exercising more political autonomy within the framework of the Canadian Confederation and, at the same time, pursuing closer economic linkages with the United States. Presently, the quest for political sovereignty is clearly not a priority for most Quebecers, but Landry remains convinced that within the foreseeable future a majority of his fellow citizens will embrace the sovereignty option.

75 per cent of its total international exports. To put the export picture in perspective, Quebec actually sends more of its goods to the United States than it does to the other nine provinces in Canada combined. However, when one factors in the size of consumer markets in the two countries, there is still room for ample growth in Quebec's trade with the United States. For example, in 2003 Quebec exported more to the western-most province of British Columbia than to neighbouring Washington, Oregon, and California combined, even though British Columbia had less than one-tenth the population of these three US states.[5] This means, in part, that the border still counts and acts as an impediment to the development

of liberalized trade relations. With the recent thickening of the border as a result of US government policies, the strengthening of the Canadian dollar vis-à-vis the US dollar, and minimal growth in the US economy, Quebec's exports to the United States actually fell in value by Can$5 billion between 2005 and 2007.

Quebec has also attracted a lower percentage of US FDI in Canada than its share of Canada's population and GDP would seem to warrant. In part, this is attributable to the concentration of so much FDI in the automobile sector in southern Ontario and in the energy sector in Alberta, and more recently, in Newfoundland and Labrador. Moreover, Quebec has historically faced some significant barriers in attracting investment from the United States. First, the dynamo of the Canadian economy has long been Ontario, which in 2007 accounted for 38 per cent of GDP and 39 per cent of population in Canada. When considering where to invest in Canada, especially in

TABLE 28.1   Quebec's Major Exports to the United States, 2003–2007 (Can$ millions)

Product	2003	2004	2005	2006	2007
Aircraft and related parts	8,244	6,684	6,925	5,212	5,629
Aluminum	3,633	3,817	4,297	5,664	5,496
Paper products and newsprint	3,803	3,985	4,135	4,125	3,315
Electricity	810	741	997	900	1,246
Electronic integrated circuits	1,327	1,432	1,880	1,140	1,181
Non-crude petroleum products	483	630	943	1,009	976
Copper wire	299	546	715	1,236	955
Lumber	1,390	1,819	1591	1,284	943
Refined copper and alloys	218	424	558	1,106	831
Furniture	1,200	1,218	1,096	977	790

Sources: Statistics Canada and l'Institut de la Statistique Québec

TABLE 28.2   Quebec's Major Exports from the United States, 2003–2007 (Can$ millions)

Product	2003	2004	2005	2006	2007
Passenger motor vehicles	3,811	3,674	3,833	3,888	4,050
Aircraft and related parts	1,680	1,623	1,583	1,464	2,811
Trucks for transport of goods	1,344	1,398	1,397	1,459	1,614
Electronic integrated circuits	805	1,333	1,827	1,029	926
Non-crude petroleum products	100	210	336	460	876
Waste and scrap metals	131	238	260	624	824
Retail pharmaceuticals	841	874	722	754	466
Printed circuits	375	442	485	416	335
Heterocyclic compounds and related products	147	261	134	142	329
Computers and peripherals	687	754	775	645	287

Sources: Statistics Canada and l'Institut de la Statistique Québec

the manufacturing sector, American executives often choose the 'Golden Horseshoe' extending from the greater Toronto area around the western end of Lake Ontario. Second, Quebec is the only officially unilingual French-speaking province in Canada and expects most corporations to conduct their business in French and most students to attend French-language schools. American corporate leaders might ask themselves why they should face a new language challenge when they can invest anywhere else in Canada and deal almost exclusively in English. Furthermore, when it comes to transferring some of their executives to Canada, the task is made easier when the children of the executives can attend English-language rather than French-language schools. Third, some of Quebec's enterprises, especially in the extractive and energy sectors, are state-owned and foreign companies often shy away from trying to compete against these enterprises, fearing that the playing field will always favour the businesses owned by the Quebec government. And lastly, Quebec has held two referendums since 1980 on whether or not it should try to separate from Canada, and the PQ still proclaims in its platform that it would like Quebec to achieve political sovereignty through the democratic process. Businesses do not like political uncertainty, and they generally try to avoid investing in a province or even a country which exhibits a high level of such uncertainty. The Snapshot box illustrates this point as it describes what happened in January 1977 when PQ Premier René Lévesque attempted to convince a New York City business audience to continue to invest in Quebec, even if Quebecers were to vote in favour of political sovereignty.

SNAPSHOT

René Lévesque and the Economic Club of New York

A major watershed in both Canadian and Quebec history occurred on 15 November 1976 with the victory of the Parti Québécois (PQ) in Quebec's provincial elections. For the first time in Canadian history, a party had been elected by voters to form a government which pledged to remove a province from the Canadian Confederation. The new PQ premier was René Lévesque, a charismatic and widely respected political leader among Quebec's French-speaking population (see Biography box in Chapter 22).

Lévesque's first major speech outside of Canada was given on 25 January 1977 at the Economic Club of New York. Approximately 1,700 business, financial, and government representatives gathered to hear Lévesque's vision on the future of Quebec and Quebec–US relations. Lévesque was fluent in English and for a long time had widely admired the United States and had even served as a liaison officer and foreign correspondent in the US armed forces during the latter part of the Second World War. He also professed a preference for travelling in the United States over travelling in other parts of Canada outside of Quebec.

In his speech, Quebec's Premier emphasized that his desire to achieve political sovereignty would be strictly democratic and based on a referendum voted on by Quebecers. If the referendum question passed, Lévesque hoped to maintain an economic association with the rest of Canada. He also assured his audience that nothing would change in Quebec–US economic relations other than that the key asbestos industry, then controlled mostly by US and British companies, would be nationalized and fair compensation be paid to the foreign-based owners.

Afterwards, Lévesque referred to his speech as a 'monumental flop'. To be fair, his audience was already skeptical before he even uttered his first word. The Cold War between the United States and its allies on one side, and the Soviet Union and its allies on the other, still dominated international relations. Many business people in the United States feared that a 'socialist' government in neighbouring Quebec would weaken Canada and the Western alliance. Some PQ representatives exacerbated the situation by being non-committal on whether a sovereign Quebec would remain a member of the North Atlantic Treaty Organization (NATO) or what is now called the North American Aerospace Defense Command (NORAD). Some alarmists in the United States even predicted that a sovereign Quebec would become the 'Cuba of the North'.

Lévesque hoped that the US government and the American business and financial communities would not pass judgment on what was developing in Quebec and would remain neutral. He understood the vital importance of US markets and investors for Quebec's economic well-being. He also realized that his task of achieving a majority vote in the referendum would become more difficult if the Quebecers felt a 'yes' vote would result in an exodus of US investment from the province and create more barriers to trade with the United States. The referendum was finally held in May 1980 and the pro-sovereignty side suffered a decisive defeat, 40 per cent in favour of sovereignty and 60 per cent opposed. Among the French-speaking voters, roughly half supported the sovereignty option.

On the other hand, the sovereignty issue, which is discussed in greater detail in other chapters, has been on the back burner for over a decade and Quebec is now at the cutting edge in the world in aeronautics, multi-media and software development, bio-pharmaceuticals, hydroelectricity, and several other commercial fields. The overall cost of doing business in the province is relatively low, and its business schools provide many highly trained and mostly multilingual graduates.[6] The commercial hub of the province, Montreal, is situated a few kilometres from the US border and is within a 1,000-kilometre radius of 110 million consumers and a 600-kilometre radius of such major population centres as New York City, Boston, and Toronto. With its abundance of hydroelectricity, the province provides among the best energy rates in North America to business enterprises and its corporate taxation structure, and research and development tax incentives are among the most competitive on the continent. Investissement Québec, the government agency responsible for facilitating FDI, also offers a wide array of financial and other incentives to foreign investors. Although the province faces major challenges from US and other Canadian jurisdictions in an effort to attract domestic, US, and international direct investment, the overall economy has grown steadily in Quebec through much of the current decade, and Quebec's provincial governments have been very favourable toward most FDI activity and business development in general. Furthermore, US multinational companies are accustomed to doing business overseas in languages other than English, and Quebec's Charter of the French Language, which mandates the use of French in the workplace for large companies, should not be considered as major impediment to investment by these major US enterprises.[7]

Tourism linkages between Quebec and the United States, although robust when compared with other international destinations, have recently been under some duress. For the past several decades, the vast majority of all international visitors to Quebec have come from the United States, and the Quebec government hoped to attract a record number of US visitors in 2008 as Quebec City celebrated the four-hundredth anniversary of its founding by Samuel de Champlain. Unfortunately, a perfect storm gathered which kept US visits below expectations. First, the price of gasoline and airfares spiralled upward through the critical summer tourism period. Second, the Canadian dollar traded for most of the year at historically high levels against the US dollar. Third, the complicated and costly US passport requirements dissuaded Americans from coming northward. And fourth, some US travellers perceived that the long border delays to re-enter the United States by car were simply not worth the effort. Of course, many of these problems encountered in 2008 may be short term. Energy prices have already moderated, border inspections may become streamlined, a greater number of Americans will procure 10-year passports or special ID cards, and the value of the Canadian dollar will continue to fluctuate against the US dollar. The challenge then facing Quebec's tourism industry is to convince Americans that the *belle province* is an exciting place to visit. More

Americans visit Mexico every year than Canada, in part because of Mexico's sunshine, warm temperatures, nice beaches, and Mayan and Aztec historical sites. Quebec, in contrast, is stereotyped by many Americans as being rather staid with cold weather and nondescript cities. In reality, Quebec may be the most European among all North American destinations; it has great ski resorts, vibrant urban areas in Montreal and the historic walled enclave of Quebec City, and its French *joie de vivre* is perhaps unparalleled. It is also a safe place to visit with very low levels of crime. Nevertheless, with tourism representing such a significant percentage of jobs and GDP in Quebec, much more must be done to alter the perceptions of Americans in order to entice a higher percentage of US residents to venture northward.

THE QUEBEC GOVERNMENT'S EFFORTS TO SOLIDIFY ECONOMIC TIES

The government of Quebec established its first office in the United States almost 70 years ago in 1940, and as Louis Balthazar points out in Chapter 27, Quebec now maintains six delegations or bureaus in the United States, more than the number of consulates operated there by the national governments of Ireland, Hungary, Bulgaria, Egypt, Ethiopia, Singapore, and 70 other nation-states.[8] In the economic realm, Quebec's delegations in the United States work to create more export opportunities for their business community back home, entice American companies to make direct investments in the province, facilitate the efforts by Quebec enterprises to secure more US venture-capital financing and to enter into marketing and licensing arrangements with US firms, and convince Americans in general that Quebec is a great place to visit and spend their tourist dollars. Quebec's representatives work directly with state government officials and business executives, with each delegation given responsibility for specific geographic areas. For example, the Quebec delegation in Boston considers that its role 'is to foster and consolidate relations between the Government of Quebec and the six New England States, by negotiating multi-sector

agreements and conducting activities in fields of recognized importance such as energy, the environment, security and transportation'.[9] The delegation's official brochure adds that 'in the fields of culture, education and tourism, the Office strives to promote Quebec's institutions and talents through a variety of events or exchanges with Quebec's partners in Boston and throughout New England.'[10]

Using the Ministry of International Relations (Ministère des Relations internationales or MRI) and its network of offices in the United States for logistical arrangements, Quebec's premier will usually plan two to four official visits to the United States annually, and other ministers will make numerous trips to make or renew the acquaintance of federal and state officials and business leaders, and to participate in trade shows, conventions, or specialized conferences. In June 2008, Premier Jean Charest led a trade mission to the Southeast United States as a follow-up to a meeting in Montreal nearly a year earlier which established the Southeastern US–Canadian Provinces Alliance. Also in 2008, Charest announced that Quebec has joined the Western Climate Initiative to reduce greenhouse gas emissions. The other partners in this cross-border initiative are Arizona, California, Montana, New Mexico, Oregon, Utah, and Washington, plus British Columbia, Manitoba, and Ontario.

Quebec also has a wide range of regional or bilateral arrangements with its neighbouring states, with the most high profile being the periodic Quebec–New York economic summit bringing together the Premier and the Governor. In 1999, these two governments established a trade-corridor project to upgrade their economic relationship, and the 2008 summit resulted in a pledge to make that corridor 'greener' with an emphasis on cross-border renewable energy projects. In addition, over the past few years, the Quebec Federation of Chambers of Commerce has entered into partnership arrangements with business associations in Vermont and New Hampshire aimed at strengthening cross-border trade, transportation, research and development, tourism, energy, and environmental co-operation.

By far, the Quebec government maintains the deepest and most expansive ties to the United States of any provincial government in Canada, or, for that matter, any other subnational government in the world. In economic terms, it is easy to understand the rationale for the Quebec government's involvement in the United States. Other than the United States as a whole, New York was the leading destination in the world for Quebec's exports in 2007. Indeed, Quebec would export more that year to the individual states of New York, Texas, Pennsylvania, Tennessee, Illinois, Vermont, Ohio, Michigan, New Jersey, and Massachusetts, than it would to its second-leading national export partner, the United Kingdom. Commercial ties to the United States are, without any doubt, vital for job creation, business diversification, and overall economic modernization and competitiveness in the province of Quebec.

FUTURE CHALLENGES AND OPPORTUNITIES IN THE BILATERAL ECONOMIC RELATIONSHIP[11]

The Quebec government's 2006 International Policy report emphasizes that the United States is a major priority for Quebec. This is spelled out in priority two, strengthening and increasing economic exchanges with the United States and Europe, and in priority three, contributing to the security of the North American continent. Since the report was released, the government has increased its resources devoted to the United States through upgrading several of its US offices.[12]

One goal of the Quebec government will be to ensure that NAFTA is respected by all of its constituent members, because the free movement of goods, services, and investment has helped to strengthen Quebec's economy and make it more competitive within North America and around the world. In the aggregate, the past 20 years of free trade beginning with the implementation of the FTA in 1989 have been very good for Canada and Quebec. Canada's GDP at the end of 2007 was US$1.3 trillion, ranking it as the ninth-largest economy in the world. This is a remarkable achievement because each of the eight nations ahead of Canada and the five nations immediately behind it has a much larger population base, with Canada having only the thirty-fifth–largest population among the world's nations. Canada's

economic growth rate over the past several years has been near the top of the major Western countries, it has enjoyed net job creation for 15 consecutive years through 2007, and its unemployment rate fell to a 33-year low in mid-2008. For Quebec, the unemployment rate has been near a three-decade low and job creation has been robust. Quebec's employment participation rate also hit 61 per cent during 2007, the highest ever recorded in the province.

NAFTA was fully implemented in 2008. Its goals have been limited and focused, with the intent 'to eliminate, progressively, tariff and non-tariff barriers, to trade in goods and services, to establish clear rules for investment, and to strengthen intellectual property rights, and, in the process, to create effective dispute settlement mechanisms'.[13] Most of these objectives have been achieved, and perhaps a new Canada–US economic agenda with more ambitious goals will be negotiated in the future as North America gears up for even greater competition from across the Atlantic and the Pacific and even within the Western hemisphere. As clearly manifested by a century and a half of on-again, off-again Canada–US bilateral trade negotiations, Ottawa, along with Quebec City and other provincial capitals, will likely take the lead in introducing any new cross-border economic agenda.

The Quebec government will also pursue other policies aimed at solidifying its commercial interests with the United States. It already supports the development of fast and efficient border controls at the forty-ninth parallel, which would allow goods and people to cross with minimum disruption. It would like its natural resources and energy sources such as lumber and hydro-power to enter the United States without any impediments. It would like to attract private investment and new technological innovations from the United States in order to expand and modernize the province's infrastructure and business sector. It would like more Americans to spend their tourist dollars in Quebec rather than in other foreign destinations, and would appreciate Washington not imposing even more rigorous passport and identification requirements which might dissuade Americans from leaving their country. It would also like to sustain robust economic expansion while at the same time producing a cleaner and greener environment.

The people of Quebec are among the relatively few who actually share a border with the United States. Some might argue that, in an era of globalization and multi-level interdependence, this close proximity carries its own burdens and risks, such as the pervasive influence of American culture and the necessity of competing against US business enterprises which are usually much larger than any counterparts found in Quebec.

On the other hand, Quebec's companies enjoy a comparative advantage in having the world's largest consumer market on their doorstep. Travel to Quebec's major cities is also much easier for Americans than travel to Europe, Asia, or South America. Venture capitalists and American investors in general are within close proximity to Quebec, with neighbouring New York state being home to one of the two largest financial markets in the world.

During recessions, Quebec's export, direct investment, and tourism linkages to the United States naturally struggle to grow. However, recessions generally last for several months, whereas economic growth tends to last for several years. Under conditions of economic growth, Quebec is still in very good shape to benefit substantially from being situated right next door to the world's largest national economy. The Quebec government's very sophisticated and expansive international policies toward the United States, including its network of permanent delegations scattered throughout the United States, help solidify prospects for a growing bilateral economic relationship.

QUESTIONS FOR CONSIDERATION

1. Should provincial governments such as Quebec engage in international economic relations with other countries, or should this responsibility be reserved to Canada's national government in Ottawa?

2. Some argue that Quebec should play a major role in pushing for a new economic arrangement between Canada and the United States, and perhaps even Mexico, which would go beyond NAFTA and perhaps lead to a common currency, a customs union which harmonizes tariffs on exports from other countries, and also permits the free movement across the border of skilled labour. What would be the potential advantages and disadvantages for Quebec of pursuing such a policy option?

3. Why do so many Americans seem to know so little about Quebec, and should the Quebec government attempt to 'educate' Americans about the many positive features of Quebec society?

NOTES

1. Stephen Blank, 'Trade Corridors and North American Competitiveness,' *The American Review of Canadian Studies* 38 (Summer 2008): 231.

2. Aaron Sydor, 'An Index of Canada-U.S. Economic Integration,' in *Foreign Affairs and International Trade Canada Analytic Paper Series*, June 2008.

3. Bernard Landry, *La cause du Québec* (Montréal: VLB éditeur, 2002), 205–9.

4. The original French version stated: 'dans la nouveau contexte mondial, la souveraineté n'est plus seulement une question de survie, de prospérité et de rayonnement international des peuples, c'est la qualité meme de leur vie démocratique qui est mise en cause par cette nouvelle donne qui constitue la mondialisation.'

5. Développement économique, Innovation et Exportation Québec, 'Les relations économique entre le Québec et les États-Unis,' *Note sur le commerce extérieur*, 4 July 2007, 1.

6. The *Economist* Intelligence Unit designates Canada as the top-ranked nation among the G-7 countries for doing business between 2008 and 2012 (see www.investcanada.gc.ca/en/advantage-canada/business_environment.aspx). Over the past several years, KMPG has ranked both Quebec City and Montreal as having much lower overall business costs than neighboring US cities such as Boston, New York City, and Philadelphia. See www.competitivealternatives.com/results/results.asp.

7. The language issue as related to Frito-Lay, a division of US-based PepsiCo, is discussed at www.cslf.gouv.qc.ca/publications/PubC132/C132.html.

8. US Department of State, *Consular Offices in the United States* (Washington, DC: Government Printing Office, 2006).

9. Ministry of International Relations, Government of Quebec, *Quebec Government Office in Boston*, 2007.
10. Ibid.
11. Specific policy recommendations for the Quebec government to improve its economic relations with the 50 US state governments are found in Earl H. Fry, 'Quebec's Relations with States in the U.S. Federal System: Challenges and Opportunities,' paper presented at the Biennial Conference of the American Council for Quebec Studies, Quebec, 15 November 2008.
12. Ministry of International Relations, Government of Quebec, *La politique internationale du Québec: Plan d'action 2006–2009* (Quebec: Government of Quebec, 2007), 31.
13. These are the words of US Assistant Secretary of State E. Anthony Wayne in praising NAFTA as a success story. See 'NAFTA: A Ten Year Perspective and Implications for the Future,' Hearing before the Subcommittee on International Economic Policy, Export, and Trade Promotion, Committee on Foreign Relations, US Senate, 24 April 2004.

RELEVANT WEBSITES

MINISTRY OF INTERNATIONAL RELATIONS / MINISTÈRE DES RELATIONS INTERNATIONALES:
www.mri.gouv.gc.ca
Numerous statistics, addresses, and contacts for Quebec offices in the United States, and historical data on development of Quebec–US relations.

INSTITUT DE LA STATISTIQUE QUÉBEC:
www.stat.gouv.qc.ca
A wide range of economic data on Quebec–US commercial interactions.

TOURISME QUÉBEC: www.bonjour.quebec.com
Information for tourists coming to Quebec and some tourism-related statistics.

INVESTISSEMENT QUÉBEC: www.investquebec.com
Statistics on foreign direct investment activity within the province and lists incentives which might be available to US and other foreign companies considering investing in Quebec.

STATISTICS CANADA: www.statcan.gc.ca
Data related to Canada–US and Quebec–US economic relations.

SELECT BIBLIOGRAPHY

Balthazar, Louis, and Alfred Hero, Jr. *Le Québec dans l'espace américain*. Montreal: Éditions Québec Amérique, 1999.

———, Louis Bélanger, Gordon Mace, et al. *Trente ans de politique extérieure du Québec 1960–1990*. Quebec: Centre québécois de relations internationales et Les editions de Septentrion, 1993.

Bernier, Luc. *De Paris à Washington: la politique internationale du Québec*. Quebec: Presse de l'Université du Québec, 1996.

Blank, Stephen. 'Trade Corridors and North American Competitiveness,' *The American Review of Canadian Studies* 38 (Summer 2008): 231–37.

Fry, Earl H. 'Quebec's Relations with the United States.' *The American Review of Canadian Studies* 32 (Summer 2002): 323–42.

———. *The Role of Sub-National Governments in North American Integration*. Montreal: Institute for Research on Public Policy, 2004.

Gagné, Gilbert. 'Cultural Sovereignty, Identity and North American Integration: On the Relevance of the U.S.-Canada-Quebec Border,' *Quebec Studies* 36 (Fall/Winter 2003–4): 29–49.

Landry, Bernard. *La cause du Québec*. Montreal: VLB éditeur, 2002.

Lisée, Jean-François. *In the Eye of the Eagle*. Toronto: HarperCollins, 1990.

Ministry of International Relations, Government of Quebec. *La politique internationale du Québec: Plan d'action 2006–2009*. Quebec: Government of Quebec, 2007.

———. *Quebec's International Policy: Working in Concert*. Quebec: Government of Quebec, 2006.

CHAPTER 29

Quebec Theatre: New Dynamics between the Local and the International

Sylvain Schryburt, University of Ottawa

— TIMELINE —

1948 Production of *Tit-Coq* by Gratien Gélinas premieres, directed by Fred Barry.

1951 Théâtre du Nouveau Monde presents its first show, Molière's *L'Avare* (*The Miser*), directed by Jean Gascon.

1954 Conservatoire d'art dramatique de Montréal founded. Conservatoire d'art dramatique de Québec and Theatre School of Canada (Montreal) follow in 1957 and 1960, respectively.

1958 Association canadienne du théâtre amateur (ACTA) founded by Guy Beaulne. Name changed in 1972 to Association québécoise du jeune théâtre (AQJT).

1965 Centre d'essai des auteurs dramatiques (CEAD) founded, today called Centre des auteurs dramatiques.

1968 *Les Belles-sœurs* by Michel Tremblay premieres, directed by André Brassard.

1981 First Conference on State of Professional Theatre in Quebec.

1982 Denis Marleau founds Théâtre UBU, today known as UBU compagnie de création.

1985 Festival de théâtre des Amériques (FTA) founded (later to become Festival TransAmériques, in 2007).

1987 Théâtre Repère's *Trilogie des dragons* (*The Dragons' Trilogy*), directed by Robert Lepage, triumphs at second edition of FTA.

1994 Robert Lepage founds Ex Machina.

1995 Usine C, multidisciplinary creative and stage production space, officially opens. Debut performance is a retrospective of work of Gilles Maheu and his company, Carbone 14 (1981–2005).

1997 Théâtre UBU's *Nathan le Sage* performed in Cour d'honneur of Palais des Papes at 51st Festival d'Avignon. Directed by Denis Marleau.

2007 Second Conference on State of Professional Theatre in Quebec.

2009 Wajdi Mouawad named 'Associated Artist' of 63rd Festival d'Avignon.

Because it is a living and therefore transitory art form, Quebec theatre, like any other national[1] theatre, is still rarely seen outside its birthplace. This historical trend has held true within the province. For example, local Quebec City productions are seldom performed in Montreal, and vice versa. On a larger, international scale, the same trend has held true in that, apart from a few noteworthy figures, knowledge of Quebec's theatrical activity is still marginal among foreign audiences and scholars alike. Against the current of this prevailing trend, since the 1980s some directors and playwrights have managed to break through and claim the world stage. Today, directors like Marie Brassard, Robert Lepage, Gilles Maheu, and Denis Marleau, and playwrights like Daniel Danis, Carole Fréchette, Wajdi Mouawad, and the long-established Michel Tremblay may be said to epitomize Quebec theatre abroad.

This chapter discusses the relatively new phenomenon of the international distribution of Quebec theatre and focuses more specifically on the handful of playwrights and directors who have succeeded in sharing their works through prestigious international venues and distribution networks. To situate our discussion within its wider context, we review the far-reaching changes that have taken place in the writing, institutions, and aesthetics of Quebec theatre since the mid-1960s, when it definitively embraced modernity. These points of reference will be helpful in understanding the enduring new dynamics of theatre ushered in during the 1980s: gradually, the local 'theatrical field'[2] in Quebec made links to the international theatrical field, where some of the most respected figures of Quebec contemporary theatre presented their productions, unfettered by borders or local artistic dynamics. By establishing themselves as players both at home (during the regular theatre season in Quebec City and Montreal) and abroad (working within international networks), the most celebrated artists of contemporary Quebec theatre developed simultaneously within these two theatrical fields, a 'double social inscription'[3] that I believe broadly constitutes the configuration of theatre in the Western world in our times.

From Assertions of Identity to Experiments with Form: 1965 to 1980

The rare scholarly works that offer a diachronic reading of modern and contemporary Quebec theatre usually bracket their studies between 1965 and 1980. It was in 1965 that the Centre d'essai des auteurs

dramatiques (CEAD[4]) was founded, charged with the mandate (which it still maintains today) of supporting, disseminating, and promoting the work of Quebec and Franco-Canadian playwrights. For theatre historians, the arrival of CEAD heralded (or confirmed) the genesis of a long dreamt-of autonomous national theatre, theatre that (for a change) would not be derived from models imported from France but would resonate with the national assertions of identity that were the quintessence of the Quiet Revolution.

The drive to make the language of dramatic literature more autonomous, pioneered by young artists of the baby-boom generation, registered its first popular and critical successes with Michel Tremblay's *Les Belles-sœurs* in 1968, followed by the collective creation, *T'es pas tannée, Jeanne d'Arc?* by Grand Cirque Ordinaire, one year later. On one hand, the 1970s saw the rapid growth of creative theatre collectives in pursuit of 'the words to express ourselves',[5] a goal very typical of the artistic approach of the period in Quebec. The use of *joual*, a distinctively Québécois French vernacular, previously deemed too unrefined for the theatre, was reclaimed in the scripts of this era as the authentic and legitimate popular voice of Quebec. On the other hand, the unprecedented boom of locally written material was so voluminous that it soon accounted for a good half of all theatre productions on offer across the province.[6] The number of both government-subsidized and private theatre companies[7] snowballed during this period, putting significantly more plays on Quebec stages. In Montreal alone, theatre productions quadrupled between 1960 and 1980, propelled from 30 to 120 productions per season.[8]

Born of the burgeoning and imperative need for self-expression that reigned during this era, Quebec playwriting was conceptualized as a locus for new creations rather than as a repertoire to invest in and revisit. As a result, of all the playwrights mentioned in Jean Cléo Godin and Laurent Mailhot's two-volume *Le Théâtre québécois* (containing selected plays performed and published from 1940 to 1980), Réjean Ducharme, Claude Gauvreau, and Michel Tremblay are the only authors whose plays are still regularly performed on the contemporary Quebec stage.[9]

At the beginning of the 1980s, following a decade of excitement and somewhat frenzied development, the theatre community was faced with the first growing pains of its history. As their numbers mushroomed, companies soon saturated their limited local markets, underfunded[10] by public authorities who were criticized for their inadequate cultural policies.[11] It was in this chaotic context that the First Conference on the State of Professional Theatre in Quebec was held in November 1981 and culminated in the formation of some 10 professional associations and groupings. These new entities would lay the groundwork for professional practices in Quebec theatre, but they would also splinter the theatre community into pressure groups whose interests sometimes clashed.[12] Whereas the 1970s had been a time of expansion, in the 1980s Quebec theatre would consolidate its institutions and stabilize its assets.

While the intense focus on national identity had lent a measure of uniformity to Quebec playwriting since the Quiet Revolution, it was succeeded in the 1980s and 1990s by a sweeping diversification of aesthetics. From introspective scripts that questioned our roles as individuals in society (Carole Fréchette) and dark, dream-like poetical prose (Daniel Danis), to realist or urban writing (François Archambault), fragmented texts with postmodern slants (Normand Chaurette, René-Daniel Dubois), and works about exile verging on the tragic (Wajdi Mouawad), high-profile playwrights of the times used many approaches and spoke with many voices. Amid all of these voices, the vernacular of *joual,* which had been indispensable to nationalist theatre of the 1960s and 1970s, lost its subversive powers and came to be regarded as just another stylistic device.

Along with this diversification of voices in Quebec theatre during the 1980s and beyond, stage directing broke free of the printed script. Some directors (often those who made their mark on the international stage) distanced themselves from strictly script-centric theatrical traditions and made greater use of stage imagery, actors' bodies, new media and technology, intermediality[13] and interdisciplinarity, hybrids of different stage traditions, or compelling and architecturally complex set designs. These creative thinkers, who were emblematic of an entirely new conception of theatrical performance, would become the main Quebec players in what I call the 'internationalization of theatre'.

THE INTERNATIONALIZATION OF QUEBEC THEATRE

Faced with saturated local markets and following the First Conference on the State of Professional Theatre in Quebec (1981), an increasing number of theatre producers decided to try their luck abroad. From then onwards, international tours by small Quebec companies became commonplace and some began to carve out a niche for themselves.[14] Robert Lepage was among the first directors to distinguish himself to foreign audiences. For over a quarter century now, Lepage has been creating compelling imagistic theatre, an aesthetic greatly enhanced by the use of new technology (especially video projection) since he founded the Ex Machina production company in 1994 (see Biography box). Denis Marleau, founding director of the theatre company UBU (1981–), distinguished himself in another vein entirely, with a body of work that initially drew its inspiration from the historical avant-garde movements and used the performative resources of voice, but later focused on major modern European writers (for example, Maeterlinck, Beckett, Pessoa, and Fosse) and used what would become his trademark projections of visuals. Last but not least on this very short list, Gilles Maheu's company, Carbone 14 (1980–2005), stood out as the first Quebec theatre company to commit to interdisciplinarity, producing unequivocally postmodern works that deliberately blurred the boundaries between dance, theatre, and performance.

These three international figureheads of theatre directing have shared world acclaim with a number of other theatre artists and companies that tour somewhat regularly abroad, including: Marie Brassard's theatre company Infrarouge; Paula de Vasconcelos's theatre-dance troupe, Pigeons International, and the now defunct Théâtre Ô Parleur, whose former guiding light, Wajdi Mouawad (of Au carré de l'hypoténuse) is now pursuing a solo career. There is also the particularly active sector of theatre for young audiences, spearheaded by Les Deux Mondes, Le Carrousel, Théâtre des Confettis, Théâtre Bouches Décousues, and Théâtre de l'Œil, whose productions are also seen on their countless regular international tours.

ROBERT LEPAGE

Quebec director and actor Robert Lepage in October 2009

The Canadian Press/
Darren Calabrese

Robert Lepage is one of the few directors in Quebec who has made a name for himself well beyond a limited local sphere of aficionados. A genuine international superstar, he has piqued interest and stirred enthusiasm in theatre, film, and opera for nearly three decades running—a rare achievement in these highly competitive milieus, prone as they are to the whims of fashion and fads. Throughout his career, Lepage has shown an exceptional ability to keep pace with and, at times, outstrip trends in contemporary dramatic arts, making him a major celebrity in theatre abroad, and all the more so at home.

Born 12 December 1957, Lepage earned a certificate in acting from the Conservatoire de Québec (1975–8), rounding out his education with Alain Knapp in Paris. Upon his return to Quebec, he joined Théâtre Repère in 1982, and quickly rose to the position of Artistic Co-director and Principal Director. *Circulations* (1984) and the solo work, *Vinci* (1986) built his reputation as a director in Quebec. But it was through his second production of *La Trilogie des dragons* (*The Dragons' Trilogy*) (1987), a six-hour saga, that he broke into the relatively closed world of international theatre. Reworked versions of this landmark play toured internationally for five years—an unparalleled achievement in the history of Quebec theatre that would become the norm for most of Lepage's later works.

Le Polygraphe (*Polygraph*) (1987) and *Plaques tectoniques* (*Tectonic Plates*) (1988) followed, establishing Lepage's modus operandi: the layering of works in progress, the use of improvisation and epic devices in developing shows and playwriting, multilingualism and multiculturalism, experimentation with new technologies, playing with audience perception and perspective, and imagistic theatre. In Lepage's shows, recurring situations and themes also emerge. Leitmotifs include characters from Quebec who set out to discover the world, historical characters, misunderstood or maladjusted intellectuals, the quest for identity, the intertwining of major historical events and everyday life stories, drug use, and the juxtaposition of pop and high culture.

After leaving the helm at Théâtre Repère, Lepage became Artistic Director for the Théâtre français from 1989 to 1993 at the National Arts Centre (NAC) in Ottawa. There he presented *Les Aiguilles et l'opium* (1991) (*Needles and Opium*), the second in a series of one-man shows. During this period, Lepage made regular forays into the Shakespearean repertoire (for example, French-language versions of *Macbeth*, *Coriolanus*, and *The Tempest*), and multiplied his collaborative efforts with some of the most prestigious theatres in Europe and elsewhere. Indeed, whereas Lepage's previous efforts had been entirely focused on creating new works, during this period he tackled a classic European repertoire, sometimes presenting bold rereadings, such as a 1992 version of *A Midsummer Night's Dream* performed entirely in a sea of mud. Along similar lines, he directed plays by Brecht, Dürrenmatt, and Strindberg, and made his first forays into opera (*Erwartung* and *Le Château de Barbe-Bleue* [*Bluebeard's Castle*], 1992), emphasizing the spectacular aspects of these works.

In 1994, following his tenure with the Théâtre français at the NAC, Lepage founded Ex Machina. The company's first show, *Les Sept branches de la rivière Ota* (*The Seven Streams of the River Ota*) (1994), and a number of later productions (*Le Polygraphe* [*Polygraph*], 1996, and *La Géométrie des miracles* [*Geometry of Miracles*], 1998), revisited the great sagas of Théâtre Repère. The solo shows Lepage created at Ex Machina made more complex use of new technologies, as in *Elseneur* (*Elsinore*) (1995), a solo version of *Hamlet* that completed the Shakespearean circle he began some years earlier. Despite Lepage's ever-increasing use of leading-edge technology, the aesthetics of most of the company's productions remained firmly rooted in simple theatricality. His sense of wonder and humour, delight in play, and inventiveness, and his ingenious, understated metonymic devices that seamlessly compress and expand time and space make Lepage an artist who is well loved by the masses and aficionados alike.

The fresh start Lepage made by founding of Ex Machina also marked his foursquare debut as a multidisciplinary artist. Besides his work in opera, still an area of occasional experimentation, he was appointed Commissioner of the show *Métissages* (2000) at the Musée de la civilisation de Québec. He directed the Cirque du Soleil show, *Kà* (2004) in Las Vegas and designed *Moulin à images* (*The Image Mill*) (2008), an ambitious outdoor projection in the Port of Québec on an imposing horizon of 81 grain silos to recount Quebec City's 400-year history in sound and images. Lepage has also launched a highly acclaimed career as a filmmaker, directing five films between 1995 and 2003, mostly adaptations of his stage works.

Throughout his career, Lepage has demonstrated a strong attachment to his birthplace, Quebec City. It was there, in 1997, that he opened La Caserne, creative hub and home to Ex Machina's archives and offices. This facility also includes a stage space where the company's productions in progress are sometimes presented. The numerous awards Lepage has garnered include the Order of Canada (1994), Ordre national du Québec (1999), and the Europe Theatre Prize (2007).

In many respects, Robert Lepage's career path reflects that of contemporary theatre, which has veered away from its past 'script-centricity' to explore forms that play freely with the boundaries of the dramatic arts. In so doing, stage direction has proclaimed independence from the script, which has come to be regarded as one tool among many at the service of performances whose meaning is unpacked and constructed beyond the printed word. While Lepage's detractors have justifiably attacked the drawbacks to this pragmatic approach to playwriting, in which the script no longer speaks for itself but serves as a simple pretext for directors to explore their personal aesthetic vision, it remains that Lepage's inimitable approach has helped free theatre from the literary rut it was in.

Given the prestige and the symbolic capital garnered from their international reach and their endorsement by foreign audiences, most of these companies enjoy exceptional status in the theatrical fields of Montreal and Quebec City. Often cited as examples to prove the vitality of Quebec theatre, these ambassadors of culture have become a source of national pride for Quebec and their achievements abroad seem to reflect well on the Quebec arts community as a whole. While the international presence of Quebec theatre is a sign of its artistic maturity, this presence also raises the question of how these companies (being part of both the dynamics of regular theatre seasons at home and of the highly competitive environment in major world theatre festivals) are socially inscribed. In other words: How have they established themselves on a sociological level?

To answer this question, we can begin by examining the balance struck between local productions and those designed for international competition. This examination will allow us to analyze and understand the new dynamics that, over and above the artistic merit of these creators, seem to define the distinctive character of contemporary Quebec theatre. Two concepts may be helpful in characterizing the far-reaching paradigm shifts in the dynamics of Quebec theatre: the well-known concept of 'field', as defined by French sociologist Pierre Bourdieu,[15] and the concept of what we will call 'festival theatre', which allows us to consider the theatrical means of production, the scope of audience expectations, and the aesthetic parameters that guide the development and appreciation of productions.

LOCAL THEATRICAL FIELD—
INTERNATIONAL THEATRICAL FIELD

The notion of 'field', as proposed by Pierre Bourdieu, divides society into dynamic spaces in which social agents struggle to impose their views on the economy, politics, culture, and other areas of public life. In the realm of the arts, artists are ultimately struggling to impose their own 'legitimate' definition of art and thus define the very boundaries of the field in which they have agency. The notion of 'field' in the realm of theatre (as in dance and other living arts) must take into consideration the fact that performance (by nature a unique and ephemeral event) has no real manifestation or existence outside of the local community of artists and theatregoers or outside of its occasional dissemination through reviews or rumours. So while we might be tempted to conceptualize Quebec's theatrical field as a function of a 'national space', it is more logical to conceptualize it according to the geographical boundaries of its performers, audiences, and main 'instances of consecration'[16] — in other words, we should scale back our theatrical field to focus on the major cities likely to produce viable theatre communities. Unlike literature or film, theatre, being a stage-based art, is rarely seen outside the city where it is produced, since touring productions require complex logistics, seasoned distribution networks, and above all, financial investment that is often prohibitive. Thus, the province of Quebec really has only two theatrical fields that are sufficiently developed to support a community of theatre professionals and a relatively diversified spectrum of companies: one in Montreal, the other in Quebec City, each with its own flagship institutions, sites of cultural dissemination (performance venues), and theatre critics.

In Montreal, theatrical hub of the province of Quebec, the local theatrical field is dominated by a dozen or so prestigious companies that possess a high degree of 'consecration'. They manage their own theatres and, most importantly, occupy a specific market niche, catering to a target public, which consists mainly of season-ticket holders. For instance, Théâtre du Rideau Vert (1949–), the doyen of Quebec theatre companies, offers mostly light, popular entertainment (variety shows, comedies, and musicals); Théâtre du Nouveau Monde (1951–), the city's most prestigious

theatre, presents mainly classic and modern plays from European repertoires; Théâtre d'Aujourd'hui (1968–) is entirely devoted to the work of Quebec playwrights; the Compagnie Jean Duceppe (1973–) specializes in canonical American drama (e.g., Albee, Miller); Théâtre de la Manufacture (1975–) presents realist theatre by English-language playwrights (in translation) and Quebec French-language playwrights; and Espace GO (1990–) leans towards the contemporary, presenting mostly European plays. Today, it is the full-time artistic directors of these institutional companies who define their specific aesthetic and 'social inscription', rather than the contractual theatre artists hired to produce one of the four or five shows on the season roster.

Alongside these more firmly institutionalized companies, we find about a hundred smaller players, of whom 15 or so show a high degree of specific consecration, constituting what Bourdieu calls 'restricted subfields of production'.[17] These small companies are usually founded and run by directors whose respective idiosyncrasies are their sole guarantee of aesthetic specificity. Inscribed within the theatrical field of Montreal, their plays are produced in part thanks to the capital provided by national governments,[18] and they compete for consecration through provincial 'instances of legitimation',[19] such as annual awards from the Association québécoise des critiques de theatre (1995–) and (previously) the Masques Awards from the Académie québécoise du théâtre (an umbrella organization for all Quebec's theatre professionals from 1993 to 2008). Quebec companies that frequently tour abroad also compete for the same grants, sometimes using the same distribution network, and vie with less famous companies from Quebec for the backing of the same instances of legitimation. Indeed, their institutional inscription resembles that of companies whose work is exclusively destined for local consumption.

Clearly, a local market the size of Montreal has its limitations for most of the few companies, whose work, without necessarily being avant-garde, is too innovative or challenging to hope to reach more than a limited audience. At last count in the theatrical field of Montreal, companies like Denis Marleau's UBU, Paula de Vasconcelos's theatre-dance company Pigeons International, and Gilles Maheu's (now defunct) Carbone 14 depended upon a public that rarely exceeded three or four thousand spectators. The limited opportunities at home partly explain why these producers, while still inscribed in the local theatrical field and still an integral part of the regular metropolitan theatre season, would also attempt to access the circuit of the international theatrical field for its expanded pool of theatre-goers with 'cultivated dispositions', its own sites of dissemination, and distinctive marks of consecration (for example, opening for the illustrious Festival d'Avignon or appearing in special issues of European arts magazines showcasing Quebec theatre artists).

Of course the transition from one theatrical field to another, from the local to the international, is no accident. This transition depends on aesthetic affinities between local Quebec artists and the major international distributors (theatre festivals). Success abroad also depends on the logistical ability to enter an extremely selective, restricted distribution network and access foreign capital, often essential to the complex funding arrangements required for touring abroad. The transition from the local to the international field is all the more daunting since the highly coveted 'originality' factor, characteristic of 'festival theatre', is measured on an international scale, where the struggle to be distinctive is undisputedly fiercer than in the less competitive environment of Montreal.

The institutional and economic difficulties faced by theatre companies who wish to break into the international touring network are different from those facing playwrights. A number of Quebec writers have often had their works performed abroad, either in translation or in the original language. For these theatre artists, penetrating the international market largely depends on individual affinities, as foreign artistic directors or stage directors are generally in charge of choosing which plays will be produced and bankrolling the attendant local costs from their regular operating budgets. Such is not the case for festival theatre, as I define the term.

FESTIVAL THEATRE

Quebec productions destined for markets abroad may seem radically new when presented at home (compared to the rest of the season's roster), but it is important to understand that they are governed by different standards, as are most of the productions selected for the major festival tours that establish international reputations. Festival theatre has its own funding formulas and networks, sites of dissemination, and instances of legitimation. The shows developed within this framework have the peculiarity of being funded by the national organizations from several countries and are developed as co-productions, courtesy of various instances (for example, festivals or national theatres), some of which later provide venues for tours and may even put their name on the productions they host.

Robert Lepage's one-man play, *The Far Side of the Moon*, is a case in point. First performed in Quebec City in February 2000, it has now been presented in over 50 cities, straddling four continents. Produced by Lepage's company, Ex Machina, which is itself partly funded by federal, provincial, and municipal governments in Canada, *The Far Side of the Moon* also received financial backing from more than 30 foreign co-producers, most of them international festivals.[20] Naturally, all of the festivals involved in subsidizing this venture hosted the production for one of its many stopovers, thereby not only providing financial support for Ex Machina, but also guaranteeing the company a sizeable distribution network and invaluable logistical assistance to promote the show. Although this may be an extreme example, it is not an isolated case: in reality, local governments are apt to provide only part of the real costs of productions destined for audiences outside of Quebec. Therefore, somewhat predictably, the Quebec theatre productions best known abroad are in fact those supported by international producers and distributors.

But festival theatre cannot be reduced to a sociological phenomenon, an economic fact, or a particularly well-developed network for the distribution and dissemination of culture. On an aesthetic level, it generates and upholds very specific standards, as evidenced by the manifest similarities among the plays produced in or for the international network. It may even be said that a degree of conformism has been established in these productions, which (as mentioned earlier) are paradoxically seen as avant-garde in the local field.

When contemporary Quebec artists ascend to the international theatrical field, it also reflects the fact that their approach has entered into an aesthetic dialogue that reifies a vision that is shared to some extent with the social agents in this field.

As recent research on post-dramatic theatre by Hans-Thies Lehmann makes clear,[21] the international contemporary theatre scene that has welcomed Quebec companies such as Ex Machina, Marie Brassard, Carbone 14, and to a lesser extent, UBU, favours theatre that incorporates intermediality and interdisciplinarity, the mixing of cultures, traditions, and genres of theatre, using the image as the principle of narrative construction, a non-linear treatment of the plot line (if there is a plot line), multilingualism, and the fragmentation of dramatic action or of the performative aspect of the theatrical event. All of these characteristics apply in varying degrees to both the Quebec companies that tour most frequently abroad and the foreign companies with whom they share billing in the programming of major international theatre festivals. It is precisely this kinship of aesthetic approaches, more than any other factor, which enables Quebec productions to tour abroad, performing in venues receptive to these forms of theatre, before audiences accustomed to these codes 'of cultivated disposition'.

THE PRESENCE OF THE INTERNATIONAL THEATRICAL FIELD WITHIN MONTREAL AND QUEBEC CITY'S THEATRICAL FIELDS

Today, the presence of international theatre is not the exception in Quebec but actually represents a new standard that has redefined theatre itself. The reasons behind this paradigm shift are clear. Quebec spectators have had the opportunity to acquaint themselves with the codes of international theatre because they frequent festivals that feature it almost exclusively. Quebec City and (to a greater extent) Montreal have become part of the vast distribution network of the international theatrical field through two major events: Montreal's Festival TransAmériques (FTA), founded in 1985 as the Festival de Théâtre des Amériques, and Quebec

City's more recent Carrefour international de théâtre (CIT), founded in 1991. These events, (which are, in principle, annual) not only enable a select number of hand-picked Quebec producers to present their latest work, but also bring in most of the leading European and American figures on the international circuits, such as Romeo Castellucci, Peter Brook, Alain Platel, Ariane Mnouchkine, and Frank Castorf.

More recently, Montreal's local theatrical field has incorporated the Usine C stage, which operates like a permanent branch of festival theatre. Designed first and foremost as a space for the dissemination and support of new creative work by artists-in-residence, Usine C is now the primary, if not the only, home-away-from-home for international artists touring on the major festival circuits. Ever since it opened in 1994, Usine C has made itself available to the FTA's two-week festival, held from late May to early June, following hot on the heels of the regular yearly institutional theatre season in Montreal. This multidisciplinary performance space is unusual in that it offers entire seasons of theatre and dance (for which season tickets are available), featuring some of the most celebrated names of the world stage. Throughout the year, audiences are regaled by the likes of Eugenio Barba's Odin Teatret, Claude Régy, or Peter Brook. Thanks to Usine C, Montreal's discerning and (most certainly) selective festival theatre public can now see shows that used to be the exclusive preserve of major international theatre festivals.

Even more importantly for the dynamics in Montreal's theatrical field, Usine C also serves as a dedicated site of dissemination for local companies whose work embraces some of the aesthetic concerns of festival theatre but who have not entirely succeeded, or even attempted, to break into that select circuit. For example, Paula de Vasconcelos's Pigeons International theatre-dance company, which occasionally tours abroad, has been performing regularly at Usine C since 1995. Brigitte Haentjens's company, Sibyllines, which specializes in non-theatrical scripts (adaptations from novels), postmodern works (e.g., Heiner Müller), and stage direction that applies extreme plastic rigour, also presents its annual show at Usine C, but has not yet ventured into the international circuit.

Another particularly interesting case is that of Marie Brassard, an actor formerly close to Robert Lepage, who has pursued a remarkable solo career since 2001. Her first solo play, *Jimmy, créature de rêve*, like all of Brassard's subsequent productions, was co-produced by the FTA, where it also presented its world premiere. Following the success of this play (which was performed in 40 cities around the world), Brassard's company, Infrarouge, and the FTA have continued to pursue their collaborative efforts, along with other distributor-producers, such as the National Arts Centre in Ottawa, Berliner Festspiele in Berlin, and Wiener Festwochen in Vienna.

Thus, sites of dissemination like Usine C and the FTA not only provide windows on new creations in world theatre for Montreal audiences, but also serve as springboards that can help productions from the metropolis access the closed network of international circuits. It is through their choices in co-production and programming that these two atypical institutions from Montreal's theatrical field (one permanent and less prestigious, the other an annual event with strong 'specific capital') have acquired bona fide powers to consecrate and sanction, in the local field, legitimate hopefuls or already-consecrated players from the international field.

THE DOUBLE INSTITUTIONAL INSCRIPTION OF CONTEMPORARY QUEBEC THEATRE

Over and above the outstanding creative minds that have emerged since the early 1980s in the fields of playwriting and (especially) directing, the Quebec theatre community has seen new dynamics emerge, establishing a consecrated double inscription of its best-known productions in both the local and international theatrical fields. At the same time, the contemporary theatre on offer in Quebec has sidelined the paradigm of identity to the point that Quebec theatre is now practically indistinguishable from much pre-eminent European theatre and that of nations whose most challenging fringe theatre shares the same distribution networks and financing structures. In fact, undoubtedly the most striking characteristic of contemporary theatre is that its aesthetic displays an astonishing level of internal conformity, despite the habitual paratext of the modern stage, which thrives on subversion, audacity, and a perpetual quest for original theatrical and dramatic forms and content.

The codes of 'festival theatre', or rather the community of aesthetic concerns shared by the principal players of the international circuit (including some of the most highly renowned Quebec companies), are therefore conducive to establishing a common corpus—which is very convenient for the international community of theatre scholars. But over time, this common corpus has also empowered the collective impetus of scholars and created expectations to which the productions themselves appear to have conformed. Be they in Montreal, New York, Paris, London, or Berlin, scholars interested in cutting-edge theatre can easily enter into dialogues with their foreign colleagues, who inevitably share their reference corpus, and in so doing, also secure a knowledgeable, well-informed readership for their work. Plainly, it is no coincidence that, in Quebec as elsewhere, fashionable research on contemporary theatre includes the avenues of exile, performativity, intermediality, and new technologies. For such are also the aesthetic concerns and tools of 'festival theatre', which continues to supply the international university community with ideal case studies, not to mention examples that appear, in turn, to validate academic discourse.

In sum, although Quebec theatre companies that tour abroad remain inscribed in local dynamics, they appeal to foreign scholars and audiences alike—but not because of their specifically national, Québécois characteristics. Quebec theatre's current appeal lies more in its ability to deliver on expectations common to the public, critics, experts, and reviewers, who consume or profit by the internationalization of theatrical practice, of which Quebec is now a part. This systemic manifestation of globalization in theatre has therefore sidelined the question of national identities. In their place, we now have an enlarged community, founded on concerns and aesthetic tastes that may be regarded as a new *lingua franca* for theatre professionals and aficionados, both in and beyond Quebec.

SNAPSHOT

From Theatre Festivals to Festival Theatre

It was during the darkest days of the Great Depression that the Governor General of Canada, Lord Bessborough, first launched the idea of the Dominion Drama Festival (DDF, 1932–9, 1947–78) to support creative theatrical works in Canada.[22] The DDF was a juried, pan-Canadian, officially bilingual (English and French), amateur theatre competition. The jury of professional theatre artists and critics awarded prizes to the best regional productions, which had qualified through local competitions prior to the main event. The festival was a powerful incentive to amateur companies, eager to raise their profile by participating in this nationwide contest. Winners included the likes of André Brassard and Paul Buissonneau, directors who would go on to play major roles in Quebec theatre.

The bilingual ideal of the DDF was challenged in 1958 when Guy Beaulne founded the Association canadienne du théâtre amateur[23] (ACTA), which soon attracted the DDF's creative core of amateur francophone theatre talent and set up a competing festival, the Festival-Carrefour de l'ACTA. The first edition of the festival was held in conjunction with the cultural activities of Expo 67, the 1967 World's Fair in Montreal. As a site where theatre artists could gather, discuss, and train (through workshops and seminars), the festival discarded the competitive aspect of the DDF in favour of a more collegial approach and narrowed its scope to French-Canadian cultural space. By its second edition, the rising tide of Quebec nationalism that had reached the theatre community led to massive participation from Quebec French-language theatre troupes, which already dominated both ACTA and its festival. Consequently, the community-based concerns of troupes from outside of Quebec tended to be marginalized. Quebec theatre troupes cast off the theatrical stylings of France in their shows, and created collective productions, which grew to become the leading theatrical form among young Quebec

theatre artists during this period. Certainly, many theatre hopefuls of this new generation rejected the theatrical traditions from France, taught and promoted in Quebec's major theatre schools[24], opting instead for theatricality based on playful physical expression (sometimes approaching the bawdy American burlesque) and direct audience interaction. Thus, the sharply defined boundary between amateur and professional practice, drawn a decade earlier with the opening of major theatre schools, was effectively blurred by young artists in Quebec.

It was in this environment that ACTA became the Association québécoise du jeune théâtre (AQJT) in 1972 and turned its back once and for all on the amateur, pan-Canadian vision of the DDF and earlier editions of Festival-Carrefour. The AQJT continued its own annual festival, known as the Festival du jeune theatre. Entirely devoted to French-language creative works from Quebec, particularly in their socially collective and culturally militant (even openly revolutionary) forms, the new AQJT festival was a space for young Quebec theatre artists to meet and share ideas—and also was a subversive hotbed for debating the socio-political issues of the day. Following the tumultuous departure of the most ardently socialist and Marxist elements of the association in 1975, the Festival du jeune théâtre would remain an inward-looking Québécois cultural space, with festival programs shifting progressively toward aesthetic exploration.

The three theatre festivals we have mentioned had specific aims which underwent a number of major paradigm shifts: from official bilingualism to French unilingualism, from amateurism to professionalism, and from a Canadian to a Quebec cultural perspective. The results of the 1980 referendum on Quebec independence effectively marked the end of the Quiet Revolution and a temporary shelving of the nationalist project that had stimulated a great deal of dramatic creation up to that point. Subsequently, the AQJT and its festival spiralled into decline, and in 1985, the Festival du jeune théâtre and the AQJT met their demise.

Not coincidentally, the very year the AQJT took its final bow, the Festival de théâtre des Amériques (FTA) made its debut. Initially held every two years,[25] the artistic direction of the FTA was led by Marie-Hélène Falcon, who had earned her stripes with the AQJT and its festival. Emblematic of the increasing openness to outside influences that emerged after 1980 (after Quebec theatre's identity-based paradigm ran out of steam), the FTA was a clear departure from the festivals that had preceded it. International rather than local, multilingual rather than unilingual, the FTA stood out for its high degree of specific consecration, but perhaps most of all for its innovation and its scrupulous formal searches for productions. Once the FTA had gained respectability, it brought together a broad variety of international and local theatre artists as well as foreign critics and distributors. For contemporary theatre artists who wished to access world stages, the FTA, under Marie-Hélène Falcon's leadership, has become a near-compulsory event if only because it is a rare 'site of mediation' that functions as a junction between local and international theatre.

The FTA has introduced production companies from the local field to the aesthetics that have won festival theatre awards in the international theatrical field. Inescapably, as the local and international fields get a better look at one another, the situation is not only conducive to exchanging information but also to making comparisons between the limited offering in Montreal and Quebec City's subfields and the best offerings in theatre from abroad.[26] Arranging for both parties to get a better look at each other can inspire a dynamic of striving for excellence and motivate local theatre producers to innovate. Conversely, measuring up to the rhetoric of novelty and creation (that is the lifeblood of this event) is nonetheless an immense challenge for local producers. While foreign shows are individually selected and have already passed muster on stage, Quebec performances are often actually created during the FTA, with all of the perilous risks that such an endeavour involves. So while the FTA has been a launch pad into the international theatre market for a few innovative Quebec theatre artists, many more have lost their shine in the shadow of the greats.

Questions for Consideration

1. What are the characteristics of 'festival theatre'?

2. Describe the 'double social inscription' that director Robert Lepage and his theatre company, Ex Machina, enjoy.

3. Which factors come into play in crossing over from the local to the international theatrical field?

Notes

1. In the province of Quebec, the word *nation* often refers to Quebec rather than Canada in common parlance (especially in French). Giving voice to the fact that Quebec is a culturally distinct society, Quebec officials have long designated government agencies as 'national' bodies.

2. Pierre Bourdieu's concept of *field* will be explained in greater detail, in the theoretical portion of this chapter, under the title, 'Local Theatrical Field–International Theatrical Field'.

3. Also a Bourdieusian term, explained in the theoretical portion of this chapter.

4. The qualifier 'essai' was dropped in 1991, but the acronym (CEAD) remained the same.

5. Jean-Marc Larrue, 'La Création collective au Québec', in Dominique Lafon, ed., *Le Théâtre québécois. 1975–1995* (Montreal: Fides, 2001), 155.

6. See Godin, Jean Cléo, and Laurent Mailhot, 'Le théâtre québécois contemporain ou comment devenir classique

en une génération' in Jean Cléo Godin and Laurent Mailhot, eds., *Théâtre québécois II. Nouveaux auteurs, autres spectacles* (Montreal: Hurtubise, 1988 [1980]), 20.

7. In the province as a whole, the number of subsidized companies rose from 16 in 1968 to 71 in 1980 (see François Colbert, *Le Marché québécois du théâtre* [Quebec: Institut québécois de recherche sur la culture, 1982], 33). This is not counting the 40 or so summer theatres and the large number of companies and small producers such as café theatres, which opened their operations without any government funding. At the end of the above-mentioned period, in 1980, the number of theatre companies in Quebec was estimated at 300 (see Angèle Dagenais, *Crise de croissance : le théâtre au Québec* [Quebec City: Institut québécois de la recherche sur la culture, 1981], 7).

8. See Gilbert David, 'Un nouveau territoire théâtral. 1965-1980', in André-G. Bourassa, Gilbert David, Jean-Marc Larrue, and Renée Legris, *Le Théâtre au Québec. 1825-1980* (Montreal: VLB Éditeur/Société d'histoire du théâtre du Québec/Bibliothèque nationale du Québec, 1988), 144.

9. Authors studied by Godin and Mailhot include Jean Barbeau, Marcel Dubé, Jacques Ferron, Michel Garneau, Gratien Gélinas, Jean-Claude Germain, Éloi de Grandmont, Robert Gurik, Anne Hébert, Jacques Languirand, Françoise Loranger, Yves Sauvageau, and Yves Thériault. Their works are only occasionally performed today, usually for student audiences, in venues like the Théâtre Denise-Pelletier, for the benefit of the institutions that include them on their academic curriculum.

10. See Colbert, *Le Marché québécois du théâtre*, 70.

11. See David, 'Un nouveau territoire théâtral', 164.

12. Some of the most notable groups include the Conseil québécois du théâtre (CQT, 1983), Association des professionnels des arts de la scène du Québec (APASQ, 1984), Théâtres associés inc. (TAI, 1985), Théâtres unis enfance jeunesse inc. (TUEJ, 1986), Association des compagnies de théâtre (ACT, 1989), and the later Association québécoise des auteurs dramatiques (AQAD, 1990), which were added to the older Union des artistes (UDA, 1987) and Centre des auteurs dramatiques (CEAD, 1965).

13. In 'intermediality,' scientific and artistic presentation forms are presented together and compared. It is assumed that different media will also yield different findings in each case. This claim is further developed and differentiated in the theory of 'Art as Research', within the framework of discussions relating to terms and methods. The comparability of artistic and scientific research is being established in practice through the research of 'Intermedial Arts' and within the context of specific artistic projects.

14. See Sylvain Schryburt, *Repère signalétique des productions de compagnies théâtrales du Québec jouées à l'étranger*, cahier de recherche n° 14, Montreal: CÉTUQ, 1999.

15. See Pierre Bourdieu, *Les règles de l'art : genèse et structure du champ littéraire* (Paris: Éditions du Seuil), 1992.

16. 'These consist, on the one hand, of institutions which conserve the capital of symbolic goods, such as museums; and, on the other hand, of institutions (such as the educational system) which ensure the reproduction of agents imbued with the categories of action, expression, conception, imagination, perception, specific to the "cultivated disposition"'. Randal Johnson, ed., *Pierre Bourdieu* (New York: Columbia Press, 1993).

17. 'The subfield of restricted production is an "autonomous" grouping associated with elite culture and organized around the specific, self-contained interests of the field, in which commercial success is frowned upon and the myth of the individual producer as charismatic genius is most prevalent . . .' Joe Moran, *Star authors: Literary Celebrity in America* (London: Pluto Press, 2000), 5.

18. This occurs principally through the Canada Council for the Arts (federal government), Conseil des arts et des lettres du Québec (Quebec provincial government arts council), and the Conseil des arts de Montréal (Montreal municipal government arts council).

19. '. . . by which cultural products are recognised and ranked . . . in public and personal economies of meaning and value.' David Peters and Laura Perry, eds., *English Art, 1860–1914: Modernities and Identities*, Barber Institute's Critical Perspectives in Art (Manchester: Manchester University Press, 2000), 24.

20. In one of the rare studies on the phenomenon of international tours, Claude des Landes has emphasized the similarities between the funding arrangements required for this kind of venture and those currently in effect in the private sector. See 'D'une entreprise nationale au rayonnement planétaire', *L'Annuaire théâtral* 27, (printemps 2000): 41.

21. Hans-Thies Lehmann, *Le Théâtre postdramatique* (Paris: L'Arche, 2002).

22. For a history of the DDF, see Betty Lee, *Love and Whisky: the Story of the Dominion Drama Festival* (Toronto: McClelland & Stewart, 1973).

23. For more on ACTA, refer to the see the voluminous special issue 15, 1980, of *Cahiers de théâtre Jeu*.

24. Conservatoire d'art dramatique de Montréal (1954–), Conservatoire d'art dramatique de Québec (1958–), and National Theatre School of Canada (1960–).

25. In 2007, the FTA became an annual event, the Festival TransAmériques, a name that reflects the festival's new openness to the world of contemporary dance and, more generally, to performances that play with the boundaries between the living arts.

26. Sometimes this juxtaposition is achieved through more or less separate categories, such as the 'Nouvelles scenes' category, launched in 1997 to promote emerging local theatre artists.

RELEVANT WEBSITES

ASSOCIATION QUÉBÉCOISE DES AUTEURS DRAMATIQUES (AQAD): www.aqad.qc.ca/

ASSOCIATION QUÉBÉCOISE DES CRITIQUES DE THÉÂTRE (AQCT): www.aqct.qc.ca/historique.html

CANADIAN THEATRE ENCYCLOPEDIA: www.canadiantheatre.com/

CARREFOUR INTERNATIONAL DE THÉÂTRE DE QUÉBEC: www.carrefourtheatre.qc.ca/

CENTRE DES AUTEURS DRAMATIQUES (CEAD): www.cead.qc.ca/

CONSEIL QUÉBÉCOIS DU THÉÂTRE (CQT): www.cqt.ca/

FESTIVAL TRANSAMÉRIQUES (FTA): www.fta.qc.ca/

OBSERVATOIRE DE LA CULTURE ET DES COMMUNICATIONS DU QUÉBEC (STATISTIQUES): www.stat.gouv.qc.ca/observatoire/

QUEBEC DRAMA FEDERATION (QDF): www.quebecdrama.org/

SELECT BIBLIOGRAPHY

Beauchamp, Hélène. *Les théâtres de création au Québec, en Acadie et au Canada français.* Montreal: VLB Éditeur, 2005.

———, and Gilbert David, eds. *Théâtres québécois et canadiens-français au XXe siècle. Trajectoires et territoires.* Montreal: Presse de l'Université du Québec, 2003.

Benson, Eugene, and L. W. Conolly, eds. *Oxford Companion to Canadian Theatre.* Toronto: Oxford University Press, 1989.

Donohoe, Joseph I., and Jonathan M. Weiss, eds. *Essays on modern Quebec Theatre.* East Lansing: Michigan University Press, 1995.

———, and Jane M. Koustas, eds. *Theatre sans frontières : essays on the dramatic universe of Robert Lepage.* East Lansing: Michigan University Press, 2000.

Godin, Jean Cléo, and Dominique Lafon. *Dramaturgies québécoises des années quatre-vingt : Michel Marc Bouchard, Normand Chaurette, René-Daniel Dubois, Marie Laberge.* Montreal: Leméac, 1999.

———, and Laurent Mailhot. *Le Théâtre québécois I : Introduction à dix dramaturges contemporains.* Montreal: Bibliothèque Québécoise, 1995 [1970].

———, and ———. *Le Théâtre québécois II : Nouveaux auteurs, autres spectacles.* Montreal: Bibliothèque Québécoise, 1995 [1980].

Greffard, Madeleine and Jean-Guy Sabourin, *Le Théâtre québécois.* Montreal: Boréal, 1997.

Lafon, Dominique, ed. *Le Théâtre québécois. 1975-1995.* Archives des lettres canadiennes. Vol. 10. Montreal: Fides, 2001.

Vaïs, Michel, ed. *Dictionnaire des artistes du théâtre québécois.* Montreal: Cahiers de théâtre Jeu /Québec Amérique, 2008.

AFTERWORD

Quebec Studies in the United States and Canada: Trends and Tendencies[1]

Alain-G. Gagnon, Université du Québec à Montréal

— TIMELINE —

1663 Foundation of Laval University.

1821 Foundation of McGill University.

1878 Foundation of University of Montreal.

1921 Foundation of Association francophone pour le savoir (ACFAS).

1937–40 Royal Commission on Dominion-Provincial Relations (Rowell-Sirois Commission).

1949–51 Royal Commission on National Development in the Arts, Letters and Sciences (Massey-Lévesque Commission).

1953–6 Royal Commission of Inquiry on Constitutional Problems (Tremblay Commission).

1954 Foundation of Sherbrooke University.

1963–9 Royal Commission on Bilingualism and Biculturalism (Laurendeau-Dunton Commission).

1968 Foundation of Quebec University Network.

1971 Creation of Association for Canadian Studies in United States.

1974 Foundation of Concordia University.

1980 First Quebec referendum.

1981 Creation of American Council for Quebec Studies (ACQS), originally named Northeast Council for Quebec Studies.

1982–5 Royal Commission on the Economic Union and Development Prospects for Canada (Macdonald Commission).

1983 Creation of Journal *Québec Studies*.

1990–1 Commission on the Political and Constitutional Future of Quebec (Bélanger-Campeau Commission).

1991–6 Royal Commission on Aboriginal Peoples (Erasmus-Dussault Commission).

1995 Second Quebec referendum.

1997 Creation of International Association of Quebec Studies (IAQS).

1998 Creation of Globe: Revue internationale d'études québécoises.

INTRODUCTION

In an article published in 1994, Robert Schwartzwald noted that Americans had little interest for cultures other than their own. Considering Quebec's proximity to the United States, Schwartzwald felt that this obstacle could, however, be transformed into a realm of opportunities:

> In the US there is a general lack of interest for a vast majority of cultures in the world and Quebec's culture is no exception. This situation might serve well to the extent that American scholars might come to interpret Quebec culture not as the expression of a radical otherness nor as one of an exotic region, but perhaps as a matrix of relevant differences from a neighbouring territory.[2] (our translation)

Language has often represented a significant barrier for Americans, as they feel more at ease working within their own vernacular. Evolving within a high-status language, Americans, as a whole, have not been predisposed to learn languages spoken by other national communities and continued to expand their influence in a vast range of domains. In academia, the net result has been the relegation of studies of Quebec, or of Canada for that matter, to a secondary status.

This phenomenon applies with little dissonance in the fields of culture, economy, business, and politics. Writing in 1993, Earl Fry and Stephen Blank stated that 'During the last twenty years few scholars in the United States have written about Québec business issues and fewer still cited French language sources as research references . . . . the interesting developments in Québec's business sector have largely been ignored, as the relevant francophone literature.'[3]

A similar point was made by Louis Balthazar in reflecting on the American perspective: 'Being English-speaking and culturally much closer to English Canada than to Quebec, in spite of their real sympathy and friendship for Quebecers, do they not tend to view things through the prism of English-speaking Canadians' stand-point? Moreover the bulk of their information comes from Anglophone sources like the Toronto-based *Globe and Mail* and *Maclean's* magazine.'[4]

This condition reveals some troubling observations that apply both to the United States and anglophone Canada. As this volume of essays is dedicated to examining a range of significant Quebec-focused questions, this Afterword examines how and when Quebec became a legitimate field of study in both

Canada and the United States. It also identifies key challenges and current opportunities that will influence the future direction of Quebec Studies.

FROM HIGH DEPENDENCY TO FRAIL DEVELOPMENT

The field of social sciences in Quebec had been highly dependent on American, British, and French scholarship prior to acquiring its own autonomous standing relative to those intellectual communities. English-speaking Canadians, due to their stronger ties with the anglophone world, were quicker to impose their influence in the fields of economic history and the social sciences more generally, while francophone Quebecers tended to be highly dependent on others to secure the professional development of the field until the Quiet Revolution. Until the 1960s, the field of social sciences in Quebec was precarious.

Anthropologist Horace Miner and sociologist Everett Hughes each made a major effort at casting Quebec as a modernizing society. Miner's 1936 *Saint-Denis: A French-Canadian Parish* and Hughes' 1943 *French Canada in Transition* brought attention to studying rural regions and developing a new paradigm. Both of those books were made accessible in French by Jean-Charles Falardeau, a former student of Hughes at Chicago, and he was instrumental in bringing Hughes to Laval University in 1942–3.[5]

Miner, Hughes, and their followers, including Alfred Hero, Earl Fry (see Chapter 28), Marc Levine, and Charles Doran have contributed to advancing the study of Quebec in the United States. In some ways, they have paved the way for us to enter US classrooms and libraries. In Canada, without a doubt, the works of political scientist Kenneth McRoberts and historian Brian Young are particularly noteworthy in making Quebec studies a pertinent field of research.

In a matter of 70 years since the publication of Miner's study, Quebec has emerged as a legitimate field of research: first as a subset of American culture and then as a by-product of Canadian studies. Gradually, Quebec studies has become a field in and of itself. Initially grounded in anthropology and sociology, research interests started to shift toward

Kenneth McRoberts

Kenneth McRoberts in his principal's office at Glendon College, York University

Printed by the permission of Evan Dion www.evandion.com

Born and raised in Vancouver, British Columbia, Kenneth McRoberts acquired his bachelor's degree from the University of California, Santa Barbara, and his master's and doctoral degrees in political science from the University of Chicago. In addition to a very successful career as a professor of Political Science in the Faculty of Arts at York University, Kenneth McRoberts served terms as Director of the Graduate Program in Political Science and Director of the Robarts Centre for Canadian Studies. In 1999, he was appointed Principal of Glendon College, York University's bilingual Arts faculty. His leitmotif since beginning this position has been 'to help Glendon become a truly national institution that would allow Anglophones and Francophones to meet, [and] that would serve as a bridge between Quebec and the rest of Canada'.[6]

McRoberts' contribution to language politics, Canadian federalism, and above all Quebec studies at home and abroad is simply outstanding. He has written many journal articles and book chapters on a variety of topics including Quebec politics and constitutional questions.

Kenneth McRoberts is one of the leading anglophone scholars who have contributed in giving Quebec studies its credentials. His knowledge of Quebec politics is probably unparalleled. McRoberts is author of *Quebec: Social Change and Political Crisis* (1999). He edited *Beyond Quebec: Taking Stock of*

Canada (1995) and co-edited *The Charlottetown Accord, the Referendum and the Future of Canada* (1993). These books have very successful and constitute a solid basis for readers seeking for a balanced interpretation of the Quebec–Canada conundrum.

He has contributed significantly to reframing the terms of debate on Canadian unity. His book entitled *Misconceiving Canada: The Struggle for National Unity* (1997) is a clear illustration of his commitment. His most recent book published, *Catalonia: Nation-building without a State* (2001) is another example of his broad understanding of comparative politics. In recognition of his work and influence, the French government in 2004 named Professor McRoberts 'Officier de l'Ordre des Palmes académiques'. Within Québécois academic circles, he was awarded an honorary doctorate by Laval University the same year.

His experience as a teacher, a scholar, an author, and an administrator were also invested in the *International Journal of Canadian Studies* where he served a six-year term as Editor-in-Chief. He has served as President of the Canadian Political Science Association, and has been an active member of the Canadian section of the International Association of Quebec Studies for several years.

In addition to his academic rigour, intellectual prowess, and prolific publications, Kenneth McRoberts is to be celebrated for his professional commitment to serving as a bridge between Canadian and Quebec scholars. To that end, in his numerous English- and French-language publications that have resonated within North American and international networks, he has faithfully presented the works of Québécois scholars, Quebec nationalist perspectives, and the national and linguistic struggles of francophones that continue to animate contemporary Canadian federalism.

literature and cultural studies. This has remained an enduring trait.

With a growing presence of political culture as an emerging field of research in the United States and

Canada as a whole, Quebec was bound to gain some exposure and to find a niche in some centres of studies and research networks over time. In the United States, the works of Seymour Martin Lipset, Gabriel

Almond (a Chicago product), and Sidney Verba contributed to expanding the field of comparative research in their attention to the cultural roots of democracy and political stability. The United States was then portrayed as a model to be emulated and exported worldwide.

The principal reference for what is deemed worthy to study and write about, to this day, continues to come from the United States. To acquire prestige within academia, most scholars have had to replicate the research model undertaken in American universities. As a result, it is highly improbable that either Canadian or Quebec scholars could make significant inroads on the other side of the border unless they reproduce American scholarship.

A TALE OF TWO NATIONS: FROM STATE AWARENESS TO INTELLECTUAL LEADERSHIP

The 1950s and 1960s revealed a desire on the part of both the Canadian and the Quebec states to promote their respective autonomy. With Quebec on the verge of shaking the Canadian establishment, the conditions were propitious for a major consolidation of the social sciences.

A series of Royal Commissions examined how to strengthen Canadian identity, as it was increasingly challenged from above (American imperialism) and from below (Quebec nationalism). Social scientists were called to the rescue as the Massey-Lévesque Commission on National Development in the Arts, Letters and Sciences (1949–51) recommended the implementation of a series of public policies to ensure Canadian autonomy from the United States. Here is what the commissioners had to say:

Apart from the work of a few brilliant persons, there is a general impression that Canadian scholarly work in the humanities and social sciences is slight in quantity and in quality. We have, it seems, some able scholars, but no consistent and representative Canadian scholarship emanating from the country as a whole and capable of making its contribution to Canadian intellectual life and to that of the western world.[7]

Those were the years during which both Quebec and Canada as a whole were highly dependent on American and European scholars, or externally trained scholars, to staff their universities countrywide. The following period would witness a major transformation on that front as Canadian universities would make significant efforts in developing graduate programs and promoting higher education.

The members of the Massey-Lévesque Commission also identified the language barrier as the major cultural obstacle to the development of Canadian Studies and, by extension, Quebec Studies.

Another special factor has affected Canadian work in the social sciences and perhaps even more in the humanities. The existence of two main languages representing two distinct cultures initially constitutes a delaying factor. Ultimately, this variety must add to the value of the Canadian contribution, but in the early stages, by placing certain inevitable barriers between members of a group of scholars already small and scattered enough, it has caused a lessening of force and vigour.[8]

In order to put in place tools and institutions to support Canadian research in the humanities and social sciences, and to build a more autonomous curriculum from the United States, the Commission recommended the creation of the National Library, the Canada Council for the Arts, funding agencies for the universities, bursary programs for students, and the like. These initiatives were largely emulated by the Quebec government, as it set up its own funding agency, and more recently its own National Library.

Indeed, these recommendations were to give structure to the emergence of more autonomous Canadian- and Quebec-based research. The language divide enticed the Quebec government to assert itself, develop university programs, and gain the momentum to finance research initiatives.

More Royal Commissions followed. In Quebec, the most notable were the Parent Commission on Education (1961–6), the Rioux Commission on Public Art Education (1966–8), and the Gendron Commission on the Situation of the French Language (1969–72). In Canada, this period produced the Laurendeau-Dunton Commission on Bilingualism and

Biculturalism (1963–8), the Macdonald Commission on the Economic Union and Development Prospects for Canada (1982–5), and the Erasmus-Dussault Commission on Aboriginal Peoples (1991–6). Such initiatives also contributed to fostering a sense of identity among Canadians, Quebecers, and Aboriginals through the implementation of reforms in education, language acquisition, establishment of academic centres of excellence, and funding research through various agencies. As a result, public funding helped assert the scientific autonomy of Canadian and Quebec Studies internally and externally, and contributed to the development of a spirit of unprecedented leadership in the humanities and the social sciences.[9]

INSTITUTIONALIZATION OF THE FIELD

Canada's central government, for its part, sought to impose an all-encompassing national culture that would buttress its own sense of nationhood. Almost nothing was neglected in attempts to achieve this objective. The best rendering of the range of initiatives undertaken by Ottawa is particularly well-documented in Doug Owram's book *The Government Generation: Canadian Intellectuals and the State 1900–1945.*[10] Moreover, Stephen Brooks and I have analyzed the period stretching from 1945 to the mid-1980s in *Social Scientists and Politics in Canada: Between Clerisy and Vanguard.*[11] Those two volumes further explored the tensions between English and French intellectuals, as well as dynamics between the two principal governing communities in the country.

The Canadian government, for instance, has been steadfastly interested in courting American scholars through its support of The Association for Canadian Studies in the United States (ACSUS), founded in 1971. This support comprises annual grant competitions, which provide funds to sponsor conferences, study and exchange programs, various publications, the activities of regional Canadian Studies associations (there are five in the United States), and the like. Ottawa has invested significantly more to support Canadian Studies south of the border than has Quebec.

Quebec Studies specialists in the United States, beginning in the late 1970's, launched a series of initiatives aimed at attracting dedicated funding from the Quebec government. State University of New York College at Plattsburgh (SUNY Plattsburgh) was successful on that front, organizing in 1979 the first Quebec Summer Seminar for US-based academics interested in Quebec. A year later, the year of the first Quebec referendum, we witnessed the establishment of the Northeast Council for Quebec Studies, renamed The American Council for Quebec Studies (ACQS) in 1984. ACQS serves, much as ACSUS does for the Canadian Studies academic community in the United States, as the national multidisciplinary academic association for Quebec Studies in the United States. The institutionalization of Quebec Studies was furthered with the launching of the scientific journal *Quebec Studies*. This journal has proven to be a very successful initiative.

The election of Lucien Bouchard as Premier of Quebec ushered in key changes for Quebec specialists in the United States, as government sources of funding, most especially those provided by the Ministry of International Relations, were dramatically curtailed or eliminated (albeit briefly).

The setting up of the International Association for Quebec Studies (IAQS) in 1997 brought some much needed oxygen. Initially the association was not warmly received, however, by either American Canadianists or American *Québécistes*. This new institution helped remove an obstacle to the development of Quebec studies in the United States, since previously research on Quebec was the purview of a few specialists. Following the creation of the IAQS, and after a couple of years of hesitation, American specialists on Quebec began to renew their interests in Quebec Studies and are now connected to a much wider network of researchers. Several academic grant programs are also now underwritten by the Quebec government to support the work of US-based academics, adding new sources of financing for a variety of structuring projects.

The last few years have seen a major realignment in research topics stretching from Aboriginal issues (Erasmus-Dussault Commission, Signing of the Paix des Braves between Crees and Quebec government, Aboriginal land claims), reengineering and modernization of the state, security (post-9/11), the environment (Kyoto), energy security, immigration, trade,

SNAPSHOT

Association internationale des études québécoises (AIEQ)
International Association for Quebec Studies (IAQS)

Quebec Studies has grown steadily within North America over the past three decades, beginning with the first Quebec Summer Seminar in 1979. The establishment of the Northeast Council for Quebec Studies was consolidated in Radford, Virginia, to be renamed The American Council for Quebec Studies in 1984. But the institutionalization of Quebec Studies as a formal area of social science research did not really begin to coalesce until the launching of *Québec Studies* journal in 1983. The 1980s and 1990s were packed with a series of political events in Quebec as its people were being invited to consider seceding from Canada. Several Quebec government-funded programs were initiated to stimulate further interest in Quebec politics, economy, culture, and society.

Following the failed referendum on sovereignty-partnership in October 1995, and Quebec's subsequent cutbacks to fight a growing deficit, support for Quebec studies programs at the international level started to suffer. Several Quebec delegations and bureaus were being closed by the Parti Québécois government under the leadership of Premier Lucien Bouchard. In reaction to this politics of retrenchment, a small group of Quebec social scientists mobilized to revamp the field of Quebec Studies.

More long-term prospects for Quebec Studies began in earnest with the establishment of the International Association for Quebec Studies (IAQS) in 1997. At the time, *Québécistes* were few and their interactions limited. Although the association's initial reception by American Canadianists and *Québécistes* was lukewarm, it has since gained recognition for the unique opportunities it offers to an increasingly international cross-section of scholars working on Quebec. This was in part due to a 'politics of containment' led by senior federal Canadian officials who made a number of attempts to have Canadian embassies block the creation of the IAQS. In the end, academics felt those initiatives were improper and refuse any interference in their own affairs.

The IAQS has often played a central role in bringing both the perspectives of Quebec Studies researchers and the diversity of viewpoints within Quebec society itself to the international stage where they can be heard and understood. One of its first achievements was the compilation of a directory of students, teachers, academics, and researchers around the world whose works focus on Quebec. In 2007, the IAQS counted over 1,200 members from 65 countries, bringing together more than 40 academic disciplines. In addition to its formal membership, the IAQS network serves as a hub of intellectual exchange for close to 3,000 Quebec specialists, 60 per cent of whom are outside Quebec. For example, October 2008 saw the establishment of the Japanese Association of Quebec Studies, an important entry point in Asia.

Celebrating its tenth anniversary in 2007, this international hub of social inquiry on Quebec society has worked to expand and diversify sources of information on Quebec, to support research excellence, and to promote knowledge transfer among diverse academic disciplines, teachers, policy specialists, and practitioners. This has been achieved through its publications, roundtables, workshops, and conferences organized in conjunction with numerous Quebec and French-Canadian universities, along with associations for Quebec and Canadian Studies and various government agencies. These interdisciplinary conversations and international exchanges on the vibrancy, specificities, and challenges of Quebec society have significantly benefited from financial support through the Ministère des Relations internationales du Québec (MRI), as well as the Ministère de la Culture et des Communications du Québec (MCC).

The IAQS is a crucial international meeting ground for academic research in sociology, economics, and political science, and also in literature, culture, and theatre. It has enabled a much broader dissemination and awareness of the contributions of Quebec specialists in a variety of scientific fields as well as of experts outside of Quebec in the expanding field of Quebec studies.

and so forth. Besides the fact that these topics constitute added opportunities for research, at the same time, they represent legitimate domains of inquiry in and of themselves. It is to these developments that this essay now turns its attention.

IMPEDIMENTS AND OPPORTUNITIES

An exploration into two flagship journals featuring Quebec-focused research in the United States, *Québec Studies* and *The American Review of Canadian Studies*, provides a clearer picture of salient subjects in American academic circles. One notes in *Québec Studies* an overwhelming proportion of articles between 1995 and 2005 pertaining to literature and culture (117 out of 179 articles), followed by political theory (27) and public policies (22). The picture is somewhat reversed in *The American Review of Canadian Studies* with nearly half of its articles during this same period dealing with public policies (116 out of 252), followed by political theory (55), and literature (42). As a political scientist, I can appreciate such a strong interest in literature and public policies but lament the rarity of material on political economy, political science, sociology, anthropology, and business.

It is possible to assess, at least on the surface, the presence of Quebec studies in the United States and Canada from a vantage point that stresses trends and tendencies during the last half-century. The 1960s and 1970s were characterized by a strong focus on literature and culture that continues (although it is slightly less dominant) well into the beginning of the new century. Both Canada and Quebec were 'lamenting for a nation'[12] and thus funded the humanities and social

sciences with renewed conviction. Quebecers tended to identify with the worldwide movement of decolonization and in it found inspiration for their cause.[13] During this time, Margaret Atwood published *Survival*, a cry alerting Canadians to challenges she saw emerging and the need to free Canadians from American hegemony.

The period stretching from 1980 to 2000 was marked by a series of major events, including two Quebec sovereignty referendums and debates on North American free trade. Growing (inter)dependency between the US and the Canadian economies, especially in transportation, energy and water supply, trade, and commerce all contributed to a new momentum in Quebec and Canadian Studies in the United States. Both the Canadian and the Quebec governments were keen to finance research in those areas. In particular, pressure was applied to the journal *Québec Studies* to publish in such subjects as well; special issues were published, for example, on the shared St Lawrence–Great Lakes water resources and on North American borders, which were aimed at broadening the journal's reach beyond its more traditional areas of culture, literature, cinema, and the like—areas that had contributed to making the journal a reference in the humanities and the social sciences.

Following 11 September 2001, new issues came to the fore. From this point onward, salient issues have been the management of borders and immigration policies, as well as homeland security and political stability. These matters have been frequently addressed in the *American Review of Canadian Studies* but have been generally absent from *Québec Studies* (see Table 2).

Beyond its traditional subjects, *Québec Studies* has had some difficulty in expanding its fields of interest and, at times, gives the impression of being disconnected from the major cultural, economic, historical, and political debates occurring in Quebec. Indeed, topics that have occupied centre stage in Quebec during the last decade—such as Quebec nationalism, citizenship, national diversity, electoral reform, the history curriculum, multinational federalism, and reasonable accommodation—have left little imprint either in this publication or in academia more generally.

TABLE 1 Published Journal Articles by Subjects, 1995–2005

	Québec Studies	The American Review of Canadian Studies
Literature	117	42
Public Policies	22	116
Security Issues	0	19
Political Theory	27	55
History and Geography	13	20
Total	179	252

TABLE 2 Trends and Tendencies in Quebec Studies in the United States

Trends		Tendencies	
1960–70s	1980–90s	2001–	2001–
Literature and Culture	Socio-economic Studies	Security Issues	Diversity Issues
identity in a literary perspective	free trade	immigration policies	federalism
postcolonial interpretation	environmental issues	border control	interculturalism
feminist studies	energy supply		
	transport		
	fresh water supply		

IMPEDIMENTS AND OPPORTUNITIES: INNOVATING AND CONNECTING

In this final section, I discuss key obstacles faced by Quebec Studies specialists, especially in diffusing their work in English-speaking Canada and in the United States. Three main obstacles can be identified.

The first obstacle remains the language barrier. Even among specialists of Canadian politics, there is a well-ensconced view that learning French is not essential to becoming an accomplished specialist in Quebec Studies or even Canadian Studies for that matter. American scholars renowned for their work on Quebec, such as Earl Fry and Stephen Blank, admit, as I noted in the introduction, that their colleagues pay little consideration to Quebec's input in their research. They often prefer to rely secondary anglophone sources that proceed from a significant distance from the community they study. Jane Moss refers to a lack of proficiency in French to account for this phenomenon.[14]

The second obstacle is that there is increasingly less incentive to write scholarly works in French. Briefly stated, publishing in French does not improve a researcher's international profile, as sources cited tend to be written in English. Moreover, it is quite disturbing to note that even when francophones write in English, their works still tend not to be cited. Two recent studies clearly show this bias, one by political scientist François Rocher and the other by legal expert Jean-François Gaudreault-Desbiens. Rocher examined 79 books in the field of Canadian politics

published by English-speaking political scientists in Canada between 1995 and 2005, and found that references to the work of francophones accounted for only 4.9 per cent (median) of all bibliographical sources.[15]

Third, there is also a tendency to subsume research on Quebec under that on Canada in general, therefore limiting the *potential for autonomy* of Quebec Studies as a genuine field distinct from Canadian Studies. A good illustration of this phenomenon is found in a book entitled *Constitutional Design for Divided Societies* (2008) in which the Basque Country, Biafra, Bosnia and Herzegovina, Catalonia, Corsica, Scotland, Fiji, Macedonia, Papua, and Quebec are discussed at length. In the index, however, Quebec is the only one of these not listed as a primary entry—it is listed in a secondary entry under 'Canada'.[16]

There is no easy solution to counter these trends. An obvious avenue is to diversify entry points in scientific journals published in English, and to continue to show the high relevance of Quebec research in a variety of domains. Another one is to make works on Quebec Studies accessible in a variety of languages and in international forums. Considering that Quebec Studies is highly relevant to policy in many federal states and states inspired by federal practices, scholars studying Quebec can aspire to having their works widely known and read. Scholars in areas such as constitutional design in federal states, liberal nationalism, nations without states, multinational federalism, language politics as applied to specific host societies, continental economic integration, accountability of party politics, referendum, and so on, have much to gain by exploring contributions made by Quebec Studies specialists over the years.

Why Put Quebec in Your Curriculum?

Quebec has demonstrated the extent to which positive action on language use has helped to elevate the status of the French language in Canada and in the Americas. Quebec is considered in this regard to be a model to be emulated by many other societies, such as Galicia, Scotland, Wallonia, and Catalonia. Indeed, Catalonia has developed its own language policy following the example set by Quebec's language laws. Quebec has also become a reference for nations seeking more prominence in international affairs and wanting to provide an added liberal model for their respective political community within their own region.

Specialists in Quebec Studies have major contributions to make in a variety of other domains. Colleagues such as Peter Graefe writing on the Quebec model of economic development, Raffaele Iacovino and Charles-Antoine Sévigny discussing models of managing diversity, Marie McAndrew debating the place of education and diversity in Quebec, and Mark Rosseau and Jody Neathery-Castro examining the role of Quebec in the Francophonie, are, through their essays in this book, making significant contributions about the leadership role Quebec plays in the Americas and in Western democracies. Indeed, Quebec can be seen as a world leader in societal cohabitation, economic and cultural management, political leadership, language promotion, citizenship engagement, and intercultural practices.

The field of Quebec Studies, though vibrant in Quebec and highly policy-relevant for nations without states, remains nonetheless a young field of research with an impressive potential that this book can only strengthen.

Conclusion

What can be done to advance, in the United States and throughout the international community, the academic field we call Quebec Studies? Major efforts have been undertaken during the last 20 years by two organizations, the American Council for Quebec Studies and the Association internationale d'études québécoises, through their support of a variety of research initiatives. At this juncture, however, the field of Quebec Studies requires a significant boost that can only come from a series of structured engagements involving universities, research centres, and states, and from personal commitments of scholars.

Quebec Studies remains a young field of research that has gained in strength over the years, yet much more can be achieved. Given current tensions in the international political system, it has become clear that the world needs more Quebec. Indeed, Quebec has demonstrated a commitment to expanding the democratic participation of its citizens through two peaceful referendums on the future of its political association with Canada. It has been capable of developing its own model of cultural integration through the recognition of a policy of interculturalism that invites *all* Quebec citizens to get involved in shaping the orientations of their society. Quebec has also acted as a world leader in developing a national culture that is genuinely attached to liberal values, building on both procedural and communitarian principles, and is taken as an example by many societies including Catalonia, Galicia, Flanders, Scotland, and Wallonia. These areas and many others provide fertile territory for the growth of Quebec Studies into the foreseeable future.

Questions for Consideration

1. Identify and discuss three factors that helped the development and institutionalization of Quebec studies.
2. Since the beginning of the 1980s, why has Quebec, as field of research, become increasingly relevant for scholars studying political autonomy, federalism, and liberal nationalism?
3. What could or should be done to facilitate the reception and diffusion of Quebec and Canadian studies in the United States and in English-speaking Canada?

Notes

1. I wish to thank Olivier De Champlain and Jackie Steele who have assisted with the preparation of tables and inserts, as well as the two anonymous commentators.
2. Robert Schwartzwald, 'Le rôle des universités américaine dans la diffusion de la culture francophone en Amérique du Nord', in Claude Poirier, ed., *Langue, espace, société : Les variétés du français en Amérique du Nord*, (Sainte-Foy: Les Presses de l'Université Laval, 1994), 123.
3. Earl Fry and Stephen Blank, 'The Business Sector', in Karen Gould, Joseph T. Jockel, and William Metcalfe, eds., *Northern Exposures: Scholarship on Canada in the United States*, (Washington: Association for Canadian Studies in the United States, 1993), 350.
4. Louis Balthazar, 'Within the Black Box: Reflections From a French Quebec Vantage Point', *American Review of Canadian Studies* 25, 4, (Winter 1995): 519.
5. The connection with Chicago remained significant over the years as several Canadians and Quebecers would be educated there, such as Guy Rocher, Daniel Latouche, and, closer to us, Guy Lachapelle, Louis Imbeau, Antonia Maioni, Pierre Martin, and Luc Bernier.
6. Andrew McRae, 'York University Political Science Professor Kenneth McRoberts appointed principal of Glendon College effective July 1, 1999' *York University Gazette*, 9 June 1999.
7. Commission on National Development in the Arts, Letters and Sciences, chapter XIV, art. 13.
8. Massey-Lévesque Commission, chapter XIV, art. 15.
9. In addition, the Quebec government twice decided to launch major debates with respect to its future in Canada. The Bélanger-Campeau Commission (1990–1) is a good illustration as commissioners canvassed Quebec's opinions. These democratic exercises contributed to raising awareness among Canadians about what made them different from other countries and spearheaded unprecedented interest of Quebec as a subject of study in Canada, the US, and worldwide.
10. Doug Owram, *The Government Generation: Canadian Intellectuals and the State 1900–1945* (Toronto: University of Toronto Press, 1986).
11. Stephen Brooks and Alain-G. Gagnon, *Social Scientists and Politics in Canada: Between Clerisy and Vanguard* (Montreal and Kingston: McGill-Queen's University Press, 1988).
12. George Grant, *Lament for a Nation: The Defeat of Canadian Nationalism* (Montreal and Kingston: McGill-Queen's University Press, 1965); Marcel Rioux, *La question du Québec* (Montreal: L'Hexagone, 1970).
13. Hubert Aquin, *Prochain Episode*. Ottawa, Cercle du livre de France, 1965; Margaret Atwood, *Survival* (Toronto: Anansi, 1972), followed by *Surfacing* (Toronto: McClelland & Stewart, 1972) in which she studied Canada's national psyche.
14. Jane Moss, 'Les études québécoises aux États-Unis' *Globe. Revue internationale d'études québécoises* 4, 2 (2001): 379.
15. François Rocher, 'The End of the "Two Solitudes"? The Presence (or Absence) of the Work of French-speaking Scholars in Canadian Politics', *Canadian Journal of Political Science* 40, 4 (2007): 833–57; Jean-François Gaudreault-Desbiens, *Les solitudes du bijuridisme au Canada* (Montreal: Thémis, 2007).
16. Daniel Latouche had noted something similar in a text published in 1993: 'Quebec, see Under Canada'. Latouche was quoting from the index entry in Eric J. Hobsbawn, *Nations and Nationalism since 1780* (Cambridge: Cambridge University Press, 1990).

Relevant Websites

American Council for Quebec Studies: www.acqs.org/qc_studies_journal/index.html

Canada Research Chair in Quebec and Canadian Studies: www.creqc.uqam.ca

Canada Research Chair in Democracy and Sovereignty: www.uqac.ca/crcds/

Centre de recherche interdisciplinaire sur la diversité au Québec: www.cridaq.uqam.ca

Globe: revue internationale d'études québécoises: www.revueglobe.uqam.ca/index_an.asp?section

Panorama sur le Québec: www.panorama-quebec.com/cgi-cs/cs.waframe.content?topic=26645&lang=1

Research Group on Plurinational Societies: www.creqc.uqam.ca

Select Bibliography

Dickinson, John A., and Brian Young. *A Short History of Quebec*, 4th edn. Montreal and Kingston: McGill-Queen's University Press, 2003.

Gagnon, Alain-G. *Québec. World Bibliographical Series*, Vol. 211. Oxford and Santa Barbara, Calif.: Clio Press, 1998.

————, ed. *Quebec: State and Society.* 3rd edn. Toronto: University of Toronto Press, 2003.

————, and Mary Beth Montcalm. *Quebec: Beyond the Quiet Revolution.* Toronto: Nelson Canada, 1989.

Hughes, Everett. *French Canada in Transition.* Chicago: University of Chicago Press, 1943.

Latouche, Daniel. *Politique et société au Québec.* Montreal: Boréal, 1993.

Levine, Marc. *The Reconquest of Montreal: Language Policy and Social Change in a Bilingual City.* Philadelphia: Temple University Press, 1990.

McRoberts, Kenneth. *Quebec: Social Change and Political Crisis.* 3rd edn. Toronto: McClelland & Stewart, 1993.

Miner, Horace. *Saint-Denis: A French-Canadian Parish.* Chicago: University of Chicago Press, 1939.

Index

Union Act of 1840, 126, 161
union federations, 362, 363, 366, 377
Union internationale de la presse francophone (UPF), 404
Union internationale des journalistes et de la presse de langue française (UIJPLF), 404, 411
union movement, 366
Union Nationale, 53, 76, 163, 170, 346, 360; 1962 election, 352; health insurance and, 329
Union Saint-Joseph, 69
United Nations Educational, Scientific and Cultural Organization (UNESCO). *See* UNESCO
United States, 387; Americanization and, 81; delegations in, 423, 439; Department of Homeland Security, 433; dollar, 434, 435; economic downturn, 433; economic relations with Quebec, 384, 430–41, 432–3, 434–9, 440; exports to Canada, 432; exports to Quebec, 375; feminism and, 320; freedom of worship in, 126; imports from Quebec, 374; investment in Canada, 436; investment in Quebec, 376; Quebec's political presence in, 416–27; states and Quebec, 439; trade with Canada, 372–3, 432; visitors to Canada from, 432
universities, 296, 308
Upper Canada: Loyalists in, 190; union with Lower Canada, 35
Usine C stage, 450
Us-Them dichotomy, 279, 281

values, secularization of, 124
Vandal, Thierry, 341
Vasconcelos, Paula de, 445, 448, 450
Vaugrante, Béatrice, 412
Verba, Sidney, 459
Verrazzano, Giovanni de, 5
'vertical mosaic', 273
Victoria Charter, 54, 58
Viger, Jacques, 157
Vigneault, Gilles, 216, 222
Villers, Marie-Éva de, 164
visible minorities, 269, 270; education and employment and, 272–3
Voice of Women, 240

War Measures Act, 58, 335
War of Independence (US), 27, 31, 82
War of the Austrian Succession, 13, 14
War of the Spanish Succession, 13, 14
Wartime Prices and Trade Board, 240
Washington: Canada's embassy in, 423; Quebec delegation in, 419
Washington 'mantra', 425
Waterman, Jack, 104
Weinstock, Daniel, 228
'welcoming class' model, 294–5
welfare state, 316, 361
Wells, Clyde, 57
Westmoreland-Traoré, Juanita, 274–6
White Paper of 1969, *Statement on Indian Policy*, 113, 349
White Paper on Quebec's Language Policy, 174
women, 228; in colonial Quebec, 8; legal status of married, 228; motherhood and, 236–7; pay equity and, 318–19; in post-war workforce, 241; power over, 44; in religious communities, 41, 237–9; right to vote, 239, 311; support payments for, 317–18; training, 318; twentieth century, 231–45; waged labour and, 235–6, 241
women's centres, 368
women's groups, 362; activism and, 314–15; funding for, 314; Quebec government and, 310
women's liberation movement, 312, 313, 314, 363, 366
workforce: immigrants in, 272–3; women in, 235–6, 241
Workman, Nanette, 216
World March of Women (WMW), 310, 319, 366, 368
World Trade Organization (WTO), 406, 409
worship: equality of, 126; freedom of, 125–6
writers (French-Canadian): in France, 100; radio and, 97–8

yé-yé movement, 151, 215, 216, 218
Young, Brian, 457
Young Women's League, 240
Yvette affair, 244–5, 316

Zeliotis, George, 333